THE POEMS OF
SHELLEY

– Volume 5 –

1821–1822

EDITED BY

CARLENE ADAMSON, WILL BOWERS,
JACK DONOVAN, KELVIN EVEREST,
MATHELINDA NABUGODI and
MICHAEL ROSSINGTON

Founding Editor of *The Poems of Shelley*
GEOFFREY MATTHEWS

LONDON AND NEW YORK

Cover image: *The Columns of the Parthenon on the Acropolis, Athens* (*c.*1858–60), albumen print on cardboard by Dimitrios Constantin (active *c.*1858–70). Source: Rijksmuseum, Amsterdam.

First published 2024
by Routledge
4 Park Square, Milton Park, Abingdon, Oxon OX14 4RN

and by Routledge
605 Third Avenue, New York, NY 10158

Routledge is an imprint of the Taylor & Francis Group, an informa business

© 2024 selection and editorial matter, Carlene Adamson, Will Bowers, Jack Donovan, Kelvin Everest, Mathelinda Nabugodi and Michael Rossington

The right of Carlene Adamson, Will Bowers, Jack Donovan, Kelvin Everest, Mathelinda Nabugodi and Michael Rossington to be identified as the authors of the editorial material and for the selection of the text has been asserted in accordance with sections 77 and 78 of the Copyright, Designs and Patents Act 1988

All rights reserved. No part of this book may be reprinted or reproduced or utilised in any form or by any electronic, mechanical, or other means, now known or hereafter invented, including photocopying and recording, or in any information storage or retrieval system, without permission in writing from the publishers.

Trademark notice: Product or corporate names may be trademarks or registered trademarks, and are used only for identification and explanation without intent to infringe.

British Library Cataloguing-in-Publication Data
A catalogue record for this book is available from the British Library

ISBN: 978-1-138-01664-4 (hbk)
ISBN: 978-1-032-68726-1 (pbk)
ISBN: 978-1-315-77987-4 (ebk)

DOI: 10.4324/9781315779874

Typeset in Minion Pro and New Baskerville
by Newgen Publishing UK

THE POEMS OF SHELLEY
VOLUME FIVE

Percy Bysshe Shelley (1792–1822) was one of the major poets of the English Romantic period. This is the fifth volume of a six-volume edition of *The Poems of Shelley*, which aims to present all of Shelley's poems in chronological order and with full annotation. Date and circumstances of composition are provided for each poem and all manuscript and printed sources relevant to establishing an authoritative text are freshly examined and assessed. Headnotes and footnotes furnish the personal, literary, historical and scientific information necessary to an informed reading of Shelley's varied and allusive verse.

Most of the poems in the present volume were composed between late summer 1821 and late January 1822. They include *Hellas*, a lyrical drama written in support of the Greek War of Independence, composed in September–November 1821 and published in February–March 1822, his unfinished tragedy *Charles the First* which he had been planning for several years, as well as important shorter poems such as 'The Indian Girl's Song', 'Autumn: a Dirge' and his 'Epitaph' for John Keats.

In addition to accompanying commentaries, there are extensive bibliographies to the poems, a chronological table of Shelley's life and publications, and indexes to titles and first lines. Now completed, this is the most comprehensive edition of Shelley's poetry available to students and scholars.

Carlene Adamson was formerly Assistant Professor of English at Vesalius College, Vrije Universiteit Brussel, Belgium.

Will Bowers is Senior Lecturer in Eighteenth-Century Literature and Thought at Queen Mary University of London, UK.

Jack Donovan was formerly Reader in English at the University of York, UK.

Kelvin Everest is A. C. Bradley Professor Emeritus at the University of Liverpool, UK.

Mathelinda Nabugodi is Lecturer in Comparative Literature at University College London, UK.

Michael Rossington is Professor of Romantic Literature at Newcastle University, UK.

LONGMAN ANNOTATED ENGLISH POETS
General Editors: Paul Hammond, Michael Rossington and Cathy Shrank
Founding General Editors: F. W. Bateson and John Barnard

Recent titles in the series include:

SHELLEY: SELECTED POEMS
Edited by Carlene Adamson, Will Bowers, Jack Donovan, Cian Duffy, Kelvin Everest, Geoffrey Matthews, Mathelinda Nabugodi, Ralph Pite and Michael Rossington. Selected and revised by Kelvin Everest (2023)

THE POEMS OF SHELLEY, VOLUME FIVE: 1821–1822
Edited by Carlene Adamson, Will Bowers, Jack Donovan, Kelvin Everest, Mathelinda Nabugodi and Michael Rossington (2024)

THE POEMS OF SHELLEY, VOLUME SIX: 1822
Edited by Carlene Adamson, Will Bowers, Jack Donovan, Kelvin Everest, Mathelinda Nabugodi and Michael Rossington (2024)

THE POEMS OF W. B. YEATS, VOLUME THREE: 1899–1910
Edited by Peter McDonald (2023)

THE POEMS OF LORD BYRON: VOLUME FOUR
Don Juan, Cantos I–VI
Edited by Jane Stabler and Gavin Hopps (2024)

THE POEMS OF LORD BYRON: VOLUME FIVE
Don Juan, Cantos VII–XVII
Edited by Jane Stabler and Gavin Hopps (2024)

THE COMPLETE POEMS OF SAMUEL JOHNSON
Edited by Robert D. Brown and Robert DeMaria, Jr. (2024)

For more information about the series, please visit: www.routledge.com/Longman-Annotated-English-Poets/book-series/LAEP

Shelley's manuscript of lines 1–18 of *Autumn: a Dirge*, from a loose sheet in the Bodleian Library (see Note on Illustrations).

Source: Bodleian MS. Shelley adds. c. 4 f. 99ʳ, black and white. Reproduced by kind permission of The Bodleian Libraries, University of Oxford.

Contents

Note by the General Editors	xi
Note on Illustrations	xiii
Preface to Volume Five	xv
Acknowledgements	xvii
Chronological Table of Shelley's Life and Publications	xix
Abbreviations	xxvii

THE POEMS

409	'In the great morning of the world'	3
410	'As the sunrise to the night' [Fragment: To Italy]	5
411	Hellas	7
411 Appendix	Lines connected with Hellas	203
412	The Indian Girl's Song [Lines to an Indian Air]	260
413	'Which like a crane, its distant home pursuing'	268
414	'An archer stood upon the Tower of Babel'	271
415	Autumn: a Dirge	273
416	'Unfathomable Sea! whose waves are years' [Time]	279
417	'The flower that smiles today' [Mutability]	282

418	'A fresh fair child stood by my side' [Love, Hope, Desire, and Fear] (Translation of Brunetto Latini, *Il Tesoretto* xxi 82–156)	284
418	Appendix Brunetto Latini, *Il Tesoretto* xxi 82–156	290
419	'A capering, squalid, squalling one'	292
420	Epitaph [On Keats]	297
421	The Zucca	302
422	'Rough wind that moanest loud' [A Dirge]	312
423	'Alas, if I could feign'	314
424	'There was a star when Heaven was young'	315
425	'Though thou scatterest their ashes'	316
426	Charles the First	319
426	Appendix Lines connected with Charles the First	479
427	'A widowed bird sate mourning for her love' [A Song]	482
428	'Art thou pale for weariness' [To the Moon]	485
429	Lines to — [Sonnet to Byron]	488

Appendix A: The Order of the Poems in *1822*	499
Appendix B: '[?] / As when within a chasm of [?mighty] seas'	501
Appendix C: 'O thou whose cold hand tears the veils from error' (Translation of Petrarch, *Africa* vi 901–2)	503
Index of Titles	507
Index of First Lines	508

Note by the General Editors

The Longman Annotated English Poets series was launched in 1965 with the publication of Kenneth Allott's edition of *The Poems of Matthew Arnold*. F. W. Bateson wrote then that the 'new series is the first designed to provide university students and teachers, and the general reader with complete and fully annotated editions of the major English poets'. That remains the aim of the series, and Bateson's original vision of its policy remains essentially the same. Its 'concern is primarily with the meaning of the extant texts in their various contexts'.

Accordingly, the annotation which the various editors provide ranges from the glossing of obscure words and references to the evocation of the cultural, social, and political contexts within which the poems were created and first received. The editions draw on recent scholarship but also embody the fruits of the editors' own new research. The aim, in so far as this is possible through the medium of editorial annotation, is to place the modern reader in a position which approximates that enjoyed by the poems' first audience.

The treatment of the text has varied pragmatically from edition to edition; some have provided modernised texts where the original conventions of spelling and punctuation were likely to create problems for a reader, whereas others retain the original accidentals—the spelling, punctuation, italics, and capitals.

Most of the poems in this, the fifth volume of the six-volume edition of *The Poems of Shelley*, were composed between late summer 1821 and January 1822. The volume includes *Hellas*, the last major poem of Shelley's published in his lifetime, which was composed to raise awareness of the Greek struggle for independence from the Ottoman Empire. This lyrical drama contains some of the finest Choruses in the poet's oeuvre. Also in this volume are Shelley's unfinished tragedy, *Charles the First*, and several important shorter poems such as 'The Indian Girl's Song', 'Autumn: a Dirge' and his 'Epitaph' for John Keats.

Paul Hammond
Michael Rossington
Cathy Shrank

Note on Illustrations

The cover image is *The Columns of the Parthenon on the Acropolis, Athens* (*c*.1858–60), albumen print on cardboard by Dimitrios Constantin (active *c*.1858–70). Source: Rijksmuseum, Amsterdam.
The image on the page preceding the Contents shows Bodleian MS. Shelley adds. c. 4 (*Box 1*) f. 99^r. This single leaf contains the probable final draft of *Autumn: a Dirge* (no. 415) ll. 1–18 (with the remaining four lines continuing on *Box 1* f. 99^v) which S. composed in the last quarter of 1821. S. had begun drafting the poem across the free upper endpaper verso and the first flyleaf recto of the second volume of his Euripides, *Euripidis Tragœdiæ Viginti, cum variis lectionibus*, ed. Josuae Barnes, 6 vols bound as three (1811–12), and then in an intermediate draft, which starts on MS. Shelley adds. e. 7 (*Nbk 21*) p. 143, continues on p. 142, and ends on p. 141. The final draft in *Box 1* f. 99 was originally on a page in Bodleian MS. Shelley adds. e. 7 between p. 154 and p. 155 where there is now a stub. The removal of the page from the notebook, the clean text with few cancellations, and the folds on the leaf, suggest that this final draft of *Autumn: a Dirge* may have been enclosed in a letter. The neatness of the draft, and Shelley's care over the indentation of lines, allows this manuscript page to express the formal ingenuity and metrical dexterity that is typical of Shelley's last lyrics.

The image facing *Charles the First* (no. 426) on p. 318 shows Bodleian MS. Shelley adds. e. 17 (*Nbk 19*) p. 181 rev., which contains *Charles the First* Act 1, scene i, lines 2–15. 'Jan. 5.' is written at the top of the page in Shelley's hand, which appears to date the first writing on this page to 5 January 1822, possibly the third day of a sustained composition period of around two to three weeks, beginning *c*.3 January. The page is covered in cancellations, ink blots, and insertions, and the differences in thickness and tone of these layered insertions suggest S.'s revisions occurred over multiple periods of composition. The roughness of the page displays the daunting task that *Charles the First* poses for a textual editor. The page also hints at Shelley's formidable reading of seventeenth-century sources (begun in summer 1820), and the 'Young Man's' question about a 'quaint masque' (l. 2) is underpinned by his reading of the account of the masque presented by the Inns of Court in February 1634 in Bulstrode Whitelocke's *Memorials of the English Affairs* [...] *from the beginning of the Reign of King Charles the First, to King Charles the Second His Happy Restauration* (1682).

Preface to Volume Five

This is the fifth volume of what has become a six-volume edition of Shelley's poems. It includes poetry that Shelley composed between late August 1821 and late January 1822 as well as nos 409 and 410, which the editors date to May 1821. In the Preface to Volume 4 (2013) the editors signalled their decision that five volumes, rather than four, would be necessary to accommodate the texts of, and commentaries on, Shelley's poems written between late summer 1821 and his death on 8 July 1822. Since then it has become clear that two volumes are required for the final ten months or so of Shelley's life, the present one and the sixth that comprises poems composed between late January 1822 and early July 1822 as well as appendices that include *Poetical Essay on the Existing State of Things* (1811) and translations from Goethe, Aeschylus and Homer that date from between 1815 and 1817. The principles of this edition were laid out in the Introduction to Volume 1 (1989) and reinforced in the Preface to Volume 2 (2000). The Preface to Volume 3 (2011) offered an account of the particular challenges involved in editing many of the poems written between summer 1819 and autumn 1820 which also applies to a large number of poems in Volumes 4–6. The expansion of the editorial team for Volumes 5 and 6 to include Carlene Adamson, Will Bowers and Mathelinda Nabugodi has been of immeasurable benefit to all aspects of this project and they have been essential to its completion. In the present volume Carlene Adamson has had editorial responsibility for no. 411 Appendix (with the exception of Appendices A, D, G and K), no. 426, no. 426 Appendix and Appendix C; Will Bowers for no. 413, no. 414, no. 415, and Appendix B; Jack Donovan for no. 411 Appendix K, no. 412, no. 416, no. 417, no. 418, no. 418 Appendix, no. 421, no. 424, no. 425, and no. 429; Kelvin Everest for no. 411 Appendices A, D and G, no. 420 and no. 422; and Michael Rossington for no. 409, no. 410, no. 419 and no. 428. Michael Rossington has had responsibility for the text, textual notes and headnote to no. 411 (except for the sections on form, by Kelvin Everest, and criticism post-1945, by Will Bowers); the non-textual notes were done by Carlene Adamson, Will Bowers, Kelvin Everest and Michael Rossington, with some notes on Spanish and German sources by Mathelinda Nabugodi, and on Greek and Latin sources by Phillip Bone; Bruce Barker-Benfield made numerous helpful comments on the final draft, especially on the manuscript evidence section of the headnote. Carlene Adamson and

Michael Rossington have had joint responsibility for nos 423 and 427. The editors remain indebted to the wisdom and expertise of the founding editor, Geoffrey Matthews, to whose unpublished research on Shelley in the Matthews-Shelley Collection they have had access, courtesy of University of Reading, Special Collections.

Acknowledgements

It is with pleasure that the editors record special thanks to the following: Paul Hammond, David Hopkins and Cathy Shrank, general editors of the Longman Annotated English Poets series; Ruth Berry, Polly Dodson, Jasmine Erice-Harling, Zoë Meyer, Karen Raith and Chris Ratcliffe at Routledge; B. C. Barker-Benfield and Stephen Hebron of the Bodleian Libraries, University of Oxford and Elizabeth C. Denlinger, Doucet Devin Fischer and Charles Cuykendall Carter of the Carl H. Pforzheimer Collection of Shelley and His Circle, New York Public Library; †Donald H. Reiman, general editor of the 'Bodleian Shelley Manuscripts' and 'Manuscripts of the Younger Romantics: Shelley' series, and his fellow editors; Phillip Bone, David Constantine, Gregory Hutchinson, Ian Maclachlan, Jonathan Thacker and Valentina Varinelli, for advice concerning Shelley's translations from, and reading in, French, German, Greek, Latin, Spanish and Italian.

In addition, gratitude is extended to the following individuals for advice and support of various kinds: John Barnard, †Gerald Bevan, Stephanie Coane, Helen Constantine, Nora Crook, Elizabeth Davies, Chris Fletcher, Neil Fraistat, Alexandra Franklin, Nicholas Halmi, Paul Hamilton, James Harriman-Smith, Nick Havely, Sue Hodson, Hamish Ironside, Lucy Keating, Henrike Lähnemann, Anne Laurence, Fabienne Leclère, James McLaverty, †Michael O'Neill, Mark Philp, Francesco Rognoni, Joel Silver, Adam Swift, Raffaele Vigliante, Patrick Vittet-Philippe and Jeff Wilson.

Michael Rossington expresses thanks to the following institutions, without whose generous support the completion of Volumes 5 and 6 would not have been possible: All Souls College, Oxford; the Huntington Library (for an Andrew W. Mellon Foundation Fellowship in 2014); the Modern Humanities Research Association (for a Research Associateship in 2014–15); the Rector and Fellows of Exeter College, Oxford (for a Visiting Fellowship in Michaelmas Term, 2015–16); the Master and Fellows of Trinity College Cambridge (for a Visiting Scholarship in September 2016); the School of English Literature, Language and Linguistics at Newcastle University (for a Research Excellence Academy Postdoctoral Award from February 2017 to July 2019, one semester of research leave in 2015–16 and another in 2019–20), and help with financial costs from the Research Support Fund; the Taylor and Francis Group.

The editors of Volume 5 are grateful to staff at the following institutions for access to manuscript, print and digitized material in their collections and, where stated, permission to cite from such material: Bibliothèque nationale de France (no. 411); The Bodleian Libraries, University of Oxford (no. 409, no. 410, no. 411, no. 411 Appendix, no. 412, no. 413, no. 415, no. 416, no. 417, no. 418, no. 419, no. 420, no. 421, no. 422, no. 426, no. 426 Appendix, no. 427, no. 428, no. 429, Appendix C); The British Library (no. 429); The Carl H. Pforzheimer Collection of Shelley and His Circle, New York Public Library (no. 419, no. 426); The English Faculty Library, University of Oxford; the Provost and Fellows of Eton College (no. 414, no. 415, Appendix B); Fondation Martin Bodmer, Cologny (Genève) (no. 412); Houghton Library, Harvard University (no. 412); The Huntington Library, San Marino, California (no. 411, no. 423, no. 424, no. 425, no. 426); John Murray Archive, National Library of Scotland (Appendix C); Lilly Library, Indiana University (no. 411 Appendix); Morgan Library & Museum, New York (no. 412); Newcastle University Library; Special Collections, Senate House Library, University of London (no. 411); Special Collections, The Claremont Colleges Library, Claremont, California (no. 419); Taylor Institution Library, University of Oxford.

Chronological Table of Shelley's Life and Publications

1792	(*4 August*) S. born at Field Place, near Horsham, Sussex, eldest son of Timothy Shelley, landowner and Whig MP (Baronet, 1806).
	(*7 September*) Baptized at Warnham, Sussex.
1798	Studies with Warnham clergyman Rev. Evan Edwards.
1802–4	At Syon House Academy, Isleworth, near London. Attends lectures by Adam Walker on natural philosophy.
1804–10	At Eton, where he is bullied. Develops scientific as well as literary interests.
1806	Possible date of composition for earliest poems in *Esd*.
1808	Begins correspondence with Harriet Grove, his cousin; relationship ended in 1810 by religious prejudices of her family.
1810	(*Spring*) Publishes Gothic novel, *Zastrozzi*.
	(*Summer*) Submits *WJ*, his earliest long poem, for publication; it is rejected (eventually published in 1829 as a series of extracts; published as a whole, but abridged, in 1831).
	(*September*) Publishes *Original Poetry by Victor and Cazire*, written with his sister Elizabeth. Withdrawn following the discovery that one of the poems had been plagiarized from M. G. ('Monk') Lewis.
	(from *October*) At University College, Oxford, where he meets Thomas Jefferson Hogg.
	(*November*) Publishes *Posthumous Fragments of Margaret Nicholson*.
	(*December*) Publishes second Gothic novel, *St. Irvyne* (dated 1811).
1811	(*January*) Meets Harriet Westbrook.
	(*March*) Publishes *Poetical Essay on the Existing State of Things* in support of Peter Finnerty, a radical Irish journalist imprisoned for libel in February.
	(*25 March*) Expelled in his second term at Oxford for refusing to answer questions about a sceptical pamphlet written with Hogg, *The Necessity of Atheism* (published February). Hogg also expelled.

	(*July*) Visits Cwm Elan in Radnorshire, Wales.
	(*August*) Elopes with Harriet Westbrook, and marries her in Edinburgh (29 August).
	(*November*) Quarrels with Hogg over his attempted seduction of Harriet.
	(*December*) Meets Southey in the Lake District.
1812	(*January*) Begins correspondence with William Godwin. Unsuccessful attempt to meet Wordsworth.
	(*January–August*) Writes a number of poems in *Esd*.
	(*February–March*) Campaigns for political reform in Ireland.
	(*February*) Writes *An Address, to the Irish People* and *Proposals for an Association of ... Philanthropists*.
	(*March*) Prints *Declaration of Rights*. Adopts vegetarianism.
	(*6 April*) Returns to Wales, then moves to Devon where he is kept under surveillance by Government agents.
	(*June–July*) Writes *A Letter to Lord Ellenborough*.
	(*July–August*) Revises *The Devil's Walk* for distribution as a broadsheet.
	(*mid-July*) Elizabeth Hitchener joins Harriet and Harriet's sister Eliza in S.'s domestic circle.
	(*August*) His servant, Daniel Healy, is imprisoned for distributing the *Declaration* and *The Devil's Walk*.
	(*September*) Goes to Tremadoc, North Wales, where he is involved in further political activity.
	(from *September*) Works on *Q Mab*.
	(*4 October–13 November*) Thomas Love Peacock introduced to S. by Thomas Hookham.
	(*October*) Meets William Godwin and John Frank Newton in London.
	(*November–December*) Copies out *Esd*.
	(*November*) Elizabeth Hitchener leaves household.
1813	(*27 February*) Flees from Tremadoc after mysterious incident at Tan-yr-allt in which S. is supposedly attacked at night.
	(*March*) Visits Dublin and Killarney.
	(*5 April*) Returns to London.
	(*May*) *Q Mab* privately published; *A Vindication of Natural Diet*, one of the notes to *Q Mab*, is published shortly before.
	(*23 June*) Ianthe Shelley born.
	(*July*) Moves to Bracknell in Berkshire. Joins expatriate pro-revolutionary French and English circle centred on Mrs Boinville and the Newtons.

	(*December*) Writes *A Refutation of Deism* (privately published in early 1814).
1814	(*March*) Remarries Harriet to ensure her legal status as his wife, but spending time apart with the Boinvilles.
	(*May–June*) Visiting Godwin in London; growing estrangement from Harriet.
	(*28 July*) Elopes with Mary Godwin, daughter of William Godwin and Mary Wollstonecraft. They travel to Switzerland accompanied by Claire Clairmont (daughter of Godwin's second wife by a previous relationship).
	(*13 September*) Returns to England.
	(*30 November*) Charles Shelley born to Harriet.
	(*December*) Review of Hogg's *Memoirs of Prince Alexy Haimatoff* published in the *Critical Review*.
1815	(*6 January*) S.'s grandfather Sir Bysshe Shelley dies.
	(*late January–early February*) Briefly involved with Irish radical George Cannon ('Erasmus Perkins') and plans for monthly paper, the *Theological Inquirer; or, Polemical Magazine*.
	(*22 February*) Mary's first child born (dies 6 March).
	(*July*) S. receiving annual income of £1000 (of which £200 is made over to Harriet). Gives large sums of money to Godwin.
	(*May–Sept*) The opening scenes of Goethe's *Faust* ('They approach you again, fluctuating Shapes!') probably translated in this period.
	(*early August*) Moves to cottage at Bishopsgate, next to Windsor Park.
	(*late August–early September*) River excursion up the Thames with Mary, Peacock and Charles Clairmont.
	(*10 September–14 December*) Writes *Alastor*.
1816	(*24 January*) William Shelley born to Mary.
	(*February*) *1816* published.
	(*3 May*) Leaves for Continent with Mary and Claire.
	(*25 May–29 August*) Stays with Mary and Claire in Switzerland; meets Lord Byron.
	(*June*) Writes *Hymn to Intellectual Beauty* (published in the *Examiner* in January 1817).
	(*July*) Writes *Mont Blanc* (published in *1817*), begins *R&H* (late July).
	(*8 September*) Returns to England.

(*9 October*) Suicide of Mary's half-sister Fanny Imlay (Wollstonecraft's daughter by Gilbert Imlay).
(*9 November*) Suicide of Harriet Shelley by drowning in the Serpentine (discovered 10 December).
(*December*) Meets John Keats and Horace Smith through friendship with Leigh Hunt.
(*15 December*) Receives news of Harriet's suicide.
(*30 December*) Marries Mary.

1817 (*12 January*) Allegra, Claire's daughter by Byron, born at Bath.
(*late January–early February*) Drafts *Declaration in Chancery*.
(*February*) Further meetings with Keats. Writes *A Proposal for Putting Reform to the Vote* (published March).
(*2 March*) Moves to Albion House, Marlow.
(*4 March*) Habeas Corpus suspended (until 1 February 1818).
(*27 March*) Lord Eldon, Lord Chancellor, denies S. custody of his two children by Harriet.
(*March-September*) Writes *L&C*.
(*July*) Mary transcribes his viva voce translation of Aeschylus' *Prometheus Bound*.
(*September*) Works on *R&H*.
(*2 September*) Clara Shelley born.
(*?September–December*) Drafts *On Christianity*.
(*November*) *1817* published anonymously. Writes, and probably prints, *An Address to the People on the Death of the Princess Charlotte* (published c.1843).
(*December*) *L&C* published (with 1818 on the title-page) and suppressed. Writes *Ozymandias*.

1818 (*January*) *L&C* reissued in a revised version as *RofI*.
(*12 March*) Leaves England for Italy with Mary, Claire and children.
(*4 April*) Arrives in Milan.
(*28 April*) Sends Allegra to Byron.
(*9 May*) Meets John and Maria Gisborne and Henry Reveley, Maria's son by her first marriage, at Livorno.
(*June–July*) Moves to Bagni di Lucca (11 June). Translates Plato's *Symposium*, writes *On Love* and *A Discourse on the manners of the Ancient Greeks relative to the subject of Love* (the latter not published in full until 1931).
(*first half of August*) Finishes *R&H*.
(*17 August*) Travels to Venice with Claire to meet Byron.

	(*late August–5 November*) Stays at the Villa I Capuccini in Este, near Venice. Begins *J&M* and writes *Lines Written among the Euganean Hills, October, 1818*.

(*31 August*) Mary travels to Venice with William and Clara.
(*24 September*) Clara Shelley dies, aged one.
(*October*) Writes Act I of *PU*.
(*November*) Travels to Rome, visiting Ferrara and Bologna en route (in Rome 20–27 November).
(*December*) Goes on to Naples (1 December). Visits surrounding classical sites and volcanic scenery, writes *Stanzas written in dejection – December 1818, near Naples*.
(*27 December*) Birth of Elena Adelaide Shelley.

1819 (*February*) Further visits to Pompeii and Paestum and other classical sites.
(*27 February*) Birth of Elena Adelaide Shelley registered at Naples.
(*March–April*) Returns to Rome (arrives 5 March). Writes *PU* Acts II and III.
(*Spring*) *1819* published.
(*May*) Finishes *J&M* (first published in *1824*).
(*7 June*) William Shelley dies, aged three and a half.
(*17 June*) Moves to Livorno.
(*8 August*) *The Cenci* completed at Villa Valsovano. Printed at Livorno in September.
(*August–December*) Completes a fourth act of *PU*.
(*September*) Receives news of the Peterloo Massacre (5 September). Writes *MA* (not published until 1832), and other political poems.
(*October–November*) Moves to Florence (2 October). Writes *Ode to the West Wind*, *PB3* (first published in *1840*) and a letter to the *Examiner* on the trial of Richard Carlile (published in part in 1880 and in full in 1926).
(*c.15 October–23 December*) Writes *England in 1819*.
(*November–December*) Begins *PVR* (not published until 1920), writes *On Life*.
(*10 November*) Sophia Stacey first meets the Shelleys.
(*12 November*) Percy Florence Shelley born.
(*December*) British Parliament passes repressive 'Six Acts'.

1820 (*26 January*) Moves to Pisa.
(*29 January*) George III dies.

(*March*) Constitutional monarchy established in Spain. Writes *SP*. *The Cenci* published in London.
(*May–November*) Translates Plato's *Phaedo* (MS lost).
(*May–June*) Writes *OL*.
(*9 June*) Elena Adelaide Shelley dies in Naples, aged one and a half.
(*15 June*) Moves to Livorno.
(*15 June–early July*) Writes *LMG* (first published in *1824*), *To a Sky-Lark*.
(*July*) Constitutional revolution in Naples.
(*August*) Moves to Casa Prinni at Bagni di San Giuliano, near Pisa. Writes *WA*, *Ode to Naples* and begins *OT*. *1820* published.
(*20 October*) Claire goes to live with the Bojti family in Florence.
(*22 October*) Medwin arrives at Bagni di San Giuliano.
(*29 October*) Returns to Pisa.
(*21 November*) Claire returns to Pisa to stay with S. and Mary.
(*early December*) First visits Teresa Viviani ('Emilia') at the Convent of St Anna. S., Mary and Claire continue to visit and correspond with her until her marriage on 8 September 1821.
(*before mid-December*) *OT* published and suppressed.
(*last two weeks of December*) S. suffers a bout of ophthalmia which prevents him from reading and writing.
(*23 December*) Claire returns to the Bojtis in Florence.

1821
(*19 January*) Edward and Jane Williams first meet the Shelleys.
(*January–early March*) William Clark publishes an unauthorised edition of *Q Mab*.
(*late January–early February*) Writes *Epipsychidion*.
(*late January–20 March*) Writes *DP* (not published until 1840) in response to Peacock's *The Four Ages of Poetry* (published in 1820 in the first and only issue of *Olliers Literary Miscellany*).
(*23 February*) Keats dies in Rome.
(*27 February*) Medwin departs for Rome.
(*1 April*) Receives news of revolution against Ottoman rule in Greece.
(*11 April*) Receives news of Keats's death in a letter from Horace Smith dated 28 March. Smith's letter also contains news of the unexpected stoppage of S.'s income.

(*May-June*) Writes *Adonais* (published at Pisa in July).
(*May*) *Epipsychidion* published anonymously.
(*4 May*) Invites Byron to Pisa for the summer.
(*5 May*) Death of Napoleon Bonaparte. The news is not reported until early July.
(*8 May*) S. and Mary return to Bagni di San Giuliano.
(*19-22 June*) Claire with S. and Mary in Pisa and Bagni di San Giuliano.
(*23 June*) Claire removes to Livorno for the summer.
(*July*) Writes *Written on hearing the news of the death of Napoleon*.
(*21-27 July*) Claire with S. and Mary in Pisa and Bagni di San Giuliano.
(*3 August*) Visits Claire at Livorno.
(*4 August*) Leaves for Ravenna via Florence and Bologna to meet Byron.
(*6 August*) Arrives at Ravenna. In talking all night with Byron, learns of circulation of scandalous rumours about him by Richard Belgrave Hoppner, the British Consul at Venice. Returns to Pisa by 22 August.
(*26 August*) Writes to Hunt mentioning Byron's plans for *The Liberal*.
(*late September-early November*) Writing *Hellas*.
(*5-15 September*) Claire with S. and Mary in Bagni di San Giuliano and the Bay of Spezia.
(*9-31 October*) Claire with S. and Mary in Pisa, Bagni di San Giuliano and Pugnano.
(*25 October*) S. and Mary return to Pisa.
(*1 November*) Byron moves to Pisa. Claire returns to the Bojtis in Florence.
(*11 November*) *Hellas* sent to Ollier for publication.
(14 November) Medwin returns to the Shelleys at Pisa.

1822 (*early January*) Begins to draft *Charles the First*.
(*14 January*) Edward John Trelawny arrives in Pisa.
(*mid-January-February*) Translates the *Walpurgisnacht* scene from Goethe's *Faust*.
(*late January-March*) Translates passages from Calderón's *El mágico prodigioso*.
(*late January-June*) Writes lyrics to Jane Williams.
(*late February-late March*) *1822* published.

(*March*) Translates the *Prolog im Himmel* scene from Goethe's *Faust*.
(*9 March*) On or soon after this date, Medwin departs for Rome.
(*24 March*) S., Byron, Trelawny and Taaffe are involved in an altercation with Stefano Masi (the so-called 'Dragoon Affair').
(*20 April*) Death of Allegra Byron at a convent in Bagnacavallo.
(*30 April*) Moves with his family and Edward and Jane Williams to Casa Magni at San Terenzo on the Bay of Spezia, near Lerici.
(*12 May*) Takes delivery of his boat, the *Don Juan* (S.'s preferred name for it was the *Ariel*), at Lerici.
(*late May–late June*) Writing *TL*.
(*1 July*) Sails to Livorno with Williams to meet Leigh Hunt.
(*8 July*) Drowns with Williams when boat founders on the return voyage.
(*16 August*) Cremated on the beach between La Spezia and Livorno, in the presence of Trelawny, Byron and Hunt.
(*August*) Mary begins to transcribe unpublished MSS for publication.
(*September*) Mary and the Hunts move in together in Albaro, near Genoa.

1823	(*March*) Ashes interred in the Protestant Cemetery, Rome. (*July*) Mary returns to England.
1824	*1824* published. Suppressed at the insistence of Sir Timothy Shelley.
1829	Mary assists in the publication of *1829*.
1839	*1839* and *1840* published.

Abbreviations

Poems and Prose Works by Shelley

Alastor	*Alastor; or, The Spirit of Solitude*
Daemon	*The Daemon of the World*
DMAG	*A Discourse on the manners of the Ancient Greeks relative to the subject of Love*
DP	*A Defence of Poetry*
J&M	*Julian and Maddalo: A Conversation*
L&C	*Laon and Cythna; Or, The Revolution of the Golden City: A Vision of the Nineteenth Century. In the Stanza of Spenser*
LMG	*Letter to Maria Gisborne*
MA	*The Mask of Anarchy: Written on the Occasion of the Massacre at Manchester*
OL	*Ode to Liberty*
OT	*Oedipus Tyrannus; or, Swellfoot the Tyrant. A Tragedy, in Two Acts*
PB3	*Peter Bell the Third*
PU	*Prometheus Unbound: A Lyrical Drama in Four Acts*
PVR	*A Philosophical View of Reform*
Q Mab	*Queen Mab; A Philosophical Poem: with Notes*
R&H	*Rosalind and Helen, a Modern Eclogue*
RofI	*The Revolt of Islam; A Poem, In Twelve Cantos*
SP	*The Sensitive-Plant*
TL	*The Triumph of Life*
WA	*The Witch of Atlas*
WJ	*The Wandering Jew; or the Victim of the Eternal Avenger*

Manuscript Sources

Box 1	Bod. MS Shelley adds. c. 4: various dates.
Box 2	Bod. MS Shelley adds. c. 5: various dates.
CHPL	The Carl H. Pforzheimer Library (now known as The Carl H. Pforzheimer Collection of Shelley and His Circle).
Esd	The Esdaile Notebook, CHPL SC 372: 1810–14 (fair copies).
G1824	John Gisborne's copy of *1824*, now in the British Library, shelfmark: C. 61 c. 5.
Harvard MSS	Harvard fMS Eng. 822: various dates.

Harvard Nbk 1	Harvard MS Eng. 258.2: between August 1819 and May 1824 (fair copies).
Harvard Nbk 2	Harvard MS Eng. 258.3: mainly 1817 (fair copies).
HM 329	Press copy of *Hellas* in the Huntington Library HM 329 (in the hand of Edward Williams, with corrections by Shelley): November 1821.
L&C (PM)	The copy of *L&C* with Shelley's MS alterations made to transform the poem into *RofI*. This copy, once owned by H. Buxton Forman, and described by him in *The Shelley Library* (1886) 83–6, is now in the Morgan Library & Museum (W25A 37292).
Mary Copybk 1	Bod. MS Shelley adds. d. 7: probably autumn 1822 to autumn 1823.
Mary Copybk 2	Bod. MS Shelley adds. d. 9: autumn 1823 with additions of *c*.1839.
Mary Copybk 3	Bod. MS Shelley adds. d. 8: autumn 1823 with additions of *c*.1839.
Mary Nbk	Bod. MS Shelley d. 2: between summer 1820 and May 1824.
Montagu	Bod. MS Montagu d. 18: various dates.
Nbk 1	Bod. MS Shelley adds. e. 16: June 1816 through July 1817.
Nbk 2	Bod. MS Shelley adds. e. 19: early April 1817.
Nbk 3	Bod. MS Shelley adds. e. 10: May through September 1817.
Nbk 4	Bod. MS Shelley adds. e. 14: October 1817.
Nbk 4a	Bod. MS Shelley d. 3: October 1817.
Nbk 5	Bod. MS Shelley e. 4: late 1817 through summer 1819.
Nbk 6	Bod. MS Shelley adds. e. 11: May 1818 through April 1819.
Nbk 7	Bod. MS Shelley e. 1: April through December 1819.
Nbk 8	Bod. MS Shelley e. 2: April–May 1819.
Nbk 9	Bod. MS Shelley e. 3: April through December 1819.
Nbk 10	HM 2177 (Huntington Library): spring 1819 through spring 1820.
Nbk 11	Bod. MS Shelley adds. e. 12: January 1818 through summer 1821.
Nbk 12	HM 2176 (Huntington Library): spring 1819 through summer 1821.
Nbk 13	Bod. MS Shelley adds. e. 15: late October 1819.
Nbk 14	Bod. MS Shelley adds. e. 6: summer 1818 through early autumn 1820.
Nbk 15	Bod. MS Shelley adds. e. 9: November 1819 through summer 1821.
Nbk 16	Bod. MS Shelley d. 1: August 1819 through March 1821.

Nbk 17	Bod. MS Shelley adds. e. 8: January 1820 through May 1821.
Nbk 18	Bod. MS Shelley adds. e. 18: April 1821 through April 1822.
Nbk 19	Bod. MS Shelley adds. e. 17: November/December 1819 through late January 1822.
Nbk 20	Bod. MS Shelley adds. e. 20: February through June 1821.
Nbk 21	Bod. MS Shelley adds. e. 7: late summer 1821 through January 1822.
Nbk 22	HM 2111 (Huntington Library): late December 1821/early January 1822 through June 1822.
Relation	'Relation of the death of the family of the Cenci' in Bod. MS Shelley adds. e. 13, pp. 1–72 (in Mary Shelley's hand, probably with corrections by Shelley): April or May 1819.
SDMS	The Scrope Davies Notebook, BL Loan 70/8: 15 May–29 August 1816 (fair copies).

The following abbreviations designate MS collections, now dispersed, originally in the possession of H. B. Forman, C. W. Frederickson, the Gisbornes, Elizabeth Hitchener, T. J. Hogg, Leigh Hunt, Charles Madocks, Thomas Medwin, Charles Ollier, Sophia Stacey and E. J. Trelawny: *Forman MSS, Frederickson MSS, Gisborne MSS, Hitch. MSS, Hogg MSS, Hunt MSS, Madocks MSS, Medwin MSS, Ollier MSS, Stacey MSS, Trelawny MSS*.

Printed Sources

1811	A Gentleman of the University of Oxford, *Poetical Essay on the Existing State of Things*, London 1811 (by Shelley). Bod. [pr.] Shelley adds. d. 14.
1816	Percy Bysshe Shelley, *Alastor; or, The Spirit of Solitude: and Other Poems*, London 1816.
1817	[Anon.], *History of a Six Weeks' Tour through a Part of France, Switzerland, Germany, and Holland*, London 1817 (by Shelley and Mary Shelley).
1819	Percy Bysshe Shelley, *Rosalind and Helen, A Modern Eclogue; with Other Poems*, London 1819.
1820	Percy Bysshe Shelley, *Prometheus Unbound: A Lyrical Drama in Four Acts, with Other Poems*, London 1820.
1822	Percy Bysshe Shelley, *Hellas: A Lyrical Drama*, London 1822.
1824	*Posthumous Poems of Percy Bysshe Shelley*, [ed. Mary Shelley], London 1824.

1829	*The Poetical Works of Coleridge, Shelley, and Keats*, Paris 1829 (the Galignani edition).
1834	*The Works of Percy Bysshe Shelley*, [ed. John Ascham], 2 vols, London 1834.
1839	*The Poetical Works of Percy Bysshe Shelley*, ed. Mary Shelley, 4 vols, London 1839.
1840	*The Poetical Works of Percy Bysshe Shelley*, ed. Mary Shelley, London 1840 (a revised one-volume edition of *1839*; published in 1839).
1840 (ELTF)	Percy Bysshe Shelley, *Essays, Letters from Abroad, Translations and Fragments*, ed. Mary Shelley, 2 vols, London 1840 (published in 1839).
1846	*The Minor Poems of Percy Bysshe Shelley. A New Edition*, London 1846.
1847	*The Poetical Works of Percy Bysshe Shelley*, ed. Mary Shelley, 3 vols, London 1847.
1907	*The Poetical Works of Percy Bysshe Shelley*, ed. A. H. Koszul, 2 vols, London 1907 (the 'Everyman' edition).
1951	Shelley, *Selected Poetry, Prose and Letters*, ed. A. S. B. Glover, London 1951 (the 'Nonesuch' edition).
1964	Shelley, *Selected Poems and Prose*, ed. G. M. Matthews, Oxford 1964.
1972	*The Complete Poetical Works of Percy Bysshe Shelley*, ed. Neville Rogers (4 vols projected, only two published), vol. i, 1802–1813, Oxford 1972.
1975	*The Complete Poetical Works of Percy Bysshe Shelley*, ed. Neville Rogers, vol. ii, 1814–17, Oxford 1975.
Adonais (1821)	Percy Bysshe Shelley, *Adonais. An Elegy on the Death of John Keats, Author of Endymion, Hyperion etc.*, Pisa 1821.
Adonais (1829)	Percy Bysshe Shelley, *Adonais. An Elegy on the Death of John Keats, Author of Endymion, Hyperion, etc.*, Cambridge 1829.
Adonais (1903)	Percy Bysshe Shelley, *Adonais*, ed. William Michael Rossetti, 2nd edn, rev. with the assistance of A. O. Prickard, Oxford 1903.
Bajetta	*Peter Bell: The 1819 Texts. A Critical Edition with Commentary and Notes*, ed. Carlo M. Bajetta (Milan 2003), rev. edn 2005.
Baker	Carlos Baker, *Shelley's Major Poetry: The Fabric of a Vision*, Princeton, NJ 1948.

Barthélemy	Jean-Jacques Barthélemy, *Travels of Anacharsis the Younger in Greece*, [trans. William Beaumont] (1788), 2nd edn, 7 vols, London 1794.
Bates	E. S. Bates, *A Study of Shelley's Drama The Cenci*, New York 1908, repr. 1969.
Bieri	James Bieri, *Percy Bysshe Shelley: A Biography*, Baltimore, MD 2008.
Bieri I	James Bieri, *Percy Bysshe Shelley, A Biography: Youth's Unextinguished Fire, 1792–1816*, Cranbury, NJ 2004.
Bieri II	James Bieri, *Percy Bysshe Shelley, A Biography: Exile of Unfulfilled Renown, 1816–1822*, Cranbury, NJ 2005.
BSM	*The Bodleian Shelley Manuscripts*, gen. ed. Donald H. Reiman, 23 vols, New York 1986–2002:

vol. i, Peter Bell the Third *and* The Triumph of Life: *[parts of] Bod. MS Shelley adds. c. 5 and adds. c. 4*, ed. Donald H. Reiman, 1986 (*Box 2* and *Box 1*);

vol. ii, *Bodleian MS Shelley adds. d. 7*, ed. Irving Massey, 1987 (*Mary Copybk 1*);

vol. iii, *Bodleian MS Shelley e. 4*, ed. P. M. S. Dawson, 1987 (*Nbk 5*);

vol. iv, *Bodleian MS Shelley d. 1*, ed. E. B. Murray, 2 Parts, 1988 (*Nbk 16*);

vol. v, The Witch of Atlas *Notebook: Bodleian MS Shelley adds. e. 6*, ed. Carlene A. Adamson, 1997 (*Nbk 14*);

vol. vi, *Shelley's Pisan Winter Notebook (1820–1821): Bodleian MS Shelley adds. e. 8*, ed. Carlene A. Adamson, 1992 (*Nbk 17*);

vol. vii, '*Shelley's Last Notebook': Bodleian MS Shelley adds. e. 20, adds. e. 15 and [part of] adds. c. 4*, ed. Donald H. Reiman and Hélène Dworzan Reiman, 1990 (*Nbk 20, Nbk 13*, and *Box 1*);

vol. viii, *Bodleian MS Shelley d. 3*, ed. Tatsuo Tokoo, 1988 (*Nbk 4a*);

vol. ix, *The* Prometheus Unbound *Notebooks: Bodleian MSS Shelley e. 1, e. 2, and e. 3*, ed. Neil Fraistat, 1991 (*Nbk 7, Nbk 8* and *Nbk 9*);

vol. x, Mary Wollstonecraft Shelley, Mythological Dramas: Proserpine *and* Midas: *Bodleian MS Shelley d. 2*, ed. Charles E. Robinson (*Mary Nbk*) *and* Relation of the Death of the Family of the Cenci: *Bodleian MS Shelley adds. e. 13*, ed. Betty T. Bennett, 1992;

vol. xi, *The Geneva Notebook of Percy Bysshe Shelley: Bodleian MS Shelley adds. e. 16 and [part of] MS Shelley adds c. 4*, ed. Michael Erkelenz, 1992 (*Nbk 1* and *Box 1*);
vol. xii, *The 'Charles the First' Draft Notebook: Bodleian MS Shelley adds. e. 17*, ed. Nora Crook, 1991 (*Nbk 19*);
vol. xiii, *Drafts for* Laon and Cythna: *Bodleian MSS Shelley adds. e. 14 and adds. e. 19*, ed. Tatsuo Tokoo, 1992 (*Nbk 4* and *Nbk 2*);
vol. xiv, *Shelley's 'Devils' Notebook: Bodleian MS Shelley adds. e. 9*, ed. P. M. S. Dawson and Timothy Webb, 1993 (*Nbk 15*);
vol. xv, *The* Julian and Maddalo *Draft Notebook: Bodleian MS Shelley adds. e. 11*, ed. Steven E. Jones, 1990 (*Nbk 6*);
vol. xvi, *The* Hellas *Notebook: Bodleian MS Shelley adds. e. 7*, ed. Donald H. Reiman and Michael J. Neth, 1994 (*Nbk 21*);
vol. xvii, *Drafts for* Laon and Cythna, *Cantos V–XII: Bodleian MS Shelley adds. e. 10*, ed. Steven E. Jones, 1994 (*Nbk 3*);
vol. xviii, *The Homeric Hymns and* Prometheus *Drafts Notebook: Bodleian MS Shelley adds. e. 12*, ed. Nancy Moore Goslee, 1996 (*Nbk 11*);
vol. xix, *The* Faust *Draft Notebook: Bodleian MS Shelley adds. e. 18*, ed. Nora Crook and Timothy Webb, 1997 (*Nbk 18*);
vol. xx, *The* Defence of Poetry *Fair Copies: Bodleian MSS Shelley adds. e. 6 and adds. d. 8*, ed. Michael O'Neill, 1994 (*Nbk 14* and *Mary Copybk 3*);
vol. xxi, *Miscellaneous Poetry, Prose and Translations from Bodleian MS Shelley adds. c. 4, etc.*, ed. E. B. Murray, 1995 (mainly *Box 1*);
vol. xxii, [Additional MSS mainly in the hand of Mary Shelley], *Part One: Bodleian MS Shelley adds. d. 6, Part Two: Bodleian MS Shelley adds. c. 5* (*Box 2*), ed. Alan M. Weinberg, 2 Parts, 1997;
vol. xxiii, *A Catalogue and Index of the Shelley Manuscripts in the Bodleian Library and a General Index to the Facsimile Edition of the Bodleian Shelley Manuscripts, Volumes I–XXII* by Tatsuo Tokoo; with *Shelleyan Writing Materials in the Bodleian Library: A Catalogue*

	of Formats, Papers, and Watermarks by B. C. Barker-Benfield, 2002.
Butter (1954)	Peter Butter, *Shelley's Idols of the Cave*, Edinburgh 1954.
Butter (1970)	Percy Bysshe Shelley, *Alastor and Other Poems, Prometheus Unbound with Other Poems, Adonais*, ed. P. H. Butter, London 1970.
Byron L&J	*Byron's Letters and Journals*, ed. Leslie A. Marchand, 13 vols, London 1973–94.
Byron Prose	Lord Byron, *The Complete Miscellaneous Prose*, ed. Andrew Nicholson, Oxford 1991.
Byron PW	Lord Byron, *The Complete Poetical Works*, ed. Jerome J. McGann with Barry Weller, 7 vols, Oxford 1980–93.
Cameron (1951)	Kenneth Neill Cameron, *The Young Shelley: Genesis of a Radical* (New York 1950), 1951.
Cameron (1974)	Kenneth Neill Cameron, *Shelley: The Golden Years*, Cambridge, MA 1974.
Cenci (1819)	Percy B. Shelley, *The Cenci: A Tragedy, in Five Acts*, London 1819 (published in 1820).
Cenci (1821)	Percy Bysshe Shelley, *The Cenci: A Tragedy, in Five Acts*, 2nd edn, London 1821.
Chernaik	Judith Chernaik, *The Lyrics of Shelley*, Cleveland, OH 1972.
Claire Jnl	*The Journals of Claire Clairmont*, ed. Marion Kingston Stocking with David Mackenzie Stocking, Cambridge, MA 1968.
Clairmont Correspondence	*The Clairmont Correspondence: Letters of Claire Clairmont, Charles Clairmont, and Fanny Imlay Godwin*, ed. Marion Kingston Stocking, 2 vols, Baltimore, MD 1995.
Concordance	*A Lexical Concordance to the Poetical Works of Percy Bysshe Shelley*, compiled by F. S. Ellis, London 1892 (based on *Forman 1882*).
Cox	Jeffrey N. Cox, *Poetry and Politics in the Cockney School: Keats, Shelley, Hunt and their Circle*, Cambridge 1998.
CPPBS	*The Complete Poetry of Percy Bysshe Shelley*, ed. Donald H. Reiman and Neil Fraistat (vols i–ii, Baltimore, MD 2000, 2004), ed. Neil Fraistat

	and Nora Crook (vol. iii, Baltimore, MD 2012), ed. Nora Crook (vol. vii, Baltimore, MD 2021). Further vols in progress.
Cronin	Richard Cronin, *Shelley's Poetic Thoughts*, London 1981.
Curran (1970)	Stuart Curran, *Shelley's Cenci: Scorpions Ringed with Fire*, Princeton, NJ 1970.
Curran (1975)	Stuart Curran, *Shelley's Annus Mirabilis: The Maturing of an Epic Vision*, San Marino, CA 1975.
Darwin	Erasmus Darwin, *The Botanic Garden*, London 1791 (comprising Part I *The Economy of Vegetation*, Part II *The Loves of the Plants* (1789)).
Dawson	P. M. S. Dawson, *The Unacknowledged Legislator: Shelley and Politics*, Oxford 1980.
Donovan	*Percy Shelley: Selected Poems and Prose*, ed. Jack Donovan and Cian Duffy, London 2016.
Dowden 1890	*The Poetical Works of Percy Bysshe Shelley*, ed. Edward Dowden, London 1890.
Dowden 1891	*The Poetical Works of Percy Bysshe Shelley*, ed. Edward Dowden, London 1891.
Dowden Life	Edward Dowden, *The Life of Percy Bysshe Shelley*, 2 vols, London 1886.
Enquirer	William Godwin, *The Enquirer: Reflections on Education, Manners, and Literature, in a Series of Essays*, London 1797.
Epipsychidion (1821)	[Anon.], *Epipsychidion: Verses Addressed to the Noble and Unfortunate Lady Emilia V—— Now Imprisoned in the Convent of —*, London 1821 (by Shelley).
Esd Nbk	Percy Bysshe Shelley, *The Esdaile Notebook: A Volume of Early Poems by Percy Bysshe Shelley*, ed. Kenneth Neill Cameron (New York 1964), slightly revised, 1964.
Esd Poems	Percy Bysshe Shelley, *The Esdaile Poems*, ed. Neville Rogers, Oxford 1966.
Essays and Studies (1992)	*Percy Bysshe Shelley: Bicentenary Essays*, ed. Kelvin Everest, Cambridge 1992.
Eustace	Rev. John Chetwode Eustace, *A Classical Tour Through Italy*, 4th edn, 4 vols, London 1817.

Faust	Johann Wolfgang von Goethe, *Faust. Historisch-kritische Edition*, ed. Anne Bohnenkamp et al., with the assistance of Gerrit Brüning et al. (2018) http://faustedition.net/
Forman 1876–7	*The Poetical Works of Percy Bysshe Shelley*, ed. H. Buxton Forman, 4 vols, London 1876–7.
Forman 1880	*The Works of Percy Bysshe Shelley in Verse and Prose*, ed. H. Buxton Forman, 8 vols, London 1880.
Forman 1882	*The Poetical Works of Percy Bysshe Shelley*, ed. H. Buxton Forman, 2 vols, London 1882.
Forman 1892	*The Poetical Works of Percy Bysshe Shelley*, ed. H. Buxton Forman, 5 vols, London 1892 (the 'Aldine' edition).
Gisborne Jnl	*Maria Gisborne & Edward E. Williams, Shelley's Friends: Their Journals and Letters*, ed. Frederick L. Jones, Norman, OK 1951.
GM	Geoffrey Matthews.
GM	*Gentleman's Magazine*.
Godwin Novels	*Collected Novels and Memoirs of William Godwin*, gen. ed. Mark Philp, 8 vols, London 1992.
Godwin Writings	*Political and Philosophical Writings of William Godwin*, gen. ed. Mark Philp, 7 vols, London 1993.
Grabo (1930)	Carl Grabo, *A Newton Among Poets: Shelley's Use of Science in Prometheus Unbound*, Chapel Hill, NC 1930.
Grabo (1935)	Carl Grabo, *Prometheus Unbound: An Interpretation*, Chapel Hill, NC 1935.
Harvard Nbk (Woodberry)	*The Shelley Notebook in the Harvard College Library*. ed. George Edward Woodberry, Cambridge, MA 1929 (*Harvard Nbk 1*).
Hayward	*Faust: A Dramatic Poem, by Goethe*. [Trans. Abraham Hayward]. London 1833.
Hazlitt Works	William Hazlitt, *The Complete Works*, ed. P. P. Howe, 21 vols, London 1930–4.
Hogg	Thomas Jefferson Hogg, *The Life of Percy Bysshe Shelley*, 2 vols (two further vols announced on title-page but never published), London 1858.
Holmes	Richard Holmes, *Shelley: The Pursuit*, London 1974.

Hughes 1820	Shelley, *Poems Published in 1820*, ed. A. M. D. Hughes, 2nd edn, Oxford 1957.
Hughes	A. M. D. Hughes, *The Nascent Mind of Shelley*, Oxford 1947.
Hunt 1820	Shelley's presentation copy of *1820* to Leigh Hunt, inscribed by Hunt (now in the Huntington Library, call no. 22460).
Hunt Autobiography	*The Autobiography of Leigh Hunt; with Reminiscences of Friends and Contemporaries*, 3 vols, London 1850.
Hunt Correspondence	*The Correspondence of Leigh Hunt*, [ed. Thornton Hunt], 2 vols, London 1862.
Hunt Works	*The Selected Writings of Leigh Hunt*, gen. eds Robert Morrison and Michael Eberle-Sinatra, 6 vols, London 2003.
Huntington Nbks	*Note Books of Percy Bysshe Shelley, From the Originals in the Library of W. K. Bixby*, ed. H. Buxton Forman, 3 vols, Boston, MA 1911 (*Nbk 10*, *Nbk 12* and *Nbk 22*).
Hutchinson	*The Complete Poetical Works of Shelley*, ed. Thomas Hutchinson, Oxford 1904.
Julian	*The Complete Works of Percy Bysshe Shelley*, ed. Roger Ingpen and Walter E. Peck, 10 vols, London 1926–30 (the 'Julian' edition).
Keats Circle	*The Keats Circle: Letters and Papers, and More Letters and Poems of the Keats Circle*, ed. Hyder Edward Rollins, 2nd edn, 2 vols, Cambridge, MA 1965.
Keats L	*The Letters of John Keats, 1814–1821*, ed. Hyder Edward Rollins, 2 vols, Cambridge, MA 1958.
Kent	[Anon.], *Flora Domestica; or, The Portable Flower-Garden, with Directions for the Treatment of Plants in Pots; and Illustrations from the Works of the Poets*, London 1823 (by Elizabeth Kent).
King-Hele (1971)	Desmond King-Hele, *Shelley: His Thought and Work*, 2nd edn, London 1971.
Knerr	*Shelley's Adonais: A Critical Edition*, ed. Anthony D. Knerr, New York 1984.
K-SJ	*Keats-Shelley Journal*.
K-SMB	*Keats-Shelley Memorial Bulletin*.

K-SR	*The Keats-Shelley Review.*
L	*The Letters of Percy Bysshe Shelley*, ed. Frederick L. Jones, 2 vols, Oxford 1964.
L about S	Edward Dowden, Richard Garnett, and William Michael Rossetti, *Letters about Shelley Interchanged by Three Friends*, ed. R. S. Garnett, London 1917.
Locock Ex	C. D. Locock, *An Examination of the Shelley Manuscripts in the Bodleian Library*, Oxford 1903.
Locock 1911	*The Poems of Percy Bysshe Shelley*, ed. C. D. Locock, 2 vols, London 1911.
MA (1832)	Percy Bysshe Shelley, *The Masque of Anarchy*, ed. Leigh Hunt, London 1832.
Mac-Carthy	Denis Florence Mac-Carthy, *Shelley's Early Life*, London 1872.
Mac-Carthy (1873)	Denis Florence Mac-Carthy, *Calderon's Dramas*, London 1873.
Major Works	Percy Bysshe Shelley, *The Major Works*, ed. Zachary Leader and Michael O' Neill (Oxford 2003), reissued, 2009.
Mary Jnl	*The Journals of Mary Shelley, 1814–1844*, ed. Paula R. Feldman and Diana Scott-Kilvert, 2 vols, Oxford 1987.
Mary Jnl (Jones)	*Mary Shelley's Journal*, ed. Frederick L. Jones, Norman, OK 1947.
Mary L	*The Letters of Mary Wollstonecraft Shelley*, ed. Betty T. Bennett, 3 vols, Baltimore, MD 1980–8.
Massey	Irving Massey, *Posthumous Poems of Shelley: Mary Shelley's Fair Copy Book*, Montreal 1969 (*Mary Copybk 2*).
Medwin	Thomas Medwin, *The Life of Percy Bysshe Shelley*, 2 vols, London 1847.
Medwin (1824)	Thomas Medwin, *Conversations of Lord Byron: Noted During a Residence with his Lordship at Pisa, in the Years 1821 and 1822*, new edn, London 1824.
Medwin (1833)	*The Shelley Papers: Memoir of Percy Bysshe Shelley, by T. Medwin, Esq., and Original Poems and Papers, by Percy Bysshe Shelley, Now First Collected*, London 1833.

Medwin (1913)	Thomas Medwin, *The Life of Percy Bysshe Shelley*, ed. H. Buxton Forman, London 1913.
Morton	Timothy Morton, *Shelley and the Revolution in Taste: The Body and the Natural World*, Cambridge 1994.
MSCTS	Mary Shelley, *Collected Tales and Stories*, ed. Charles E. Robinson, Baltimore, MD 1976.
MSLL	*Mary Shelley's Literary Lives and Other Writings*, 4 vols, gen. ed. Nora Crook, London 2002.
MSW	*The Novels and Selected Works of Mary Shelley*, gen. ed. Nora Crook with Pamela Clemit, 8 vols, London 1996:

vol. i, *Frankenstein*, ed. Nora Crook, introd. Betty T. Bennett;
vol. ii, *Matilda, Dramas,* etc., ed. Pamela Clemit;
vol. iii, *Valperga*, ed. Nora Crook;
vol. iv, *The Last Man*, ed. Jane Blumberg with Nora Crook;
vol. v, *The Fortunes of Perkin Warbeck*, ed. Doucet Devin Fischer;
vol. vi, *Lodore*, ed. Fiona Stafford;
vol. vii, *Falkner*, ed. Pamela Clemit;
vol. viii, *Travel Writing, Index*, ed. Jeanne Moskal.

MWW	*The Works of Mary Wollstonecraft*, ed. Janet Todd and Marilyn Butler, 7 vols, London 1989.
MYRS	*The Manuscripts of the Younger Romantics: Shelley*, gen. ed. Donald H. Reiman, 9 vols, New York 1985–97:

vol. i, *The Esdaile Notebook*, ed. Donald H. Reiman, 1985 (*Esd*);
vol. ii, *The Mask of Anarchy*, ed. Donald H. Reiman, 1985;
vol. iii, *Hellas: A Lyrical Drama*, ed. Donald H. Reiman, 1985;
vol. iv, *The Mask of Anarchy Draft Notebook: Huntington MS HM 2177*, ed. Mary A. Quinn, 1990 (*Nbk 10*);
vol. v, *The Harvard Shelley Poetic Manuscripts*, ed. Donald H. Reiman, 1991 (*Harvard Nbk 1, Harvard Nbk 2*, and *Harvard MSS*);
vol. vi, *Shelley's 1819–1821 Huntington Notebook: Huntington MS HM 2176*, ed. Mary A. Quinn, 1994 (*Nbk 12*);

vol. vii, *Shelley's 1821–1822 Huntington Notebook: Huntington MS HM 2111*, ed. Mary A. Quinn, 1996 (*Nbk 22*);
vol. viii, *Fair-Copy Manuscripts of Shelley's Poems in European and American Libraries*, ed. Donald H. Reiman and Michael O'Neill, 1997 (includes *SDMS*);
vol. ix, *Mary Wollstonecraft Shelley: The Frankenstein Notebooks*, ed. Charles E. Robinson, 2 Parts, 1996.

New SL	*New Shelley Letters*, ed. W. S. Scott, London 1948.
Notopoulos	James A. Notopoulos, *The Platonism of Shelley: A Study of Platonism and the Poetic Mind*, Durham, NC 1949.
OSA	*Shelley: Poetical Works*, ed. Thomas Hutchinson, 2nd edn, rev. G. M. Matthews, Oxford 1970 ('Oxford Standard Authors').
OT (1820)	[Anon.], *Oedipus Tyrannus; or, Swellfoot the Tyrant. A Tragedy. In Two Acts.* London 1820 (by Shelley).
Paine Writings	*The Writings of Thomas Paine*, ed. Moncure Daniel Conway, 4 vols, New York 1894–96.
Peacock L	*The Letters of Thomas Love Peacock*, ed. Nicholas A. Joukovsky, 2 vols, Oxford 2001.
Peacock Works	*The Works of Thomas Love Peacock*, ed. H. F. B. Brett-Smith and C. E. Jones, 10 vols, London 1924–34.
Peck	Walter Edwin Peck, *Shelley: His Life and Work*, 2 vols, Boston, MA 1927.
PFMN	[Anon.], *Posthumous Fragments of Margaret Nicholson*, Oxford 1810 (by Shelley).
Political Justice	William Godwin, *Enquiry Concerning Political Justice* (1793), 3rd edn, 1798, ed. F. E. L. Priestley, 3 vols, Toronto 1946.
Prose	*Shelley's Prose; or, The Trumpet of a Prophecy*, ed. David Lee Clark (Albuquerque, NM 1954), corr. edn, Albuquerque, NM 1966.
Prose Works	*The Prose Works of Percy Bysshe Shelley*, vol. i, ed. E. B. Murray, Oxford 1993.
Recollections	E. J. Trelawny, *Recollections of the Last Days of Shelley and Byron*, London 1858.
Records	Edward John Trelawny, *Records of Shelley, Byron, and the Author*, 2 vols, London 1878.

Reflections	Edmund Burke, *Reflections on the Revolution in France* (1790), in *The Writings and Speeches of Edmund Burke*, gen. ed. Paul Langford, 9 vols, Oxford 1981–2000, vol. viii, *The French Revolution, 1790–1794*, ed. L. G. Mitchell.
Reiman (1969)	Donald H. Reiman, *Percy Bysshe Shelley*, New York 1969.
Reiman (1977)	*Shelley's Poetry and Prose*, ed. Donald H. Reiman and Sharon B. Powers, New York 1977.
Reiman (2002)	*Shelley's Poetry and Prose*, 2nd edn, ed. Donald H. Reiman and Neil Fraistat, New York 2002.
Relics	*Relics of Shelley*, ed. Richard Garnett, London 1862.
Ricci	Corrado Ricci, *Beatrice Cenci*, 2 vols, Milan 1923.
Ricci (1926)	Corrado Ricci, *Beatrice Cenci*, trans. Morris Bishop and Henry Longan Stuart, 2 vols, London 1926.
Robinson	Charles E. Robinson, *Shelley and Byron: The Snake and Eagle Wreathed in Fight*, Baltimore, MD 1976.
Rogers	Neville Rogers, *Shelley at Work: A Critical Inquiry*, Oxford 1956.
Rogers (1967)	Neville Rogers, *Shelley at Work: A Critical Inquiry*, 2nd edn, Oxford 1967.
Rognoni	Shelley, *Opere*, ed. Francesco Rognoni, Turin 1995.
Rognoni (2018a)	Percy Bysshe Shelley, *Opere poetiche*, ed. Francesco Rognoni and Valentina Varinelli, Milan 2018.
Rognoni (2018b)	Percy Bysshe Shelley, *Teatro, prose e lettere*, ed. Francesco Rognoni and Valentina Varinelli, Milan 2018.
Rossetti 1870	*The Poetical Works of Percy Bysshe Shelley*, ed. William Michael Rossetti, 2 vols, London 1870.
Rossetti 1878	*The Complete Poetical Works of Percy Bysshe Shelley*, ed. William Michael Rossetti, 3 vols, London 1878.
Ruins	Constantin-François Chasseboeuf, Comte de Volney, *The Ruins: or, A Survey of the Revolutions of Empires* (1791), 3rd edn, London 1796.
S in Eng	Roger Ingpen, *Shelley in England: New Facts and Letters from the Shelley-Whitton Papers*, London 1917.
S Memorials	*Shelley Memorials, from Authentic Sources*, ed. Lady Shelley, London 1859.
SC	*Shelley and his Circle: 1773–1822* (an edition of the manuscripts of Shelley and others in CHPL), ed. Kenneth Neill Cameron (vols i–iv, Cambridge, MA 1961–70), ed. Donald H. Reiman (vols v–viii, Cambridge, MA 1973–86), ed. Donald H. Reiman and Doucet Devin Fischer (vols ix–x, Cambridge, MA 2002). Further vols in progress.

SC followed by a number	CHPL's classification of an item in its collection.
Shelley and Mary	*Shelley and Mary*, [ed. Lady Shelley], 3 vols (sometimes 4 vols), London 1882.
Shelley Revalued	*Shelley Revalued: Essays from the Gregynog Conference*, ed. Kelvin Everest, Leicester 1983.
Shelley's Guitar	B. C. Barker-Benfield, *Shelley's Guitar: An Exhibition of Manuscripts, First Editions and Relics, to Mark the Bicentenary of the Birth of Percy Bysshe Shelley, 1792/1992*, Oxford 1992.
Shepherd 1871–5	*The Poetical Works of Percy Bysshe Shelley*, ed. R. H. Shepherd, 4 vols, London 1871–5.
Southey Life	*The Life and Correspondence of Robert Southey*, ed. Charles Cuthbert Southey, 6 vols, London 1849–50.
St Irvyne	[Anon.], *St. Irvyne; or, the Rosicrucian: A Romance*, London 1811 (by Shelley; published in 1810).
Système de la Nature	[Baron D'Holbach], *Système de la nature, ou des loix du monde physique & du monde moral* (Amsterdam 1770; attributed to Mirabaud).
Taylor	Charles H. Taylor, Jr., *The Early Collected Editions of Shelley's Poems: A Study in the History and Transmission of the Printed Text*, New Haven, CT 1958.
Thompson	*Selections from the Poems of Percy Bysshe Shelley*, ed. A. Hamilton Thompson, Cambridge 1915.
TL (GM)	'"The Triumph of Life": a New Text', ed. G. M. Matthews, *Studia Neophilologica*, xxxii (1960).
TL (Reiman)	Donald H. Reiman, *Shelley's 'The Triumph of Life': A Critical Study based on a Text Newly Edited from the Bodleian MS*, Urbana, IL 1965.
Turner	Paul Turner, 'Shelley and Lucretius', *Review of English Studies*, n. s. x (1959).
Unextinguished Hearth	*The Unextinguished Hearth: Shelley and His Contemporary Critics*, ed. Newman Ivey White, Durham, NC 1938.
V&C	[Anon.], *Original Poetry by Victor and Cazire*, Worthing 1810 (by Shelley and his sister Elizabeth; edition withdrawn).

V&C (1898)	*Original Poetry by Victor and Cazire*, ed. Richard Garnett, London 1898.
V&P	*Verse and Prose from the Manuscripts of Percy Bysshe Shelley*, ed. Sir John C. E. Shelley-Rolls and Roger Ingpen, London 1934.
Viviani della Robbia	Enrica Viviani della Robbia, *Vita di una donna (L'Emily di Shelley)*, Florence 1936.
Walker	Adam Walker, *A System of Familiar Philosophy*, London 1799.
Wasserman	Earl R. Wasserman, *Shelley: A Critical Reading*, Baltimore, MD 1971.
Webb	Timothy Webb, *The Violet in the Crucible: Shelley and Translation*, Oxford 1976.
Webb (1977)	Timothy Webb, *Shelley: A Voice Not Understood*, Manchester 1977.
Webb (1995)	Percy Bysshe Shelley, *Poems and Prose*, ed. Timothy Webb, London 1995.
White	Newman Ivey White, *Shelley*, 2 vols, New York 1940.
Woodberry 1892	*The Complete Poetical Works of Percy Bysshe Shelley*, ed. George Edward Woodberry, 4 vols, Boston, MA 1892.
Woodberry 1893	*The Complete Poetical Works of Percy Bysshe Shelley*, ed. George Edward Woodberry, 4 vols, London 1893.
Woodberry (1901)	*The Complete Poetical Works of Percy Bysshe Shelley*, ed. George Edward Woodberry, Boston, MA 1901 (the 'Cambridge' edition).
Woodberry (1909)	Percy Bysshe Shelley, *The Cenci*, ed. George Edward Woodberry, Boston, MA 1909.
Wordsworth Prose	*The Prose Works of William Wordsworth*, ed. W. J. B. Owen and Jane Worthington Smyser, 3 vols, Oxford 1974.
Worthen	John Worthen, *The Life of Percy Bysshe Shelley: A Critical Biography*, Chichester 2019.
Zillman Text	*Shelley's Prometheus Unbound: The Text and the Drafts*, ed. Lawrence John Zillman, New Haven, CT 1968.

Zillman Variorum   *Shelley's Prometheus Unbound: A Variorum Edition*, ed. Lawrence John Zillman, Seattle, WA 1959.

Further editorial abbreviations that are unique to the commentary on a poem are identified in the headnote or notes to that poem.

Unless otherwise stated, all quotations from Greek and Latin texts, and their translations, are from the most recent Loeb Classical Library edition. In the case of Theocritus, Moschus and Bion, A. S. F. Gow, ed., *Bvcolici Graeci* (1952) is used for the Greek text, and the same scholar's *The Greek Bucolic Poets* (1953) for the translation. The sources of translations from Dante's *Divina commedia* (*Inferno*, *Purgatorio* and *Paradiso*), Goethe's *Faust*, Calderón's *El mágico prodigioso* and Petrarch's lyric poems are respectively and unless otherwise stated: *The Vision of Dante* [1814], trans. Henry Cary, ed. Ralph Pite (1994); *Hayward*; *Mac-Carthy (1873)*; and *Petrarch's Lyric Poems: The Rime Sparse and Other Lyrics*, ed. Robert M. Durling (1976).

THE POEMS

409 'In the great morning of the world'

The two MS witnesses to these lines are transcripts by Mary in *Mary Copybk 1*. She copied one version as follows beneath the heading 76 on p. 46 (for a facsimile and transcription, see *BSM* ii 94–5), subsequently adding a pencilled cross to the right of the heading and an ink cross to the right of the first line:

> *In the great morning of the world*
> *The Spirit of God was moving upon chaos,*
> *And from his flag unfurled*
> *The Anarch Desolation with his [   ]*
> *Scared from their dark [   ]*
> *Fled like a flock of vultures from an [?]*

BSM conjectures the final word to be 'herse'. A second version, which is the basis of the text below, is copied overleaf on p. 47 of *Mary Copybk 1* beneath a short horizontal line in ink that separates it from her transcript of *As the sunrise to the night* (no. 410) above.

The basis of what Mary copied on p. 46 would appear to be a draft by S. that was reworked by him into the version she copied on p. 47. There would then appear to have been a subsequent reworking in a now lost fair copy of *Hellas* (no. 411) in S.'s hand that formed the basis of these lines in the press copy of *Hellas* by Edward Williams in *HM 329* p. 3 (for a facsimile, see *MYRS* iii 25):

> *In the great morning of the world*
> *The spirit of God with might unfurled*
> *The flag of Freedom over chaos*
> *And all its banded anarchs fled*
> *Like Vultures frighted from Imaus*
> *Before an Earthquake's tread. —*

The above passage, published as *Hellas* 46–51, is among the lines of the poem for which no draft in S.'s hand has been located. Given that apart from these lines, along with some (lines 52–93), that follow, all lines of the poem have a basis in drafts in the surviving leaves of *Nbk 21* (see the note to those lines, *BSM* xxiii 262–3 and *BSM* xvi pp. xxiii–xxvi), it would appear that some or all of ll. 46–93 were drafted on a leaf, or leaves, of *Nbk 21* subsequently removed and now lost. Another possibility is that some or all of them (including ll. 46–51) were drafted elsewhere. It may be inferred from

DOI: 10.4324/9781315779874-2

the position of Mary's transcript of the present lines in *Mary Copybk 1* in relation to the two poems she copied immediately before and after them in her notebook — *To Emilia Viviani* (no. 393) on pp. 45–6 and *Epithalamium* (no. 401) on pp. 47–8 — that their basis, like that of these two poems, was draft in S.'s hand in *Nbk 20*. *Nbk 20* in its present state shows evidence of many losses, making it impossible to date conclusively the period during which it was used, though the material on the notebook's leaves that survive appears to have been written between February and June 1821 (see *BSM* xxiii 53 and *BSM* vii 112–21). In the case of the two versions of the present lines in *Mary Copybk 1* there is thus some evidence to support the idea that they were not composed during the period in which *Lines connected with Hellas* (no. 411 Appendix) and *Hellas* were drafted in *Nbk 21* (i.e. between late August and October 1821). Instead they may have been composed earlier, on a leaf or leaves of *Nbk 20* which, after Mary made her transcriptions in *Mary Copybk 1* between autumn 1822 and autumn 1823 (see *BSM* xxiii 55), were removed or became detached and lost. One further piece of evidence that identifies the present lines with other writing in *Nbk 20* is the parallel between the first two of them and *Adonais* (no. 403) 166–7: 'From the great morning of the world when first / God dawned on Chaos'. One draft of the stanza (XIX) of *Adonais* containing these lines is found in *Nbk 20* f. 23^v (see *BSM* vii 276–7), another, including these exact words, is in f. 28^v (see *BSM* vii 322–3). Massey's assertion that the lines from *Adonais* 'evidently [represent] the first germ of the image' (*BSM* ii 230) implies that lines 1–2 were re-worked for *Hellas* which was drafted between late September and late October 1821. However, since *Adonais* was drafted in mid-May, S.'s lost draft of the present lines may date from that period too.

Text from *Mary Copybk 1* p. 47.

Published in *BSM* ii 96–7 (facsimile and transcription of MS).

'In the great morning of the world'

In the great morning of the world
The Spirit of God first unfurled
The flag of Freedom over chaos,
And all its million anarchs fled,

¶ 409 1–3. Cp. *Adonais* 166–7, discussed in the headnote above.
3. *Freedom*] freedom *Mary Copybk 1*. *chaos*,] chaos *Mary Copybk 1*.

5   Like vultures frightened from Imaus
    Before an Earthquake's tread.

410 'As the sunrise to the night'

[Fragment: To Italy]

The sole MS witness to this fragment is on pp. 46–7 of *Mary Copybk 1* where it appears beneath the heading 77 with an ink cross in the right margin alongside the first line (see *BSM* ii 94–5). On p. 47, the fragment ends above a short horizontal line in ink that separates it from *In the great morning of the world* (no. 409) below. Massey suggests that these lines, like *In the great morning of the world* 'may also have been part of the draftings for this chorus in *Hellas*' (*BSM* ii 231), i.e. the one that starts at *Hellas* (no. 411) 46. However, for reasons discussed in the headnote to *In the great morning of the world*, the holograph which formed the basis of Mary's transcript was probably made on a now lost leaf or leaves from *Nbk 20*, the surviving parts of which contain material dating from between February and June 1821, not during the period between late August and October 1821 when *Lines connected with Hellas* (no. 411 Appendix) and *Hellas* were composed.

These lines were first published by Richard Garnett in the 'Miscellaneous Fragments' section of *Relics* without a title and numbered 'XXV'. Garnett's date of 1819 (*Relics* 83) was accepted by late nineteenth- and early twentieth-century editors. Forman, taking the place referred to in l. 5 as authority, entitled them 'Fragment: To Italy'. In line with this characterisation of the poem, GM suggested that they were composed in February or early March

5–6. Cp. *Paradise Lost* iii 431–6:

> As when a vulture on Imaus bred,
> Whose snowy ridge the roving Tartar bounds,
> Dislodging from a region scarce of prey
> To gorge the flesh of lambs or yeanling kids
> On hills where flocks are fed, flies toward the springs
> Of Ganges, or Hydaspes, Indian streams;

5. *Imaus*] According to Pliny, *Nat. Hist.* v 27, the name of part of Mount Taurus ('Himaeus' = 'Himalaya'), an extensive mountain range in Asia. Pliny states that Imaus 'in the vernacular means "snowy"' (*Nat. Hist.* vi 64).
6. *tread.*] tread *Mary Copybk 1*; head *BSM*.

1821 to 'hail the Italian rising', that is, the struggle of the Neapolitans against the Austrians for which S. expressed hope in his letter to Claire of 18 February 1821 (*L* ii 266-7) discussed in the headnote to *Sonnet: Political Greatness* (no. 342). However, such a date is not entirely convincing given the juxtaposition of these lines in *Mary Copybk 1* with *In the great morning of the world*. Instead, it is more likely that the reference to 'Everlasting Italy' was made after the failure of the Neapolitan revolution — the army of the Neapolitan constitutionalists was defeated at Rieti on 7 March 1821 (see the headnote to *Ode to Naples* (no. 343)). A composition date of May 1821, similar to *In the great morning of the world*, is possible given that notwithstanding the suppression of the Neapolitan revolution, S. explained to Byron in a letter of 4 May 1821 that he retained hope of Italian liberty: 'This attempt in Italy has certainly been a most unfortunate business. With no strong personal reasons to interest me, my disappointment on public grounds has been excessive. But I cling to moral and political hope, like a drowner to a plank' (*L* ii 290-1).

Text from *Mary Copybk 1* pp. 46-7. Indentation follows Mary's transcript.

Published in *Relics* 83 (ll. 1-6); *Rossetti 1870* ii 326-7 (ll. 1-6); *Forman 1876-7* iv 15 (ll. 1-6, entitled 'Fragment: To Italy'); *BSM* ii 94-7 (facsimile and transcription of MS).

'As the sunrise to the night'

    As the sunrise to the night,
        As the north wind to the clouds,
    As the Earthquake's fiery flight,
        Ruining mountain solitudes,
5   Everlasting Italy,
    Be those hopes and fears on thee,
    Like a tempest on the sea,
    Like an atom of that Chaos
    Which when God first dawned
10 Drove with shafts of barbed light

¶ 410 *Title.* See headnote.
3. *Earthquake's*] earthquake's *Relics. fiery*] fury *BSM*.
4. *solitudes,*] *Relics*; Solitudes *Mary Copybk 1*.
5. *Italy,*] *Relics*; Italy *Mary Copybk 1*.
6. *those*] Written after *that* canc. in *Mary Copybk 1. thee,*] thee *Mary Copybk 1*; thee. *Relics*; thee! *Rossetti 1870*.
7. *sea,*] sea *Mary Copybk 1*.

411 Hellas

A Lyrical Drama

Date of composition. Medwin recalls that *Hellas* 'had been written during the autumn' of 1821 (*Medwin (1913)* 353). This statement accords with S.'s letter to Horace Smith of 11 April 1822 in which he describes it as 'a poem written on the Greek cause last summer' (*L* ii 411). '[T]he Greek cause last summer' suggests the poem's composition was prompted by the defeat of Alexandros Ypsilantis's Sacred Battalion at the battle of Dragatsani which took place on 7 June (according to the Julian calendar). The Greek 'Revolution', sometimes referred to as the 'war of independence', had begun in March 1821 when Ypsilantis entered Jassy, the capital of Moldavia (one of the principalities of the Ottoman Empire, in *mod.* Romania) with a small band of followers and issued a proclamation of war against the Turks. This prompted a wave of uprisings by Greeks across mainland Greece and the islands that was followed in the spring by Turkish reprisals and months of intensely violent conflict between the two sides. Newspaper reports of Ypsilantis's defeat at Dragatsani must have reached S. soon after 20 July (see note to Preface ll. 42–43) and apparently led him to believe that the publication of a poem could raise awareness among a British readership that the Revolution was in jeopardy. Composition is likely to have begun after *It is the period when all the Sons of God* (Prologue to Hellas) (*Lines connected with Hellas* (no. 411 Appendix) A) and *Lines connected with Hellas* B-G, probably drafted after S. returned from visiting Byron at Ravenna in late August, had been abandoned. Holmes suggests S. began to write between 5 and 9 October when he went to Livorno to stay with Claire (*Holmes* 677; *Claire Jnl* 249), although a late September start-date seems possible. S. informed Ollier of *Hellas* in a letter of 11 October, asking him to advertise it immediately and requesting prompt publication: 'My dramatic poem called "Hellas" will soon be ready—You may advertise it, and as the subject is in a certain degree of a transitory nature, I send it to you, instead of printing it here, in the full confidence that you will at my request not delay to send it to the press' (*L* ii 356–7). Nearly a fortnight later, in a letter of 22 October, he told John Gisborne that he 'was just finishing' the poem (*L* ii 363). On 11 November S. sent Ollier the transcript which Edward Williams had made between 6 and 10 November (*L* ii 365; *Gisborne Jnl* 110–11). S. may have drafted the Notes as late as the day before he posted the transcript to Ollier (see 'Manuscript evidence').

DOI: 10.4324/9781315779874-4

Manuscript evidence. Most lines of the poem are roughly drafted in *Nbk 21* (for indexes of the pages containing them, see *BSM* xxiii 201–5 and 261–3). However, the holograph draft of ll. 46–93 (the first Chorus) is not extant. Apart from Williams's transcript the only authority for its opening six lines, treated in the present edition as a separate item (*In the great morning of the world*, no. 409), is Mary's transcription in *Mary Copybk 1*. The sole authority for ll. 52–93 is Williams's transcript. S.'s draft of ll. 46–51 may originally have been in *Nbk 20*, given the evidence discussed in the headnote to *In the great morning of the world*. But the location of S.'s rough draft of ll. 52–93 is not possible to determine. It seems almost certain that a fair draft of the poem by S. was the basis of Williams's transcript. If so, and as surmised by E. B. Murray (*BSM* xxi 442), it may have been written on bifolia similar to the *Box 1* ff. 14–15 bifolium containing Notes 4, 6 and 7 and part of Note 8 in S.'s hand, and the mutilated *Box 1* ff. 61–2 bifolium containing a draft of the poem's title and epigraph in Williams's hand (for the material characteristics of these two bifolia, see *BSM* xxiii 82–3). Although a holograph draft of only some of the Notes survives (and Murray, using evidence from Williams's transcript, offers a credible explanation in *BSM* xxi 442 of why Note 6 follows Note 4 in *Box 1* f. 14), it seems likely that the remainder of the Notes were written on another bifolium enclosing ff. 14–15. S. headed Notes 6, 7 and 8 'Page 37' in *Box 1* f. 14^v, 'Page 48' (f. 15^r) and 'Page 49' (f. 15^v), the first two numbers corresponding to the page numbers of Williams's transcript containing the lines of the poem to which Notes 6 and 7 are keyed: 814 and 1060. There is a discrepancy between the number of the page of the transcript containing line 1090 to which Note 8 is keyed (50) and S.'s 'Page 49' in *Box 1* but this may simply have been a scribal error. There is thus strong evidence that S. drafted the Notes to *Hellas* after Williams had finished copying the poem which was on 9 November when he wrote 'Continue writing and finish' in his journal. S. may have drafted them as late as 10 November when Williams's journal records 'Finish the notes and preface to "Hellas"' (*Gisborne Jnl* 111) rather than October 1821, as Murray supposes (*BSM* xxi 442). For discussion of Williams's draft of the title and epigraph, see the notes and the headnote to *A capering, squalid, squalling one* (no. 419).

Williams's transcript remained in Ollier's family after his death in 1859 and was purchased by F. S. Ellis for Frederick Locker-Lampson at the Puttick & Simpson sale of Ollier's papers in July 1877 (William Michael Rossetti, entry for 20 March 1878, Diaries, Box 15-3, Angeli-Dennis Collection, The Library of the University of British Columbia Special Collections Division). Its whereabouts were noted in several publications of 1886 including *The Rowfant Library* (214), Forman's *The Shelley Library* (106) and an edition of *Hellas* published for the Shelley Society by Thomas Wise (*Wise*), who noted that '[t]o the textual student the preservation of this manuscript [...] must ever remain cause for sincere congratulation' (xxiii). Rossetti borrowed Williams's transcript from Locker-Lampson in October 1878 to read 'against my text line by line', commenting '[t]here is not *much* to be learned from it, yet quite enough to make the collation useful and requisite' (*Selected Letters of William Michael Rossetti*, ed. Roger W. Peattie (1990) 372 n. 3). Ollier's son, Edmund, in a note dated 25 May 1877, now in The Huntington Library, San Marino, California, commented 'not in Shelley's own writing, but with occasional corrections and additions in his hand' (HM 20104 f. 1^r). Rossetti's additional note on the same leaf shows he was the first to authenticate it: 'The handwriting of the Hellas is, to the best of my recollection, the same as that of the drama wh. Lieut. Williams composed, named *A Year, a Month, and a Day*, now in the possession of Trelawny. I therefore confidently assume that the Hellas is written by Williams' (HM 20104 f. 1^v). While the notes in *Rossetti (1878)* ii 455–6 confirm Rossetti consulted Williams's transcript, Reiman's judgement that he 'seems not to have made many serious corrections of his text on the basis of the manuscript' (*MYRS* iii 6) seems fair.

Williams's transcript was purchased at the Huntington-Bixby-Church sale in March 1916 (see https://hdl.huntington.org/digital/collection/p151 50coll7/id/10834) and is in The Huntington Library (call number: HM 329, hereafter *HM 329*). *HM 329* was first subject to scholarly scrutiny by Bennett Weaver in 'The Williams Transcription of *Hellas*', *Essays and Studies in English and Comparative Literature by Members of the English Department of the University of Michigan* (1932) 151–68, having earlier been consulted at the Huntington by Ingpen and Peck although their text of *Hellas* is based on *1822* and only in two cases adopts readings from *HM 329* (*Julian* iii 311–12). A photo-facsimile of *HM 329* (without a diplomatic transcription) with annotations and an introduction by Reiman was published in 1985 and high-quality images were made available through the Huntington Digital Library in 2015 via the URL above. Reiman describes the material characteristics, dimensions and watermarks of the laid paper of *HM 329* and the physical evidence that shows it served as press copy for *Hellas* in *MYRS* iii 11–12. His judgement that we need to 'take seriously the priority of the manuscript that Shelley had helped to prepare and that—far more than a printed volume for which he saw no proofs—has the right to be considered the best copy text for the poem' *MYRS* iii 7) is incontrovertible. While *HM 329* is in Williams's hand, there are corrections, substitutions and additions in S.'s hand. In some instances, recorded in the notes, it is difficult to say whether a revision, be it cancellation alone or cancellation and substitution, is in S.'s hand or Williams's, though S.'s interventions are usually distinctive and in darker ink. Self-corrections that are evidently in Williams's hand are not recorded in the notes below unless they have been identified as S.'s by a previous editor. *HM 329* is also of interest because it contains evidence of handling by printers (ink stains are noted by Reiman in *MYRS* iii 12) as well as words, letters and numbers in an unidentified hand or hands, probably that of a compositor or compositors (see the notes to Preface l. 44 and to ll. 298, 653 and 995). Reiman further notes that *HM 330*, Mary's transcript of *Written on hearing the news of the death of Napoleon* (no. 407), which was printed after *Hellas* in *1822*, is written on the same kind of paper as *HM 329* and S.'s letters to Byron and Horace Smith of 14 September 1821, now in CHPL (call numbers: PBS 0076 and PBS 0075; *MYRS* iii 85, 11; *L* ii 346–50).

B. C. Barker-Benfield's suggestion that the material characteristics of *HM 329* may be comparable to those of the *Box 1* ff. 14–15 and 60–1 bifolia discussed above (*BSM* xxiii 82–3) can now be verified: the *Box 1* ff. 14–15 bifolium is in exactly the same format as *HM 329*. Barker-Benfield's further comment (in 2002) that 'Although Huntington HM 329–30 now comprise singletons with torn edges, it would be interesting to investigate whether these were originally written in booklet form, or at least before the leaves were separated' (*BSM* xxiii 60 n. 3) led to a meeting in 2014 of him and the present editors in the Bodleian Library after they had consulted the originals of *HM 329* and *HM 330* at the Huntington. Together they re-constructed the original make-up of the home-made gatherings (quires) comprising thirty-five leaves containing the transcripts of *Hellas* and *Written on hearing the news of the death of Napoleon* that S. posted to Ollier on 11 November. This has enabled an alternative way of describing *HM 329* to Reiman's in *MYRS* iii 12 to be provided. It should be noted that the numbering of the folios below does not correspond to the numbering of *HM 329* where Williams inserted arabic numerals at the top of every recto and verso of each leaf of the verse and Notes, and roman numerals at the top of each recto (apart from the first) and each verso of leaves of the Preface; the arabic numerals on the recto of each leaf of the preliminaries appear to have been added subsequently, perhaps by a compositor or, as Reiman speculates (*MYRS* iii 12), after acquisition by the Huntington. Williams's numbering is noted in square brackets in what follows. The first home-made gathering of four leaves comprises the Preface (ff. 2^r-5^r [pp. [i] and ii–vii]) and the Dedication (f. 5^v); the second gathering, the title and epigraph (f. 1ʳ), Dramatis Personae (f. 1ᵛ) and lines 1–113 (ff. 6ʳ-8ᵛ [pp. 1–6]); the third gathering (ff. 9ʳ-12ᵛ [pp. 7–14]), lines 114–281; the fourth gathering (ff. 13ʳ-16ᵛ [pp. 15–22]), lines 282–469; the fifth gathering (ff. 17ʳ-20ᵛ [pp. 23–30]), lines 470–667; the sixth gathering (ff. 21ʳ-24ᵛ [pp. 31–8]), lines 668–847; the seventh gathering (ff. 25ʳ-28ᵛ [pp. 39–46]), lines 848–1022; the first single leaf (f. 29ʳ⁻ᵛ [pp. 47–8]), lines 1023–65; the second single leaf (f. 30ʳ⁻ᵛ [pp. 49–50]), lines 1066–1101; the eighth gathering (ff. 31ʳ-34ʳ [pp. 51–7]), the Notes, with f. 34ᵛ a blank; the third single leaf, comprising Mary's transcript of *Written on hearing the news of the death of Napoleon* (*HM 330*). This reconstruction allows for Williams's last-minute insertions of the Preface and Dedication (ff. 2ʳ-5ᵛ, perhaps tucked in after the title and Dramatis Personae of f. 1ʳ⁻ᵛ) and Notes (ff. 31ʳ-34ʳ, with 34ᵛ blank) in two separate gatherings at the beginning and end. The two single leaves at ff. 29 and 30 are anomalies, most likely because they are the last two leaves of the main text; their two conjoint leaves, if blank (not enough to contain the seven pages of Notes), might have been removed almost immediately, to reduce bulk in postage.

Publication. Referring to S.'s acknowledgement to Ollier in a letter of 11 April 1822 that *1822* 'in general is more correct than my other books' (*L* ii 410), Reiman comments: 'Of all the poems of Percy Bysshe Shelley that were published in England while he was living in Italy, *Hellas* is the only one about which he expressed himself satisfied with its textual accuracy.' Reiman's further assertion that 'the chief reason for the relative accuracy of Shelley's text in the *Hellas* volume' is the hand-writing of his amanuensis, 'clearer than that of either Percy or Mary W. Shelley' (*MYRS* iii 1) is persuasive. One may infer from the impatient tone of S.'s letter to Ollier of 11 November that he considered the deployment of Williams as copyist a means of expediting publication, his clear hand minimising difficulties for the printers and precluding the need for extensive intervention at proof-stage:

> I send you the Drama of Hellas, relying on your assurance that you will be good enough to pay immediate attention to my *literary* requests.—What little interest this Poem may ever excite, depends upon it's *immediate* publication; I entreat you therefore to have the goodness to send the Ms. instantly to a Printer, & the moment you get a proof, dispatch it to me by the Post. The whole might be sent at once […]. (*L* ii 365)

Because proofs had not been forthcoming, S's letter to John Gisborne of 10 April assumes (possibly correctly) that Gisborne must have taken responsibility for seeing *1822* through the press in London:

> I have received Hellas, which is prettily printed, & with fewer mistakes than any poem I ever published. Am I to thank you for the revision of the press? or who acted as midwife to this last of my orphans, introducing it to oblivion, & me to my accustomed failure? May the cause it celebrates be more fortunate than either!— (*L* ii 406)

Hellas had been published as an octavo pamphlet probably between late February and late March 1822. The dates can be surmised from Mary telling Maria Gisborne that 'We received Hellas today' on 10 April (*Mary L* i 229) — the time it took mail to travel between London and Pisa at this time was usually 'two weeks to twenty days' (*MYRS* iii 81) — and the Ollier brothers informing John Gisborne in a meeting shortly before 19 February that the poem 'will be out in a few days' (*Gisborne Jnl* 81). As noted in 'Date of composition', S. had begun to assail Ollier with demands that he publish the poem promptly on 11 October. His frustration is evident in a letter of 11 January, two months after he had posted Williams's transcript: 'I had exceedingly desired the immediate publication of "Hellas" from public no less than private reasons; but as post-day after post-day passes and I receive no proof-sheets of it as I had requested, I suppose I might as well not have relied upon your spontaneous offers to execute my commissions' (*L* ii 372). On 25 January, having asked Hunt 'if Ollier has published *Hellas*' (*L* ii 382), he informed Horace Smith that 'Ollier's conduct has at length compelled me to cashier him', acknowledging that 'I suppose this will occasion some delay in the publication of *Hellas*' (*L* ii 379). The following day he wrote to John Gisborne: 'I will have nothing more to do with Ollier on *whatever terms* or for *whatever apology*. And as the books are my property I would rather that they were burnt than that they remained in his possession' (*L* ii 387–8). He had already instructed Gisborne a fortnight earlier 'to discover whether [Ollier] has printed and published the poem of "Hellas", and if not to give it to some other publisher' (*L* ii 375). But S. was in no position to extricate himself from Ollier. As Gisborne told him in a letter of 19 February, the Olliers 'think the balance against you is from 50£. to 60£.' (*Gisborne Jnl* 80) and no alternative publisher could be found. Charles Robinson has shown that Ollier held no animus towards S. at this time but was struggling to maintain his business; *Hellas* was one of only five books published by the Ollier brothers in 1822 ('Percy Bysshe Shelley, Charles Ollier, and William

Blackwood: the contexts of early nineteenth-century publishing', *Shelley Revalued* 208). Robinson conjectures that 'Ollier, lacking operating funds in 1822, would have printed [*Hellas*] in no more than 250 copies (and perhaps no more than 100)' (*Shelley Revalued* 210). The printing of Williams's transcript, the costs of which, Robinson notes, Ollier is likely to have borne (*Shelley Revalued* 209), was of significance for the poem's textual history. A copy of *Hellas* at the Berg Collection in New York Public Library contains a pencilled note at the top of the title-page: 'Suppressed Copy. To be taken care of. C.O.'. Purchased in 1935, the Berg copy that once belonged to Ollier is one of three copies of the unexpurgated edition of *1822* (*1822 Unexpurgated*) that the present editors have examined; the other two are in the Huntington Library (the C. W. Frederickson copy, call number: 54530) and the Sterling Library, University of London (classmark: [S.L.] I [Shelley – 1817]). The differences between *1822 Unexpurgated* and *1822* show Ollier to have exceeded the instructions given by S. in his letter of 11 November: 'If any passages should alarm you in the notes, you are at liberty to suppress them; the *Poem* contains nothing of a tendency to danger' (*L* ii 365). There are three differences between *1822 Unexpurgated* and *1822*. In *1822*, the penultimate paragraph of the Preface is removed; the words in the second half of line 1091 and lines 1092–3 in the sixth stanza of the final Chorus are replaced with asterisks; and Note 8 (keyed to line 1090) is cut extensively and edited. It may have been an oversight on Ollier's part that led to the printing of Williams's transcript entire instead of the material to be suppressed being marked up for the attention of the printer before the volume went to press. But it is notable that none of the excisions of text from *1822 Unexpurgated* entailed changes to the pagination of *1822*. Costs (for S. ultimately, but more immediately for the Olliers) that would have been incurred in a major re-setting were thus avoided.

The textual history of *Hellas* between *1822* and *Reiman (2002)* is tangled in a way that is characteristic of S.'s writings. His letter to Ollier of 11 April 1822, which contained a list of errata (*Errata*), was purchased by Ellis for Frederickson at the Puttick & Simpson sale of 1877 (Seymour de Ricci, *A Bibliography of Shelley's Letters Published and Unpublished* (1927) 203; *Woodberry 1893* iii 481). The first edition of *Hellas* that mostly followed *Errata* was *Rossetti 1878* (for the exception, see the note to l. 620) while the first which incorporated them all was *Woodberry 1893*. Sold at the Frederickson sale of 1897 (de Ricci, 203), the letter was later acquired by the Huntington (call number: HM 20152).

The texts of Mary's editions of *Hellas* were obviously wanting because Ollier had in his possession *Errata* as well as Williams's transcript. After S.'s death, Peacock promised her in a letter of 2 September 1822 that he would 'procure the M.S.S. from Ollier', which Nicholas Joukovsky presumes to mean 'the MSS of works that Shelley had sent to Charles Ollier, but that Ollier had not published, including "Julian and Maddalo", "The Witch of Atlas", and a number of shorter poems' (*Peacock L* i 191 and 191 n. 9). Peacock's letter to Mary of 15 April 1823 refers to having 'sent your box a month ago' containing 'the M.S.S. from Ollier' and 'the six copies of *Hellas*' (*Peacock L* i 195). These arrived 'shortly before [Mary] left Italy' for London in July 1823 (*Taylor* 1). The manuscripts from Ollier clearly did not include either Williams's transcript or *Errata*. But among the six copies of *Hellas* to which Peacock refers were four of *1822 Unexpurgated*, if her recollection in a letter to Ollier of 13 February 1839, as she prepared her first collected edition, was correct:

> You may remember when Hellas was published certain verses & a portion of a note were omitted. A few copies containing these were struck off—four you sent to Italy—I have given or lent them & do not possess a perfect copy—Do you? If you do & would lend it me <u>immediately</u> I should feel very greatly obliged. (*Mary L* ii 310)

On the basis of his collation, Taylor supposes that it was *1829* which 'served as printer's copy for the 1839 text of *Hellas*' (*Taylor* 40). However, this claim needs some qualification. While Mary lacked a copy of *1822 Unexpurgated*, on 13 February 1839 she may have recalled writing to Cyrus Redding in September 1829 with 'a suppressed stanza of Hellas' (*Mary L* ii 86), indicating that she supplied for *1829* the words replaced by asterisks in ll. 1091–3 in *1822*. However, as the notes below demonstrate, the text of ll. 1091–3 in *1829* does not correspond with *1822 Unexpurgated* nor does the text of *1839* follow *1829*. The wording of her letter to Redding might suggest that she transcribed the words missing in *1822* from a copy of *1822 Unexpurgated* then in her possession. But if that were the case, the three substantive differences between *1829* and *1822 Unexpurgated* cannot be explained satisfactorily. While the word 'native' for 'votive' in l. 1095 could be a compositor's mis-reading of Mary's hand, 'wise' for 'bright' (l. 1091) and 'unwithstood' for 'unsubdued' (l. 1093) are all but impossible to fathom. One explanation for the *1829* readings could lie in Taylor's observation regarding *Hellas* that 'the editors of the Paris edition […] introduced […] many more variants into this text than elsewhere'

(*Taylor* 61). Another, much more convincing, is that the 'suppressed stanza' sent to Redding was imperfectly recalled by Mary which, in turn, would suggest that she no longer possessed a copy of *1822 Unexpurgated* in September 1829. To be able to supply the reading of ll. 1091–3 in *1839* (which corresponds with *1822 Unexpurgated* apart from two differences in punctuation), she could have consulted S.'s rough draft of the stanza in *Nbk 21* p. 201. But the fact that most of Note 8 as well as ll. 1091–3 in full appear in *1839* — the second volume of which, containing *Hellas*, was published by 8 March (*Taylor* 34 n. 3) — suggests that she was indeed able to obtain a copy of *1822 Unexpurgated* soon after 13 February 1839 either from Ollier or by some other means. If she did so, she chose not to publish the penultimate paragraph of the Preface and did not provide a completely unsuppressed text of Note 8. The suppressed paragraph of the Preface was restored in *Forman 1892* iv and the following year by Woodberry from the copy of *1822 Unexpurgated* 'in the possession of Mr. C. W. Frederickson' (*Woodberry 1893* iii 96). However, one word in Williams's transcript was not published in any edition of *Hellas* until 2002. In *1839* Mary replaced 'Demon' in the text of Note 8 in the unexpurgated edition with 'power', which has no authority. There it remained until *Reiman (2002)* published the only text of this Note to date that is authorised by Williams's transcript in respect of substantives. On Williams's transcript and the poem's publication history, see Michael Rossington, 'The Publication of *Hellas*', *Romanticism* xxx (2024) 81–92.

Biographical context. The familiarity of the Shelleys with Alexandros Mavrokordatos (1791–1865) between December 1820 and June 1821 is a vital context for the poem. Mary recalled them becoming friendly with this distinguished refugee in Pisa in her 'Note on Hellas':

> We had formed the acquaintance at Pisa of several Constantinopolitan Greeks, of the family of Prince Caradja, formerly Hospodar of Wallachia, who, hearing that the bowstring, the accustomed finale of his viceroyalty, was on the road to him, escaped with his treasures, and took up his abode in Tuscany. Among these was the gentleman to whom the drama of Hellas is dedicated. Prince Mavrocordato was warmed by those aspirations for the independence of his country, which filled the hearts of many of his countrymen. (*1839* ii 345)

Mavrokordatos was introduced to the Shelleys on 2 December 1820 (*Mary Jnl* i 341; *Claire Jnl* 191) by Francesco Pacchiani (1771–1835), Professor of Logic, Metaphysics and Theoretical Philosophy at the University of

Pisa and a poet. The Shelleys had become acquainted with Pacchiani on 24 November (*Claire Jnl* 187; *Mary Jnl* i 341) and he introduced Claire to Teresa Viviani on 29 November (see headnote to *Epipsychidion*, no. 391) and the Shelleys and Claire to Tommaso Sgricci on 1 December (*Claire Jnl* 190; *Mary Jnl* i 341). Mavrokordatos was nephew of Prince Ioannis Karatzas, Hospodar of the province of Wallachia and 'owed the courtesy title "prince" to his uncle' in whose administration he served (Roderick Beaton, *Byron's War: Romantic Rebellion, Greek Revolution* (2013) 69). Mavrokordatos, along with Karatzas and his family, had been forced to flee Bucharest (capital of Wallachia), for Geneva in 1818 then, in 1819, took up residence in Pisa where the influential Bishop Ignatios had become 'a magnet for young Greeks eager to study abroad' (Beaton, *Byron's War* 69). Claire noted in her journal of 1 December, 'Call with Pacchiani upon the Greek Archbishop and the Princess Argiropoli', that is, Ignatios and Karatzas's daughter, Ralou Argyropoulo whom Mary also called upon on 7 December (*Mary Jnl* i 341). It was the 1 December occasion, which marked, as Marion Kingston Stocking puts it, 'the first introduction to the group of Greek patriots who so enlivened the Shelley circle' (*Claire Jnl* 190 n. 71). In a letter to Peacock of 21 March, S. recorded his and Mary's relations with Mavrokordatos over the previous three months:

> We [...] have made a very interesting acquaintance with a Greek Prince, perfectly acquainted with antient literature & full of enthusiasm for the liberties & improvement of his country. Mary has been a Greek student several months & is reading Antigone with our turbaned friend, who in return is taught English. (*L* ii 276)

The easy familiarity between Mary and Mavrokordatos is evident from the frequency of his visits to her between 21 December and 15 June sometimes, after the Shelleys moved to Bagni San Giuliano on 8 May, with his uncle Prince Karatzas (see *Mary Jnl* i 343-70; Beaton, *Byron's War* 77). There are eighteen letters from Mavrokordatos to her, in French, the last of which is dated 25 June 1821 (Bodleian MS. Abinger c. 45 ff. 64-8, 73-98). Eight of them were published (unsatisfactorily) in *Shelley and Mary* iii [Bodleian [pr.] Shelley adds. d. 4] 581, 600-2, 621-3, 626-30, 647. Mary's esteem for Mavrokordatos is clear from her letters to Hunt of 29 December 1820 (*Mary L* i 173), Claire of 21 January 1821 (*Mary L* i 182), Maria Gisborne of *c.*14 February, *c.*21 March, 30 November and 21 December 1821 (*Mary L* i 183, 185, 210, 212-13) and Peacock of 21 March 1821 (*Mary L* i 186), as well as her touching letter to him of 22 February 1825 in which she described S. as 'your incomparable friend' (*Mary L* i

468). She copied the following sketch of his character from an article in *Le Constitutionnel, journal du commerce, politique et littéraire* cccxvi (12 November 1821) 1 into her third journal (Bodleian MS. Abinger d. 29 f. 236ʳ; *Mary Jnl* i 426):

> Alexandre Mavrocordatos réunit à la persévérance et à la fermeté de caractère l'extérieur le plus doux et le plus affable. Il a tout sacrifié pour la cause de sa nation; sa fortune tout entière a été employée à faire des préparatifs de guerre, et son seul but semble être la liberté de sa nation [Mary writes 'patrie']. Aussi jouit il déjà de l'estime générale des chefs et de toute l'affection des troupes souliotes.
>
> (Alexander Mavrocordatos combines perseverance and strength of character with the gentlest and most affable exterior. He has sacrificed everything for the cause of his nation; his entire fortune has been used in preparation for war, and his sole aim seems to be the liberty of his nation. Consequently, he already enjoys the general esteem of the leaders and the entire devotion of the Suliote troops.)

S.'s private opinion of Mavrokordatos was, by contrast, muted. On 14 May he confided to Claire: 'The Greek Prince comes sometimes, & I reproach my own savage disposition that so agreable accomplished and aimiable [a] person is not more agreable to me' (*L* ii 292); and on 8 June, a few weeks before Mavrokordatos sailed on 26 June from Livorno (*Mary Jnl* i 372) to Missolonghi via Marseille, he expressed no regret at his forthcoming departure: 'A vessel has arrived to take the Greek Prince & his suite to join the army in the Morea. He is a great loss to Mary, and *therefore* to me—but not otherwise' (*L* ii 296–7). Medwin refers to some friction in their intellectual companionship which he must have witnessed before he left Pisa on 27 February 1821:

> The life Shelley led at Pisa was one of much isolation, but not so complete as it had been. Prince Mavrocordato was his constant visitor; with him he read the *Paradise Lost*, which he infinitely admired [...] As both Shelley and Mavrocordato were great linguists, the task was rendered the easier. [...] In return, the prince read with us the *Agamemnon*, though Shelley little approved of his emendations, and would not admit that a modern Greek was a better scholiast than an English scholar. He admitted, "that he might know better the names of plants and flowers, but had no advantage over a foreigner

in correcting the faults, or supplying the *hiatuses* in the text; the best proof of which was, that with a solitary exception, Mustoxidi, to whom Monti owed his admirable Translation of Homer, modern Greece has produced no great philologist." Nor could Shelley's ears, accustomed to our pronunciation, endure Mavrocordato's, which the latter contended was the only right one. (*Medwin (1913)* 262–3)

Nevertheless, Medwin goes on to note that S. 'entertained a sincere regard for Prince Mavrocordato, who had very enlarged and enlightened views of the state of Europe' (*Medwin (1913)* 264) and S.'s letter to Horace Smith of 14 September 1821 indicates why he considered Mavrokordatos to be the obvious dedicatee for his poem:

> All public attention is now centred on the wonderful revolution in Greece. I dare not, after the events of last winter, hope that slaves can become freemen so cheaply; yet I know one Greek of the highest qualities, both of courage and conduct, the Prince Mavrocordato, and if the rest be like him, all will go well.— (*L* ii 350)

S. told Claire in a letter of 11 December, a month after the press copy of *Hellas* had been posted to Ollier for publication, that

> The news of the Greeks continues to be more & more glorious—It may be said that the Peloponnesus is entirely free, & Mavrocordato has been acting a distinguished part, & will probably fill a high rank in the magistracy of the infant republic.— (*L* ii 368)

For accounts of Mavrokordatos in the early 1820s, see: [Elizabeth Kent], *Flora Domestica* (1823) xx; Julius Millingen, *Memoirs of the Affairs of Greece* (1831) 64–8 (repr. in *Claire Jnl* 474–6); Henry Reveley, 'Notes and Observations to the "Shelley Memorials"' (after 1859) (*SC* x 1149); Herbert Huscher, 'Alexander Mavrocordato, Friend of the Shelleys', *K-SMB* xv (1965) 29–38; *Mary Jnl* ii 583–5; *Byron L&J* xi 124 and 215–16; Beaton, *Byron's War* 68–79; Will Bowers, 'On First Looking into Mary Shelley's Homer', *RES* lxix (2018) 510–31; and Mark Mazower, *The Greek Revolution: 1821 and the Making of Modern Europe* (2021) 92–114.

A further biographical context for the idealisation of Greece expressed in *Hellas* is the personal investment the Shelleys had in the struggle. Mary told Maria Gisborne in a letter of 30 November 1821 that 'If Greece be free, Shelley and I have vowed to go, perhaps to settle there, in one of those beautiful islands where earth, ocean, and sky form the Paradise—' (*Mary*

L i 210); see also *Epipsychidion* 422 and note). S. had mooted the idea of going there in letters to Byron of 20 September 1820, 'If I were to go to Levant & Greece, could you be of any service to me? If so, I should be very much obliged to you' (*L* ii 237), and 29 October 1820, to Claire Clairmont where he reported discussing with Medwin 'a plan [...] to visit Greece, Syria, and Egypt' by ship (*L* ii 242).

Sources of S.'s knowledge of the Greek revolution. In early April 1821, over seven months before S. sent *Hellas* to Ollier, Mavrokordatos had enlisted him to influence British public opinion in favour of the cause of Greek independence. S. played a significant part in an English translation of a key Greek insurrectionary text and in letters published in the *Examiner* and the *Morning Chronicle* at Mavrokordatos's behest. In her 'Note on Hellas' Mary remembered the precise date when Mavrokordatos communicated decisive news of the uprising:

> Prince Mavrocordato [...] often intimated the possibility of an insurrection in Greece; but we had no idea of its being so near at hand, when, on the 1st of April, 1821, he called on Shelley; bringing the proclamation of his cousin, Prince Ipsilanti, and radiant with exultation and delight, declared that henceforth Greece would be free. (*1839* ii 345–6)

In her journal for that day, Mary noted: 'αμ [Mavrokordatos's initials in Greek] calls with news about Greece—he is as gay as a caged eagle just free' (*Mary Jnl* i 359). She reported details in a letter to Claire the next day:

> Greece has declared its freedom! Prince Mavrocordato had made us expect this event for some weeks pas[t]. Yesterday he came <u>rayonnant de joie</u>—he had been ill for some days but he forgot all his pains—Ipselanti, a greek General in the service of Russia, has collected together 10,000 Greeks & entered Wallachia declaring the liberty of his country—The Morea—Epirus—Servia are in revolt. Greece will most certainly be free. The worst part of this news for us is that our amiable prince will leave us—he will of course join his countrymen as soon as possible—never did Man appear so happy. (*Mary L* i 186–7)

S.'s letter to Medwin of 4 April reported the same news, noting that 'Greece has risen in this moment to vindicate its freedom' (*L* ii 280). On 2 April (see *Mary Jnl* i 359), Mavrokordatos gave the Shelleys a copy of Alexander Ypsilantis's proclamation of war against the Turks which Mary described in a letter to Maria Gisborne of 5 April as 'an eloquent & Beautiful Cry of War to his countrymen' (*Mary L* i 188). A virtually complete English translation of the proclamation, in Mary's hand, with corrections in S.'s, and titled *Cry of War to the Greeks* survives in Box 2 ff. 91, 34. The two *Box 2* leaves were first identified as part of the same work by P. M. S. Dawson in 1977 (*The Unacknowledged Legislator: Shelley and Politics* (1980) 17 n. 2; *BSM* xxii, Pt 2, 412). For the standard reading text, edited by A. A. Markley, who includes it in Mary's canon among 'Part-Authored and Attributed Writings', see *MSLL* iv pp. lxxviii–lxxx and 350–3. For a complete facsimile and transcription of the *Box 2* leaves, edited by Alan M. Weinberg with commentary, see *BSM* xxii, Pt II, 29–31, 238–45 and 412–14 (there is also a transcription of a portion of it with commentary in *Shelley's Guitar* 156). *Cry of War to the Greeks* must have been written by 5 April, the date of the letters by the Shelleys published in the *Examiner* and the *Morning Chronicle* referred to below. Charles E. Robinson in 'The Shelleys to Leigh Hunt: A New Letter of 5 April 1821', *K-SMB* xxxi (1980) 52–6 (55) assumes the text of Ypsilantis's proclamation to have been in the original (i.e. modern) Greek and that S. aided Mary in its translation, 'with Mavrocordato offering his advice', and both Weinberg (*BSM* xxii, Pt II, 31) and Bowers ('On First Looking into Mary Shelley's Homer', 523–4) concur that the translation was a work of collaboration involving Mavrokordatos. However, it seems likely that Mavrokordatos had given them a French translation of the proclamation to translate into English since, referring to Mavrokordatos showing him and S. a modern Greek translation of the *Iliad*, Medwin notes that 'Shelley's knowledge of the language as at present spoken, was very superficial' (*Medwin (1913)* 264).

In a postscript to his letter to Mary of 3 April Mavrokordatos wrote:

> Je prépare un petit travail pour Mr Shelley. [I]l m'a promis de le faire insérer dans une feuille anglaise, et je compte tout-à-fait sur sa promesse, et sur son ame naturellement sensible à tout ce qui s'attache à la cause sacrée de la liberté. (Bodleian MS. Abinger c. 45 f. 82^r; *Shelley and Mary* iii [Bodleian [pr.] Shelley adds. d. 4] 602)

(I am preparing a small task for Mr Shelley. He has promised me to have it inserted in an English paper, and I have complete confidence in that promise as well as in his soul, which is by nature sensitive to all that relates to the sacred cause of liberty.)

Beaton suggests that the 'task' was to translate into English Mavrokordatos's introduction (in French) to Ipsilantis's proclamation and send it with their translation of the proclamation itself to English newspapers (*Byron's War* 73). Press copies (now lost) of their translation of the proclamation were evidently enclosed in a letter to Hunt which was published in the *Examiner* 694 (22 April 1821) 248, and a letter to James Black published in the *Morning Chronicle* 16227 (23 April 1821) 2. Their translation of the proclamation was not published because one had earlier appeared in the *Morning Chronicle* 16219 (13 April 1821) 3 and another (abridged) in the *Examiner* 693 (15 April 1821) 231–2. The letters were first attributed to the Shelleys by Charles E. Robinson who published them in 'The Shelleys to Leigh Hunt', referred to above, and 'Shelley to the Editor of the *Morning Chronicle*: a second new letter of 5 April 1821', *K-SMB* xxxii (1981) 55–8. Robinson's attributions of the *Examiner* letter to Mary and the *Morning Chronicle* letter to S. are plausible though as he notes, the inference of 'Write to Hunt' in Mary's journal entry for 4 April (*Mary Jnl* i 359) need not be that she authored the letter to the *Examiner* alone (assuming her journal refers to this letter). Beaton concurs with Robinson that S.'s opinions are recognisable in some of the wording of the *Morning Chronicle* letter (*Byron's War* 73).

Beaton's claim that 'Thanks to Shelley's connivance, Mavrokordatos was later jubilant that the *Morning Chronicle* had been the first newspaper to announce the uprising in the Peloponnese – in effect, before it had happened' (*Byron's War* 73) demands attention. Assuming that the letter published anonymously under the heading 'PRIVATE CORRESPONDENCE' in the *Morning Chronicle* of 23 April was by S. and that Mavrokordatos had a part in it, it is of significance to an understanding of *Hellas*. The mode of the poem is prophetic and originates not only in Mavrokordatos's communication of news of Ypsilantis's proclamation on 1 April but also in S.'s willingness to share in Mavrokordatos's imagining of a future for Greece very different from its present control by the Ottoman Empire. *Hellas* mediates contemporary events in Greece in order to enjoin the British public to support the insurrectionists' cause by pointing out their country's failure to do so (for example, in ll. 303–6). The poem's assertion of an outcome that is wished for but as yet unproven has parallels with the tone of S.'s letter:

PISA, APRIL 5, 1821

Having been requested by a Greek of high rank to obtain publicity for the inclosed Proclamation,* and the facts connected with it, through the medium of an English Journal, I conceive that I shall best fulfil his desire by communicating them to the Editor of *The Morning Chronicle*.

The Prince Ypsilanti, a Greek Nobleman, who had been Aid-de-camp to the Emperor of Russia, has entered the Northern boundaries of European Turkey, with a force of 10,000 men, levied from among the Greeks inhabiting the Russian Empire, and has already advanced to Bucharest. His Proclamation (which is inclosed, and for which I solicit an insertion in your Paper) has produced a simultaneous insurrection throughout Greece, or rather it has been the signal before determined on of that measure. The Greeks dispersed over Europe, whether as merchants or as students at the Universities, are hastening to join the army, or in the few cases where their affairs detain them, furnish their contingents of money. The Turks have been completely driven from the Morea, and Revolutionary movements have taken place in several of the Islands. The Suliotes have gained a victory over the Turkish army before Janina; and Ali Pacha is purchasing the assistance of the Greeks by the treasures extorted from them by his tyranny. Every circumstance seems to combine to promise probable success to an enterprise, in which every enlightened mind must sympathise, not less from the hopes than the memories with which it is connected. The Greeks express a great anxiety, lest the British Administration should be unfavourable to their cause, and lest it should secretly abet the tyranny of the Turks. They disclaim whatever views upon the Ionian Islands, and the Chiefs of the Insurrection (I speak from personal knowledge) have exerted their utmost influence to restrain the inhabitants of those Islands from any attempt to withdraw themselves from the British power. Should the Greeks succeed in their efforts to become a nation, all motives for controversy on such a question would probably be absorbed in the greater advantages which a friendly intercourse with them would render to England.

I conclude with recommending to the powerful intercession of your Paper, with public opinion in England, the cause of the Greeks—a cause respecting which I have the happiness to believe there cannot be one dissentient voice—a sacred cause, and one entwined with the sympathies of the earliest years of men of the highest education, no less than of those who consider the cause of national independence and personal liberty as more especially their own.

*The Proclamation was published in *The Morning Chronicle* of the 13th.—ED. (*Morning Chronicle* 16277 (23 April 1821) 2)

Mavrokordatos was in an authoritative position to provide S. and Mary with frequent intelligence about the Greek insurrection by letter and in person between early December 1820 and mid-June 1821. In telling Claire that 'Greece has declared its freedom' in his letter of 2 April 1821, S. added that 'Prince Mavrocordato has made us expect this event for some weeks past' (*L* ii 278). Evidence of the Shelleys' preparedness for Mavrokordatos's news of 1 April is provided by Mary's note of 'the taking of the citadel of Candia [Heraklion, capital of Crete] by the Greeks' in her journal for 16 March (*Mary Jnl* i 357). The liberation of Greece from the Ottoman Empire had been meditated since the end of the Napoleonic Wars by the *Philiki Etairia* (Society of Friends), founded in Odessa in 1814, members of whom S. refers to as 'Heteristi' in his letter to Byron of 21 October 1821 (*L* ii 358). Roderick Beaton, *Greece: Biography of a Modern Nation* (2020) 73 notes two main factors which came to a head in 1820 and, in combination, precipitated action. First, the Albanian warlord Ali Pacha (see l. 566 and note) revolted against his Ottoman masters, as reported in the *Examiner* 657 (30 July 1820): 'a war is now raging in the Turkish Dominions between the Grand Seignior and his nominal subject, the fierce ALI, Pacha of Albania' (488). Secondly, Alexandros Ypsilantis (mentioned in l. 577), son of a former Hospodar of Wallachia, who had left his homeland to join the Russian army in 1806, accepted the leadership of the *Philiki Etairia*. In autumn 1820 Ypsilantis decided to launch the uprising in the Danubian Principalities of the Ottoman Empire (Mazower 20–5). After some delay, he marched with his retainers on Jassy, capital of Moldavia, in early March 1821. An '*official* article from Laybach [Ljubljana]', where the Congress of the Quadruple Alliance (Austria, Britain, Prussia and Russia) met between late January and March 1821, reporting the proclamations which Mavrokordatos had joyfully communicated to the Shelleys for them to relay to the English press, was published in the *Examiner* 693 (15 April 1821) 229:

> Prince Ypsilanti [...] proclaimed himself the deliverer of the Greek nation from the yoke of the Ottoman government. Soon after his arrival at Jassy, the few Turks in that town were disarmed, and supposed to be put to death. The Prince, on the 17th ult., issued many proclamations.—"These proclamations," says the Laybach article, "are drawn up in the most exalted language of poetry, in which he declares himself to have been called upon by many thousands of his countrymen to undertake the work of their deliverance, describes the insurrection of all the Greek tribes as a revolution which has long been determined upon, which has been preparing for many years

by secret patriotic societies, and is now every where matured for execution[".]

The article went on to note Tsar Alexander's expulsion of Ypsilantis from the army after he had called upon Russia to support the Greek cause. A further article in the same column stated that 'Ali Pacha and Ypsilanti are ready to support each other.' However, Ypsilantis's progress was halted by the humiliating defeat of his Sacred Battalion and his capture by the Turks at Dragatsani in Wallachia on 7 June (figured as 'the battle / Of Bucharest' in *Hellas* 362–3), reports of which, as noted above, were published in newspapers in late July. Notwithstanding S.'s awareness of Greek victories elsewhere, in the Morea and the islands, in the summer and early autumn, *Hellas* responds to a precarious moment in the narrative of the revolution, entirely distinct from the excited anticipation which led to the publication of S.'s letter to the *Morning Chronicle* in April. In dramatising 'the Greek cause last summer' (*L* ii 422), as he put it the following spring, *Hellas* confronts that cause's fragility which by October had turned into a protracted struggle. Hassan's conflicted account of 'the battle / of Bucharest' (ll. 363–452) on the one hand conveys a significant setback to the rebellion by the Greeks yet on the other foregrounds their heroic refusal to surrender. In the wake of news of the defeat at Dragatsani, S.'s mood appeared to be finely balanced; he told Mary in a letter of 8–10 August from Ravenna, where he was staying with Byron, that 'We have good rumours of the Greeks here' (*L* ii 324).

S.'s acknowledgement of 'the display of newspaper erudition to which I have been reduced' (Preface ll. 35–36) shows him aware of the limited nature of his sources and of the perils of propaganda of which Mavrokordatos had made him and Mary instruments through coopting them to publish letters in London newspapers. However, the intimacy with Mavrokordatos in the early months of the insurrection, between March and June 1821, which meant that S. was ahead of published news, seems to be in play in the poem's prophetic tenor (with the Choruses, especially, suggesting that Ottoman ascendancy will only ever be temporary). Mavrokordatos's letters to Mary describe the speed with which the uprising spread to mainland Greece and the islands and the intense fighting on land and by sea as the Sultanate mobilised against the insurrectionists. They also show his investment in the Shelleys for faith in the ultimate victory of the cause which the word 'sympathy' in S.'s Dedication ('an imperfect token / of the admiration, sympathy and friendship / of / The Author') acknowledges. Between mid-June, when Mavrokordatos departed from Leghorn, and October, it must be assumed that S.'s main sources of information about events were reports in newspapers. Peacock continued to send S. the weekly *Examiner* in this period, as noted in his letter to S. of 3 June 1821 (*Peacock L* i 178), presumably following S.'s instructions to make it 'so clipped as to make as little weight as possible' (*L* ii 18). *Hellas* shows similarities with Hunt's interpretation of the Greek insurrection within the wider context of European geopolitics between April and October 1821 in the *Examiner*'s editorials (on this topic, see *Cameron (1974)* 375–93). Like Hunt, S. directly challenges Castlereagh's policy of non-intervention and criticises Britain's part in the reactionary Holy Alliance (see note to Preface ll. 45–49). Reports published in *Galignani's Messenger* (a Paris-based newspaper founded in 1814 and published daily from 1815) appear to have informed a considerable number of passages in *Hellas* (see notes). Valuable selections of such reports, or references to them, are provided by Michael Erkelenz in 'Inspecting the Tragedy of Empire: Shelley's *Hellas* and Aeschylus' *Persians*', *PQ* lxxvi (1997) 313–37 and Cian Duffy in 'Percy Shelley's "Display of Newspaper Erudition" in *Hellas, a Lyrical Drama* (1822)', *N&Q* lxi (2014) 519–23. However, despite S.'s profession of 'newspaper erudition', some sources that inform the poem may have been word of mouth, or possibly written exchanges with members of Greek expatriate communities in Pisa and Livorno. A letter dated 24 October 1821 to S. in Pisa from Costantino Argiropulo, a merchant friend of Mavrokordatos who lived in Livorno (see *Mary L* i 202–3), announces itself to be a reply to one from S. two days previously (for commentary on this letter, see Huscher, 'Alexander Mavrocordato' 30 n. 3). Argiropulo informs S. that 'Il Principe Mavrocordato era Colà passato onde procurare a formare con i primati un Governo Provvisorio' (Prince Mavrocordato went there [Tripolizza] in order to form a Provisional Government with its leaders), and offers to have 'di Lei comandi o di Lettere' (your orders or letters) for the Prince, now returned to Missolonghi, delivered through an intermediary via a cargo-ship (Bodleian MS. Abinger c. 67 f. 10^r). The contrast between 'the Greeks of *Hellas* and the Greeks of the historic revolution' (60) is addressed in Newman I. White, 'The Historical and Personal Background of Shelley's Hellas', *South Atlantic Quarterly* xx (1921) 52–60 and in the commentary to the English/Greek parallel-text edition by M. B. Raizis, *Hellas (1821) A Lyrical Drama* (1990) (*Raizis*). For recent accounts of the origins of the Greek insurrection and unfolding events between March and October 1821, see Beaton, *Greece: Biography of a Modern Nation* 15–85; *The Greek Revolution: A Critical Dictionary*, ed. Paschalis M. Kitromilides and Constantinos Tsoukalas (2021) *passim*; and Mazower 3–214.

Literary sources. Hellas resembles *PU* (no. 195) in its sub-title 'A Lyrical Drama' and the fundamental re-working of a tragedy (here *Persae* [The Persians]) by Aeschylus that is its model. The first Chorus (ll. 46-93) reprises the story of the fortunes of political liberty developed in poems S. composed and published in 1820 which responded to news that year of revolutions in Spain (*OL* (no. 322)) and the Italian peninsula (*Ode to Naples* (no. 343)). *Hellas*'s theatre of action returns to *L&C* (no. 143) 'whose scene is supposed to be laid in Constantinople & modern Greece' (S. to [a Publisher], 13 October 1817, *L* i 563). *Hellas* draws for some of its topographic and historical detail about 'modern Greece' and the Ottoman Empire on Byron's *Childe Harold's Pilgrimage*, Canto II (1812) and Thomas Hope's *Anastasius: Or, Memoirs of a Greek; Written at the Close of the Eighteenth Century*, 3 vols (1819) which he read while staying with Byron at Ravenna in August 1821 (see note to Preface ll. 73-76) and described as 'a very powerful & very entertaining novel—& a faithful picture they say of modern Greek manners.—' (*L* ii 332). In its increasingly cosmic frame of reference, it is continuous with the visionary ambition of S.'s earliest extended poem, *Q Mab* (no. 92) which also features the figure of Ahasuerus and, like *Hellas*, is explicitly indebted to Edward Gibbon, *The History of the Decline and Fall of the Roman Empire* (*Decline and Fall*), 6 vols (1776-88) (see the notes to the sounds and vision of the siege of Constantinople (1453) in ll. 814-41 and Notes 6 and 7 and notes). Mahmud shows qualities of a tragic hero in the gradual recognition that his empire will be superseded yet in his early speeches deploys the stock language of a Gothic villain (see ll. 242-4, which have echoes of Count Cenci in *The Cenci* (no. 209)) thereby recalling S.'s interest in that genre and particularly William Beckford's novel *Vathek*, first published in Samuel Henley's translation as *An Arabian Tale from an Unpublished Manuscript; with Notes Critical and Explanatory* (1786).

In a letter to John Gisborne of 22 October 1821, S. described *Hellas* as 'a sort of imitation of the *Persæ* of Æschylus, full of lyrical poetry' (*L* ii 364). Aeschylus' tragedy, first produced in 472 BCE, depicts the aftermath of the victory of the Greeks at the Battle of Salamis (480 BCE) from the perspective of the defeated Persians whose leader, Xerxes, returns at the end of the play to Susa, the Persian capital, in humiliation. S.'s 'imitation' is typically sophisticated. *Persae*, the earliest surviving European drama, was a suitable model for his poem which stages the conflict between contemporary Greece and the latest empire in the East. There are several parallels. *Hellas* comprises a similar number of lines of verse (1101) to *Persae* (1068 in Æschyli, *Tragœdiæ*, ed. C. G. Schütz (1809), S.'s copy of which survives at Bodleian [pr.] Shelley adds. g. 1). The setting of both plays is an emperor's palace in the empire's capital. Early in *Persae*, Atossa, Xerxes' widowed mother, has a terrifying dream which she asks the Chorus to interpret. Correspondingly, Mahmud's opening lines (114 ff.) show him awakening troubled by a dream then asking his aide Hassan to summon 'A Jew' (l. 133) — Ahasuerus — whose 'tribe [...] are wise interpreters of dreams' (ll. 135–6). Atossa becomes so agitated by the news of a Messenger who details the Persian humiliation at Salamis which he has witnessed that she declares ἐμοὶ γὰρ ἤδη πάντα μὲν φόβου πλέα (l. 603; 'for me now, everything is full of fear'). Mahmud, convulsed with 'idiot fear' (l. 357) becomes increasingly anxious as Hassan and then four Messengers give accounts of the Turkish fleet's losses (ll. 460–638). Both plays see the invocation of the spirits of ancestors. The ghost of Xerxes' father, Darius, is summoned by the Chorus and decrees that any further Persian imperial ambition in the west will meet with failure. Ahasuerus calls up the Phantom of Mahmud's namesake, the supremely powerful Sultan Mehmed II (1432–81) who prophesies that 'Islam must fall' (l. 887). Each tragedy thus depicts the protagonist's gradual realisation that empire is transient and that they are impotent in the face of its demise. The ghost of Darius in *Persae* and the Phantom of Mehmed in *Hellas* have special authority because they, unlike their successors, wielded military might with consummate skill. A point of difference between the two works is that whereas the Messenger in *Persae* describes Xerxes as κακῶς τὸ μέλλον ἱστορῶν (l. 454; 'reading the future badly'), in *Hellas* Ahasuerus instructs Mahmud in how to read the future well. A number of further parallels with *Persae* are discussed in the notes. The following offer useful accounts of S.'s engagement with *Persae*: Richard Ackermann, *Quellen, Vorbilder, Stoffe zu Shelley's poetischen Werken* (1890) 44–53 (which lists sources in *Decline and Fall* as well as *Persae*); Erkelenz, 'Inspecting the Tragedy of Empire'; *Raizis* 10–26 (which also summarises further literary sources); and David Ferris, 'The History of Freedom: From Aeschylus to Shelley', in *Silent Urns: Romanticism, Hellenism, Modernity* (2000) 108–33.

In describing *Hellas* to Gisborne as 'full of lyrical poetry', S. referred to its principal means of expressing what transcends particular historical crises and is unchangeable, in Ahasuerus' words, 'the One / The unborn and the undying' (ll. 768–9). The most notable departure from *Persae* is the function of the choruses. In *Persae* the Chorus of Persian elders contributes directly to the plot throughout. In *Hellas* a variety of elaborately patterned choruses serve from the beginning as a counterpoint to the dramatic action in blank verse offering a perspective that is initially remote and cryptic but, with increasing urgency, comments clearly and directly on the narrative. This culminates in the closing sequence in the Chorus replying to the Turkish '*Voice without*' that proclaims 'Victory! Victory!' (l. 912ff.) with 'O cease!' (l. 1096). The insistent invocation of the sanctity of Greece and its association with freedom is supported by allusions to 'The Isles of Greece' lyric in *Don Juan* iii (Cantos III–V of Byron's poem were published on 8 August 1821) and the Chorus's lyrical description of Colonus, near Athens, in Sophocles, *Oedipus at Colonus* 668–706. S. told Medwin that the opening scene of *Hellas* was taken from *El príncipe constante* (1636) (see note to l. 1. SD) and the specific debt reflects S.'s Spanish reading noted in his letter to Peacock of 8 November 1820: 'I have been reading nothing but Greek and Spanish. Plato and Calderon have been my gods' (*L* ii 245). Parallels include most of *El príncipe constante* being set in the court of the 'enemy' (the moslem King of Fez); the action centering on an armed conflict, in this case naval, between Christians and Muslims; and an encounter with an old African woman described as 'espíritu en forma humana' ('a spirit in human form') who delivers a prophecy (see note to ll. 137–41). Among the dialogues of Plato *Notopoulos* 302–8 notes the particular influence of *Phaedo*, *Symposium* and *Timaeus*. Bryan Shelley, *Shelley and Scripture: The Interpreting Angel* (1994) suggests the book of Daniel is a source (157–61) and lists possible echoes from the Bible exhaustively (183).

Form. S.'s lyric invention is evident in the opening choric exchanges, ll. 1–45. The first five choruses alternate seven- and six-line stanzas, the first, third and fifth ending in a triplet rhyme *ababccc*, and the second and fourth in a couplet *ababcc* (anticipating the rhyme scheme of the five-line stanzas which form the final chorus of the poem). The semichoruses in ll. 34–45 then reduce to quatrains rhyming in couplets before the more complex formal organisation of the chorus at ll. 46–93. This chorus is carefully shaped to suggest an elaborate formality which yet avoids definition, the first and third stanzas of eighteen lines and the second stanza of twelve lines deploying eight rhyme-sounds and five rhyme-sounds respectively in a shifting pattern of couplets, quatrains, and triplets which never repeats itself. The chorus at ll. 197–238 is organised differently, in three fourteen-line stanzas which use seven rhyme-words, but in a pattern tightly repeated through the three stanzas. Its forty-two lines are balanced against the closing chorus ll. 1060–1101, also of forty-two lines. The other lyric sequences in *Hellas*, at ll. 648–737, 940–7 and 952–1059, all but defy descriptive analysis in their shape-shifting variations of rhyme, again mixing couplets, triplets and quatrains, in combination with short, longer and sometimes very long lines, and a restless movement from iambic and trochaic to anapaestic and dactylic metres. These passages display something like a pure lyric intensity which is too protean in character for exact definition, particularly as the array of rhymes, metres and line-lengths are often broken across different speakers. Given this extraordinary lyric experimentation, it is not surprising that S. published *Written on hearing the news of the death of Napoleon* together with *Hellas* in *1822*; it is another poem which offers an extreme example of S.'s late virtuosity in lyric verse.

Criticism. S.'s estimate of *Hellas* was modest. Describing the poem publicly as a 'mere improvise' (Preface l. 2), he referred to it in a letter to Horace Smith of 11 April 1822 as 'a sort of lyrical, dramatic, nondescript piece of business' (*L* ii 411). Nevertheless, his letter to John Gisborne of 18 June 1822, a few weeks before his death, surveying his most recently published work, including *Adonais* (no. 403) and *Epipsychidion* was not overly dismissive: '"Hellas" too I liked on account of the subject—one always finds some reason or other for liking one's own composition' (*L* ii 434). In addition, Williams's evaluation, on completing his transcription of the poem on 10 November 1821, may in its second sentence speak of S.'s own judgement:

> It is a poem which may be called a fine improvise, but so far above the level of common apprehension (as indeed most of his writings are) that I am doubtful of its popularity. If such a poem *does* become popular we may flatter ourselves on having advanced one step further towards improvement and perfection in all things moral & political. (*Gisborne Jnl* 111)

The only full-length contemporary review was hostile. *The General Weekly Register of News, Literature, Law, Politics and Commerce* xiii (30 June 1822) 501–3 (repr. in *Unextinguished Hearth* 303–8) pronounced it 'but a bad specimen of Mr. Shelley's powers, and but ill calculated to increase the former fame of its author' (503), commenting 'we find much to censure, and but little to admire; the ideas are neither original nor poetical, the language obscure and frequently unpolished, and although the poem undoubtedly possesses some beauties, yet its defects certainly predominate' (502). An article headed 'Hellas: A Poem. By Percy Bysshe Shelley' in *The Paris Monthly Review of British and Continental Literature* ii (1822) 392–6 (repr. in *Unextinguished Hearth* 326–9) explained itself as an obituary: 'we are anxious to record our intention of reviewing the last of Mr. Shelley's productions, before we had heard the fate of the unfortunate author' (392). The critical consensus from its publication in

Mary's collected editions onwards has concurred with her singling out the choruses for praise:

> 'Hellas' was among the last of [Shelley's] compositions, and is among the most beautiful. The chorusses are singularly imaginative, and melodious in their versification. There are some stanzas that beautifully exemplify Shelley's peculiar style [...] The conclusion of the last chorus is among the beautiful of his lyrics; the imagery is distinct and majestic; the prophecy, such as poets love to dwell upon, the regeneration of mankind—and that regeneration reflecting back splendour on the foregone time, from which it inherits so much of intellectual wealth, and memory of past virtuous deeds, as must render the possession of happiness and peace of tenfold value. (*1839* ii 347)

In the audience of the staging of *Hellas* by the Shelley Society on 16 November 1886 were Oscar Wilde and Robert Browning (see Thomas Wise, 'The Performance of Hellas', *Note-book of the Shelley Society: Part I* (1888), 134–6); this production's musical setting of the choruses, by William Selle, was published by the Society in 1886. A dramatisation produced by John Theocharis for BBC Radio 3 was broadcast on 13 October 1976.

Most critical discussion of *Hellas* since 1945 has tended to appreciate the poem's relevance to two interrelated subjects: ideas of nationalism (both nascent Greek nationalism and that of places which had recently seen revolutions such as Naples and Spain), and how S.'s transposition of Greek drama to his contemporary situation plays with history and historicism. Of the many works on this subject, the best are Mark Kipperman, 'History and Ideality: The Politics of Shelley's *Hellas*', *SiR* xxx (1991) 147–69; William A. Ulmer, '*Hellas* and the Historical Uncanny' *ELH* lviii (1991) 611–32; L. M. Findlay, '"We Are All Greeks": Shelley's *Hellas* and Romantic Nationalism', *History of European Ideas* xvi (1993) 281–6; Christopher Bundock, 'Historicism, Temporalization, and Romantic Prophecy in Percy Shelley's *Hellas*', in *Rethinking British Romantic History, 1770–1845*, ed. Porscha Fermanis and John Regan (2014) 144–64; and Mathelinda Nabugodi, 'Old Anew: *Hellas*', *European Romantic Review* xxx (2022) 639–52. While many readings have tended to view *Hellas* as part of the history of ideas, welcome attempts have been made to appreciate its literary qualities, for example: Michael O'Neill, '"Wrecks of a Dissolving Dream": Shelley's Art of Ambivalence in *Hellas*', in *The Neglected Shelley*, ed. Alan M. Weinberg and Timothy Webb (2015) 239–60; and Jonathan Quayle, 'Directing the "Unfinished Scene": Utopia and the Role of the Poet in Shelley's *Hellas*', *Romanticism* xxvi (2020) 280-91. Baker 182-7, *Butter (1954)* 131-3, and *Wasserman* 374-413 all offer useful analysis.

Text from *HM* 329 except for the position of the Dedication and the list of Dramatis Personae where the arrangement in *1822* is followed. Indentation follows the MS.

Published in *1822* i-ix, 1-58 (Preface except penultimate paragraph; ll. 1-1090, part of l. 1091, 1094-1101; Notes 1-7; some of Note 8); *1829* 171-80 (Preface except penultimate paragraph; ll. 1-1101; Notes 1-7; some of Note 8); *1839* ii 281-342 (Preface except penultimate paragraph; ll. 1-1101; Notes 1-7; most of Note 8); *Forman 1892* iv 33-91 and *Woodberry 1892* iii 95-155 (Preface; ll. 1-1101; Notes 1-7; most of Note 8); *Reiman (2002)* 427-64 (complete); *MYRS* iii 13-79 (facsimile of MS).

Hellas

A Lyrical Drama

By Percy B. Shelley

ΜΆΝΤΙΣ ΈΙΜ' ἘΣΘΛΩΝ ἈΓΩΝΩΝ
Oedipus Coloneus

¶ 411 *Title*. Hellas / A Lyrical drama. / by Percy B.[ysshe] Shelley. *HM 329* (the alteration of *Bysshe* to *B*. is probably in S.'s hand); Hellas / A Lyrical Drama / By / Percy B. Shelley *1822*; Hellas; / A Lyrical Drama. *1829, 1839, 1840*. In Williams's draft design of the title-page (and perhaps the half-title too) in *Box 1* f. 61ʳ the reading is *Hellas / Hellas / a lyrical drama* (see facsimile in *BSM* xxi 16; this *Box 1* leaf is discussed in the headnote to *A capering, squalid, squalling one*, no. 419). *Hellas*] S. first refers to 'his dramatic poem' as 'called "Hellas"' in a letter to Ollier of 11 October 1821 (*L* ii 356), a month before he sent it to him. Williams's statement in his journal entry for 26 October 1821, that it was he who suggested the title to S. the previous day, may, as Reiman suggests, have been 'after the fact' (*Reiman (2002)* 428). Nevertheless, Williams's characteristically careful record of his exchange with S. is worth noting: 'He asked me yesterday what name he should give to the drama he is now engaged with. I proposed "Hellas" which he will adopt. I mention this circumstance as I was proud at being asked the question, and more so that the name pleased him' (*Gisborne Jnl* 106). 'Hellas' was a country around the river Sperchius inhabited by the Hellenes, a tribe of southern Thessaly (usually extended in meaning to cover Greece in general), referred to in *Iliad* ii 683, ix 395, 447, 478, xvi 595 and *Odyssey* xi 496. In choosing his title, S. was anglicising the word Ἑλλάς in the most important source of his poem (discussed in the Headnote ('Literary sources')), Aeschylus, *Persae* (e.g. 176–200, where Atossa dreams of figures representing 'Hellas' and 'the barbarian land' in conflict); the word is found in Herodotus, *Histories* viii 47, which mentions 'Hellas in its danger' during the account of the victory of the Greeks at the Battle of Salamis that is the context for *Persae*. S. ordered the *Histories* of Herodotus, whom he describes as a poet in *DP* (*Reiman (2002)*, para. 10), from Hookham on 27 December 1812 (*L* i 342) and Mary records him reading it in 1815 (*Mary Jnl* i 93); his notes in a copy of Herodotus now in CHPL (SC487; see *SC* vi 618–33) may date from the period 16 July-2 August 1818 when Mary records him reading *Histories* (see *L* i 26 and *Mary Jnl* i 219–21); S. also read this work between 27 September and 1 October 1820 (*Mary Jnl* i 333). Since the eighteenth century, 'Hellas' and 'Hellene' had been used to signify Greece and the Greeks by those seeking liberation from the Ottoman Empire (see Mazower xxviii–xxix). S.'s choice of title was prescient. With the encouragement of Mavrokordatos, head of the new Provisional Government (as Mary noted in her letter to Maria Gisborne of 21 December 1821, *Mary L* i 212–13), a national assembly of 'the whole liberated nation' took place in January 1822 at which 'the proclamation of the first Provisional Constitution of independent Greece [...] established the name of the new country as Hellas' (Beaton, *Greece: Biography of a Modern Nation* 84). That the word 'Hellas' had currency in political discourse at the point when S.'s title was confirmed is evident from contemporary newspapers. See, e.g., the article from *Le Constitutionnel*, a Paris-based daily, reproduced (in translation) in the *Examiner* 719 (14 October 1821) 644: 'How can any one behold the sufferings of Hellas with apathy that can read in the original the melancholy descriptions of Childe Harold or his fervid allocutions?'. *A Lyrical Drama*] The same formulation is used in the sub-title of *PU*. In the Dedication *Hellas* is referred to as a 'drama', in the Preface (l. 1) as a 'Poem'; the Preface elaborates on the description of the poem as a drama in the second paragraph (ll. 23–26).

Epigraph. 'I predict a victory in the struggle!' (*Oedipus at Colonus* 1080). The line is from a speech by the Chorus after Theseus' men have gone to rescue Antigone and Ismene, daughters of Oedipus, from kidnap by Creon. Lines 1074-84 read in full:

ἔρδουσιν ἢ μέλλουσιν; ὥς
προμνᾶταί τί μοι
γνώμα τάχ' ἀνδώσειν
τᾶν δεινὰ τλασᾶν, δεινὰ δ' εὑ-
ρουσᾶν πρὸς αὐθαίμων πάθη.
τελεῖ τελεῖ Ζεύς τι κατ' ἦμαρ.
μάντις εἴμ' ἐσθλῶν ἀγώνων.
εἴθ' ἀελλαία ταχύρρωστος πελειὰς
αἰθερίας νεφέλας κύρσαιμ' ἄνωθ' ἀγώνων
αἰωρήσασα τοὐμὸν ὄμμα.

('Are they in action, or do they delay? My mind prophesies to me that the sufferings of the girls who have endured grievous things, and have had grievous treatment from their kindred, will soon abate. This day, this day Zeus will fulfil some purpose! I predict a victory in the struggle! I wish I were a wind-swift strong-winged dove, gazing from a lofty cloud upon the contest!')

In the next few lines Antigone and Ismene return with Theseus. For the Shelleys, line 1080 had specific associations with Alexandros Mavrokordatos, to whom *Hellas* is dedicated. See S.'s letter to Peacock of 21 March 1821:

> I want you to do something for me. That is, to get me £2's worth of Tassi's gems in Leicester square, the prettiest according to your taste, among them the head of Alexander & to get me two seals engraved & set, one smaller & the other handsomer,—the device, a dove with outspread wings & this motto, round it. Μάντις εἰμί ἐσθλῶν ἀγώνων .— (*L* ii 276–7)

The unelided εἰμί here also appears in the rendition of the motto in Williams's draft title-page (*Box 1* f. 61^r): the elision of the last letter is only called for by the original metrical context of the line, and it is likely in any case that S. (and Williams) were quoting from memory. The motto (seemingly with the elision) is also found in S.'s hand at the top of *Nbk 21* p. 27 (*BSM* xvi 30), the right-hand page of an opening containing draft of *It is the period when all the Sons of God* (*Lines connected with Hellas* A) ll. 115–21. In a letter to Maria Gisborne of 21 March 1821, Mary noted, 'I have finished the two Œdipi with my Greek', 'my Greek' referring to Mavrokordatos who was teaching her Ancient Greek at this time and reading *Oedipus Tyrannus* and *Oedipus at Colonus* with her (*Mary L* i 185; see also her postscript to S.'s letter to Peacock of the same date in *Mary L* i 186). Mary cites the line in her letter to Maria Gisborne of 30 November 1821 in the context of the current situation in Greece and Mavrokordatos's role:

> Do you get any intelligence of the Greeks—Our worthy Countrymen take part against them in every possible way, yet such is the spirit of freedom, and such the hatred of these poor people for their oppressors, that I have the warmest hopes—μάντις εἴμ' ἐσθλῶν ἀγώνων.— Mavrocordato is there justly revered for the sacrifice he has made of his whole fortune to the cause, and besides for his firmness and talents. (*Mary L* i 210; the source of this citation is John Gisborne's nbk containing copies of letters from Mary to Maria Gisborne, May 1818– 18 Jan. 1822, Bodleian MS. Abinger d. 20 f. 43^v)

These instances in the writings of S. and Mary indicate that it was Mavrokordatos himself who applied this line from Sophocles to the contemporary political situation. Herbert Huscher notes that 'it is striking that the same […] line from the *Oedipus Coloneus* was also prefixed as a motto by Mavrocordato in a letter he wrote to Andreas Louriotos and other friends, then in Paris, dated Pisa, April 2, 1821' ('Alexander Mavrocordato' 30; see also Beaton, *Byron's War* 75). Oedipus Coloneus] Œdipus Coloneus. *HM 329*; ŒDIP. COLON. *1822, 1839, 1840*; ŒDIP. *Colon. 1829*; Williams follows his transliteration of the Greek in *Box 1* f. 61^r with *Soph*: but omits the Latinised title of the play. Eight Greek letters in pencil beneath the epigraph in *HM 329* may be in the hand of a compositor at the firm of S. and

R. Bentley, printers of *1822*, as suggested by Donald Reiman (*MYRS* iii 13), who notes they 'are lower-case equivalents of the Greek capital letters immediately above each, perhaps to help the compositor find the correct pieces of type.' The epigraph is echoed in l. 664 of the poem (see note to ll. 648–64.) S.'s jotting ουρανιας αχνας followed by a partial translation, *The heavenly spume*, in *Nbk 17* p. 13 (*BSM* vi 108) appears to recall part of *Oedipus at Colonus* 681 (οὐρανίας ὑπ' ἄχνας ['by dew from heaven', Loeb trans.]; for commentary on this jotting which, given the date-range of *Nbk 17*, must date from between January 1820 and May 1821, see *BSM* vi 65). Peacock translated choruses from *Oedipus at Colonus* and other tragedies between winter 1812 and autumn 1813 within which period (between 4 October and 13 November 1813), he was first introduced to S. by Hookham (see *Peacock L* i pp. cxxi–cxxii; Peacock's letter to William Roscoe of 10 January 1815 in *Peacock L* i 109, 111 and 112 n. 9; and Peacock's letters to Thomas L'Estrange of 2 May 1860 and 3 July 1860 in *Peacock L* ii 391–2, and n. 2 to the letter of 2 May).

> To
> His Excellency
> Prince Alexander Mavrocordato,
> late Secretary for Foreign Affairs
> to the Hospodar of Wallachia,
> The drama of Hellas
> is inscribed
> as an imperfect token
> of the admiration, sympathy, and friendship
> of
> The Author.

Pisa, November 1st, 1821.

Dedication. In *HM 329* the Dedication is on the verso of f. 5, the recto of which contains part of the final paragraph of the Preface. Cp. S.'s Dedication to *The Cenci* (no. 209), which is 'inscribed' to Leigh Hunt in the opening sentence and closes with the place of its composition and a precise date.

Ded. His Excellency ... The Author.] For S.'s opinion of Mavrokordatos, see Headnote ('Biographical context').

Ded. Excellency] A title of honour. This instance is cited in *OED* 'excellency' n. 3b.

Ded. Mavrocordato,] *1829, 1839, 1840*; Mavrocordato *1822*. S. corrects Williams's *Mavrocodarto* to *Mavrocordato* in *HM 329* and writes the name in full above.

Ded. Secretary ... Wallachia] Markos Karasaranis comments that Mavrokordatos was 'manager of foreign affairs to his uncle' ('Mesolonghi' in *The Greek Revolution: A Critical Dictionary* 249). Beaton refers to him as having 'risen to the rank of *megas postelnikos*, or secretary to the government' between 1812 and 1818 (*Byron's War* 69). *Foreign Affairs*] foreign affairs *HM 329*.

Ded. the Hospodar of Wallachia] Prince Karatzas, Mavrokordatos's uncle, was Hospodar (Governor) of the province of Wallachia, a region of modern-day Romania. The position is described as '"the very highest situation which a Greek can attain in the Turkish empire"' in Hope, *Anastasius*, 3 vols (1819) II, ch. vii. *Wallachia,*] *1829, 1839*; Wallachia *HM 329, 1822*; Wallachi *1840*.

Ded. The drama] The alteration of *the* to *The* in *HM 320* is probably in Williams's hand.

Ded. inscribed] inscribed, *1839, 1840*.

Ded. sympathy] Sympathy *HM 329*. *Author.*] Author. *1829*. *Pisa, November 1st, 1821.*] *1822*; Pisa November 1st 1821. *HM 329*; Pisa, November 1, 1821. *1829, 1839, 1840*. On this day Byron took up residence at the Palazzo Lanfranchi, Pisa (*Mary Jnl* i 381), near the Tre Palazzi di Chiesa where the Shelleys had moved from Bagni di San Giuliano on 25 October (*Claire Jnl* 251–2; *Gisborne Jnl* 105).

Preface

The Poem of *Hellas*, written at the suggestion of the events of the moment, is a mere improvise, and derives its interest (should it be found to possess any) solely from the intense sympathy which the Author feels with the cause he would
5   celebrate.
    The subject in its present state, is insusceptible of being treated otherwise than lyrically, and if I have called this poem a drama from the circumstance of its being composed in dialogue, the licence is not greater than that which has been
10 assumed by other poets who have called their productions epics, only because they have been divided into twelve or twenty-four books.

Preface 1-2. The Poem ... is a mere improvise] The sole surviving portion of draft of the Preface in *Nbk 21* pp. 193-4 (a torn leaf), amid draft of the final Chorus of *Hellas*, is a version of this sentence: 'This poem deserves to be regarded as little more than an improvise inspired by the uncontrollable emotions of the moment. — The admirers of Goethe will [?perhaps] recognize in the [?free] chorus of the [?] an attempt to naturalize the [?inestimable] harmony of the lyrical poetry of Faust' (for a facsimile and transcription, see *BSM* xvi 196-9; *BSM* conjectures the illegible word after 'chorus of the' to be 'irrelivoscuro'). For possible parallels with *Faust* in *Hellas*, see the notes to ll. 426, 956 and 1098.
Pref. 1. The] The alteration from *This* in *HM 329* is probably in S.'s hand. *Poem*] poem *1822, 1829, 1839*.
Pref. 2. improvise] An improvised composition (the first published instance of this noun, according to *OED*). Mary uses the word of a performance by Sgricci in her journal for 21 December 1820: 'go to the theatre & hear the Improvise of Sgricci' (*Mary Jnl* i 343). *Wasserman* 378-80 discusses it, noting that '"improvise" accurately describes *Hellas* as a recreation of *The Persians* and as a re-emergence of the original Hellenic spirit of both art and liberty' (378).
Pref. 6. subject] subject, *1822, 1839, 1840*. state,] state *1829*.
Pref. 8. drama] drama, *1840*.
Pref. 10. poets] poets, *1829, 1839, 1840*.
Pref. 11-12. epics ... twenty-four books] On S.'s view of the nature of epic, see *DP* (composed between late January and 20 March 1821):

> Homer was the first, and Dante the second epic poet: that is, the second poet the series of whose creations bore a defined and intelligible relation to the knowledge, and sentiment, and religion, and political conditions of the age in which he lived, and of the ages which followed it, developing itself in correspondence with their development. [...] none among the flock of mock-birds, though their notes were sweet,

> The *Persae* of Aeschylus afforded me the first model of my
> conception, although the decision of the glorious contest now
> 15 waging in Greece being yet suspended forbids a catastrophe
> parallel to the return of Xerxes and the desolation of the
> Persians. I have, therefore, contented myself with exhibiting

> > Apollonius Rhodius, Quintus Calaber Smyrnaeus, Nonnus, Lucan,
> > Statius, or Claudian, have sought even to fulfil a single condition of epic
> > truth. For if the title of epic in its highest sense be refused to the Æneid,
> > still less can it be conceded to the Orlando Furioso, the Gerusalemme
> > Liberata, the Lusiad, or the Fairy Queen. (*Reiman (2002)* para. 28)

Pref. 13–17. The Persae *of Aeschylus ... desolation of the Persians.*] On parallels between *Hellas* and Aeschylus' tragedy, see Headnote ('Literary sources'). Mary recorded S. reading *Persae* on 3 August 1818, the day after he finished Herodotus' *Histories* (*Mary Jnl* i 221–2). He wrote out *Persae* 93–100 in Greek (these lines normally appear after l. 113 in modern editions), and *86—Persae* alongside the last line, *reverso* in *Nbk 15* p. 376, the last page of this notebook (see facsimile and transcription in *BSM* xiv 270–1) translated in Loeb as, 'But what mortal man can escape / the guileful deception of a god? / Who is so light of foot / that he has power to leap easily away? / For Ruin begins by fawning on a man in a friendly way / and leads him astray into her net, from which it is impossible for a mortal to escape and flee'. At the foot of the same notebook page he wrote, in Greek, the Chorus's reply to Atossa, Xerxes' mother, in ll. 215–16 ('Mother, we do not wish to say what would make you either unduly fearful or unduly optimistic.') He then wrote, 'Atossa asks where is Athens / Chorus replies', a reference to l. 231 and l. 232; the latter line he writes in Greek ('Far away, near the place where the Lord Sun declines and sets'.) Overleaf on *Nbk 15* p. 375 (see facsimile and transcription in *BSM* xiv 268–9), he wrote, *reverso*, 'What treasure have they' (a rendering of Atossa's question at l. 237) and then, the first two and the last two words of Greek from the Chorus's reply at l. 238 ('They have a fountain of silver, a treasure in their soil'). Beneath he wrote, 'Atossa asks again', then, in Greek, her question at l. 241 ('And who is the shepherd, master and commander over their host?'). Finally he wrote, 'Chorus', then, in Greek, their reply at l. 242 ('They are not called slaves or subjects to any man.') These pencilled notes from *Persae* are dated '?1820–1821' by P. M. S. Dawson and Timothy Webb in *BSM* xiv p. xxxiv (see also their commentary in *BSM* xiv pp. xxiii–xxiv and 293). There are pencil lines in the margin alongside the following lines of *Persae* (Loeb lineation) in S.'s pocket edition of Aeschylus (*Æschyli, Tragœdiæ*, ed. C. G. Schütz (1809); Bodleian [pr.] Shelley adds. g. 1): 151, 388–91, 426–8, 461, 467–70, 495–502, 689–90, 821–2.
Pref. 14. decision] resolution (see *OED* 2a).
Pref. 15. suspended] suspended, *1829, 1839, 1840*.
Pref. 17–22. I have, therefore, contented myself ... social improvement] Cp. the idea of a poem anticipating revolutionary change in the final paragraph of *DP*:

a series of lyric pictures, and with having wrought upon the
curtain of futurity, which falls upon the unfinished scene,
such figures of indistinct and visionary delineation as suggest
the final triumph of the Greek cause as a portion of the cause
of civilization and social improvement.
The drama (if drama it must be called) is, however, so
inartificial that I doubt whether, if recited on the Thespian
wagon to an Athenian village at the Dionysiaca, it would have

> The most unfailing herald, companion, and follower of the
> awakening of a great people to work a beneficial change in opinion or
> institution, is Poetry. [...] Poets are the hierophants of an unappre-
> hended inspiration, the mirrors of the gigantic shadows which
> futurity casts upon the present, the words which express what they
> understand not, the trumpets which sing to battle and feel not what
> they inspire: the influence which is moved not, but moves. (*Reiman
> (2002)* para. 48)

The above passage was first drafted in *PVR* between November 1819 and January 1820; see *SC* vi 993.

Pref. 19. futurity, ... scene,] *1822, 1829, 1839*; futurity ... scene *HM 329. falls upon*] falls on *1834*.

Pref. 20. such figures of indistinct and visionary delineation] 'That is, of Ahasuerus, of Mahomet's Phantom, and of the Chorus (in part)' (*Raizis* 86).

Pref. 24. inartificial] 'constructed without art or skill, rude, clumsy' (*OED* 2). whether,] *1822, 1829, 1839, 1840*; whether *HM 329*.

Pref. 24-25. Thespian wagon] The source is probably Horace, *Ars Poetica* (The Art of Poetry) 275-6: 'Ignotum tragicae genus invenisse Camenae / dicitur et plaustris vexisse poemata Thespis' ('Thespis is said to have discovered the Tragic Muse, a type unknown before, and to have carried his pieces in wagons').

Pref. 25. an Athenian village at the Dionysiaca] The Dionysia were festivals of Dionysus for which Greek drama was written. *Dionysiaca* literally means 'relating to Dionysus' and is presumably intended as an equivalent to 'Dionysia' (Thucydides, *History of the Peloponnesian War* viii 93 has Διονυσιακὸν θέατρον, i.e. 'the Dionysiac theatre') though it may simply be an error. S. uses the word in the Preface to his translation of Plato's *Symposium* (written around 25 July 1818; see *L* ii 26), noting that the debate described therein is 'supposed to have taken place at the house of Agathon, at one of a series of festivals given by that poet, on the occasion of his gaining the prize of tragedy at the Dionysiaca' (*Notopoulos* 402; for a facsimile and transcription of the MS of this sentence in *Nbk 14* p. 63, see *BSM* v 130-1).

obtained the prize of the goat. I shall bear with equanimity any punishment greater than the loss of such a reward which the Aristarchi of the hour may think fit to inflict.

30   The only *goat-song* which I have yet attempted has, I confess, in spite of the unfavourable nature of the subject, received a greater and a more valuable portion of applause than I expected or than it deserved.

Pref. 26. the prize of the goat] See Horace, *Ars Poetica* 220: 'Carmine qui tragico vilem certavit ob hircum' ('The poet who in tragic song first competed for a paltry goat').

Pref. 28. Aristarchi] Plural of Aristarchus, the scholar-grammarian of Samothrace (*c*.216–144 BCE) whose name is synonymous with severe criticism. See, e.g., Horace, *Ars Poetica* 450: 'fiet Aristarchus' ('he will prove an Aristarchus'); Pope, *The Dunciad* (1743 edn) iv 203–4: 'Before them march'd that awful Aristarch; / Plow'd was his front with many a deep Remark'; and Godwin, *Things As They Are; or, The Adventures of Caleb Williams*, 3 vols (1794) Vol. III ch. viii (*Godwin Novels* iii 228): 'they were rejected with contempt by the Aristarchus of that place'. S. was gloomy about his prospects of success as a poet at this time. See his letter to Hogg of 22 October 1821:

> My spirits also are by no means good, & I feel sensibly la noia e l'affanno della passata vita ['the trouble and pain of my past life', recalling 'la noia e 'l mal de la passata via', line 11 of Petrarch's canzone 'Ne la stagion che 'l ciel rapido inchina'].—I have some thoughts, if I could get a respectable appointment, of going to India, or any where where I might be compelled to active exertion, & at the same time enter into an entirely new sphere of action.— (*L* ii 361)

Pref. 29–32. The only ... than it deserved.] A reference to *The Cenci* which had been published in a second edition in June 1821 (see headnote to no. 209).

Pref. 29. goat-song] goat-song *1829*. A reference to what was believed to be the etymology of the word 'tragedy': 'song of goat', from τράγος (goat) and ἀοιδή (song). This instance is cited in *OED*. *Locock 1911* cps Socrates in Plato, *Cratylus* 408: 'Well, the true part [of speech] is smooth and divine and dwells among the gods above, while the false part dwells below among the human masses, and is rough and goatish (*tragikon*); for it is here, in the tragic (*tragikon*) life, that one finds the vast majority of myths and falsehoods' (trans. C. D. C. Reeve, in Plato, *Complete Works*, ed. John M. Cooper (1997) 126).

Pref. 32. expected] expected, *1829, 1839, 1840.* than] *MYRS* states that S. corrected *that* to *than* in *HM 329*; however, it appears that having altered the *n* to a *t*, S. realised his mistake and changed it back to an *n*.

Common fame is the only authority which I can allege for the details which form the basis of the poem, and I must
35 trespass upon the forgiveness of my readers for the display of newspaper erudition to which I have been reduced. Undoubtedly, until the conclusion of the war, it will be impossible to obtain an account of it sufficiently authentic for historical materials; but poets have their privilege,
40 and it is unquestionable that actions of the most exalted courage have been performed by the Greeks, that they have gained more than one naval victory, and that their defeat in

Pref. 33. fame] talk (see *OED* 1a). For similar uses of this word (*fama*, Lat. = report, rumour), see *L&C* 1491 and *J&M* (no. 198) 233.
Pref. 36. newspaper erudition] The sole instance of this phrase recorded in *OED*. S.'s main newspaper sources appear to have been *Galignani's Messenger* and the *Examiner*; see Headnote ('Sources of S.'s knowledge of the Greek Revolution.')
reduced] Written above *compelled* canc. in *HM 329* (both cancellation and insertion appear to be in S.'s hand.)
Pref. 38. authentic] accurate (see *OED* 2a).
Pref. 39. historical] The cancellation of the previous word *the* in *HM 329* is probably in S.'s hand.
Pref. 41. Greeks, that] Greeks—that *1822, 1829, 1839, 1840*; Greeks—they *1834*.
Pref. 42. more than one naval victory] A naval victory at Mytilene on Lesbos was reported in *Galignani's Messenger* 2002 (26 July 1821) [p. 3] and 2004 (28 July 1821): 'The Greek fleet of thirty-five vessels, made a resolute attack and maintained a bloody battle which the Turks endured with the heroism of despair' [p. 4]. First noted in the *Examiner* no. 708 (29 July 1821) 468, the 'important naval victory at Mytilene' was 'confirmed' in no. 709 (5 August 1821) 485. The *Examiner* 720 (21 October 1821) reported that the Greeks 'continue masters of the sea, a circumstance which protects them in that Peninsula from maritime attack' (660).
Pref. 42–3. their defeat in Wallachia] A reference to the Battle of Dragatsani on 7 June 1821 at which Alexandros Ypsilantis's Sacred Battalion was defeated; see Headnote ('Sources of S.'s knowledge of the Greek Revolution.') The battle was reported in *Galignani's Messenger* 1997 (20 July 1821) [p. 3]:

> Prince Ypsilanti, with 5,000 men, left Rymnick on the 16th of June, and proceeded towards Drageshcen. He passed the first night at Okna; and on the 19th ult., his advanced guard, commanded by Captain Iordaki, met a detachment of about 1,000 Turks. A battle ensued when the Bulgarians immediately fled, the Pandours refused to fight, and Jordaki was left with only forty Albanians. He then fell back upon the Heteristes of the *sacred battalion*, consisting of 700 men unskilled in

Wallachia was signalized by circumstances of heroism more
glorious even than defeat.

arms. The Turks pursued, and fell upon them with such impetuosity,
that this battalion was utterly annihilated.

The *Examiner* 509 (5 August 1821) 485 noted that 'Prince YPSILANTI and the northern Greeks are said to have been totally defeated and dispersed, owing to the cowardice of the Arnaut and Walachian auxiliaries'. S. described the support of the Tuscan government for the defeated Etairists in a letter to Byron of 21 October 1821: 'The other day a number of Heteristi, escaped from the defeat in Wallachia, past through Pisa, to embark at Leghorn & join Ipsilanti in Livadia. It is highly to the credit of the actual government of Tuscany, that it allowed these brave fugitives 3 livres a day each, & free quarters during their passage through these states' (*L* ii 358; Williams records this account of S.'s in his journal entry for that date (*Gisborne Jnl* 103); S. repeats it in his letter to John Gisborne of the following day, *L* ii 364).
Pref. 43–44. circumstances of heroism more glorious even than defeat] Possibly a reference to the actions of a Greek Priest recounted by S. (from an unidentified source) and recorded by Williams in his journal entry for 21 October 1821:

It is worthy of remark, that a Greek Priest unable to repress his emotions during this retreat, seized a sword from the grasp of one of his dying countrymen, and rushing into the Turkish ranks performed prodigies of valour, and causing a panic amongst the troops, whom he scattered on all sides, actually cut his way thro' to an Austrian outpost, to whom, tired with slaughter, he delivered himself! A detachment of Turks was sent to demand him; and being given to their custody & within a very short distance of the Turkish army, having in some measure regained his strength, he attacked his guards, and again escaped; but, unhappily, relied too fully on Austrian generosity. These wretches were barbarous enough to give the poor fellow *bound* to his enemies, under whose hands he died, in the fine spirit of his forefathers, after three days of savage and unparalleled torture. May the blood of this Grecian martyr be as an offering to God to defend their cause. (*Gisborne Jnl* 103–4)

The idea that the *defeat* in Wallachia was *glorious* may have been expressed when the Shelleys dined with the Williamses on 21 October 1821; Williams refers to 'Greeks who were at the memorable battle, or rather glorious retreat of Bucharest' (*Gisborne Jnl* 103). In the phrase *heroism more glorious even than defeat* there is possibly an echo of 'the heroism of despair' in the article in *Galignani's Messenger* 2004 cited in the note to Preface l. 42 above.
Pref. 43. heroism] 1822, 1829, 1839, 1840; heroism, HM 329.
Pref. 44. defeat] victory *eds*. A careted, encircled cross at the end of this sentence in HM 329 f. 3^r, is keyed to a barely legible note (unrecorded in *MYRS*) at the top of f. 2^r. The decipherable portion of the note reads: 'Sh$^{d.}$ not "victory" be read inst$^{d.}$

45   The apathy of the rulers of the civilized world to the
     astonishing circumstance of the descendants of that nation
     to which they owe their civilization rising as it were from the

---

of "defeat" at [encircled cross]'. (All markings are in pencil). The note is initialled
'J.M.'. The markings may be the work of a compositor, perhaps the one responsible
for the Greek letters on the title-page (see note to Epigraph).
Pref. 45–49. *The apathy ... this mortal scene.*] Cp. the lead article in the *Examiner*
713 (2 September 1821) 545–6 ('The Political Examiner' no. 699, 'The Greeks—
Russia, Turkey, and the Rest of Europe'), especially the following passage on 546:

> If France or England,—or either of them,—would play the part pointed
> out by honesty and prudence, justice would be done to a people
> trampled upon for centuries—the unnatural junction of two nations
> of hostile character dissolved—the Turks would be driven entirely out
> of Europe (the end so long desired)—and a most dangerous acqui-
> sition of territory withheld from Russia.—Utopian! cry the men of
> ledgers and counters. Alarming principles! shout the secret longers
> after simple despotism. It is indeed objected, that the new Greek state,
> in its infancy, would be inadequate to support itself against Russian
> encroachment. No easy task certainly; but surely infinitely more likely
> than that the incongruous parts of the Turkish Empire could be long
> held together by any means whatever. The *canting* objection is, that
> the long-oppressed people are not *fit* to govern themselves. Therefore
> the kind souls who make the objection would doom them to a new
> 100 years' lease of *protection!* But we say, Let them try: they must *gain*
> by change of any sort: it requires no great cleverness to govern decently,
> when the good of the many *must* be consulted; and six months' experi-
> ence would correct all the mere errors of novelty.

††

Pref. 45. *world*] world, *1829, 1839, 1840.*
Pref. 47–48. *civilization ... ruin*] civilization— ... ruin, *1822, 1829, 1839, 1840.*
rising ... from the ashes of their ruin] An allusion to the phoenix, a mythical bird
periodically consumed by fire then reborn. Cp. *An Address, to the Irish People*
(1812): 'these claims have for their basis, truth and justice, which are immut-
able, and which in the ruin of Governments shall rise like a Phœnix from their
ashes' (*Prose Works* 35). There may also be echoes of the account of the ruins of
Pompeii in Bk XI ch. iv of de Staël's *Corinne ou l'Italie* (1807) which S. read at
Naples in December 1818 (*Mary Jnl* i 243): 'Le volcan qui a couvert cette ville
de cendres l'a préservée des outrages du temps' ('The volcano that covered this
city with ashes preserved it from the ravages of time' (trans. Avriel Goldberger
(1987)).

ashes of their ruin is something perfectly inexplicable to a mere spectator of the shows of this mortal scene. We are all

Pref. 48–49. a mere spectator of the shows of this mortal scene] Cp. *TL* (no. 452) 305–6.
Pref. 49. this mortal scene] The phrase is found in Godwin, *St Leon*, 4 vols (1799) Vol. I ch. x. See also *Q Mab* i 88.
Pref. 49–54. We are all Greeks ... savages and idolaters;] Cp. *DMAG* (probably drafted late July 1818), especially: 'What the Greeks were, was a reality, not a promise. And what we are and hope to be, is derived, as it were, from the influence and inspiration of these glorious generations' (*Notopoulos* 407). S.'s encouragement of support among British readers for the modern Greeks by reminding them of their ancestors has parallels with the lead article in the *Examiner* 718 (7 October 1821) 625–7 ('The Political Examiner', no. 704, 'The Greeks'):

> But the Greeks! the Greeks! what do we not owe them? If the mere sympathy with one's fellow beings can fill men with impatient longings to take the part of an ordinary nation, what ought we not to feel in behalf of a country, to whose former inhabitants we are indebted for some of the noblest parts of our knowledge, and even our daily amusements? We wonder for our parts, that a subscription has not started up in every possible place where the word Greek is understood; [...] If we know any thing at all of the Greeks, we can hardly help being reminded of them at every turn of our lives. We can hardly open a book,—we cannot look at a school-boy,—we cannot use a term of science but we read of the Greeks, or have thoughts that may be traced to them, or speak their very language. We are Greek when we speak of nautical matters with the sailor, of arithmetic with the merchant, of stratagems with the soldier, of theatres and dramas with the play-goer, of poetry and philosophy with the man of letters, of theology with the churchman, of cosmetics with the fine lady. Our mechanics cannot perform some of their commonest and most necessary operations without being indebted to Greek ingenuity. Greek mythology is the religion of our poetry, the peopler of our starry sphere. All that is best in our very dress and fashions comes from Greece; the draperies of our women; and the heads, rescued from the powderer and the peruke-maker, of our men. [...] In short, we cannot exercise the art of reasoning, we cannot indulge the faculties of memory and imagination, we cannot employ the every day arts of life, we cannot set before us noble examples, we cannot converse, we cannot elegantly amuse ourselves, we cannot paint, sculpture, write poetry or music, we cannot be school-boys, be patriots, be orators, be useful or ornamental members of society, be human beings in a high state of cultivation, be persons living and moving and having their being in other wordls [sic] besides those of the idiot who only sees before him, without having a debt of gratitude to the Greeks:—and shall we not pay what we can for all this obligation?' (626–7)

50   Greeks — our laws, our literature, our religion, our arts have their root in Greece. But for Greece, Rome, the instructor, the conqueror, or the metropolis of our ancestors would have spread no illumination with her arms, and we might still have been savages and idolaters; or, what is worse, might have
55   arrived at such a stagnant and miserable state of social institution as China and Japan possess.
      The human form and the human mind attained to a

Pref. 50. Greeks — our] Greeks. Our *1822, 1829, 1839, 1840.* A small *o* is written over a capital in *HM 329*, whether in S.'s hand or Williams's is uncertain. *arts*] arts, *1822, 1829, 1839, 1840.*
Pref. 51. Greece,] Greece— *1822, 1829, 1839, 1840.*
Pref. 52. ancestors] ancestors, *1822, 1829, 1839, 1840.*
Pref. 54. savages] *1822, 1829, 1839, 1840*; savages, *HM 329.*
Pref. 55-56. such a stagnant ... as China and Japan possess] For the expression of similar views towards the countries of east Asia, cp. *PVR*:

> It was principally [by] a similar quietism that the populous & extensive nations of Asia have fallen into their existing decrepitude; and that anarchy insecurity ignorance & barbarism, the symptoms of the confirmed disease of monarchy have reduced nations in the most delicate physical & intellectual organization, & under the most fortunate climates of the globe to a blank in the history of man (*SC* vi 1057)

See also: 'I imagine however that before the English Nation shall arrive at that point of moral & political degradation now occupied by the Chinese, it will be necessary to appeal to an exertion of physical strength' (*SC* vi 1064).
Pref. 55-56. social institution] social institutions *1839, 1840*. social order; for 'institution', see *OED* 2a: '[t]he giving of form or order to a thing; orderly arrangement; regulation'.
Pref. 56. possess.] Written above *enjoy.* canc. in *HM 329* (both cancellation and insertion appear to be in S.'s hand.)
Pref. 57-58. The human form and the human mind attained to a perfection in Greece] Cp. *DMAG* where the Ancient Greeks are described as 'on the whole, the most perfect specimens of humanity of whom we have authentic record' (*Notopoulos* 407); and Marie-Jean-Antoine-Nicolas Caritat, Marquis de Condorcet, *Esquisse d'un tableau historique des progrès de l'esprit humain* [Sketch for a historical picture of the progress of the human mind] (L'an III [1795]), Quatrième Époque; Progrès de l'esprit humain dans la Grèce, jusqu'au temps de la division des sciences, vers le siècle d'Alexandre [The fourth stage; the progress of the human mind in Greece up to the division of the sciences about the time of Alexander the Great]:

60   perfection in Greece which has impressed its image on those
         faultless productions whose very fragments are the despair of
         modern art, and has propagated impulses which cannot cease,

> A cette époque des premières lueurs de la philosophie chez les Grecs, et de leurs premiers pas dans les sciences, les beaux arts s'y élèverent à un degré de perfection qu'aucun peuple n'avoit encore connu, qu'à peine quelques-uns ont pu atteindre depuis. (98)

> ('At this stage, marked for the Greeks by the dawn of philosophy, and the first advances in the sciences, the fine arts attained a degree of perfection that no other people had known before and that scarcely any has since achieved.'; trans. June Barraclough (1955) 53)

Pref. 58–60. those faultless productions ... modern art] Cp. *DMAG*: 'The wrecks and fragments of those subtle and profound minds, like the ruins of a fine statue, obscurely suggest to us the grandeur and perfection of the whole' (*Notopoulos* 404).
Pref. 59. productions] productions, 1822, 1840.
Pref. 60–63. has propagated impulses ... the race] Cp. A. W. Schlegel's *Vorlesungen über dramatische Kunst und Literatur* (1808), which S. read aloud to Mary and Claire *en route* to Italy between 16 and 21 March 1818 (*Mary Jnl* i 198–9) in John Black's translation, *A Course of Lectures on Dramatic Art and Literature*, 2 vols (1815), i 45–6:

> What is the best means of becoming imbued with the spirit of the Greeks, without a knowledge of their language? I answer without hesitation,—the study of the antique [...] These models of the human form require no interpretation; their elevated character is imperishable, and will always be recognized throughout every succession of ages, and in every clime, where a noble race of men related to the Greek (which the European undoubtedly is) shall exist [...] Respecting the inimitable perfection of the antique in its few remains of a first rate character, there is but one voice throughout the whole of civilized Europe; and if ever their merit was called in question, it was in times when the plastic art of the moderns had sunk to the lowest degree of mannerism. Not only all intelligent artists, but all men of any degree of feeling, bow with the most enthusiastic adoration to the masterly productions of ancient sculpture.

Schlegel goes on, 'The best key to enter this sanctuary of beauty, by deep and self-collected contemplation, is the history of art of our immortal Winckelmann' (i 46). S. read Johann Joachim Winckelmann's *Geschichte der Kunst des Alterthums* (1764)

65 through a thousand channels of manifest or imperceptible operation, to ennoble and delight mankind until the extinction of the race: the modern Greek is the descendant of those glorious beings whom the imagination almost refuses to figure to itself as belonging to our kind, and he inherits much of their sensibility, their rapidity of conception, their enthusiasm and their

aloud to Mary in a French translation between 24 December 1818 and 3 January 1819 (*Mary Jnl* i 246–7). S. appears to have assented to Winckelmann's claim that, 'With regard to the constitution and government of Greece, freedom was the chief reason for their art's superiority' (Johann Joachim Winckelmann, *History of the Art of Antiquity*, trans. Harry Francis Mallgrave, introd. Alex Potts (2006), 187).
Pref. 61–62. operation,] *1822, 1829, 1839, 1840*; operation *HM 329*.
Pref. 63. race: the modern Greek] race. The modern Greek *1822, 1829, 1839, 1840*. The new sentence marks the start of a new paragraph in eds. The compositor of *1822* may have been disconcerted by *HM 329* where Williams first indented the sentence, then added and cancelled *the* in the space at the start of the line. Finally, *The* is altered to *the* and, while the full stop after *race* is unaltered, two stops appear to have been written over the final two letters of this word (it is not certain in whose hand these last markings are made).
Pref. 63–4. those glorious beings] Cp. S.'s letter to John Gisborne of 16 November 1819:

> Were not the Greeks a glorious people? What is there, as Job says of the Leviathan, like unto them? If the army of Nicias had not been defeated under the walls of Syracuse, if the Athenians had, acquiring Sicily held the balance between Rome & Carthage, sent garrisons to the Greek colonies in the south of Italy, Rome might have been all that its intellectual condition entitled it to be, a tributary not the conqueror of Greece; the Macedonian power would never have attained to the dictatorship of the civilized states of the world. Who knows whether under the steady progress which philosophy & social institutions would have made, (for in the age to which I refer their progress was both rapid & secure,) among a people of the most perfect physical organization, whether the Christian Religion would have arisen, or the barbarians have overwhelmed the wrecks of civilization which had survived the conquests & tyranny of the Romans.—What then should we have been? (*L* ii 156)

Pref. 65. kind,] kind; *1829, 1839, 1840*.
Pref. 66. enthusiasm] enthusiasm, *1822, 1829, 1839, 1840*.

courage. If in many instances he is degraded by moral and
political slavery to the practice of the basest vices it engenders,
and that below the level of ordinary degradation, let us reflect
70   that the corruption of the best produces the worst, and that
habits which subsist only in relation to a peculiar state of social
institution may be expected to cease so soon as that relation
is dissolved. In fact, the Greeks, since the admirable novel of

---

Pref. 67–70. If in many instances he is degraded ... the worst] See S.'s letter to Mary
of 8–10 August 1821 from Ravenna in which he cites Aeschylus, *Agamemnon*
758–60:

> We have good rumours of the Greeks here & [of] a Russian war.
> I hardly wish the Russians to take any part in it—My maxim is with
> Æschylus τὸ δυσσεβὲς-μετὰ μὲν [με *canc*., correctly, after an apparent
> dittography] πλείονα τίκτει, σφετέρᾳ δ' εἰκότα γέννᾳ (it is the impious
> [deed — a translation of the equivalent Greek word omitted from S.'s
> quotation] that breeds more to follow resembling their progenitors)—
> There is a Greek exercise for you.—How should slaves produce any
> thing but tyranny—even as the seed produces the plant.— (*L* ii 324–5)

See also his letter to Horace Smith of 14 September 1821 in which he noted that 'All
public attention is now centred on the wonderful revolution in Greece.' S. went on
to remark, with reference to the defeat of the revolutions in Naples and Piedmont by
the Austrians in March, 'I dare not, after the events of last winter, hope that slaves
can become freemen so cheaply' (*L* ii 350). According to Medwin, S. 'admitted
that a long course of political slavery under their Mahomedan masters, had so
demoralised and bastardised the [modern Greek] nation, that important changes
must be undergone before it could be regenerated' (*Medwin (1913)* 353).
Pref. 67. degraded] *1829, 1839, 1840*; degraded, *HM 329, 1822*.
Pref. 68. slavery] Followed by a cancelled comma in *HM 329* (the cancellation is
probably in S.'s hand.)
Pref. 68–69. engenders, ... degradation,] *1834*; engenders, ... degradation; *HM 329,
1822, 1829, 1839*.
Pref. 71–2 social institution] See Preface ll. 55–6, above, and note.
Pref. 72. cease so soon] cease, as soon *1829, 1839, 1840*; cease as soon *1834*.
Pref. 73–4. the admirable novel of Anastasius ... *most important changes*] On S.'s
reading of *Anastasius: Or, Memoirs of a Greek; Written at the Close of the Eighteenth
Century*, 3 vols (1819) by Thomas Hope (1769–1831), see Headnote ('Literary
sources'). S. told Mary in a letter of 11 August: 'I am reading Anastasius.—One
would think that Albè had taken his idea of the 3 last cantos of Don Juan from
this book. That of course has nothing to do with the merit of this latter: poetry
having nothing to do with the invention of facts.—' (*L* ii 332). After its anonymous
publication in 1819, *Anastasius* appeared under Hope's name in a second edition

	Anastasius could have been a faithful picture of their manners,
75	have undergone most important changes; the flower of their youth returning to their country from the universities of Italy, Germany and France have communicated to their fellow citizens the latest results of that social perfection of which their ancestors were the original source. The university of Chios

in 1820 which was followed by a third in the same year. Hope's picaresque novel was based on 'what must have been the grandest of grand tours' (David Watkin, *Thomas Hope 1769-1831 and the Neo-Classical Idea* (1968) 5) between 1787 and 1795, and in the dedication to the second edition of 1820, he claimed, in language echoed by S. that 'the historical and statistical parts are (as far as my knowledge extends) strictly correct, and [...] the fictitious superstructure—founded on personal observation—is as conformable as I could make it to the manners of the nations whom it was my aim to describe' (vi). Claire read the novel between 30 August and 1 September 1821 (*Claire Jnl* 247), Mary on 5, 9, 19 September 1821 and 13-17 February 1822 (*Mary Jnl* i 379, 397-8). As S. implies in 'the Greeks ... have undergone most important changes', the novel's portrayal of Greeks in the late eighteenth century purported to be realistic. For example, in Vol. 1 ch. iii, the character of Mavroyeni states: 'When patriotism, public spirit, and pre-eminence in arts, science, literature, and warfare were the road to distinction, the Greeks shone the first of patriots, of heroes, of painters, of poets, and of philosophers. Now that craft and subtlety, adulation and intrigue are the only paths to greatness, these same Greeks are—what you see them!' (i 84).

Pref. 74. Anastasius] *Dowden 1890*; "Anastatius" *HM 329, 1822, 1829, 1839, 1840*; "Anastasius" *Forman 1876-7*.

Pref. 75-77. *their youth returning to their country from the universities of Italy, Germany and France*] The most likely source of this information is S.'s knowledge of the Greek expatriate community at Pisa, which extended beyond Alexandros Mavrokordatos. Cp. the Shelleys' anonymous letters, dated 'Pisa, April 5, 1821', published in London newspapers discussed in the Headnote ('Sources of S.'s knowledge of the Greek revolution'): 'The Greek students dispersed in the various Universities of Europe are hastening to assist in the struggles of their country' (*Examiner* 694 (22 April 1821) 248); 'The Greeks dispersed over Europe, whether as merchants or as students at the Universities, are hastening to join the army' (*Morning Chronicle* 16227 (23 April 1821) 2).

Pref. 76. *universities*] *1822, 1829, 1839, 1840*; Universities *HM 329*.

Pref. 77. *Germany and France*] Germany, and France, *1822, 1840*; Germany and France, *1829, 1839*.

Pref. 77-78. *fellow citizens*] fellow-citizens *1822, 1829, 1839, 1840*.

Pref. 79. *Chios*] The native island of the protagonist in Hope's *Anastasius*, 3 vols (1819); see vol. I, ch. i. Raizis states that 'Chios had always had excellent educational institutions and flourishing cultural and artistic activities on account of its wealth' (*Raizis* 86). William St Clair notes that 'The revival of Greek education had

80   contained before the breaking out of the Revolution eight
      hundred students, and among them several Germans and
      Americans. The munificence and energy of many of the Greek
      princes and merchants, directed to the renovation of their
      country with a spirit and a wisdom which has few examples, is
85   above all praise.
         The English permit their own oppressors to act according
      to their natural sympathy with the Turkish tyrant, and to
      brand upon their name the indelible blot of an alliance

---

gone further in Chios than elsewhere in Greece and many Sciotes lived abroad in Western Europe maintaining close links with their homeland' (*That Greece Might Still Be Free: The Philhellenes in the War of Independence*, rev. edn (2008) 79).

Pref. 80. Revolution] revolution *1822, 1829*; revolution, *1839, 1840*.

Pref. 82. Americans] A reference to Americans attending Greek universities is found in the Proclamation of the Messenian Senate at Kalamata to the Citizens of the United States signed by Petros Mavromihalis in the *Morning Chronicle* 16405 (16 November 1821) 2: 'No, the country of Penn, of Franklin, and of Washington cannot refuse her aid to the descendants of Phoclon, Thrasybulus, Aratus, and Philopœmen. You have already evinced your confidence in them, by sending your children to their schools.'

Pref. 82–85. The munificence ... of the Greek princes ... is above all praise.] An apparent reference to Alexandros Mavrokordatos; see Headnote ('Biographical context').

Pref. 83. princes] Princes *1829*. *merchants,*] *1822, 1829, 1839, 1840*; merchants *HM 329*.

Pref. 84. examples,] Followed by *and* canc. in *HM 329*. The comma, the cancellation of *and* and the extension to the descender of the *p* in *examples* are probably all in S.'s hand (as *MYRS* suggests); 'examples' = precedents (this instance is cited in *OED* 'example' *n.* 5a).

Pref. 86–90. The English permit ... civilization] S. echoes Hunt who frequently describes the British government's lack of support for the Greek cause as endorsing un-Christian Turkish tyranny:

> The great question for Englishmen is, What is the true policy of this country at the crisis? [...] The insurrection and partial success of the Greeks have created a new interest, which totally changes our situation and duties. We were wont to aid the Ottoman Government, because that was the only way of checking the Russian. But now we cannot do so without contributing to bring back a people struggling for liberty under the barbarous and unjust yoke of usurping fanatics. ('The Greeks—Russia, Turkey, and the Rest of Europe', 'The Political Examiner', no. 699 in the *Examiner* 713 (2 September 1821) 545).

with the enemies of domestic happiness, of Christianity and
90   civilization. Russia desires to possess, not to liberate Greece, and
is contented to see the Turks, its natural enemies, and the
Greeks, its intended slaves, enfeeble each other until one or
both fall into its net. The wise and generous policy of England
95   would have consisted in establishing the independence of

Pref. 89. *Christianity*] Christianity, *1834, 1840*.
Pref. 91–94. *Russia desires to possess ... into its net*] The hostility towards Russia and its Tsar, Alexander, was strongly evident in the *Examiner* from spring to autumn 1821. See, e.g., the opening of 'The Greeks—Russia, Turkey, and the Rest of Europe':

> The situation of Europe is a very singular and critical one in regard to the anticipated Turkish war. Russia has long had a hankering after the possession of the neighbouring provinces of Turkey, and more particularly of Constantinople and the Dardanelles. Her whole foreign commerce to and from the Black Sea is dependant on the power which holds that capital and the Straits. Imagine what prodigious advantages would accrue to Russia from the possession of that entrance into the Mediterranean, and the consequent inlet to the South of Europe,— commanding as she also does the navigation of the Baltic in the North. Then again the Russians profess a religion in common with the Greeks, and have a common fanatical hatred to the Mahometan oppressors of the latter. ('The Political Examiner', no. 699 in the *Examiner* 713 (2 September 1821) 545).

Pref. 91. *Russia*] Russia, *1834. possess,*] *1822, 1829, 1839, 1840*; possess *HM 329*. *liberate*] liberate, *1834. Greece,*] Greece; *1822, 1829, 1839, 1840*.
Pref. 92–93. *Turks, ... enemies, ... Greeks, ... slaves,*] *1822, 1829, 1839, 1840*; Turks ... enemies ... Greeks ... slaves *HM 329*.
Pref. 93. *other*] other, *1829, 1839, 1840*.
Pref. 94–97. *The wise and generous policy ... generous or just?*] In 'Percy Shelley's "display of newspaper erudition"' 521, Duffy suggests that S. here engages with an editorial from the *New Times* reprinted in *Galignani's Messenger* 2082 (29 October 1821) [p. 1] which denies that Britain should support the Greek cause:

> still less can we be expected to contribute to the success of the Greek cause, when our own engagements and interests are recollected. We are the allies of Turkey, who cordially co-operated with us when we had an enemy in Egypt; it would be a faithless return to aggravate intestine war, and support revolted subjects against a Sovereign, who (whatever may be his religion, or his barbarism), has never violated faith with us. But if we assist the Greeks, what are we to do with them? [...] Then,

Greece, and in maintaining it both against Russia and the
Turk; — but when was the oppressor generous or just?
   Should the English people ever become free, they
will reflect upon the part which those who presume to
100 represent their will have played in the great drama of the
revival of liberty, with feelings which it would become them
to anticipate. This is the age of the war of the oppressed

> let us consider the interest of Great Britain, her treaties, and her true
> policy, rather than squander our superabundant wealth to support civil
> war, and embroil the pacific state into which the affairs of the world are
> gradually subsiding.

As Duffy notes, S.'s criticism of British neutrality echoes that of Hunt in the *Examiner* 713 (2 September 1821) 546 cited in the note to Preface ll. 45–49.
Pref. 96. Greece,] Greece *1829*.
Pref. 97. Turk] Turks *1839, 1840*.
Pref. 98–112. Should the English ... and dread.] Omitted in *eds* before *Forman 1892* iv 40–1 and *Woodberry 1892* iii 100–1 (see Headnote ('Publication')).
Pref. 98–102. Should the English people ... become them to anticipate] Cp. Mary's letter to Leigh Hunt of 17 April 1821:

> I send you the latest news from Greece—you see what a pretty part We
> English are acting—but we are so moral & religious that there can be
> no wonder that we help Turks & Tyrants against Xtians & the Would-
> be-free. (*Mary L* i 189)

Pref. 98. free,] *1822 Unexpurgated*, *Forman 1892*, *Woodberry 1892*; free *HM 329*.
Pref. 100. their will] *Forman 1892, Woodberry 1892*; their will, *HM 329, 1822 Unexpurgated*.
Pref. 102–103. the war of the oppressed against the oppressors] Cp. Robert Emmet's speech at his trial on 19 September 1803 after one of Lord Norbury's interruptions: 'What, my Lord, shall you tell me on my passage to the scaffold [...] that I am accountable for all the blood that has and will be shed in this struggle of the oppressed against the oppressor?' (R. R. Madden, *The United Irishmen; their Lives and Times*, 3rd ser., iii (1846) 244). On S. and Emmet, see *On Robert Emmet's Tomb* (no. 72). The 'oppressed'/'oppressors' collocation is frequent in S.'s writings; see *L&C* 3333; *PB3* 253; *The Cenci* III i 284, V iii 75; and the present poem l. 897.

against the oppressors, and every one of those ringleaders
of the privileged gangs of murderers and swindlers called
105   Sovereigns, look to each other for aid against the common
enemy, and suspend their mutual jealousies in the presence
of a mightier fear. Of this holy alliance all the despots of

Pref. 103–112. those ringleaders ... foresee and dread] In this attack on monarchy, there are echoes of Hunt's article 'The Greeks' ('The Political Examiner' no. 704) in the *Examiner* 718 (7 October 1821) 625:

> The Monarchs [...] long to put down the Turks; they long to appropriate Greece; they long to shew themselves worthy members of the Holy Christian Alliance; but they fear the Greek *people*; they fear their own people; their Christianity and their Legitimacy are at issue. Inasmuch as the Greeks are *Christians* who have risen against *Turks*, they would assist them with all their orthodoxy; but inasmuch as the Greeks are Christians who have *risen* against Turks, they would put them down with their tyrannodoxy.

S.'s hostility towards the institution of monarchy evinced in this passage was evident in other writings he published in the summer of 1821. He defended the right to criticise it in a letter 'To the Editor of the Examiner' dated '*Pisa, June* 22, 1821', published in the *Examiner* 706 (15 July 1821) 443 (and the *Morning Chronicle* 16299 (16 July 1821) 3), further to learning that a piracy of *Q Mab* had recently been published:

> Whilst I exonerate myself from all share in having divulged opinions hostile to existing sanctions, under the form, whatever it may be, which they assume in this poem; it is scarcely necessary for me to protest against the system of inculcating the truth of Christianity and the excellence of Monarchy, however true or however excellent they may be, by such equivocal arguments as confiscation, and imprisonment, and invective, and slander, and the insolent violation of the most sacred ties of nature and society.

Pref. 104. swindlers] swindlers, Woodberry 1892.
Pref. 105. Sovereigns] sovereigns Woodberry 1892.
Pref. 107–112. this holy alliance ... tyrants foresee and dread] In her 'Note on Hellas', Mary commented: 'the Holy Alliance was alive and active in those days, and few could dream of the peaceful triumph of liberty' (*1839* ii 344). A 'Holy Alliance' had been signed in September 1815 by Alexander, Tsar of Russia, Francis 1, Emperor of Austria, and Frederick William III, King of Prussia, 'to deal with each other and other peoples on the basis of the Christian gospel' (Robert Gildea,

the earth are virtual members. But a new race has arisen
throughout Europe, nursed in the abhorrence of the
110   opinions which are its chains, and she will continue to

Barricades and Borders: Europe 1800–1914, 3rd edn (2003) 60). A meeting of the Alliance at the Congress of Laibach in January-March 1821 had been used by Metternich to authorise the Austrian suppression of the uprisings in Naples and Piedmont in March. The report in the *Examiner* 700 (3 June 1821) 340 of a 'CIRCULAR DISPATCH' by 'the three Monarchs' 'dated *Laybach, May* 12' clarifies the intent of the Holy Alliance at this time:

> The Monarchs [...] talk of the 'vast conspiracy against all Established Power;' and say of its object, that 'Pure Monarchies, limited Monarchies, Federative Constitutions, Republics, all are comprehended, all are engulphed, in the proscriptions of a sect who brand as an *oligarchy* every thing, of whatever kind, that rises above the level of a chimerical equality.' [...] The Allies next lay down their own leading principle—'*to preserve what is legally established.*' * * * '*Useful or necessary changes in legislation, and in the administration of States, ought only to emanate from the free will, and the intelligent and well weighed conviction of those whom God has rendered responsible for power.*[1]

The basis of Mary's contempt for the Holy Alliance is clear from her letter to Hunt of 17 April 1821:

> Russia & Austria have both joined in a declaration that they disapprove of the Revolt of the Greeks—Austria would if she dared declare openly for the Turks—as it is she refuses passports to allow the Greeks dispersed in Europe to pass through her territories to Wallachia— They must therefore wait until the army of Ipsilanti coming south the whole of Greece [   ] so that Prince Mavrocordato is not yet gone, & the poor Ex-Ospodaro here who thought to return not to his principality but to his estates in Wallachia is obliged to wait. They stop all letters also—Thus at once avowing their wicked hypocrisy with regard to religion, and as their own policy suits them declaring for the crescent against the Cross—Why I am a better Xtian than they. (*Mary L* i 189)

Pref. 111–112. that destiny which tyrants foresee and dread] Cp. Mahmud's encounter with the Phantom in ll. 879–85.

produce fresh generations to accomplish that destiny which tyrants foresee and dread.

The Spanish peninsula is already free. France is tranquil in the enjoyment of a partial exemption from the abuses which
115   its unnatural and feeble government are vainly attempting to revive. The seed of blood and misery has been sown in Italy and a more vigorous race is arising to go forth to the harvest. The world waits only the news of a revolution of Germany to see the Tyrants who have pinnacled themselves
120   on its supineness precipitated into the ruin from which they shall never arise. Well do these destroyers of mankind know their enemy when they impute the insurrection in Greece to

Pref. 113. The Spanish peninsula is already free.] A reference to the uprising in Cadiz on 1 January 1820 that led Ferdinand VII to restore the Spanish Constitution of 1812. See *OL. peninsula*] Peninsula *1822, 1829, 1839, 1840.*

Pref. 113–116. France is tranquil ... to revive] A reference to the state of France following the death of Napoleon Bonaparte in May 1821; see *Written on hearing the news of the death of Napoleon.* The Bourbon monarchy under Louis XVIII had been restored in May 1814 (after the abdication of Napoleon the previous month) and S. appears to refer here to anti-Liberal measures by the government following the murder of the Duc de Berri, nephew of the king, in February 1820.

Pref. 115. feeble] enfeebled *1834.*

Pref. 117. Italy] Italy, *1822, 1829, 1839, 1840.*

Pref. 119. Germany] Germany, *1829, 1839, 1840.* Tyrants] tyrants *1822, 1829, 1839, 1840.*

Pref. 121–127. Well do these destroyers ... from their grasp. —] *Donovan* cps Hunt's article 'The Greeks' in the *Examiner* 718 (7 October 1821) 625:

> the Governments of Europe [...] see the Greek insurrection forerunning a Prussian insurrection, an Italian insurrection, insurrection every where; and they think they would rather be acknowledged vassals to ALEXANDER, and pay him tribute for keeping their crowns on, than run a risque so horrible to be imagined.

Pref. 122. enemy] enemy, *1822, 1829, 1839, 1840.*

125 the same spirit before which they tremble throughout the rest of Europe, and that enemy well knows the power and the cunning of its opponents, and watches the moment of their approaching weakness and inevitable division to wrest the bloody sceptres from their grasp. —

Pref. 124. Europe,] Europe; *1829, 1839, 1840.*
Pref. 124–125. and the cunning] and cunning *1829, 1834, 1839, 1840.*
Pref. 125–127. the moment ... grasp. —] This passage is added in S.'s hand in HM 329.
Pref. 126. division] division, *1829, 1839, 1840.*

DRAMATIS PERSONAE

MAHMUD.
HASSAN.
DAOOD.
AHASUERUS, a Jew.
Chorus of Greek captive women.
Messengers, Slaves, and Attendants.

SCENE. *Constantinople.*
TIME, Sunset.

Dramatis Personae. In *HM 329* the Dramatis Personae is on the verso of f. 1 of the preliminaries, the recto of which contains the title-page. The omission of PHANTOM OF MAHOMET THE SECOND in *1822* is noted in 'Additional Errata' in *Wise* (lvi); Rossetti added this character in the Dramatis Personae in *Rossetti 1870* ii 109 (see *Rossetti 1878* ii 455).

Dramatis Personae. MAHMUD] In the Dramatis Personae in *HM 329* f. 1ᵛ the regnal number *2ⁿᵈ* after *Mahmud* is cancelled. In 'Percy Shelley's "display of newspaper erudition"' 522, Duffy suggests that the 'sympathetic portrait which Shelley draws of the Ottoman sultan Mahmud II [...] was no doubt informed by the biographical sketch of Mahmud II carried in *Galignani's Messenger*'. Duffy refers to the article headed 'The Ottoman Empire' in no. 1996 (19 July 1821) [p. 2]:

> In the present condition of the Ottoman empire, it may prove, in some degree, interesting to direct our attention to the reigning Sovereign:—
> "Mahmud the Second, mounted the throne on the 11th of August, 1808, at a time when the affairs of the empire presented the most unfavourable aspect. Intestine commotions, and an unsuccessful war, carried on against the Servians and Russians, seemed to prognosticate its approaching dissolution. By his prudent exertions he allayed the storm. Constrained at first to sign a disadvantageous treaty of peace, he contrived to draw from it an opportunity for successively reducing the revolted Pachas. The repression of the sect of Wahabis, and the conquest of Servia, are proofs of the political talents of this Monarch. Finally, the line of conduct he has pursued in situations of a delicate nature with regard to European Powers, do equal honour to

the clearness of his understanding. It was worthy of remark, that the Princess of Wales should be received in his own residence (the admission of a female being contrary to the usage of this Court) at the very moment the English squadron was bombarding Algiers.

"Mahmud exercises his internal administration with excessive rigour. The depredators of the finances were lately terrified with examples of justice administered with equal severity and expedition. A tendency of but rare occurrence amongst Sultans, to the amelioration and reform so unhappily attempted by Selim III is remarked in this Prince, whose character, in some respects, resembles that of Soliman II.

"Mahmud may be frequently seen, followed by an immense retinue, passing through the streets of Constantinople to prayers on a Friday. He always rides a white horse, caparisoned with tissue of gold and pearls. He is about thirty-three years old, his countenance pale, but his features are noble and regular. As he passes, he surveys his people with his full black eyes; his glance is awaited in the most profound silence, and he is at a distance before the brow of the faithful Mussulman touches the dust. In 1817, by a dreadful conflagration (the only right of petition with the Turks), during which, respect for the laws of the Harem did not permit the assistance of the men who hastened to extinguish it to be accepted, Mahmud lost his mother, a Princess of a good understanding and amiable disposition, who possessed great influence with him. One of his sons also perished in the flames. To the qualities of the understanding and heart which distinguish him, Mahmud joins all the advantages of a prepossessing exterior."

Dramatis Personae. HASSAN] 'Hassan, a not uncommon Turkish name, might mean to recall the celebrated Grand Admiral Cezayirli Gazi Hasan, who commanded the Ottoman navy 1774–89, subdued Egypt and served as Grand Vizier from 1789 until his death in 1790' (*Donovan* 826). S. may have had the depiction of this commander in Hope's *Anastasius*, 3 vols (1819) in mind in his characterisation of Hassan. The death of 'Ghazi Hassan' on 20 March 1790 is recorded in Vol. II ch. xv where the narrator offers the following eulogy:

Of Hassan, nothing now remains save his memory. This however will endure in all its splendor while the Turkish empire lasts. The single cloud which dims the setting sun cannot produce forgetfulness of the many hours during which it shed its undiminished radiance! As a youth, I witnessed Hassan's expedition to the Morea. More matured, I followed him in that to Egypt. His history, his achievements exerted over my destinies that remote but unceasing influence which the luminary of the world exerts alike over all the living things of the earth, whether he directly gladdens them with his aspect, or whether, lighting up other regions, he be hidden from their view. As I beheld the meridian glory, so I beheld the last refulgence of his dazling career; and not only while Hassan lived did my fate remain indirectly linked to his fortunes, but even at his death did the mournful chill which pervaded the empire, extend its benumbing influence to my remote and narrow orbit. Of the bright beams which he poured forth in his zenith, a few had been reflected upon my humble person, and the long shadow he left at his decline, involved my fate likewise in its wide extending darkness.

Dramatis Personae. AHASUERUS, a Jew] Ahasuerus, or the Wandering Jew, figures in several of S.'s early writings: *WJ* (no. 11) 609–705; *The Wandering Jew's Soliloquy* (no. 48); *Q Mab* vii 49–275 and note to vii 67; *Alastor* 675–81. Historically Ahasuerus is identified as Xerxes I (485–464 BCE). According to *Esther* i 1, he ruled 'from India even unto Ethiopia'.

Dramatis Personae. captive women] Captive Women *1822, 1839, 1840*; captive Women *1829*.

TIME, Sunset] S.'s drama observes the classical unities of time, place and action, and opens at the sunset both of the day, and of the Ottoman Empire.

Hellas,
A Lyrical Drama

SCENE. *A terrace on the Seraglio.*
MAHMUD, *sleeping, an Indian slave sitting beside his couch.*

Chorus of Greek Captive Women
We strew these opiate flowers
On thy restless pillow, —
They were stripped from Orient bowers,
By the Indian billow.
5   Be thy sleep
Calm and deep,

SCENE. *Seraglio*] The apartments in the Sultan's palace where the women of the Harem were kept in seclusion. MAHMUD] See notes to *Dramatis Personae*.
1. SD. *Chorus of Greek Captive Women*] Medwin states: 'The opening Chorus of *Hellas* is taken from the *Principe Costante* of Calderon, as Shelley pointed out to me' (*Medwin (1913)* 353). S. read Calderón's *El príncipe constante* (The Constant Prince) with Maria Gisborne in the summer of 1819 (*L* ii 105, *L* ii 154); as discussed in the headnote to *Cyprian* (no. 441), the edition in which S. read the play is likely to have been *Sexta Parte de Comedias del Celebre Poeta Español, Don Pedro Calderon de la Barca*, ed. Vera Tassis (1683). Calderón's play opens with a series of choruses sung by 'Christian captives', in dialogue with 'Zara'; S.'s conception for his chorus clearly derives from this, but there are no substantive verbal parallels. GM noted an affinity between S.'s opening chorus and the exchanges between Electra and the Chorus by the sleeping Orestes at the opening of Euripides, *Orestes* (140–210). The repetition of 'low, low' in lines 27, 31 and 33 may echo similar doubled instructions for quiet in Euripides: σῖγα σῖγα ('hush, hush'; 140, 183), ἀτρέμας, ἀτρέμας ('softly, softly'; 149). *Raizis* 22 observes that the chorus 'secures a Greek voice and view point in an entirely Turkish environment'.
1-45. The opening choric exchanges are a good example of S.'s lyric invention throughout *Hellas*. The first four choruses alternate seven- and six-line stanzas, the first and third ending in a triplet rhyme *ababcc*, and the second and fourth in a couplet *ababcc* (thereby anticipating the rhyme scheme of the five-line stanzas which form the final chorus of the poem). In the fifth Chorus, like the first and third of seven lines and ending with a triplet rhyme, the first four lines rhyme *aabb*. The semichoruses in ll. 34–45 then reduce to quatrains rhyming in couplets before the more complex formal organisation of the chorus at ll. 46–93 (see notes below).
3. bowers,] bowers *1829*.
6. deep,] *1822, 1829, 1839, 1840*; deep *HM 329*.

Like theirs who fell, not ours who weep!

Indian
Away, unlovely dreams!
Away, false shapes of sleep!
10   Be his, as Heaven seems,
Clear and bright and deep!
Soft as love, and calm as death,
Sweet as a summer night without a breath.

Chorus
Sleep, sleep! our song is laden
15   With the soul of slumber;
It was sung by a Samian maiden
Whose lover was of the number

7. *theirs*] their's *1822. fell,*] fell— *1822, 1829, 1839, 1840. ours*] our's *1822.*
9. *Away,*] *1822, 1829, 1839, 1840;* Away *HM 329. sleep!*] sleep: *1829.*
10. *Heaven*] heaven *1829. seems,*] *1822, 1829, 1839, 1840;* seems *HM 329.*
11. *Clear and bright*] Clear, and bright, *1822, 1839, 1840;* Clear, bright *1829, 1834.*
12. *love,*] love *1829. death,*] *1822, 1829, 1839, 1840;* death *HM 329.*
13. *summer night*] summer-night *1829.*
15. *slumber;*] *1822, 1829, 1839, 1840;* slumber, *HM 329.*
16–20. *Samian maiden ... shall weep*] Samos is a Greek island in the Eastern Aegean Sea, close to Turkey. In Ancient Greece it was a powerful centre of Ionian culture, but had been under Ottoman rule since the late fifteenth century; it joined the Greek uprising in April 1821 (cp. l. 287 below). 'Samian wine' is part of the recurring refrain in stanzas 9–16 of Byron's lyric 'The Isles of Greece' in Byron, *Don Juan* Canto iii. The motif of (Persian) women deprived of their lovers is a strong focus of the chorus of Aeschylus' *Persae*, for example at 133–9:

λέκτρα δ' ἀνδρῶν πόθῳ
πίμπλαται δακρύμασιν·
Περσίδες δ' ἁβροπενθεῖς ἑκάστα πόθῳ φιλάνορι
τὸν αἰχμάεντα θοῦρον εὐνατῆρ' ἀποπεμψαμένα
λείπεται μονόζυξ.

('And beds are filled with tears because the men are missed and longed for: Persian women, grieving amid their luxury, every one, loving and longing for her husband, having sent on his way the bold warrior who was her bedfellow, is left behind, a partner unpartnered.')

16. *maiden*] maiden, *1822, 1829, 1839, 1840.*

                    Who now keep
                    That calm sleep
20   Whence none may wake, where none shall weep.

                        Indian
                 I touch thy temples pale!
                 I breathe my soul on thee!
                 And could my prayers avail,
                    All my joy should be
25   Dead, and I would live to weep
            So thou might'st win one hour of quiet sleep.

                        Chorus
                    Breathe low, low,
            The spell of the mighty mistress now!
            When Conscience lulls her sated snake
30   And Tyrants sleep, let Freedom wake.

20. *where*] The alteration from *whence* in *HM 329* is probably in Williams's hand not, as *MYRS* suggests, S.'s. *wake,*] wake *1840*.
23. *avail,*] *1822, 1829, 1839, 1840*; avail (the alteration from *prevail* in *HM 329* is probably in Williams's hand not, as *MYRS* suggests, S.'s.).
25. *weep*] weep, *1822, 1829, 1839, 1840*.
26. *might'st*] mightst *1829*.
27-8. *low, low, … now!*] *1829, 1839, 1840*; low low … now — *Nbk 21*; low, low! … now *HM 329*; low, low … now! *1822*.
27. *Breathe low, low*] Cp. (also ll. 31, 33) with Coleridge, 'Fire, Famine, & Slaughter' (first pub. in 1798, repr. in *The Annual Anthology*, 2 vols (1799-1800) ii 231-5), ll. 17-18:

        Whisper it, Sister! so and so!
        In a dark hint, soft and low.

S. knew this poem well. See headnotes to *Falsehood and Vice: A Dialogue* (no. 76), *Lines Written among the Euganean Hills, October 1818* (no. 183) and *PU* I 74, 105, 504 and notes.
29. *Conscience lulls her sated snake*] In the context of Electra and Orestes (see note to l. 1 SD above), the 'sated snake' recalls Clytaemnestra's dream of giving birth to and suckling a serpent, which bites and wounds her breast, in Aeschylus, *Libation Bearers* 526-50. Orestes interprets the dream to mean that he is to kill her, as eventually he does: ἐκδρακοντωθεὶς δ' ἐγὼ/ κτείνω νιν, ὡς τοὔνειρον ἐννέπει τόδε (549-50; 'for I, turned serpent, am her killer, as this dream declares'). Orestes' sleep at the opening of Euripides' *Orestes* is set after the death of his mother. *Conscience*] conscience *1829*. *snake*] snake, *1822, 1829, 1839, 1840*.

Breathe! low — low!
The words which like secret fire shall flow
Through the veins of the frozen earth — low, low!

Semichorus 1st
Life may change, but it may fly not;
35 Hope may vanish, but can die not;
Truth be veiled but still it burneth;
Love repulsed, — but it returneth!

Semichorus 2nd
Yet were Life a charnel where
Hope lay coffined with despair;
40 Yet were Truth a sacred lie;
Love were Lust —

Semichorus 1st
If Liberty
Lent not Life its soul of light,
Hope its iris of delight,
Truth its prophet's robe to wear,
45 Love its power to give and bear.

31. *Breathe! low — low!*] Breathe low—low *1822*; Breathe low, low, *1829, 1839, 1840*.
32-3. *The words ... earth*] S. frequently invokes volcanic activity as a metaphor for political revolution; see, e.g., *PU* II ii–iii and notes, *OL* 182-7 and *Ode to Naples* ll. 3-8.
32. *words which ... fire*] words which, ... fire, *1822, 1829, 1839*; words, which, ... fire, *1840*.
36. *veiled*] veil'd, *1822*; veiled, *1829, 1839, 1840*. *burneth;*] *1822, 1829, 1839, 1840*; burneth *HM 329*.
38. *Life*] life *1822, 1829, 1839, 1840*. *charnel*] charnel, *1829, 1839, 1840*.
39. *despair*] Despair *1822, 1839, 1840*.
40. *Truth*] truth *1822, 1829, 1839, 1840*. *lie;*] lie, *1822, 1829, 1839, 1840*.
41. *Lust*] lust *1822, 1829, 1839, 1840*.
42. *Life*] life *1822, 1829, 1839, 1840*. *light,*] *1822, 1829, 1839, 1840*; light *HM 329*.
43. *iris*] rainbow; in Greek mythology Iris was the goddess of the rainbow.
44. *prophet's*] *1822, 1829, 1839, 1840*; prophets *HM 329*.

> *Chorus*
> In the great morning of the world,
> The spirit of God with might unfurled
> The flag of Freedom over chaos,
> And all its banded anarchs fled
> 50   Like vultures frighted from Imaus

46–93. No holograph of these lines survives. It is possible that some or all of them were drafted on a leaf or leaves of *Nbk 21* subsequently removed and lost; for discussion of the make-up of this notebook including quires with missing leaves and a stray, see *BSM* xxiii 53–4 and *BSM* xvi pp. xvii, xxi–xxii. The chorus offers a condensed version of *OL*, which is itself effectively a poetic rendering of S.'s historical-political analysis in *PVR* (see headnote to *OL*); but the outline of political developments here is much more narrowly focused on the Greek struggle in its European context, and with an eye to an English audience. The chorus is formally complex, the first and third stanzas of eighteen lines and the second stanza of twelve lines deploying eight rhyme-sounds and five rhyme-sounds respectively in a shifting pattern of couplets, quatrains, and triplets which never repeats.
46–51. For transcriptions in *Mary Copybk 1* of versions of these lines that S. may have composed during the period when he was drafting *Adonais* in May 1821, i.e. prior to the composition of *Hellas*, see *In the great morning of the world*.
46–8. Cp. *Adonais* 166–7: 'From the great morning of the world when first / God dawned on Chaos'.
46. world,] *1822, 1829, 1839, 1840*; world *HM 329*.
47–8. Cp. Byron, *Childe Harold's Pilgrimage* IV (1818) xcviii ll. 1–2: 'Yet, Freedom! yet thy banner, torn, but flying, / Streams like the thunder-storm *against* the wind'.
48. flag] The final letter of this word appears to have been overwritten by S. in *HM 329* (perhaps to distinguish it from *play*). *over*] The first letter appears to have been overwritten by S. in *HM 329* (perhaps to distinguish it from *ever*). *chaos,*] *Rossetti 1870*; chaos *HM 329*; Chaos, *1822, 1829, 1839, 1840*.
49. banded anarchs] 'banded' = 'leagued' but also 'blindfolded'; cp. *An Ode ('Arise, arise, arise!')* (no. 244) 20: 'Lift not your hands in the banded war', and *A Vision of the Sea* (no. 321) l. 119 and note. 'Anarchs' is S.'s usual term for monarchs and tyrants, as at ll. 879 and 934 below, and cp. e.g. *Ode to Naples* 77, 137, *OL* 43, *TL* 237. *fled*] fled, *1822, 1829, 1839, 1840*.
50–1. Cp. *Paradise Lost* iii 431–6:

> As when a vulture on Imaus bred,
> Whose snowy ridge the roving Tartar bounds,
> Dislodging from a region scarce of prey
> To gorge the flesh of lambs or yeanling kids
> On hills where flocks are fed, flies toward the springs
> Of Ganges, or Hydaspes, Indian streams;

50. vultures] *1822, 1829, 1839, 1840*; Vultures *HM 329*. *Imaus*] Imaus, *1822, 1829, 1839, 1840*. According to Pliny, *Nat. Hist.* v 98, the name of part of Mount Taurus

>   Before an earthquake's tread. —
>   So from Time's tempestuous dawn
>   Freedom's splendour burst and shone. —
>   Thermopylae and Marathon
> 55   Caught, like mountains beacon-lighted,
>   The springing Fire. — The winged Glory

('Himaeus' = 'Himalaya'), an extensive mountain range in Asia. Pliny states that Imaus 'in the vernacular means "snowy"' (*Nat. Hist.* vi 64).

51. *earthquake's*] *1822, 1829, 1839, 1840*; Earthquake's *HM 329.* tread. —] tread — *1829.*

52-75. The journey of the light of freedom echoes that of the beacon fires signalling the capture of Troy in Clytaemnestra's speech in Aeschylus' *Agamemnon* (281-314), to which 'like mountains beacon-lighted' (l. 55) draws attention. S.'s reworking of the beacon journey begins by substituting Aeschylus' locations for the sites of famous Greek battles against the Persians ('Thermopylae and Marathon', l. 54). S. read *Agamemnon* with Lady Mountcashell ('Mrs Mason') in April 1820 (*L* ii 186) and with Alexandros Mavrokordatos and Medwin (see *Medwin (1913)* 263). This latter reading, also referred to by Medwin in the Preface to his translation of *Prometheus Unbound* (1832) iv, must have taken place between 1 December 1820 when the Shelleys were introduced to Mavrokordatos (*Claire Jnl* 190) and 27 February 1821 when Medwin departed for Rome (*Mary Jnl* i 354). S. transcribed *Agamemnon* 1-38 in *Nbk 19* pp. 1-2 (facsimile and transcription in *BSM* xii 8-11) and made transcriptions from and notes on many passages in the play in *Nbk 12* ff. *38ʳ rev.-*41ᵛ rev. (facsimile and transcription in *MYRS* iv 320-35), observing of Clytaemnestra's speech 'The description is wonderfully magnificent of this beaconing' (f.*38ᵛ rev.; *MYRS* iv 320-1). These transcriptions and notes could have been written between December 1820 and February 1821 but, according to Mary Quinn (*MYRS* iv p. xxxi) and Nora Crook (*BSM* xii pp. xxxviii-xxxix), a late 1819 date is more plausible.

53. *shone.* —] shone:— *1822, 1829, 1839, 1840.*

54. Thermopylae and Marathon were military engagements in which Greek heroism triumphed over daunting odds. The plain of Marathon was the site in 490 BCE of an Athenian victory over a much greater Persian army under Darius the First; the narrow Pass of Thermopylae had in 480 BCE seen the heroic defeat of Leonidas and the Spartans by the Persians under Darius' son Xerxes, in which the vastly outnumbered Spartans held out for three days, until all were killed.

55. *mountains*] *1822*; mountain's *HM 329.* *beacon-lighted,*] *1822, 1829, 1839, 1840*; beacon-lighted *HM 329.*

56. *The springing Fire*] Cp. Aeschylus' description of the beacon fire as ὑπερθοροῦσα ('leaping', 'springing') in *Agamemnon* 297. *Glory*] glory *1822, 1829, 1839, 1840.* The alteration from *glory* to *Glory* in *HM 329* is probably in Williams's hand.

56-93. *The winged Glory … or a grave*] On the eagle's association with freedom, see Milton's vision of England in *Areopagitica* (1644):

On Philippi half alighted,
   Like an eagle on a promontory.
   Its unwearied wings could fan
60   The quenchless ashes of Milan. (1)
   From age to age, from man to man
      It lived; and lit from land to land
      Florence, Albion, Switzerland.

Methinks I see in my mind a noble and puissant Nation rousing herself like a strong man after sleep, and shaking her invincible locks: Methinks I see her as an Eagle muing her mighty youth, and kindling her undazl'd eyes at the full midday beam; purging and unscaling her long abused sight at the fountain it self of heav'nly radiance; (*Complete Prose Works of John Milton* (1959) ii 557–8)

See also: *Mighty Eagle, thou that soarest* (no. 136) and headnote; *L&C* 2182–4; *Like an eagle hovering* (no. 220) and headnote; *OL* 8–9; *An eagle floating in the golden [glory]* (no. 338) and headnote; and *Adonais* 147–9 and note.

57. *On Philippi half alighted*] Julius Caesar's heirs Mark Antony and Octavian defeated the forces of his assassins Brutus and Cassius at the Battle of Philippi on the plain to the west of the Greek city in October of 42 BCE. Philippi was then developed as a Roman colony. In *Ode to Naples* l. 124 S. laments 'the high prize lost on Philippi's shore', referring to the republican cause, 'lost' with the suicide of high-minded Brutus after his defeat. *half alighted*] *Rossetti 1870*; half-alighted *HM 329, 1822, 1829, 1839, 1840*. *Half alighted*, perhaps, because of the bipartite nature of the Battle of Philippi: the 'Liberators', the faction opposed to Octavian, held their own in the first part of the battle (3rd October) before being finally defeated in the second part (23rd October).

58. *eagle*] *1822, 1829, 1839, 1840*; Eagle *HM 329*.

60. *Milan.*(1)] *1822, 1829, 1839, 1840*; Milan(1) *HM 329* (a cross alongside the bracketed number is keyed to a note in Williams's hand at the foot of the page (p. 4) which reads: 'reference to notes.') See S.'s Note 1.

61. *to man*] to man, *1822*.

62. *to land*] to land, *1822*.

63–4. The omission of a stanza-division between these lines in *1822* is recorded in *Errata*.

63. Florence and Switzerland exemplify virtuous non-monarchical states illuminated by the 'springing fire' of Freedom. 'Albion' however uses the ancient name for England — with the poem's potential English audience in mind — to evoke the reign of King Alfred (848/9–899), a figurehead of Whig oppositional discourse in the eighteenth century, and widely celebrated by libertarians in the period following the French Revolution as the founder of English Freedom; see *OL* 123 and note. *Switzerland.*] Switzerland: *1829*.

	Then night fell — and, as from night,
65	Reassuming fiery flight,
	From the west swift Freedom came,
	Against the course of Heaven and doom,
	A second sun arrayed in flame,
	To burn, to kindle, to illume.
70	From far Atlantis its young beams
	Chased the shadows and the dreams.
	France, with all her sanguine steams,
	Hid, but quenched it not; again
	Through clouds its shafts of glory rain
75	From utmost Germany to Spain.

As an eagle fed with morning

64. *fell* —] fell; *1822, 1829, 1839, 1840*. *and, ... night,*] *1822, 1839, 1840*; and ... night *HM 329, 1829*.
65. *flight,*] *1822, 1829, 1839, 1840*; flight *HM 329*.
66-8. *From ... A*] Of the position of these two words in *HM 329* Reiman comments: 'PBS has indicated the proper metrical alignment of the stanzaic pattern by canceling the initial words "From" and "A" and rewriting them further to the left' (*MYRS* iii 26); however, the revisions in the MS appear to be in Williams's hand rather than S.'s.
66. *west*] West *1822, 1829, 1839, 1840*. Whether the alteration from *West* in *HM 329* is in S.'s hand or Williams's is uncertain. *came,*] *1822, 1829, 1839, 1840*; came *HM 329*.
67. *Heaven*] heaven *1829, 1839, 1840*. *doom,*] *1822, 1839, 1840*; doom *HM 329, 1829*.
68. *flame,*] *1822, 1839, 1840*; flame *HM 329*; flame; *1829*.
69. *illume.*] illume, *1829*.
70. *far Atlantis*] The United States of America.
71. *dreams.*] *1829, 1839, 1840*; dreams *HM 329, 1822*.
72. *France, ... steams,*] *1822*; France ... steams *HM 329*. *sanguine steams*] bloody exhalations, i.e. The French Revolution (cp. *PU* I 567-77 and notes); 'steams' = vapours or fumes (see *OED* 1a and 1b).
73. *Hid,*] *1822*; Hid *HM 329*.
74. *rain*] ran *1834*.
75-6. The omission of a stanza-division between these lines in *1822* (recorded in Errata), is explained by the fact that line 75 is written at the foot of the page (p. 4) in *HM 329*.
75. This line is in S.'s hand in *HM 329*. S. was inspired by the popular insurgency in Spain in 1819 and 1820 (see headnotes to *An Ode ('Arise, arise, arise!')* and *OL*). He was also aware of pro-independence unrest in parts of Germany (see *OL* 200-2 and note).

>   Scorns the embattled tempest's warning
>   When she seeks her aerie hanging
>   In the mountain-cedar's hair,
> 80   And her brood expect the clanging
>   Of her wings through the wild air,
>   Sick with famine — Freedom so
>   To what of Greece remaineth now
>   Returns; her hoary ruins glow
> 85   Like orient mountains lost in day.
>   Beneath the safety of her wings
>   Her renovated nurslings prey,
>   And in the naked lightnings
>   Of truth they purge their dazzled eyes.
> 90   Let Freedom leave, where'er she flies,
>   A Desert, or a Paradise;
>   Let the beautiful and the brave
>   Share her glory, or a grave.

77. *tempest's*] *1822, 1829, 1839, 1840*; tempests *HM 329, 1822*. *warning*] warning, *1822, 1829, 1839, 1840*.
79. *mountain-cedar's*] mountain cedar's *1829*. *hair,*] *1822, 1829, 1839, 1840*; hair *HM 329*.
80. *her*] Written over *the* in *HM 329* in what appears to be S.'s hand. *clanging*] Cp. Alexander Pope's description of two eagles in his translation of Homer's *Odyssey* (1725) ii 175-6: 'Above th' assembled Peers they wheel on high, / And clang their wings, and hovering beat the sky'.
81. *air,*] *1822, 1829, 1839, 1840*; air *HM 329*.
82-4. *Freedom ... Returns*] 'So Freedom now (i.e. in autumn 1821) returns to what remains of Greece.'
82. *famine —*] famine:— *1822*; famine; — *1839, 1840*. *Freedom*] Freedom, *1822, 1839, 1840*.
85. *orient*] Orient *1822, 1829, 1839, 1840*. *day.*] day; *1822, 1829, 1839, 1840*.
86-9. Eagles were believed to be able to look directly at the sun; young eagles were made by their parents to stare into the sun, and were discarded if unable to do so. See *TL* 131 and note, and, e.g., Lucan, *Pharsalia* ix 1057-61 and Pliny, *Nat. Hist.* x 10.
87. *prey*] play *1829, 1834, 1839, 1840*.
88. *lightnings*] The metre requires a trisyllable.
90. *leave,*] leave— *1822*. *flies,*] *1822, 1829, 1839, 1840*; flies *HM 329*.
91. *Paradise;*] *1829, 1839, 1840*; Paradise *HM 329*; Paradise: *1822*.

Semichorus 1st
With the gifts of gladness
95   Greece did thy cradle strew —

Semichorus 2nd
With the tears of sadness
Greece did thy shroud bedew!

Semichorus 1st
With an orphan's affection
She followed thy bier through Time;

Semichorus 2nd
100   And at thy resurrection
Reappeareth, like thou, sublime!

Semichorus 1st
If Heaven should resume thee,
To Heaven shall her spirits ascend;

Semichorus 2nd
If Hell should entomb thee,
105   To Hell shall her high hearts bend.

95. *thy*] I.e. 'Freedom's'. *strew* —] strew; *1822, 1839, 1840.* strew. *1829.*
97. *bedew!*] bedew. *1829*; bedew; *1839, 1840.*
99. *Time;*] *1822*; Time *HM 329* (whether the alteration from *time* is in S.'s hand, or Williams's is uncertain); time; *1829*; time! *1839, 1840.*
102. *resume thee*] take you back. *thee,*] *1822, 1829, 1839, 1840*; thee *HM 329.*
103. *spirits*] spirit *1822, 1829, 1839, 1840.* Whether the insertion of the final (barely visible) letter of this word in *HM 329* is in S.'s hand or Williams's is uncertain; the reading is *spirits* in *Nbk 21* p. 109 (see *BSM* xvi 114–5). *ascend;*] *1822, 1829, 1839, 1840*; ascend *HM 329.*
104. *Hell*] Whether the alteration from *Heaven* in *HM 329* is in S.'s hand or Williams's is uncertain. *thee,*] *1822, 1839, 1840*; thee *HM 329*; thee; *1829.*
105. *bend.*] *1822, 1829, 1839, 1840*; bend *HM 329.*

> *Semichorus 1st*
> If Annihilation —
>
> *Semichorus 2nd*
> Dust let her glories be!
> And a name and a nation
> Be forgotten, Freedom, with thee!
>
> *Indian*
110 His brow grows darker — breathe not — move not!
> He starts — he shudders; — ye that love not,
> With your panting loud and fast,
> Have awakened him at last.
>
> *Mahmud*   [*Starting from his sleep.*
> Man the Seraglio-guard! — make fast the gate.
115 What! from a cannonade of three short hours?
> 'Tis false! that breach towards the Bosphorus

106. Annihilation] *1822, 1829, 1839, 1840*; annihilation *HM 329*. The initial letter of this word is capitalised in *Nbk 21* p. 109 (see *BSM* xvi 114–5).
107. be!] be; *1829, 1839, 1840.*
108. name] name, *1829.*
111. shudders; —] *1829, 1839, 1840*; shudders — *HM 329, 1822.*
112. fast,] fast *1829, 1839, 1840.*
114–121. Mahmud awakes from a dream in which his palace is about to be breached by an attacking force, which he plans to oppose by sparking an explosion which would destroy both defenders and attackers. This fearful dream of overthrow by invaders suggests the original capture of Constantinople, then the capital of the Byzantine Empire, by Mahmud's predecessor Mehmed II in 1453; Mahmud rehearses this event in his dialogue with Ahasuerus at ll. 814–41 below. Mahmud's speech recalls that of Richard III waking agitatedly from his dream on the eve of the Battle of Bosworth Field in *Richard III* V iii 177ff.
114. The punctuation of this line in *HM 329* is unresolved. It appears that Williams first wrote *Man the Seraglio, guard — make fast the gate.* Then, a small equals sign (which, in Williams's hand, indicates a hyphen) was inserted above the comma and an exclamation mark after *guard* but the comma is uncancelled. *Seraglio-guard! — make*] Seraglio-guard! make *1822, 1829, 1839, 1840.* Seraglio-guard] The only instance of this noun cited in *OED. gate.*] *1822, 1829, 1839, 1840*; gate *HM 329.*
116. Bosphorus] The strait which runs from the Sea of Marmora to the Black Sea, separating Asia from Europe; Constantinople (mod. Istanbul) was on the Western side.

Cannot be practicable yet — who stirs?
Stand to the match! that when the foe prevails,
One spark may mix in reconciling ruin
120   The conqueror and the conquered! Heave the tower
Into the gap — wrench off the roof!
                                                       [*Enter* HASSAN.
                                                  Ha! what!
The truth of day lightens upon my dream
And I am Mahmud still. —

117. practicable] I.e. 'cannot yet be a viable gateway into the palace'. *who*] Who *1829, 1839, 1840*.
118–20. Stand to ... the conquered!] Erkelenz ('Inspecting the Tragedy of Empire' 326 and 335 n. 35) notes that Mahmud's command echoes a report in *Galignani's Messenger* (3 July 1821) [p. 4] of Ali Pasha 'threatening precisely this course of action to keep at bay the Turkish army besieging Yanina (Ioannina)': 'He still defended himself in a fortress of the Lake of Joannina, where he had collected 400 barrels of gunpowder, with the resolution, if overpowered, of destroying himself and all his followers.' For Ali Pasha, see l. 566 and note.
118. Stand to the match] I.e. 'Get ready to detonate an explosion' (*Concordance* glosses 'match' as 'fuse' and 'stand to' as 'attend to' or 'remain near'). *match!*] match; *1822, 1829, 1839, 1840. prevails,*] *1829, 1839, 1840*; prevails *HM 329, 1822*.
119–20. One spark ... the conquered!] Locock 1911 ii 468 cps *PU* III i 78–9.
121. roof!] roof. *1822, 1829, 1839, 1840.* Mahmud's speech continues as follows in *HM 329* p. 7 (see *MYRS* iii 29) until the entrance of Hassan; it is cancelled, whether by S. or Williams is difficult to determine:

                            Ibrahim,
Stab that pernicious slave who talks of fear.
All is not lost! I can yet fight until
The flesh be hacked from these too weary bones;
Give me my pistols! Hassan, Youssouff, Daoud,
All false as Greeks? Thou here true Fatima —
One kiss, and if thou lovest God and me
Go, drown thyself — within an hour at most
We two will meet in Paradise

The above passage reworks lines from *Nbk 21* pp. 59–60 which appear in this edition as *Ibrahim — / Stab that pernicious slave who talks of fear* (*Lines connected with Hellas* H); its notes include a collation with the cancelled lines in *HM 329*.
122. dream] dream, *1829, 1839, 1840*.
123. I am Mahmud still] *Major Works* cps Webster, *Duchess of Malfi* IV ii 142, 'I am Duchess of Malfi still'. Webster is mentioned in Godwin's letter to S. of 10 December 1812, which had a powerful influence on S.'s reading; see *L* i 341 n. *Mahmud still.* —] Mahmud, still — *HM 329*; Mahmud still. *1822, 1829, 1839, 1840. sublime highness*] Sublime Highness *1822, 1829, 1839, 1840*.

Hassan
                              Your sublime highness
        Is strangely moved.

Mahmud
                        The times do cast strange shadows
125   On those who watch and who must rule their course
      Lest they, being first in peril as in glory,
      Be whelmed in the fierce ebb — and these are of them.
      Thrice has a gloomy vision hunted me
      As thus from sleep into the troubled day;
130   It shakes me as the tempest shakes the sea,
      Leaving no figure upon memory's glass.
      Would that — no matter — thou didst say thou knewest
      A Jew, whose spirit is a chronicle

123-4. *Your sublime ... moved*] Cp. *The Tempest* IV i 143-4: 'This is strange. Your father's in some passion / That works him strongly.' Cf. also *The Tempest* IV i 146: 'You do look, my son, in a mov'd sort'.
124-7. *The times ... are of them*] The 'strange shadows' of Mahmud's dream are characteristic products of 'The times' (l. 124); i.e. powerful leaders are as likely to be swept away by momentous events, as they are to be able to control them.
125. *course*] Nbk 21; course, 1829, 1839, 1840; course. HM 329, 1822.
126. *they, ... glory,*] 1822, 1829, 1839, 1840; they ... glory HM 329.
127. *ebb —*] ebb:— 1822, 1829, 1839, 1840. *and these are of them*] Cp. *Macbeth* I iii 79-80: 'The earth hath bubbles, as the water has, / And these are of them.'
128. *Thrice*] The alteration from *There* in HM 329 is in S.'s hand. *has ... hunted me*] Cp. *Persae* 176-7: πολλοῖς μὲν αἰεὶ νυκτέροις ὀνείρασι / ξύνειμ' ('I have been ever haunted by many a dream'). *hunted*] haunted 1829, 1834. The alteration of *haunted* to *hunted* in HM 329 is probably in S.'s hand. The reading in *Nbk 21* p. 61 is *hunted* although *BSM* gives 'haunted' (see *BSM* xvi 66-7).
132. *matter — thou*] matter. Thou 1822, 1829, 1839, 1840. *knewest*] The alteration of the third letter from an *o* to an *e* and the overwriting of the first letter in *HM 329* are probably in S.'s hand.
133. *A Jew*] Ahasuerus, the Wandering Jew; see notes to *Dramatis Personae* above. He makes his appearance at l. 737.

Of strange and secret and forgotten things.
135 I bade thee summon him — 'tis said his tribe
Dream, and are wise interpreters of dreams.

Hassan
The Jew of whom I spake is old — so old
He seems to have outlived a world's decay;
The hoary mountains and the wrinkled ocean
140 Seem younger still than he — his hair and beard
Are whiter than the tempest-sifted snow.

135. *I bade*] *I'd* was altered to *I* and *bade* written over an indecipherable word (possibly *bid*) in HM 329, then both words were cancelled and *I bade* written beneath; the alterations appear to be in S.'s hand. *him* —] him:— *1822, 1829, 1839, 1840*.
137-41. Cp. the description of an old African woman who appears before Phenix and delivers a prophecy in Calderón, *El príncipe constante* Act II 1005-1014:

> Atenta me puse y vi
> una caduca africana,
> espíritu en forma humana,
> ceño arrugado y esquivo,
> que era un esqueleto vivo
> de lo que fue sombra vana;
> cuya rústica fiereza,
> cuyo aspecto esquivo y bronco
> fue escultura hecha de un tronco
> sin pulirle la corteza. (Text from *El príncipe constante*, ed. Isabel Hernando Morata (2015) 186-7)

('I attentive looked, and saw / An ancient dame of Africa— / A spirit in a human form, / Marked with all that can deform— / Wrinkles, scowling, haggard, dark— / A living skeleton, a shade; / But as if with features made / Of a tree's trunk, rude and stark, / Wrapt in rough, unpolished bark; trans. Denis Florence M'Carthy, *Dramas of Calderon, Tragic, Comic, and Legendary*, 2 vols (1853) (hereafter *Mac-Carthy (1853)*) i 42).

137. *is old* —] is old,— *1822, 1829, 1839, 1840*.
138. *decay;*] *1822, 1829, 1839, 1840*; decay *HM 329*.
140. *he* —] he;— *1822, 1829*; he; *1839, 1840*.
141. Cp. *PU* II iii 36-8 and *The Cenci* V ii 170-1. *snow.*] snow; *1822, 1829, 1839, 1840*.

His cold pale limbs and pulseless arteries
Are like the fibres of a cloud instinct
With light, and to the soul that quickens them
145 Are as the atoms of the mountain-drift
To the winter wind — but from his eye looks forth
A life of unconsumed thought which pierces
The present, and the past, and the to-come.
Some say that this is he whom the great prophet
150 Jesus, the son of Joseph, for his mockery
Mocked with the curse of immortality. —
Some feign that he is Enoch, — others dream
He was pre-Adamite and has survived

143. instinct] Stressed on the second syllable, as usual in the adjectival use of this word. *Concordance* glosses as 'animated, filled'.
144. quickens] gives life to.
146. wind —] wind:— *1822, 1829, 1839, 1840.*
147. unconsumed] *Concordance* glosses as 'inexhaustible'. *thought*] thought, *1829, 1839, 1840.*
148. present,] present *1840.*
149–51. In legend the Wandering Jew taunted Jesus on the way to his crucifixion, and then was cursed to walk the earth until the Second Coming.
150. mockery] mockery, *1840.*
151. Mocked] *Concordance* glosses as 'punished scornfully'. *immortality.* —] immortality. *1822, 1829, 1839, 1840.*
152. feign] I.e. 'pretend', or possibly 'conjecture'. *Enoch,* —] *Nbk 21*; Enoch — *HM 329*; Enoch: *1822*; Enoch; *1829, 1839, 1840.* Cp. *Genesis* v 21–4: 'And Enoch lived sixty and five years, and begat Methuselah: And Enoch walked with God after he begat Methuselah three hundred years, and begat sons and daughters: And all the days of Enoch were three hundred sixty and five years: And Enoch walked with God: and he *was* not; for God took him.' The biblical text has been interpreted to mean that Enoch never died, but entered Heaven alive.
152–3. dream / He was pre-Adamite] S. was familiar with scientific speculation which offered a material basis for the *pre-Adamite* theological belief that humans, or other intelligent life, had existed before Adam, the 'first man' of the Bible. The implications of the fossil record were the subject of wide debate in S.'s day, particularly under the influence of the anti-evolutionist Georges Cuvier, whose *Recherches sur des ossements fossiles de quadrupèdes* (1812) argued that the evidence for extinct species pointed to a series of catastrophic events in the earth's history causing massive land upheavals and floods that destroyed entire species. These and related ideas concerning the evidence for numerous pre-historic cycles of life are explored in detail in *PU* IV; see especially *PU* IV 270–318 and notes.
153. pre-Adamite] pre-adamite, *1829, 1839, 1840.*

Cycles of generation and of ruin.
155 The sage, in truth, by dreadful abstinence
And conquering penance of the mutinous flesh,
Deep contemplation, and unwearied study
In years outstretched beyond the date of man,
May have attained to sovereignty and science
160 Over those strong and secret things and thoughts
Which others fear and know not.

Mahmud

                                    I would talk
With this old Jew.

Hassan

                Thy will is even now

155–61. This passage suggests S.'s own poetic accounts of figures in ascetic search of secret knowledge; see e.g. *Alastor* 20–49, *Hymn to Intellectual Beauty* (no. 123) 49–60.
155. abstinence] abstinence, *1840*.
157. contemplation,] Nbk 21, *1822, 1829, 1839, 1840*; contemplation *HM 329*. *study]* study, *1822, 1829, 1839, 1840*.
158. date] term of life (see *OED* 1). man,] *1822, 1829, 1839, 1840*; man *HM 329*.
159. attained to] obtain'd to *1829, 1834*. I.e. 'achieved'.
160. those strong ... thoughts] Cp. *Mont Blanc. Lines written in the Vale of Chamouni* (no. 124) Text B ll. 139–40: 'The secret strength of things / Which governs thought'.
161. others] Nbk 21, *1822, 1829, 1839, 1840*; other *HM 329*.

Made known to him, where he dwells in a sea cavern
'Mid the Demonesi, less accessible
165 Than thou or God! He who would question him
Must sail alone at sunset where the stream
Of ocean sleeps around those foamless isles,
When the young moon is westering as now,
And evening airs wander upon the wave;
170 And when the pines of that bee-pasturing isle,
Green Erebinthus, quench the fiery shadow
Of his gilt prow within the sapphire water,
Then must the lonely helmsman cry aloud,

163–184. where he dwells … The Jew appears] Cian Duffy, '"Less accessible than thou or God": Where does Percy Shelley locate Ahasuerus in *Hellas*?', *N&Q* lxi (2014) 517–9 identifies the setting:

> it is possible to place Ahasuerus' residence quite precisely on Sedef Adası (Mother-of-Pearl Island), one of the Prince Islands (Kızıl Adar), to which Patriarch Ignatius of Constantinople was exiled in 857 AD […] the Prince islands, known in Classical writing as the Demonesi, are nine in number, and lie just off the coast, southeast of Istanbul, in the Sea of Marmara. This sea (known in Classical literature as the Propontis) is almost entirely landlocked, hence "ocean sleeps around those foamless isles" [l. 167]. The Greek name for Sedef Adası is Terebinthos ("Erebinthus" in l. 171) which suggests an association with the terebinthine, or terebinth tree, the resin of which is highly attractive to bees, and hence "that bee-pasturing isle" in l. 170. No single source for Shelley's knowledge of the region has been identified, but his decision to fix Ahasuerus' residence there might have been influenced by Strabo, *Geography* XVI ii 39, which mentions a prophet Achaecarus (Ἀχαΐκαρος) living amongst the Bosporeni (Βοσπορηνοίς).

163. sea cavern] sea-cavern *1822, 1829, 1839, 1840*.
165. He who would] He would *1834*.
166–7. the stream / Of ocean] Cp. *L&C* 337–8: 'a shoreless stream / Wide ocean rolled' and note to l. 337.
166. sunset] sunset, *1822*; sun-set, *1829, 1839, 1840*.
167. ocean] Ocean *1822*. The small *o* is unambiguous in *HM 329*. *foamless isles*] Cp. *Epipsychidion* 412. *isles,*] isles *1829, 1839, 1840*.
168. the young moon is westering] I.e. the new moon is close to setting. *now,*] *1822, 1829, 1839, 1840*; now *HM 329*.
170. isle,] *1822, 1829, 1839, 1840*; isle *HM 329*.
172. water,] *1822, 1839, 1840*; water. *HM 329*; water; *1829*. Whether the alteration of *water* to *waters* in *HM 329* is in S.'s hand or Williams's is uncertain.
173. aloud,] aloud *1822, 1829*.

'Ahasuerus!' and the caverns round
175   Will answer 'Ahasuerus!' If his prayer
      Be granted, a faint meteor will arise,
      Lighting him over Marmora, and a wind
      Will rush out of the sighing pine forest,
      And with the wind a storm of harmony
180   Unutterably sweet, and pilot him
      Through the soft twilight to the Bosphorus:
      Thence at the hour and place and circumstance
      Fit for the matter of their conference
      The Jew appears. Few dare, and few who dare
185   Win the desired communion —
                                          [*A shout within.*
                              but that shout
      Bodes —

174–5. *'Ahasuerus!'* ... *'Ahasuerus!'*] Rossetti 1870; Ahasuerus! ... Ahasuerus! *HM 329, 1822, 1829, 1839, 1840.*
175. *answer*] answer, *1829, 1839, 1840.* *If*] *1822, 1829, 1839, 1840;* if *HM 329.*
176. *arise,*] *1829, 1839;* arise *HM 329, 1822;* arise. *1840.*
177–80. *a wind ... Unutterably sweet*] Cp. *PU* II i 156–9:

>   A wind arose among the pines; it shook
>   The clinging music from their boughs, and then
>   Low, sweet, faint sounds, like the farewell of ghosts,
>   Were heard:

177. *Marmora*] The Sea of Marmora is the inland sea which connects the Black Sea with the Aegean, via the Bosporus to the east and the Dardanelles straits to the west (see notes to ll. 116 and 162–84 above).
178. *pine forest,*] pine-forest, *1822, 1829, 1839, 1840;* pine forest *HM 329.*
181. *Bosphorus:*] *1822, 1829, 1839, 1840;* Bosphorus *HM 329.*
182. *Thence*] Thence, *1829, 1839, 1840.*
183. *conference*] conference, *1829, 1839, 1840;* meeting for conversation (see *OED* 4b).
184. *Few dare,*] *1822, 1829, 1839, 1840;* Few dare *HM 329.* *who dare*] who dare, *1829, 1839, 1840.*
185. *SD. [A shout within.*] In *HM 329* and *eds* the *SD* is positioned after *Bodes —*.
185. *Win*] Written after [?*Him* canc.] in *HM 329.*

Mahmud
                    Evil, doubtless, like all human sounds.
            Let me converse with spirits.

Hassan
                                    That shout again?

Mahmud
            This Jew whom thou hast summoned —

Hassan
                                            Will be here —

186. *Evil, doubtless,*] Evil doubtless, *Nbk 21*; Evil doubtless *HM 329*; Evil, doubtless; *1822, 1829, 1839, 1840*. *sounds.*] *1822, 1829, 1839, 1840*; sounds *HM 329*.
187. *spirits.*] *1822, 1829, 1839, 1840*; spirits *HM 329* (a comma after *spirits* is cancelled). The remainder of Mahmud's speech in *HM 329* is cancelled, whether by S. or Williams is uncertain. The cancelled passage reads thus:

                                            or with men
                Who have put off those filthy general rags
                Which make the soul leprous

These cancelled lines have parallels with *Charles the First* (no. 426) I i 153-4. *again?*] again. *1822, 1829, 1839, 1840*.
188. *Will be here*] One of a number of places in *Hellas* in which S. seems to imitate Greek tragic style in the way in which he employs *antilabê*, where a line of verse is shared between two speakers. The use of *antilabê* is common in Sophocles and Euripides but does not occur at all in Aeschylus (see also the note to l. 373). Here, as often in Greek tragedy, the *antilabê* constitutes an interruption of subsequently unfinished syntax. Cp. e.g. *Oedipus at Colonus* 1170-1:

                            ΟΙΔΙΠΟΥΣ
            μή μου δεηθῇς—
                            ΘΗΣΕΥΣ
                        πράγματος ποίου; λέγε.
                            ΟΙΔΙΠΟΥΣ
                ἔξοιδ' ἀκούων τῶνδ' ὅς ἐσθ' ὁ προστάτης.

                            ('*Oedipus*
                Do not ask of me …
                            Theseus
                        What thing? Tell me!
                            Oedipus
                I know well, from hearing it from these, who the suppliant is.')

Mahmud
    When the omnipotent hour to which are yoked
190 He, I, and all things, shall compel — enough!
    Silence those mutineers — that drunken crew
    That crowd about the pilot in the storm.
    Aye! strike the foremost shorter by a head. —
    They weary me and I have need of rest.
195 Kings are like stars — they rise and set, they have
    The worship of the world but no repose.
                                                    [*Exeunt severally.*

189-90. to which are yoked ... all things] Cp. Aeschylus, *Agamemnon* 218: ἀνάγκας [...] λέπαδνον ('the yokestrap of necessity').
189. hour] hour, *1829, 1839, 1840*. Written after *power* canc. in *HM 329*.
190. things,] *1829, 1839, 1840*; things *HM 329, 1822*. *enough!*] enough. *1822, 1829, 1839, 1840*.
191-2. that drunken ... storm.] Woodberry (1901) 638 and Notopoulos 303 cp. Plato, *Republic* vi 488b-c:

> The sailors are quarrelling with one another about steering the ship, each of them thinking that he should be the captain, even though he's never learned the art of navigation, and cannot point to anyone who taught it to him, nor to a time when he learned it. Indeed, they claim that it isn't teachable, and are ready to cut to pieces anyone who says that it is. They're always crowding around the shipowner, begging him and doing everything possible to get him to turn the rudder over to them. And sometimes, if they don't succeed in persuading him, they execute the ones who do succeed or throw them overboard, and then, having stupefied their noble shipowner with drugs, wine, or in some other way, they rule the ship, using up what's in it and sailing while drinking and feasting, in the way that people like that are prone to do. (Trans. G. M. A. Grube, rev. C. D. C. Reeve, in Plato, *Complete Works*, ed. John M. Cooper (1997) 1111)

191. crew] crew, *1822*.
193. Aye!] Ay! *1822, 1829, 1839, 1840*. head. —] head! *1822, 1829, 1839, 1840*.
194. me] me, *1822, 1829, 1839, 1840*.
195-6. Rossetti *1870* ii 555 cps Bacon, *Essayes* (1612), Essay xix, 'Of Empire': 'Princes are like to heavenly bodies, which cause good or evil times; and which have much veneration, but no rest' (Francis Bacon, *The Major Works*, ed. Brian Vickers (1996) 379).
196. world] world, *1822, 1829, 1839, 1840*.

Chorus (2)
Worlds on worlds are rolling ever

197–238. This forty-two line chorus is balanced against the closing chorus ll. 1060–1101, also of forty-two lines. However, the 'Worlds on worlds' chorus is differently organised, in three fourteen-line stanzas which use seven rhyme-words in a pattern tightly repeated through the three stanzas. *Thompson* 184–5 offers commentary.
197–210. This stanza has its origin in S.'s draft lines *Suns and stars are rolling ever*; see *Lines connected with Hellas* C. In this remodelled and completed rendering, S. contrasts the perpetual flux in the material world with the immortally successive incarnations of creative human intellect; 'material worlds are continually disintegrating, while human minds undergo reincarnation (Shelley's note explains that this is poetic conjecture, not a statement of belief)' (GM). Cp. Pindar, Second *Olympian Ode* 68–70:

> ὅσοι δ' ἐτόλμασαν ἐστρὶς
> ἑκατέρωθι μείναντες ἀπὸ πάμπαν ἀδίκων ἔχειν
> ψυχάν, ἔτειλαν Διὸς ὁδὸν παρὰ Κρόνου τύρσιν

> (And they, that thrice, above, below
> This earth, with transmigrating entity
> Have stood their trial, passing to and fro;
> And from th' unjust society
> Have kept their souls aloof and free:
> They take the way which Jove did long ordain
> To Saturn's ancient tower ...) (*Specimens of the Classic Poets*, trans. Sir Charles Elton, 3 vols (1814) i 184–5)

Also Edward Young, *Night Thoughts* (1742), ed. Stephen Cornford (1989), Night VII:

> And is there nought on Earth,
> But a long Train of transitory Forms,
> Rising, and breaking, Millions in an Hour?
> Bubbles of a fantastic Deity, blown up
> In Sport, and then in Cruelty destroy'd? (ll. 867–71)

197–200. S.'s 'Worlds on worlds' suggests successive cycles of human existence, but there is also a possible embodiment of his understanding of contemporary scientific ideas concerning the atomic structure of matter; see *PU* IV 236–68 and notes, and cp. also *Adonais* 379–87:

> He is a portion of the loveliness
> Which once he made more lovely: he doth bear

>   From creation to decay,
>   Like the bubbles on a river
> 200   Sparkling, bursting, borne away.
>   But they are still immortal
>   Who through Birth's orient portal

> His part, while the one Spirit's plastic stress
> Sweeps through the dull dense world, compelling there,
> All new successions to the forms they wear;
> Torturing th' unwilling dross that checks its flight
> To its own likeness, as each mass may bear;
> And bursting in its beauty and its might
> From trees and beasts and men into the Heaven's light.

197–8. GM suggests S. may be recalling Cicero, *De Natura Deorum* i 67: 'But where is the truth to be found? I suppose in an infinite number of worlds, some coming to birth and others hurled into ruin at every minutest moment of time?'.
197. SD.[(2)]] See S.'s Note 2.
199–200. Cp. Lucian, *Charon, or the Inspectors* 19:

> Let me tell you, Hermes, what I think men and the whole life of man resemble. You have noticed bubbles in water, caused by a streamlet plashing down—I mean those that mass to make foam? Some of them, being small, burst and are gone in an instant, while some last longer and as others join them, become swollen and grow to exceeding great compass; but afterwards they also burst without fail in time, for it cannot be otherwise. Such is the life of men; they are all swollen with wind, some to greater size, others to less; and with some the swelling is short-lived and swift-fated, while with others it is over as soon as it comes into being; but in any case they all must burst.

199. river] river, *1829, 1839, 1840.*
200. away.] away; *1829.*
201–10. Cp. *With a guitar. To Jane* (no. 446) ll. 27–39. Notopoulos 304 cps Plato, *Phaedo* 87–8, where the soul's outlasting of a number of human bodies through the repeated process of metempsychosis is compared to a human body's outlasting of a number of garments during its lifetime: '[One] might say that each soul wears out many bodies [just as each body outlives many coats]' (87d), trans. G. M. A. Grube in Plato, *Complete Works*, ed. John M. Cooper (1997) 76. S.'s translation of *Phaedo*, made between May and November 1820, is lost; it is referred to in his letter to Hogg of 22 October 1821 (*L* ii 360).
202. Who] Who, *1822, 1829, 1839, 1840. Birth's*] birth's *1822, 1829, 1839, 1840, 1964. portal*] portal, *1829, 1839, 1840.*

	And Death's dark chasm hurrying to and fro,
	Clothe their unceasing flight
205	In the brief dust and light
	Gathered around their chariots as they go;
	New shapes they still may weave,
	New Gods, new Laws receive,
	Bright or dim are they as the robes they last
210	On Death's bare ribs had cast.

    A Power from the unknown God,
      A Promethean Conqueror came;
    Like a triumphal path he trod
    The thorns of death and shame.

---

203. Death's] death's *1822, 1839, 1840, 1964.*
205. brief dust and light] 'Thinking beings, "to use a common and inadequate metaphor, *clothe themselves in matter*" (Shelley's note)' (GM).
207. still] I.e. 'ever' (GM).
208. Gods,] gods, *1822, 1964. Laws*] laws *1822, 1829, 1839, 1840, 1964. receive,*] receive; *1829.*
209–10. 'Their stage of perfection depends on what they did with their last lives and with the institutions they last inherited' (GM).
209. are they] are they, *1829, 1839, 1840.*
210. had] The alteration from *have* in HM 329 is probably in S.'s hand.
211–24. These lines posit Christianity to be a stronger religion than Islam in the context of the Greek war against the Turks.
211. A Power] 'Jesus Christ' (GM). *Power*] power *1822, 1829, 1839, 1840. the unknown God*] See *Acts* xvii 23: 'For as I passed by, and beheld your devotions, I found an altar with this inscription, TO THE UNKNOWN GOD. Whom therefore ye ignorantly worship, him declare I unto you.' *God,*] God; *1829, 1839, 1840.*
212. Promethean Conqueror] S. was doubtless aware of a tradition of reading Prometheus as an image of Christ. See, e.g., Alexander Ross, *Mystagogus Poeticus, Or The Muses Interpreter*, 5th edn (1672) 367–70 who offers fourteen allegorical meanings for Prometheus including that Christ 'nailed to the Cross upon mount Calvary' recalls '*Prometheus* [...] nailed to a Cross on the hill *Caucasus*' (370). *Conqueror*] conqueror *1822, 1829, 1839, 1840, 1964.* While the initial capital in HM 329 is not particularly clear, it is unambiguous in *Nbk 21* p. 165 (*BSM* xvi 168–9).
214. shame.] *1822, 1829, 1839, 1840;* shame *HM 329.*

215	A mortal shape to him
	Was like the vapour dim
	Which the orient planet animates with light;
	Hell, Sin and Slavery came
	Like bloodhounds mild and tame,
220	Nor preyed, until their Lord had taken flight;
	The moon of Mahomet
	Arose, and it shall set
	While blazoned as on Heaven's immortal noon
	The cross leads generations on.
225	Swift as the radiant shapes of sleep
	From one whose dreams are Paradise

217. *the orient planet*] Venus as the morning star; the planet Venus is so bright that it is the first 'star' to appear after sunset (when it is known as the evening star, or Hesperus), and the last to disappear before sunrise (when it is the morning star).
218. *Sin*] Sin, *1822, 1839, 1840, 1964. came*] HM 329; came, *1822, 1829, 1839, 1840.*
219. *tame,*] *1822, 1829, 1839, 1840, 1964*; tame HM 329.
220. *preyed,*] preyed *1829, 1839, 1840. flight;*] flight. *1829, 1839, 1840.*
221-24. 'Mohammed lived six centuries after Christ, but the religion he founded (its emblem is a crescent moon) will die before Christianity' (GM). S.'s 'Mahomet' is Muhammad (c.570-632 CE), the divinely inspired prophet who founded Islam. The cross 'blazoned as on Heaven's immortal noon' recalls the 'Cross of Constantine'; according to Eusebius, *Life of Constantine*, before the Battle of the Milvian Bridge in Rome the Emperor Constantine saw a vision of a cross of light above the sun, and the Greek words (ἐν) τούτῳ νίκα (lit. 'by this, conquer') written on it (see ll. 601-3 and l. 829 and note). Constantine used this sign in battle, and won a victory which made him sole ruler of the Roman Empire, and set him on the path to his conversion to Christianity.
222. *set*] set: *1822, 1829, 1839, 1840.*
223. *Heaven's*] heaven's *1822, 1829, 1839, 1840.*
225-38. 'Christianity represents "Truth" [l. 234] compared with the dream-world of the ancient gods, but error compared with the "golden years" [l. 238] to come—a source of bloodshed and suffering (*turned*, in l. [237], is a participle). This is a "revision" of Milton's *On the Morning of Christ's Nativity*, whose metre it imitates' (GM). It is, however, also possible that S.'s sense is 'nature ('Our hills and seas and streams', l. 235), with the coming of Christianity (and all the bloodshed and suffering which has ensued) and the passing of the pagan gods, lamented the loss of its innocence in the Saturnian "golden age" of Greek mythology'.
226. *Paradise*] paradise, *1829, 1839, 1840.*

>   Fly, when the fond wretch wakes to weep
>   And Day peers forth with her blank eyes,
>   So fleet, so faint, so fair
> 230 The Powers of earth and air
>   Fled from the folding-star of Bethlehem:

227. *Fly,*] Fly *1829. fond wretch*] Cp. *Adonais* 416; 'fond' = foolish. *wakes to weep*] Cp. *J&M* 335–7: 'as one from dreaming / Of sweetest peace, I woke, and found my state / Such as it is'; and *The flower that smiles today* (no. 417) ll. 19–21. The phrase is common in S.'s verse; other examples include *R&H* (no. 144) 775, *Charles the First* I iii 33–4 and *TL* 334, 460. *wakes*] Whether the alteration from *makes* in *HM 329* is in S.'s hand or Williams's is uncertain. *weep*] weep, *1822, 1829, 1839, 1840*.
228. *Day*] day *1822, 1829, 1839, 1840. eyes,*] eyes; *1822, 1839, 1840*; eyes! *1829*.
229. *fleet, ... faint,*] *1822, 1829, 1839, 1840, 1964*; fleet ... faint *HM 329. fair*] fair, *1822, 1829, 1839, 1840*.
230–8. Webb (1995) 443 cps *On the Devil, and Devils*:

> The Sylvans and Fauns, with their leader the great Pan, were most poetical personages, and were connected in the imagination of the Pagans with all that could enliven and delight. They were supposed to be innocent beings not greatly different in habits from the shepherds and herdsmen of which they were the patron saints. But the Christians contrived to turn the wrecks of the Greek mythology, as well as the little they understood of their philosophy, to purposes of deformity and falsehood. (*Julian* vii 103)

230. *The Powers of ... air*] Cp. *The Cloud* (no. 319) l. 69 ('the Powers of the Air') and note. *Powers*] powers *1829*. The alteration from *powers* in *HM 329* is probably in S.'s hand.
231. Christ's birth at Bethlehem was a new morning for Christianity, but sunset for the ancient gods. *folding-star of Bethlehem*] Cp. *Epipsychidion* 374 and note. The 'folding-star' is Venus as the evening star, 'The star that bids the shepherd fold' his sheep (Milton, *Comus* 93). *Bethlehem:*] *1822, 1829, 1839, 1840*; Bethlehem, *HM 329*.
232–8. Cp. Milton, 'On the Morning of Christ's Nativity' 173–96:

>   XIX
>   The oracles are dumb,
>   No voice or hideous hum
>   Runs through the arched roof in words deceiving.
>   Apollo from his shrine
>   Can no more divine,

        Apollo, Pan, and Love,
        And even Olympian Jove
Grew weak, for killing Truth had glared on them;
        Our hills and seas and streams
        Dispeopled of their dreams,
Their waters turned to blood, their dew to tears,

With hollow shriek the steep of Delphos leaving.
No nightly trance, or breathed spell,
Inspires the pale-eyed priest from the prophetic cell.

XX
The lonely mountains o'er,
And the resounding shore,
    A voice of weeping heard, and loud lament;
From haunted spring, and dale
Edged with poplar pale,
    The parting genius is with sighing sent,
With flower-inwoven tresses torn
The nymphs in twilight shade of tangled thickets mourn.

XXI
In consecrated earth,
And on the holy hearth,
    The lars, and lemures moan with midnight plaint,
In urns, and altars round,
A drear and dying sound
    Affrights the flamens at their service quaint;
And the chill marble seems to sweat,
While each peculiar power forgoes his wonted seat.

232. *Love*,] *1822, 1829, 1839, 1840, 1964*; Love *HM 329*.
234. *them*;] them. *1829, 1839, 1840*.
235. *hills ... seas ... streams*] hills, ... seas, ... streams, *1829, 1839, 1840*.
236. *dreams*,] *1822, 1829, 1839, 1840, 1964*; dreams *HM 329*.
237. *Their waters turned to blood*] Cp. *Exodus* vii 17: 'behold, I will smite with the rod that is in mine hand upon the waters which are in the river, and they shall be turned to blood.' See also *Exodus* vii 20 and *Revelation* xi 6. *tears*,] *1822, 1829, 1839, 1840, 1964*; tears *HM 329*.

Wailed for the golden years.

[*Enter* MAHMUD, HASSAN, DAOOD, *and others.*]

Mahmud
More gold? our ancestors bought gold with victory,
240 And shall I sell it for defeat?

238–9. *golden ... gold*] The words of the Chorus link with the entrance of Mahmud and his retinue discussing the Janizars' demands for payment, illustrating a theme central to *Hellas*. In *Nbk 21* p. 69, S. inscribes at the top of the page, above drafts for ll. 409–13, a Greek word Χρυσοκρατια, apparently his neologism, meaning 'rule by gold'. (The Latinised version — *Chysocracy*— appears, centred and underlined on p. 66.) It seems likely that *Persae* with its recurring references to gold and material wealth prompted S.'s word play. See, e.g., *Persae* 1–9:

> Τάδε μὲν Περσῶν τῶν οἰχομένων
> Ἑλλάδ᾽ ἐς αἶαν πιστὰ καλεῖται,
> καὶ τῶν ἀφνεῶν καὶ πολυχρύσων
> ἑδράνων φύλακες, κατὰ πρεσβείαν
> οὓς αὐτὸς ἄναξ Ξέρξης βασιλεὺς
> Δαρειογενὴς
> εἵλετο χώρας ἐφορεύειν.
> ἀμφὶ δὲ νόστῳ τῷ βασιλείῳ
> καὶ πολυχρύσου στρατιᾶς […]

('Of the Persians, who have departed / for the land of Greece, we are called the Trusted, / the guardians of the wealthy palace rich in gold, / whom our lord himself, King Xerxes / son of Darius, chose by seniority to supervise the country. Yet as regards the return of our King and of his host, so richly decked out in gold […]' [Gk text and translation from Herbert W. Smyth's 1926 Loeb edition; the most recent Loeb edition (ed. Alan H. Sommerstein, 2008) emends l. 9's MS reading πολυχρύσου, 'so richly decked in gold' to πολυάνδρου, 'comprised of many men'])

238. *the golden years*] This phrase is repeated in l. 1061. GM cps the Solitary in Wordsworth, *The Excursion* (1814) iii 756–8 recalling how he greeted the French Revolution:

> I sang Saturnian rule
> Returned,—a progeny of golden years
> Permitted to descend, and bless mankind.

239. *victory,*] *1822, 1829, 1839, 1840*; victory *HM 329*.

Daood

                                    The Janizars
       Clamour for pay —

Mahmud
                      Go! bid them pay themselves
With Christian blood! Are there no Grecian virgins
Whose shrieks and spasms and tears they may enjoy?
No infidel children to impale on spears?
245 No hoary priests after that Patriarch ⁽³⁾
Who bent the curse against his country's heart
Which clove his own at last? — Go! bid them kill;
Blood is the seed of gold.

240. *Janizars*] The Janissaries (literally 'new soldiers' in Ottoman Turkish) were elite infantry troops of the Sultan's household, and from the fourteenth century formed the first modern European standing army. Originally,

> they had been recruited from the Christian population. Young boys had been forcibly removed from their families, converted to Islam and brought up to an austere life in barracks. Janissaries had been forbidden to marry, so that they would know no other loyalty than to their sovereign. (Beaton, *Greece* 52)

But by the time of Mahmud II they had become a corrupt and reactionary force resistant to all change, recruited from the privileged Ottoman classes and a constant source of unrest and conflict within the Sultanate. They were eventually forcibly disbanded by Mahmud in 1826. The word 'Janizar' is found in Byron's *The Siege of Corinth* (1816) l. 659.
241. *pay* —] pay. *1822, 1829, 1839, 1840*.
245-7. *No hoary ... at last?*] See note to S.'s Note 3.
245. *after*] like (*OED* 10b). *Patriarch*] patriarch *1829*. ⁽³⁾] See S.'s Note 3.
246. *bent*] I.e. 'aimed', or 'directed' (see *OED* 'bend' 17). Locock *1911* ii 469 cps *R&H* 861. *heart*] heart, *1822, 1829, 1839, 1840*.
247. *last? — Go!*] last — Go! *HM 329*; last? Go! *1822, 1829, 1839, 1840*. *kill;*] kill *HM 329*; kill, *1822*; kill: *1829, 1839, 1840*.
248. *Blood is the seed of gold.*] I.e. wealth, and the power it brings, has its origins in violence. The association of blood and gold is a frequent motif in S.'s poetry: cp. e.g. *Q Mab* iv 195, *L&C 1843*, *Mazenghi* (no. 166) 19-20, *PU* I 531, *MA* (no. 231) 65,

Daood
                                  It has been sown,
    And yet the harvest to the sicklemen
250 Is as a grain to each.

Mahmud
                               Then take this signet,
    Unlock the seventh chamber in which lie
    The treasures of victorious Solyman.
    An Empire's spoil stored for a day of ruin.
    O spirit of my sires! is it not come?
255 The prey-birds and the wolves are gorged and sleep
    But these, who spread their feast on the red earth,

298, *England in 1819* (no. 255) l. 10, *OL* 43, *WA* (no. 341) 191, *Written on hearing the news of the death of Napoleon* l. 35, *Charles the First* I i 71, *TL* 287. See also *An Address to the People on the Death of the Princess Charlotte* (1817): 'Kings and their ministers have in every age been distinguished from other men by a thirst for expenditure and bloodshed' (*Prose Works* 235); and S.'s letter to Peacock, 17 July 1816: 'Leave Mammon and Jehovah to those who delight in wickedness and slavery—their altars are stained with blood or polluted with gold, the price of blood' (*L* i 490). sown,] *1822, 1829, 1839, 1840*; sown *HM 329*.

249. *the harvest ... sicklemen*] Cp. *The Tempest* IV i 134: 'You sunburn'd sicklemen, of August weary'. sicklemen] *1822*; sickleman *HM 329*; sickle-men *1829, 1839, 1840*. In *Nbk 21* p. 44 *sickleman* is altered to *sicklemen* (see *BSM* xvi 50–1). While the usual meaning is 'reapers', here it refers to scimitar-bearing Ottoman warriors. See also l. 383.

250. each.] *1822, 1829, 1839*; each *HM 329*. Then] *1840*; Then, *HM 329, 1822, 1829, 1839*. signet,] *1822, 1839, 1840*; signet. *HM 329*; signet: *1829*.

251. chamber] chamber, *1829, 1839, 1840*.

252. *Solyman*] Suleiman I (1494–1566), known as the 'Magnificent', was the longest-reigning Sultan (1520–66), and presided over the Ottoman Empire at the height of its extent, and the peak of its political, military, artistic and cultural power.

253. *Empire's*] Empires' *HM 329*; empire's *1822, 1829, 1839, 1840*. spoil] spoils *1829, 1834, 1839, 1840*. ruin.] ruin— *1829*.

254. sires!] *Nbk 21, 1822, 1829*; sires *HM 329*.

255. prey-birds] Cp. *Charles the First* I iii 73. sleep] sleep; *1822, 1839, 1840*; sleep, *1829*.

256. these] Referring to 'The Janizars' (l. 240).

Hunger for gold, which fills not — see them fed,
Then lead them to the rivers of fresh death.
[*Exit* DAOOD.

O, miserable dawn after a night
260 More glorious than the day which it usurped!
O, faith in God! O power on earth! O word
Of the great prophet, whose o'ershadowing wings
Darkened the thrones and idols of the West
Now bright! — for thy sake cursed be the hour,
265 Even as a father by an evil child,
When th'orient moon of Islam roll'd in triumph
From Caucasus to white Ceraunia!
Ruin above, and anarchy below;
Terror without, and treachery within;
270 The chalice of destruction full, and all

257. *not — see*] not.—See *1822, 1829, 1839, 1840. fed,*] fed; *1822, 1829, 1839, 1840.*
258. *Then*] *1829, 1839, 1840*; Then, *HM 329, 1822. death.*] *1822, 1829, 1839*; death *HM 329.*
259. *O,*] O! *1822*; Oh! *1829, 1839, 1840. dawn*] dawn, *1822, 1829, 1839, 1840.*
261. *O power*] O, power *1822, 1829, 1839, 1840. O word*] O, word *1822, 1829, 1839, 1840.*
262. *prophet,*] *1822*; prophet *HM 329*; Prophet, *1829, 1839, 1840. o'ershadowing*] *1822*; o'er-shadowing *HM 329*; overshadowing *1829, 1834, 1839, 1840.*
263. *West*] West: *HM 329*; West, *1822*; west, *1829, 1839, 1840.*
264–5. *hour, ... child,*] *1822, 1829, 1839*; hour ... child *HM 329.*
264. *bright*] Written above *veiled* canc. in *HM 329* in S.'s hand. *for*] For *1822, 1829, 1839, 1840.*
266. *th'orient*] the Orient *1822*; the orient *1829, 1839, 1840.*
267. The 'Caucasus' is the mountainous region between the Black Sea and the Caspian Sea, and 'white Ceraunia' the Acroceraunian mountains, the Kanalit range running along the north-west coast of Epirus and the south-west coast of Albania; the two areas roughly designate the East-to-West extent of the Ottoman Empire in the early nineteenth century. Cp. *Arethusa Arose* (no. 311) l. 3, and *Lines connected with Hellas* A l. 201. *white*] White *1822.*
270–2. Cp. the closing stanza 16 of 'The Isles of Greece' in *Don Juan* iii:

> Place me on Sunium's marbled steep,
>   Where nothing, save the waves and I,
> May hear our mutual murmurs sweep;
>   There, swan-like, let me sing and die:
> A land of slaves shall ne'er be mine—
> Dash down yon cup of Samian wine!

270. *chalice*] Chalice *1822.*

Thirsting to drink; and who among us dares
To dash it from his lips? and where is hope?

Hassan
The lamp of our dominion still rides high;
One God is God — Mahomet is his prophet.
275 Four hundred thousand Moslems from the limits
Of utmost Asia, irresistibly
Throng, like full clouds at the Sirocco's cry,
But not like them to weep their strength in tears;
They bear destroying lightning and their step
280 Wakes earthquake to consume and overwhelm

271. drink;] 1822, 1829, 1839, 1840; drink, *HM 329.*
272. hope] Hope *1822, 1829, 1839, 1840.*
273. high;] 1822, 1829, 1839, 1840; high, *HM 329.*
274. prophet] Prophet *1829, 1839, 1840.*
275-7. Four hundred thousand ... Throng] Duffy, 'Percy Shelley's "display of newspaper erudition"' 521 notes that a report in *Galignani's Messenger* 1919 (18 April 1821) [p. 1] stated the total size of Ottoman forces to be 406,400 (181,000 cavalry and 225,400 infantry).
275. Moslems] Moslems, *1829, 1839, 1840.*
276. Asia,] Asia *1829, 1839, 1840.*
277. Sirocco's] 1829, 1839; Sairocco's *1822;* Scirocco's *HM 329, 1840.* The *1822* reading is explained by the fact that the alteration of *Sirocco's* to *Scirocco's* in S.'s hand in *HM 329* is unclear (also the first letter is possibly altered from a majuscule to a minuscule). The reading is *Scirocco's* in *Nbk 21* p. 47 (see *BSM* xvi 52-3). The Sirocco is a wind which blows south-easterly from the Sahara, bringing Mediterranean storms, and warm wet weather to Southern Europe; it is noted among other winds in *Paradise Lost* x 703-6:

> thwart of these as fierce
> Forth rush the Lévant and the ponent winds
> Eurus and Zephir with their lateral noise,
> Sirocco, and Libecchio.

cry,] cry; *1822.*
278. tears;] 1829, 1839, 1840; tears, *HM 329;* tears: *1822.*
279. bear] have *1829, 1834, 1839, 1840. lightning]* lightning, *1822, 1829, 1839, 1840.*
280. earthquake] earthquake, *1829, 1839, 1840.* Whether the cancellation of the final letter of *earthquakes* in *HM 329* is in S.'s hand or Williams's is uncertain; the reading is *earthquake* in *Nbk 21* p. 47 (see *BSM* xvi 52-3). *overwhelm]* overwhelm, *1822, 1829, 1839, 1840.*

And reign in ruin. Phrygian Olympus,
Tmolus and Latmos and Mycale roughen
With horrent arms; and lofty ships even now,
Like vapours anchored to a mountain's edge,
285 Freighted with fire and whirlwind, wait at Scala
The convoy of the ever-veering wind.
Samos is drunk with blood; — the Greek has paid
Brief victory with swift loss and long despair.
The false Moldavian serfs fled fast and far

281-2. Phyrgian ... Mycale] Tmolus, Latmos and Mycale are all mountains in Western Anatolia, an ethnic heartland of the Ottoman Empire. Olympus (mod. Tahtali Dagi, near Antalya) is also a mountain in Anatolia — 'Phrygia' in the ancient world — which Mahmud refers to as 'Phrygian Olympus' to distinguish it from Mount Olympus in north-eastern Greece (home of the ancient Greek gods). *281. Olympus,]* *1822, 1829, 1839, 1840*; Olympus *HM 329.*
282. Tmolus] Tmolus, *1822, 1829, 1839, 1840*; Tymolus, *1829, 1834.* Cp. *Song of Pan* (no. 318) l. 11 and note. *Latmos ... Mycale]* Latmos, and Mycale, *1822, 1829, 1839, 1840.*
283. horrent arms;] horrent arms, *1829, 1839, 1840.* Cp. *Paradise Lost* ii 512-4: 'him round / A globe of fiery seraphim enclosed / With bright emblazonry, and horrent arms'; 'horrent' = 'rough with bristling points' (*OED* 1). *ships]* ships, *1829, 1839, 1840. now,]* *1822, 1829, 1839, 1840*; now *HM 329.*
284. edge,] *1822, 1829, 1839, 1840*; edge *HM 329.*
285. whirlwind,] *1822, 1829, 1839, 1840*; whirlwind *HM 329. Scala]* The last four letters of this word appear to have been overwritten by S. in *HM 329.* Scala Nuova, on the eastern coast of mod. Turkey, where Turkish troops boarded vessels bound for Samos, as reported in *Galignani's Messenger* 2040 (10 September 1821) [p. 4].
286. convoy] conveyance (see *OED n.* 8).
287-94. See note to ll. 361-85 below.
287-8. The Greeks under the leadership of Georgios Logothetis (1772-1850) had overthrown Turkish rule on Samos in April 1821 (see note to ll. 16-20). Intending to 'quash any revolutionary movement in the Eastern Aegean' the Turks laid siege to the island on 3 July 1821 and subsequently attempted to land; they were, however, successfully repelled (see Christos Landros, 'Samos' in *The Greek Revolution: A Critical Dictionary* 319). As Erkelenz notes ('Inspecting the Tragedy of Empire' 335 n. 28), the Greek 'victory' (l. 288) was reported in *Galignani's Messenger* 2040 (10 September 1821) [p. 4].
288. despair.] Reiman may be correct that 'PBS wrote the final word "despair" (apparently to fill in a blank in the holograph text from which EEW transcribed)' in *HM 329* (*MYRS* iii 37); the full stop is altered from a semi colon.
289. Moldavian serfs] See note to ll. 361-85 below. *far]* far, *1822.*

290 When the fierce shout of 'Allah-illa-allah!'
    Rose like the war-cry of the northern wind
    Which kills the sluggish clouds, and leaves a flock
    Of wild swans struggling with the naked storm.
    So were the lost Greeks on the Danube's day!
295 If night is mute, yet the returning sun
    Kindles the voices of the morning birds;
    Nor at thy bidding less exultingly
    Than birds rejoicing in the golden day,

290. *'Allah-illa-allah!'*] Allah illa allah *Nbk 21*; Allah-illa-allah! *HM 329*; Allah-illa-Allah! *1822, 1829, 1839, 1840*; 'Allah-illa-Allah!' *Locock 1911*. The phrase is translated by Hassan as 'One God is God' in l. 274. Hope glosses the phrase in *Anastasius* i 62 as 'Mohammedan [form] of prayer or invocation to the Supreme Being' (i 360). There is a version of this phrase ('"La Ilah illa Alla!"') in *Vathek* (1786) where it is glossed as *'there is no God but God'* (77, 150; page references are to the 1816 edn, ed. Roger Lonsdale (1970)). Of the fall of Constantinople, Gibbon states in *Decline and Fall* Vol. VI (1788), ch. lxviii that, 'the camp re-echoed with the Moslem shouts of, "God is God, there is but one God, and Mahomet is the apostle of God"' (David Womersley, ed., 3 vols (1995) iii 958–9).
291. *wind*] wind, *1829, 1839, 1840*.
294. A reference to the defeat of Ypsilantis's 'Sacred Battalion' at Dragatsani in the Danubian Principality of Wallachia on 7 June 1821; see Headnote ('Sources of S.'s knowledge of the Greek Revolution').
296. *the morning birds*] eds; y̰e morning birds *HM 329*. The reading is *the morning birds* in *Nbk 21* p. 47 (see *BSM* xvi 52–3). Reiman ascribes the careted y̰e, inserted in pencil after *of* in *HM 329*, to S. (*MYRS* iii 37). It is notable, however, that all other corrections and additions in S.'s hand in *HM 329* are in ink, and the only other pencil markings appear to be those of a compositor (see notes to Epigraph and Preface l. 44). birds;] *1822, 1829, 1839, 1840*; birds *HM 329*.
297. *exultingly*] The reading is *exaltingly* in *Nbk 21* p. 47 (see *BSM* xvi 52–3).
298. This line is marked off in ink in the margin of *HM 329* p. 15 with 'C17' above. As Reiman notes (*MYRS* iii 12, 37), these markings are those of the printer, noting this line to be the first on p. 17 in *1822*, i.e. the beginning of signature C. *day,*] *1822, 1829, 1839*; day *HM 329*.

The Anarchies of Africa unleash
300 Their tempest-winged cities of the sea
To speak in thunder to the rebel world.
Like sulphurous clouds half shattered by the storm
They sweep the pale Aegean, while the Queen
Of Ocean, bound upon her island-throne,
305 Far in the west sits mourning that her sons
Who frown on Freedom spare a smile for thee:

299–301. See *Galignani's Messenger* 2005 (31 July 1821) [p. 4]:

A correspondent at Smyrna informs us, that three Naval officers, sent by the Porte to the three Barbarian Regencies [the North African port cities of Algiers, Tripoli and Tunis, then under the control of the Ottoman Empire] to invite them to join their maritime forces to the Ottoman fleet, had embarked from that port in the early part of June. He adds the strongest squadron of the Greek fleet is stationed at the entrance of the Sea of Crete, and the largest vessels are at anchor in the roads of the Isle of Milos, to watch the motions of the Barbarians, who can enter the Archipelago by no other way.

299. Anarchies] anarchies *1829.*
300. tempest-winged cities of the sea] warships. *Locock 1911* ii 469 cps *PU* II iv 93. *sea]* sea, *1822, 1829, 1839, 1840.*
302. sulphurous] sulphureous *1829, 1834, 1839, 1840. clouds]* clouds, *1822. half shattered]* half-shattered *1822, 1829, 1839, 1840. storm]* storm, *1822, 1839, 1840.*
303–6. Queen ... smile for thee] The *Queen / Of Ocean ... in the west* is Great Britain, whose failure to intervene on behalf of the Greek Insurrection is lamented by her people; see Headnote ('S.'s sources of knowledge of the Greek revolution').
304. island-throne,] 1822; island-throne *HM 329;* island throne, *1829, 1839, 1840.*
305. west] West *1822;* West, *1839, 1840.* The reading in *Nbk 21* p. 47 is *west* although *BSM* reads *West* (see *BSM* xvi 52–3). *sons]* sons, *1829, 1839, 1840.*
306. Freedom] Freedom, *1829, 1839, 1840. thee:] 1822, 1829, 1839, 1840;* thee *HM 329.*

Russia still hovers as an eagle might
Within a cloud, near which a kite and crane
Hang tangled in inextricable fight

307–20. Russia, like Great Britain, declined to intervene either for or against the Ottoman Empire, with both powers mindful of their broader imperial interest; Austria likewise, newly dominant in Central Europe following the post-Napoleonic 'balance of powers' established by the Congress of Vienna in 1814–5, was not hostile to the Ottoman suppression of the Greek revolt. Cp. the *Examiner* 704 (1 July 1821) 407–8:

> Turkey is now the only theatre of events which excite any immediate interest among the other nations of Europe. The contest between the old despotism of the bigoted Mussulmen, and the new attempt at freedom of the long oppressed owners of the glorious name of Greeks,—continues bloody in its progress, and doubtful as to its event. As would naturally be expected, the Greeks, who were always the sailors of the Ottoman Empire, have got the mastery at sea. Their fleets, fitted out from the numerous islands of the Archipelago, ride triumphant in the Ionian seas, destroying the Turkish commerce, threatening to straiten Constantinople itself by cutting off its Egyptian supplies of corn, and promising to drive the remaining Turkish garrisons in the Morea to surrender, by the deprivation of aids from the capital. Thus, though the Insurgent cause is said to have lost ground greatly in Moldavia and Walachia, it is not improbable, that the Morea, the ancient Peloponnesus, may be enabled by this maritime superiority, to complete and maintain its independence against the ill-assorted and distracted dominions of the GRAND SEIGNOR.
>
> In the mean time, Austrian and Russian forces are assembling on the Turkish frontier; and the Emperor of AUSTRIA has formally admitted the Grand Turk to be a Member of the Holy Alliance, by declaring the Insurrection against the Sublime Porte 'no less criminal,' than that against his own imperial usurpations in Italy. [...] How rapidly are all the old jealousies and hatreds of courts giving way to the greater alarm of the general diffusion of anti-despotic principles!

307. Russia still hovers as an eagle] A black two-headed eagle was the symbol of Imperial Russia; see ll. 948–9 and note. *hovers*] hovers, *1822, 1829, 1839, 1840*. *eagle*] Nbk 21, *1822, 1829, 1839, 1840*; Eagle *HM 329*.
308–9. near ... fight] Ackermann, *Quellen* (1890) 51, Woodberry (1901) and Locock 1911 ii 469 all cp. *Persae* 207–12 although the parallels are quite tenuous. *tangled in inextricable fight*] Cp. *L&C* 193 and *PU* III i 73.
309. Hang] Inserted above *Are* canc. in *HM 329* in S.'s hand. *fight*] fight, *1822, 1829, 1839, 1840*.

310   To stoop upon the victor — for she fears
      The name of Freedom even as she hates thine.
      But recreant Austria loves thee as the Grave
      Loves Pestilence, and her slow dogs of war,
      Fleshed with the chase, come up from Italy
315   And howl upon their limits; for they see
      The panther Freedom fled to her old cover
      'Mid seas and mountains, and a mightier brood
      Crouch round. What anarch wears a crown or mitre,
      Or bears the sword, or grasps the key of gold,
320   Whose friends are not thy friends, whose foes thy foes?
      Our arsenals and our armouries are full,
      Our forts defy assault — ten thousand cannon
      Lie ranged upon the beach, and hour by hour

310. *stoop*] 'Of a hawk or other bird of prey: To descend swiftly on its prey, to swoop' (*OED* 6a); cp. *Charles the First* I iii 71. *victor* —] victor;— *1822, 1829, 1839*; victor; *1840*.
311. *Freedom*] Freedom, *1822, 1829, 1839, 1840*. *thine.*] thine; *1829, 1839*; thine: *1840*.
312. *recreant*] I.e. 'false; unfaithful'; cp. *Paradise Regained* iii 138: 'recreant to God, ingrate and false'. *Grave*] grave *1829*. The capital written over the small *g* in *HM 329* appears to be in Williams's hand not, as *MYRS* suggests, S.'s.
313–4. war, ... chase,] *1822, 1829, 1839, 1840*; war ... chase *HM 329*.
313. *Pestilence*] pestilence *1829*. *dogs of war*] Cp. *Julius Caesar* III i 273: 'let slip the dogs of war'.
314. *Italy*] Italy, *1822, 1829, 1839, 1840*.
316. *panther Freedom*] panther, Freedom, *1822*. In *HM 329*, *freedom* is altered to *Freedom*, whether by S. or Williams is uncertain. *cover*] cover, *1822, 1839, 1840*.
317. *'Mid*] Amid *1822, 1829, 1839, 1840*. *mountains,*] *1822, 1829, 1839, 1840*; mountains *HM 329*.
318. *round*] around *1829, 1834, 1839, 1840*. *What anarch wears a crown or mitre*] Cp. *TL* 209–10. *anarch*] Anarch *1822, 1839, 1840*. Recalling Milton's *Paradise Lost* ii 988 where 'the anarch' (ruler) in question is Chaos. Milton's is the earliest recorded instance of this word in *OED*. *or*] Inserted above *and* canc. in *HM 329* by Williams not, as *MYRS* suggests, S.
318–20. *What anarch ... thy foes?*] 'What ruler ("anarch"), whether monarch, religious leader ("the key of gold" symbolises the Vatican), or military general, is not going to side with the Ottomans, sharing as they do their friends and their enemies?.'
321. *full,*] full *HM 329*; full; *1822, 1829, 1839, 1840*.
322. *assault* —] assault; *1822*; assaults; *1829, 1834, 1839, 1840*.

Their earth-convulsing wheels affright the city;
325 The galloping of fiery steeds makes pale
The Christian merchant; and the yellow Jew
Hides his hoard deeper in the faithless earth.
Like clouds and like the shadows of the clouds
Over the hills of Anatolia,
330 Swift in wide troops the Tartar chivalry
Sweep — the far flashing of their starry lances
Reverberates the dying light of day.
We have one God, one King, one hope, one law,
But many-headed Insurrection stands

324. As Reiman notes of *HM 329*, Williams 'had copied "Their" and possibly "earth"; the rest of the line ("-convulsing … the city;") was added by PBS' (*MYRS* iii 39).
326. *merchant;*] merchant, *1829*, *1839*, *1840*.
328. *Like clouds*] Like clouds, *1822*, *1829*, *1839*, *1840*. *the clouds*] the clouds, *1822*, *1839*, *1840*.
329. *Anatolia,*] *1822*, *1829*, *1839*, *1840*; Anatolia *HM 329*. Anatolia (mod. Southern Turkey), the central plain of Asia Minor.
330. *Tartar chivalry*] I.e. high-ranking troops from Tartary, the blanket term for a vast area of Asia bounded by the Caspian Sea, the Ural Mountains, the Pacific Ocean, and the Northern borders of China, India and Persia. By the early nineteenth century Ottoman influence had ceased so far East, but the region's diverse population included ethnic Turks.
331. *Sweep —*] Sweep;— *1822*, *1829*, *1839*, *1840*. *far flashing*] far-flashing *1829*, *1839*, *1840*. A hyphen between these two words appears to be cancelled in *HM 329*, whether by S. or Williams is uncertain. *their*] The word *thier* is inserted in S.'s hand above *whose* canc. in *HM 329*.
332. *Reverberates*] I.e. 'reflects'.
333. *Major Works* cps *MA* 37 'to gauge S's irony here':

> And he [Anarchy] wore a kingly crown,
> And in his grasp a sceptre shone;
> On his brow this mark I saw —
> 'I AM GOD, AND KING, AND LAW.' (34–37)

hope] Hope *1822*, *1829*, *1839*, *1840*. *law,*] law *HM 329*; Law; *1822*, *1839*, *1840*; Law, *1829*.
334–5. 'The manyheaded Greek Revolution, without a central command, planning or coordination' (*Raizis* 184).
334. *many-headed*] A reference to the Hydra, a many-headed snake in Greek mythology whose heads grew again as soon as they were cut off, eventually destroyed by Heracles. The Hydra is traditionally associated with the unruly multitude; see, e.g., *Coriolanus* III i 93 and Dryden, *Absalom and Achitophel* (1681) 541–2.

335   Divided in itself, and soon must fall.

Mahmud
      Proud words when deeds come short are seasonable;
      Look, Hassan, on yon crescent moon emblazoned
      Upon that shattered flag of fiery cloud
      Which leads the rear of the departing day,
340   Wan emblem of an empire fading now.

336. *words ... short*] words, ... short, *1822, 1829, 1839, 1840. seasonable;*] *1840*; seasonable *HM 329*; seasonable: *1822, 1829, 1839*. The word carries bitter irony (cp. *Charles the First* I i 92). *Concordance* glosses 'what may be expected' but 'unsuitable' is implied.
337–41. These lines allude to the flag of the Ottoman Empire: a crescent moon and an eight-pointed star against a red background. Cp. the preoccupation with flags, crosses and crescent moons as symbols for power in Calderón's *El príncipe constante*, e.g. Act I 187–96 where Muley describes the Christian 'occupation' of Ceuta:

> y en oprobrio de las armas
> nuestras sabemos agora
> que pendones portugueses
> en sus torres se enarbolan,
> teniendo siempre a los ojos
> un padrastro que baldona
> nuestros aplausos, un freno
> que nuestro orgullo reporta,
> un Cáucaso que detiene
> al Nilo de tus vitorias [...] (Text from *El príncipe constante*, ed.
> Isabel Hernando Morata (2015) 143–4)

('Which, opprobrium of our valour! / Now a foreign ruler hath. / Where we tamely gape and gaze at, / Where our slavish eye-sight sees, / Floating from its topmast turrets, / Banners of the Portuguese. / 'Neath our very eyes prescribing / Limits that our arms deride— / 'Tis a mockery of our praises, / 'Tis a bridle to our pride, / 'Tis a Caucasus, which, lying / Midway, doth the stream detain; / Back thy Nile of victory turning [...]; trans. *Mac-Carthy (1853)* i 11)

337. *Look, Hassan,*] *1822, 1829, 1839, 1840*; Look Hassan *HM 329*. *moon*] moon, *1822, 1829, 1839, 1840*.
338. *shattered flag*] 'floating fragment' (*Concordance*).
339. *day,*] *1829, 1839, 1840*; day *HM 329*; day; *1822*.
340. *Wan emblem*] Wan-emblem *1822*. *now.*] now *HM 329*; now! *1822, 1829, 1839, 1840*.

See! how it trembles in the blood-red air
And like a mighty lamp whose oil is spent
Shrinks on the horizon's edge, while from above
One star with insolent and victorious light
345 Hovers above its fall, and with keen beams,
Like arrows through a fainting antelope,
Strikes its weak form to death.

Hassan
                                  Even as that moon
    Renews itself —

Mahmud
                    Shall we be not renewed!
Far other bark than ours were needed now
350 To stem the torrent of descending time;
The spirit that lifts the slave before his lord
Stalks through the capitals of armed kings
And spreads his ensign in the wilderness,
Exults in chains, and when the rebel falls,

---

341. See!] See *1822, 1829, 1839, 1840. air*] air, *1822, 1829, 1839, 1840.*
342. spent] spent, *1829, 1839, 1840.*
343. edge,] *1822, 1829, 1839, 1840*; edge *HM 329. while*] while, *1822, 1829, 1839, 1840. above*] above, *1822, 1829, 1839, 1840.*
344. One star] Venus (see note to l. 217). *insolent … light*] Cp. *The Cenci* II i 180.
345–6. beams, … antelope,] *1822, 1829, 1839, 1840*; beams … antelope *HM 329.*
347. moon] moon, *1822.*
349. ours] our's *1822.*
350. time;] time: *1822, 1829, 1839, 1840.*
351–8. Cp. the attack on monarchy in the Preface ll. 104–113 and the note to those lines which cites Hunt's article, 'The Greeks', in the *Examiner* 718 (7 October 1821) 625.
351. his] its *1829, 1834, 1839, 1840.*
352. kings] kings, *1822, 1829, 1839, 1840.*
353. wilderness,] wilderness *HM 329*; wilderness: *1822*; wilderness; *1829, 1839, 1840.*
354. chains,] chains; *1822, 1829, 1839, 1840. and*] and, *1822. falls,*] *1822, 1829, 1839, 1840*; falls *HM 329.*

355 Cries like the blood of Abel from the dust;
And the inheritors of the earth, like beasts
When earthquake is unleashed, with idiot fear
Cower in their kingly dens — as I do now.
What were Defeat when Victory must appal?
360 Or Danger when Security looks pale?
How said the messenger who from the fort
Islanded in the Danube saw the battle
Of Bucharest? — that —

Hassan
                              Ibrahim's scimitar
Drew with its gleam swift victory from heaven
365 To burn before him in the night of battle,

---

355. *dust;*] *1822, 1829, 1839, 1840;* dust *HM 329*. Cp. *Genesis* iv 8–10: 'And Cain talked with Abel his brother: and it came to pass, when they were in the field, that Cain rose up against Abel his brother, and slew him. And the Lord said unto Cain, Where *is* Abel thy brother? And he said, I know not: *Am* I my brother's keeper? And he said, What hast thou done? the voice of thy brother's blood crieth unto me from the ground.'
356. *of the earth*] of earth *1829, 1834, 1839, 1840*.
357. *unleashed,*] *1822, 1829, 1839, 1840;* unleashed *HM 329*. *idiot*] Whether the alteration of the third letter from *e* to *i* and the overwriting of the first and fourth letters in *HM 329* are in S.'s hand, or Williams's, is uncertain.
359. *Defeat*] Defeat, *1829, 1839, 1840*.
360. *Danger*] Danger, *1822, 1829, 1839, 1840*. *pale?*] pale?— *1822*.
361–85. *How said the messenger ... Grew weak and few*] In this passage Hassan recounts the sequence of events leading to the defeat of the Sacred Battalion under Alexandros Ypsilantis at the Battle of Dragastani on 7 June 1821. See Headnote ('Sources of S.'s knowledge of the Greek revolution').
361. *messenger*] messenger— *1822, 1829, 1839, 1840*. *who*] who, *1822*.
362. *Danube*] Danube, *1822, 1829, 1839, 1840*.
363. *Ibrahim's*] A Turkish commander by the name of 'Ibrahim Pacha' is mentioned in a report published in *Galignani's Messenger* 2043 (13 September 1821) [p. 4]. A cancelled passage in *HM 329* p. 7 referring to 'Ibrahim' is supplied in the note to l. 121 above. *scimitar*] The curved blade sword typically carried by the Turkish soldiers. See also note to l. 249.
364. *heaven*] heaven, *1822, 1829, 1839, 1840*. The reading in *Nbk 21* p. 58 is *Heaven* (see *BSM* xvi 64–5).
365. *battle,*] battle— *1822, 1829, 1839, 1840*.

A light and a destruction —

Mahmud

Was ours — but how? —

Aye! the day

Hassan

The light Wallachians,
The Arnaut, Servian, and Albanian allies

366. *destruction* —] destruction. *1822, 1829, 1839, 1840. Aye!*] Ay! *1822, 1829, 1839, 1840*; Ah! *1834*.
367. *ours* —] our's: *1822*; ours; *1829, 1839, 1840*.
367–401. *The light Wallachians … in triumphant death*] What follows bears some similarity to *Persae* 441–71 where the messenger tells Atossa of the fate of the Persians stationed on an island at Salamis. Cp. the Greeks described by Hassan in ll. 399–401 ('So these survivors … Met in triumphant death') with the Persians described in *Persae* 441–4:

> Περσῶν ὅσοιπερ ἦσαν ἀκμαῖοι φύσιν,
> ψυχήν τ᾽ ἄριστοι κεὐγένειαν ἐκπρεπεῖς,
> αὐτῷ τ᾽ ἄνακτι πίστιν ἐν πρώτοις ἀεί,
> τεθνᾶσιν αἰσχρῶς δυσκλεεστάτῳ πότμῳ.

('All those Persians who were in their bodily prime, outstanding in courage, notable for high birth, and who always showed the highest degree of loyalty to the person of the King, have perished shamefully by a most ignoble fate.')

The messenger of the *Persae* goes on to describe the Greeks encircling the Persian survivors and killing them with a combination of missiles and hand-to-hand combat. Cp. *Hellas* 378–85 ('Our baffled army […] gave them space but soon / From the surrounding hills the batteries blazed, / Kneading them down with fire and iron rain; / Yet none approached till […] The band, intrenched in mounds of Turkish dead, / Grew weak and few') with *Persae* 457–64:

> ὅπλοισι ναῶν ἐξέθρῳσκον, ἀμφὶ δὲ
> κυκλοῦντο πᾶσαν νῆσον, ὥστ᾽ ἀμηχανεῖν
> ὅποι τράποιντο. πολλὰ μὲν γὰρ ἐκ χερῶν
> πέτροισιν ἡράσσοντο, τοξικῆς τ᾽ ἄπο
> θώμιγγος ἰοὶ προσπίτνοντές ὤλλυσαν·
> τέλος δ᾽ ἐφορμηθέντες ἐξ ἑνὸς ῥόθου
> παίουσι, κρεοκοποῦσι δυστήνων μέλη,
> ἕως ἁπάντων ἐξαπέφθειραν βίον.

('[The Greeks] leaped off their ships, and landed all around the island,

Fled from the glance of our artillery
370 Almost before the thunderstone alit.
One half the Grecian army made a bridge
Of safe and slow retreat with Moslem dead,
The other —

Mahmud

    Speak — tremble not. —

Hassan

        Islanded
By victor myriads, formed in hollow square

---

so that the Persians had no idea which way to turn. They were being heavily battered by hand-thrown stones, and hit and killed by arrows shot from the bowstring, until finally the Greeks charged them in a simultaneous rush and struck them down, hacking the wretched men's limbs until they had extinguished the life of every one of them.')

Xerxes, the messenger reports, had placed his finest troops in the position in which they met this fate, with the express intention of killing any Greeks who had survived shipwreck in the Battle of Salamis (*Persae* 450–4). Hassan's description here of the 'triumphant' (l. 401) deaths forms a sort of realisation of Xerxes' intended scenario.

368. *allies*] allies, *1829, 1840*.
370. *thunderstone*] I.e. cannon-ball. *alit*.] alit; *1829, 1839, 1840*.
372. *retreat*] retreat, *1822, 1829, 1839, 1840*. *dead,*] dead *HM 329*; dead; *1822, 1829, 1839, 1840*.
373. *Speak — tremble not.* —] Another 'tragic' *antilabê* (see note to l. 188 above): often in Greek tragedy characters artificially delay the revelation of information by interjecting attempts to encourage or speed up their interlocutors. *not.* —] not— *1829, 1839, 1840*.
374. *victor*] 'victorious, conquering' (*Concordance*). *myriads,*] *1822, 1829, 1839, 1840*; myriads *HM 329*. 'Countless multitudes' (*OED n.* 3a). The word, also found in l. 463 and Note 8 l. 20, is used in the description of Mahomet transporting his navy over land in *Decline and Fall* Vol. VI ch. lxviii: 'the deficiency of art was supplied by the strength of obedient myriads' (Womersley, ed., iii 955). *hollow square*] 'a defensive formation of fusiliers, with a double or triple line of infantry on each side and, of course, an empty center. Their well-aimed fire from all four sides kept the attacking ene[m]y, cavalry o[r] infantry, at bay; if the attackers were to finally fall on the square, they would have to face the bayonettes of the massed defenders, too' (*Raizis* 186).

375 With rough and steadfast front, and thrice flung back
     The deluge of our foaming cavalry;
     Thrice their keen wedge of battle pierced our lines.
     Our baffled army trembled like one man
     Before a host, and gave them space but soon
380 From the surrounding hills the batteries blazed,
     Kneading them down with fire and iron rain;
     Yet none approached till, like a field of corn
     Under the hook of the swart sickleman,
     The band, intrenched in mounds of Turkish dead,
385 Grew weak and few — then said the Pacha, 'Slaves —

375–6. *thrice ... foaming cavalry*] An ironic echo of the confident description of the Persian army by the Chorus in *Persae* 87–92:

δόκιμος δ' οὔτις ὑποστὰς
μεγάλῳ ῥεύματι φωτῶν
ὀχυροῖς ἕρκεσιν εἴργειν
ἄμαχον κῦμα θαλάσσας.
ἀπρόσοιστος γὰρ ὁ Περσᾶν
στρατὸς ἀλκίφρων τε λαός.

('No one can be counted on to withstand this great flood of men and be a sturdy barrier to ward off the irresistible waves of the sea: none dare come near the army of the Persians and their valiant host.')

377. The Theban general Epaminondas defeated the Spartans at the Battle of Leuctra in 371 BCE by the use of a 'wedge' or echelon formation of troops to penetrate the Spartan cavalry (see *Raizis* 186).
379. space] space; *1822, 1829, 1839, 1840. but*] Inserted above *and* canc. in *HM 329*, whether in S.'s hand or Williams's is uncertain. *soon*] soon, *1822, 1829, 1839, 1840*.
380. hills] hills, *1822, 1829, 1839, 1840. blazed,*] *1822, 1829, 1839, 1840*; blazed *HM 329*.
381. Omitted in *1834. Kneading ... down*] 'smashing or crushing' (*Concordance*). Cp. *PU* I 614 and IV 342. *rain;*] rain *HM 329*; rain: *1822*; rain. *1829, 1839, 1840*.
382. approached] approached; *1822, 1829, 1839, 1840. till,*] *1822, 1829, 1839*; till *HM 329, 1840*.
383. swart] dark skinned. *sickleman,*] *1822, 1829, 1839, 1840*; sickleman *HM 329*. See note to l. 249.
384. band,] bands *1829, 1834, 1839, 1840. dead,*] dead *1829*.
385. few — then] few.—Then *1822, 1829, 1839, 1840. Pacha*] Commander; 'Pasha' = 'the highest official title of honour in the Ottoman Empire' (*OED* 1). *Slaves —*] *Nbk 21*; Slaves *HM 329*; Slaves, *1822, 1829, 1839*.

Render yourselves — they have abandoned you,
What hope of refuge, or retreat or aid? —
We grant your lives' — 'Grant that which is thine own!'
Cried one, and fell upon his sword and died!
390   Another — 'God, and man, and hope abandon me;
But I to them and to myself remain
Constant' — he bowed his head and his heart burst.

386. Render] Surrender (*OED* 6c). *yourselves* —] yourselves!— *1829. they]* They *1829. you,]* you— *1822, 1829, 1839, 1840.*
387. retreat] retreat, *1822, 1829, 1839, 1840. aid?* —] aid? *1822, 1829, 1839, 1840.*
388–401. Grant that which is thine own! ... triumphant death] The suicides of the three Greek soldiers in this passage recall 1 *Samuel* xxxi 3–6 where Saul and his followers choose to die by their own hands rather than those of the Philistine victors:

> And the battle went sore against Saul, and the archers hit him; and he was sore wounded of the archers. Then said Saul unto his armourbearer, Draw thy sword, and thrust me through therewith; lest these uncircumcised come and thrust me through, and abuse me. But his armourbearer would not; for he was sore afraid. Therefore Saul took a sword, and fell upon it. And when his armourbearer saw that Saul was dead, he fell likewise upon his sword, and died with him. So Saul died, and his three sons, and his armourbearer, and all his men, that same day together.

388. We] 1822. The portion of p. 19 on which this word is written in *HM 329* is torn away, although the tail of an *e* is visible. Reiman states that "We" appears on the fragment folded back (visible on p. 20), due to a triangular tear at the left margin' (*MYRS* iii 41); however, no 'fragment folded back' was evident to the editors when they consulted *HM 329* in 2014. The reading in *Nbk 21* p. 67 is *I* (see *BSM* xvi 72–3). *lives'* —] lives.' *1822*; lives.'— *1829, 1839, 1840. own!]* own, *1829, 1839, 1840.* Whether the careted insertion of *own* in *HM 329* is in S.'s hand, or Williams's is uncertain.
390. Another—'God, man, hope, abandon me; Rossetti 1870. Rossetti regarded the *1822* reading 'as a clear and indisputable case of oversight; like the "alexandrine in the middle of a stanza" pointed out by Shelley himself as an erratum in the *Revolt of Islam*' (Rossetti 1870 ii 555). *me;]* 1822, 1829, 1839, 1840; me *HM 329.*
391. them ... myself] them, ... myself, *1822.*
392. Constant' —] Constant —' *HM 329*; Constant:'— *1822*; Constant;'— *1829*; Constant;' *1839, 1840*. This word — arresting in its trochaic measure at the caesura and poised dramatically as the last word of the first Greek soldier to die — may allude to Calderón's *El príncipe constante* which contains repeated instances of characters sacrificing their lives, hopes and desires for a higher morality. See l. 1 SD and note. *head]* head, *1822, 1829, 1840.*

A third exclaimed — 'There is a refuge, tyrant,
Where thou darest not pursue and canst not harm
395   Should'st thou pursue; there we shall meet again.'
Then held his breath and after a brief spasm
The indignant spirit cast its mortal garment
Among the slain; — dead earth upon the earth!
So these survivors, each by different ways,
400   Some strange, all sudden, none dishonourable,
Met in triumphant death; and when our army
Closed in, while yet wonder and awe and shame

393. exclaimed —] exclaimed, *1822, 1829, 1839, 1840*.
394. pursue] pursue, *1822, 1829, 1839, 1840*. *canst not*] The alteration from *cannot* in *HM 329* appears to be in S.'s hand. *harm*] harm, *1822, 1829, 1839, 1840*.
396. breath] breath, *1822, 1829, 1839, 1840*. *and*] and, *1822, 1829, 1839, 1840*. *spasm*] spasm, *1822, 1829, 1839, 1840*.
398. slain; —] slain— *1822, 1829, 1839, 1840*. *dead earth upon the earth*] Repeats *MA* 131, as noted in *Locock 1911* ii 469. The phrase recalls 'The Order for the Burial of the Dead' in *The Book of Common Prayer*: 'we therefore commit his body to the ground, earth to earth, ashes to ashes, dust to dust'. The phrase that follows, 'in sure and certain hope of resurrection to eternal life', is echoed in the speech of the fourth Greek warrior in ll. 412–24.
399–401. So these survivors … triumphant death] Cp. Muley's account of the drowning enemy sailors who chose not to be saved by their foes in Act I 326–9 of Calderón, *El príncipe constante*:

> si bien otros les baldonan
> diciéndoles que el vivir
> eterno es morir con honra,
> –y aun así se resistieron … (Text from *El príncipe constante*, ed. Isabel Hernando Morata (2015) 151)

> ('But the rest, resisting, cried,
> "Life is but to live with honour!"—; trans. *Mac-Carthy (1853)* i 14)).

399. each] As Reiman notes of *HM 329*: 'Probably EEW [Edward Ellerker Williams] had canceled "each" and written "all" above the line; PBS then canceled "all" and rewrote "each" heavily in large letters' (*MYRS* iii 42). *by*] Whether the partial overwriting of this word in *HM 329* is in S.'s hand or Williams's is uncertain.
400. dishonourable,] The comma is overwritten in *HM 329*.
401. army] army, *1829*.
402. yet wonder] yet wonder, *1822, 1839, 1840*; yet in wonder, *1829, 1834*. *awe*] awe, *1822, 1829, 1839, 1840*. *shame*] shame, *1822, 1829*.

Held back the base hyenas of the battle
That feed upon the dead and fly the living,
405 One rose out of the chaos of the slain
And if it were a corpse which some dread spirit
Of the old saviours of the land we rule
Had lifted in its anger wandering by; —
Or if there burned within the dying man
410 Unquenchable disdain of death, and faith
Creating what it feigned; — I cannot tell —
But he cried — 'Phantoms of the free, we come!
Armies of the Eternal, ye who strike
To dust the citadels of sanguine Kings,
415 And shake the souls throned on their stony hearts
And thaw their frostwork diadems like dew; —

405–51. One rose ... to oblivion] Much of this passage derives from S.'s initial attempt to address the Greek struggle for independence in *It is the period when all the Sons of God* (*Lines connected with Hellas* A). The speech by the fourth dying Greek warrior begins by invoking Greece's glorious past, 'Phantoms of the free, we come!' (l. 412) and, after cursing the enemy, 'ye, weak conquerors!' (l. 425), prophesies their annihilation.
405. slain] slain: *1822*; slain; *1829, 1839, 1840*.
406–9. And if ... Or if] 'as if ... Or as if'.
408. anger wandering by; —] *1822*; anger wandering, by; — *HM 329*; anger wandering by, — *Nbk 21*; anger, wandering by; *1829, 1839, 1840*.
410–11. faith ... Creating what it feigned] Locock 1911 ii 469 cps *PU* IV 573–4: 'till Hope creates / From its own wreck the thing it contemplates'. Locock notes '"what it feigned" [l. 411] is the power of resurrection.'
411. tell —] tell, *1829*; tell: *1839, 1840*.
412–24. Phantoms of the free! ... yet to come!] A single sentence punctuated by the dying soldier's repeated addresses to the 'Armies of the Eternal' (l. 413) and 'Progenitors' (l. 421). He requests of them one action: 'Ascribe to your bright senate ... us, your Sons —' (ll. 422–3).
412. cried —] cried, *1822, 1829, 1839, 1840*.
413. Eternal,] eternal, *1829*.
414. sanguine] 'Causing or delighting in bloodshed' (*OED* 2b). *Kings*] kings *1822, 1829, 1839, 1840*.
415–6. shake ... like dew] Cp. *MA* 153 and 374.
415. hearts] hearts, *1822, 1829, 1839, 1840*. The final two letters of this word are torn away in *HM 329* p. 20 (this tear is recorded in the note to l. 388 above). The reading is *hearts* in *Nbk 21* p. 70 (see *BSM* xvi 76–7).
416. frostwork] 'unsubstantial as the forms of frost' (*Concordance*). *dew; —*] dew! — *1829*.

> O ye who float around this clime, and weave
> The garment of the glory which it wears,
> Whose fame, though earth betray the dust it clasped,
> 420 Lies sepulchred in monumental thought, —
> Progenitors of all that yet is great,
> Ascribe to your bright senate, O accept
> In your high ministrations, us, your Sons —
> Us first, and the more glorious yet to come!
> 425 And ye, weak conquerors! giants who look pale
> When the crushed worm rebels beneath your tread,

417. *clime,*] *1822, 1829, 1839, 1840*; clime *HM 329*.
418. *wears,*] *1822, 1829*; wears *HM 329*; wears; *1839, 1840*.
419–20. 'The fame of which clime [l. 417], though earth expose to view the mortal remains which it (earth) clasped, lies sepulchred, etc.' (*Locock 1911* ii 469).
419. *fame,*] *1822, 1829, 1839, 1840*; fame *HM 329*. *clasped,*] *1822, 1829, 1839, 1840*; clasped *HM 329* (inserted in S.'s hand above an illegible cancelled word).
420. *thought, —*] thought;— *1822, 1839, 1840*; thought! *1829*.
421. Progenitors] Literally, 'ancestors' but figuratively, 'spiritual, political, or intellectual predecessors; persons who are taken as a model or inspiration by another' (*OED* 2a). *great,*] *1822, 1829, 1839, 1840*; great *HM 329*.
422. Ascribe to] Enroll among (see *OED* 3). *your bright senate*] Cp. *Lines connected with Hellas* A ll. 1–2.
423. ministrations] 'renderings of service' (see *OED* 1a). *Sons —*] *1822*; Sons. *HM 329*; sons— *1829, 1839, 1840*.
425. ye, weak] ye weak *1840*.
426. *the crushed worm ... your tread*] Cp. Goethe, *Faust* 653–5:

> Dem Wurme gleich' ich, der den Staub durchwühlt;
> Den, wie er sich im Staube nährend lebt,
> Des Wandrers Tritt vernichtet und begräbt.

('I am like the worm, which drags itself painfully through the dust,— which, as it seeks its living in the dust, is crushed and buried by the step of the passenger.'; trans. *Hayward* 17)

Cp. also *3 Henry VI* II ii 17: 'The smallest worm will turn, being trodden on'. The image recurs in S.'s verse. See, e.g.: *J&M* 412–3 ('Even the instinctive worm on which we tread / Turns, though it wound not —') and *Lines to —* (no. 429) ll. 13–14 and notes. *tread,*] *1822*; tread *HM 329*; tread— *1829, 1839, 1840*.

The vultures and the dogs, your pensioners tame,
Are overgorged, but like oppressors still
They crave the relics of destruction's feast;
430 The exhalations and the thirsty winds
Are sick with blood; the dew is foul with death;
Heaven's light is quenched in slaughter: thus, where'er
Upon your camps, cities, or towers, or fleets,
The obscene birds the reeking remnants cast
435 Of these dead limbs, — upon your streams and mountains,

427. The vultures and the dogs] Perhaps a recollection of the birds and dogs feasting on carrion in Sophocles, *Antigone* 1016–17: βωμοὶ γὰρ ἡμῖν ἐσχάραι τε παντελεῖς/ πλήρεις ὑπ᾽ οἰωνῶν τε καὶ κυνῶν βορᾶς ('for our altars and our braziers, one and all, are filled with carrion brought by birds and dogs'). In this context, *Are sick with blood* (l. 431) might recall the statement in *Antigone* 1015 that the city of Thebes νοσεῖ ('is sick'). Erkelenz cps ll. 432–42 with *Antigone* 1015–20 in 'Inspecting the Tragedy of Empire' 315 and 333 n. 7. *vultures*] vultures, *1829, 1839, 1840. dogs,*] *1822, 1829, 1839, 1840*; dogs *HM 329. pensioners*] 'mercenaries' (*Donovan*); see *OED* 'pensioner' 2a: 'a dependent; a person in the pay of another, a hireling'. *tame,*] *1822, 1829, 1839, 1840*; tame *HM 329.*
428. overgorged,] overgorged; *1822, 1829, 1839, 1840. but ... oppressors*] but, ... oppressors, *1822, 1829, 1839, 1840.*
429. relics] relic *1822, 1829, 1839.* Whether the final letter of *relic* was added in *HM 329* in S.'s hand or Williams's is uncertain. The reading in *Nbk 21* p. 71 is relicks (see *BSM* xvi 76–7). *destruction's*] Destruction's *1822, 1839, 1840. feast;*] feast. *1822, 1829, 1839, 1840.*
430–9. The exhalations ... light] The contamination of 'winds' (l. 430) 'dew' (l. 431) and 'light' (l. 432) by the slaughter brings the dying Greek to his last action, a curse beginning 'thus' (l. 432). In ll. 437–9, the 'winds', 'dews', and 'light' re-appear, only to bring ruin to the world of the 'conquerers' (l. 425).
431. death;] death— *1829, 1839, 1840.*
432. thus,] Thus *1829, 1839, 1840.*
433. fleets,] *1822, 1829, 1839, 1840*; fleets *HM 329.*
434. obscene] 'loathsome' (*OED* 2) and 'inauspicious' (*OED* 3). The latter sense of this word might constitute a further echo of the scene of dogs and birds in *Antigone* (see above, note on l. 427), where their feasting on flesh is said to compromise the birds' use as givers of omens: κότ᾽ οὐ δέχονται θυστάδας λιτὰς ἔτι/ θεοὶ παρ᾽ ἡμῶν οὐδὲ μηρίων φλόγα,/ οὐδ᾽ ὄρνις εὐσήμους ἀπορροιβδεῖ βοάς,/ ἀνδροφθόρου βεβρῶτες αἵματος λίπος (1019–22; 'And the gods are no longer accepting the prayers that accompany sacrifice or the flame that consumes the thigh bones, and the cries screamed out by the birds no longer give me signs for they have eaten fat compounded with a dead man's blood').
435. limbs, —] limbs *1829*; limbs, *1839, 1840. mountains,*] *1822, 1829, 1839, 1840*; mountains *HM 329.*

Upon your fields, your gardens, and your house tops,
Where'er the winds shall creep or the clouds fly
Or the dews fall or the angry sun look down
With poisoned light — Famine and Pestilence
440 And Panic shall wage war upon our side;

436. *house tops,*] house tops *HM 329*; house-tops, *1822, 1829, 1839, 1840.*
437–42. *Where'er ... Against ye*] *Chernaik* 120 n. 19 sees '[t]he idea of Nature defending her own against the enemy' as part of 'the standard political rhetoric of the time' and cps these lines with Coleridge, *Ode on the Departing Year* (1796) ll. 93, 97–9:

> Avenger, rise! [...]
> And on the darkling foe
> Open thine eye of fire from some uncertain cloud!
> O dart the flash! O rise and deal the blow! (1834 text)

and Byron, *The Prophecy of Dante* (1821) ii 101–7:

> Oh! when the strangers pass the Alps and Po,
> Crush them, ye rocks! floods, whelm them, and forever!
> Why sleep the idle avalanches so,
>   To topple on the lonely pilgrim's head?
> Why doth Eridanus but overflow
> The peasant's harvest from his turbid bed?
>   Were not each barbarous horde a nobler prey?

437. *creep*] creep, *1822, 1829, 1839, 1840. fly*] fly, *1822, 1829, 1839, 1840.*
438. *fall*] fall, *1822, 1829, 1839, 1840.*
439–43. *Famine ... rebels*] The dying Greek names new and greater adversaries 'upon our side' (l. 440) who are assembling to destroy the enemy. Cp. the prophetic voice of Christ foretelling the destruction of the temple and Jerusalem in *Luke* xxi 11: 'And great earthquakes shall be in divers places, and famines, and pestilences; and fearful sights and great signs shall there be from heaven.'
439. *Famine*] Famine, *1829, 1839, 1840. Pestilence*] Pestilence, *1822, 1829, 1839, 1840.*
440–2. *side; ... ye; — ... foam;*] The punctuation, in dark ink in *HM 329*, appears to be in S.'s hand.
440. *Panic*] Panic, *1822, 1829, 1839, 1840. side;*] side! *1822, 1829, 1839, 1840.*

Nature from all her boundaries is moved
Against ye; — Time has found ye light as foam;
The Earth rebels; and Good and Evil stake
Their empire o'er the unborn world of men
445 On this one cast; — but ere the die be thrown,
The renovated Genius of our race,
Proud umpire of the impious game, descends,

442. *Against ye; —*] Against ye: *1822, 1829, 1839, 1840. foam;*] foam. *1822, 1829, 1839, 1840.*
443-7. *and Good ... game*] An extended gaming metaphor ('stake', 'this one cast', 'the die be thrown', 'umpire', and 'impious game') where 'Good and Evil' are the players. It is, however, a game played for naught with 'The renovated Genius of our race' being the ultimate judge or 'umpire'. Cp. *Lines connected with Hellas* A ll. 32-3.
443-5. *stake / ... On this one cast*] 'chance ... on this one throw of dice'.
443. *Earth*] earth *1840. stake*] Inserted in S.'s hand above *set* canc. in *HM 329*.
445. *cast; —*] cast *1829, 1839, 1840.* The alteration (in dark ink) in *HM 329* of a comma to a semi colon followed by a dash is probably in S.'s hand. *the die be thrown*] The phrase supposedly spoken by Caesar once he had decided to cross the Rubicon, as recorded in Plutarch, *Life of Pompey* lx 2: 'ἀνερρίφθω κύβος' ('Let the die be cast'); and Suetonius, *Divus Iulius* ([Lives of the Caesars, Book I:] The Deified Julius) 32: 'Iacta alea est' ('The die is cast'). *thrown,*] *1822, 1829, 1839;* thrown *HM 329.*
446. *Genius*] genius *1822, 1829, 1839, 1840.* Whether the alteration of the small *g* to a capital in *HM 329* is in S.'s hand or Williams's is uncertain. 'Guardian spirit' (Donovan); a reference to 'Victory' (l. 448; see note). *race,*] *1822, 1829, 1839, 1840;* race *HM 329.*
447-50. *descends ... all things*] Cp. *Lines connected with Hellas* A ll. 115-18.
447. *descends,*] descends *1822, 1829, 1839, 1840.*

         A seraph-winged Victory, bestriding
         The tempest of the Omnipotence of God,
450   Which sweeps all things to their appointed doom,
         And you to oblivion' — more he would have said
         But —

Mahmud
                  Died — as thou should'st ere thy lips had painted
         Their ruin in the hues of our success —
         A rebel's crime gilt with a rebel's tongue!
455   Your heart is Greek, Hassan.

448–9. The (female) personification of Victory was often represented as winged. See S.'s description of the relief on the Arch of Titus in the Forum in his letter to Peacock of 23 March 1819 from Rome:

> The keystone of these arches is supported each by two winged figures of Victory, whose hair floats on the wind of their own speed, & whose arms are outstretched bearing trophies, as if impatient to meet. They look as it were borne from the subject extremities of the earth on the breath which is the exhalation of that battle & desolation which it is their mission to commemorate. (*L* ii 86)

See also *The Arch of Titus*, probably contemporaneous with the above letter: 'Behind [Titus] stands a Victory, eagle-winged' (Nora Crook, 'Shelley's Jewish "Orations"', *K-SJ* lix (2010) 43–64 (59)). An oracle credits Nike, the Greek goddess of Victory, with defeat of the Persians at Salamis in Herodotus, *Histories* viii 77: '"But Zeus far-seeing, and hallowed Victory then shall grant that Freedom dawn upon Hellas".' Cp. *Charles the First* I i 166: 'Canopied by Victory's eagle-wings outspread' and note to ll. 165–7.
449. God,] *1822, 1829, 1839, 1840*; God *HM 329*.
450. doom,] *1822, 1829, 1839, 1840*; doom *HM 329*.
451. oblivion' — more] oblivion!'—More *1822, 1839, 1840*; Oblivion!'—More *1829*. said] said, *1822, 1829, 1839, 1840*.
453. success —] success. *1822, 1829, 1839, 1840*.
454. crime] crime, *1829, 1839, 1840*.
455. *Your heart is Greek, Hassan*] Cp. Mahmud's anger, provoked by Hassan's moving account of the 'triumphant death' (l. 401) of the Greeks, with that of the King in Calderón, *El príncipe constante* Act I 381–4 after Muley recounts the impressive sight of the Portuguese armada:

Hassan
                    It may be so.
A spirit not my own wrenched me within
And I have spoken words I fear and hate;
Yet would I die for —

Mahmud
            Live! O live! outlive

Calla, no me digas más,
que, de mortal furia lleno,
cada voz es un veneno
con que la muerte me das. (Text from *El príncipe constante*,
ed. Isabel Hernando Morata (2015) 154)

('Silence! do not speak the rest, / For my heart such wrath is feeling, / That each word is like the stealing / Of strong poison through my breast'; trans. *Mac-Carthy (1853)* i 16)

Your] Thy *Rossetti 1870, Rossetti 1878.* Rossetti justifies his emendation thus: 'The drama of *Hellas* is, for all practical purposes, consistent in using the pronoun "thou" and its congeners throughout, instead of "you;" save in this instance' (*Rossetti 1870* ii 555–6). *so.*] so: *1822, 1829, 1839, 1840.*
456. Cp. *PU* I 254: 'A spirit seizes me and speaks within'; Coleridge, 'The Rime of the Ancyent Marinere' (1798) l. 578: 'Forthwith this frame of mine was wrench'd'; and Wordsworth, *The Excursion* (1814) vii 872: 'Of twelve ensuing days his frame was wrenched'. *within*] within, *1822, 1829, 1839, 1840.*
457. *words I fear and hate;*] *1822, 1829, 1839, 1840*; words, I fear, and hate, *HM 329.*

Me and this sinking empire. — But the fleet? —

Hassan
460 Alas! —

459-76. But ... their voice!] With reference to Rossetti's punctuation of the end of l. 461 (see note below), Forman comments: 'Although the opening of this speech of Mahmud [ll. 460-1], which is here pointed according to the first edition, might seem at first sight to be an accidentally unfinished sentence, I do not think there is really any imperfection; nor should I take it to be what Mr. Rossetti makes it (the first of the series of exclamatory sentences), by subsituting a note of admiration for a full-stop after *banner*. It seems to me that Mahmud begins to draw Hassan to speak of the fleet,—that when he says "But the fleet" he means "But what do you say about the fleet?"—and, that, on Hassan's exclaiming "Alas!"—he finishes his own question with an amplifying affirmation in lines 460 and 461, and then, knowing something about the matter, bursts out in angry exclamations, to come back at last in line 476 to his demand on Hassan as narrator' (*Forman 1876-7* iii 66 n. 1).
459. empire. — But] empire. But *1822*; empire:—but *1829, 1839, 1840. But the fleet?*] Cp. Atossa's impatient questioning of the messenger about the fate of the Persian fleet in *Persae* 350-1:

> ἀρχὴ δὲ ναυσὶ συμβολῆς τίς ἦν, φράσον·
> τίνες κατῆρξαν, πότερον Ἕλληνες, μάχης [...];

('But tell me how the naval battle began. Who started the fight? Was it the Greeks [...]?')

fleet? —] fleet— *1822, 1829, 1839, 1840*.
460-5. The fleet ... servile fear!] Cp. Mahmud's bitter irony with the Messenger in *Persae* 338-43 who implies that Xerxes should have defeated the Greeks given the superior size of the Persian navy:

> πλήθους μὲν ἂν σάφ' ἴσθ' ἕκατι βάρβαρον
> ναῦς ἂν κρατῆσαι. καὶ γὰρ Ἕλλησιν μὲν ἦν
> ὁ πᾶς ἀριθμὸς εἰς τριακάδας δέκα
> ναῶν, δεκὰς δ' ἦν τῶνδε χωρὶς ἔκκριτος·
> Ξέρξῃ δέ, καὶ γὰρ οἶδα, χιλιὰς μὲν ἦν
> ὧν ἦγε πλῆθος, αἱ δ' ὑπέρκοποι τάχει
> ἑκατὸν δὶς ἦσαν ἑπτά θ'· ὧδ' ἔχει λόγος.

('I assure you that, so far as numbers are concerned, the fleet of the Easterners would have prevailed. The Greeks had a grand total of about three hundred ships, and ten of these formed a special select squadron; whereas Xerxes—I know this for sure—had a thousand under his command, and those of outstanding speed numbered two hundred and seven. Such is the reckoning')

Mahmud
> The fleet which like a flock of clouds
> Chased by the wind flies the insurgent banner.
> Our winged castles from their merchant ships!
> Our myriads before their weak pirate bands!
> Our arms before their chains! our years of Empire
> 465 Before their centuries of servile fear!
> Death is awake, Repulse is on the waters;

While the size of the Greek fleet was modest in summer 1821, it was well organised, as noted in the *Examiner* 717 (30 September 1821) 614:

> The Greek fleet is said in a continental paper to consist of 150 vessels, carrying each from 15 to 40 guns; of a great number having fewer than 15; and of 500 which are armed with from 2 to 5 guns. The larger class of vessels is divided into four squadrons. The first cruises at the mouth of the Dardanelles; the second is stationed near the Cyclades; the third protects the isles of Hydra, Spezza, and Psara; and the fourth is in the Ionian Sea.

460. *Alas!* —] Alas! *1829, 1839, 1840*. *The fleet ... clouds*] Cp. *Charles the First* I iii 18: 'Mark too that fleet of fleecy winged cloud'. *which*] which, *1822, 1829, 1839, 1840*.
461. *Chased*] Alt. in S.'s hand from ?*Charged* to *Chaced* in *HM 329*; the reading in *Nbk 21* p. 74 is *Chased* (in pencil). *by*] The second letter may be overwritten by S. in *HM 329*. *wind*] wind, *1822, 1829, 1839, 1840*. *flies*] Locock's gloss — 'flies from' — is convincing but he acknowledges the ambiguity of this word, suggesting that Forman in his interpretation of ll. 459–76 (see note to those lines above) 'would seem to take "flies" in its other sense' (*Locock 1911* ii 469). *banner.*] banner; *1829*; banner! *Rossetti 1870*; banner— *Locock 1911*.
462. *winged castles*] winged-castles *1822*. 'large war ships' (*Concordance*). *merchant ships*] The highly effective mercantile fleet was crucial to the Greek cause, as noted by Katerina Galani and Gelina Harlaftis: 'It was privately owned ships from the Aegean islands, designated for grain trade and armed with several canons, that acted as warships in the uprising' ('Aegean Islands and the Revolution at Sea', *The Greek Revolution: A Critical Dictionary* 148).
463. *myriads*] See note to l. 374.
464. *our*] Our *1829, 1839, 1840*. *Empire*] empire *1822, 1829, 1839, 1840*.
466. *awake,*] awake! *1822, 1829, 1839*. *Repulse is on*] Repulsed on *1822, 1829, 1839, 1840*. In *Errata* S. told Ollier: 'this error is of so much consequence that it would be worth while to cancel the leaf' (*L* ii 411). Rossetti gave the correct reading in *Rossetti 1878* ii 398 noting 'a correction of special moment' in *Errata* (see *Rossetti 1878* ii 455). *Repulse* = 'the act of repelling a hostile force' (*OED* 'repulse' *n*. 2a). *waters;*] waters *HM 329*; waters, *1822, 1829, 1839, 1840*.

> They own no more the thunder-bearing banner
> Of Mahmud, but like hounds of a base breed
> Gorge from a stranger's hand and rend their master.
>
> *Hassan*
> 470   Latmos, and Ampelos and Phanae saw
> The wreck —
>
> *Mahmud*
>   The caves of the Icarian isles
> Told each to the other in loud mockery,
> And with the tongue as of a thousand echoes,
> First of the sea-convulsing fight — and, then, —

467–9. 'Many Greek crews of Turkish warships refused to fight against their compatriots' (*Raizis* 186).
467. *thunder-bearing banner*] The insertion of the hyphen and the overwriting of the first letter of *banner* in *HM 329* are probably in S.'s hand.
468. *Mahmud,*] Mahmud; *1822, 1829, 1839, 1840*. *but*] but, *1822*. *breed*] breed, *1822, 1829, 1839, 1840*.
469. *hand*] hand, *1822, 1829, 1839, 1840*. *rend*] 'tear to pieces' (see *OED* 5c); cp. *J&M* 357. *master.*] *1822, 1829, 1839, 1840*; master *HM 329*.
470. *Latmos … Ampelos … Phanae*] Elevated locations that overlook the Aegean Sea from the east. *Latmos*] A mountain in Caria (mod. south-eastern Turkey) where Endymion was seduced by the goddess Selene; mentioned in Keats, *Endymion: A Poetic Romance* (1818) i 63. *Ampelos*] Ampelos, *1822, 1829, 1839, 1840*. A mountain range on Samos. *Phanae*] Phanae, *1822, 1829, 1839, 1840*. The high southern tip of Chios.
471. *wreck*] 'The vaguely reported "wreck" must be the blowing up of a Turkish two-decker off Eressos [on the island of Lesbos] by Demetrios Papanikolis' (*Raizis* 186) which took place on 24 May 1821 (Nikolas Pissis, '"Little Malta": Psara and the Peculiarities of naval warfare in the Greek Revolution', *Open Military Studies* ii (2022) 186). *Icarian isles*] The island of Icaria is to the west of Samos. The other 'isles' referred to are presumably those which lie in the Icarian Sea: the closest to Icaria are Thymaina and Phournoi.
472. *Told*] Hold *1822, 1829, 1839, 1840*. S. noted the misprint in *Errata*. Rossetti guessed the correct reading in *Rossetti 1870* ii 122 (see *Rossetti 1870* ii 556) then gave it in *Rossetti 1878* ii 398 having consulted *HM 329* and *Errata* (see *Rossetti 1878* ii 455). *loud*] Written over *wild* in *HM 329* in S.'s hand.
473. *echoes,*] *1822*; echoes *HM 329, 1829, 1839, 1840*.
474. *sea-convulsing*] *1822, 1829, 1839, 1840*; sea convulsing *HM 329*. *and, then, —*] and then *1829, 1839, 1840*.

475   Thou darest to speak — senseless are the mountains;
      Interpret thou their voice!

Hassan   My presence bore
      A part in that day's shame. The Grecian fleet

475-6. *senseless ... their voice*] Cp. *Mont Blanc* Text B ll. 80-4:

> Thou has a voice, great Mountain, to repeal
> Large codes of fraud and woe; not understood
> By all, but which the wise, and great, and good
> Interpret, or make felt, or deeply feel.

475. *mountains;*] *1822, 1829, 1839*; mountains *HM 329*; mountains, *1840*.
477-88. *The Grecian fleet ... victory*] Echoing in some respects *Persae* 353-442 in which a messenger recounts details of the Battle of Salamis to the Persian queen Atossa. Lines 408-23 seem to have been an especially rich source of inspiration for S. (in particular, see note on l. 486):

> εὐθὺς δὲ ναῦς ἐν νηὶ χαλκήρη στόλον
> ἔπαισεν· ἦρξε δ' ἐμβολῆς Ἑλληνικὴ
> ναῦς, κἀποθραύει πάντα Φοινίσσης νεὼς
> κόρυμβ', ἐπ' ἄλλην δ' ἄλλος ηὔθυνεν δόρυ.
> τὰ πρῶτα μέν νυν ῥεῦμα Περσικοῦ στρατοῦ
> ἀντεῖχεν· ὡς δὲ πλῆθος ἐν στενῷ νεῶν
> ἤθροιστ' ἀρωγὴ δ' οὔτις ἀλλήλοις παρῆν,
> αὐτοὶ δ' ὑπ' αὐτῶν ἐμβολαῖς χαλκοστόμοις
> παίοντ', ἔθραυον πάντα κωπήρη στόλον,
> Ἑλληνικαί τε νῆες οὐκ ἀφρασμόνως
> κύκλῳ πέριξ ἔθεινον· ὑπτιοῦτο δὲ,
> σκάφη νεῶν, θάλασσα δ' οὐκέτ' ἦν ἰδεῖν,
> ναυαγίων πλήθουσα καὶ φόνῳ βροτῶν·
> ἀκταὶ δὲ νεκρῶν χοιράδες τ' ἐπλήθυον,
> φυγῇ δ' ἀκόσμῳ πᾶσα ναῦς ἠρέσσετο,
> ὅσαιπερ ἦσαν βαρβάρου στρατεύματος.

('At once one ship began to strike another with its projecting bronze beak; the first to ram was a Greek ship, which sheared off the whole stern of a Phoenician vessel, and then each captain chose a different enemy ship at which to run his own. At first the streaming Persian force resisted firmly; but when our masses of ships were crowded into a narrow space, they had no way to come to each other's help, they got struck by their own side's bronze-pointed rams, they had the whole of their oarage smashed, and the Greek ships with careful coordination, surrounded them completely and went on striking them. The hulls of our ships

Bore down at day-break from the North, and hung
As multitudinous on the ocean line
480 As cranes upon the cloudless Thracian wind.
Our squadron convoying ten thousand men
Was stretching towards Nauplia when the battle

> turned keel-up, and the sea surface was no longer visible, filled as it was with the wreckage of ships and the slaughter of men; the shores and reefs were also full of corpses. Every remaining ship of the Eastern armada was being rowed away in disorderly flight.')

478–9. hung ... on the ocean line] Cp. L&C 4805 and note.
479–80. Assembled Greek forces are also compared to cranes at the start of Homer's 'Catalogue of Ships' (*Iliad* ii 459–66).
479. the ocean line] the ocean line, *1822*.
480. Thracian] Thrace is the region encompassing the northern coast of the Aegean Sea and the western coast of the Black Sea. This is the part of Europe closest to Anatolia.
481. squadron] squadron, *1822, 1829, 1839, 1840. men*] men, *1822, 1829, 1839, 1840*.
482–6. Was stretching ... Dashed] The references to 'Nauplia' (l. 482) and 'Hydriote barks' (l. 485) recall Alexandros Mavrokordatos's report of Greek naval success against the Turks in his letter to Mary of 14 May 1821:

> On dit aussi que la flotille des Hydriotes s'est emparée d'une corvette et d'un bric Turc dans la mer Ægée. C'est une nouvelle encore que je ne vous donne pas pour sûre. ... Une dame de l'Ile de Spécia, situé vis-à-vis la côte orientale du Péleponèse, devant la Golfe de Nauplion, veuve d'un très riche négociant, a équipée en guerre 5 batimens appartenant jadis à son mari. Elle a déclaré le port de Nauplion en état de blocus, et c'est déjà emparée de quelques batimens Turcs. (Bodleian MS. Abinger c. 45 ff. 83ᵛ-84ʳ; *Shelley and Mary* iii [Bodleian [pr.] Shelley adds. d. 4] 623).

> (It is reported as well that the Hydriote fleet has seized a fleet escort and a Turkish brig in the Aegean sea. This is news of which I am not yet certain. ... A woman from the island of Spetses opposite the eastern coast of the Peloponnese before the bay of Nafplion, the widow of a very wealthy merchant, has equipped for war 5 ships once owned by her husband. She has declared the port of Nafplion in a state of blockade, and has already seized several Turkish ships.)

Although Raizis does not refer to the above letter, he implies that S. was aware of 'the naval activities of Lascarina Bouboulina' (*Raizis* 188), the 'widow' who 'equipped' ships 'for war'. Eleni Angelomatis-Tsougarakis notes that Bouboulina (1781–1825) 'took part in the blockade of Nafplio onboard *Agamemnon*, her newly built eighteen-cannon ship, and three smaller ships of her own' ('Women', *The*

Was kindled. —
   First through the hail of our artillery
485 The agile Hydriote barks with press of sail
   Dashed — ship to ship, cannon to cannon, man

Greek Revolution: A Critical Dictionary 426). Mavrokordatos confirmed the above events as well as further attacks on Turkish ships in a letter to Mary of 27 May 1821:

> Les batimens Hydriotes, Spéziotes et Psariotes, au nombre de 120 voiles équipées en guerre, furent divisés en quatre escadres séparées, dont l'une se porte contre la flotille Turcque stationée dans la mer Ionienne, qui est déjà dégarnie de matelots à cause de la désertion; l'autre partit pour croiser à la hauteur de l'Ile de Ténédos, à l'embouchure des Dardanelles. La troisième est destinée à protéger et à sécourir le mouvement insurrectionnel manifeste dans l'Ile de Candie, et elle parvint déjà à s'emparer d'une frégate et des deux bricks, et à bruler un [?] Turcs, qui portaient des secours aux Musulmans de cette île. (Bodleian MS. Abinger c. 45 ff. 90^v-91^r; *Shelley and Mary* iii [Bodleian [pr.] Shelley adds. d. 4] 629-30).

(The Hydriote, Speziote and Psariote ships, numbering 120 war ships, were divided into four separate squadrons, of which one confronted the Turkish flotilla stationed in the Ionian sea, which has already lost sailors through desertion; the second squadron left to make its crossing alongside the isle of Tenedos at the mouth of the Dardanelles. The third is destined to protect and assist the insurrection movement on the isle of Candia, and it has already succeeded in seizing a frigate and two brigs, and a [?] of the Turks, who were bringing aid to the Musulmen of this island.)

482. *Nauplia*] mod. Nafplion, a strategically significant fortessed port in the Gulf of Argolis in the Peloponnese.
485. *Hydriote barks*] Ships from the island of Hydra off the eastern coast of the Peloponnese, and just to the South of the Saronic Gulf (in which the Battle of Salamis took place). The *Examiner* 718 (7 October 1821) 629 noted:

> Hydra, with only 20,000 inhabitants, has fitted out several formidable squadrons, since the commencement of hostilities, and is celebrated throughout the Mediterranean for the excellence as well as bravery of its seamen, whose intrepidity could not have been exceeded by the heroes of Salamin and Mycale.

press of sail] 'as many sails as possible hoisted, to increase speed' (*OED* 'press' *n.^{1}* 11b).
486. *Dashed* —] Dashed:— *1822, 1829, 1839, 1840*. Cp. *Persae* 408-9: 'At once one ship began to strike another with its projecting bronze beak' (the original of this translation and the one in the next note are given in the note to ll. 477-88 above). *ship to ship*] Cp. *Persae* 410: 'each captain chose a different enemy ship at which to run his own'.

To man were grappled in the embrace of war,
Inextricable but by death or victory; —
The tempest of the raging fight convulsed
490 To its crystalline depths that stainless sea
And shook Heaven's roof of golden morning clouds
Poised on a hundred azure mountain-isles.
In the brief trances of the artillery
One cry from the destroyed and the destroyer
495 Rose, and a cloud of desolation wrapt
The unforeseen event, till the north wind
Sprung from the sea, lifting the heavy veil

487. *man*] man, *1840. war,*] *1822, 1829, 1839, 1840*; war *HM 329*.
488. *Inextricable*] *1822*. This word is cancelled in *HM 329* p. 23 but no replacement is inserted above. Since the alteration on p. 23 recorded in the note to l. 472 is in ink and a penstroke similar to this one, it seems likely that the cancellation was S.'s and that he overlooked supplying an alternative in error. *victory; —*] victory *HM 329*; victory. *1822, 1829, 1839, 1840*.
490. *sea*] sea, *1822, 1829, 1839, 1840*.
491. *Heaven's*] heaven's *1829, 1839, 1840. clouds*] clouds, *1822*.
492. *a*] an *1822, 1829, 1839, 1840. mountain-isles.*] *1822, 1829, 1839, 1840*; mountain-isles *HM 329*.
493. *trances*] The final letter of this word in *HM 329* appears to have been added in S.'s hand. 'intervals, pauses' (*Concordance*). *artillery*] artillery, *1829, 1839, 1840*.
494. The joint cry of the two sides echoes that of *Persae* 400–7, where the Persian cry answers its Greek counterpart:

>   δεύτερον δ' ὁ πᾶς στόλος
> ἐπεξεχώρει, καὶ παρῆν ὁμοῦ κλύειν
> πολλὴν βοήν, 'ὦ παῖδες Ἑλλήνων ἴτε,
> ἐλευθεροῦτε πατρίδ', ἐλευθεροῦτε δὲ
> παῖδας, γυναῖκας, θεῶν τέ πατρῴων ἕδη,
> θήκας τε προγόνων· νῦν ὑπὲρ πάντων ἀγών.'
> καὶ μὴν παρ' ἡμῶν Περσίδος γλώσσης ῥόθος
> ὑπηντίαζε.

('Next their whole army pressed on against us, and at the same time a loud shout met our ears: "On, you men of Hellas! Free your native land. Free your children, your wives, the temples of your fathers' gods, and the tombs of your ancestors. Now you are fighting for all you have." Then from our side arose in response the mingled clamor of Persian speech.')

496. *event,*] *1822, 1829, 1839, 1840*; event *HM 329*; 'outcome' (*OED* 1).
497. *sea,*] *1822, 1829, 1839, 1840*; sea *HM 329*.

Of battle-smoke — then Victory — Victory!
  For, as we thought, three frigates from Algiers
500 Bore down from Naxos to our aid, but soon
  The abhorred cross glimmered behind, before,
  Among, around us; and that fatal sign
  Dried with its beams the strength in Moslem hearts,
  As the sun drinks the dew — What more? We fled! —
505 Our noonday path over the sanguine foam
  Was beaconed, — and the glare struck the sun pale —
  By our consuming transports; the fierce light
  Made all the shadows of our sails blood red
  And every countenance blank. Some ships lay feeding
510 The ravening fire even to the water's level;

498. *Victory — Victory!*] victory—victory! *1822, 1829, 1839, 1840*.
499–500. *three frigates ... aid*] Cp. the report in *Galignani's Messenger* 2073 (18 October 1821) p. 4: 'the Turkish fleet, united to those of Egypt and Algiers, had arrived at Calamata in the Morea, with provisions and ammunition for the Ottoman garrisons'.
499. *For,*] *1822, 1829, 1839, 1840*; For *HM 329. thought,*] *1822, 1829, 1839, 1840*; thought *HM 329. Algiers*] The North African port was part of the Ottoman Empire at this time.
500. *Naxos*] Largest island of the Cyclades.
503. Cp. *Persae* 391–2: φόβος δὲ πᾶσι βαρβάροις παρῆν/ γνώμης ἀποσφαλεῖσιν: ('All we Easterners were terrified because we had been deceived in our expectation'). *in*] of *1829, 1834, 1839, 1840*.
504. *dew —*] dew. — *1822, 1829, 1839, 1840. What more?*] In *HM 329 what more?* is inserted in S.'s hand. *What*] *1822, 1829, 1839, 1840*; what *HM 329. fled! —*] fled! *1829, 1839, 1840*.
505–14. Cp. the scene of broken and capsized ships at *Persae* 418–21: 'The hulls of our ships turned keel-up, and the sea surface was no longer visible, filled as it was with the wreckage of ships and the slaughter of men; the shores and reefs were also full of corpses' (the original of this translation is given in the note to ll. 477–88 above).
506. *beaconed, —*] beacon'd, *1829*; beaconed, *1839, 1840. pale —*] pale *1822, 1829, 1839*; pale, *1840*.
507. *transports;*] transports: *1822, 1829, 1839, 1840*. 'excitement' (*Concordance*); see *OED* 'transport' *n*. 3.
508. *blood red*] blood-red, *1822, 1829, 1839, 1840*.
510. *ravening*] voracious (*OED* 1). *fire*] fire, *1822. even to the water's level*] 'until they sank' (*Locock 1911*). *water's*] *1822, 1829, 1839, 1840*; waters *HM 329. level;*] level: *1829, 1839, 1840*.

Some were blown up — some settling heavily
Sunk; and the shrieks of our companions died
Upon the wind that bore us fast and far,
Even after they were dead — nine thousand perished.
515 We met the vultures legioned in the air
Stemming the torrent of the tainted wind;
They, screaming from their cloudy mountain peaks,

511. *up* —] up; *1822, 1839, 1840*; up: *1829. some*] some, *1822, 1829, 1839, 1840. heavily*] heavily, *1822, 1829, 1839, 1840.*
512–14. *and the shrieks ... perished*] Cp. the account the Messenger gives to Atossa in *Persae* 426–32:

οἰμωγὴ δ' ὁμοῦ
κωκύμασιν κατεῖχε πελαγίαν ἅλα,
ἕως κελαινὸν νυκτὸς ὄμμ' ἀφείλετο.
κακῶν δὲ πλῆθος, οὐδ' ἂν εἰ δέκ' ἤματα
στοιχηγοροίην, οὐκ ἂν ἐκπλήσαιμί σοι.
εὖ γὰρ τόδ' ἴσθι, μηδάμ' ἡμέρᾳ μιᾷ
πλῆθος τοσουτάριθμον ἀνθρώπων θανεῖν.

('And a mixture of shrieking and wailing filled the expanse of the sea, until the dark face of night blotted it out. Our sufferings were so multitudinous that I could not describe them fully to you if I were to talk for ten days on end: you can be certain that never have so vast a number of human beings perished in a single day.')

In the copy of S.'s Aeschylus in the Bodleian ([pr.] Shelley adds. g. 1) the first three lines of the above passage are marked in the margin with a vertical pencil stroke.
512. *died*] became fainter and fainter (see *OED* 'die' $v.^1$ 11).
513. *wind*] wind, *1822, 1829, 1839, 1840. far,*] *1822, 1829, 1839, 1840*; far *HM 329*.
514. *dead — nine*] dead. Nine *1822, 1829, 1839, 1840. nine thousand perished*] Possibly referring to a report in *Galignani's Messenger* 2044 (14 September 1821) [p. 4] which included the following information:

> The news from sea is not less favourable to the cause of the Greeks, for out of 9000 men that the Ottoman fleet was carrying out to make a descent upon the Morea, more than two thirds have been taken and drowned by the Greeks, who made themselves masters of the transport vessels.

perished.] perished! *1822, 1829, 1839, 1840.*
515. *legioned*] 'innumerable' (*Concordance*). *air*] air, *1829, 1839, 1840.*
516. *wind;*] wind: *1829, 1839, 1840.*
517. *peaks,*] *1822, 1839, 1840*; peaks *HM 329*; peak *1829, 1834.*

Stooped through the sulphurous battle-smoke and perched
Each on the weltering carcase that we loved,
520 Like its ill angel or its damned soul,
Riding upon the bosom of the sea.
We saw the dog-fish hastening to their feast,
Joy waked the voiceless people of the sea,
And ravening Famine left his ocean cave
525 To dwell with war, with us and with despair.
We met Night three hours to the west of Patmos,
And with night, tempest —

518. *sulphurous*] sulphureous *1829, 1834, 1839, 1840. battle-smoke*] battle-smoke, *1829, 1839, 1840.*
519. *weltering carcase*] Cp. Scott, *The Lady of the Lake* (1810) VI xx 41: 'A weltering corse beside the boats'; 'weltering' = 'tossed or tumbled about' (*OED* 'welter' *v.¹* 3b). *loved,*] *1822, 1829, 1839, 1840;* loved *HM 329.*
520. *ill*] evil. *soul,*] soul. *1829, 1834, 1839, 1840.*
521. *sea.*] sea, *1829, 1834, 1839, 1840.*
522–5. *We saw ... with war*] S.'s vision of the underwater aftermath of the sea battle recalls Endymion's wanderings in the 'deep, deep water-world' (101) in Keats, *Endymion* iii 119–126:

> Far had he roamed,
> With nothing save the hollow vast, that foamed,
> Above, around, and at his feet—save things
> More dead than Morpheus' imaginings:
> Old rusted anchors, helmets, breast-plates large
> Of gone sea-warriors; brazen beaks and targe;
> Rudders that for a hundred years had lost
> The sway of human hand;

522. *dog-fish*] small sharks. Cp. *To S[idmouth] and C[astlereagh]* (no. 252) l. 11 and note and *A Vision of the Sea* l. 56. *feast,*] feast. *1822, 1829, 1834, 1839, 1840.*
523. *the voiceless people of the sea*] ocean life.
524. *ravening*] See l. 510 and note. *Famine*] famine *1829, 1839, 1840. ocean cave*] ocean-cave *1829, 1839, 1840.*
525. *us*] us, *1822, 1829, 1839, 1840.*
526. *Night*] night *1822, 1829, 1839, 1840.* The first letter is altered to a capital and the second overwritten in S.'s hand in *HM 329. Patmos,*] *1822, 1829, 1839, 1840;* Patmos *HM 329.* The northernmost island of the Sporades, to the south west of Samos.
527. *And*] As *1839, 1840. Cease!* —] Cease! *1822, 1829, 1839, 1840. sublime*] Sublime *1822, 1829, 1839, 1840. Highness,*] *1822, 1829, 1839, 1840;* Highness *HM 329.*

Mahmud
                              Cease! —
                                              [*Enter a Messenger.*]
Messenger
                              Your sublime Highness,
That Christian hound, the Muscovite Ambassador,
Has left the city — if the rebel fleet
530   Had anchored in the port, had Victory

528–9. *Muscovite … left the city*] The departure of the Russian Ambassador, Baron de Stroganoff [G. A. Stroganov] (1770–1857) was noticed in the *Examiner* 705 (5 August 1821) 484:

> Accounts just received from Petersburgh state, that the Emperor of Russia had given a categorical answer to the complaints of the Ottoman Porte against the Baron de Strogonoff, and had demanded complete satisfaction for the insults offered to his Ambassador, to be given within eight days, otherwise the Ambassador was to quit Constantinople, and the Russian troops were to enter Moldavia.

A report of his departure was published in *Galignani's Messenger* 2031 (30 August 1821) [p. 4]:

> Yesterday intelligence arrived up to the 30th ult.:—It announces, that on the 28th, two days after the time fixed by the Emperor of Russia, Baron Strogonoff, finding that the Divan gave him no satisfactory answer, declared that his mission was at an end, and demanded of the Reis-Effendi [Minister for Foreign Affairs] the passports necessary for himself and the persons of the Embassy. At first, the Grand Seignior refused to comply with this demand, but, at length, upon the interference of the Foreign Ambassadors, a verbal message was sent to the Commander of the port, to allow the vessel to pass in which the Ambassador would embark at Bujukdere. Contrary winds prevented the departure of the Embassy up to the 30th, but it is supposed that it sailed on the 31st for Odessa.

Strogonoff's removal from Constantinople was also reported in the *Examiner* no. 713 (2 September 1821) 548.
528. *hound,*] *1822, 1829, 1839, 1840*; hound *HM 329*. *Muscovite*] *1822, 1829, 1839*; muscovite *HM 329*. *Ambassador,*] Ambassador *HM 329*; ambassador, *1822, 1829, 1839, 1840*.
529. *city — if*] city.—If *1822*; city. If *1829, 1839, 1840*.
530. *Victory*] victory *1822, 1829, 1839, 1840*.

> Crowned the Greek legions in the hippodrome,
> Panic were tamer. — Obedience and Mutiny,
> Like Giants in contention planet-struck,
> Stand gazing on each other — there is peace
> 535 In Stamboul. —
>
> *Mahmud*
>   Is the grave not calmer still?
> Its ruins shall be mine!

531. *hippodrome,*] *1829*; hippodrome *HM 329*; Hippodrome, *1822, 1839, 1840*. The arena for horse and chariot racing at Constantinople, described in *Anastasius* (1819) Vol. I ch. xii:

> Thus enjoying the command of the fleetest horses and the most active grooms, I took care that neither should want exercise[.] I devoted my whole time to drawing the bow, and slinging the Djereed. In no place was I seen, but at the Oc-meidan and in the Hippodrome […]

In the Notes to Vol. I, Hope states that it is 'still called by the Turks At-Meidan, or the place of horses'. Gibbon refers to the hippodrome in the 'Return and Triumph of Belisarius' in 534 CE in *Decline and Fall* Vol. IV (1788) ch. xli: 'From the palace of Belisarius, the procession was conducted through the principal streets to the hippodrome' (Womersley, ed., ii 640).
532. *Panic were tamer*] 'there would be less panic than there is now' (*Locock 1911* ii 470). *tamer.* —] *1822, 1829, 1839, 1840*; tamer — *HM 329. Mutiny,*] *1822, 1839, 1840*; Mutiny *HM 329*; mutiny, *1829*.
533. *Like … planet-struck*] *Major Works* cps *Coriolanus* II ii 113-4: 'And with a sudden reinforcement struck / Corioles like a planet'. The usual sense of 'planet-struck' is 'Stricken or afflicted, as by paralysis or other sudden physical disorder, as a result of the supposed malign influence of a planet' (*OED*); here the meaning is 'perhaps literally struck by a meteor or thunderbolt' (*Locock 1911*). *Giants*] giants *1822, 1829, 1839, 1840*.
534. *other — there*] other.—There *1822, 1829, 1839, 1840*.
535. *Stamboul.* —] *1822, 1829, 1839, 1840*; Stamboul — *HM 329*. Mod. Istanbul. According to Hope, in a Note to *Anastasius* Vol. I ch. iii, 'the Turkish corruption of the Greek εἰς τὴν πόλιν [to the city], pronounced by them ees teen bolin; and used to denote their going to the City κατ' ἐξοχὴν [*par excellence*]' (i 361).
536. *Its*] Stamboul's. *mine!*] *Nbk 21*; mine *HM 329*; mine. *1822, 1829, 1839, 1840*. *Fear not the Russian*] The *Examiner* 713 (2 September 1821) 545 noted that while 'the Russians profess a religion in common with the Greeks', they had no interest in the Greek cause except in so far as it destabilised the Ottoman

Hassan
                    Fear not the Russian;
    The tiger leagues not with the stag at bay
    Against the hunter — cunning, base, and cruel,
    He crouches, watching till the spoil be won,
540 And must be paid for his reserve in blood.
    After the war is fought, yield the sleek Russian
    That which thou canst not keep, his deserved portion
    Of blood, which shall not flow through streets and fields,
    Rivers and seas, like that which we may win,
545 But stagnate in the veins of Christian slaves!
                                    [*Enter Second Messenger.*
    Second Messenger
    Nauplia, Tripolizza, Mothon, Athens,
    Navarin, Artas, Monembasia,

Empire. Nevertheless Russia 'has long had a hankering after the possession of the neighbouring provinces of Turkey, and more particularly of Constantinople and the Dardanelles', and in the summer of 1821 threatened to invade Moldavia (see note to ll. 528–9). *Russian;*] *1829, 1839, 1840*; Russian *HM 329*; Russian: *1822*.
538. *hunter — cunning*] hunter.—Cunning *1822, 1829, 1839, 1840*. cruel,] *1822, 1829, 1839, 1840*; cruel *HM 329*.
539. *crouches,*] *1822, 1829, 1839, 1840*; crouches *HM 329*. won,] *1822, 1829, 1839, 1840*; won *HM 329*.
540. *reserve*] 'restraint' (see *OED* 6b) or, more precisely, 'non-interference' (*Concordance*). blood.] *1822, 1829, 1839, 1840*; blood *HM 329*.
541. *fought,*] *1822, 1829, 1839, 1840*; fought *HM 329*. *sleek*] 'Oily, fawning, plausible, specious' (*OED* 3a).
543. *fields,*] *1822, 1839, 1840*; fields *HM 329, 1829*.
546–8. *Nauplia ... by assault*] Most, but not all, places in the Morea (Peloponnese) taken by the Greeks between spring and early autumn 1821. Newspapers published reports between June and October that were largely positive about the progress of the Greek cause. The *Examiner* 702 (17 June 1821) stated that 'The Peloponnesus or Morea is almost wholly delivered from the power of the Turks' (372). A report published in *Galignani's Messenger* 1995 (18 July 1821) [p. 4] stated: 'The troops at Livadi, Thebes, Athens, and their dependancies now form the advanced guard. Mezara and the villages of the isthmus of Corinth are organized in the second line, and the Greek Navy having the preponderance at sea, all announce that the Peloponnesus will soon be entirely free.' See also the *Examiner* no. 718 (7 October 1821) 631:

> Accounts of the successes of the Greeks become more abundant and probable every day. There are letters from Leghorn, dated the 18th of September, stating, that a vessel which came from Syria, and others

which had left Constantinople the 16th, 18th, 20th and 22d August, and arrived at different times and at different ports, all agreed in their accounts of a naval victory obtained by the Greeks over the combined Turkish and Egyptian fleets […]

546. *Nauplia*] See note to l. 482. Alexandros Mavrokordatos reported 'la forteresse […] de Nauplium était sur le point de se rendre' (the fortress of Nauplia was on the verge of surrender) in his letter to Mary of 31 May (Bodleian MS. Abinger c. 45 f. 92ᵛ). *Tripolizza*] *1822, 1839*; Tripolizzia *HM 329*; Tripolizzi *1829*. The reading is *Tripolizza* in *Nbk 21* p. 98 (see *BSM* xvi 104–5). The capital of the Morea. The *Examiner* 702 (17 June 1821) published a report from Leipzig dated 24 May stating 'Tripoliza' among other fortresses of the Morea had 'been taken by the Greeks by storm, and with great slaughter' (372). However, S. was almost certainly referring to a later report — noted by Erkelenz ('Inspecting the Tragedy of Empire' 335 n. 28) — in *Galignani's Messenger* 2040 (10 September 1821) [p. 4] which stated that the city 'has just been reduced.' *Mothon*] Modon (Methoni), a port on the western coast of the Peloponnese. *Athens*] A report of 15 May describing the revolt against the Turks at Athens was published in the *Examiner* 707 (22 July 1821) 456:

> The Standard of the Cross floats on the Parthenon. The Turks, who had placed part of their families in Negropont, saw a body of 2,000 Greeks approach from Marathon. On seeing it, they fired an alarm-gun, and placed themselves on the ramparts uttering horrible cries. […] But they were driven from the ramparts by the Greeks the first day, who occupied the town without loosing a man. The next day the citadel began to fire and some houses were damaged; but it was reduced on the 10th, the Greeks having received some artillery from Hydra. The Turks capitulated on condition of being sent to Negropont.

547. All places mentioned in a report published in *Galignani's Messenger* 2078 (24 October 1821) [p. 4]:

> The central government of the Greeks at Modon, have published several bulletins of the advantages gained by their troops. These bulletins announce a decisive victory over the Turks encamped before the fortress of Navarin, and the capture of Artas, *Coron*, Monembasia, Bikajour, and several small fortresses.

Navarin] Navarino, a port on the western coast of the Peloponnese, north of Modon. *Artas*] Arta, a town in Thessaly. *Monembasia*] Mowenbasia *1829, 1834*. A fortress on the south east coast of the Peloponnese. The *Examiner* 718 (7 October 1821) noted 'news of the taking of Malvasia or Monambasia, the strongest port in the Morea, and containing abundance of warlike stores' (631). This followed the publication of a report in *Galignani's Messenger* 2040 (10 September 1821) [p. 4], noting that 'The fortress of Monembaza has recently been reduced'.

Corinth and Thebes are carried by assault
And every Islamite who made his dogs
550   Fat with the flesh of Galilean slaves
Passed at the edge of the sword; the lust of blood
Which made our warriors drunk, is quenched in death,
But like a fiery plague breaks out anew
In deeds which make the Christian cause look pale
555   In its own light. The garrison of Patras
Has store but for ten days, nor is there hope

548. *Corinth*] Corinth, *1839*. A port on the eastern coast of the Morea separated from mainland Greece by a narrow isthmus. As noted by Erkelenz ('Inspecting the Tragedy of Empire' 335 n. 28), *Galignani's Messenger* 2010 (4 August 1821) [p. 1] reported that 'the Greeks are in possession of the whole of the Peloponnesus, and of its key and great fortress, the citadel of Corinth.' *Thebes*] Thebes, *1840*. A town in Rumeli. Though Thebes had surrendered to the Greeks in April 1821 (see Markos Karasarinis, 'Rumeli', *The Greek Revolution: A Critical Dictionary* 302), S. is almost certainly referring — as Erkelenz notes ('Inspecting the Tragedy of Empire' 335 n. 28) — to the report that 'Thebes and the fortress of Livadia have fallen into the hands of the Greeks' in *Galignani's Messenger* 2044 (14 September 1821) [p. 4]. *assault*] assault, *1822*; assault; *1829, 1839, 1840*.
550. *Galilean*] Christian; see *OL* 119 and note. *slaves*] slaves, *1829, 1839, 1840*.
551. *Passed at the edge of the sword*] Cp. *Luke* xxi 24: 'And they shall fall by the edge of the sword'. *Passed*] 'killed, slain' (*Concordance*). *sword;*] sword: *1822, 1829, 1839, 1840*. *blood*] blood, *1840*.
552. *death,*] death. *HM 329*; death; *1822, 1829, 1839, 1840*.
553. *anew*] anew, *1829*.
554. *make*] makes *1829, 1834*.
555. *Patras*] A town on the northern coast of the Peloponnese.
556-7. *nor is ... Briton*] Possibly a reference to an article published in *Galignani's Messenger* 2021 (18 August 1821) [pp. 3-4] in which British assistance for the Turks was roundly criticised:

> The solemn declaration of neutrality made by the English Government to the Greeks, has proved but empty words.—From the beginning, the English Consuls and vessels have afforded considerable succour to the Turks, without which they could not have held out so long in their fortresses in the Morea. On the 4th of April, when the Greeks proclaimed their independence at Patras, the Turks set fire to two quarters of that town, and then retired into the citadel. The next day the Greeks descended in arms from Mount Calvito, and united with the peasants to make an assault. Aided by the English at Patras, and by means of the packet *Sliften*, the Turks

But from the Briton; at once slave and tyrant
His wishes still are weaker than his fears,
Or he would sell what faith may yet remain
560 From the oaths broke in Genoa and in Norway;

> informed the Captain Bey who was cruising near Prevesa, of their situation, and received his answer through the same medium. In the night of the 14th or 15th, 500 Turkish Cavalry disembarked before Patras, and the besieged encouraged by this succour made a sally; a moment after a Turkish brig of war fired upon the town from the road; the English then reported that 8000 Turks had arrived, which so intimidated the Greeks that they retreated to the mountains, the Turks took possession of Patras and put all to the fire and sword. During this period the English Consul General remained totally inactive.

Galignani's Messenger 2040 (10 September 1821) [p. 4], reiterating the above report, stated that a 'circular has just been published in the Peloponnesus, upon the conduct of Mr W. P. Green, the English Consul at Patras. It charges him with having violated the neutrality proclaimed by the Government of the Ionian Islands, by furnishing provisions to the Turkish forces in the Morea.'
557. *Briton;*] Briton: *1822, 1829. slave ... tyrant*] The cancellations of the final letters of *slaves* and *tyrants* in HM 329 are probably in S.'s hand. *tyrant*] tyrant, *1829, 1839, 1840.*
558. *fears,*] *1822;* fears HM 329; fears; *1829, 1839, 1840.*
560. Cp. the attack on the Holy Alliance in the article entitled 'Death of Napoleon Bonaparte' in the *Examiner* 705 (8 July 1821) 419:

> What a spectacle! NAPOLEON—the great-minded, the conqueror, the liberal patron of art and science—the elected Ruler of his people,—sent into exile and confinement, *on a moral principle*, by the hypocrites who had partitioned Poland, torn away Finland, dismembered Saxony, sold Norway, betrayed Genoa, broken their often repeated promises and oaths, hanged and dungeoned those who only wanted them to be just and decent!

As a result of the Congress of Vienna (1814–15), Genoa, which had been an independent republic prior to its annexation by Napoleon in 1805, became part of the Kingdom of Sardinia. Its betrayal by Britain was noted in a report of a debate in Parliament in the *Examiner* 703 (24 June 1821) 389: 'the King of Sardinia added Genoa to his continental dominions, in opposition to the positive engagement of the British authorities, that Genoa should be restored to independence.' [O]*aths broke* may also refer to the failure of the uprising and proclamation of

And if you buy him not, your treasury
Is empty even of promises — his own coin. —
The freedman of a western poet chief ⁽⁴⁾
Holds Attica with seven thousand rebels
565 And has beat back the Pacha of Negropont. —
The aged Ali sits in Yanina,

---

the Spanish Constitution in Genoa and elsewhere in Piedmont in March 1821 after Charles Albert, the Prince Regent, abandoned the constitutionalists' cause (see the *Examiner* 692 (8 April 1821) 211). In 1814 Norway had been ceded to Sweden, but S. may have had in mind Britain's connivance, through the Holy Alliance, in the actions of the Swedish King reported in the *Examiner* 714 (9 September 1821) 567:

> The northern part of Europe seems almost in as agitated a state as the southern. The disputes between the Parliament of Norway and the King of Sweden are as far from adjustment as ever, and the advance of Swedish troops to the Norwegian frontiers has given rise to considerable apprehension. It is supposed that, in insisting, contrary to the general wish of the Norwegians, for the power of creating Nobles, the King is not so much influenced by the dictates of his own judgment, as by communications which he has received on this subject by the Holy Alliance.

Norway;] *1822, 1840*; Norway *HM 329*; Norway: *1829, 1839*.
561. *not,*] *1822, 1829, 1839, 1840*; not *HM 329*.
562. *coin.* —] coin. *1822, 1829, 1839, 1840*.
563. *freedman*] freeman *1829, 1834, 1839, 1840*. The sense appears to be 'former servant'. *a western poet chief*] Byron. ⁽⁴⁾] See S.'s Note 4. Whether the correction of the number from 5 in *HM 329* p. 26 is in S.'s hand or Williams's is uncertain.
564. *Attica*] The region encompassing Athens and its surroundings. *rebels*] rebels, *1822, 1829, 1839, 1840*.
565. *the Pacha of Negropont*] *Raizis* 190 identifies this individual as Omer Pasha (of Euboea). *Negropont.* —] *Nbk 21*; Negropont *HM 329*; Negropont: *1822*; Negropont; *1829, 1839, 1840*. Also known as Euboea, a large island in the Aegean Sea to the east of mainland Greece.
566. *The aged Ali*] Ali Pasha (1741–1822) to whom Byron had been introduced during his travels in Albania; see his Note to *Childe Harold's Pilgrimage* II xxxviii l. 5 (*Byron PW* ii 192–3; and also the note to ll. 574–8 below). Byron described him in a letter to his mother of 12 November 1809 as 'a remorseless tyrant, guilty of the most horrible cruelties, very brave & so good a general, that they call him the Mahometan Buonaparte' (*Byron L&J* i 228). An article in the *Examiner* 441 (9

A crownless metaphor of empire;
His name, that shadow of his withered might,
Holds our besieging army like a spell
570 In prey to Famine, Pest, and Mutiny;
He, bastioned in his citadel, looks forth
Joyless upon the sapphire lake that mirrors
The ruins of the city where he reigned
Childless and sceptreless. The Greek has reaped

June 1816) 360-1 noted that 'The progress of this enterprising chief has been long viewed with jealousy and alarm; but the Porte was never in a condition to hazard driving him into open rebellion' (361). A few years later the *Examiner* 657 (30 July 1820) 489 reported that 'it appears that [ALI] distrusted the Turks at Jannina his capital, and had deprived them of their arms, filling the ranks of his army, by the help of very large bounties, with Greeks'. His defiance of the Sultan, which facilitated the Greek uprising of April 1821, was noted in the *Examiner* 693 (15 April 1821) 232 ('ALI PACHA still defies the Turkish arms') and 713 (2 September 1821) 545 ('ALI PACHA has long withstood in Albania the most powerful efforts of the Sultan'). His death in February 1822 was reported by Mary to Maria Gisborne in a letter of 6-10 April 1822 (*Mary L* i 229).

566-71. *Yanina ... his citadel*] *1829, 1839, 1840*; Yanina *HM 329, 1822*. Ioannina, a city in Epiros (northern Greece); Ali Pasha's base was a fortress there.

567. *metaphor*] 'empty representation' (*Concordance*). *empire;*] *1829, 1839, 1840*; empire *HM 329*; empire: *1822*. Locock proposes a 'trisyllabic scansion' (*Locock 1911* ii 470).

568. *name,*] *1822, 1829, 1839, 1840*; name *HM 329*. *might,*] *1822, 1829, 1839, 1840*; might *HM 329*.

570. *Famine*] famine *1822, 1829, 1839, 1840*. *Pest*] pest *1822, 1829, 1839, 1840*; pestilence. *Mutiny;*] mutiny; *1822*; mutiny: *1829, 1839, 1840*.

572-3. *sapphire lake ... city*] Mod. Lake Pamvotis, commonly known as the Lake of Ioannina, a large lake to the east of Ioannina, referred to as 'Acherusia's lake' in Byron, *Childe Harold's Pilgrimage* II xlvii l. 1.

572. *mirrors*] The final letter, in dark ink in *HM 329*, may have been added by S.

573. *reigned*] A comma after this word in *HM 329* appears to have been cancelled, whether by Williams or S. is uncertain.

574. *Childless*] S. appears to allow the Messenger licence; Ali Pasha's sons were widely known. Byron refers to his second son, Veli Pasha, as 'one of the most powerful men in the Ottoman empire' in his letter to his mother of 12 November 1809 (*Byron L&J* i 226).

574-8. *Greek ... Indian gold*] See Mary's letter of 5 April published in the *Examiner* 694 (22 April 1821) 248: 'ALI PACHA is purchasing [the Sulliotes'] assistance by the treasures which his tyranny before extorted from them', and S.'s similar wording in a letter of the same date published in the *Morning Chronicle* 16227 (23 April 1821) 2: 'Ali Pacha is purchasing the assistance of the Greeks by the treasures

575   The costly harvest his own blood matured,
      Not the sower, Ali — who has bought a truce
      From Ypsilanti with ten camel loads
      Of Indian gold.
                              [*Enter a Third Messenger.*]

extorted from them by his tyranny'. In a letter of 1 January 1821, early in her acquaintance with Alexandros Mavrokordatos Mary told Hunt that he 'was done up by some alliance I believe with Ali Pacha' (*Mary L* i 173). S.'s lines may recall Byron, *Childe Harold's Pilgrimage* II xlvii ll. 417–23:

> And onwards did his further journey take
> To greet Albania's chief, whose dread command
> Is lawless law; for with a bloody hand
> He sways a nation, turbulent and bold:
> Yet here and there some daring mountain-band
> Disdain his power, and from their rocky hold
> Hurl their defiance far, nor yield, unless to gold.

Byron's note to 'To greet Albania's chief', refers to him as 'The celebrated Ali Pacha' (*Byron PW* ii 288).
575. *matured,*] *1822, 1829, 1839, 1840*; matured *HM 329*.
576–7. *Ali … Ypsilanti*] The *Examiner* 693 (15 April 1821) 227 reported that 'Ali Pacha and Ypsilanti are ready to support each other.'
577. *Ypsilanti*] Ypsilanti, *1839, 1840. camel loads*] camel-loads *1840*.
578. *Indian gold*] 'Gold bullion (rather than currency) from India or, perhaps, South America; possibly a popular term for opium' (*Donovan*). *Indian*] The first letter is overwritten in dark ink in *HM 329*, whether in S.'s hand or Williams's is uncertain. *gold.*] *1822, 1829, 1839, 1840*; gold — *HM 329*.
578–80. *The Christian tribes … revolt*] Duffy, 'Percy Shelley's "display of newspaper erudition"' 521 suggests the source of these lines is an extract 'of a letter from the coast of Syria' published in *Galignani's Messenger* 2003 (27 July 1821) [p. 4]:

> The Syrian Christians have united with the Druses, the descendants of the Crusaders […] As soon as these warriors heard that the church of the Holy Sepulchre had been destroyed, that fire and sword had been carried into all the churches, and that the Christians themselves had been driven from their habitations, and pursued upon the barren mountains that surround them, they collected the small number that had escaped the Turks, and rose against the Sultan.—We anticipate that the union of these brave men with the Christians of Greece and Syria, of Armenia, Diarbekir and Peryamo, may be the means of saving part of the Christian population of Asia from the extermination to which they have been condemned by the Mahometan sect Osmanli.

Mahmud
                    What more?

Third Messenger
                                  The Christian tribes
    Of Lebanon and the Syrian wilderness
580   Are in revolt — Damascus, Hems, Aleppo
    Tremble — the Arab menaces Medina,

580-1. Damascus, Hems, Aleppo / Tremble] Disturbances in two of these places were reported in a letter from Alexandria of 10 June published in *Galignani's Messenger* 2006 (1 August 1821) [p. 4]:

> A vessel arrived yesterday from Acre, which announces that, at the time of its departure, the Christians of Libanus and Anti-Libanus, were in a state of insurrection, declaring that they would not pay tribute to a Government capable of murdering their Patriarch. In vain the Pacha of Syria endeavoured to bring them back to their duty; the detachments sent against them were beaten and routed.—It is said, that a formidable persecution has arisen at Damascus and Aleppo, and that some of the Christians have been massacred.

580. revolt —] revolt;— *1822, 1829, 1839, 1840. Hems*] Mod. Homs, a city in western Syria referred to in *Anastasius* (1819) Vol. III ch. xi. *Aleppo*] Aleppo, *1829, 1839, 1840.*
581. Tremble —] Tremble;— *1822, 1829, 1839, 1840. the Arab menaces Medina*] Medina is an Islamic holy city, second in significance only to Mecca, where the prophet Muhammed is buried; under Ottoman rule since 1517, it is in mod. Saudi Arabia. Among the reasons cited in the *Examiner* 693 (15 April 1821) why 'The Ottoman Empire is in a condition singularly favourable to an attempt of this sort [i.e. the Greek Insurrection]' was that 'a tribe in Arabia called Wechabites are again growing troublesome' (232). 'Wechabites' appears to refer to 'the sect of Wahabis' whom Mahmud II is said to have repressed in the report in *Galignani's Messenger* of July 1821 quoted in the note to *Dramatis Personae.* MAHMUD above. Founded by Muhammad ibn 'Abd al-Wahhab (1703-92) this Sunni sect had launched military raids against Ottoman cities in mod. Syria, Iraq and Saudi Arabia (including Mecca). S. summarises their beliefs in *PVR*:

> In Syria & Arabia the [great questions] of human [intellect] have aroused a sect of people called the Wahabees who maintain the Unity of God, & the equality of man, & their enthusiasm (goes on, "conquering & to conquer—") even if it must be repressed in its present shape. (*SC* vi 988-9)

Medina,] *1822*; Medina *HM 329*; Medina; *1829, 1839, 1840.*

The Ethiop has intrenched himself in Senaar
And keeps the Egyptian rebel well employed
Who denies homage, claims investiture
585   As price of tardy aid — Persia demands

582. Two reports of unrest in Abyssinia in early 1821 were published in *Galignani's Messenger* 2063 (6 October 1821) [p. 2]:

> On the 22d February, accounts arrived, from Judda, announcing the success of the Turkish army in Abyssinia, under Ishmael Pasha, which stated that they had taken possession of Sennar, the capital, after a battle, in which 3000 Turks and 500 Nubians were slain. Salutes were fired at Judda on the receipt of this intelligence.
>
> A letter from a native merchant at Judda states, that Hamed Pasha, with an army of Turks and Bedouins of 8,000 men, were advancing to Yemen, to demand from the Imaun of Sennar 18,000 dollars, being an old debt, and the arrears for the annual tribute of coffee. They threaten to take possession of the sea-coast from Loheia to Mocha, and then advance upon the capital of Yemen.

Senaar] Sennaar, *1822, 1829, 1839, 1840*. A city in mod. Sudan.
583–5. *the Egyptian rebel ... tardy aid*] The draft of these lines in *Nbk 21* p. 100 reads: *The Egyptian rebel claims investiture / As price of tardy aid* (see *BSM* xvi 106–7).
583. *Egyptian rebel*] Crook's assertion that this is 'clearly' a reference to Muhammad Ali Pasha ('Shelley's "Jewish Orations"' 51 n. 33) is supported by the following reports of tensions between the Pacha of Egypt and the Ottoman government in the summer of 1821: the *Examiner* 693 (15 April 1821): 'MAHOMET ALI, Pacha of Egypt, has been disgusted at his treatment by the Divan of Constantinople' (232); *Galignani's Messenger* 2011 (6 August 1821): 'The Porte is said to be deserted by his nominal subjects of the Barbary States and of Egypt. They have refused all aid, to the most earnest solicitations'; *Galignani's Messenger* 2029 (28 August 1821): 'It appears that the Pacha of Egypt favours the Greeks' [p. 3]. *employed*] employed, *1822, 1839, 1840*; employ'd: *1829*.
584. *homage, claims*] I.e. 'homage, and claims'. *homage*] allegiance (to the Sultan). *investiture*] 'appointment to a dignity' (*Concordance*).
585–6. *Persia ... Tigris*] *Galignani's Messenger* 2082 (29 October 1821) [p. 4] reported growing tension between Persia and the Porte: 'One of the principal Banking Houses received a letter on Saturday, which stated that hostilities had commenced between the Turks and the troops of the Schah of Persia, and that the latter had the advantage.'
585. *tardy aid*] The sense seems to be that the Ottoman Empire was dilatory in supporting the Pacha of Egypt's efforts to suppress rebellion in Ethiopia. *aid —*] aid. *1822, 1829, 1839, 1840*.

The cities on the Tigris, and the Georgians
Refuse their living tribute. Crete and Cyprus,
Like mountain-twins that from each other's veins
Catch the volcano-fire and earthquake spasm,
590   Shake in the general fever. Through the city
Like birds before a storm the Santons shriek

586-7. *the Georgians ... tribute*] Forman glosses *living tribute* as 'tribute paid in slaves,—in this case, I believe, selected virgins sent annually to the harem of the Sultan' (*Forman 1876-7* iii 72 n.). S. may have recalled the female Georgian slaves with whom the narrator finds himself on a ship in *Anastasius* Vol. I ch. xv. The proverbial beauty of Georgians was discussed in sources familiar to S. including Buffon, *Histoire naturelle, générale et particulière,* 15 vols (1749-67) iii 433-7 and Gibbon, *Decline and Fall* Vol. IV ch. xlii:

> It is in the [...] climates of Georgia, Mingrelia, and Circassia, that nature has placed, at least to our eyes, the model of beauty, in the shape of the limbs, the colour of the skin, the symmetry of the features, and the expression of the countenance. (Womersley, ed., ii 717)

A note in Beckford's *Vathek* states that 'The incursions of robbers in the confines of Circassia, afford the means of supplying the seraglio, even in times of peace' (ed. Lonsdale, 135), while 'the beauty of Georgia' is referred to in *Anastasius* Vol. III ch. i.
587-90. *Crete ... general fever*] Cp. the Mediterranean revolutionary upheaval in *OL* 182-7:

> as with its thrilling thunder
> Vesuvius wakens Aetna, and the cold
> Snow-crags by its reply are cloven in sunder:
> O'er the lit waves every Aeolian isle
> From Pithecusa to Pelorus
> Howls, and leaps, and glares, in chorus

587. *Cyprus,*] 1822, 1829, 1839, 1840; Cyprus *HM* 329.
588. *other's*] 1822, 1829, 1839, 1840; others *HM* 329.
589. *Catch the volcano-fire*] Cp. *MA* 364-7 and note.
590. *general*] widespread. *city*] city, 1822, 1829, 1840.
591. *storm*] storm, 1822, 1829, 1840. *Santons*] santons 1829. Beckford glosses 'santons' as '[a] body of religionists who were also called *abdals*, and pretended to be inspired with the most enthusiastic raptures of divine love. They were regarded by the vulgar as *saints*' (*Vathek*, ed. Lonsdale, 144). Hope describes 'Turkish Santon' as 'an itinerant saint, of the sort that travel about, living upon the credulity and superstition of the lower orders' (*Anastasius* iii 455). Byron refers to 'Slaves, eunuchs, soldiers, guests and santons' in Byron, *Childe Harold's Pilgrimage* II (1812) lvi l. 7. *shriek*] shriek, 1822, 1829, 1839, 1840.

> And prophesyings horrible and new
> Are heard among the crowd — that sea of men
> Sleeps on the wrecks it made, breathless and still.
> 595 A Dervise, learned in the Koran, preaches
> That it is written how the sins of Islam
> Must raise up a destroyer even now.
> The Greeks expect a Saviour from the West [(5)]
> Who shall not come, men say, in clouds and glory,
> 600 But in the omnipresence of that spirit
> In which all live and are. Ominous signs

592. Cp. *Macbeth* II iii 57–9:

> And prophesying, with accents terrible,
> Of dire combustion and confus'd events
> New hatch'd to th' woeful time.

593. *crowd* —] crowd: *1822*; crowd; *1829, 1839, 1840*.
595–7. Duffy, 'Percy Shelley's "display of newspaper erudition"' 521 cps the following report in *Galignani's Messenger* 2036 (5 September 1821) [p. 4]:

> On the 28th [of July], an old man appeared in the streets, who gave himself out for a prophet, and by an explication of some passages of the Coran, foretold the destruction of the Ottoman Empire. Nothing could exceed the alarm of the superstitious populace, except their fury. They sought fresh victims, but an armed force dispersed these bands of murderers and arrested the prophet.

595. *Dervise,*] *1822, 1829, 1839, 1840*; Dervise *HM 329*. Beckford notes that '[t]he term *dervich* signifies a *poor man*, and is the general appellation by which a Mahometan monk is named' (*Vathek*, ed. Lonsdale, 144). The word is frequent in Byron's poetry; see: *The Giaour, A Fragment of a Turkish Tale* (1813) 340; *The Corsair; A Tale* (1814) ii 49 and *passim*; *Don Juan* III (1821) xxix 6. *Koran,*] *1822, 1840*; Koran *HM 329*; koran, *1829, 1839*.
598–9. *Major Works* cps *Mark* xiii 26: 'And they shall see the Son of man coming in the clouds with great power and glory.'
598. *Saviour from the West*] See the note to S.'s Note 5. *West*] west, *1822, 1829, 1839*; west; *1840*. [(5)] See S.'s Note 5. Whether the correction of the number from 4 to 5 in *HM 329* p. 28 is in S.'s hand or Williams's is uncertain.
599. *in clouds and glory*] See *Matthew* xxiv 30: 'And then shall appear the sign of the Son of man in heaven: and then shall all the tribes of the earth mourn, and they shall see the Son of man coming in the clouds of heaven with power and great glory'; and see note to ll. 598–9 above. *glory,*] *1822, 1829, 1839, 1840*; glory: *HM 329*.
600–1. *the omnispresence ... are*] The idea is Platonic, as noted in *Raizis* 190.

Are blazoned broadly on the noonday sky.
One saw a red cross stamped upon the sun;
It has rained blood, and monstrous births declare
605   The secret wrath of Nature and her Lord.
The army encamped upon the Cydaris
Was roused last night by the alarm of battle
And saw two hosts conflicting in the air,
The shadows doubtless of the unborn time
610   Cast on the mirror of the night; — while yet
The fight hung balanced, there arose a storm

601-12. Donovan cps *Julius Caesar* II ii 17-24.
601-5. Ominous signs ... Lord] Cp. *Luke* xxi 25: 'And there shall be signs in the sun, and in the moon, and in the stars; and upon the earth distress of nations, with perplexity; the sea and the waves roaring'.
601-3. Ominous signs ... sun] An echo of Constantine's vision; see ll. 221-4 and l. 829 and notes.
602. noonday] noon-day *1822, 1829, 1839, 1840. sky.*] sky: *1822;* sky; *1829, 1839, 1840.*
603. sun;] *1822, 1829, 1839, 1840;* sun *HM 329.*
604. blood,] blood; *1822, 1829, 1839, 1840.*
606. Cydaris] *1829, 1839, 1840;* Cydaris, *HM 329, 1822.* A tributary of an inlet of the Bosporus known as the Golden Horn which divides the north of mod. Istanbul from the south. James Dallaway refers to it in *Constantinople Ancient and Modern, with Excursions to the Shores and Islands of the Archipelago and to the Troad* (1797): 'Of the vast cisterns, mentioned by Gyllius, those now worthy inspection are two made by the emperor Constantine, and that of Philoxenus. One of the former is now occasionally full, as it receives the brook Cydaris' (110). S.'s father had engaged Dallaway (1763-1834), an antiquarian and traveller, to advise S. in the composition of a poem on the subject of the Parthenon for a University competition at Oxford in 1811 (see S.'s letter to Timothy Shelley of 17 February 1811, *L* i 53 and the headnote to *Poetical Essay on the Existing State of Things*, Appendix A of Volume 6 in the present edition).
607. battle] battle, *1822, 1829, 1839, 1840.*
608. air,] *1822;* air *HM 329;* air,— *1829, 1839, 1840.*
609-10. The shadows ... night] The 'two hosts conflicting' (l. 608) are 'shadows', in the sense of 'Ominous signs' (l. 601), of war in the future ('the unborn time') that are cast on the moon ('the mirror of the night'). The phraseology echoes *DP* where poets are described as 'the mirrors of the gigantic shadows which futurity casts upon the present' (*Reiman (2002)* para. 48).
609. doubtless] An adverb ('undoubtedly') rather than an adjective qualifying 'shadows'. *time*] time, *1829, 1839, 1840.*
610. night; — while] night. While *1822, 1829, 1839, 1840.*
611. balanced,] *1822, 1829, 1839;* balanced *HM 329.*

        Which swept the phantoms from among the stars.
        At the third watch the spirit of the plague
        Was heard abroad flapping among the tents;
615 Those who relieved watch found the sentinels dead.
        The last news from the camp is that a thousand
        Have sickened, and —
                                    [*Enter a Fourth Messenger.*

Mahmud
                    And thou, pale ghost, dim shadow
        Of some untimely rumour — speak!

Fourth Messenger
                              One comes
        Fainting with toil, covered with foam and blood;
620 He stood, he says, on Chelonite's

613–17. The situation of plague afflicting such large numbers of fighting men in their tents recalls that of *Iliad* i, in which the Greek army encamped on the Trojan shore is ravaged by a plague sent by Apollo.

613. *the third watch*] One of the 'watches' or 'vigils' of the night which are calculated in different ways in various traditions. See *Luke* xii 37–8: 'Blessed *are* those servants, whom the lord when he cometh shall find watching […] And if he shall come in the second watch, or come in the third watch, and find *them* so, blessed are those servants.' The period of darkness before dawn is associated with weakness. Jesus foretold that Peter would betray him at this time: 'And he said, I tell thee, Peter, the cock shall not crow this day, before that thou shalt thrice deny that thou knowest me' (*Luke* xxii 34).

614. *tents;*] *1822*; tents *HM 329*; tents: *1829, 1839, 1840*.

615. *dead.*] *1822, 1829, 1839, 1840*; dead *HM 329*.

616. *last*] latest. *is*] is, *1822, 1829, 1839, 1840*.

617. *And*] *1822, 1829, 1839, 1840*; And, *HM 329*.

618–38. *One comes … abhorred cross*] The Third Messenger delivers news of battles on land and in aerial visions (ll. 578–617); the Fourth reports a sea-battle which the witness ('One', l. 618) 'saw, or dreamed he saw' (l. 634). Both use prophetic, biblical language, and the battles described seem more mystical than actual.

618. *rumour —*] rumour, *1822, 1829, 1839, 1840*.

619. *blood;*] *1829, 1839, 1840*; blood *HM 329*; blood: *1822*.

620–1. *Chelonite's / Promontory … isles*] See Strabo, *Geography* VIII iii 4: 'the promontory Chelonatas, the most westerly point of the Peloponnesus. Off Chelonatas lies an isle […]'. The 'isle' to which Strabo refers is likely to be Zante (Zakynthos) to the south west of the promontory and one of the Ionian islands (see note to ll. 621–2). *Rossetti 1870* ii 556 notes that 'there is a promontory so named nearly opposite Cephallenia'; Cephallenia (mod. Cephalonia) is the largest of the Ionian islands and lies northwest of the promontory.

Promontory, which o'erlooks the isles that groan
Under the Briton's frown, and all their waters
Then trembling in the splendour of the moon —
When, as the wandering clouds unveiled or hid
625   Her boundless light, he saw two adverse fleets
Stalk through the night in the horizon's glimmer
Mingling fierce thunders and sulphureous gleams,
And smoke which strangled every infant wind
That soothed the silver clouds through the deep air.

620. The line is hypometric. on Chelonite's] Errata; upon Chelonile's *HM 329* (written in S.'s hand in *HM 329* above and alongside Williams's *on the Cleonite's* which is cancelled; S. must have intended to write a *t* instead of a second *l*); upon Clelonite's *1822;* upon Clelonites *1829, 1834;* upon Clelonit's *1839, 1840;* upon Chelonites' *Rossetti 1870, Rossetti 1878.* The reading in *Nbk 21* p. 212 is impossible to decipher with confidence (see *BSM* xvi 208–9).
621-2. isles … Briton's frown] The Ionian islands, to the west of mainland Greece. The British had taken these islands from the French between 1809 and 1814 and the Treaty of Paris (1815) established them under British protection. In his letter of 5 April 1821 published in the *Morning Chronicle* 16227 (23 April 1821), S. advanced the Greek cause by presenting it as of no threat to British interests in these islands:

> The Greeks express a great anxiety, lest the British Administration should be unfavourable to their cause, and lest it should secretly abet the tyranny of the Turks. They disclaim whatever views upon the Ionian Islands, and the Chiefs of the Insurrection (I speak from personal knowledge) have exerted their utmost influence to restrain the inhabitants of those Islands from any attempt to withdraw themselves from the British power. Should the Greeks succeed in their efforts to become a nation, all motives for controversy on such a question would probably be absorbed in the greater advantages which a friendly intercourse with them would render to England.

623. moon —] moon, *1822, 1829;* moon; *1839, 1840.*
624. When,] 1839, 1840; When *HM 329, 1822, 1829.*
626. glimmer] glimmer, *1822, 1829, 1839, 1840.*
627. sulphureous] 1822, 1829, 1839, 1840; sulphurious *HM 329. Major Works* comments: 'S. uses this form of "sulphurous" (see l. 8[30]) for the metre.' *gleams,] 1822, 1829, 1839, 1840;* gleams *HM 329.*

630　At length the battle slept, but the Sirocco
　　　Awoke and drove his flock of thunder-clouds
　　　Over the sea-horizon, blotting out
　　　All objects — save that in the faint moon-glimpse
　　　He saw, or dreamed he saw, the Turkish admiral
635　And two the loftiest of our ships of war,
　　　With the bright image of that Queen of Heaven
　　　Who hid, perhaps, her face for grief, reversed;
　　　And the abhorred cross —
　　　　　　　　　　　　　　　　　　　　[*Enter an Attendant.*
Attendant
　　　　　　　　　　　　Your Sublime Highness,
　　　The Jew, who —

Mahmud
　　　　　　　　　Could not come more seasonably:

630. *Sirocco*] Scirocco *1840*. See note to l. 277.
631. *Awoke*] Awoke, *1822, 1829, 1839, 1840*. *thunder-clouds*] *1822, 1829, 1839, 1840*; thunder clouds *HM 329*.
633. *the faint moon-glimpse*] I.e. the intermittent light of the moon through cloud. The sense is evident from the draft of ll. 633–4 in *Nbk 21* p. 213: *Is known, but that the glimpses of the moon* / [*Revealed*] [*the Turkish admiral*] *sailing by* (see *BSM* xvi 208–9).
634. *he saw,*] he saw *1829, 1839, 1840*. *admiral*] flagship (ship bearing an admiral's flag) (*OED* 3).
635. *war,*] *1822, 1829, 1839, 1840*; war *HM 329*.
636. *that Queen of Heaven*] I.e. the moon, referred to as such in *Epipsychidion* 281. The crescent moon is the symbol of the Ottoman Empire. *Queen*] queen *1829*. *Heaven*] heaven, *1829*; Heaven, *1839, 1840*.
638. SD. *Attendant*] *1822*. The speaker is omitted in *HM 329*.
638. *Sublime Highness,*] *1829, 1839, 1840*; sublime highness *HM 329*; Sublime Highness *1822*.
639. *The Jew*] Ahasuerus; see *Dramatis Personae* note and note to ll. 163–84. *seasonably:*] *1822, 1829, 1839, 1840*; seasonably *HM 329*.

640   Bid him attend — I'll hear no more! too long
      We gaze on danger through the mist of fear,
      And multiply upon our shattered hopes
      The images of ruin — come what will!
      Tomorrow and tomorrow are as lamps
645   Set in our path to light us to the edge
      Through rough and smooth, nor can we suffer aught
      Which he inflicts not in whose hand we are.
                                                            [*Exeunt.*

              Semichorus 1st
         Would I were the winged cloud

640. *attend* —] attend. *1822, 1829, 1839, 1840.*
643. *ruin — come*] ruin. Come *1822, 1829, 1839, 1840.*
644-5. Cp. *Macbeth* V v 19-23:

>   To-morrow, and to-morrow, and to-morrow,
>   Creeps in this petty pace from day to day,
>   To the last syllable of recorded time;
>   And all our yesterdays have lighted fools
>   The way to dusty death.

646. *smooth,*] smooth; *1829, 1839, 1840.* nor] The middle letter is overwritten in darker ink in *HM 329*, whether in S.'s hand or Williams's is uncertain.
648-737. This choral interlude of 90 lines, set just over half way through the drama, responds to the previous speeches of Mahmud, Hassan and the Messengers but also anticipates the dialogue between Mahmud and Ahasuerus which follows. In this thematically organised chorus, the first four stanzas (ll. 648-81) express the desire to join the Greek cause curtailed by the hold that 'Slavery' (l. 676) has on that desire. The next four stanzas (ll. 682-710) are a paean to Greece, geographically, historically and culturally. The last four (ll. 711-37) open with the abstraction of 'Destiny' (l. 712), relentless and unknowable, and close with the imperative of choosing love over 'Revenge and wrong' (l. 729). The emotional arc follows those themes, opening with anger and anguish; these are then followed by joy and pride in Greece but tempered by reflection. The final dramatic stanzas open with confusion and fear but ultimately conclude with understanding and a commanding call for action. Lyrically, all stanzas but one move swiftly with tetrameters and dimeters; the single stanza of the Chorus (ll. 676-81) begins with two pentameters, and then resolves into tetrameters and a single dimeter. While the first two stanzas share the same rhyme scheme — except for the last line of the second stanza (l. 670) — all other stanzas are unique and no clear patterns

Of a tempest swift and loud,
650   I would scorn
The smile of morn

---

emerge. Further erosion to pattern occurs because of interruptions to the speaker. For example, in the seventh stanza (ll. 693–703), the last line of Semichorus 1 is interrupted when Semichorus 2 concludes it with 'Hear ye the blast' (l. 703), the final word rhyming with 'past' (l. 701) in Semichorus 1. No rhyming counterpart to *blast* occurs in Semichorus 2, so it is an anomaly in that stanza. These disruptions to sound patterns signal a growing sense of confusion and urgency although that instability is somewhat resolved by the final stanza's neatly finished lines and simple rhyme-scheme of *abaab*.

648–70. *Would I ... Tyranny!*] These stanzas mark the first impulse in the Greek women's response to the events of the preceding lines. Semichorus 1st rejects all possibilities for pleasure and comfort in 'The smile of morn, the moon-rise', or 'the deep blue noon divine'. The second Semichorus then asks 'Whither to fly?'. The answer, recalling the cloud imagery throughout the battle-scene of the Fourth Messenger's speech (ll. 624, 629, 631), is to fly to 'th' Aegean', site of the violent struggle for liberty — 'battle paean / Of the free, the Grecian slain, the bloody main' — ringing a 'thunder knell' to mark the end of 'Tyranny'.

648–64. Erkelenz, 'Inspecting the Tragedy of Empire' 327–8 cps ll. 648–9 and 660–4 of the first Semichorus with ll. 1044–8 and 1080–4 of the Chorus in *Oedipus at Colonus*:

εἴην ὅθι δαΐων
ἀνδρῶν τάχ' ἐπιστροφαὶ
τὸν χαλκοβόαν Ἄρη
μείξουσιν

('I wish I were where the enemy will soon wheel about and join the brazen din of battle')

μάντις εἴμ' ἐσθλῶν ἀγώνων.
εἴθ' ἀελλαία ταχύρρωστος πελειὰς
αἰθερίας νεφέλας κύρσαιμ' ἄνωθ'
ἀγώνων αἰωρήσασα τοὐμὸν ὄμμα.

('I predict a victory in the struggle! I wish I were a wind-swift strong-winged dove, gazing from a lofty cloud upon the contest!')

Line 664 echoes *Oedipus at Colonus* 1080, the epigraph of S.'s poem.

648–59. The rhyme scheme for this 11–line stanza and single line interruption by the second Semichorus is *aabbbcccdde*, then *e*. The stanza is bookended by 'Would I' and 'would, — not I'.

649. *loud,*] loud! *1822, 1829, 1839, 1840*.
651. *morn*] morn, *1829, 1839, 1840*.

And the wave where the moon-rise is born!
I would leave
The spirits of eve
655 A shroud for the corpse of the day to weave
From other threads than mine!
Bask in the deep blue noon divine
Who would, — not I.

Semichorus 2nd
Whither to fly?

Semichorus 1st
660 Where the rocks that gird th' Aegean

652. *moon-rise*] *1829, 1839, 1840*; moon rise *HM 329, 1822*.
653. This line is marked off in ink in the margin of *HM 329* p. 30 with 'D32' alongside. As Reiman comments (*MYRS* iii 12, 52), these markings are those of the printer, noting this line to be the first of p. 32 in *1822*, i.e. the beginning of signature D.
655. Cp. *Song: To the Men of England* (no. 292) l. 31 and note.
656. *other*] others' *1829, 1834*.
657. *deep blue noon*] *Errata*; blue noon *HM 329, 1822, 1829, 1839, 1840*; deep-blue noon *Rossetti 1878*. *Rossetti 1878* is the first edition of *Hellas* which takes note of *Errata* but there is no authority for its hyphen (see *Rossetti 1878* ii 403, 456). The reading is *calm blue noon* in *Nbk 21* p. 135 (*BSM* xvi 136-7).
658. *would,* —] would, *1822, 1829, 1839, 1840*.
660-4. Cp. the description of the Greeks' singing before the Battle of Salamis at *Persae* 388-94:

> πρῶτον μὲν ἠχῇ κέλαδος Ἑλλήνων πάρα
> μολπηδὸν ηὐφήμησεν, ὄρθιον δ' ἅμα
> ἀντηλάλαξε νησιώτιδος πέτρας
> ἠχώ· φόβος δὲ πᾶσι βαρβάροις παρῆν
> γνώμης ἀποσφαλεῖσιν· οὐ γὰρ ὡς φυγῇ
> παιᾶν' ἐφύμνουν σεμνὸν Ἕλληνες τότε,
> ἀλλ' ἐς μάχην ὁρμῶντες εὐψύχῳ θράσει·

('there rang out loudly a joyful sound of song from the Greeks, and simultaneously the echo of it resounded back from the cliffs of the island. All we Easterners were terrified, because we had been deceived in our expectation: the Greeks were now raising the holy paean-song, not with a view to taking flight, but in the act of moving out to battle, with confidence'.)

660. *th' Aegean*] the Ægean *1829*.

	Echo to the battle paean
	Of the free —
	I would flee,
	A tempestuous herald of Victory;
665	My golden rain
	For the Grecian slain
	Should mingle in tears with the bloody main,
	And my solemn thunder knell
	Should ring to the world the passing bell
670	Of Tyranny!

                   Semichorus 2nd
                Ha king! wilt thou chain

661. *paean*] song of victory.
663. *flee,*] Locock 1911; flee *HM 329, 1822, 1829, 1839, 1840.*
664. See note to ll. 648–64 above. *Victory;*] Victory. — *Nbk 21*; Victory, *HM 329*; victory! *1822, 1829, 1839, 1840.*
666. *For*] Written over an indecipherable word in *HM 329*, whether in S.'s hand or Williams's is uncertain.
667. *the ... main,*] *1822*; the ... main *HM 329*; the ... main; *1829, 1839, 1840.* The sea.
668. *thunder knell*] *1822*; thunder knell, *HM 329*; thunder-knell *1829, 1839, 1840.*
669. *the passing bell*] passing-bell *1829, 1839, 1840.* The 'bell tolled to announce a death' (*OED* 2); cp. *The Cenci* V iii 143.
670. *Tyranny*] tyranny *1822, 1829, 1839, 1840.*
671–3. *wilt thou ... hurricane?*] The imagery of chaining the forces of the natural world recalls Xerxes' famous 'yoking' of the Hellespont. Cp. *Persae* 745–8:

      ὅστις Ἑλλήσποντον ἱρὸν δοῦλον ὣς δεσμώμασιν
      ἤλπισε σχήσειν ῥέοντα, Βόσπορον ῥόον θεοῦ,
      καὶ πόρον μετερρύθμιζε, καὶ πέδαις σφυρηλάτοις
      περιβαλὼν πολλὴν κέλευθον ἤνυσεν πολλῷ στρατῷ·

('He thought he could stop the flow of the Hellespont, the divine stream of the Bosporus, by putting chains on it, as if it were a slave; he altered the nature of its passage, put hammered fetters upon it, and created a great pathway for a great army.')

671. *Ha*] Ah *1822, 1829, 1839, 1840.*

>   The rack and the rain?
>   Wilt thou fetter the lightning and hurricane?
>   The storms are free,
> 675   But we?
>
>   *Chorus*
>   O Slavery! thou frost of the world's prime,
>   Killing its flowers and leaving its thorns bare!
>   Thy touch has stamped these limbs with crime,
>   These brows thy branding garland bear,
> 680   But the free heart, the impassive soul,
>   Scorn thy control!
>
>   *Semichorus 1st*
>   'Let there be light!' said Liberty,
>   And like sunrise from the sea,

672. *rack*] 'A mass of cloud moving quickly, esp. above lower clouds' (*OED* 3a); cp. *The Cloud* 33 and *WA* 48. *rain?*] *1822, 1829, 1839, 1840*; rain *HM 329*.
674. *free,*] *1822, 1829, 1839, 1840*; free *HM 329*.
675. *we?*] we— *1822, 1829, 1839, 1840*.
676–81. In this Chorus the question posed by the female slaves in l. 675 is answered. Just as the 'king' (l. 671) cannot fetter nature, so 'the free heart' (l. 680) scorns control by 'Slavery' (l. 676).
676. *prime,*] *1822, 1829, 1839, 1840*; prime *HM 329*. Spring, i.e. the first age (see *OED n.*[1] 6b and 7).
677. *its flowers*] *1822, 1829, 1839, 1840*; it's flowers *HM 329*.
678–9. *stamped ... garland bear*] A reference to the physical marks of chattel slavery; *Concordance* glosses 'garland' as a 'wreath of disgrace'. *bear,*] bear; *1829, 1839, 1840*.
678. *crime,*] *1822, 1829, 1839, 1840*; crime *HM 329*.
680. *impassive*] 'not liable to be disturbed by passion, serene' (*OED* 3). *soul,*] *1829, 1839, 1840*; soul *HM 329, 1822*.
682–6. *'Let there be light!' ... states*] Cp. Athens' illuminating effects in *OL* 61–90.
682. *'Let there be light!'*] Rossetti 1870; Let there be light! *HM 329, 1822, 1829, 1839, 1840*. Cp. Genesis i 3: 'And God said, Let there be light: and there was light.' *Liberty,*] *1822*; Liberty *HM 329*; Liberty; *1829, 1839, 1840*. Liberty speaks, unlike its antithesis *Slavery* in the previous strophe.
683. *sunrise*] Alt. from *sun rise* in *HM 329*, whether in S.'s hand or Williams's is uncertain.

	Athens arose! — around her born,
685	Shone like mountains in the morn,
	Glorious states, — and are they now
	Ashes, wrecks, oblivion?

> *Semichorus 2nd*
> Go,
> Where Thermae and Asopus swallowed
> Persia, as the sand does foam.
> 690 Deluge upon deluge followed, —
> Discord, Macedon and Rome,

684. *Athens arose!*] Repeats *OL* 61. *around*] Around *1822, 1829, 1839, 1840*.
685. *Shone*] Shone, *1829*. *morn,*] *1829, 1839, 1840*; morn *HM 329, 1822*.
686. *states, —*] states;— *1822, 1829, 1839, 1840*.
687. *Go,*] Go *1829, 1839, 1840*. The cancellation of an exclamation mark and insertion of the comma after *Go* in *HM 329* may be in S.'s hand, as *MYRS* suggests.
688. *Thermae and Asopus*] A reference to two battles: 'The battle of Thermopylae (Hot Gates) was fought in 480 BCE by the Thermae (Hot Springs). It bought the Greeks time to unite, prepare, and give Mardonius' Persians a final and fatal blow at Plataea (495 BCE) by the river Asopus' (*Raizis* 192). Herodotus refers to Asopus throughout his Plataea narrative in Book IX of *Histories* and mentions θερμὰ λουτρά ('hot springs for bathing') in his description of the site of Thermopylae (vii 176). For Thermopylae see l. 54 and note.
689. *foam.*] foam, *1829*.
690. *followed, —*] follow'd, *1822, 1829*; followed, *1839, 1840*.
691. Further references to devastating wars and the rise and fall of empires. 'Macedon' and 'Rome' seem to have been selected as the largest empires of the European Classical world. Macedon was finally defeated by the Romans in a series of terrible losses; the end of the battle at Pydna is described thus in J. Lemprière, *Classical Dictionary* 8th edn (1812) ('MACEDONICUM BELLUM'): 'The victory sided with the Romans, and 20,000 of the Macedonian soldiers were left on the field of battle'. Eventually, the Roman empire fell to the Goths, led by Alaric in the fifth century CE. Both empires also suffered significant internal strife (the Wars of Alexander's Successors and the many civil wars of the Romans) and it may be to this that 'Discord' refers. *Macedon*] Macedon, *1822, 1829, 1839, 1840*. *Rome,*] *Nbk 21*; Rome. *HM 329*; Rome: *1822, 1829, 1840*.

And lastly Thou!

   Semichorus 1st
   Temples and towers,
  Citadels and marts, and they
  Who live and die there, have been ours,
695 And may be thine, and must decay,
  But Greece and her foundations are
  Built below the tide of war,
  Based on the crystalline sea
  Of thought and its eternity;

692-5. Cp. *The Tempest* IV i 152-4:

> The cloud-capp'd tow'rs, the gorgeous palaces,
> The solemn temples, the great globe itself,
> Yea, all which it inherit, shall dissolve [...]

See also *Lines connected with Hellas* A ll. 38-44.
692. *And lastly*] And, lastly, *1829, 1839, 1840*. *Thou!*] thou! *1822, 1829, 1839, 1840*. Either Mahmud (the 'king' of l. 671) or, as *Donovan* suggests, 'the Ottoman Empire'. *towers,*] *1822, 1829, 1839*; towers *HM 329*.
693. *marts,*] *1822, 1829, 1839, 1840*; marts *HM 329*. Marketplaces.
694. *ours,*] *1822, 1829, 1839, 1840*; ours. *HM 329*.
695. *decay,*] decay; *1822, 1829, 1839, 1840*.
696-9. Cp. *Paradise Lost* vii 269-72:

>   so he the world
> Built on circumfluous waters calm, in wide
> Crystálline ocean, and the loud misrule
> Of Chaos far removed

Mary comments of these lines that they offer 'the assertion of the intellectual empire which must be for ever the inheritance of the country of Homer, Sophocles, and Plato' (*1839* ii 347).
696-8. Cp. the description of Athens in *OL* 64-5 ('the ocean-floors / Pave it') and 76-9 and note.
696. 'The main metaphysical idea of the poem, the primacy of thought and its sole reality, begins here' (*Woodberry 1901*). *foundations*] foundation *1834*.
697. *war,*] *1822, 1829, 1839, 1840*; war *HM 329*.
698. Cp. *Revelation* iv 6: 'And before the throne *there was* a sea of glass like unto crystal'.

700   Her citizens, imperial spirits,
         Rule the present from the past,
         On all this world of men inherits
         Their seal is set. —

              Semichorus 2nd
                  Hear ye the blast
         Whose Orphic thunder thrilling calls
705   From ruin her Titanian walls?
         Whose spirit shakes the sapless bones

700-1. Her citizens … from the past] Albert S. Cook, 'Notes on Shelley', *MLN* xx (1905) 161-2 cps Manfred's recollection of the legacy of Ancient Rome while at the Coliseum in *Manfred* III iv 40-1: 'The dead, but sceptred sovereigns, who still rule / Our spirits from their urns.—' See also *Lines connected with Hellas* A ll. 8-10.
700. citizens, imperial spirits,] citizens' imperial spirits *1829. imperial*] The sense appears to be 'capable of governing (themselves and others)' (see *Sonnet: Political Greatness* (no. 342) ll. 10-14 and note).
701. past,] *1822, 1839, 1840*; past *HM 329*; past; *1829*.
702. On all this] I.e. on all that this.
703. Their seal is set] The phrase (frequent in S.'s poems; see, e.g., *Epipsychidion* 139-40 and *Adonais* 453) has Biblical resonances; see, e.g., *John* iii 33: 'He that hath received his testimony hath set to his seal that God is true'. A 'seal', used figuratively, is 'something that authenticates or confirms' (*OED* 'seal' $n.^2$ 1b). *set.* —] *Nbk 21*; set — *HM 329*; set. *1822, 1829, 1839, 1840. blast*] blast, *1822, 1829, 1839, 1840.*
704. Orphic] 'oracular' (see *OED* 1); Orpheus represents the mythical beginnings of poetry and therefore prophecy in *PU* IV 415 (see note). *thunder thrilling*] resounding thunder.
705. Titanian] Of the Titans, the oldest generation of Greek gods who mark the earliest reaches of Greek civilisation (before their 'modern' gods, the Olympians), i.e. 'ancient'; since the Titans were giant in size, Donovan suggests 'immense' also.
706-7. sapless bones … Slavery?] The bones of 'Slavery' (the state of subjection generally rather than the chattel slavery specifically referred to in l. 679) are devoid of sap, i.e. it is dying.
706. spirit] spirits *1834*.

Of Slavery? Argos, Corinth, Crete
Hear, and from their mountain thrones
The daemons and the nymphs repeat
The harmony.

Semichorus 1st
710   I hear! I hear!

Semichorus 2nd
The world's eyeless charioteer,
Destiny, is hurrying by!

707-8. Argos, Corinth, Crete / Hear] Insurrections in all of these places were favourable to the Greek cause. *Argos*] Argos, a town in the south east of the Peloponnese whose bishop headed the siege of 'Nauplia' (l. 482); see note to that line and Dionysis Tzakis, 'Morea', trans. Alexandra Douma, in *The Greek Revolution: A Critical Dictionary* 263. *Corinth*] See l. 548 and note. *Crete*] Crete, *1829, 1839, 1840*. Known at this time as Candia. The *Examiner* 695 (29 April 1821) 262 reported:

> The troops which the Porte has successively sent from Constantinople to the Isle of Candia have been vanquished. The insurgents, after making great carnage, took possession of all the forts in the island, on which they have hoisted the independent flag.

In addition, Mavrokordatos reported assistance for the insurrectionists on the island in his letter to Mary of 27 May cited in the note to ll. 482–6 above.
709. daemons] Spirits who mediate between Gods and men.
710. harmony.] *1822, 1829, 1839, 1840*; harmony *HM 329*.
710-12. I hear! I hear! ... hurrying by] Cp. Marvell, 'To His Coy Mistress' (1681) 21–2: 'But at my back I always hear / Time's wingèd chariot hurrying near'.
711-12. charioteer, / Destiny,] *1822, 1829, 1839, 1840*; charioteer / Destiny *HM 329*.
711. eyeless charioteer] See *Lines connected with Hellas* A l. 135: 'art thou eyeless like old Destiny'. Mathilde Blind, in her review of *Rossetti 1870* in *Westminster Review* xxxviii (1870) 95 identifies this charioteer with the one in *TL* 99–100. However, A. C. Bradley, 'Notes on Shelley's "Triumph of Life"', *MLR* ix (1914) 447, cautions that the 'charioteer' in *TL* 99 is not eyeless, rather its 'four faces [...] / Had their eyes banded' (99–100). Bradley sees 'Destiny' as interchangeable with 'Necessity' which is described as having 'sightless strength' in *L&C* 3708.

What faith is crushed, what empire bleeds
Beneath her earthquake-footed steeds?
715 What eagle-winged victory sits
At her right hand? what shadow flits
Before? what splendour rolls behind?
  Ruin and Renovation cry
'Who but We?'

    Semichorus 1st
  I hear! I hear
720 The hiss as of a rushing wind,
The roar as of an ocean foaming,
The thunder as of earthquake coming.

---

714. earthquake-footed steeds] Horses whose tread is as destructive as earthquakes. For other compound adjectives combined with 'earthquake', see *PU* I 167 and II iv 152.

715–16. eagle-winged victory sits / ... right hand] Cp. *Paradise Lost* vi 762–3: 'at his right hand Victory / Sat eagle-winged'; see also l. 448 and note to ll. 448–9. *eagle-winged*] *1822, 1829, 1839, 1840*; eagle winged *HM 329*.

716. At] Written over *On* in what appears to be S.'s hand in *HM 329*. *shadow*] shadows *1834*.

718. Renovation] renovation *1822*. *cry*] cry, *1829, 1839, 1840*.

719. 'Who but We?'] Who but We? *HM 329, 1822*; Who but we? *1829, 1839, 1840*; 'Who but we?' *Rossetti 1870*. We is written over *he* in *HM 329* in what appears to be S.'s hand. *I hear! I hear*] I hear! I hear! *1822, 1829, 1839, 1840*.

720–8. The hiss ... a small still voice] Cp. Elijah's encounter with the Lord in *I Kings* xix 11–12:

> And he said, Go forth, and stand upon the mount before the LORD. And, behold the LORD passed by, and a great and strong wind rent the mountains, and brake in pieces the rocks before the LORD; *but* the LORD *was* not in the wind: and after the wind an earthquake; *but* the LORD *was* not in the earthquake: And after the earthquake a fire; *but* the LORD *was* not in the fire: and after the fire a still small voice.

720–1. Cp. *Come thou Awakener of the spirit's Ocean* (no. 218) l. 1 and note.

720. wind,] *1822, 1829, 1839, 1840*; wind *HM 329*.

721. foaming,] *1822, 1829, 1839, 1840*; foaming *HM 329*.

722. coming.] coming, *1829, 1839, 1840*.

> I hear! I hear!
> The crash as of an empire falling,
725 　The shrieks as of a people calling
> 'Mercy! Mercy!' — how they thrill!
> Then a shout of 'kill! kill! kill!'
> And then a small still voice, thus —
>
> 　　　　Semichorus 2nd
> 　　　　　　　　　　For
> Revenge and wrong bring forth their kind,

724–5. *The crash ... The shrieks*] Cp. Gibbon's account of the assault on Constantinople in *Decline and Fall* Vol. VI (1788) ch. lxviii:

> The cries of fear and of pain were drowned in the martial music of drums, trumpets, and attaballs; and experience has proved, that the mechanical operation of sounds, by quickening the circulation of the blood and spirits, will act on the human machine more forcibly than the eloquence of reason and honour. (Womersley, ed., iii 961)

724. *falling,*] *1822, 1829, 1839, 1840*; falling *HM 329*.
726. *'Mercy! Mercy!'* —] *Rossetti 1870*; Mercy! Mercy! *HM 329*; Mercy! mercy!— *1822*; Mercy! Mercy!— *1829, 1839, 1840*. *how*] How *1822, 1829, 1839, 1840*. *thrill*] 'sound piercingly' (*Concordance*).
727. Cp. *King Lear* IV vi 187: 'Then kill, kill, kill, kill, kill, kill!'. '*kill! kill! kill!*'] 'Kill! kill! kill!' *1829, 1839, 1840*.
728–30. *For ... parents are*] As first noted by Richard Garnett in *Select letters of Percy Bysshe Shelley* (1882) 249, the source of these lines appears to be *Agamemnon* 758–60:

> τὸ δυσσεβὲς γὰρ ἔργον
> μετὰ μὲν πλείονα τίκτει,
> σφετέρᾳ δ' εἰκότα γέννᾳ.

('it is the impious deed
that breeds more to follow,
resembling their progenitors;')

S. reproduces this passage in the original Greek and applies it to the situation in Greece at the time in his letter to Mary of 8–10 August 1821 from Ravenna (see note to Preface ll. 66–70).
728. *For*] Fear *Rossetti 1870, Forman 1876–7*. Rossetti justifies his emendation in *Rossetti 1870* ii 556–7 and retracts it, having consulted *HM 329*, in *Rossetti 1878* ii 456.
729. *kind,*] *1822, 1829, 1839, 1840*; kind *HM 329*.

730   The foul cubs like their parents are,
          Their den is in the guilty mind
          And Conscience feeds them with despair. —

                    Semichorus 1st
          In sacred Athens, near the fane
          Of Wisdom, Pity's altar stood. —

730. Cp. Aeschylus *Agamemnon* 727–8: ἀπέδειξεν ἦθος τὸ πρὸς τοκέων ('displayed the character / inherited from its parents').
731. *the*] their *1829, 1834, 1839, 1840. mind*] mind, *1822, 1829, 1839, 1840*.
732. *despair. —*] despair. *1822, 1829, 1839, 1840*.
733–7. *In ... for blood!*] Webb (1977) 151, 155 cps Pausanias, *Description of Greece* I xvii 1:

> In the Athenian market place among the objects not generally known is an altar to Mercy, of all divinities the most useful in the life of mortals and in the vicissitudes of fortune, but honoured by the Athenians alone among the Greeks. And they are conspicuous not only for their humanity but also for their devotion to religion.

733. *fane*] temple.
734–7. *Pity's altar ... blood!*] See ll. 1094–5 below. Cp. Paul's address to the Athenians on Mars' hill in *Acts* xvii 22–5:

> Ye men of Athens, I perceive that in all things ye are too superstitious. For as I passed by, and beheld your devotions, I found an altar with this inscription, TO THE UNKNOWN GOD. Whom therefore ye ignorantly worship, him declare I unto you. God that made the world and all things therein, seeing that he is Lord of heaven and earth, dwelleth not in temples made with hands; Neither is worshipped with men's hands, as though he needed any thing, seeing he giveth to all life, and breath, and all things;

Major Works comments 'Paul can identify God; S.'s Chorus suggests that God remains "unknown".'
734. *stood. —*] stood *HM 329*; stood: *1822*; stood; *1829, 1839, 1840*.

735   Serve not the unknown God in vain,
      But pay that broken shrine again,
      Love for hate and tears for blood!

                              [*Enter* MAHMUD *and* AHASUERUS.

Mahmud
      Thou art a man, thou sayest, even as we.

Ahasuerus
      No more!

Mahmud
                   But raised above thy fellow men
740   By thought, as I by power.

Ahasuerus
                                  Thou sayest so.

Mahmud
      Thou art an adept in the difficult lore

---

736. *again,*] again *1829, 1839, 1840.*
737. *hate*] hate, *1829, 1839, 1840. blood!*] blood. *1822, 1839, 1840.*
738. *man, thou sayest,*] Nbk 21, *1839, 1840;* man thou sayest HM 329, *1822;* man, thou sagest, *1829, 1834. we.*] *1822;* we HM 329; we — *1829, 1839, 1840.*
739. *fellow men*] fellow-man *1829;* fellow-men *1839, 1840.*
741–91. The shape of the start of this episode recalls that of the confrontation between Oedipus and the prophet Tiresias in Sophocles' *Oedipus Tyrannus* 300ff. Mahmud begins by praising his interlocutor's prophetic skill, as does Oedipus in ll. 300–1: ὦ πάντα νωμῶν Τειρεσία, διδακτά τε ἄρρητά τ' οὐράνιά τε καὶ χθονοστιβῆ ('Tiresias, you who dispose all things, those that can be explained and those unspeakable, things in heaven and things that move on earth'). He is then confused by his interlocutor's words at 786–91 as Oedipus is at l. 330: τί φής; ξυνειδὼς οὐ φράσεις; ('What are you saying? You know, but you will not tell us[?]'), and l. 359: ποῖον λόγον; λέγ' αὖθις, ὡς μᾶλλον μάθω ('To say what? Tell me again, so that I can understand it better!').
741. *an adept*] 'a person who has been initiated into any system of spiritual knowledge' (*OED*).

Of Greek and Frank philosophy; thou numberest
The flowers, and thou measurest the stars;
Thou severest element from element;
745 Thy spirit is present in the past, and sees
The birth of this old world through all its cycles
Of desolation and of loveliness,
And when man was not, and how man became
The monarch and the slave of this low sphere,
750 And all its narrow circles — it is much —
I honour thee, and would be what thou art
Were I not what I am; — but the unborn hour,
Cradled in fear and hope, conflicting storms,
Who shall unveil? nor thou, nor I, nor any
755 Mighty or wise. I apprehended not
What thou hast taught me, but I now perceive
That thou art no interpreter of dreams;

742. *Frank*] 'A name given by the nations bordering on the Levant to an individual of Western nationality' (*OED n.* 2), here used as an adjective to mean 'Western, non-Greek'. This Levantine usage is supported by the comparison in *Rognoni (2018a)* with a line from Byron's 'The Isles of Greece': 'Trust not for freedom to the Franks' (*Don Juan* iii 766). *numberest*] 'takest note of' (*Concordance*).
747. *loveliness,*] loveliness; *1829, 1839, 1840.*
750. *its narrow circles —*] Inserted by S. in *HM 329* above *that it inherits —* canc. The cancelled reading is found in *Nbk 21* p. 111 (see *BSM* xvi 116–17). *much —*] much. *1829, 1839, 1840.*
752–3. *the unborn / … hope*] Locock 1911 cps *PU* IV 61–2.
752. *am; —*] am — *HM 329*; am; *1822, 1829, 1839, 1840.*
754–5. *nor thou, nor I, nor any / Mighty or wise.*] Inserted with a caret in *HM 329* in S.'s hand.
754. *nor thou,*] nor thou *HM 329*; Nor thou, *1822, 1829, 1839, 1840.*
755. *apprehended*] *Errata, Rossetti 1878*; apprehend *HM 329, 1822, 1829, 1839, 1840.* Forman guessed the correct reading in *Forman 1876–7* iii 79.
756. *I now*] now I *1834.*
757. *dreams;*] *1822, 1829, 1839, 1840*; dreams *HM 329.*

Thou dost not own that art, device, or God,
Can make the future present, — let it come!
760 Moreover thou disdainest us and ours;
Thou art as God whom thou contemplatest.

Ahasuerus
Disdain thee? not the worm beneath thy feet!
The Fathomless has care for meaner things
Than thou canst dream, and has made Pride for those
765 Who would be what they may not, or would seem
That which they are not. — Sultan! talk no more
Of thee and me, the future and the past;

758-9. *Thou ... present*] These lines require another 'that' to make their syntax work: 'Thou dost not own that art, device, or God, / [that] Can make the future present'.
758. In *HM 329 then* is altered to *that*, and the *a* of *that* is overwritten in dark ink, possibly in S.'s hand.
759. *present, —*] present — *1822, 1829, 1839, 1840*.
760-1. Mahmud suggests that while Ahasuerus has the haughtiness and superiority of God ('thou disdainest us and ours'), he only appears to be ('art as') like him. Cp. *PU* I 450 and note.
760. *Moreover*] Moreover, *1829*. *ours;*] *1822, 1839*; ours *HM 329*; ours: *1829*; ours! *1840*.
761. *God*] God, *1822, 1829, 1839, 1840*.
762. Cp. the words of 'the mangled man' in *The Assassins* (1814-15) ch. iii: '"The great Tyrant is baffled even in success ... Joy! Joy to his tortured foe! Triumph to the worm whom he tramples under his feet!"' (*Prose Works* 134). *thee?*] thee?— *1822, 1829, 1839, 1840*. *worm beneath thy feet*] Cp. l. 426 and note. *thy*] my *1829, 1834, 1839, 1840*.
763-4. *The ... dream*] Cp. Hamlet's retort to Horatio at *Hamlet* I v 166-7: 'There are more things in heaven and earth, Horatio, / Than are dreamt of in your philosophy.' Byron used these lines as the epigraph to *Manfred*.
763. *The Fathomless*] *Concordance* glosses 'Almighty God, the Deity'. But Ahasuerus refers to a divine force that is neither possible to define nor to name; cp. Demogorgon's 'the deep truth is imageless' (*PU* II iv 116).
764. *Pride*] pride *1822, 1829, 1839, 1840*.
766. *not. —*] *Nbk 21*; not— *HM 329*; not. *1822, 1829, 1839, 1840*.

> But look on that which cannot change — the One,
> The unborn and the undying. Earth and ocean,
770 Space, and the isles of life or light that gem
> The sapphire floods of interstellar air,
> This firmament pavilioned upon chaos,
> With all its cressets of immortal fire,
> Whose outwall, bastioned impregnably

768. *change* —] *Nbk 21, 1822, 1829, 1839, 1840*; change *HM 329. the One*] Partially overwritten in *HM 329*, possibly in S.'s hand. Cp. *Adonais* 460 and note. *One,*] *Rossetti 1870*; One *HM 329, 1822, 1839, 1840*; one *1829*.
769-71. *Earth ... air*] Cp. *Fragments of an Unfinished Drama* (no. 436) 28-9: 'And lastly light whose interfusion dawns / On the dark space of interstellar air —'.
769. *unborn*] unborn, *1829, 1839, 1840*. *and the undying*] and undying *1829, 1834*. *ocean,*] *1822, 1829, 1839, 1840*; ocean *HM 329*.
770. *Space,*] *Nbk 21, 1822, 1829, 1839, 1840*; Space *HM 329*.
771. Cp. *Lines connected with Hellas* A l. 21. *air,*] *1822, 1829, 1839, 1840*; air *HM 329*.
772-3. See 'A star has fallen upon the Earth — a torch' (*Lines connected with Hellas* L) ll. 5-6.
772. *chaos,*] *1822, 1829, 1839, 1840*; chaos *HM 329*.
773-4. *cressets ... outwall*] Cp. Lucretius, *De Re. Nat.* i 73: 'flammantia moenia mundi' ('the flaming walls of the world'); *Turner* 278 notes part of this parallel.
773. *cressets of immortal fire*] stars; a 'cresset' is a 'vessel of iron or the like, made to hold grease or oil [...] to be burnt for light; usually mounted on the top of a pole or building, or suspended from a roof' (*OED* 1a). *fire,*] *1822, 1829, 1839, 1840*; fire — *Nbk 21*; fire *HM 329*.
774-5. *Whose outwall ... thoughts*] Cp. Lucretius, *De Re. Nat.* iii 14-17:

> nam simul ac ratio tua coepit vociferari
> naturam rerum, divina mente coortam,
> diffugiunt animi terrores, moenia mundi
> discedunt [...]

('For as soon as your reasoning begins to proclaim the nature of things revealed by your divine mind, away flee the mind's terrors, the walls of the world open out [...]').

774. *outwall,*] *Nbk 21, 1822, 1840*; outwall *HM 329*; outwalls, *1829, 1834, 1839*. 'An outer wall of a building or enclosure' (*OED* 1), here used figuratively. *bastioned impregnably*] See *Charles the First* I iii 55 and note.

775 Against the escape of boldest thoughts, repels them
    As Calpe the Atlantic clouds — this Whole
    Of suns, and worlds, and men, and beasts, and flowers,
    With all the silent or tempestuous workings
    By which they have been, are, or cease to be,

775. *Against ... escape ... boldest*] Written above *Beyond ... flight ... speediest* canc. in S.'s hand in *HM 329*. The reading is *Against ... flight ... boldest* in *Nbk 21* p. 114 (see *BSM* xvi 120–1).

776. *As Calpe the Atlantic clouds*] The Romans referred to the Rock of Gibraltar as *Mons Calpe*; it is referred to by this name in Byron, *Childe Harold's Pilgrimage* II (1812) xxii l. 1: 'Through Calpe's straits survey the steepy shore'. S.'s image of the Rock repelling Atlantic clouds refers to a meteorological phenomenon known as the 'Gibraltar levanter' (after the easterly wind called the Levant) whereby an orographic banner cloud is created over the Rock. The phenomenon makes it appear as if the Rock is preventing the clouds moving from the Atlantic to mainland Spain. For another intricate meteorological image, see *TL* 155–7. *Whole*] whole *1829, 1839, 1840*. The initial capital is overwritten in *HM 329* probably in S.'s hand.

776–85. *this Whole ... to be.*] Ahasuerus' lines have similarities to Prospero's speech in *The Tempest* IV i 148–58:

>   These our actors
> (As I foretold you) were all spirits, and
> Are melted into air, into thin air,
> And like the baseless fabric of this vision,
> The cloud-capp'd tow'rs, the gorgeous palaces,
> The solemn temples, the great globe itself,
> Yea, all which it inherit, shall dissolve,
> And like this insubstantial pageant faded
> Leave not a rack behind. We are such stuff
> As dreams are made on; and our little life
> Is rounded with a sleep.

There are also parallels in the speech of Charon in Lucian, *Charon, or the Inspectors* 19 (quoted in the note to ll. 199–200 above). See also Young, *Night Thoughts* 'Night VII' 862–71 (quoted in part in the note to ll. 197–210 above). There may also be echoes here of Sigismundo's speech at the end of Act II of Calderón's *La vida es sueño* (Life is a dream) and Plato, *Republic* 476c; for discussion of these two passages, see the headnote to Appendix E (*It is a singular world we live in — and*) in Volume 6 of the present edition.

777. *flowers,*] *1822, 1829, 1839, 1840*; flowers *HM 329*.
779. *be,*] *1822, 1829, 1839, 1840*; be *HM 329*.

780   Is but a vision — all that it inherits
      Are motes of a sick eye, bubbles and dreams;
      Thought is its cradle and its grave, nor less
      The future and the past are idle shadows
      Of thought's eternal flight — they have no being.
785   Nought is but that which feels itself to be.

Mahmud
      What meanest thou? Thy words stream like a tempest
      Of dazzling mist within my brain — they shake
      The earth on which I stand, and hang like night
      On Heaven above me. What can they avail?
790   They cast on all things surest, brightest, best,
      Doubt, insecurity, astonishment.

Ahasuerus
      Mistake me not! All is contained in each.
      Dodona's forest to an acorn's cup

780. *vision —*] vision;— *1822, 1829, 1839, 1840.*
781. *motes of a sick eye*] 'motes' are literally particles of dust or, figuratively, faults (see *OED* 1a, 2a). Cp. *Matthew* vii 3–4 ('And why beholdest thou the mote that is in thy brother's eye, but considerest not the beam that is in thine own eye? Or how wilt though say to thy brother, Let me pull out the mote out of thine eye; and, behold, a beam *is* in thine own eye?') and *Hamlet* I i 112 ('A mote it is to trouble the mind's eye'). *bubbles and dreams;*] Cp. Queen Margaret in *Richard III* IV iv 88: 'A dream of what thou wast, a garish flag / To be the aim of every dangerous shot; / A sign of dignity, a breath, a bubble'. In *HM* 329 bubbles *&* dreams; is inserted in S.'s hand. *bubbles*] bubbles, *1840*.
784. *thought's*] The apostrophe is in darker ink in *HM* 329 and may have been inserted by S. *being.*] being: *1822*; being; *1829, 1839, 1840.*
785. *Donovan* cps *DP*: 'All things exist as they are perceived: at least in relation to the percipient' (*Reiman (2002)* para. 42); see also, in the same paragraph, S.'s claim that poetry 'compels us to feel that which we perceive, and to imagine that which we know.' *which*] it *1829, 1834, 1839, 1840.*
786. *Thy*] *1822*; thy *HM 329, 1829, 1839, 1840. stream*] Inserted in S.'s hand above *are* canc. in *HM 329*.
788. *hang like*] The careted insertion of the word *hang* and the overwriting of *like* in *HM 329* are both in S.'s hand.
790. *things*] things, *1829, 1839, 1840.*
791. Cp. *Hymn to Intellectual Beauty* A l. 31: 'Doubt, Chance and mutability'.
792-5. *All is … present.*] *Locock 1911* cps S.'s letter to Peacock of [?2] May 1820 where he recalls 'a theory I once imagined, that in everything any man ever wrote,

Is that which has been, or will be, to that
795　Which is — the absent to the present. Thought
　　　Alone, and its quick elements, Will, Passion,
　　　Reason, Imagination, cannot die;
　　　They are, what that which they regard appears,
　　　The stuff whence mutability can weave

---

spoke, acted, or imagined, is contained, as it were, an allegorical idea of his own future life, as the acorn contains the oak' (*L* ii 192). These lines recall *Ecclesiastes* i 9 ('The thing that hath been, it *is that* which shall be; and that which is done *is* that which shall be done: and *there is* no new *thing* under the sun') and iii 15 ('That which hath been is now; and that which is to be hath already been; and God requireth that which is past.')
792. *each.*] each, *1829, 1839.*
793. *Dodona's forest*] Dodona is a city in Epirus in the northwest of mainland Greece. An oak forest outside the city was home to the oracle of Zeus. Ahasuerus' reference to Dodona's forest is significant for three reasons: first, Dodona was supposed to be the oldest of the oracular sites (in contrast to the youth of 'an acorn's cup'); second, because, like Ahasuerus, the oaks themselves were thought to have prophetic qualities, as mentioned in *Odyssey* xiv 327–8 and *Argonautica* i 526–7, which describes the use of oak from Dodona as part of the construction of the Argo that is itself presented elsewhere in that poem as having prophetic abilities (and to which S. refers in l. 1072); and finally because in a discussion about floods in *Meteorologica* I 352a-b, Aristotle claims:

> the so-called flood of Deucalion took place largely in the Hellenic lands and particularly in old Hellas, that is, the country round Dodona and the Acheloüs, a river which has frequently changed its course. Here dwelt the Selloi and the people then called Greeks and now called Hellenes.

Thus Dodona is a particularly apt choice for Ahasuerus' image as it is the original land of the Hellenes. Dodona is referred to in Byron, *Childe Harold's Pilgrimage* II liii ll. 1–2: 'Oh! where, Dodona! is thine aged grove, / Prophetic fount, and oracle divine?'. *cup*] cup, *1829.*
794. *been,*] been *1829, 1839, 1840.*
795–7. *Thought ... Imagination*] Locock notes '[t]he same five abstractions are mentioned together' in *PU* II iv 10–12 (*Locock 1911* ii 471).
798. *are,*] are *1829, 1839, 1840.* regard] *1822, 1829, 1839, 1840;* regard, *HM 329.* appears,] *1822, 1829, 1839, 1840;* appears *HM 329.*
799–800. *mutability ... dominion o'er*] Cp. The first of Spenser's 'Two Cantos of Mutabilitie' in *Faerie Queene* VII vi 4 ll. 1–2: 'So likewise did this *Titanesse* aspire, / Rule and dominion to her selfe to gaine'.

800   All that it hath dominion o'er, worlds, worms,
      Empires and superstitions — what has thought
      To do with time or place or circumstance?
      Wouldst thou behold the future? — ask and have!
      Knock and it shall be opened — look, and lo!
805   The coming age is shadowed on the past
      As on a glass.

Mahmud
                    Wild — wilder thoughts convulse
      My spirit — did not Mahomet the Second
      Win Stamboul?

Ahasuerus
                    Thou wouldst ask that giant spirit
      The written fortunes of thy house and faith.
810   Thou wouldst cite one out of the grave to tell
      How what was born in blood must die. —

800. *o'er,*] o'er,— *1829, 1839, 1840.*
801. *Empires*] Empires, *1822, 1829, 1839, 1840. superstitions — what*] superstitions. What *1822, 1829, 1839, 1840.*
802. *time or place*] time, or place, *1822, 1829, 1839, 1840.*
804. *Knock and it shall be opened*] See *Matthew* vii 7 (also *Luke* xi 9): 'Ask, and it shall be given you; seek, and ye shall find; knock, and it shall be opened unto you'. *look, and*] *Nbk 21, 1829, 1839, 1840*; look and, *HM 329, 1822.*
805. *past*] past, *1839, 1840.*
806. *glass*] mirror. Cp. l. 131 and *Macbeth* IV i 119 where Macbeth sees in a mirror successive generations of Banquo's family on the throne. *Wild —*] Wild, *1822, 1829, 1839, 1840.*
807-8. *did not Mahomet ... Stamboul*] Mehmed II, known as 'the Conqueror', ruled the Ottoman Empire 1444-46 and 1451-81. He captured Constantinople on 29 May 1453 after a fifty-three day siege and made it the Ottoman capital under the name Stamboul. See ll. 814-46 and note for an account of this siege.
807. *did*] Did *1822, 1829, 1839, 1840.*
811. *die. —*] *Nbk 21;* die — *HM 329;* die. *1822, 1829, 1839, 1840.*

Mahmud

           Thy words
  Have power on me! — I see —

Ahasuerus

         What hearest thou?

Mahmud
  A far whisper —
  Terrible silence —

Ahasuerus
      What succeeds?

Mahmud

           The sound ⁽⁶⁾
815 As of the assault of an imperial city —
  The hiss of inextinguishable fire, —
  The roar of giant cannon; — the earthquaking
  Fall of vast bastions and precipitous towers,
  The shock of crags shot from strange engin'ry,

---

812. *me! —*] me! *1822, 1829, 1839, 1840. hearest*] *1822, 1829, 1839, 1840*; hearest, HM 329.
814–46] As S.'s Note 6 attests (see notes), the description of the 1453 Ottoman siege of Constantinople is based on Gibbon, *Decline and Fall*, Vol. VI ch. lxviii (Womersley, ed., iii 941–67). For a summary of the verbal parallels, see Ackermann, *Quellen* 53.
814–15. *sound* ⁽⁶⁾ *... city*] sound ( ) ... city *1822*. See S.'s Note 6.
814. *silence —*] silence. *1822, 1829, 1839, 1840.*
815. *city —*] city, *1822, 1829, 1839, 1840.*
816. *fire, —*] fire, *1822, 1829, 1839, 1840.*
817. *cannon; —*] cannon; *1822*. Gibbon makes much of the Ottoman cannons, devoting a paragraph to a description of 'The Great Cannon of Mahomet' in *Decline and Fall* Vol. VI (1788) ch. lxviii (see Womersley, ed., iii 943–4).
819. As Gibbon notes in *Decline and Fall* Vol. VI ch. lxviii, the Ottomans also used older siege weapons: 'The cannon were intermingled with the mechanical engines for casting stones and darts' (Womersley, ed., iii 952). *crags*] 'broken lumps of rock' (*Concordance*). *engin'ry,*] *1822, 1839, 1840*; engin'ry HM 329; enginery *1829*. Cp. *Paradise Lost* vi 553; also *LMG* (no. 325) 107 and *Charles the First* I i 43.

820   The clash of wheels, and clang of armed hoofs
      And crash of brazen mail as of the wreck
      Of adamantine mountains — the mad blast
      Of trumpets, and the neigh of raging steeds,
      And shrieks of women whose thrill jars the blood
825   And one sweet laugh, most horrible to hear,
      As of a joyous infant waked and playing
      With its dead mother's breast, and now more loud
      The mingled battle-cry; — ha! hear I not
      'Εν τουτώ νικη' — 'Allah, Illah, Allah'?

820. *hoofs*] hoofs, *1822, 1829, 1839, 1840.*
821. *mail*] mail, *1829, 1839, 1840.*
822–4. *the mad blast ... jars the blood*] 'The cries of fear and of pain were drowned in the martial music of drums, trumpets, and attaballs' (*Decline and Fall*, Vol. VI (1788) ch. lxviii; Womersley, ed., iii 961).
822. *adamantine*] 'unable to be broken or dissolved; unbreakable; impenetrable' (*OED* 1a).
824. *thrill*] 'piercing sound' (*Concordance*). *blood*] blood, *1822, 1829, 1839, 1840.*
825. *laugh,*] *Nbk 21, 1822, 1829, 1839, 1840;* laugh *HM 329. hear,*] *1822, 1829, 1839, 1840;* hear *HM 329.*
826. *waked*] waked, *1840.*
827. *breast,*] breast; *1829, 1839, 1840.*
828. *The mingled battle-cry*] I.e., with reference to l. 829, the battle cries of both the Christian defenders and the Islamic attackers. *battle-cry; —*] battle cry; — *HM 329;* battle-cry,— *1822;* battle-cry— *1829, 1839, 1840.*
829. 'Εν τουτώ νικη'] *Rossetti 1878;* Εν τουτώ νικη — *HM 329, Nbk 21* p. 118; Ἐν τούτω νίκη. *1822, 1829, 1839, 1840.* The Greek phrase (ἐν) τούτῳ νίκα (the final letter of the third word should be an alpha rather S.'s eta) is usually translated as *in hoc signo vinces* or 'by this sign you will conquer' (lit. 'by this, conquer'). It is associated with Constantine's vision before his victory at the Battle of the Milvian Bridge as described by the Christian historian Eusebius in *Life of Constantine* i 28:

> About the time of the midday sun, when day was just turning, he said he saw with his own eyes, up in the sky and resting over the sun, a cross-shaped trophy formed from light, and a text attached to it which said, 'By this conquer'. (Trans. Averil Cameron and Stuart G. Hall (1999) 81)

Gibbon describes Constantine's vision in *Decline and Fall* Vol. II (1781) ch. xx (Womersley, ed., i 741); cp. *Q Mab* vii 219 and note. The battle-cry of the defenders

Ahasuerus
830   The sulphurous mist is raised, thou seest —

Mahmud
                                                      A chasm,
      As of two mountains in the wall of Stamboul;
      And in that ghastly breach the Islamites,
      Like giants on the ruins of a world,
      Stand in the light of sunrise. In the dust
835   Glimmers a kingless diadem, and one
      Of regal port has cast himself beneath
      The stream of war. Another proudly clad

---

of Constantinople in Mahmud's vision thus recalls ironically, at the end of the remnants of the Christian Roman Empire, its beginnings under Constantine. (For Constantine as the initiator of Roman Christianity see *TL* 284 and note.) S. additionally may have been aware that the flag of Ypsilantis's Sacred Battalion bore on one side an image of Constantine and his mother along with the words EN TOYTΩ NIKA ('by this, conquer'). The phrase is also found in the original Greek in [Charles Maturin], *Melmoth the Wanderer: A Tale*, 4 vols (1820) Vol. III ch. xii: 'The Suprema, though looking pale, bated not a jot of his pride. "These are my arms!" he exclaimed, pointing to the crucifixes, "and their inscription is εν-τουτω -νικα. I forbid a sword to be drawn, or a musket to be levelled. On, in the name of God."' '*Allah, Illah, Allah'?*] Allah, Illah, Allah! *HM 329, 1822, 1829*; Allah-illah-Allah! *1839, 1840*; 'Allah-illa-Allah'? *Rossetti 1878*. See l. 290 and note.

830. SD. Ahasuerus] Ahasueras *HM 329, 1822*.

830. sulphurous] sulphureous *1829, 1834, 1839, 1840*. raised,] *Nbk 21*; raised *HM 329*; raised— *1822, 1829, 1839, 1840*.

831. mountains] mountains, *1829, 1839, 1840*. Stamboul;] *1822, 1829, 1839, 1840*; Stamboul *HM 329*.

832-3. Islamites, ... world,] *1822, 1829, 1839, 1840*; Islamites ... world *HM 329*.

835-7. and one ... war] *Raizis* 196 notes: 'This may be Constantine Paleologus, the last Greek Emperor of Byzantium.' Palæologus' death during the assault of Constantinople by the Turks on 29 May 1453 is described thus by Gibbon in *Decline and Fall* Vol. VI ch. lxviii: 'Amidst these multitudes, the emperor, who accomplished all the duties of a general and a soldier, was long seen, and finally lost. [...] The prudent despair of Constantine cast away the purple: amidst the tumult he fell by an unknown hand, and his body was buried under a mountain of the slain' (Womersley, ed., iii 962).

837. stream] steam *1834*. *Another*] Another, *1829, 1839, 1840*.

In golden arms spurs a Tartarian barb
Into the gap, and with his iron mace
840   Directs the torrent of that tide of men,
And seems — he is, — Mahomet! —

Ahasuerus
                                   What thou seest
Is but the ghost of thy forgotten dream.
A dream itself, yet less, perhaps, than that
Thou callst reality. Thou mayst behold
845   How cities, on which Empire sleeps enthroned,
Bow their towered crests to Mutability.
Poised by the flood, e'en on the height thou holdest,
Thou mayst now learn how the full tide of power
Ebbs to its depths — inheritor of glory,

837–41 Another ... Mahomet!] Cp.: 'The sultan himself on horseback, with an iron mace in his hand, was the spectator and judge of their valour: he was surrounded by ten thousand of his domestic troops, whom he reserved for the decisive occasions; and the tide of battle was directed and impelled by his voice and eye' (*Decline and Fall*, ed. Womersley, iii 960–1).

838. *arms*] arms, *1829, 1839, 1840*. *Tartarian barb*] 'barb' is a term for a 'horse of the breed imported from Barbary and Morocco, noted for great speed and endurance' (*OED n.*³ 1); here the horse is from Tartar (the region of central Asia extending eastward from the Caspian Sea).

839–40. *gap, ... men,*] *1822, 1829, 1839, 1840*; gap ... men *HM 329*.

841. *is, —*] *Nbk 21*; is, *HM 329*; is— *1822, 1829, 1839, 1840*. *Mahomet! —*] Mahomet! *1822, 1839, 1840*; Mahomet. *1829*.

842. *dream.*] dream; *1829, 1839, 1840*.

843. *yet*] *1822, 1829, 1839, 1840*; yet, *HM 329*. *less*] I.e. 'less a dream' (*Locock 1911* ii 471).

844. *callst*] *Nbk 21*; callest *HM 329*; call'st *1822, 1829, 1839, 1840*. *reality*] The correction of *reallity* to *reality* in *HM 329* is possibly in S.'s hand.

845. *Empire*] *1822*; empire *HM 329, 1829, 1839, 1840*. The word *Empire* is cancelled and underlined (indicating restitution) in *Nbk 21* p. 214 (see *BSM* xvi 210–11).

846. *Mutability*] mutability *1822, 1829, 1839, 1840*. The small initial letter is overwritten with a capital in Williams's hand in *HM 329*; the reading is *Mutability* in *Nbk 21* p. 214 (see *BSM* xvi 210–11).

847. *flood, ... holdest,*] *1822, 1829, 1839, 1840*; flood ... holdest *HM 329*.

849. *depths —*] depths.— *1822, 1829, 1839, 1840*. *inheritor*] Inheritor *1822, 1829, 1839, 1840*. In *HM 329* a small *i* is written in what appears to be S.'s hand over the capital *I*. The reading is *inheritor* in *Nbk 21* p. 214 (see *BSM* xvi 210–11). *glory,*] *1822, 1829, 1839, 1840*; glory *HM 329*.

850 Conceived in darkness, born in blood, and nourished
   With tears and toil, thou seest the mortal throes
   Of that whose birth was but the same. The Past
   Now stands before thee like an incarnation
   Of the To-come; yet wouldst thou commune with
855 That portion of thyself which was ere thou
   Didst start for this brief race whose crown is death;
   Dissolve, with that strong faith and fervent passion
   Which called it from the uncreated deep,
   Yon cloud of war, with its tempestuous phantoms
860 Of raging death; and draw with mighty will
   The imperial shade hither —

                                    [*Exit* AHASUERUS.

852–4. *The Past ... To-come*] Cp. Lines connected with Hellas A l. 189.
852. *Past*] Alt. from *past* by S. in *HM 329*.
853. *incarnation*] Incarnation *1822, 1829, 1839, 1840*. In *HM 329* a small *i* is written over the capital *I* in what appears to be S.'s hand.
854. *To-come;*] Alt. from *to-come*, in what appears to be S.'s hand in *HM 329*.
856. *death;*] *1829, 1839, 1840*; death *HM 329*; death, *1822*.
857. *Dissolve,*] *Nbk 21*; Dissolve *HM 329, 1822, 1829, 1839, 1840. and*] Inserted (in the form of an ampersand) in *HM 329* in what appears to be S.'s hand.
858. *it*] Inserted above *them* canc. in *HM 329* in what appears to be S.'s hand. *uncreated*] 'Not brought into existence by a special act of creation; of a self-existent or eternal nature' (*OED* 1); a usage found in *Paradise Lost* ii 150: 'In the wide womb of uncreated night'. *deep,*] *1822, 1829, 1839, 1840*; deep *HM 329*. 'An indefinable abyss of thought, imagination, space or time' (*Concordance*). Cp. *PU* I 462, II iii 54, 80.
859. *war,*] *Nbk 21, 1822, 1829, 1839, 1840*; war *HM 329*.
861. *SD*. After '*Exit* Ahasuerus', Rossetti adds the SD 'The Phantom of Mahomet the Second *appears*' in *Rossetti 1870* and *Rossetti 1878* (see *Rossetti 1878* ii 456). *Woodberry (1901)* suggests analogies with the Phantasm of Jupiter in *PU* I 240 ff. Douglas Bush, *Mythology and the Romantic Tradition in English Poetry* (1937) 163 cps Lucan, *Pharsalia* vi 776 ff. where the witch Erichtho commands a dead man to speak.
861. *hither* —] hither. *1822, 1829, 1839, 1840*.

Mahmud
                              Approach!

Phantom
                                          I come
Thence whither thou must go! The grave is fitter
To take the living than give up the dead;
Yet has thy faith prevailed and I am here.
865 The heavy fragments of the power which fell
When I arose, like shapeless crags and clouds,
Hang round my throne on the abyss, and voices
Of strange lament soothe my supreme repose,
Wailing for glory never to return. —
870   A later Empire nods in its decay:
The autumn of a greener faith is come,
And wolfish Change, like winter, howls to strip

862–4. *The grave … here*] Cp. the Ghost of Darius in *Persae* 689–92: χοὶ κατὰ χθονὸς θεοὶ / λαβεῖν ἀμείνους εἰσὶν ἢ μεθιέναι. / ὅμως δ' ἐκείνοις ἐνδυναστεύσας ἐγὼ / ἥκω. ('the gods below the earth are better at taking people in than at letting them go; nevertheless, holding as I do a position of power among them, I have come here.')
862. *whither*] The second letter of this word is inserted in what appears to be S.'s hand in *HM 329*. *The*] *Nbk 21, 1822, 1829, 1839, 1840*; the *HM 329*.
863. *living*] living, *1829, 1839, 1840*. *dead;*] *1822, 1829, 1839, 1840*; dead. *Nbk 21*; dead *HM 329*.
864. Cp. Edmund in the final scene of *King Lear*: 'The wheel is come full circle, I am here' (V iii 175). *prevailed*] prevail'd, *1822, 1829*; prevailed, *1839, 1840*. *here.*] *Nbk 21, 1822, 1829, 1839, 1840*; here *HM 329*.
866. *arose,*] *1822, 1829, 1839, 1840*; arose *HM 329*. *clouds,*] *1822, 1829, 1839, 1840*; clouds *HM 329*.
868. *repose,*] *Nbk 21, 1822, 1829, 1839, 1840*; repose *HM 329*.
869. *return. —*] *1822, 1829, 1839, 1840*; return — *HM 329*.
870. *1829* omits the indentation. *decay:*] *1822*; decay *HM 329*; decay; *1829, 1839, 1840*.
871. *come,*] *1822, 1829, 1839, 1840*; come *HM 329*.
872. *Change,*] change, *1822, 1829, 1839, 1840*. *winter,*] *1822, 1829, 1839, 1840*; winter *HM 329*.

The foliage in which Fame, the eagle, built
Her aerie, while Dominion whelped below.
875 The storm is in its branches, and the frost
Is on its leaves, and the blank deep expects
Oblivion on oblivion, spoil on spoil,
Ruin on ruin — thou art slow, my son;
The Anarchs of the world of darkness keep
880 A throne for thee round which thine empire lies
Boundless and mute, and for thy subjects thou,
Like us, shalt rule the ghosts of murdered life,
The phantoms of the powers who rule thee now,
Mutinous passions, and conflicting fears

873-4. *The foliage ... Her aerie*] The mention of 'foliage' recalls the following description in Pope, *The Temple of Fame* (1715) 137-40:

> The Temple shakes, the sounding Gates unfold,
> Wide Vaults appear, and Roofs of fretted Gold:
> Rais'd on a thousand Pillars, wreath'd around
> With Lawrel-Foliage, and with Eagles crown'd

At the beginning of the third book of Chaucer's *The House of Fame*, on which Pope's poem is based, the narrator has been transported to the House of Fame by an eagle.
877. *oblivion, ... on spoil,*] *1822, 1829, 1839*; oblivion ... on spoil *HM 329*.
878. *ruin — thou*] ruin:—Thou *1822*; ruin:—thou *1829*; ruin: thou *1839, 1840*. *slow,*] *1822, 1829, 1839, 1840*; slow *HM 329*. *son;*] son; *1822, 1829, 1839, 1840*; son *HM 329*.
879-80. Locock 1911 ii 471 cps *PU* I 195 ff. (see note to this passage).
879. *Anarchs*] anarchs *1829*. The alteration of the first letter to a capital in *HM 329* is probably in S.'s hand.
880. *thee*] thee, *1822, 1829, 1839, 1840*.
881. *Boundless and mute*] Cp. *Ozymandias* (no. 145) ll. 12-13 'Round the decay / Of that colossal Wreck, boundless and bare'. *mute,*] mute; *1822, 1829, 1839, 1840*. *thou,*] *1822, 1829, 1839, 1840*; thou *HM 329*.
882. *shalt*] shall *1829, 1834, 1839, 1840*. *life,*] *1822, 1829, 1839, 1840*; life *HM 329*.
883. *now,*] now— *1822, 1829, 1839, 1840*.
884. *passions,*] passions *1839, 1840*. *fears*] fears, *1822, 1829, 1839, 1840*.

885 And hopes that sate themselves on dust and die,
Stripped of their mortal strength, as thou of thine.
Islam must fall, but we will reign together
Over its ruins in the world of death —
And if the trunk be dry, yet shall the seed
890 Unfold itself even in the shape of that
Which gathers birth in its decay. — Woe! woe!
To the weak people tangled in the grasp
Of its last spasms.

Mahmud
                      Spirit, woe to all! —
Woe to the wronged and the avenger! Woe
895 To the destroyer, woe to the destroyed!
Woe to the dupe, and woe to the deceiver!
Woe to the oppressed, and woe to the oppressor!
Woe both to those that suffer and inflict,
Those who are born and those who die! but say,

---

885. *die,*] die!— *1822*; die! *1829, 1839, 1840*. The compositor of *1822* appears to have read the comma after *die* in *HM 329* together with the dot above the *i* of *thine* in l. 886 as an exclamation mark.
887. *Islam must fall*] Cp. ll. 221-4 and the note to ll. 211-24. *together*] together, *1829*.
888. *death —*] death:— *1822, 1829, 1839, 1840*.
891. *its*] *1822, 1829, 1839, 1840*; it's *HM 329* (the insertion of the redundant apostrophe is probably in S.'s hand). *decay. —*] decay — *HM 329*; decay. *1822, 1829, 1839, 1840*.
893. *all!* —] all! *1822, 1829, 1839, 1840*.
894. This line is inserted with a caret in *HM 329* in S.'s hand. *avenger! Woe*] *1822, 1829, 1839, 1840*; avenger! woe *HM 329*.
895. *destroyer,*] *1822, 1829, 1839, 1840*; destroyer; *HM 329*.
896. *dupe,*] *1822, 1829, 1839, 1840*; dupe; *HM 329*.
897. *oppressed,*] *1822, 1829, 1839, 1840*; oppressed; *HM 329*.
898. *inflict,*] inflict. *HM 329*; inflict; *1822, 1829, 1839, 1840*.
899–900. *say, … am,*] *1822, 1829, 1839*; say … am *HM 329*; say … am, *1840*.
899. *born*] born, *1829, 1839, 1840*. *die! but*] die! But *1829, 1839, 1840*.

900 Imperial shadow of the thing I am,
When, how, by whom, Destruction must accomplish
Her consummation?

Phantom
Ask the cold pale Hour,
Rich in reversion of impending death,
When he shall fall, upon whose ripe grey hairs
905 Sit Care and Sorrow and Infirmity,
The weight which Crime, whose wings are plumed with years,

900. 'That is, as long as he lives Mahmud, too, is what Mahomet II was once' (*Raizis* 196).
902–9. *Ask ... Fond wretch!*] Cp. *PU* I 772–9 and note.
902–3. *Hour, ... death,*] 1822, 1829, 1839, 1840; Hour ... death *HM 329*.
902. *Hour*] 'any particular moment or period of time' (*Concordance*). Cp. *PU* III iii 69 and *Adonais* 4–9 (and see note to these lines).
903. 'The Hour will be enriched by what reverts to it on Mahmud's death' (*Major Works*). 'reversion' = 'The state of being to be possessed after the death of the present possessor' (Johnson, *Dictionary of the English Language* (1755) 1).
904. *he*] he 1822, 1839, 1840. *fall,*] Nbk 21; fall *HM 329, 1822, 1829, 1839, 1840*.
905–6. *Care ... Sorrow ... Infirmity, / ... Crime,*] Care ... Sorrow ... Infirmity / ... Crime *HM 329*; Care, ... Sorrow, ... Infirmity— / ... Crime, 1822; care, ... sorrow, ... infirmity— / ... crime, 1829; care, ... sorrow, ... infirmity— / ... Crime, 1839, 1840. The small initial letters of *care* and *crime* are capitalised and the initial capitals of *Sorrow* and *Infirmity* are overwritten in darker ink in *HM 329*, whether in S.'s hand or Williams's is uncertain.
906–7. *Crime, ... to heart*] A sort of perversion of Eros as described in Plato, *Symposium* 195b and 195e (see the note to *PU* I 772–9 referenced in the note to ll. 902–9 above); the translations below are S.'s:

> he escapes with the swiftness of wings from old age; a thing in itself sufficiently swift, since it overtakes us sooner than there is need; and which Love, who delights in the intercourse of the young, hates[.] (*Notopoulos* 434)

> For Love walks not upon the earth, nor over the heads of men, which are not indeed very soft; but he dwells within, and treads on the softest of existing things, having established his habitation within the souls and inmost nature of Gods and men; (*Notopoulos* 435)

906. *years,*] 1822, 1829, 1839, 1840; years *HM 329*.

    Leaves in his flight from ravaged heart to heart
    Over the heads of men, under which burden
    They bow themselves unto the grave. Fond wretch!
910 He leans upon his crutch and talks of years
    To come, and how in hours of youth renewed
    He will renew lost joys, and —

Voice without

                        Victory! Victory!
                              [*The Phantom vanishes.*

Mahmud
    What sound of the importunate earth has broken
    My mighty trance?

Voice without

                        Victory! Victory!

Mahmud
915 Weak lightning before darkness! poor faint smile
    Of dying Islam! Voice which art the response
    Of hollow weakness! Do I wake and live?
    Were there such things, or may the unquiet brain,
    Vexed by the wise mad talk of the old Jew,

---

909. *grave. Fond*] *Rossetti 1870*; grave. fond *HM 329*; grave: fond *1822, 1829, 1839, 1840*. *wretch!*] *1822, 1829, 1839, 1840*; wretch *HM 329*.
910. *crutch*] crutch, *1822, 1829, 1839, 1840*.
912. *Victory! Victory!*] Victory victory! *1829, 1839, 1840*.
914. *trance?*] *1822, 1829, 1839, 1840*; trance. *HM 329*. *Victory! Victory!*] Victory! victory! *1829, 1839, 1840*.
918-20. *Were there ... fear?*] *Major Works* cps *Macbeth* I iii 81-3:

> Were such things here as we do speak about?
> Or have we eaten on the insane root
> That takes the reason prisoner?

918. *things,*] *1822*; things *HM 329*; things? *1829, 1839, 1840*. *brain,*] *1822, 1829, 1839, 1840*; brain *HM 329*.
919. *Jew,*] *1822, 1829, 1839, 1840*; Jew *HM 329*.

920 Have shaped itself these shadows of its fear?
     It matters not! — for nought we see or dream,
     Possess or lose or grasp at can be worth
     More than it gives or teaches. Come what may,
     The future must become the Past, and I
925 As they were, to whom once this present hour,
     This gloomy crag of Time to which I cling
     Seemed an Elysian isle of peace and joy
     Never to be attained. — I must rebuke
     This drunkenness of triumph ere it die,

920. *these*] Alt. from *the* in S.'s hand in *HM 329*.
921. *not! —*] *1822, 1829, 1839, 1840*; not — *Nbk 21*. The punctuation after *not* in *HM 329* is unclear; there is a dash with a vertical line above but no dot beneath. *dream,*] *1829, 1839, 1840*; dream *Nbk 21, HM 329, 1822*.
922. *Possess ... lose ... at*] Possess, ... lose, ... at, *1822, 1829, 1839, 1840*. A comma after *lose* is cancelled in *HM 329*.
923. *may,*] *1829, 1839, 1840*; may *HM 329, 1822*.
924–30. There is no draft of these lines in *Nbk 21*.
924. *must ... and I*] These words appear to have been inserted in *HM 329* and may be in S.'s hand. *Past,*] past, *1822, 1829, 1839, 1840*.
925. *were,*] *1839, 1840*; were *HM 329, 1822, 1829*. *hour,*] *1822, 1829, 1839, 1840*; hour *HM 329*.
926. Woodberry (1901) cps *The Cenci* III i 247 (see the note to III i 247–57). *Time*] time *1822, 1829, 1839, 1840*. *to ... cling*] The careted insertion of the word *to* and the insertion of *cling* above *inhabit* canc. in *HM 329* are in S.'s hand. *cling*] cling, *1822, 1829, 1839, 1840*.
927. *Seemed*] Inserted in *HM 329* above *Was* canc. in S.'s hand. *Elysian isle*] Cp. *Epipsychidion* 539. 'Elysian' refers to the habitation of the blessed dead in Greek mythology.
928–30. *I ... slaves!*] Inserted (apart from the comma after *die*) in *HM 329* in S.'s hand. Cp. *PVR*:

> The Turkish Empire is in its last stage of ruin, & it cannot be doubted but that the time is approaching when the deserts of Asia Minor & of Greece will be colonized by the overflowing population of countries less enslaved & debased, & that the climate & the scenery which was the birthplace of all that is wise & beautiful will not remain forever the spoil of wild beasts & unlettered Tartars. (*SC* vi 988)

929. *die,*] *1822, 1829, 1839, 1840*; die *HM 329*.

930   And dying, bring despair. Victory? poor slaves!
                                                    [*Exit* MAHMUD.

Voice without
      Shout in the jubilee of death! the Greeks
      Are as a brood of lions in the net
      Round which the kingly hunters of the earth
      Stand smiling. Anarchs, ye whose daily food
935   Are curses, groans and gold, the fruit of death
      From Thule to the girdle of the world,
      Come, feast! the board groans with the flesh of men —

930. despair. Victory?] despair. Victory! *1822*; despair.—Victory!— *1829, 1839, 1840*.
930. *SD*. The SD *(exit Mahmud)* is inserted in S.'s hand in *HM 329*.
931. *jubilee*] An 'occasion of joyful celebration or general rejoicing' (*OED* 4). *Greeks*] The Greeks *1822, 1829, 1839, 1840*.
932. *lions in the net*] For a possible allusion to Aeschylus' *Agamemnon*, see note to ll. 937–9. *net*] net, *1829, 1839, 1840*.
934. *Anarchs,*] Nbk 21, *1822, 1829, 1839, 1840*; Anarch *HM 329*.
935. *groans*] groans, *1822, 1829, 1839, 1840. gold,*] *1822, 1829, 1839, 1840*; gold *HM 329. death*] death, *1829, 1839, 1840*.
936. *Thule*] The ancient name for the most northerly region of the world (thought variously to be Norway, the Shetland Isles, Denmark, and Iceland). Thule is first mentioned by Polybius in his disagreement with Pytheas in *Histories* xxxiv 5. *girdle of the world,*] *1822, 1829, 1839, 1840*; girdle of the world *Nbk 21*; Girdle of the World *HM 329*. I.e. the equator.
937–9. These lines have parallels with Aeschylus' *Agamemnon*, which S. studied in 1820–1 (see note to ll. 52–75). See Aegisthus' speech in *Agamemnon* 1577–1611 where he describes his father, Thyestes, being served δαῖτα παιδείων κρεῶν (l. 1593, 'with a meal of his children's flesh') by Atreus. After this meal that was ἄσωτον [...] γένει (l. 1597, 'ruinous for the family'), Thyestes μόρον δ' ἄφερτον Πελοπίδαις ἐπεύχεται (l. 1600, 'called down an unendurable fate on the house of Pelops'), to which Aegisthus contributes through murdering Agamemnon, son of Atreus. In this context, the 'lions in the net' in l. 932 might recall Agamemnon's ensnarement with an ἀμφίβληστρον (net) to facilitate his murder in *Agamemnon* 1382 (he is elsewhere in the play described as a lion, e.g. at *Agamemnon* 1259). There may also be echoes here of another feast of human flesh: see note to l. 939.
937. *board groans*] board of groans *1834. men —*] Nbk 21, *1829, 1839, 1840*; men *HM 329*; men; *1822*.

The cup is foaming with a nation's blood,
Famine and Thirst await. Eat, drink and die!

Semichorus 1st
940   Victorious Wrong, with vulture's scream,
Salutes the risen sun, pursues the flying day!
I saw her, ghastly as a tyrant's dream,
Perch on the trembling pyramid of night
Beneath which earth and all her realms pavilioned lay
945   In visions of the dawning undelight. —

938. Cp. the Sibyl in *Aeneid* vi 86-7: 'bella, horrida bella / et Thybrim multo spumantem sanguine cerno' ('Wars, grim wars I see, and the Tiber foaming with streams of blood'). blood,] *Nbk 21*, *1822*, *1829*, *1839*, *1840*; blood *HM 329*.
939. *Famine and Thirst await*] Perhaps evoking the eternal posthumous punishment of Tantalus, tormented in the afterlife by unreachable fruit and water in retribution for his own feast of 'the flesh of men', when he served the flesh of Pelops to the gods: this punishment is described, for example, at *Odyssey* xi 582-92. *await. Eat, drink and die!*] await — eat, drink and die. *Nbk 21*; await. eat drink & die! *HM 329*; await! eat, drink, and die! *1822*; await:—eat, drink, and die! *1829*, *1839*; await: eat, drink, and die! *1840*. In *HM 329* the word *feast* (the first letter of which is barely legible) appears to have been altered to *eat*, whether in S.'s hand or Williams's is uncertain. *Eat, drink and die!*] See *Isaiah* xxii 13: 'let us eat and drink; for to morrow we shall die.'
940. *Wrong, ... scream,*] *1822*, *1829*, *1839*; Wrong ... scream *HM 329*. *vulture's*] vultures *Nbk 21*; vulture *HM 329*, *1822*, *1829*, *1839*, *1840*.
942. The commas inserted in dark ink in *HM 329* may be in S.'s hand. *her,*] her *1829*, *1839*, *1840*. *tyrant's*] *1822*, *1829*, *1839*, *1840*; tyrants *HM 329*.
943. *pyramid of night*] The conical shape of the earth's shadow in space. Cp. *Paradise Lost* iv 776 ('Now had night measured with her shadowy cone'), Earth in *PU* IV 444-5 ('I spin beneath my pyramid of night, / Which points into the heavens') and *TL* 22-3 ('the stars that gem / The cone of night'). *night*] night, *1822*, *1829*, *1839*, *1840*.
945. *visions*] *Nbk 21*, *1822*, *1829*, *1839*; Visions *HM 329*. *undelight. —*] undelight. *1822*, *1829*, *1839*, *1840*. Cp. *Ginevra* (no. 398) ll. 14-16: 'the weary glare / [Lay] like a chaos of unwelcome light / Vexing the sense with gorgeous undelight' and *Paradise Lost* iv 285-6: 'where the fiend / Saw undelighted all delight'. E. Marsh's suggested emendation to 'underlight' in the *London Mercury* ix (1924) 413 was refuted by Fabian Colenutt in the subsequent issue (527); the reading *undelight* in *Nbk 21* p. 171 and *HM 329* p. 43 is clear.

> Who shall impede her flight?
> Who rob her of her prey?
>
> *Voice without*
> Victory! Victory! Russia's famished eagles
> Dare not to prey beneath the crescent's light.
> 950 Impale the remnant of the Greeks! despoil!
> Violate! make their flesh cheaper than dust!
>
> *Semichorus 2nd*
> Thou Voice which art
> The herald of the ill in splendour hid!
> Thou echo of the hollow heart

948–51. These lines accord with the view that Russia was no ally to the Greeks in their struggle for independence, seeing the insurrection merely as a welcome means of destabilising the Ottoman Empire. Mary had noted in her letter to Hunt of 17 April that 'Russia & Austria have both joined in a declaration that they disapprove of the Revolt of the Greeks' (*L* i 189). On S.'s view of Russian involvement in the Greek uprising against the Ottoman Empire, see his letter to Mary of 8–10 August 1821 cited in the note to Preface ll. 66–70 above.

948–9. Russia's famished … light.] A reference to the flags of the warring nations. The various Russian Imperial standards from 1462 to 1917 all feature a double-headed eagle and the various flags of the Ottoman Empire from the 1720s to 1922 all feature a crescent moon. Mary calls the Greek War of Independence 'The war of the Cross against the Crescent' in her letter to the *Examiner* 694 (22 April 1821) 248; she also describes the struggle in these terms in letters to Maria Gisborne of 5 April and to Leigh Hunt of 17 April 1821 (*Mary L* i 188, 189).

948. Victory! Victory!] Victory! victory! *1829, 1839, 1840.* eagles] *Nbk 21, 1822, 1829, 1839, 1840*; Eagles *HM 329.*

949. crescent's] *1822, 1829, 1839, 1840*; crescents *HM 329.* light.] *1822, 1829, 1839, 1840*; light *HM 329.*

951. This line is inserted in S.'s hand in *HM 329.*

952–9. Cp. The imagery of *Bound in my hollow heart they lie* (no. 345).

952. Voice] voice *1822, 1829, 1839, 1840.* Whether the overwriting of the small initial letter with a capital in *HM 329* is in S.'s hand or Williams's is uncertain; the reading at *Nbk 21* p. 184 is *Voice* (see *BSM* xvi 188–9).

955   Of monarchy, bear me to thine abode
      Where Desolation flashes o'er a world destroyed.
      O bear me to those isles of jagged cloud

956. Where Desolation flashes] Cp. *Prolog im Himmel* from Goethe's *Faust* l. 263: 'Da flammt ein blitzendes Verheeren' which S. translates in *Prologue in Heaven* (no. 447) ll. 21–2 as 'A flashing desolation there / Flames'. *Where*] When *1822, 1829, 1839*. It is sometimes difficult to differentiate between 'When' and *Where* in Williams's hand, as it is in S.'s. In comparison with other instances of *When* and *Where* in Williams's hand at the start of lines in *HM 329*, the printing of 'When' in *1822* in this instance is understandable. However, an early draft of ll. 955–6, *Bear me to thy abode / Where Ruin broods over a world* in *Nbk 21* p. 184 (see *BSM* xvi 184–5), suggests that the intermediate fair copy from which Williams was presumably making his transcription may have read *Where*. This could therefore be an example of Williams mistranscribing S.'s fair copy and S. overlooking the need for correction. *Desolation*] desolation *1822, 1829, 1839, 1840*. *destroyed*.] destroyed: *1822*.

957–62. Cp. the language of the following speeches by Antony and Prospero respectively:

> Sometime we see a cloud that's dragonish,
> A vapor sometime like a bear or lion,
> A [tower'd] citadel, a pendant rock,
> A forked mountain, or blue promontory
> With trees upon't that nod unto the world,
> And mock our eyes with air. Thou hast seen these signs,
> They are black vesper's pageants. (*Antony and Cleopatra* IV xiv 2–8)

>   I have bedimm'd
> The noontide sun, call'd forth the mutinous winds,
> And 'twixt the green sea and the azur'd vault
> Set roaring war; to the dread rattling thunder
> Have I given fire, and rifted Jove's stout oak
> With his own bolt; the strong-bas'd promontory
> Have I made shake (*The Tempest* V i 41–7)

957–8. jagged cloud ... like mountains] *Turner* 279 cps the description of clouds taking the shape of mountains in Lucretius, *De Re. Nat.* iv 138–9: 'interdum magni montes avolsaque saxa / montibus anteire et solem succedere praeter' ('sometimes great mountains and rocks torn from the mountains [appear] to go before and to pass by the sun').
957. O] Oh, *1822*; Oh *1829, 1839*. *jagged cloud*] Cp. *PU* IV 227–8 'as a storm is poured / From jagged clouds'.

                Which float like mountains on the earthquake, mid
                The momentary oceans of the lightning,
960   Or to some toppling promontory proud
                Of solid tempest whose black pyramid
                Riven, overhangs the founts intensely brightening
                Of those dawn-tinted deluges of fire
                Before their waves expire,
965   When Heaven and Earth are light, and only light
                In the thunder night!

Voice without
                Victory! Victory! Austria, Russia, England
                And that tame serpent, that poor shadow, France,
                Cry Peace, and that means Death when monarchs speak.

958. *earthquake*] earthquakes *1829, 1834, 1839, 1840*.
959. *lightning,*] lightning; *1829, 1839, 1840*. Metre and rhyme scheme require a trisyllable (the word rhymes with *brightening* in l. 962). See l. 88 and note.
961. *tempest*] tempest, *1829, 1839, 1840*. *pyramid*] pyramid, *1822, 1829, 1839, 1840*.
962. *Riven,*] Riven *Nbk 21*. *founts*] Written over another word (possibly *fount*) in S.'s hand in *HM 329*. *brightening*] brightning *1822*.
963. *fire*] fire, *Nbk 21*.
964. *expire,*] *1822, 1829, 1839, 1840*; expire *HM 329*.
965. *Heaven … Earth*] heaven … earth *1822, 1829, 1839, 1840*.
966. *thunder night*] thunder-night *1829, 1839, 1840*. The first three letters of *night* are overwritten in *HM 329* in dark ink and are probably in S.'s hand.
967. *Victory! Victory!*] Victory! victory! *1839, 1840*. *England*] England, *1822, 1829, 1839, 1840*.
968. *tame serpent … poor shadow*] Apparently referring to France's diminished significance in Restoration Europe following the defeat and exile to St Helena in 1815 of Napoleon Bonaparte, news of whose death on 5 May 1821 S. addressed in *Written on hearing the news of the death of Napoleon* which was published with *Hellas* in 1822. serpent,] *1822, 1829, 1839, 1840*; serpent *Nbk 21*; Serpent, *HM 329*. shadow,] *1822, 1829, 1839, 1840*; Shadow, *Nbk 21*; shadow *HM 329*. France,] *1822, 1829, 1839, 1840*; France. *HM 329*.
969. *Peace, … Death*] peace, … death *1822, 1829, 1839, 1840*. speak.] *1822, 1839, 1840*; speak *HM 329*; speak! *1829*. *Reiman (2002)* cps the British chieftain Calgacus' description of the Romans in a speech to his troops reported in Tacitus, *Agricola* 30: 'auferre trucidare rapere falsis nominibus imperium, atque ubi solitudinem faciunt, pacem appellant' ('They call stealing, slaughter and plunder by the false name of empire, and when they make a wasteland they call it peace.') See also Byron, *The Bride of Abydos. A Turkish Tale* (1813) ii 430–1: 'Mark! where his carnage and his conquests cease— / He makes a solitude—and calls it—peace!'.

970 Ho, there! bring torches, — sharpen those red stakes;
    These chains are light, fitter for slaves and poisoners
    Than Greeks. Kill, plunder, burn! let none remain.

   Semichorus 1st
   Alas for Liberty!
  If numbers, wealth or unfulfilling years
975   Or fate can quell the free!
   Alas for Virtue, when
  Torments or contumely, or the sneers
   Of erring judging men
  Can break the heart where it abides.
980 Alas if Love, whose smile makes this obscure world splendid,
  Can change with its false times and tides
   Like hope and terror —
   Alas for Love!
  And Truth, who wanderest lone and unbefriended,

---

970. torches, —] torches, *1822, 1829, 1839, 1840. red*] Perhaps because bloodstained. *stakes;*] stakes *HM 329*; stakes, *1822*; stakes! *1829, 1839, 1840.*
971. poisoners] The second and third letters are written in S.'s hand in *HM 329*; Reiman suggests that S. altered the word from *prisoners* (*MYRS* iii 66). The reading in *Nbk 21* p. 182 is *poisoners* (see *BSM* xvi 186–7).
972. Kill, plunder,] Kill! plunder! *1822, 1829, 1839, 1840.*
973. Alas for Liberty!] *1829, 1839, 1840*; Alas for Liberty *Nbk 21*; Alas! for Liberty! *HM 329, 1822.*
974. wealth] wealth, *1822, 1829, 1839, 1840. years*] years, *1822, 1829, 1839, 1840.*
975. Or] Of *1834. fate*] fate, *1822, 1829, 1839, 1840. free!*] free; *1829, 1839, 1840.*
976. Alas for Virtue,] *Nbk 21*; Alas! for Virtue *HM 329*; Alas! for Virtue, *1822*; Alas for Virtue! *1829, 1834, 1839, 1840.*
977. Torments or contumely,] *Nbk 21*; Torments or contumely *HM 329*; Torments, or contumely, *1822, 1829, 1839, 1840*. 'contumely' = insolent abuse.
979. abides.] *1822, 1829, 1839, 1840*; abides *HM 329.*
980. Alas] *Nbk 21*; Alas! *HM 329, 1822, 1829, 1839, 1840. Love, … splendid,*] *1822, 1829, 1839, 1840*; Love … splendid *HM 329. world*] more *1829, 1834.*
981. change] change, *1829, 1839, 1840. tides*] tides, *1822, 1829, 1839, 1840.*
982. terror —] *Nbk 21, 1829, 1839, 1840*; terror *HM 329*; terror,— *1822.*
984. unbefriended,] *1822, 1829, 1839, 1840*; unbefriended *HM 329.*

985   If thou canst veil thy lie-consuming mirror
         Before the dazzled eyes of Error,
         Alas for thee! Image of the Above.

             Semichorus 2nd
         Repulse, with plumes from Conquest torn,
         Led the Ten Thousand from the limits of the morn
990   Through many an hostile Anarchy!
         At length they wept aloud and cried, 'the sea! the sea!'
         Through exile, persecution and despair,
            Rome was, and young Atlantis shall become,
            The wonder, or the terror or the tomb

985–6. lie-consuming mirror … Error] Cp. the shield that Prince Arthur employs to dazzle his enemies in *Faerie Queene* I vii 33–4 and viii 20. Locock *1911* ii 471 also cps *Ode to Naples* ll. 78–9.
986. Error,] *1822*; Error *HM 329*; error. *1829*; Error. *1839, 1840*. There are other personifications of Error in S.'s verse at *OL* 138, *WA* 51, *Epipsychidion* 168.
987. Image of the Above.] 'The "Image" is Liberty, the phrasing Platonic' (*Major Works*). *Above*] above *1829*.
988–91. A summary of Xenophon's *Anabasis*, which records the return to Greece of the Ten Thousand, a mercenary force led by Xenophon, after betrayal left them deep in Persian territory at the turn of the fourth century BCE. When the soldiers saw the sea from a vantage point on Mount Theches, on the northern Anatolian coast, they famously shouted θάλαττα θάλαττα ('The Sea! The Sea!'; *Anabasis* IV vii 24).
988. Repulse] See the note to l. 466. *Conquest*] conquest *1822, 1829, 1839, 1840*.
989. Ten Thousand] ten thousand *1822, 1829, 1839, 1840*. Although this reference is to the mercenaries led by Xenophon, Alexandros Ypsilantis's army was of the same number according to Mary's letter to the *Examiner* 694 (22 April 1821) 248: 'Prince YPSILANTI […] has entered Wallachia, declaring the liberty of Greece, with a force of 10,000 Greeks'. *from the limits of the morn*] I.e. from the very far east, as far as the exact point where the sun rises.
990. an] a *1834*.
991. aloud] aloud, *1822*. *cried,*] *1822, 1829, 1839, 1840*; cried *HM 329*. *'the sea! the sea!'*] 'the Sea! the Sea!' *1822*; 'The sea! the sea!' *1829, 1839, 1840*.
992. persecution] persecution, *1822, 1829, 1839, 1840*. *despair,*] *1822, 1829, 1839, 1840*; despair *HM 329*.
993. young Atlantis] America. See l. 70 and note. *become,*] become *1822, 1829, 1839, 1840*.
994. terror] terror, *1822, 1829, 1839, 1840*.

995	Of all whose step wakes Power lulled in her savage lair;
	But Greece was as a hermit child
	Whose fairest thoughts and limbs were built
	To woman's growth, by dreams so mild,
	She knew not pain or guilt;
1000	And now — O Victory, blush! and Empire tremble
	When ye desert the free —
	If Greece must be
	A wreck, yet shall its fragments reassemble
	And build themselves again impregnably
1005	In a diviner clime
	To Amphionic music on some cape sublime
	Which frowns above the idle foam of Time.

Semichorus 1st
Let the tyrants rule the desert they have made —
Let the free possess the paradise they claim,

---

995. This line is marked off in ink in the margin of *HM 329* p. 45 with 'E49' above. As Reiman notes (*MYRS* iii 12, 67), these markings are those of the printer, noting this line to be the first of p. 49 in *1822*, i.e. the beginning of signature E. *Power*] power *1822, 1829, 1839, 1840. lair;*] lair: *1822, 1829, 1839, 1840.*
996. *hermit child*] hermit child, *1822, 1829, 1839, 1840.* I.e. solitary child.
998. *growth,*] growth *1829. mild,*] mild *1839, 1840.*
999. *or*] nor *1834.*
1000. *now — O*] now — o *HM 329*; now, O *1822, 1829, 1839, 1840.* The insertion of the dash, the alteration of O to o, the alteration of the initial letter of *victory* to a capital, and the overwriting of the second and third letters of *victory* in *HM 329* all appear to be in S.'s hand. *Empire*] Empire, *1829, 1839, 1840. tremble*] tremble, *1829, 1839, 1840.*
1001. *free —*] free! *1829, 1839, 1840.*
1003. *reassemble*] re-assemble, *1822*; reassemble, *1829, 1839, 1840.*
1005. *a*] Written above *some* canc. in *HM 329*, whether in S.'s hand or Williams's is uncertain. *clime*] clime. *1822*; clime, *1829, 1839, 1840.*
1006. *Amphionic*] 'Of or relating to Amphion, one of the twin sons of Zeus and Antiope in Greek mythology; [...] melodious' (*OED*). See *L&C* 88 and note. *music*] music, *1829, 1839, 1840. some*] Written above *the* canc. in *HM 329*, whether in S.'s hand or Williams's is uncertain. *cape*] Cape *1822, 1839, 1840. sublime*] sublime, *1822, 1829, 1839, 1840.*
1008. *made —*] made; *1822, 1829, 1839, 1840.*
1009. *claim,*] claim; *1822, 1829, 1839, 1840.*

1010   Be the fortune of our fierce oppressors weighed
         With our ruin, our resistance and our name!

Semichorus 2nd
         Our dead shall be the seed of their decay —
         Our survivors be the shadow of their pride,
         Our adversity a dream to pass away —
1015   Their dishonour a remembrance to abide!

Voice without
         Victory! Victory! The bought Briton sends
         The keys of Ocean to the Islamite —
         Now shall the blazon of the cross be veiled
         And British skill directing Othman might,
1020   Thunderstrike rebel Victory. O keep holy

1010. *oppressors*] Written above a cancelled word in *HM 329* that Reiman plausibly reads as *possessors* (*MYRS* iii 68), probably in Williams's hand rather than S.'s.
1011. *resistance*] resistance, *1822, 1829, 1839, 1840*.
1012. *decay* —] *Nbk 21*; decay *HM 329*; decay, *1822, 1829, 1839, 1840*.
1013. *shadow*] shadows *1829, 1839, 1840*.
1016–17. A reference to British support for the Turkish navy. *Galignani's Messenger* 2021 (18 August 1821) [p. 4] reported: 'We are informed that the English furnish secret supplies to the Turks. Two Turkish ships being chased by the Greeks took refuge in a narrow Bay, where the latter blockaded them, when some English vessels came to their succour and delivered them.'
1016. *bought*] bribed.
1017. *Ocean*] ocean *1822, 1829, 1839, 1840. Islamite* —] Islamite.— *1822*; Islamite. *1829, 1839, 1840*.
1018. *Now*] Nor *1829, 1834. veiled*] veiled, *1822, 1839, 1840*; veil'd *1829*. The second letter is overwritten in dark ink in *HM 329*.
1019. *Othman*] The third letter is overwritten in dark ink in *HM 329*. Ottoman, Turkish. See Byron, *The Giaour* (1813) l. 810: 'Yet seems he not of Othman race'. *might,*] *1822, 1829, 1839, 1840*; might *HM 329*.
1020. *Thunderstrike*] Thunder-strike *1822, 1829, 1839, 1840*. 'Strike as with "thunder"' (*OED* 2). Cp. Byron, *Childe Harold's Pilgrimage* IV (1818) clxxxi l. 1: 'The armaments which thunderstrike the walls'. See also *L&C* 115–17, and *And what art thou, presumptuous, who profanest* (no. 257) 15 and note. *Victory*] victory *1822, 1829, 1839, 1840*. Alt. from *victory* in *HM 329*, whether in S.'s hand or Williams's is uncertain.

This jubilee of unrevenged blood! —
Kill, crush, despoil! Let not a Greek escape!

    Semichorus 1st
  Darkness has dawned in the East
  On the noon of Time. —
1025 The death-birds descend to their feast
  From the hungry clime. —
  Let Freedom and Peace flee far
  To a sunnier strand,
  And follow Love's folding-star
1030 To the Evening-land!

    Semichorus 2nd
  The young moon has fed
  Her exhausted horn
  With the sunset's fire.

1021. jubilee] See note to l. 931. *blood!* —] *Nbk 21*; blood *HM 329*; blood— *1822*; blood! *1829, 1839, 1840*. The mark after *blood* in *HM 329* p. 46, which the compositor of *1822* appears to have read as a dash, is show-through from the dash inserted in l. 1000 on the reverse of the leaf (see note to l. 1000).
1022. Kill,] Kill; *HM 329*; Kill! *1822, 1829, 1839, 1840. crush,*] crush! *1822, 1829, 1839, 1840*.
1024. Time. —] Time *HM 329*; time: *1822, 1829, 1839, 1840*. The reading is [*of time* canc.]. — in *Nbk 21* p. 178 (see *BSM* xvi 182–3).
1025. death-birds] Carrion-feeding birds (*Concordance*). See *The Devil's Walk: A Ballad* (no. 83) and *PU* I 340. *feast*] *Nbk 21*; feast, *HM 329, 1822, 1829, 1839, 1840*.
1026. clime. —] clime. *1822, 1829, 1839, 1840*.
1029. Love's folding-star] I.e. Venus (the god of love) as the evening star; see ll. 231 and 1038–41 and notes. *folding-star*] folding star! *1840*.
1030. Evening-land!] Evening land! *1822, 1839, 1840*; evening land! *1829*. Woodberry (1901) suggests: 'Here and in the following lines, America appears to furnish the elements of the idealized new age, which soon changes imaginatively into a glorification of a newly arisen ideal Greece'.
1032. horn] horn, *1822*. The horn is 'each of the pointed extremities of the moon as she appears in her first and last quarters' (*OED* 18a).
1033. fire.] fire: *1822, 1829, 1839, 1840*.

>   The weak day is dead
> 1035   But the night is not born,
>   And like Loveliness panting with wild desire
>   While it trembles with fear and delight,
>   Hesperus flies from awakening night
>   And pants in its beauty and speed, with light
> 1040   Fast flashing, soft and bright.
>   Thou beacon of love, thou lamp of the free!
>   Guide us far, far away,

1034–40. Cp. a similar analogy between erotic passion and the sunset in *Epithalamium* (no. 401) C ll. 3–8 (and see the note to l. 6):

> Never smiled the inconstant Moon
>   On a pair so true—
> Haste coy Hour and quench all light,
> Lest eyes see their own delight—
> Haste swift Hour, and thy loved flight
>   Oft renew.

1034. Locock 1911 ii 471 cps *PU* IV 493. *dead*] dead, *1822, 1829, 1839, 1840.*
1035. born,] born; *1822, 1829, 1839, 1840.*
1036. And] And, *1822, 1829, 1839, 1840. Loveliness*] loveliness *1822, 1829, 1839, 1840. desire*] desire, *1829, 1839, 1840.*
1038–41. Hesperus ... free!] Hesperus is the Latin name for Venus as the evening star, also known as the 'folding star' (see l. 1029 and note), as opposed to Venus' other guise as the Morning star (*Lat.* Lucifer). S.'s idea of Hesperus as a symbol of freedom may be related to Hazlitt's claim in a letter published in the *Morning Chronicle* 13957 (28 January 1814) [p. 3] that,

> He who has seen the evening-star set over a poor man's cottage, or has connected the feeling of hope with the heart of man, and who, although he may have lost the feeling, has never ceased to reverence it—he, Sir, with submission, and without a nickname, is *the true Jacobin*. (See *Hazlitt Works* vii 370)

See also *TL* 414–23 and note.
1038. night] night, *1822, 1839, 1840*; might, *1829, 1834.*
1039. speed,] *Nbk 21*; speed *HM 329, 1822, 1829, 1839, 1840.*
1040. Fast flashing,] *1822*; Fast flashing *HM 329*; Fast-flashing *1829, 1839, 1840. soft*] soft, *1822, 1829, 1839, 1840. bright.*] *1822, 1829, 1839, 1840*; bright, *HM 329.*
1041. love,] love! *1822, 1829, 1839, 1840.*
1042–9. Cp. *Charles the First* I iii 26–32.

	To climes where now veiled by the ardour of day
	Thou art hidden
1045	From waves on which weary noon
	Faints in her summer swoon,
	Between Kingless continents sinless as Eden,
	Around mountains and islands inviolably
	Pranked on the sapphire sea.

Semichorus 1st

1050	Through the sunset of Hope
	Like the shapes of a dream,
	What Paradise islands of glory gleam!
	Beneath Heaven's cope,
	Their shadows more clear float by —
1055	The sound of their oceans, the light of their sky,
	The music and fragrance their solitudes breathe,
	Burst, like morning on dream or like Heaven on death,
	Through the walls of our prison;
	And Greece which was dead, is arisen!

1043. now ... day] now, ... day, *1829, 1839, 1840.*
1045–6. From waves ... summer swoon] The Mediterranean. Locock *1911* ii 471 cps *OWW* (no. 259) ll. 29–30. *noon ... swoon]* Cp. *A schoolboy lay near a pond in a copse* (no. 444) l. 4: 'When the languid noon breathed so hard in its swoon'.
1045. noon] noon, *1822;* Noon *1829.*
1046. swoon,] *1822, 1829, 1839, 1840;* swoon *HM 329.*
1047. Between] Inserted in S.'s hand above *Amid* canc. in *HM 329. Kingless continents sinless as Eden]* Cp. *Charles the First* I iii 7–8 and 26–32. The reference is to America; see note to l. 1030. *Kingless]* kingless *1829, 1839, 1840. continents]* continents, *1829, 1839, 1840. sinless]* Written over *sacred* in dark ink in *HM 329* in S.'s hand; *sacred* is cancelled in the draft of this line in *Nbk 21* p. 188 (see *BSM* xvi 192–3).
1049. Pranked] 'Set like a gem' (*OED* 'prank' $v.^4$ 4). Cp. the image in ll. 770–1.
1050. Hope] hope, *1822, 1829, 1839, 1840.*
1051. dream,] *1822, 1829, 1839, 1840;* dream *HM 329.*
1052–3. gleam! ... cope,] gleam ... cope. *1829, 1834, 1839, 1840.*
1053. cope] 'the over-arching canopy or vault of heaven' (*OED n.¹* 7). Cp. *L&C* 4457.
1056. breathe,] *1829, 1839, 1840;* breathe *HM 329, 1822.*
1057. Burst,] Burst *1829, 1839, 1840. dream]* dream, *1822;* dreams, *1829, 1834, 1839, 1840. death,]* *1829, 1839, 1840;* death *HM 329, 1822.*
1059. Greece] Greece, *1822, 1829, 1839, 1840. dead,]* *Nbk 21, 1822, 1829, 1839, 1840;* dead *HM 329.*

Chorus

1060   The world's great age begins anew,[7]
         The golden years return,
         The earth doth like a snake renew

1060–1101. GM suggests this final Chorus alludes to the doctrine of the 'Great Year', when all celestial objects return to their original positions, referred to in Plato, *Timaeus* 39d; Cicero, *De Natura Deorum* ii 51–2 ('On the diverse motions of the planets the mathematicians have based what they call the Great Year, which is completed when the sun, moon and five planets having all finished their courses have returned to the same positions relative to one another'); and *Paradise Lost* v 583 ('heaven's great year').
1060. Cook, 'Notes on Shelley' 162 cps Virgil, *Eclogue* iv 5: 'magnus ab integro saeclorum nascitur ordo' ('The great line of the centuries begins anew.') Cook notes that 'the earlier part of this chorus has a certain resemblance to' the close of Act II of Seneca, *Medea* (ll. 364–79); see especially ll. 375–9:

> Venient annis saecula seris,
> quibus Oceanus vincula rerum
> laxet, et ingens pateat tellus,
> Tethysque novos detegat orbes
> nec sit terris ultima Thule.

> ('There will come an epoch late in time
> when Ocean will loosen the bonds of the world
> and the earth lie open in its vastness,
> when Tethys will disclose new worlds
> and Thule not be the farthest of lands.')

[7]] See S.'s note.
1061. Cook, 'Notes on Shelley' 162 cps Virgil, *Eclogue* iv 9: 'surget gens aurea mundo' ('and a golden race [shall] spring up throughout the world!'). *The golden years*] See l. 238 and note.
1062–3. Cp. Corisca's song in Fanshawe's 1647 translation of Guarini's *Il Pastor Fido* III v 2593–2600, esp. 2595–6:

> 'Let us use it whilst wee may;
> 'Snatch those joyes that haste away.
> 'Earth her winter-coat may cast,
> 'And renew her beauty past;
> 'But, our winter come, in vain
> 'We sollicite spring again:

                Her winter weeds outworn;
                Heaven smiles, and faiths and empires gleam
1065   Like wrecks of a dissolving dream.

        A brighter Hellas rears its mountains

> 'And when our furrows snow shall cover,
> 'Love may return, but never Lover.
>
> (*A Critical Edition of Sir Richard Fanshawe's 1647 translation of Giovanni Battista Guarini's Il pastor fido*, ed. Walter F. Staton, Jr. and William E. Simeone (1964) 81)

Cook, 'Notes on Shelley' 162 cps Ovid, *Ars amatoria* (The Art of Love) iii 77: 'Anguibus exuitur tenui cum pelle vetustas' ('Serpents put off their age with their frail skins'), noting further references to snakes casting off their skins in Statius, *Thebaid* iv 93–8:

> Ecce inter medios patriae ciet agmina gentis
> fulmineus Tydeus, iam laetus et integer artus,
> ut primae strepuere tubae: ceu lubricus alta
> anguis humo verni blanda ad spiramina solis
> erigitur liber senio et squalentibus annis
> exutus laetisque minax interviret herbis

('See, bolt-like Tydeus in the midst rouses the hosts of his countrymen, happy now and sound of body, as the first trumpets bray; like a slippery snake rising at the coaxing breath of vernal sunshine from deep earth, free of mould and stripped of musty years—a green threat among the lush grasses')

See also Pliny, *Nat. Hist.* VIII xli: 'anguis, hiberno situ membrana corporis obducta, feniculi suco inpedimentum illud exuit nitidusque vernat' ('When a snake's body gets covered with a skin owing to its winter inactivity it sloughs this hindrance to its movement by means of fennel-sap and comes out all glossy for spring').
1063. *winter weeds*] 'clothes worn, or suitable to be worn, in winter' (*OED* 'winter weed' *n.¹*); 'weeds' also carries the sense of clothes 'customarily worn by a widow during a period of mourning for her spouse' (see *OED* 'weed' *n.²* 6a). *outworn;*] outworn: *1822, 1829, 1839, 1840*.
1064. *smiles*] smiled *1834*. *gleam*] gleam, *1822*.
1066–71. *A ... deep*] S.'s geographical image of a revived 'brighter Hellas' attempts to encompass the whole Greek mainland and some of its islands. 'Peneus' is the major river of the plain of Thessaly which flows eastwards from the Pindus mountains in north west Greece, through the vale of 'Tempe', and out on to the Aegean sea, with its waters, S. claims, flowing in the direction of the 'Cyclads' (the island

>   From waves serener far,
>   A new Peneus rolls his fountains
>   Against the morning-star;
> 1070   Where fairer Tempes bloom, there sleep
>   Young Cyclads on a sunnier deep.
>
>   A loftier Argo cleaves the main

---

group known as the Cyclades, which includes Naxos and Santorini). The easterly progress of 'Peneus' across mainland Greece is opposed to that of the 'morning-star' (the planet Venus as Lucifer) which rises in the west.

1067. *far,*] far; *1822, 1829, 1839, 1840.*

1068-9. See the cancelled lines discussed in the note to *Could Arethusa to her fountain run* (*Lines connected with Hellas* K) ll. 3-4.

1068. Cp. *Song of Pan* (no. 318) l. 13 and note to ll. 13-15. *his*] its *1829, 1834, 1839, 1840.*

1069. *morning-star;*] morning-star, *HM 329*; morning-star. *1822, 1829, 1839, 1840.* The planet Venus as Lucifer.

1070. J. B. Pryor, 'Shelley's Metre', *The Shelley Society's Papers* Pt ii (1891) 260 commented, 'I do not see the sense of saying [*"*]*Where* fairer Tempes bloom[*"*] […] I believe Shelley wrote "here."'; a claim refuted by *Nbk 21* p. 196 as well as *HM 329* p. 49.

1071. *Cyclads*] Cyclads, *1829. deep.*] *1822, 1839, 1840*; deep *HM 329*; deep; *1829.*

1071-2. The omission of the stanza-break between these lines in *1822* is noted in *Errata*. The compositor apparently overlooked a centred horizontal line in *HM 329* p. 49 signalling the close of the stanza that begun at l. 1066; Williams copied ll. 1070-1 in the left margin at right angles to the rest of his transcript and indicated their position after l. 1069 with a carefully-drawn line and manicule pointing to a cross above the centred horizontal line. The stanza-break is first observed in *Rossetti 1870.*

1072-7. Cook, 'Notes on Shelley' 162 cps ll. 1072-3 and 1076-7 with Virgil, *Eclogue* iv 34-6:

>   alter erit tum Tiphys et altera quae vehat Argo
>   delectos heroas; erunt etiam altera bella
>   atque iterum ad Troiam magnus mittetur Achilles.
>
> ('A second Tiphys will then arise, and a second Argo to carry chosen heroes; a second war will be fought, and great Achilles be sent again to Troy.')

Cook also cps ll. 1074-5 with *Eclogue* iv 55-6: 'non me carminibus vincet nec Thracius Orpheus nec Linus' ('Then shall neither Thracian Orpheus nor Linus vanquish me in song'). This part of the choral song of renewal chooses three

            Fraught with a later prize;
            Another Orpheus sings again,
1075   And loves, and weeps, and dies;
            A new Ulysses leaves once more
            Calypso for his native shore.

famous mythological episodes, at least two of which constitute 'beginnings' of a sort: the hero's first journey recounted in the *Odyssey* is his departure in Book V from the nymph Calypso who had detained him for seven years, while in antiquity the Argo was often considered to be the first ship, for example in Catullus LXIV 11: 'illa rudem cursu prima imbuit Amphitriten' ('That ship [the Argo] first hanselled with voyage Amphitrite [the sea] untried before'). It might also be noted that Orpheus' singing acts as the starting-point for the Argonautic expedition in Apollonius of Rhodes's *Argonautica* (i 496–511). In classical mythology Orpheus, whose parents were Apollo and one of the Muses, has extraordinary singing powers and is associated with prophecy (see l. 704 and note). S. was reading the *Argonautica* in August 1820 (see *Mary Jnl* i 329–30).

1072. Argo] 1840; Argos *Nbk 21, HM 329, 1822, 1829, 1834, 1839. the main] the* main, *1822, 1829, 1839, 1840.* The sea.

1073. Loaded with a more recent trophy than the golden fleece.

1075. dies;] dies. 1829, 1839, 1840.

1076. A new Ulysses] As noted by W. E. J. in 'Shelley's FINAL CHORUS from HELLAS', *The Explicator* iv.1 (Oct. 1945), Margaret Armstrong, *Trelawny: A Man's Life* (1941) 283–4 suggests this is a reference to the Greek military leader Odysseas Androutsos (1788–1825). Mavrokordatos refers to him in his letter to Mary of 21 May 1821:

> Un autre corps Grec commandé par Odysseus (capitaine connu par sa bravure, et par un contraste singulier Γλῶσσαν μὲν ἀργήν, χεῖρα δ' ἔχων ἐργάτιν) a proclamé la liberté dans la Livadia et s'est avancé jusques à Athènes. (Bodleian MS. Abinger c. 45 f. 87ʳ; *Shelley and Mary* iii [Bodleian [pr.] Shelley adds. d. 4] 627; the Greek words are a line from a speech by Odysseus in Sophocles' *Philoctetes* 97 in which he describes himself in his less wise youth, before he understood the power of words).

> (Another Greek troop commanded by Odysseus (a captain who is well known for his bravery, and for a peculiar contrast 'with a lazy tongue, but a hardworking hand') has proclaimed liberty in Livadia, and has advanced as far as Athens.)

Galignani's Messenger 2012 (7 August 1821) [p. 4] reported that 'Ulysses, chief of the Greeks, had defeated the Turks in Thessaly' and the following day gave

O, write no more the tale of Troy
If earth Death's scroll must be!
1080 Nor mix with Laian rage the joy
Which dawns upon the free;
Although a subtler Sphinx renew
Riddles of death Thebes never knew.

Another Athens shall arise
1085 And to remoter time
Bequeath, like sunset to the skies,
The splendour of its prime —
And leave, if nought so bright may live,

---

details of his victory over the Turks under Omer Vrioni at the battle of Gravia in May 1821 (no. 2013 [p. 4]). He was co-signatory of the proclamation of liberty in Macedonia published in *Galignani's Messenger* 2037 (6 September 1821) [p. 4].
1078–9. 'Let us have no more *Iliads*, if more wars are needed to furnish subjects for them' (GM).
1078. O,] O *1829, 1839, 1840. Troy]* Troy, *1822, 1829, 1839, 1840.*
1080–3. 'Perhaps: "Don't corrupt your new freedom with hatred and revenge, no matter what terrible problems may face you in the future"' (GM). A reference to Sophocles' *Oedipus Tyrannus*, in which Oedipus' anger is an important driver of the plot. His rage causes him to kill his father Laius in a fight when the two meet as strangers on the road: τὸν τροχηλάτην,/ παίω δι' ὀργῆς ('[i]n anger I struck the driver [Laius]', ll. 806–7). Oedipus' role as king of Thebes in the play stems from his successful solving of the riddle set by the sphinx troubling the city: φανερὰ γὰρ ἐπ' αὐτῷ πτερόεσσ' ἦλθε κόρα ποτέ, καὶ σοφὸς ὤφθη βασάνῳ θ' ἡδύπολις (ll. 507–10; 'for in sight of all the winged maiden came against him once, and he was seen to be wise and approved as dear to the city').
1080. Laian] Adjective derived from Laius (see note to ll. 1080–3).
1081. free;] free: *1822, 1829, 1839, 1840.*
1082. subtler Sphinx] subtle sphinx *1829, 1834;* subtler sphinx *1839, 1840.*
1083. knew.] knew, *1829, 1834.*
1084. arise] arise, *1822, 1829, 1839, 1840.*
1087. prime —] Nbk 21; prime. *HM 329, 1822;* prime; *1829, 1839, 1840;* prime, *1964.*

All earth can take or Heaven can give.

1090 Saturn and Love their long repose [8]
Shall burst, more bright and good
Than all who fell, than One who rose,
Than many unsubdued;
Not gold, not blood, their altar dowers
1095 But votive tears and symbol flowers.

O cease! must hate and death return?
Cease! must men kill and die?
Cease! drain not to its dregs the urn

1089. Heaven] heaven *1829, 1839, 1840*.
1090. Saturn and Love] '"deities of a real or imaginary state of innocence and happiness" (Shelley's note), before Jupiter's usurpation ended the Age of Gold' (GM).
1091–3. more bright ... unsubdued;] These lines were first published in *1829* (see Headnote); in *1822* the words are replaced with lines of asterisks.
1091. bright] wise *1829, 1834*.
1092. all who fell] '"the Gods of Greece, Asia, and Egypt" [Shelley's note], superseded by Jesus Christ (*One who rose*)' (GM). *One*] one *1829, 1834*.
1093. many unsubdued] '"the monstrous objects of the idolatry of China, India," &c. [Shelley's note], not yet discredited' (GM). *unsubdued;*] unsubdued: *1822 Unexpurgated, 1839, 1840*; unwithstood— *1829, 1834*.
1094. Not gold, not blood] See l. 248 and note. *blood,*] *1822, 1829, 1839, 1840*; blood *HM 329. dowers*] 'furnishes with' (see *OED* 'dower', *v* 2). dowers, *1829, 1839, 1840*.
1095. votive tears] tears that are 'promised or vowed' (*Concordance*). *votive*] native *1829, 1834. tears*] tears, *1829, 1839, 1840. symbol flowers*] flowers that have symbolical significance.
1096–8. O cease! ... Cease! ... Cease!] 'a direct answer of the Chorus to the words of hatred and catastrophe uttered by the offstage Voices — which, certainly, are Turkish and rejoice at the mistreatment of the Greeks' (*Raizis* 42).
1098. drain ... urn] Cp. *May-day Night* (no. 440) 295: 'So is the world drained to the dregs'.

                Of bitter prophecy.
1100   The world is weary of the past,
                O might it die or rest at last!

1099. bitter prophecy] 'i.e. of renewed bloodshed, in Virgil's Fourth Eclogue: "the reign of Saturn returns ('redeunt Saturnia regna' l. 6)... all traces that remain of our iniquity will be effaced and, as they vanish, free the world from its long night of horror ('si qua manent sceleris vestigia nostri,/ inrita perpetua solvent formidine terras' ll. 13-14) ... yet will a few traces of old-time sin live on ('pauca tamen suberunt priscae vestigia fraudis' l. 30)... a second war will be fought, and great Achilles be sent again to Troy ('erunt etiam altera bella/ atque iterum ad Troiam magnus mittetur Achilles' ll. 35-6)"' (GM). See the notes to S.'s Note 7.
1100. past,] *1822, 1839, 1840*; past — *Nbk 21, 1829*; past *HM 329*.
1101. 'I.e. if the earth is *never* to achieve peace, it might as well perish' (GM).

NOTES

Note 1.

[60.] *The quenchless ashes of Milan*

Milan was the centre of the resistance of the Lombard league against the Austrian tyrant. Frederic Barbarossa burnt the city to the ground, but Liberty lived in its ashes and it rose like an exhalation from its ruin. See Sismondi's *Histoire des Républiques Italiennes*, a book which has done much towards awakening the Italians to an imitation of their great ancestors.

¶ *Note 1*. The heading 'Note 1' is omitted in *HM 329*.
Note 1. 1. the Lombard league] A coalition of northern Italian cities — the largest of which was Milan — founded in 1167 to resist Frederick I. Cp. *PVR*: 'The Republics & municipal governments of Italy opposed for some time a systematic & effectual resistance to the all-surrounding tyranny' (*SC* vi 964) and *OL* 124-35 and note.
Note 1. 2. the Austrian tyrant] 'applied to Frederick Barbarossa and the emperors of his line' (*Rossetti 1870* ii 557); Rossetti calls this one 'of the unnumbered loosenesses so characteristic of Shelley', another being the mistaken date in Note 6.
Note 1. 2-4. Frederic ... ruin] Frederick I ('Barbarossa'; *c*.1123-90), Holy Roman Emperor from 1152, conquered Milan in 1158 and razed it to the ground in 1162. But he was defeated at the Battle of Legnano (1176), as *PVR* notes: 'The Lombard League defeated the armies of the despot in open field' (*SC* vi 964). *Frederic*] Frederick *1839, 1840*. *Liberty*] liberty *1822, 1829, 1839, 1840*. *ashes*] ashes, *1822, 1829, 1839, 1840*. *ruin*.] ruin.— *1829, 1839, 1840*.
Note 1. 4-5. See Sismondi's Histoire ... Italiennes] In his *Histoire des républiques italiennes du moyen âge*, 2nd edn, 16 vols (1809-18), J. C. L. Simonde de Sismondi noted that 'Milan et Tortone, que Frédéric avoit voulu détruire, se relevoient plus florissantes de leur ruine' (ii 173; Milan and Tortona, which Frederick wanted to destroy, recovered more flourishing from their ruin). Of the Lombard League, Sismondi commented: 'Tant il est vrai que dans les petits états, où le sentiment de la patrie a toute sa force, l'amour de la liberté est une arme puissante contre le despotisme! (ii 176; Thus it is true that in small states, where patriotic sentiment has such strength, the love of liberty is a powerful weapon against despotism!). In a letter of 22 January 1819 from Naples, Mary told Maria Gisborne 'we are all reading "Sismondi's Histoire des Republiques Italiennes du moyen âge"' (*Mary L* i 85). Sismondi's work was a source for *Mazenghi* (no. 166).

Note 2.

[*197. SD.*] *The Chorus*

The popular notions of Christianity are represented in this chorus as true in their relation to the worship they superseded, and that which in all probability they will supersede, without considering their merits in a relation more universal. The first stanza contrasts the immortality of the living and thinking beings which inhabit the planets, and to use a common and inadequate phrase, *clothe themselves in matter* with the transience of the noblest manifestations of the external world.

The concluding verses indicate a progressive state of more or less exalted existence according to the degree of perfection which every distinct intelligence may have attained. Let it not be supposed that I mean to dogmatize upon a subject concerning which all men are equally ignorant, or that I think the Gordian knot of the origin of evil can be disentangled by

Note 2. 6–7. and to] and, to *1829, 1839, 1840*.
Note 2. 7–8. clothe themselves in matter] clothe themselves in matter, *1829, 1834, 1839, 1840*.
Note 2. 9. world.] *1822, 1829, 1839*; world *HM 329*.
Note 2. 11. existence] existence, *1822, 1829, 1839, 1840*.
Note 2. 13. dogmatize] 'speak authoritatively or imperiously (*upon* a subject) without reference to argument or evidence' (*OED* 2a) *subject*] subject, *1822*.
Note 2. 15. Gordian knot] A matter of extreme difficulty; the phrase refers to '[a]n intricate knot tied by Gordius, king of Gordium in Phrygia. The oracle declared that whoever should loosen it should rule Asia, and Alexander the Great overcame the difficulty by cutting through the knot with his sword' (*OED* 1a). *the origin of evil*] S. reflected on this matter in *On the Devil, and Devils* (1819):

> the Greek Philosophers [...] accounted for evil by supposing that what is called matter is eternal, and that God in making the world, made not the best that he, or even inferior intelligence could conceive; but that he moulded the reluctant and stubborn materials ready to his hand, into the nearest arrangement possible to the perfect archetype existing in his contemplation. (*Julian* vii 88–9)

that or any similar assertions. The received hypothesis of a
Being resembling men in the moral attributes of his nature,
having called us out of non-existence, and after inflicting on
us the misery of the commission of error, should superadd
20   that of the punishment and the privations consequent upon
it, still would remain inexplicable and incredible. That there
is a true solution of the riddle and that in our present state
that solution is unattainable by us, are propositions which
may be regarded as equally certain; meanwhile, as it is the
25   province of the poet to attach himself to those ideas which
exalt and ennoble humanity, let him be permitted to have

Note 2. 16–21. *The received ... incredible.*] Cp. *On Christianity* (1817):

> It is not to <be> believed that a person of such comprehensive views as Jesus Christ could have fallen into so manifest a contradiction as to assert that men would be tortured after death by that being whose character is held up as a model to human kind because he is incapable of malevolence or revenge. (*Prose Works* 259)

a Being] that Being *1834. nature,*] *1822, 1829, 1839, 1840*; nature *HM 329. non-existence, and*] non-existence, who, *Rossetti 1870. the commission*] *1822, 1829, 1839, 1840*; the commission, *HM 329* (*the* alt. from *this*, whether in S.'s hand or Williams's is uncertain.) *should*] *Forman 1876–7* comments: 'This brusque change of construction is a really unfortunate oversight, apparently resulting from Shelley's haste; but, as it is impossible to say what part of the sentence he would have altered had he discovered his mistake, I can see nothing for it but to leave things as they are' (iii 95 n.). *superadd*] add to what has already been added (*OED* 1a). *Forman 1892* comments: 'The lamentable break-down of syntax is of course attributable to the haste with which Shelley threw off his book and the lack of opportunity to see proofs of it. That Williams and Gisborne both passed the slip is astonishing. I do not venture to substitute *superadding* for *should superadd*, because Shelley would not improbably have remedied the error by changing the construction of the sentence, had he seen it in print' (iv 89 n.). *incredible.*] *1822, 1829, 1839, 1840*; incredible *HM 329.*
Note 2. 22–28. *riddle*] riddle, *1822, 1829, 1839, 1840. that solution*] the solution *1839, 1840. certain;*] certain: *1822. meanwhile, ... humanity,*] *1822, 1829, 1839, 1840*; meanwhile ... humanity *HM 329. it is the province of the poet ... impelled*] Cp. *DP*:

> Poets, according to the circumstances of the age and nation in which they appeared, were called in the earlier epochs of the world legislators or prophets: a poet essentially comprises and unites both these characters. For he not only beholds intensely the present as it is,

conjectured the condition of that futurity towards which we are all impelled by an inextinguishable thirst for immortality. Until better arguments can be produced than sophisms
30   which disgrace the cause, this desire itself must remain the strongest and the only presumption that eternity is the inheritance of every thinking being.

       and discovers those laws according to which present things ought to be ordered, but he beholds the future in the present, and his thoughts are the germs of the flower and the fruit of latest time. (*Reiman (2002)* para. 4)

Note 2. 28. *an inextinguishable thirst for immortality*] Cp. Diotima's words to Socrates in Plato's *Symposium* 208d-e:

       Far otherwise; all such deeds are done for the sake of ever-living virtue, and this immortal glory which they have obtained; and inasmuch as any one is of an excellent nature, so much the more is he impelled to attain this reward. For they love what is immortal. (S.'s trans., *Notopoulos* 447)

Note 2. 29–32. *Until better arguments ... thinking being*] Cp. *On Life*:

       man is a being of high aspirations "looking both before and after," whose "thoughts that wander through eternity," disclaim alliance with transience and decay, incapable of imagining to himself annihilation, existing but in the future and the past, being, not what he is, but what he has been, and shall be. Whatever may be his true and final destination, there is a spirit within him at enmity with change and extinction [nothingness and dissolution]. (*Reiman (2002)* 506)

sophisms] fallacious arguments. *cause*,] *1822, 1829, 1839*; cause *HM 329*.

Note 3.

[245.] *No hoary priests after that Patriarch*

The Greek Patriarch after having been compelled to fulminate an anathema against the insurgents was put to death by the Turks.

Note 3. Title. priests] *1839, 1840; priest HM 329, 1822.* The *HM 329* reading shows S. to misquote l. 245 (see *Forman 1876-7* iii 95 n.).
Note 3. 1-3. The Greek ... by the Turks.] Gregorios V, Greek Patriarch of Constantinople, was hanged on 22 April 1821, as reported in *Galignani's Messenger* 1951 (26 May 1821) [p. 4]:

> On the morrow, the Greek Patriarch, Gregory, just at the moment after celebrating divine service, was arrested by the guard, thown into prison, and at five o'clock in the evening this venerable old man was hanged at the door of his own palace. Six Ecclesiastics of high rank shared his fate. The writing which, as usual, accompanied these corpses to the grave, accused the deceased of complicity in the Greek plot. Private letters add that the death of the Patriarch the more sensibly affected the Greeks, as they view with peculiar horror so infamous and ignoble a death. The Patriarch was 74 years of age, and he had himself pronounced a few days before an anathema against the insurgents.

Galignani's Messenger 2019 (15 August 1821) [p. 4] noted that '[t]his Prelate had not taken the least share in the insurrection of the Greeks' and that while his anathema was 'dictated [...] by the Mussulman's sabres', it was 'uttered to prevent the effusion of blood, and the massacre of the Greek Christians.' The Patriarch's death was also reported in the *Examiner* 700 (3 June 1821) 344 but S. probably learned of it through Alexandros Mavrokordatos's letter to Mary of 24 May 1821: 'Les lettres du hier nous confirment l'exécution du Patriarche de Constantinople et de trois archevêques, elles ne désignent pas les Princes Moresi et Mavrocordato; mais elles disent que plusieurs personnages [?manquans] furent décapités' (Bodleian MS. Abinger c. 45 f. 88^r; Yesterday's letters confirm for us the execution of the Patriarch of Constantinople and three archbishops; they do not refer to the Princes Moresi and Mavrocordato; but they say that several [? missing] individuals were beheaded). Mary mentions the beheadings laconically in a letter to Maria Gisborne of 28 May: 'The Greeks are getting on finely, except that the Patriarch and four Bishops, and some Princes have been decapitated in Constantinople' (*Mary L* i 200). *Patriarch ... insurgents*] Patriarch, ... insurgents, *1829, 1839, 1840. fulminate*] pronounce violently. *anathema*] curse; see *OED* 'anathema' *n.^{1}* 2b: 'In the Roman Catholic and Orthodox churches: a formal curse

>   Fortunately the Greeks have been taught that they cannot buy
> 5   security by degradation, and the Turks, though equally cruel,
>   are less cunning than the smooth-faced Tyrants of Europe.
>   As to the anathema, his Holiness might as well have thrown
>   his mitre at Mount Athos for any effect that it produced. The
>   Chiefs of the Greeks are almost all men of comprehension
> 10 and enlightened views on religion and politics.

---

excommunicating a person or denouncing a doctrine, etc.; the formal act or formula of excommunication.'

Note 3. 5. by degradation] by debasing themselves (see *OED* 3); cp. Byron, *Don Juan* iii 541-3:

> and such like things, that gain
> Their bread as ministers and favourites—(that's
> To say, by degradation)—mingled there

Note 3. 5-7. Turks, ... cruel,] *1822, 1829, 1839, 1840*; Turks ... cruel *HM 329*. *smooth-faced Tyrants of Europe.*] The governments of Restoration Europe are routinely referred to thus in the *Examiner*; see, e.g., 693 (15 April 1821) 231: 'The Greeks have risen in arms! What an inspiring sound! The other nations of Europe have been struggling with their several tyrannies for ages'. *Tyrants*] tyrants *1822, 1829, 1839, 1840*.

Note 3. 7-8. As to ... produced] This sentence begins a new paragraph in *1829, 1839, 1840*. *Mount Athos*] Mountain on a peninsula of the Macedonian coast, the location of several Orthodox monasteries. According to *Galignani's Messenger* 2019 (15 August 1821) [p. 4], the Patriarch was twice banished there from Constantinople by the Turkish Government. The claims of the monks of Mount Athos to have experienced divine visions are mocked as 'folly' by Gibbon in *Decline and Fall* Vol. VI ch. liii (Womersley, ed., iii 784).

Note 3. 8-10. The Chiefs ... politics] Cp. the *Examiner* 718 (7 October 1821) 631 which, in 'some friends of ours', refers to the Shelleys:

> The chief leaders of the Greeks have not only known "the world" in its ordinary sense, which means the bad and half-knowing part of it;— they have known misfortune; they have been wanderers; they have been witnesses, in Europe, of the sorry effects of retaliation, and the victorious ones of a generous self-possession [...] of another [of them], ALEXANDER MAVROCORDATO, nephew of PRINCE CARAYA, we heard a short time since in Italy, where he was reading Greek with some friends of ours, and doubtless cultivating those mutual dispositions which end in making men conquerors and pardoners.

Chiefs] chiefs *1822, 1829, 1839, 1840*. *on religion*] of religion *1834*. *politics.*] *1822, 1829, 1839*; politics *HM 329*.

Note 4.

[563.] The freedman of a western poet chief

A Greek who had been Lord Byron's servant commands the insurgents in Attica. This Greek, Lord Byron informs me, though a poet and an enthusiastic patriot, gave him rather the idea of a timid and unenterprising person. It appears that circumstances make men what they are, and that we all contain the germ of a degree of degradation or of greatness whose connection with our character is determined by events.

Note 4. Title. western poet chief] Western Poet Chief *HM 329*.
Note 4. 1-2. A Greek ... Attica.] 'His name (as notified in Moore's *Life of Byron*) was Demetrius Zograffo' (*Rossetti 1870* ii 557; Rossetti refers to Thomas Moore, *Letters and Journals of Lord Byron: with Notices of his Life*, 2 vols (1830) i 280 n.). commands] commanded *1829, 1834*.
Note 4. 2-7. This Greek ... by events] Cp. Byron's letter to Lady Byron of 14 September 1821:

> The Chief of the Athenian Insurgents is Demetrius Zograffo—who was my Servant for a long time—and with me in London—when I first knew you in 1812.—He was a clever but not an enterprising man—but circumstances make men. (*Byron L&J* viii 211)

Parallels between S.'s note ('unenterprising ... circumstances make men') and Byron's letter suggest the latter may have told S. about Zograffo during S.'s stay at Ravenna in August 1821. Byron appraises Zograffo in similar terms in 'Detached Thoughts' (15 October 1821-18 May 1822; see *Byron L&J* ix 23). Greek, ... me, ... patriot,] *Box 1, 1822, 1829, 1839, 1840*; Greek ... me ... patriot *HM 329*. they are,] *1822, 1829, 1839, 1840*; they are *HM 329*. or of greatness] or of greatness, *1829*; or greatness, *1834, 1839, 1840*.

Note 5.

[598.] *The Greeks expect a Saviour from the West*

It is reported that this Messiah had arrived at a sea-port near Lacedaemon in an American brig. The association of names and ideas is irresistibly ludicrous, but the prevalence of such a rumour strongly marks the state of popular enthusiasm in Greece.

Note 5. 1–2. It is reported … brig] As noted in Duffy, 'Percy Shelley's "display of newspaper erudition"' 522, the source of the report was *Galignani's Messenger* 2009 (3 August 1821) [p. 1]:

> 'The Greeks have long expected, with impatience and anxiety, the arrival of a mysterious personage, who was to deliver them, and give them permanent independence. This Prophet—this Messiah, is at length among them, and they fancy themselves at the summit of prosperity. No positive and authentic data respecting this person can be given.—Under circumstances like the present, it is difficult, nay impossible, to come at the truth, amidst a thousand extravagant fictions.—Every one reasons after his own manner. A person who does not know how lively, I may say, how volcanic, the imagination of the inhabitants of these countries is, can form no idea of the enthusiasm which the arrival of this person has excited in Greece. All that appears certain is, that an American ship, of 18 guns, brought him hither. This vessel was pursued all the way from the Cape of Good Hope by several English ships, but the American was such a good sailer that they could not overtake it. It has overcome all difficulties, and gliding over the waves with the rapidity of a bird, has arrived happily in the harbour of Rovarino[.] This is all I can now tell you. Little circumstances often produce great effects, and, in a political view, there is nothing indifferent in the conflict of human passions.—'

Lacedaemon] Lacedemon *1839, 1840*. The ancient name of Sparta, a city in the south of the Peloponnese.

Note 5. 2–4. The association … in Greece] Cp. the editorial commentary on the above report (on the same page of *Galignani's Messenger*):

> The strange narrative contained in the following article, dated Zante, we must leave to make its own impression upon the credulity or scepticism of our readers. If it be true that the Greeks cherish the superstitious expectations of a Prophet or Messiah one day appearing among them, to break their chains and restore them to liberty, it is not improbable that at a crisis, like the present, some enterprising impostor may start up, and avail himself of that notion, to rally under him the whole Greek population. We must confess, however, that the idea of an American brig bringing this mysterious personage from the Cape of Good Hope, and pursued all the way by several English ships, which strove, in vain, to overtake the sacred vessel, is a little difficult to be believed.

Note 6.

[*814–15.*] *The sound*
As of the assault of an imperial city

For the vision of Mahmud of the taking of Constantinople in 1453, see Gibbon's *Decline and Fall of the Roman Empire*, Vol. 12, p. 223. The manner of the invocation of the Spirit of Mahomet
5 the Second will be censured as over subtle. I could easily have made the Jew a regular conjuror, and the phantom an ordinary ghost. I have preferred to represent the Jew as disclaiming all pretension or even belief in supernatural agency, and as tempting Mahmud to that state of mind in which ideas may

Note 6. Title. As of the assault of an imperial city] *is of an Assault of an Imperial City. 1822.*
Note 6. 2–3. Vol. 12, p. 223] Vol 12 p. 223 *HM 329*; Vol. 12 p. 223 &c. *Box 1.* The volume and page numbers suggest S. refers to the 12–vol. edn of *Decline and Fall* published by Cadell and Davies in 1807 which he said he owned in his letter to [?Lackington, Allen & Company] of 26 September 1815 (*L* i 433); see *L* i 342 and the note to S.'s footnote to l. 35 of his Note to *Q Mab* v 189. Vol. 12 p. 223 is part of the paragraph in the section of ch. lxviii entitled 'Preparations of the Turks for the general assault, May 26'; the page begins 'chiefs; and dispersed' and ends 'visited the tents,' (see Womersley, ed., iii 957–8). *1453*] *Rossetti 1870*; 1445 *Box 1, HM 329, 1822, 1829, 1834, 1839, 1840.* The reason S. wrote '1445' rather than '1453' in *Box 1* is not clear.
Note 6. 4–6. manner] Written above *mode* canc. in *Box 1. Spirit*] *Box 1*; spirit *HM 329, 1822, 1829, 1839, 1840. over subtle.*] overdrawn *1829, 1834, 1839, 1840.* The full stop is followed by *But why should every one write according to the* canc. in *Box 1.*
Note 6. 6. Jew] jew *1829. regular*] 'formally trained' (*OED* 6b). *phantom*] phantasm *Box 1*; Phantom *1822.*
Note 6. 7–12. Jew] jew *1829. pretension*] pretension, *1822, 1829, 1839, 1840. belief*] belief, *1822, 1829, 1839, 1840. agency,*] *Box 1, 1822, 1829, 1839, 1840*; agency *HM 329. ideas may be supposed … creations of imagination*] The language is Wordsworthian. Cp. *Tintern Abbey* 102 ('all objects of all thought') and the Preface to *Lyrical Ballads* (1800): 'Poems to which any value can be attached, were never produced on any variety of subjects but by a man who being possessed of more than usual organic sensibility had also thought long and deeply. For our continued influxes of feeling are modified and directed by our thoughts' (*Wordsworth Prose* i 126). *sensations*] sensations, *Box 1, 1829*; sensation, *1834, 1839, 1840. and the excess*] and excess *1839, 1840. of imagination*] of the imagination *1839, 1840.*

10   be supposed to assume the force of sensations through the confusion of thought with the objects of thought, and the excess of passion animating the creations of imagination.

        It is a sort of natural magic, susceptible of being exercised in a degree by any one who should have made himself master
15   of the secret associations of another's thoughts.

Note 6. 13–15. It is ... thoughts.] The following draft after this sentence in *Box 1* is cancelled: *The vision of Mahmud is* and *No reader will be so severe as to insist upon the imagery of such a poem as Hellas* au pied du lettre. *there is an ideal possibility.* The phrase *au pied de la lettre* = 'literally'. *natural magic*] 'magic involving the manipulation of supposed occult properties of the natural world (usually excluding the conjuration of personal spirits)' (*OED* 'magic', *n.* 1b). S. refers to his youthful 'fondness for natural magic' in a letter to Godwin of 3 June 1812 (*L* i 303) and uses the phrase to explain the plot of *Zastrozzi* in a letter to John Joseph Stockdale of 14 November 1810: 'Ginotti, as you will see did *not* die by Wolfstein's hand, but by the influence of that natural magic which when the secret was imparted to the latter, destroyed him' (*L* i 20). *any one ... another's thoughts*] Cp. *The Cenci* where Giacomo acknowledges that Orsino has made himself master of his thoughts (V i 19–24) and Orsino fears Beatrice discovering his motives and thereby gaining mastery over him (I ii 83–7). See also S.'s letter to Mary of 8–10 August 1821 from Ravenna reflecting on his uneasy relationship with Byron: 'What is passing in the heart of another rarely escapes the observation of one who is a strict anatomist of his own—' (*L* ii 324). *made himself master of*] The words *made himself master* are written above *discovered* canc. in *Box 1*. *thoughts*] Written after *ideas* canc. in *Box 1*.

Note 7.

[*1060. SD.*] *Chorus*

The final chorus is indistinct and obscure as the event of the living drama whose arrival it foretells. Prophecies of wars, and rumours of wars &c., may safely be made by poet or prophet in any age, but to anticipate, however darkly, a
5   period of regeneration and happiness is a more hazardous exercise of the faculty which bards possess or feign. It will remind the reader 'magno, *nec* proximus intervallo' of Isaiah

Note 7. Title. *Chorus*] *1839, 1840*; omitted in *HM 329* and *1822*.
Note 7. 1. *chorus*] Chorus *1822. obscure*] obscure, *1822. event*] outcome.
Note 7. 2-6. *Prophecies ... feign*] This sentence begins a new paragraph in *1840. wars &c.,*] wars &ca, *HM 329*; wars, &c. *1822, 1839, 1840*; wars, etc. *1829. age,*] age; *1829, 1839, 1840. anticipate, ... darkly,*] anticipate ... darkly *1822, 1829, 1839, 1840. happiness*] happiness, *1829, 1839, 1840*.
Note 7. 6-11. *It*] I *1829. reader*] reader, *1829, 1839, 1840*. '*magno,* nec *proximus intervallo*'] Modelled on Virgil, *Aeneid* v 230, 'longo sed proximus intervallo' ('but next by a long distance'), which describes the order of runners in a footrace. There is some doubt as to how S. intends his version to be read. The more obvious meaning of his Latin would be 'and not next by a great distance', i.e. suggesting, by a slight alteration of a Virgilian phrase, that the resemblance of his chorus to Isaiah and Virgil will strike readers as an especially close one. It has also been suggested by E. B. Murray that we are to understand S.'s phrase as meaning 'not near, <but> at a great interval' (*BSM* xxi 443), i.e. (in complete contrast to the above) admitting that the resemblance of his chorus to Isaiah and Virgil, whether in style or quality, is not exceptionally close. This requires a less obvious reading of the Latin, however, even if the comma which S. places after *magno* could be thought to make such a reading easier. Although Murray's reading is persuasive, it might also be pointed out that this second option would have been far more clearly expressed by an exact quotation of the Virgilian phrase although S. is, of course, capable of misquotation, as the reference to Isaiah later in this sentence shows. *magno,*] magno *eds*; the reading *magno,* is also found in *Box 1*. nec] nec *1829, 1834, 1839, 1840. intervallo'*] intervallo,' *1829. Isaiah and Virgil ... 'omnis feret omnia tellus'*] Cp. Gibbon's account of Constantine's discourse on *Eclogue* iv in *Decline and Fall* Vol. II (1781) ch. xx:

> Forty years before the birth of Christ, the Mantuan bard, as if inspired by the celestial muse of Isaiah, had celebrated, with all the pomp of Oriental metaphor, the return of the Virgin, the fall of the serpent, the approaching birth of a godlike child, the offspring of the great Jupiter, who should expiate the guilt of human kind, and govern the peaceful

and Virgil, whose ardent spirits overleaping the actual reign
of evil which we endure and bewail, already saw the possible
10   and perhaps approaching state of society in which the '*lion
shall lie down with the lamb*' and 'omnis feret omnia tellus'. Let
these great names be my authority and my excuse.

universe with the virtues of his father; the rise and appearance of a heavenly race, a primitive nation throughout the world; and the gradual restoration of the innocence and felicity of the golden age. The poet was perhaps unconscious of the secret sense and object of these sublime predictions, which have been so unworthily applied to the infant son of a consul, or a triumvir: but if a more splendid, and indeed specious, interpretation of the fourth eclogue contributed to the conversion of the first Christian emperor, Virgil may deserve to be ranked among the most successful missionaries of the gospel. (Womersley, ed., i 744)

spirits] spirits, *1840*. 'lion shall lie down with the lamb'] '*lion shall lie down with the lamb,*' *Box 1, 1822*; 'lion shall lie down with the lamb,' *1829, 1834, 1839, 1840*. The alteration of *lay* to *lie* in *Box 1* is repeated in *HM 329* (with the last two letters overwritten), whether in S.'s hand or Williams's is uncertain. A misquotation of *Isaiah* xi 6: 'The wolf also shall dwell with the lamb, and the leopard shall lie down with the kid'. '*omnis feret omnia tellus*'] 'every land will bear all fruits' (*Eclogue* iv 39). *tellus'*.] tellus.'— *Box 1, 1822, 1829*; tellus' *HM 329*; tellus. *1839*; tellus.' *1840*. Note 7. 12. and my excuse.] and excuse *1829, 1834, 1839, 1840*.

Note 8.

[*1090–1.*] *Saturn and Love their long repose*
Shall burst

Saturn and Love were among the deities of a real or imaginary state of innocence and happiness. *All* those *who fell,* or the gods of Greece, Asia, and Egypt; *the One who rose* or Jesus Christ, at whose appearance the idols of the Pagan world were amerced
5   of their worship; and *the many unsubdued,* or the monstrous objects of the idolatry of China, India, the Antarctic islands and the native tribes of America certainly have reigned over the understandings of men in conjunction or in succession, during periods in which all we know of evil has been in a state
10   of portentous, and, until the revival of learning and the arts,

Note 8. 1. Saturn and Love] See note to l. 1090.
Note 8. 2-10. All ... who fell ... the One who rose ... the many unsubdued] All ... who fell ... the One who rose ... the many unsubdued *1829, 1834.* All *those* who fell] See note to l. 1092. *gods*] Gods *1822, 1829, 1834, 1839, 1840. Asia,*] Asia *1829. Egypt;*] Egypt, *1829.* the One who rose ... *their worship*] This passage was first published in *1839* (see Headnote ('Publication')). Cp. *DP*: 'Christianity, in its abstract purity, became the exoteric expression of the esoteric doctrines of the poetry and wisdom of antiquity [...] no nation or religion can supersede any other without incorporating into itself a portion of that which it supersedes' (*Reiman (2002)* para. 25). rose] *rose, 1822 Unexpurgated, 1839, 1840.* amerced *of*] deprived of. *worship;*] worship: *1822 Unexpurgated.* many unsubdued] See note to l. 1093. unsubdued, *or*] *1822, 1839;* unsubdued or, *HM 329;* unsubdued, or *1829; unsubdued* or *1840. islands*] islands, *1822, 1829, 1839, 1840. America*] America, *1822, 1829, 1839, 1840. portentous*] the sense may be 'prodigious' (*OED* 2) rather than 'ominous' (*OED* 1). *and, until*] *1822, 1829, 1839, 1840;* and until *HM 329. until the revival of learning and the arts*] Cp. *PVR*: 'Many native Indians have acquired a competent knowledge in the arts & philosophy of Europe, & Locke & Hume & Rousseau are familiarly talked of in Brahminical society. But the thing to be sought is that they should, as they would if they were free attain to a system of arts & literature of their own' (*SC* vi 987–8).
Note 8. 11-13. gods] Gods *1829, 1834, 1839, 1840. said*] said, *1822. that*] that, *1829, 1839, 1840. concerned*] concerned, *1822, 1829, 1839, 1840.*

perpetually increasing activity. The Grecian gods seem indeed to have been personally more innocent, although it cannot be said that as far as temperance and chastity are concerned they gave so edifying an example as their successor. The sublime
15 human character of Jesus Christ was deformed by an imputed identification of it with a Demon, who tempted, betrayed and punished the innocent beings who were called into existence by his sole will; and for the period of a thousand years the spirit of this the most just, wise and benevolent of men has
20 been propitiated with myriads of hecatombs of those who approached the nearest to his innocence and his wisdom, sacrificed under every aggravation of atrocity and variety of torture. The horrors of the Mexican, the Peruvian, and the Indian superstitions are well known.

Note 8. 14–23. *so edifying an example ... of torture.*] Prior to *1839* when most of this passage was first published in unexpurgated form (see Headnote ('Publication')), it was replaced with the words 'very edifying examples.'
Note 8. 16–20. *of it with a Demon*] with a power *1839. betrayed*] betrayed, *1822 Unexpurgated, 1839, 1840. years*] years, *1839, 1840. this the most*] this most *1839, 1840. just, wise*] just wise *HM 329*; just, wise, *1822 Unexpurgated, 1839, 1840. men*] men, *1839, 1840. hecatombs*] sacrifices. Cp. *PU* I 7 and *A Letter to Lord Ellenborough* (1812): 'the Demon to whom savage nations offer human hecatombs is less barbarous than the Deity of civilized society' (*Prose Works* i 65).
Note 8. 23–24. *The horrors of ... the Indian superstitions are well known*] See *PVR*:

> Revolutions in the political & religious state of the Indian peninsula, seem to be accomplishing, & it cannot be doubted but the zeal of the missionaries of what is called the Christian faith, will produce beneficial innovation there, even by the application of dogmas & forms of what is here an outworn incumbrance. The Indians have been enslaved & cramped in the most severe & paralysing forms which were ever devised; some new enthusiasm ought to be kindled among them to consume it & leave them free, and even if the doctrines of Jesus do not penetrate through the darkness of that which those who profess to be his followers call Christianity, there will yet be a number of social forms modelled upon those European feelings from which it has taken its colour, substituted to those according to which they are at present cramped, & from which, when the term for complete emancipation shall arrive, their disengagement may be less difficult, & under which their progress to it may be less imperceptibly slow. (*SC* vi 987)

Indian] Indian, *1839.*

411 Appendix

Lines connected with Hellas

The verses in this Appendix are all located in *Nbk 21* and range from a text that consists of one and a half lines to one which runs to 201 lines. Although they differ widely in prosodic invention and rhetorical strategies, it seems that they are all concerned with Greece in 1821, her struggle for independence, and S.'s hope for an international response to that struggle. Appendices A-G include *It is the period when all the Sons of God* (Appendix A, described by previous editors as the 'Prologue to *Hellas*') and verses which appear to be preludes to, or part of, that sustained work. The next group of texts, Appendices H–J, are verses that are integrated into the drafts of *Hellas* (no. 411) but were ultimately omitted when S. stitched together the final version of his lyrical drama. The assigning of lines to these two groups is occasionally conjectural for sometimes a passage is found in drafts for *It is the period* as well as *Hellas*. Unlike the first two groups which appear only right way up on pages in the forwards direction of *Nbk 21* as now paginated, the last group of texts, Appendices K–M, while still attached to the theme of the Greek struggle, are all inscribed *reverso* on pages in the present reversed direction of the notebook and appear to belong to a different compositional impulse. It is possible that this last group of texts could be post-*Hellas* compositions. The fact that all of the *Hellas* material is written in the notebook's forwards direction — a singular feature of this notebook unlike the more widely and evenly distributed right way up and *reverso* movements in other notebooks — suggests that it was purchased with the express purpose of composing a work addressed to the Greek war of independence. Of the 264 extant pages in *Nbk 21*, 185 of them, all right way up, contain *Hellas*-related materials (Appendices A–J). Only 27 pages contain *reverso*-inscribed texts; those pages include Appendices K–M, the epitaph on Keats (*Epitaph* (no. 420)), and the reading notes for *Charles the First* (no. 426). The most likely date for the writing of the epitaph and the *Charles* reading notes is November–December 1821, and given the proximity of Appendices K-M to those texts, a late autumn date seems a likely period for their composition as well.

Mary transcribed and published (in *1840*) part of only one of these texts, *I would not be a King: enough* (Appendix J). Richard Garnett published several more passages in *Relics* (1862), the longest and most important of these being what he termed 'an unfinished prologue to

DOI: 10.4324/9781315779874-5

"Hellas'" (2). In 1886 Thomas Wise printed 'for private distribution only' an edition of the 'Prologue to Hellas' section of *Relics*. It included a Postscript by Garnett (cited in the headnote to Appendix A) and notes by Wise. This edition was reproduced in the Shelley Society's edition of *Hellas* in the same year (2nd edn 1886, 3rd edn 1887), with Garnett's Postscript incorporated into his introductory note. Sir John Shelley-Rolls and Roger Ingpen published a group of eleven fragments in 1934 (*V&P* 49–52), as well as further lines to Garnett's so-called 'Prologue' (47–8), clarifying this addition in a note: 'Garnett printed practically all of the Prologue. We give a further portion of the dialogue between Christ and Satan' (147–8). In 1994, Donald H. Reiman and Michael J. Neth edited *Nbk 21* with complete transcriptions in *BSM* xvi. The piecemeal publication history of these verses has meant that contiguous passages have been separated; cancelled and in some cases abandoned passages have gained an authority over other more finished versions. Many of the freshly edited texts here show S. devising rigorous formal structures coupled with freedom and inventiveness, features which were not revealed in earlier editions. The effort in the present edition has been, first, to re-examine the MS evidence, which has resulted in numerous new readings, and secondly, to represent as nearly as possible the latest state of a text with some attention given to previous versions. Individual headnotes indicate the texts' likely relationship to *Hellas* and details of previous publication, where applicable.

A: 'It is the period when all the Sons of God'
[Prologue to Hellas]

This substantial fragment represents S.'s first sustained attempt to write a poem on the Greek War of Independence, a project which found its completed form in *Hellas* (see headnote to no. 411). It is drafted roughly in *Nbk 21* pp. 13–37, where it is preceded in the order of items in the forwards direction of that notebook as now paginated (see *BSM* xvi p. xxvii) by other shorter passages of draft obviously also intended for the work which became *Hellas*: *Youngest of the Destinies* (Appendix B), *Suns and stars are rolling ever* (Appendix C), and *We pass, outspeeding the thunder* (Appendix D). S.'s draft of *Hellas* itself almost immediately follows this long fragment in *Nbk 21*, and it is clear that his original conception for the form of his poem, as represented here, was abandoned when he decided to recast it as a drama modelled on the *Persae* of Aeschylus. S. was writing

Hellas in its published form in late September and October of 1821, so the present lines must have been drafted in the immediately preceding period, some time between late August when S. returned from his visit to Byron in Ravenna, and late September when he changed his mind about the form of the work.

The lines were first published under the title 'Prologue to Hellas' by Richard Garnett in *Relics*, where in a prefatory note he described the challenges presented by the draft in *Nbk 21*:

> Few even of Shelley's rough drafts have proved more difficult to decipher or connect; numerous chasms will be observed, which, with every diligence, it has proved impossible to fill up; the correct reading of many printed lines is far from certain; and the imperfection of some passages is such as to have occasioned their entire omission. (*Relics* 3)

This does not overstate the challenges of S.'s draft, which combines extensive cancellation and frequent doubtful or illegible readings with a series of perplexing issues concerning the intended order of lines. Garnett's editorial redaction represents a considerable achievement in itself, and has provided the sole source of the text for all subsequent editions of S.'s poetry until the present one. The manuscript was published in a photo-facsimile with a diplomatic transcription in *BSM* xvi (edited by Donald Reiman and Michael Neth) in 1994, and that volume's work represents the only published editorial attention given to *It is the period when all the Sons of God* since Garnett's efforts more than 130 years earlier. The *BSM* transcription improves many of Garnett's readings, and has greatly benefitted the text of the present edition, which has also drawn on the transcription of *Nbk 21* made by GM in the early 1960s.

The *BSM* editors argue that a comparison of their transcription of pp. 25–8 of *Nbk 21* with Garnett's published text (corresponding to ll. 87–119 of the text in *Hutchinson* and ll. 97–133 of the present text),

> reveals that Garnett took considerable liberties in rearranging these lines and transposing sections of several pages out of sequence in order to construct a text that appears to have Christ drawing ready and facile parallels between the "Golden Age" of high Athenian culture in the fifth and fourth centuries B.C.E. and his own martyrdom to renewed ignorance centuries later. In fact, however, PBS's several closely related and canceled false starts on pp. 23–8 indicate that he became bogged down

at this point — and for good reason, if one considers the implications of his ideas [i.e. S.'s ideas, concerning what the *BSM* editors characterise as an emerging conflict in the draft between on the one hand Destiny, and on the other human will, as the means to determine the outcome of the revolutionary war]. (*BSM* xvi p. xxxvi)

However, these strictures seem harsh on Garnett, who was attempting to produce a readable editorial redaction which respected S.'s intentions, so far as these could be inferred from the relative chaos of the draft. It is true that Garnett's text does not entirely follow the page sequence in *Nbk 21*, and that he made decisions about how to place in relatively coherent sequence passages of draft separated one from another on the page or on different pages. But the draft itself is evidently working towards coherence, in a way which characteristically involves rapid composition with copious cancellation and redrafting, second and third thoughts, passages reworked in different places, and uncertain connections between spatially disparate lines. The present text differs in various ways from Garnett's redaction, but it too is based on reasoned decisions concerning the order of the lines, in the service of a readable text, and is mainly in broad agreement with many of his choices (see e.g. notes to ll. 107–31 below).

The approach to the subject of the struggle for Greek Independence which S. adopted in *It is the period when all the Sons of God* was to place it in a transhistorical and cosmic context, where the opening lines address rulers of all past ages, and envision the earth as one of countless planets wandering through interstellar space, before turning to the fate of Greece since classical times. As the *BSM* editors note, its conception seems to hover undecidedly between epic and dramatic modes, with a noticeable Miltonic influence (*BSM* xvi 'Introduction' pp. xxxiii–xxxiv). The idea of a grand dialogue between supernatural protagonists as they comment on worldly events also strongly suggests the opening chapters of the Book of Job, a work which had long been of interest to S. Another possible model is the opening 'Prolog im Himmel' of Goethe's *Faust*, which S. translated in early 1822 (see *Prologue in Heaven* (no. 447)); however, it should be noted that S. avoids one of the most controversial aspects of Goethe's scene by not giving God a speaking part in *It is the period when all the Sons of God*. It was presumably the perceived influence of *Faust* which prompted Garnett to his title 'Prologue to Hellas', although the fragment was almost certainly not intended as a Prologue to the published work, but rather represents an abandoned first approach to the subject.

Wise's 1886 edition of the 'Prologue to Hellas' section of *Relics* included the following Postscript by Garnett:

> Besides the evident imitation of the Book of Job, the resemblance of the first draft of "Hellas" to the machinery of Dryden's intended epic is to be noted. "He gives," says Johnson, summarising Dryden's preface to his translation of Juvenal, "an account of the design which he had once formed to write an epic poem on the actions of either Arthur or the Black Prince. He considered the epic as necessarily involving some kind of supernatural agency, and had imagined a new kind of contest between the guardian angels of kingdoms, of whom he conceived that each might be represented zealous for his charge without any intended opposition to the purposes of the Supreme Being, of which all created minds must in part be ignorant.
> This is the most reasonable scheme of celestial interposition that ever was formed."

The passage Garnett cites is from Johnson's life of 'Dryden' (see Samuel Johnson, *The Lives of the Most Eminent English Poets; with Critical Observations on their Works* (1781), ed. Roger Lonsdale, 4 vols (2006) ii 106–7); Johnson is referring to Dryden's 'A Discourse Concerning the Original and Progress of Satire' (1693) (see John Dryden, *Of Dramatic Poesy and other critical essays*, ed. George Watson, 2 vols (1962), ii 91–2). Although *The Vision of Judgment* (1822) cannot have been an influence on *It is the period when all the Sons of God*, since 'almost all of the poem was written between 20 September and 4 October 1821' (*Byron PW* vi 669), and S. only read it (probably in proof) on 9 November (*Gisborne Jnl* 111), Byron had begun composing it on 7 May of that year (*Byron PW* vi 668) and it can be seen as a parallel endeavour which Byron may have discussed with S. at Ravenna in August.

Critical accounts of *It is the period* are offered in *BSM* xvi pp. xxxiii–xxxvii and Cian Duffy, 'Percy Bysshe Shelley's Other Lyrical Drama and the Inception of *Hellas*', *SEL* lv (2015) 817–40, esp. 827–34.

Text from *Nbk 21* pp. 13–37.

Published in *Relics* 4–11 (ll. 1–4, 6–17, 20–25, part of 29, 30, part of 31, part of 32, part of 34, 35–43, 45–50, 52–58, part of 59, 60–3, 67–71, part of 72, 73–7, 79–81, part of 82, part of 83, 84–9, 94–5, 98–114, 116–56, part of 157, 158–174, part of 175, part of 188, 189–195, 197–201; *V&P* 47–8 (ll. 175–90); *BSM* xvi 16–41 (facsimile and transcription of MS).

'It is the period when all the Sons of God'

Herald of Eternity
It is the period when all the Sons of God
Meet in the roofless Senate House, whose floor
Is Chaos, and the immoveable abyss
Frozen by his word to steadfast hyaline.
5   Impenetrable hate sits there enthroned,
The shadow of God — and delegated Cause
Of that, before whose breath the Universe
Is as a point of dew —
                Hierarchs and Kings
Who from your thrones pinnacled in the past

¶ **411 Appendix A** *1–2*. Cp. *Job* i 6: 'Now there was a day when the sons of God came to present themselves before the Lord, and Satan came also among them.'
1. period] day *Relics*. Written above *day* canc. in *Nbk 21. Sons*] sons *Relics*.
2. Meet] Wait *Relics. Senate House*] senate-house *Relics*. Written above *palace* canc. in *Nbk 21*.
4. Frozen by His steadfast word to hyaline *Relics*. S. first wrote *solid hyaline* in *Nbk 21*, then cancelled *solid* and wrote alternatives above and below, read by *BSM* as 'firm' and 'abiding'; *steadfast* is written above but a little to the left, prompting Garnett to attach it to *word. hyaline*] 'a poetic term for the smooth sea, the clear sky, or any transparent substance' (*OED*). Cp. *Paradise Lost* vii 617–19:

> Witness this new-made world, another heaven
> From heaven gate not far, founded in view
> On the clear hyaline, the glassy sea

Milton's reference is to the 'sea of glass like unto crystal' (θάλασσα ὑαλίνη) of *Revelation* iv 6; S. uses the word in *PU* (no. 195) II v 21.
5. This line is omitted in *Relics* and represented by a line of asterisks. *Impenetrable*] *Insuperable*, on the preceding (and facing) page in *Nbk 21* (p. 12), may be intended as an alternative.
6. God —] God, *Relics. delegated Cause*] delegate *Relics*.
7. that,] that *Relics. Universe*] universe *Relics*.
8. point] print *Relics*, *BSM*. S. first wrote *As an autumn leaf* in *Nbk 21*, then cancelled *autumn* and wrote *point of dew* above, then *Is* to the left of *As*; he omitted to alter *an* to *a* in this series of emendations. *dew* —] dew. *Relics. Hierarchs*] Those who 'have rule or authority in holy things' (*OED* 1). The word is Miltonic (see *Paradise Lost* v 468, xi 220) and is also found in *Charles the First* (no. 426) iv 60. *Kings*] kings *Relics*.
9. your] yon *Forman 1876–7. in*] on *Relics*.

10 Rule the reluctant present — ye who sit
   Pavilioned in the radiance or the gloom
   Of mortal thought, which like an exhalation
   Steaming from earth, [?curtains] the [?light] of Heaven
   Which gave it [being] ... assemble here ...
15 Before [her] father's throne the swift decree
   Yet hovers ... but the [fiery] incarnation
   Is yet withheld, in which will be arrayed
   The power, [
                                                 ]
   Shall arbitrate the instant [?hours'] [?count]. —
20 The fairest of yon wandering isles that gem
   The purple space of interstellar air,
   That green and azure [sphere], that Earth, is wrapt

10. Rule] Sway *Relics*; Mark *BSM*. Sway is written as an uncancelled alternative above *Rule* in *Nbk 21. present* —] present, *Relics*.
11. in] on *Relics*.
12-13. an exhalation / ... from earth] Cp. *Paradise Lost* i 710-11: 'Anon out of the earth a fabric huge / Rose like an exhalation'.
13. [?curtains]] conceals *Relics*; [?darkens] GM; [?conceals] *BSM*. Written beneath *blots* canc. and *conceals* canc. in *Nbk 21. [?light]]* [?fire] GM. Written above *lamp* canc. in *Nbk 21* (*BSM* reads '[limits]'). *Relics* leaves a blank space. *Heaven]* heaven *Relics*.
14. Which gave it birth,   assemble here Relics. [being] ...] [being] .. Nbk 21.
15. Before your Father's throne; the swift decree *Relics. Before]* Written above *Yet at* canc. in *Nbk 21. father's]* fathers *Nbk 21*; Father's *Relics. throne]* throne; *Relics*.
16. hovers ... but] hovers, and *Relics. [fiery]]* The word *fiery* in ink is cancelled in pencil; it is apparently replaced by an indecipherable word in pencil at the foot of *Nbk 21* p. 14.
17-19. Relics reads 'Is yet withheld, clothed in which it shall', followed by a line of blank space except for the word 'annul' (which has no basis in the *Nbk 21* draft).
18-19. The draft of these lines in *Nbk 21* p. 15 is confused and unresolvable. It includes the words: *clothed in which might* and *[The unconquerable Might ... whose]*.
19. [?hours']] [?hours] *Nbk 21. [?count]]* [?out] GM; [?spent] *BSM*.
20. yon] those *Relics*. Written above *those* canc. in *Nbk 21*.
21. Cp. 'the dark space of interstellar air' in *Fragments of an Unfinished Drama* (no. 436) l. 29. *purple space]* sapphire space *Relics*. Written above *azure depths* canc. in *Nbk 21* (with *space* alt. from *spaces*); one uncancelled alternative to *purple* is *liquid*, the other, undecipherable, is presumably what Garnett read as 'sapphire'. *air,]* *Relics*; air *Nbk 21*.
22. green and azure [sphere]] Locock 1911 ii 466 cps *PU* IV 459. *Earth, is wrapt]* earth inwrapt *Relics*.

>   Less in the beauty of its tender light
>   Than in an atmosphere of living [?]
>   25   Which interpenetrating all things, [?]
>   Its [?heart's] inhabitants to Heaven;
>   Like sparks and smoke contending as they burst
>   Out of a deluge of circumfluous fire
>   Tempestuously it sweeps from realm to realm

24. S. first wrote *Than in a spirit* in *Nbk 21*, then cancelled *spirit* and wrote *atmosphere*, omitting to change *a* to *an*. [?]] spirit *Relics*. The cancelled word *spirit* is overwritten in *Nbk 21* with an indecipherable word in ink, also cancelled; above, the cancelled alternative in ink and the uncancelled one in pencil are both indecipherable.

25–36. These lines in *Nbk 21* are represented in *Relics* as follows:

>   Which interpenetrating all the
>   it rolls from realm to realm
>   And age to age, and in its ebb and flow
>   Impels the generations
>   To their appointed place,
>   Whilst the high Arbiter
>   Beholds the strife, and at the appointed time
>   Sends his decrees veiled in eternal

25. [?]] One word appears to be written over another and then cancelled in *Nbk 21*. GM reads '[?lifts]'.

26. The draft in *Nbk 21* is tangled and apparently unresolved; '[?heart's]' is a debatable reading (the apostrophe is editorial), and *Heaven* is squeezed downwards against the right margin, with a possible semi-colon written below and, below that, an illegible word read by *BSM* as 'rise', making a kind of grammatical sense if 'which' is understood before 'rise' (i.e. the plural subject of the verb would be 'the inhabitants of the Earth's heart').

28. circumfluous] surrounding; the idea of a 'deluge of … fire' draws on the literal meaning of 'circumfluous': 'flowed around, surrounded by water' (*OED*). See *Paradise Lost* vii 269–71: 'so he the world / Built on circumfluous waters calm, in wide / Crystalline ocean'.

29. sweeps] Written above *rolls* canc. in *Nbk 21*.

30　And age to age, and in its ebb and flow
　　Impels the generations, whom it [?hurries]
　　To their appointed place —
　　　　　　　　　　　Evil and good
　　Like adverse whirlwinds still [?embroil] the storm
　　Whilst the high arbiter whose voice [　?　]
35　Beholds the strife — and at the [?fatal] [?hour]
　　Sends his Decrees veiled in eternal [light].
　　Within the circuit of this pendulous orb
　　There lies an antique region, on which fell
　　The dews of thought in the world's golden dawn,
40　Earliest and most benign; and from it sprung
　　Temples and cities and immortal forms
　　And harmonies of wisdom and of song
　　And thoughts, and deeds worthy of thoughts so fair
　　As flowers and herbs beneath bright April tears. —
45　And when the Sun of its dominion failed
　　And when the Winter of its glory came,

32. *their appointed place* —] Cp. 'th' appointed place' in *May-day Night* l. 3. The dash following *place* is written over three suspension points in *Nbk 21* and would appear to make redundant the dash before *Evil* in the line below.
33. *still*] Written above *more* uncanc. in *Nbk 21*. *[?embroil]*] Evil God *BSM*.
34. [　?　]] This word is compressed into the bottom corner of *Nbk 21* p. 16; *BSM* reads '[?groans]' above *I am* canc.
35. GM's reading of the tangled draft in *Nbk 21*. *BSM* reads '[are]' for *and*, and '[fated] [?heirs]' for [*?fatal*] [*?hour*].
36. *Decrees*] Decree's *Nbk 21*. *[light].*] [light] *Nbk 21*.
37. *pendulous*] pendant *Relics*. I.e. 'hanging or floating in the air or in space' (*OED*). See *Paradise Lost* iv 1000-1: 'The pendulous round earth with balanced air / In counterpoise'.
38. *an antique region*] I.e. Greece.
39. *world's*] *Relics*; worlds *Nbk 21*. *dawn,*] dawn *Nbk 21*, *Relics*.
40. *benign;*] benign, *Relics*. S.'s punctuation mark in *Nbk 21* is ambiguous and could be read as a colon (as it is in *BSM*).
42. *song*] song, *Relics*.
43. *thoughts,*] *Relics*; thoughts *Nbk 21*. *fair*] fair. *Relics*.
44. The line is omitted in *Relics*. *bright April tears.* —] S. first wrote *the tears of May* in *Nbk 21* then cancelled *the tears of* and wrote *bright April tears.* — beneath.
45. *Sun*] sun *Relics*. *dominion failed*] dominion failed, *Relics*; domain fail *BSM*.
46. *Winter*] winter *Relics*. *came,*] *Relics*; came *Nbk 21*.

The winds that stripped it bare, blew on and swept
That dew into the utmost wildernesses
In wandering clouds of sunny rain, that thawed
50   The unmaternal bosom of the North
And paved the torrid South with orient [?flame].

Haste, Sons of God — [   ] for ye beheld,
Reluctant or consenting or astonished,
The three Decrees go forth which pour on Greece
55   Ruin and Degradation and despair ...
A fourth now waits. — Assemble, Sons of God,
To speed or to prevent or to suspend,
If, as ye dream, such power be not withheld
The unaccomplished Destiny. —

47. *bare,*] bare *Relics*.
49. *In*] The *BSM*. *rain,*] rain *Relics*.
50. *North*] North. *Relics*.
51. This line is omitted in *Relics*. Beneath the ink draft of it in *Nbk 21* p. 18 are the pencilled words: *Fertilizing the desolation*. *South*] Written above *dust* canc. in *Nbk 21. orient*] Written above *eastern* canc. in *Nbk 21. [?flame].*] [?flame] *Nbk 21*; forms *BSM*.
52. S. left a blank space before drafting this line at the bottom of the page (p. 18) in *Nbk 21*, and then tried to complete it at the top of the next and facing page (p. 19); however, it is not clear from the draft how to resolve a metrical line. *Haste,*] *Relics*; Haste *Nbk 21*. *Sons of God* —] sons of God, *Relics*. *beheld,*] *Relics*; beheld *Nbk 21*.
53. *Reluctant or consenting*] Reluctant, or consenting, *Relics*. *astonished,*] *Relics*; astonished *Nbk 21*.
54. The stern decrees go forth, which heaped on Greece *Relics*. *three*] stern *BSM*. *pour*] Written above *to heap* canc. in *Nbk 21*. *on*] Alt. from *of* in *Nbk 21*.
55. Ruin and degradation and despair. *Relics*. *despair ...*] despair ...... *Nbk 21*.
56. A fourth now waits: assemble, sons of God, *Relics*. *Assemble, Sons*] assemble Sons *Nbk 21*. *God,*] God *Nbk 21*.
57. *suspend,*] *Relics*; suspend *Nbk 21*.
58. *If, as ye dream,*] *Relics*; If as ye dream *Nbk 21*. *withheld*] witheld *Nbk 21*; withheld, *Relics*.
59. There is a stop after *Destiny* in *Nbk 21*, followed by three suspension points and a dash that appears to cancel them. *Mahomet* is centred clearly in *Nbk 21* p. 19 and indicates a new speech, but below *By the spear* there is a long centred dash, and below it, a single apparently unconnected line, *The world must bleed*

          Mahomet
                              By the spear

                    * * * * *

60   The curtain of the universe
            Is rent and shattered ...
        The splendour-wingèd worlds disperse
            Like wild doves scattered,
        As earthquake splits a screen of crag
65   And the snow and dust in many a jag
            Cling in the astonished air. —

---

from all its gaping wounds, with another dash centred below it as if to mark it off clearly from other draft on the page. *BSM* conjectures that it may be meant for insertion into the draft material on the facing p. 18, possibly as an alternative to ll. 47–50 above. *Relics* omits *By the spear. Destiny.* —] destiny. *Relics.*
60–89. S. moves from blank verse to lyric in these lines, anticipating the alternation between dramatic and choric passages in *Hellas*; however, in this draft the lyric movement never quite settles to a definite pattern, seeming to experiment with line-lengths and rhymes as the poetry develops. There is no authority in *Nbk 21* for *Relics* attributing these lines to a 'Chorus'.
60–1. Next to the tangled draft of these lines in *Nbk 21* p. 20, S. drew eight short vertical lines (three above five), presumably representing a syllable-count for the eight-syllable first line of the lyric interlude (there are similar marks on p. 22).
60. universe] Universe *Relics.*
61. shattered ...] shattered, *Relics.*
63. scattered,] scattered — *Nbk 21*; scattered. *Relics.*
64–6. These lines are omitted in *Relics.*
66. astonished air —] Written in pencil beneath *vacant [air]* — in *Nbk 21*, with *sky* canc. followed by three suspension points written beneath *air* canc. (the punctuation mark after *air* may be a full stop rather than a dash). This phrase is used in *Charles the First* I i 140.

     The space is roofless and bare —
    In the midst a cloudy shrine
     Dark [amid] thrones of light; —
70 Through the thin floor of hyaline
    Golden worlds [revolve] and shine
     In unwearied flight; —
  From every point of the infinite,
  Like a thousand dawns on a single night,
75   The Splendours rise and spread.

  Through thunder and darkness dread
  Light and music are radiated —
  And the ether from God's own spirit fed;
  And in their pavilioned chariots led
80 By [?living] wings far overhead
  The giant Powers move

67–70. In *Relics* these lines read as follows:

> Space is roofless and bare,
> And in the midst a cloudy shrine,
> Dark amid thrones of light.
> In the blue glow of hyaline

67. The two centred horizontal lines (enclosing some cancelled false starts) above the draft of this line at the top of *Nbk 21* p. 21 appear to indicate a stanza-break.
68. *In*] Written over *And* in *Nbk 21*.
69. *light; —*] light — *Nbk 21*.
70. *Through*] Written beneath *And* canc. in *Nbk 21*, with *and* uncanc. above. *hyaline*] See note to l. 4 above.
71. *[revolve]*] Written above *move* canc. in *Nbk 21*; '[revolve]' is preferred here on metrical grounds.
72. In   flight *Relics. flight; —*] flight — *Nbk 21*.
73. *infinite,*] infinite *Nbk 21*; Infinite, *Relics*.
74. *night,*] night *Nbk 21*, *Relics*.
75. *Splendours*] splendours *Relics. spread. —*] spread — *Nbk 21*; spread; *Relics*. There is a large gap in *Nbk 21* before the next line, perhaps to indicate a stanza-break.
76. *Through*] And through *Relics*. *Through* is written after *And* canc. in *Nbk 21*.
77. Following this line in *Nbk 21* at the bottom of the page (p. 21) is rough draft for an unresolved line, read by *BSM* as 'And Hymen and love [divine]' and by GM as 'Led By awe and love [driven]'. The draft as rendered here then continues with l. 78 at the top of the next page (p. 22). *radiated —*] radiated. — *Nbk 21*; radiated, *Relics*.
78. This line is omitted in *Relics*. *God's*] Gods *Nbk 21*. *fed;*] fed *Nbk 21*.
80. *[?living]*] [?loving] *BSM*. *far*] high *Relics*; *far* is written in pencil above *high* canc. in *Nbk 21* (*high* is written in ink and cancelled in pencil).
81. *move*] move, *Relics*.

> From the worlds they rule to the thrones they fill
> Gloomy or bright or invisible ...
> Built on glassy ocean.
>
> 85 The senate of the Gods is met,
> There is silence and space;
> Each in his rank and station set —
> Lo! Satan and Christ and Mahomet
> [Start] from their places:
> 90 Desolation and love and fate
> Are burning in mute debate
> Whilst they prone! —

82–5. In *Relics* these lines are represented as a single line: 'Gloomy or bright as the thrones they fill.'; this is followed by a row of stops (presumably to indicate a hiatus), then 'A chaos of light and motion / Upon that glassy ocean.'
83. invisible ...] invisible .... *Nbk 21.*
84. ocean.] ocean *Nbk 21.* Below this line in *Nbk 21* S. placed a horizontal dash, and below that wrote a single line in ink: *A chaos of light & of motion.* This is followed by confused draft in pencil, presumably made at a later time, which resolves at the bottom of the page to ll. 85–6 of the present text, then skips the following p. 23, which is occupied by *There are two fountains in which spirits weep* in ink (Appendix G, presumably also intended for *Hellas*), before continuing in pencil on p. 24. Near the bottom of p. 22 are eight short vertical strokes, S.'s syllable-count for the line immediately below (l. 85).
85–9. In *Relics* these lines read as follows:

> The senate of the Gods is met,
> Each in his rank and station set;
> There is silence in the spaces—
> Lo! Satan, Christ, and Mahomet
> Start from their places!

85. *met,*] met *Nbk 21.*
86. *space*;] space *Nbk 21.*
88. *Lo!*] Lo *Nbk 21.*
89. *places:*] places *Nbk 21.*
90–2. Omitted in *Relics.*
91. *mute*] Written above [*?fierce* canc.] in *Nbk 21.*
92. *Whilst they prone*] Christ thy name *BSM.*
93–7. There is a horizontal centred line beneath l. 92 in *Nbk 21* p. 24, with l. 93 written beneath it, and, squeezed in between the horizontal and l. 93, the cancelled word *Satan* is centred (apparently indicating a new speaker). The word *Christ* is centred immediately beneath l. 93 in faint pencil. The rest of the draft (mostly in pencil but

> [*Satan*]
> Victory to the weak!
>
> *Christ*
> Almighty Father, be the Decree
> 95 Now kneeling at the feet of Destiny
> [?   ]
> Once more arise out of the sea of hope
> The Aurora of the nations — by this brow
> Whose pores wept tears of blood ... by these wide wounds
> 100 [And] by this imperial crown of [agony]
> Whose thorns with leaves [and flowers] shall never more

---

with some overwriting in ink) on p. 24, continuing on the following p. 25, is tangled, with much cancellation and apparently unresolved lines, before it settles to a somewhat less difficult passage from l. 97. A tidied-up transcription of the uncancelled lines reads: *Spirited in Thee ... or be thou supreme power / And [?] and contempt of death and [pain] / And love to create, and strength to over[throw] / And patience to end[ure] and [?]*.
93. *weak!*] weak *Nbk 21*.
94–5. In *Relics* these lines are represented as follows:

> CHRIST.
> Almighty Father!
> Low-kneeling at the feet of Destiny

They are followed by a row of asterisks (presumably to indicate a hiatus), and then follow seven lines representing Garnett's rendering of the lines beginning *There are two fountains in which spirits weep* (see note to l. 84 above, and Appendix G).
97. This line is omitted in *Relics*.
98. The Aurora of the nations. By this brow *Relics*. A long dash after *nations* in *Nbk 21* and a short one before *by* in the line below clearly indicates that this line is split by a paragraph break, although it is not clear why, unless the tangled draft conceals an intention to introduce a different speaker between the beginning of Christ's speech and its continuation at this point (however this seems unlikely). *The Aurora of the nations*] 'Hellas' (*Locock 1911* ii 466).
99. *blood ... by these wide wounds*] blood, by these wide wounds, *Relics*.
100. By this imperial crown of agony, *Relics*. See note to ll. 132–4 below.
101–2. These lines are omitted in *Relics*. Between them is another virtually complete line, that began as *Its shadow to the palms* but was then emended to *Its shelter to the* [?] [?] *shade*.

In the green gardens of Jerusalem —
By thy infamy and solitude and death
For these I underwent ... and by the pain
105 Of pity for those [   ] who felt for me
The unenvied joy of [hatred] and revenge;
For this I felt — by Plato's sacred light
Of which my spirit was a burning mirror,
By Greece and all she cannot cease to be,
110 Her quenchless words, sparks of immortal truth,
[?Their] [?brighter] deeds — her harmonies and forms,

103. death] death, *Relics*.
104. underwent ... and] underwent, and *Relics*. *underwent*] Written beneath *suffered* canc. in *Nbk 21*.
105-6. Relics reads:

> Of pity for those who would   for me
> The unremembered joy of a revenge,

105. The pencil draft at this point on p. 25 of *Nbk 21* is confused and difficult to resolve.
106. revenge;] revenge *Nbk 21*.
107-31. The order of this sequence is conjectural (see headnote). Line 107 is initially drafted at the bottom of p. 25 in *Nbk 21* as *For this I felt — I do compel thee*, but the draft at the top of the following p. 26 is not a continuation of this sense; S. appears to complete l. 107 with the phrase *by Plato's sacred light*, which is drafted half-way down p. 27, positioned to indicate that it forms the second half of an iambic pentameter, preceded on the top half of the page by tangled and unresolved ink draft, and set apart by a page-wide horizontal stroke. Relatively clear draft then follows on the rest of the page, all cancelled by three long vertical lines; this cancelled draft seems to have been reworked to produce ll. 108-114 from rougher draft half-way down on the preceding facing p. 26 (i.e. positioned next to the cancelled draft on the facing p. 27), incorporating at l. 113 the phrase *I do compel thee* which had initially completed l. 103. Lines 115-18 are drafted clearly at the top of p. 26, and apparently continue from l. 119 on p. 28.
107. light] light, *Relics*.
108. mirror,] mirror *Nbk 21*; morrow— *Relics*.
109. be,] *Relics*; be *Nbk 21*.
110. truth,] *Relics*; truth *Nbk 21*.
111. [?Their] [?brighter] deeds] *Shelley's Guitar*; Stars of all night *Relics*. The reading in *Shelley's Guitar* (166) is of uncancelled words above a cancelled line above *Stars of all night* canc. in *Nbk 21*. *forms,*] *Relics*; forms *Nbk 21*.

> Echoes and shadows of what love adores
> In power. — I do compel thee, Fate, send forth
> Thy irrevocable child — ... she shall descend,
115 The Destiny of Greece — [let] it descend,
> A seraph-wingèd Victory, and [?start]
> The tempest of the omnipotence of God
> Which sweeps through all things ... from republic,
> From hollow league, and from tyranny which arms

112–18. Relics reads:

> Echoes and shadows of what Love adores
> In thee, I do compel thee, send forth Fate,
> Thy irrevocable child: let her descend
> A seraph-wingèd victory [arrayed]
> In tempest of the omnipotence of God
> Which sweeps through all things.

113. In power. —] In *Nbk 21* (p. 27) S. first wrote *In thee ... and by her deeds, and her* then cancelled all but the first word and wrote *power* below the beginning of the line. *thee,*] thee *Nbk 21*.
114. child — ...] child — .. *Nbk 21. descend,*] descend *Nbk 21*.
115–18. [let] it descend ... all things] Cp. the final words of the dying Greek soldier recalled by Hassan in *Hellas* 445–51:

> [']but ere the die be thrown,
> The renovated Genius of our race,
> Proud umpire of the impious game, descends,
> A seraph-winged Victory, bestriding
> The tempest of the Omnipotence of God,
> Which sweeps all things to their appointed doom,
> And you to oblivion'

115. Greece —] Greece. — *Nbk 21. descend,*] descend *Nbk 21*.
116. seraph-wingèd] seraph winged *Nbk 21. [?start]*] stand *BSM*.
117–18. the omnipotence ... all things] Cp. *Adonais* (no. 403) 381–2: 'the one Spirit's plastic stress / Sweeps through the dull dense world'.
119–121. These lines are drafted at the top of p. 27 in *Nbk 21*; the sequence of lines 115–122 as printed here therefore runs across the top part of three successive notebook pages: ll. 115–118 on p. 26, ll. 119–121 on p. 27 (where line 121 is ruled off from the draft below it of ll. 107–114), and l. 122 on p. 28.
118. republic,] republic *Nbk 21*.
119. league, and from tyranny] leagues, from Tyranny *Relics*.

120 Adverse miscreeds and emulous anarchies
To stamp as on a wingèd serpent's seed
Upon [   ] name of freedom. — From the storm
Of faction which like earthquake shakes and sickens
The solid heart of enterprise — from all
125 By which the holiest dreams of highest spirits
Are stars beneath [?her] dawn — She shall arise
Victorious as the world arose from Chaos
And as the Heavens and the Earth arrayed

120. miscreeds] miseries *BSM*. A 'miscreed' is 'a mistaken or false creed' (*OED*); as well as the present instance, *OED* illustrates the meaning through Keats's 'How fevered is the man who cannot look' (1819) l. 14. *emulous*] rivalrous; see *Paradise Lost* vi 820–2: 'since by strength / They measure all, of other excellence / Not emulous, nor care who them excels'. See also *PU* III iii 168.
121. stamp ... seed] stamp, ... seed, *Relics. wingèd serpent's*] *Relics*; winged serpents *Nbk 21*.
122. Upon the name of Freedom; from the storm *Relics*. This line is at the top of p. 28 in *Nbk 21*, where S. first wrote *The liberty name of*, then cancelled it and wrote *Upon* beneath, followed, after a space, by *name of freedom. — from the storm*.
123. faction] faction, *Relics*.
124. enterprise —] enterprise; *Relics*. *Concordance* defines the word in this context as 'energy, daring'.
126. Relics gives this line as follows:

> Are stars beneath the dawn
>
> She shall arise

However, there is no reason to indicate a new verse paragraph; in *Nbk 21 She shall arise* is set lower than *beneath the dawn*, and to its right, but this is simply to avoid draft of the preceding line. *Are* is written faintly above a cancelled half-line, and *stars beneath the dawn* is squeezed in small writing between the cancelled half-line and the line beneath. *[?her]*] the *Relics, BSM*.
127. Chaos] Chaos! *Relics*.
128–30. And as the Heavens ... O Father] Cp. *Genesis* i 1–3: 'In the beginning God created the heaven and the earth. And the earth was without form, and void; and darkness *was* upon the face of the deep. And the Spirit of God moved upon the face of the waters. And God said, Let there be light: and there was light.'
128–32. the Earth ... the abyss] Cp. *PU* IV 519–22:

> Thou Earth, calm empire of a happy soul,
>   Sphere of divinest shapes and harmonies,
>   Beautiful orb! gathering as thou dost roll
> The Love which paves thy path along the skies

Their [presence] in the beauty and the lips
130 Of thy first smile, O Father ... as they gather
The [spirit] of thy love which paves [?like light]
Their path over the abyss — till every sphere
Shall be one living spirit — so [shall] Greece.

Satan
Be as all things beneath this empyrean:
135 Mine! — art thou eyeless like old Destiny,
Thou mockery King crowned with a wreath of thorns
Whose sceptre is a reed, — the broken reed
Which pierces thee! whose throne a chair of scorn —
For seest thou not beneath this crystal floor
140 The innumerable worlds of golden fire
Which are my empire? And the [least] of them

129. lips] light *Relics, BSM.*
130. smile, O Father ...] smile o Father ... *Nbk 21*; smile, O Father, *Relics.*
131. [?like light]] for them *Relics.* The present reading is doubtful; the words are written squeezed against the right margin in *Nbk 21* p. 28 and sloping downwards; *BSM* records the last word as illegible.
132-3. Relics reads:

>   Their path o'er the abyss, till every sphere
>   Shall be one living Spirit, so shall Greece—

133. Greece.] Greece *Nbk 21*; Greece— *Relics.*
134. this empyrean:] this empyrean *Nbk 21*; the empyrean, *Relics.* The 'empyrean' is 'the highest or most exalted part or sphere of Heaven' (*OED*); there are six instances of the word in *Paradise Lost* (ii 771, iii, 57, vi 833, vii 73, vii 633 and x 321).
135. Mine! —] Mine! *Relics. Destiny,] Relics*; Destiny *Nbk 21.* Following this line in *Nbk 21* is a complete uncancelled line *O thou, whose sceptre is a broken reed*; omitted here (and in *Relics*) because clearly replaced by l. 137 below.
136-8. Cp. *Matthew* xxvii 29: 'And when they had platted a crown of thorns, they put *it* upon his head, and a reed in his right hand: and they bowed the knee before him, and mocked him, saying, Hail, King of the Jews!'; see also *Mark* xv 17-19.
136. Thou mockery-king, crowned with a wreath of thorns? *Relics.* The phrase 'mockery King' is found in *Richard II* IV i 260: 'O that I were a mockery king of snow'. *thorns]* thorns? *Relics.*
137. reed, —] reed, *Relics.*
138. scorn —] scorn *Nbk 21*; scorn; *Relics.*
139. For] [Or] *BSM.* Written beneath *And* canc. in *Nbk 21.*
140. fire] light *Relics.* Written in small writing above *golden light* in *Nbk 21*; *BSM* reads *light* as cancelled.
141. empire? And] empire: and *Nbk 21*; empire, and *Relics.*

How dearly wouldst not thou redeem from me
Or knowest thou not, these are by portion mine,
[Or] wouldst thou waken the primeval strife
145 Which our great father then did arbitrate
When he assigned to his competing Sons
Each his apportioned realm —
                          Thou [?],
Thou who art mailed in the omnipotence
Of him who sends thee forth! ... whatever thy task,

142-7. Relics reads as follows:
                    which thou wouldst redeem from me?
                  Know'st thou not them my portion?
                  Or wouldst rekindle the   strife
                  Which our great Father then did arbitrate
                  When he assigned to his competing sons
                  Each his apportioned realm?
                            Thou Destiny,

142. This line is conjectural. S. began by writing *One* in *Nbk 21*, then cancelled it and wrote *How dearly of which thou w*^{dst} *redeem from* (with *ye* canc. above *thou*); he then wrote *wd not* (i.e. 'would not') in small writing beneath *wouldst*. *BSM* reads *from* as *power*.
143. *by*] My *BSM*. *mine,*] mine *Nbk 21*.
144. *waken*] *rekindle*, an uncancelled alternative, is written above *waken* in *Nbk 21*. *primeval*] *old*, an uncancelled alternative, is written above *primeval* in *Nbk 21*.
146. *When*] Which *Hutchinson*.
147. There is a long sloping dash beneath *realm* in *Nbk 21*; this usually indicates a change of speaker in S.'s drafts for dramatic works, but it is difficult to understand what other speaker could be intended at this point. The line seems to continue with a word conjectured by GM as 'powers', and read by *BSM* as 'from'. *Thou* and a word following are positioned below so as to indicate that they complete the iambic pentameter, but the final word is illegible. [?],] [?] *Nbk 21*. GM conjectured this word to be 'Destiny', *BSM* offers 'Divine', but apart from the definite initial capital letter the word is too sketchily formed to read.
149-155. Relics reads as follows:
                Of Him who sends thee forth, whate'er thy task,
                Speed, spare not to accomplish, and be mine
                Thy trophies, whether Greece again become
                The fountain in the desert whence the earth
                Shall drink of freedom, which shall give it strength
                To suffer, or a gulph of hollow death
                To swallow all delight, all life, all hope.

149. *task,*] task *Nbk 21*.

150 Speed! spare not to accomplish. — And be [?mine]
     Thy triumphs, whether [Greece again] becomes
     The fountain in the deserts; whence the earth
     Shall drink of freedom ... And may draw new strength
     To suffer; or a gulf of [hollow] death
155 To swallow all delight, all life, all hope ...
     Go, thou Vicegerent of my will, no less
     Than of the Father ... [thou a]rt swift
     [?   ] but lest thou shouldst be frail
     The wingèd hounds, famine and pestilence,
160 Shall fawn on thee; the hundred-footed Snake,
     Insatiate Superstition, shall still mine

150. accomplish. — And] accomplish. — and *Nbk 21*.
151. triumphs] temples *BSM*.
153. freedom ...] freedom . . *Nbk 21*.
155. life,] life *Nbk 21*.
156. Go,] *Relics*; Go *Nbk 21*. *Vicegerent*] 'A deputy or delegated ruler' (*Concordance*). The word is used adjectivally in *Paradise Lost* v 609 and x 56.
157–8. *Relics* presents these two lines as one: 'Than of the Father's; but lest thou shouldst faint,'.
158. The beginning of this line, among several lines of rough draft at the top of *Nbk 21* p. 31, is unresolved.
159–170. In *Relics* this passage reads as follows (see note to ll. 167–9 below):

> The wingèd hounds, Famine and Pestilence,
> Shall wait on thee, the hundred-forkèd snake,
> Insatiate Superstition, still shall
> The earth behind thy steps, and War shall hover
> Above, and Fraud shall gape below, and Change
> Shall flit before thee on her dragon wings,
> Convulsing and consuming, and I add
> Three vials of the tears which demons weep
> When virtuous spirits through the gate of Death
> Pass triumphing over the thorns of life,
> Sceptres and crowns, mitres and swords and snares,
> Trampling in scorn, like Him and Socrates.

159. hounds, ... pestilence,] hounds ... pestilence *Nbk 21*.
160–1. Snake, / ... Superstition,] Snake / ... Superstition *Nbk 21*.
160. fawn on thee] S. first wrote *wait on thee* in *Nbk 21*, then cancelled *wait on* and wrote *fawn* above (read by *BSM* as '[?pounce]'), followed by *on thee. hundred-footed*] hundred footed *Nbk 21. thee;*] thee — *Nbk 21. Snake*] Cancelled and underlined to indicate reinstatement in *Nbk 21* with *scorpion* canc. above.

The earth behind thy steps — and War shall boil
Above; and Fraud shall gape below, and Change
Shall flit before thee on her dragon wings
165 Convulsing and consuming ... So I add
Three vials ... they are the tears [which demons] weep
When virtuous spirits o'er the thorns of life,
Sceptres and crowns, mitres, and swords and snares,
Trample in scorn [ ] through the [gate] of Death
170 Pass triumphing, like thou and Socrates.
The first is anarchy ... when power and pleasure
Glory and science and security
On freedom hang like fruit on the green tree —
Then pour it forth, and men shall gather ashes;

163–5. Change ... consuming] Cp. *Adonais* 348–50: 'We decay / Like corpses in a charnel; fear and grief / Convulse us and consume us day by day'.
164. her] his *BSM*.
166. [which demons]] which daemons *Forman 1876–7, Hutchinson*.
167–9. o'er the thorns ... scorn] These lines are written vertically in the left margin of p. 31 in *Nbk 21*, obviously for insertion, though at what exact point is debatable; Garnett placed them after the half-line 'When virtuous spirits', l. 167 of the present text (see note to ll. 159–170 above). S. first wrote *When virtuous spirits through the gate of death / Pass triumphing, like thou and Socrates* (*BSM* reads 'trampling' for *triumphing*). He then wrote *oer the thorns* above *gate of death*, indicating the most likely insertion point for the marginal lines.
167. o'er] oer *Nbk 21*.
168. snares,] snares *Nbk 21*.
169. S.'s reworking of the line appears to end up omitting a necessary connective between 'scorn' and 'through', e.g. 'then'. Cp. *Job* xxxviii 17: 'Have the gates of death been opened unto thee? or hast thou seen the doors of the shadow of death?'.
170. Socrates.] Socrates — *Nbk 21*.
171. The first is Anarchy; when Power and Pleasure, *Relics*.
172. science] Written after *light* canc. in *Nbk 21*. *security*] security, *Relics*.
173–4. like fruit ... gather ashes] Cp. *Paradise Lost* x 564–6: 'they fondly thinking to allay / Their appetite with gust, instead of fruit / Chewed bitter ashes'.
173. freedom] Freedom *Relics*. *green*] Written above *full* canc. in *Nbk 21*. *tree* —] tree, *Relics*.
174. ashes;] ashes *Nbk 21*; ashes. *Relics*.

175   The second tyranny — terror shall reign
      And darkness; but before the [?   ]
      Unseal the third: custom, the poison [?dew]
      Which aye [?   ] upon the blighting cloud
      And press its slow, sullen, perpetual rain
180   Until it fall in lurid drops, and strike
      The towered crests of mightiest states, and stain
      Their purest shrines, until a [?slimy] [?lichen]
      Shall spread and clasp and cling to them, [?   ]
      In the deep growth of its hoar rottenness,

175-88. terror shall reign ... hew their thrones. —] *Relics* omits these lines, treating the first three words of l. 175 as the beginning of a line completed by the opening words of Christ's speech in l. 188.
175. tyranny] Tyranny *Relics, V&P.*
176. darkness;] *V&P*; darkness *Nbk 21.* before the [?   ]] before   *V&P.* After several cancelled attempts in *Nbk 21,* the draft of the end of the line is not resolved.
177. third:] third, *V&P. custom, the poison [?dew]*] custom the poison *V&P.* Written above *the poison of all poisons* canc. in *Nbk 21 (the* is alt. from *a); BSM* reads [?dew] as 'dart'.
178. Which is written above two attempts to start this line in *Nbk 21,* then below S. continues with a slight indent followed by a dash; *BSM* reads 'age' for *aye,* and 'brightning' for *blighting. Which aye [?   ]*] Which!— Aye out *V&P.*
179. slow, sullen,] *V&P*; slow sullen *Nbk 21.*
180. strike] [?shrine] *BSM.* Written above *stain* canc. in *Nbk 21. lurid drops,*] hurried drops *V&P.*
181. states,] states *V&P.*
182-4. until a [?slimy] [?lichen] ... hoary rottenness] This passage, at the foot of *Nbk 21* p. 32 (ll. 182-3) and the top of p. 33 (l. 184), appears to be reworked at the foot of p. 33: *and stagnate in their courts / And breed leprous lichens which shall creep / [Till from its rank corruption a] / Till from. BSM* reads '[?lemings]' for *leprous.*
182. purest] firmest *GM*; fairest *BSM. [?slimy] [?lichen]*] slimy lichen *V&P. V&P* offers the correct stress pattern and syllable count but is a debatable reading of the draft; *BSM* reads '[sky] [?   ] leeches'.
183. them, [?   ]] their towers *V&P;* these [?high] [?towers] *GM;* them, cover *BSM.*
184. growth] Written above *ruin* canc. in *Nbk 21. hoar rottenness,*] hoar rottenness *Nbk 21.* Written after *growth* canc. in *Nbk 21* (with *hoar* alt. from *hoary). hoar* means grey from the absence of foliage (see *OED* 4a).

185 The Senate house, the altar and the hearth,
     Till Heaven shall weep and from her frozen tears —
     As from a mine of [perfect] diamond —
     My slaves shall hew their thrones. —

                         Christ
                                    Obdurate Spirit,
     Thou seest but the past in the to-come. —
190 Pride is thy error and thy punishment.
     Boast not thine empire! dream not that thy worlds
     Are more than furnace sparks or rainbow drops
     Before the Power that wields and kindles them ...
     True greatness asks not space, true excellence

185. Senate] senate *BSM. house,*] *V&P*; house *Nbk 21. altar*] altar, *V&P. hearth,*] hearth *Nbk 21*; hearth. *V&P.*
186. Till] Idle *V&P. frozen tears* —] frozen tears *Nbk 21*; frozen tears, *V&P*; prayers tears *BSM.*
187. of [perfect] diamond —] of [perfect] diamond *Nbk 21*; of diamonds, *V&P.*
188. slaves] Slaves *V&P. hew*] have *BSM, V&P. thrones.* —] thrones. *V&P. Spirit,*] *V&P*; Spirit *Nbk 21*; spirit! *Relics.*
189. past] Past *Relics. to-come.* —] to come. — *Nbk 21*; To-come. *Relics*; to-come, *V&P*; to come *BSM.*
190. S.'s attempt to continue Christ's speech after this line breaks down in *Nbk 21* into cancelled draft filling much of the bottom half of p. 33. The presentation of a selection of this draft as follows in *V&P* 47–8 is somewhat misleading in that *Since* is uncancelled and *who has that now* is cancelled:

> [Since thou art blind, but to the thing thou art,]
> So is not the Decree ... who has that now
> [To do our will, and his in whom we are]

The following page of *Nbk 21* (p. 34) contains draft identified persuasively by Garnett in his *Relics* text as a new speech by Mahomet (see below), and he also surmised that Christ's speech begun on p. 33 in fact continues in relatively neat draft four pages further on (on p. 37). *punishment.*] *Relics*; punishment *Nbk 21, V&P.*
191–5. These lines in *Nbk 21* p. 37 seem partly to rework material more roughly drafted on the facing p. 36.
191. empire!] empire, *Relics.*
192. furnace sparks or rainbow drops] furnace-sparks or rainbow-drops *Relics.*
193. them ...] them. *Relics.*

195   Lives in the spirit of all things that live. —

[?*Mahomet*]
   Arise, O sister of my spirit

195. live. —] live, *Relics*; Garnett read the comma because he follows this line with another: 'Which lends it to the worlds thou callest thine.' S.'s stop and dash are however clear in *Nbk 21*. The first two words of the line represented in *Relics* are cancelled in *Nbk 21*, suggesting that S. may have first thought to continue to develop ll. 191–5, but then decided not to and punctuated l. 195 with a strong period. [*Which lends*] *it to the worlds thou callest thine* is followed by a further three lines in *Nbk 21*, all cancelled with a wavy line, which were first published as follows in *V&P* 48:

> And as one thought of Plato's mind outlives
> The Palaces of Athens, and with light
> Gilds their oblivion—so

The *V&P* transcription is accurate save for 'Plato's' and 'Palaces' where the *Nbk 21* readings are *Platos* and *palaces* respectively. *BSM* reads 'in' for 'of' in the first line, 'like night' for 'with light' in the second, and 'this' for 'their' in the third.

196–201. Garnett assigned this speech to Mahomet in *Relics* 11 on the persuasive grounds that its perspective is obviously Islamic and anti-Christian. It is on *Nbk 21* p. 34, immediately following the beginning of Christ's speech (ll. 188–190 above), drafted on the preceding p. 33. Mahomet's speech is drafted similarly but differently (less resolved and with more cancellation), on p. 35 as follows (text minimally tidied; see *BSM* xvi 39 for an alternative transcription): *Wake Sister of my spirit ... wake thou* [?*Word*] / *Of God, and from the throne of Destiny* / *Even to the utmost limit of thy way* / *May triumph* [*pave*] *thy tread: and whensoeer* / *Thou tramplest those proud infidels,* [*whose*] *creed* / [*Divides and multiplies the one high God*] / [*May their blood nourish, like a chosen dew*]. Below are three uncancelled lines which attempt a reworking: *Be thou a curse on them, whose creed* / *Divides and multiplies the one high God* / *Be thou a curse on theirs* —. *Relics* presents the following redaction of these lines after l. 201 of the present text:

>   Wake, thou Word
>   Of God, and from the throne of Destiny
>   Even to the utmost limit of thy way
>   May Triumph
>   *   *   *   *   *
>   Be thou a curse on them whose creed
>   Divides and multiplies the most high God.

196. The line is left unfinished in *Nbk 21*. *Arise, O*] Arise o *Nbk 21*.

Haste thee and fill the waning Crescent [?]
With beams as keen as those which pierced the shadow
Of Christian night rolled back upon the West
200 When the orient moon of Islam rolled in triumph
From Tmolus to th' Acroceraunian snow

B: 'Youngest of the Destinies'

These lines are drafted in *Nbk 21* pp. 7–8, mostly in ink; the last two lines as well as an emendation in l. 17 are in pencil. What appears to be a centred speaker heading, *Des*, presumably an abbreviation for 'Destiny', separates the two stanzas; the speaker of the second stanza would thus be the figure addressed in the first stanza. The rhyme scheme provides a further link between the two stanzas: the un-rhymed 'd' ('born') of the first stanza becomes the 'a' rhyme ('Morn', 'born') of the second stanza. Because these verses were entered early in *Nbk 21* among passages related to *It is the period when all the Sons of God* (Appendix A), they are undoubtedly related to that text and perhaps intended as a choral interlude to be interjected in the debate among the 'Sons of God'. Thirty-three pages later, on p. 40, S. recopies the first two lines of the first stanza, but he then cancels *Youngest* and adds *Fairest* above the cancelled word. The next five lines are completely revised, although S. retains the stanza's rhyme pattern of *aabccbd*. (See *And like that star, the Shepherd of true stars* (Appendix F)).

197. thee] thou *Relics. waning Crescent* [?]] waning crescent *Relics*; waning Crescent [?light] GM; waning crescent! [?moon] *BSM*.
199. West] West[ern] *BSM*.
200–1. These lines, in which Mahomet celebrates the westward advance of the Islamic empire, are adapted in *Hellas* 266–7: 'When th'orient moon of Islam roll'd in triumph / From Caucasus to white Ceraunia!'.
200. rolled] rode *Relics*.
201. Beneath two cancelled lines after this line in *Nbk 21* is a complete line, *And planets [?turn] the enemies of God* which appears related in sense to ll. 190–4, but grammatically dislocated from them because of the tense. *Tmolus*] In classical times Sardis, the ancient capital of Lydia, was at the foot of Mount Tmolus (now Boz Dag in Izmir Province, Turkey), east of the Aegean coast. It is named in *Hellas* 282. *th' Acroceraunian*] the'Acroceraunian *Nbk 21*; the Acroceraunian *Relics*. The Acroceraunian mountains are the Kanalit range, running along the north-west coast of Epirus (Ipeiros) and the southwest coast of Albania. S. references the Acroceraunian mountains in *Arethusa arose* (no. 311) l. 3. *snow*] snow. *Relics*.

The upper third of Nbk 21 p. 7, just above the first stanza, contains a prose passage, possibly stage directions for *It is the period* which reads:

The golden cloud is coloured with the sound of them — *& sweet music and a [veiled] form with a spear & a balance comes [forth] forth*

The passage is then cancelled with six diagonal strokes. These stage directions would seem to introduce the figure addressed in the next stanza. Because the *form* carries a spear and a balance, Reiman and Neth conjecture that perhaps S. is referencing 'one of the three Moirae or Fates' (*Republic* x 617b–621a) who 'are sometimes conflated with the Horae or Seasons' (*BSM* xvi 11).

These two abandoned stanzas are an indication of S.'s continually evolving vision of Destiny and her role in his poetic response to the Greek crisis. Destiny appears personified in *It is the period*: 'Now kneeling at the feet of Destiny' (l. 95). Several lines later in this same speech, Christ says:

> I do compel thee, Fate, send forth
> Thy irrevocable child — ... she shall descend,
> The Destiny of Greece — [let] it descend,
> A seraph-wingèd Victory (ll. 113–16)

This passage retains the father/child relationship of the fragment where 'Fate' is perhaps the equivalent of the 'great Sire' (l. 5). Later in *It is the period*, Satan asks of Christ, 'art thou eyeless like old Destiny' (l. 135). Such an image is a far cry from the speaker's request addressed to the 'Youngest of the Destinies' to '[d]isarray thy dazzling eyes'. By the time of the composition period of *Hellas*, Destiny is now still 'eyeless' and possesses a fearful power:

> The world's eyeless charioteer,
>   Destiny, is hurrying by!
> What faith is crushed, what empire bleeds
> Beneath her earthquake-footed steeds? (*Hellas* 711–14)

While lines 19–20 do have affinities with the weapon and hunting images of the preceding lines, it is not clear whether the last three lines (ll. 18–20) belong to this fragment or if they represent a different composing impulse altogether. GM suggested that l. 18 ('Like an owl midday bewildered') was recycled the following year in the presentation copy of *1820* that S. gave to Trelawny in 1822 which is now in the Lilly Library, Indiana University (call no.: PR5416 1820). On the fly leaf facing the last page of verse in *1820*, which contains the final stanza of *OL* (no. 322), are the pencilled lines: *Truth is too bright for human [eyes] sight. When it comes suddenly before them, their eyes blink like the owl's at the midday sun.* (For images of these lines, see the page facing p. 24 of *K-SMB* xv (1964) and Rebecca Baumann, *Frankenstein 200: The Birth, Life, and Resurrection of Mary Shelley's Monster* (2018) 22). However, while the title-page of the volume is undoubtedly inscribed in S.'s hand with the words *Edw Trelawny / from his friend / P B Shelley / Lerici / July 1822*, the editors of the present edition dispute the claim made by Louise Schutz Boas and, according to her, supported by GM, in 'Shelley: Three unpublished lines' (*N&Q* xi (1964) 178) that the pencilled lines are in S.'s hand and that they are verse.

Text from *Nbk 21* pp. 7–8. A comma has been added in l. 1. Indentation follows the MS.

Published in *V&P* 50 (ll. 8–18 only, as Fragments V and VI); *BSM* xvi 10–13 (facsimile and transcription of MS).

'Youngest of the Destinies'

  Youngest of the Destinies,
   Disarray thy dazzling eyes …
  Let the world behold the sign
   [Which] in hieroglyphic fire
5 [Burn]s, where the great Sire
  Touched with lips divine
  Thy front, his youngest born —

¶ **411 Appendix B** 3. *sign*] sigh *Nbk 21, BSM*. The final letter in *Nbk 21* begins with an ascender stroke, but it seems likely that it was a mis-stroke for 'n'; the rhyme pattern requires that it rhyme with 'divine' in l. 6.
4–5. Although the first two words of each line are lightly cancelled, no alternatives are evident in the MS.
4. *hieroglyphic*] 'Of the nature of a hieroglyph; having a hidden meaning; symbolical, emblematic' (*OED* 2).
7. *front*] i.e. 'forehead'.

Destiny
  The keenest shaft which azure Morn
    Elects from her quiver
10 When she goes forth to chase the shadows of night —
  And the gold Sun forever borne
    On the speed of unwearied light ...
    And Night with his herds
    Of terrors and dreams and slumbers
15   Sinks like a [?floundering] bird
  On the forests and lakes and meadows

8–18. *V&P* publishes these lines found in *Nbk 21* pp. 7–8 as two separate fragments: 'Fragment V' (ll. 8–12) and 'Fragment VI' (ll. 13–18). The pattern of MS lineation and the rhyme formula for ll. 8–17 indicate that this is a single stanza. See note to l. 18.
8. *SD*. Centred between ll. 7 and 8 is *Des* presumably an abbreviation for 'Destiny'; see headnote.
8. *which azure Morn*] which Morn *V&P*; which arise [?morn] *BSM*.
9. Elects from within her quiver *V&P*.
10. *shadows*] chadows *Nbk 21*. S. inadvertently repeated the consonant blend of 'ch' in 'chase'. *of night* —] Of night— *V&P*. *of night* is squeezed in at the top of *Nbk 21* p. 8. *V&P* assumes that the phrase represents a new line start and attached it to the beginning of l. 11; however, the minuscule *o* in *of* and the deep indent of this phrase indicate it concludes l. 10 drafted at the bottom of p. 7.
11. *And*] and *V&P*. (See note to l. 10.) *Sun*] Sun, *V&P*.
12. On the swift speed of never-ceasèd light. *V&P*.
15. *[?floundering] bird*] falling foe *V&P*; [?flaming] [birds] *BSM*. S. first wrote *Fall like* [?floundering] *birds*. The conjectural *floundering* was overwritten by *wounded* which was then cancelled; added above was *eagle* [?] which was also cancelled. A stroke skims underneath *floundering birds* and another short stroke appears to cancel the terminal *s* of *birds*. Following *like*, the article *a* was added above required by the singular *bird*. In the event that S. forgot to cancel the article in the series of emendations, a possible alternative line might be 'Sinks like floundering birds' which provides a more perfect rhyme with 'herds' above in l. 13.
16. *forests*] wastes *V&P*.
17. *dim*] Inserted above *pool* and in pencil, *dim* overwrites another pencilled word which was cancelled. This emendation may have occurred at the same time that the two pencilled ll. 19–20 were drafted at the bottom of this page (*Nbk 21* p. 8). *river* —] river *V&P*.

   And every dim pool and river —

  Like an owl midday bewildered

   For far swifter is thy shaft —
20 Far deeper the fall of my foe ...

C: 'Suns and stars are rolling ever'

The drafts for these three stanzas are composed in ink and found near the beginning of *Nbk 21* on pp. 2–6, 9–11. The first two stanzas both have multiple versions that are finally resolved in the stanzas found on pp. 9–10. The third stanza developed as a single version on pp. 10–11. *V&P* published several of the early drafts of the first two stanzas as short independent fragments, truncating the two stanzas and omitting the third stanza. Such a presentation obscured S.'s resolved versions of the first two stanzas and concealed entirely the existence of the third stanza. Collations in the accompanying notes are only supplied for the more or less complete set of stanzas on pp. 9–11.

  S. constructed a nine-line stanza form with a regular rhyming pattern for all three stanzas (*ababcdcdd*) with the first quatrain in tetrameters, the second quatrain shortened to trimeters and dimeters, and the rhyming refrain — *Thou art still thyself alone!* — resuming the tetrameter. The first stanza shows an indication, however, of S.'s irresolution with this pattern: at a later moment he added a new short line between the two

---

18. Above this line are a series of line starts and emendations; the only uncancelled version reads: *Like a dizzy owl*. In a distinctly different pen-cut and ink, S. returned and wrote *Like like an owl mid day bewildered* suggesting the uncancelled version was now abandoned. Given the deliberate, large space between l. 17 and l. 18, it is clear that l. 18 does not belong to the preceding stanza (ll. 8–17). Moreover, it is uncertain that l. 18 is textually sequential: it might represent an entirely independent text. *Like*] Distressed like *V&P*; Sinks like *BSM*. S. wrote *Like like*, an apparent slip in composition. *midday bewildered*] mid day bewildered *Nbk 21*; midday-bewildered. *V&P*; amid day bewildered *BSM*. Cp. *Venus & Adonis* 177: 'And Titan, tired in the midday heat'.
19–20. These two lines are drafted in pencil.
19. The line originally read: *Far [brighter] keener & far swifter is thy lance*. S. altered the *a* to *o* making *For*, then cancelled *keener* and *lance* adding *shaft* just below.
20. *deeper*] [Swifer] *BSM*.

quatrains that has no rhyme within the stanza nor with either of the next two stanzas.

The cosmic scenario containing spiritual entities — 'Spirits' and 'Angels' — as well as terrestrial beings — 'man' and 'worm' — could possibly be regarded as a stage-setting choral interlude for the 'Herald of Eternity' who summons the meeting in *It is the period when all the Sons of God* (Appendix A), a text which follows these stanzas on p. 13 in *Nbk 21*. This possibility is supported by the fact that S. had introduced *It is the period* even earlier, directly below the last line of the third stanza on p. 11 but cancelled it and began another verse *We pass, outspeeding the thunder* (Appendix D). The refrain (ll. 10, 19 and 28) emphasises the choric nature of these three stanzas, reinforcing their rhythmic and prosodic coherence. S. had employed refrains in a similar fashion in such poems as *Song of Proserpine* (no. 315), *Song of Pan* (no. 318), and *A Lament ('O World, O Life, O Time')* (no. 399). The language of this refrain, however, had previous incarnations as a statement of forlorn isolation or unwavering autonomy. A draft of *Sonnet: 'Lift not the painted veil'* (no. 173) (see note to ll. 11-14) located in *Nbk 11* pp. 22-3 concludes with the following lines:

> Like an unheeded shadow he did move
> Among the careless crowd that marked him not
> I should be happier had I never known
> This mournful man — he was himself alone

In another sonnet but with a different context, S. employs a variation of the phrase:

> Man, who man would be,
> Must rule the empire of himself; in it
> Must be supreme, establishing his throne
> On vanquished will; quelling the anarchy
> Of hopes and fears; being himself alone. (*Sonnet: Political Greatness* (no. 342) 10-14)

Beyond Wasserman's comment that '"Being himself alone" was S.'s standard phrase for self-possession' (*Wasserman* 181), the repeating 'alone' in *Suns and stars* functions as a powerful lyric device in its tonal reverberation. Located among the drafts of *It is the period*, these stanzas of supplication would seem to be addressed to God. The mortality of the speakers and the ephemeral nature of the 'Suns and stars', 'the bubbles', 'the dew of morn' are contrasted with immortal figures, 'Spirits', 'Angels' and 'Thou' who transcend time and space. The incomplete stanzas, particularly in the final three lines of the second and third, are evidence of their being abandoned with one important exception. The first quatrains of the first and second stanzas were adapted and developed for the *Chorus* in *Hellas* 197-203. Evidence for this transformation is found much later in this notebook in two places. The first re-working occurs in *Nbk 21* p. 186, where ll. 1-4 and 11-15 are initially brought together as consecutive stanzas. (The bottom quarter of the page is torn away.) Although this draft is cancelled, these verses are recognisable as draft of *Hellas* 197-203. The final transformation occurs on page 233, where lines 2, 11, 13-14 are reworked once again, more closely identifiable as the final stage for the *Chorus* for *Hellas*. (See notes to lines 1-4 and 11-15 below.)

Text from *Nbk 21* pp. 2-6, 9-11. Indentation follows the MS.

Published in *V&P* 49-50 (ll. 5-10, part of 11, part of 13-14, 15-17, 19); *BSM* xvi 6-15 (facsimile and transcription of MS).

'Suns and stars are rolling ever'

Suns and stars are rolling ever,
   From their birth to their decay;

¶ **411 Appendix C** *1-4*. These four lines were initially drafted in *Nbk 21* p. 3; the revised draft on p. 9 is the source of the lines published here. During the later composing period of *Hellas*, on p. 186, S. copied, with several emendations, these lines, along with ll. 11-15; this version reads:

> *Suns & stars are rolling ever*
>   *From their birth to their decay —*
> *Like the bubbles on a river*
>   *Sparkling, bursting, borne away!*

This quatrain along with the quatrain based on ll. 11-15 were cancelled with a single vertical stroke. Then, on p. 233, S. inscribed yet another version of l. 2 — *From creation to decay* — perhaps as a reminder of this quatrain which is the basis for the Chorus in *Hellas* 197-200. The most substantial difference between the text published here and the lines in *Hellas* is the substitution of 'Worlds on worlds' for 'Suns and stars'. Mahmud's exit line, just before the Chorus is 'The worship of the world' (l. 196) possibly prompting the revision of the Chorus's first line at 197.

>   As the bubbles on a river
>   Sparkling, bursting, borne away
> 5   By the torrent sea
>   Like the dew of morn

3. *As* appears to overwrite *Like*.
5–10. In composing, S. wrote two evolving drafts on *Nbk 21* pp. 2–3 which culminated in a more or less stable third draft on p. 9. *V&P* 49 published the first two of the rough drafts as two independent fragments (see note to ll. 6–9):

>   I
>   Like the spherèd star of morn
>   When the eye of day looks down,
>   All must die and all are born,
>   In thy smile and in thy frown
>   Thou art still thyself alone!
>
>   II
>   By the torrent sea,
>   Like the dew of morn,
>   When day looks down,
>   They die and are born
>   In thy smile and thy frown—
>   Thou art still thyself alone!

5. This is the only line not to have been drafted among the earlier versions on *Nbk 21* pp. 2–3. Written in a much smaller hand and squeezed in between l. 4 and l. 6 on p. 9, the line appears to be a late addition to the stanza, making it ten lines rather than the nine lines found in the two succeeding stanzas. Additionally, this is the only unrhymed line-ending. *V&P* publishes this line as the first line of Fragment II along with four more lines from *Nbk 21* p. 2.
6–9. Based on two versions drafted on *Nbk 21* pp. 2–3, this quatrain is carefully re-worked and rewritten on p. 9; *V&P* publishes the first draft version as Fragment I (see note to ll. 5–10), mostly based on the p. 3 version (along with l. 5 found on p. 9; see note to l. 5). The MS (p. 3) reads:

>   [Like]*As the sphered dew of morn*
>   *When the eye of day looks down*
>   *All* [must] *things die/perish & all are born*
>   *In thy smile & in thy frown*

V&P publishes the second version drafted on the facing page 2 as Fragment II (along with l. 5 found on p. 9; see note to l. 5). The MS (p. 2) reads:

>   *Like/As the dew of morn*
>   *When the* [Sun] *day looks down*
>   *They die & are born*
>   *In thy smile & thy frown*

With each successive revision, S. simplifies and reduces the lengths of the lines.

>   When Day looks down —
>   They die and are born
>   In thy smile and frown —
> 10   Thou art still thyself alone!
>
>   But those Spirits are immortal
>   Which like ours adore thee now. . .
>   Hurrying [between] Birth's orient portal
>   And Death' s dark gate, to and fro

10. This line, drafted at the top of *Nbk 21* p. 4 and rewritten on p. 9, serves as the refrain for the next two stanzas. A wavy centred line separates the completed first and second stanzas on p. 9.

11-15. Like the first stanza, two preliminary drafts of these lines are found roughly worked on *Nbk 21* pp. 4-6; a more finished version on p. 9 is the basis for the present edition. On p. 186, is yet another version which reads:

> *But the spirits are immortal*
> *Which behold[s] them as they flow;*
> *[Hurrying through Births orient portal]*
> *And death[?s] dark porch, to & [?fro]*

These lines are then cancelled; see note to ll. 1-4. On p. 233, these four lines are reworked yet again in a state recognisable as *Hellas* 201-3. It is the second rough draft found on pp. 5-6 that *V&P* publishes as Fragment IV. A partial transcription of that draft reads:

> *But th[ee]y Spirit is immortal*
> *Which beholds them as they flow*
> *All who through Births orient portal*
> *And Deaths dark gate pass to & fro*
> *Live as thou must. — all on whom*
> *Thy secret breath has oer blown*
> *[?Fell] know behold thee — 'tis then doom*
> *To be a portion, every one,*
> *Of thee — Thou art thyself alone!*

12. adore] above BSM. now ...] now .. *Nbk 21*.
13.*[between]]* S. tried several other alternatives including *from* and possibly *toward*, but all are cancelled. Birth's] Births *Nbk 21*.
14. Death's] Deaths *Nbk 21*.

15   All the living millions
                Far aroun[?d] thy throne. —
             Power and Love pavilions
                [?] [?] [the] Like ...
     Thou art still thyself alone.

20   Mid the Angels thou art love
        In stars and storms thou art motion

15-19. Line 15 is reasonably legible but the next four lines, written at the top of *Nbk 21* p. 10, are incomplete and problematic: scraps of words for l. 18 are all cancelled. Only the refrain (l. 19) is certain. Ignoring the problem of the intended but absent l. 18 (see note to l. 18), *V&P* publishes four lines as Fragment III:

   All the living millions
   Far around thy throne,
   Power and love pavilions—
   Thou art thyself alone!

V&P's decision to omit S.'s clear full-stop and dash and to accept the ungrammatical singular verb form 'pavilions' means a more or less coherent passage emerges, but it is a solution which assumes S. made multiple slips.
16. *Far*] For *BSM*. *For* is possible; on the other hand, *Far* would seem to be confirmed by the full-stop and long dash at the end of the line. *aroun[?d]*] Conjectural because no terminal *d* is apparent; what might be perceived as *d* is in fact the descender stroke of the *y* in [*thy*] above.
17. While *pavilions* might be a verb, the compound *Power and Love* on the other hand would require the plural verb form *pavilion*.
18. The first attempt at this line was cancelled, and *Like* is possibly a new start to the line. S. concluded with four spaced-out dots as a reminder to return to complete the line and are not to be considered suspension points. *BSM* suggests conjecturally 'It was' *canc.* as a possible reading of the illegible words at the beginning of the line. *Like ...*] Like .... *Nbk 21*.
19. Below the line is a centred dash, indicating the stanza division.
21. *storms*] stress *BSM*.
22. For this line, *BSM* gives 'Thou the morn thy father move', indicating that *thy father* is underlined and *move* is cancelled in *Nbk 21*. S. first wrote *In the worm thy pulses move* and then cancelled *In*, adding what seems to be *Thru* (or GM's suggestion, 'Thro'), an abbreviation for 'Through'. Above *thy pulses move* is an illegible cancelled phrase ending with *thou art*. *BSM* suggests 'all illness thou art' noting that the last three of these words are cancelled. The thin stroke skimming under *thy pulses* but cancelling part of *move* might be a stet rather than a cancel.
23. *th' emotion*] the'emotion *Nbk 21*; the [?conception] *BSM*. Below this line is a tangle of cancelled layers in ink, mostly illegible, but which overwrite a pencilled phrase, conjecturally, *Of liberty*. The rest of the stanza is continued at the top of the facing page, *Nbk 21* p. 11.
24. *heart*] heart. *Nbk 21*.

>   [?Through] the worm [thy pulses move]
>   And in man thou art th' emotion
>   With which his panting heart
> 25   [Bursts its icy zone].
>   Then   thou art
>   Freedom ... yet we [?must] own
>   Thou art still thyself alone. —

D: 'We pass, outspeeding the thunder'

These lines are drafted in ink in *Nbk 21* pp. 11–12, where they follow S.'s abandoned but organised draft of *Suns and stars are rolling ever* (Appendix C). They appear to represent an attempt at a choral lyric in the voice of 'Years', i.e. time past, passing and to come, intended either for *It is the period* or the poem that became *Hellas* which, like *PU* (no. 195), is characterised formally by alternation between lyric choruses and dialogue in blank verse.

These lines were first published by Sir John Shelley-Rolls and Roger Ingpen in 1934 in *V&P*, where they are titled as 'VIII' of the 'Fragments Written for Hellas'.

Text from *Nbk 21* pp. 11–12. Indentation follows the MS.

Published in *V&P* 51; *BSM* xvi 14–17 (facsimile and transcription of MS).

'We pass, outspeeding the thunder'

> *Years*
> We pass, outspeeding the thunder,
>   Oblivion and [?death] pursuing. —

25. S. cancelled this line, but the addition above of an uncancelled *its* (replacing *the* beneath) suggests that the line was to be retained. zone.] zone *Nbk 21*.
27. S. initially wrote [*Liberty* ... *o*]; after its cancellation, the new l. 27 was added below. *[?must]*] [?silent] *BSM*.
28. Below this line is a long horizontal stroke; below that is a cancelled speaker heading *Herald of eternity*. Thus l. 28 would seem to conclude this three-stanza passage.

¶ **411 Appendix D** *SD*. S. first wrote *Herald of Eternity* as a centred speech heading in *Nbk 21* (cp. the opening of *It is the period when all the Sons of God*), then cancelled it and wrote *Years* centred beneath, suggesting that these lines were conceived as a choral lyric in the voice of passing time.
1. Written beneath *It is the day* canc. in *Nbk 21* (*It* is written over *The*). pass,] pass *V&P*. thunder,] *V&P*; thunder *Nbk 21*.
2. [?death]] fate *V&P*; dust *BSM*. S. first wrote *fate* in *Nbk 21* then cancelled it and wrote a word above, conjectured here to be *death*, which is faint and obscured by the ascenders of *fate. pursuing.* —] pursuing, *V&P*.

     The hoar deep is [?groaning] under
     The world's roof is torn asunder
5   And pours down a rain of ruin.
     To the dust and the slime of annihilation
     We are beaten down and we rise no more

E: 'Like an exhalation'

These four lines, drafted in the middle of *Nbk 21* p. 12, are written in an ink consistent with that of the verses drafted above on this page, the last two lines of *We pass, outspeeding the thunder* (Appendix D). Such consistency of medium suggests a contemporaneous composing period. On the facing p. 13 are the opening lines to *It is the period when all the Sons of God* (Appendix A). The quatrain shares the lyric features and imagery found in the choruses of both *It is the period* and *Hellas*.

These lines were first published by Sir John Shelley-Rolls and Roger Ingpen in 1934 in *V&P*, where they are titled as 'IX' of the 'Fragments Written for Hellas'.

Text from *Nbk 21* p. 12.

Published in *V&P* 51; *BSM* xvi 16–17 (facsimile and transcription of MS).

'Like an exhalation'

     Like an exhalation
          Wandering along a woody shore
     Lifted by the airs of dawn
          Over the white Ocean floor

3. *[?groaning] under*] gaining under, *V&P*; [?yawning] under GM; groaning under *BSM*. S. first wrote the words *convulsed asunder* in *Nbk 21*, then cancelled them and wrote [?*groaning*] above and the rhyme word *under* beneath.
4. *world's*] worlds *Nbk 21*; woody *V&P*. Written above *vast* canc. in *Nbk 21*.
5. *ruin.*] ruin *V&P*.
6. There are several abandoned starts to this line in *Nbk 21*: [This] / [We are] [?*earth*] / [We are s] / [The whirlwind drives us afar, afar]. *annihilation*] annihilation; *V&P*. Written beneath [?*nought*] in *Nbk 21*.
7. *we rise no more*] we rise no more. *V&P*; are [?risen] [?] *BSM*.

¶ **411 Appendix E** *1–4.* Above the first line is a centred dash separating this stanza from *We pass, outspeeding the thunder*. The bottom half of *Nbk 21* p. 13 is blank except for a single word, *Insuperable* (see *It is the period when all the Sons of God*, note to l. 5).
1. *exhalation*] Cp. *It is the period when all the Sons of God* 12–13: 'which like an exhalation / Steaming from earth' and note.
2. *shore*] shore, *V&P*.
4. *Over*] On *V&P*. *Ocean*] ocean *V&P*.

F: 'And like that star, the Shepherd of true stars'

The present edition concurs with the view of *V&P* that the two facing pages, *Nbk 21* pp. 38 and 39, are meant to be woven together into a single stanza. It seems likely, however, that verses drafted overleaf, at the top of p. 40, are a continuation of the pp. 38–9 material. Composing in the lower halves of pp. 38–9, S. perhaps began on the left-hand p. 38 with the *star* and *Shepherd* images which were followed by several attempts to develop the *gild / gilt* idea. (See note to l. 2 for these cancelled drafts.) Once ll. 2–3 were resolved, S. apparently left off writing, but then returned to complete the stanza on facing p. 39 in a distinctly different ink and pen-cut. On p. 38, a single word *That* appears below l. 3; it is possibly a linking device to l. 4 on facing p. 39 beginning with another relative pronoun *Which*. Line 6 with the suspension at the caesura and the reiteration of *now* from l. 4 appears to signal a change in the speech act: overleaf, on p. 40, is the apostrophe beginning [*Youngest*] *Fairest of the destinies* a stanza of seven lines which is recycled and emended from verses on p. 7. (See Appendix B, *Youngest of the Destinies*). Their likely continuation from the ll. 1–6 passage seems supported by cancelled phrases in the drafts of that passage on pp. 38–9. On p. 38, for example, a cancelled line following l. 1 is *Which smiled upon its ruin*. The 'smile' theme appears in l. 11. On that same page, following the last line there (l. 3) is the cancelled phrase *That destiny comes*. The arrival of the 'Fairest of the destinies' evokes the first stanza's images of 'stars' with a web of illuminated features: 'dazzling', 'lightnings', and 'light'. Fitted in among material for both *It is the period* (Appendix A) and *Hellas*, it is possible that these unused lines represent a moment when S. was reassessing the models and rhetorical strategies for his lyrical drama.

Text from *Nbk 21* p. 38–40.

Published in *Relics* 12 (ll. 7–13); *V&P* 51 (ll. 1–6 as Fragment VII); *BSM* xvi 42–5 (facsimile and transcription of MS).

'And like that star, the Shepherd of true stars'

And like that star, the Shepherd of true stars
Gilt the departure [of] its glory and still

¶ **411 Appendix F** *1. Shepherd of true stars*] shepherd of the stars *V&P*. The 'Shepherd' presumably is Hesperus, the so-called evening star — actually the planet Venus — that appears at twilight just before the appearance of the 'true stars'. Given its proximity to the sun, Venus is also called the morning star for it is the last celestial object to remain illuminated before dawn.
2. Three other cancelled drafts of this successful line were *Gilded its fall, outlived its night* then *Which gilt its [twilight] evening, outlived its* and *Gilt its hoar ruin,*

Is shining now, that like the incarnate Dawn,
Which [beckons] the Day out of her orient [cave],
5   Outlived the death of light, — and shall attend
The second dawn ... even now the Dawn is here.

   Fairest of the destinies,
    Disarray thy dazzling eyes ...
   Keener far their lightnings are

& outlived. All these attempts echo two similar attempts on the facing p. 39. The successful line, *Gilt [its] [oblivion] the departure of its [light] glory and still* finally emerged. *[of] its glory]* of its joy *V&P*. The pale cancel stroke through *of* could be understood as making for another plausible reading if 'its glory' is viewed as an appositive to 'departure'.

3-4. *the incarnate ... orient [cave]]* Cp. *TL* (no. 452) 343-4: 'the bright omnipresence / Of morning through the orient cavern flowed'.

3. *shining now,]* shining, now *Nbk 21. the incarnate Dawn,]* the incarnate of Dawn *Nbk 21*; the tint of dawn *V&P*. For the line ending, S. first wrote *the Spirit of Dawn*; then *Spirit* was cancelled and replaced by *Grace*, which was also cancelled, and *incarnate* added above. With these changes, the *of* is no longer necessary. *incarnate]* 'Light pink or crimson' (OED 3).

4. *Which [beckons]]* Which [Beckons] *Nbk 21*; Which leads *V&P*. The cancellation of *Beckons* — which at one point began the line — was emended to *Which [wins]* added just above. With the cancellation of *wins* another stroke seems to have been added to *Beckons*, perhaps to reinstate it. Another later emendation shows *leaves*, in pencil, above *[wins]*, accounting perhaps for *V&P*'s 'leads'. *[cave],]* [cave] *Nbk 21*; cave; *V&P*. Lightly cancelled with pencil, *cave* was replaced by *tombs* added above in pencil, but that too was cancelled. It seems likely that S. returned to his first choice.

5. *Outlived]* Outlasts *V&P*. S. first wrote *Outlivest* but overwrote the *st* with a *d* that could account for *V&P*'s reading. *light, —]* light *V&P*.

7-13. First published in *Relics* 12, this stanza occurs overleaf, in the upper half of *Nbk 21* p. 40; in the lower half are lines related to *Hellas* 21-26. The characteristics of the media are quite different, and the two sets of verse on this page are separated by a long, centred dash and what appears to be the numeral 2.

7. *destinies]* Destinies *Relics, Locock 1911*.

8. *eyes ...]* eyes: *Relics, Locock 1911*.

9. *Keener]* See OED 'keen' (3a): 'Of weapons, cutting instruments, and the like: Having a very sharp edge or point; able to cut or pierce with ease' but also (4c): 'Of sound, light, scent: Sharp, piercing, penetrating; shrill; vivid; clear; strong'.

| 10 | Than the wingèd reeds thou bearest
And the smile thou wearest
Would wreathe thee, as a star
Is wrapt in light — |

G: 'There are two fountains in which spirits weep'

These lines are drafted in ink in *Nbk 21* p. 23. They are written out relatively neatly filling the middle third of the page, and although there are cancellations (notably S.'s alteration of *three* to *two* in ll. 1 and 3) they could well have been copied from a rough draft now lost. The lines are on the right-hand page (p. 23) of an opening, where they interrupt S.'s rough draft of *It is the period when all the Sons of God* (Appendix A) on the facing page (p. 22). S.'s draft of *It is the period* on p. 22 is mainly in ink, and represents a stage in that draft where he was clearly beginning to have difficulty in continuing. There are numerous cancellations and unresolved lines as the verse breaks down at a point corresponding to ll. 79–85 of the text in the present edition. In the middle of this page pencilled draft is added, and near the bottom the draft is entirely in pencil; it then skips p. 23 with the much neater ink draft of *There are two fountains* and continues in pencil through the three following pages (pp. 24–6), strongly suggesting that *There are two fountains* was written or copied into *Nbk 21* before the pencil draft was entered (although perhaps not before the ink draft on p. 22).

10. *wingèd*] winged *Nbk 21*. *reeds*] [bolts] *Relics*; illegible in *Locock 1911*; seeds *BSM*. S.'s 'r' and 's', at the start of a word can often look very similar; see *Charles the First* (no. 426) I iii 99 and *Box 1* f. 136^r (reproduced in *BSM* xii 122–3) for a similar confusion between 'reed' and 'seed'. Although S. used the image of 'wingèd seeds' in *OWW* (no. 259) 7, the arrow imagery here is more consistent with the rest of this passage; 'reed' for 'arrow' is common in literary contexts (see *OED* 'reed' *n.*^{1} 7b). In this case, the 'wingèd reeds' are compared to the keenness of the 'lightnings' from her eyes.
12. *Would wreathe thee,*] Wraps thee *Relics, Locock 1911*. Multiple emendations and cancels make decipherment challenging. In a darker ink, *wreathe* overwrites several layers of words. While the word *wrapt* does appear — just below the tangle in the core line — it is clearly cancelled to avoid repetition with *wrapt* in l. 13.
13. Below this line is a centred long dash separating this seven-line stanza from what appears to be two attempts at a start for a new speaker: [*The brightest star which Night*] / [?Ha] *where is the star* [*so swift of flight*] [*so burning*] [*fiery bright*]. The persistent attempts to rhyme 'light' in l. 13 suggests that these mostly cancelled lines were sequential to l. 13. *light* —] light. *Relics, Locock 1911*.

It is therefore a reasonable inference that these lines are not to be considered as integral with the draft of *It is the period* but represent an abandoned attempt at a separate conception, although still connected with S.'s preliminary drafts for *Hellas*. Garnett in his *Relics* text of 'Prologue to Hellas' (i.e. *It is the period*) decided otherwise and printed ll. 1–7 of the text between his renderings of what is now ll. 95 and 98 in the present edition's text of *It is the period*; Garnett omits ll. 96–7.

Text from *Nbk 21* p. 23.

Published in *Relics* 7 (ll. 1–7); *BSM* xvi 26–7 (facsimile and transcription of MS).

'There are two fountains in which spirits weep'

  There are two fountains in which spirits weep
  When mortals err … Discord and Slavery named. —
  [And] with their bitter dew two destinies
  Filled each th' irrevocable urns … the third,
5 Fiercest and mightiest, mingled both, and added
  Chaos, and Death, and slow Oblivion's [lymph],
  And hate and terror; and the poisoned rain
  Fell, like

¶ **411 Appendix G** *1. two*] Written above *three* canc. in *Nbk 21*.
2. A cancelled start to this line in *Nbk 21* reads *One Discord and one Slavery* (with *Tyranny* canc. written above *Slavery* canc.). *mortals err* …] mortals err, *Relics*; mortals err. *BSM*. *Discord and Slavery*] S. first wrote *one, discord & one Slavery* in *Nbk 21* then cancelled *one*, and *one. named.* —] named, *Relics*.
3. *[And]*] And *Relics*. *bitter*] Alt. from *better* in *Nbk 21*. *two*] Written over *three* in *Nbk 21*. *destinies*] Destinies *Relics*.
4. *each*] Written above *their* canc. in *Nbk 21*. *th' irrevocable urns* …] their irrevocable urns; *Relics*; the irrevocable urns … *BSM*. The sense is that these destinies cannot be revoked. *third,*] *Relics*; third *Nbk 21*.
5. *Fiercest … mightiest*] Alt. from *Fiercer* and *mightier* in *Nbk 21*. *mightiest, mingled*] *Relics*; mightiest mingled *Nbk 21*; mightiest-migled *BSM*.
6. *Chaos, and Death,*] Chaos, and death; *Nbk 21*; Chaos and Death, *Relics*. Written above *The rain rain of chaos,* canc. in *Nbk 21* (with the second *rain* altered from *rains*). *Oblivion's [lymph],*] *Relics*; Oblivion's lymph *Nbk 21*. *Oblivion's* is written above *Lethes* canc. in *Nbk 21* and the cancellation of 'lymph' is in pencil. 'Lymph' = stream (see *OED* 1a). Cp. *Darwin* i 117 (*The Economy of Vegetation* iii 29–30): 'Call from the crystal cave the Naiad-Nymph, / Who hides her fine form in the passing lymph'.
7. *terror;*] terror, *Relics*.

H: 'Ibrahim — / Stab that pernicious slave who talks of fear'

These nine lines found on pp. 59-60 in *Nbk 21* were apparently revised elsewhere by S. and then copied by Williams in *HM 329* p. 7 (see *MYRS* iii 29) and subsequently cancelled, whether by S. or Williams is difficult to determine (see the note to *Hellas* 121). *V&P* published eight lines of draft in *Nbk 21* as Fragment XI with the sub-heading '[*After line* 114]'. The press copy of *Hellas* (*HM 329*), however, demonstrates that these lines followed l. 121; the present edition of the text recovers the last foot of what was originally the conclusion to l. 121: 'Into the gap — wrench off the roof!'. Once these lines were cancelled in *HM 329*, the new conclusion to l. 121, *Ha! what!* replaces the cancelled *Ibrahim*, completing the line's metrical sufficiency and at the same time allowing Mahmud to acknowledge the entrance of Hassan.

Perhaps the reason for the exclusion of these lines from *Hellas* is that introducing Fatima as a character with potential for action and speech — which this passage would allow for — could only distract from the central characters and the focus of *Hellas*. Furthermore, by the time of its completion, Fatima's name and role were reduced to 'Indian Slave', a cipher in keeping with the choral conventions of Greek drama as in S.'s model, Aeschylus' *Persae*. (For the possibility that a similar rationale led to the excision of another draft passage, see the headnote to Appendix J, *I would not be a King: enough*.)

Text from *Nbk 21* pp. 59-60.

Published in *V&P* 52 (ll. 2-9); *BSM* xvi 64-67 (facsimile and transcription of MS).

'Ibrahim — / Stab that pernicious slave who talks of fear'

      Ibrahim —
Stab that pernicious slave who talks of fear.
'Tis something yet [that] I can fight until
The flesh be hacked from these too weary bones;

¶ **411 Appendix H** *1. Ibrahim* —] Ibrahim, *HM 329*; omitted in *V&P*. In *Nbk 21*, *Ibrahim* is struck through several times, while a series of dots skims under it and continues past the word. Such elaborate notations are generally a signal in S.'s dialogues confirming a speaker or an addressee.
2-9. V&P encloses these lines in single quotation marks.
2-4. Stab ... weary bones] Cp. *Macbeth* V iii 32, 36: 'I'll fight, till from my bones my flesh be hack'd. / [...] / Hang those that talk of fear'.
2. pernicious] Janizar *V&P*; passionless *BSM*. *fear*.] peace *BSM*.
3. [All is not lost! I can yet fight until] *HM 329*. '*Tis*] Tis *Nbk 21*. [*that*]] that *V&P*.
4. hacked] hackèd *V&P*. Because *V&P* omitted the *too* inserted between ll. 3 and 4, the editors added a grave accent to 'hacked', apparently to compensate for a missing syllable. *too*] omitted in *V&P*; the *BSM*. *bones;*] bones *Nbk 21*; bones, *V&P*.

5   Give me my pistols ... Hassan, Youssouff, Daood,
    All false as Greeks ... thou here, true Fatima,
    One kiss — and if thou lovest God and me
    Go drown thyself. — Within an hour at most
    We two will meet in Paradise. —

I: 'The clouds of every heart and every mind'

Drafted in pencil in the lower half of *Nbk 21* p. 89, these four lines are set off from the surrounding material by large spaces. On the facing p. 88 are rough drafts for *Hellas* 184–94; several of those lines are also in pencil. At the top of p. 89 is the draft for the two concluding lines for Mahmud's speech (ll. 195–6):

> *Kings are like stars; they rise & set, they have*
> *The worship of the world, but no repose. —*

These two lines are followed by a SD: *Exit Mahmud & Hassan.* Conjecturally, these four lines might have characterised Mahmud's state of mind before becoming unsettled by 'a gloomy vision'; they seem to describe his imperviousness to the suffering of humankind. S.'s decision to focus on Mahmud's disquiet at the drama's outset could thus explain his decision to omit these lines.

Text from *Nbk 21* p. 89.

5–6. Having just awakened from his disturbing sleep, Mahmud finds himself surrounded by threatening disaster and treachery, even to the point of suspecting that his trusted servants are disloyal.
5. *pistols* ...] pistols . . *Nbk 21*; pistols! *HM 329*; pistols, *V&P*. Hassan, Youssouff, Daood,] Hassan Youssouff Daood, *Nbk 21*; Hassan, — Youssouff, Daood, *HM 329*; Hassan; transport Davod; *V&P*.
6. *All false as Greeks*] Perhaps an allusion to *Aeneid* ii 49: 'timeo Danaos et dona ferentes' ('I fear the Greeks, even when bringing gifts'). *as Greeks* ...] as Greeks . . *Nbk 21*; as Greeks? *HM 329*; are Greeks ... . *V&P*; like Greeks . . *BSM. thou here, true Fatima,*] thou here true Fatima *Nbk 21*; Thou here true Fatima — *HM 329*; Thou here, true Fatima *V&P*.
7. *kiss* —] kiss, *HM 329*; kiss, *V&P*.
8. *Go*] Go, *HM 329. thyself. — Within*] thyself. — within *Nbk 21*; thyself — within *HM 329*; thyself within *V&P. most*] most; *V&P*.
9. *Paradise. —*] Paradise *HM 329*; Paradise!' *V&P*.

Published in *BSM* xvi 94–5 (facsimile and transcription of MS).

'The clouds of every heart and every mind'

The clouds of every heart and every mind,
Death and the massy darkness which imprisons
The embryon phantoms of the absent [?hour]
To him, are as thin air to the Sun's gaze

J: 'I would not be a King: enough'

Lines 1–43 are written mostly in ink with some words in pencil in *Nbk 21* pp. 90–5. These six pages are sandwiched between drafts for *Hellas*; some *Hellas* lines are also present at the foot of pp. 90–1. The last six lines of this fragment (ll. 44–50), found on *Nbk 21* pp. 149–51, have, until the present edition, been thought to represent a separate and independent verse composition. Newly deciphered words and passages, both cancelled and uncancelled, suggest that they are a continuation of the lines on pp. 90–5 and that the whole is a single though incomplete poetic composition. The conjecture of the editors of *BSM* xvi, Donald Reiman and Michael Neth, that the pp. 90–5 material is possibly related to the opening Choruses of *Hellas* comprising the Greek captive women and the Indian slave seems to be correct. The Indian slave's overwhelming concern for Mahmud and her total absorption in his well-being are reflected in the drafts here as is the Greek women's concentration on the power of greater forces at work such as 'Freedom', 'Chaos' and 'Time'.

At the top of p. 90 in *Nbk 21*, S. inscribed *Maidens*, in pencil, and then a little below that, *Fatima*, in ink, just before the first lines, suggesting that he contemplated a harem scene for *Hellas*. Two speeches (ll. 1–11, 28–39) bear the stamp of Fatima's mournful devotion and can, with some certainty, be ascribed to her. (Elsewhere in the *Nbk 21* drafts of *Hellas*, S. assigned *Fatima* as a speaker heading (p. 63), and in another passage, Mahmud directly

¶ **411 Appendix I** *1. mind,*] mind *Nbk 21*.
2. *massy*] 'Of an immaterial thing: great, substantial, dense, impressive' (*OED* 4). Cp. Ann Radcliffe, *The Mysteries of Udolpho*, 3 vols (1794) I ch. ix: 'the massy darkness of the woods'.
3. *embryon*] For 'embryon', a rare usage, see *Fragments of an Unfinished Drama* (no. 436) l. 214 and note. *[?hour]*] [desire] *BSM*. In a note for this word, *BSM* xvi 95 also proposes 'hour' as another possible reading.
4. *To him*] O Min[d] *BSM*. Although written in faint pencil, the upper looping stroke of the *T* is just visible and is followed by a minuscule *o*. Admittedly, the ascender stroke of the *h* in *him* is a little shortened, but the rest of the word seems legible.

addresses her by name; see *Ibrahim — Stab that pernicious slave who talks of fear* (Appendix H)). S. provided no further indications of speaker designations with one exception: in *Nbk 21* p. 92, S. squeezed in a centred speaker heading which the editors of *BSM* xvi conjecturally read as *Semi*, an indication of a choric convention. The other speeches, lacking any speaker heading, are characterised by their references to Judeo-Christian narratives and a focus on 'equal love' accompanied by freedom. The spacing, lineation, indentations and symbols of these speeches in the MS make it clear that they belong to a Maiden speaker, of which there are at least two, and that the final speech (ll. 40–51) belongs to a chorus of *Maidens*. The present edition indicates these separate speeches with 'Maiden' or 'Maidens'. Elsewhere in the *Nbk 21* drafts of the women's speeches for *Hellas*, S. is clear-cut in attributing speaker assignments. For example, on p. 136 of *Nbk 21*, S. inscribes *Semi — 2* and *Semi . 1* for draft of *Hellas* ll. 659–60. (Other similar instances are found in *Nbk 21* pp. 135, 137 and 162–3.) Without such clear designations, this abandoned passage perhaps represents a moment when S. decided to forego individualised speakers. The abandonment of these lines reflects his decision to focus on the political aspects of the Greek struggle; a scene with clearly identified women speakers of the harem voicing more intimate, domestic concerns could only distract from the principal goals of his lyrical drama. The *HM 329* press copy in Williams's hand shows the shift towards the anonymity of the female characters and is in keeping with the choral conventions of S.'s model from Aeschylus' *Persae*.

The transcription of ll. 1–11 in *Mary Copybk 2* p. 77 (see *Massey* 186), under the heading 'III' with an ink cross alongside, would appear to be in Mary's later hand, and was probably made when she was preparing her collected editions for the press in 1838–9. Lines 1–11 were first published in *1840* as no. 'XX' in the 'Fragments' section of 'Poems written in MDCCCXXII'.

Text from *Nbk 21* pp. 90–5, 149–51. Indentation follows the MS.

Published in *1840* 321 (ll. 1–11); *Massey* 292 (transcription of *Nbk 21* pp. 90–1, ll. 1–11); *BSM* xvi 96–101, 150–153 (facsimile and transcription of MS).

¶ **411 Appendix J** *1–11*. Granville Bantock (1868–1946) published a choral part-song entitled *On Himalay* based on these lines in 1908.
1. SD. *Fatima* is inscribed just above the first line. Because this is the only time S. wrote in her speaker heading, the second speaker heading for her is conjectural.

'I would not be a King: enough'

Fatima
I would not be a King: enough
Of woe it is to love.
The path to Power is steep and rough
And tempests reign above;
5   I would not climb ... The [imperial] throne
Is built on ice, which Fortune's sun
Thaws in its height of noon. —
Then farewell, King! yet I were one,
Care could not come so soon!
10 Would he and I were far away,
Keeping flocks on Himalay. —

1. *I would not be a King*] This phrase is a quote from William Cowper, *The Task* (1785) v 359: 'I would not be a king to be beloved'. *be*] Mary Copybk 2, 1840; be, Nbk 21. *King:*] King, Nbk 21; king — Mary Copybk 2, 1840. For this phrase's ending, S. first wrote *Queen* canc., and then added *Queen* above but cancelled that as well; *King* is then added below.
2. The word *one* is written at the end of this line and of l. 4 in Nbk 21. *woe*] Mary Copybk 2, 1840; woe, Nbk 21. *love.*] love Mary Copybk 2; love; 1840.
3. *Power*] power Mary Copybk 2, 1840. *rough*] rough, 1840.
4-5. Mary Copybk 2 and 1840 insert a space between these two lines, but the MS gives no indication of such a space; rather, lines 1–11 form a single stanza.
4. See note to l. 2. *above;*] above Mary Copybk 2; above. 1840.
5. *climb ... The*] climb ... the Nbk 21; climb the Mary Copybk 2, 1840. *throne*] throne; 1840.
6. *Is built*] I built Nbk 21; Tis built Mary Copybk 2; 'Tis built 1840. A likely slip in the MS because the first draft of this line on facing p. 90 in Nbk 21 gives *Is built*. *ice,*] ice Mary Copybk 2, 1840. *Fortune's*] Fortunes Nbk 21, Mary Copybk 2; fortune's 1840.
7. *its*] the 1840. *noon.* —] noon. 1840.
8. *Then farewell, King!*] Then farewel King! Nbk 21; Then farewell king — Mary Copybk 2; Then farewell, king, 1840. Cf. Richard II III ii 170: 'and farewell king!'. See also *It is the period* (Appendix A), l. 136 and note for another echo of *Richard II*. *I were*] were I Mary Copybk 2, 1840. *one,*] 1840; one Nbk 21, Mary Copybk 2.
9. Mary Copybk 2 follows the indentation of this line in Nbk 21 but 1840 does not. *could*] would Mary Copybk 2, 1840. *soon!*] soon Mary Copybk 2; soon. 1840.
10. *away,*] away Mary Copybk 2, 1840.
11. *Himalay.* —] Himaläy. — Nbk 21; Himelay Mary Copybk 2; Himelay! 1840. The diacritical dash in the MS over the second 'a' of Himaläy is also found in the MS of *Fragments of an Unfinished Drama* (no. 436) l. 180 in Nbk 18 p. 136 *reverso*; there, it is spelled *Himaläh*.

Maiden
Judith loved not her enslaver.
My virgin heart beats high to know
Such bridal joys as hers were never,
15   Soft Indian, dreamed by such as thou.

Maiden
Shall the slave love the master?

12. SD. A new speaker here is indicated by the space between lines 11 and 12 as well as the dash at the end of line 11. Rather than a chorus of Maidens, the speaker is a single female voice.
12–15. The 'Maiden' speaker, one of the captive Greek women, recounts a Judeo-Christian story where the heroine feigns love to deceive a powerful Assyrian general thus gaining freedom for herself and the people of Israel. The speaker also seems to recognise that Fatima, the 'Soft Indian', could never imagine such actions or freedom.
12. Judith] *The Book of Judith* in *The Apocrypha* recounts the siege of Bethulia by Holofernes, a general of King Nabuchodonosor. To force the Jewish town to surrender, Holofernes blocks its access to water; rather than fight, the leaders of the town accept this fate with the expectation that God will somehow intervene and save them. Dismissing their assumptions of God's future action and at the same time rejecting any notion of surrender, Judith, a wealthy and righteous widow, devises a secret plan to thwart Holofernes' deadly siege. Entering his camp, she claims that she can help Holofernes defeat the 'hill country, without losing the body or life of any one of his men' (*Judith* x 13). In time, she enchants Holofernes with her wisdom and beauty and is rewarded by his trust: he invites her to dine with him where he drinks 'much more wine than he had drunk at any time in one day since he was born' (xii 20). Left alone with the inebriated sleeping commander, Judith 'smote twice upon his neck with all her might, and ... took away his head from him' (xiii 8). Her return to Bethulia with the head of Holofernes inspires the town to fight and resist; Holofernes' head is hung from the city walls provoking disarray and fear in the surrounding Assyrian army, which is eventually defeated.
13. high to know] [high] to [?sorrow] *BSM*.
14. never,] never *Nbk 21*.
15. BSM seems to suggest that this line is incomplete, but emendations to its second half in *Nbk 21* staircase down below completing it and the rhyme pattern, *abab*. *thou*.] thou *Nbk 21*; thee *BSM*.
16. SD. See headnote for speaker designations. Centred mid-page in *Nbk 21* p. 92, *BSM* conjecturally reads 'Semi'. A symbol — possibly the numeral *2* or merely a squiggle — is centred above the level of the last two words of l. 16; a similar notation occurs again, just before l. 19.

Maiden
                                    Aye, when
The lion lies down with the doe
And the babe in the basilisk's den.

Maiden
Yet Love him not, no love can be
20   Holy between him and thee;
Love lives only with the free ...
Those whom equal love unite
In their common country's sight
Of equal years and rank and mind
25   To equal duties yoke and bind —
[?While] laws, religion, friends approve

---

16. master?] master? oh no *Nbk 21*. *BSM* follows the MS here with 'oh no', and cites the following cancelled line in its partial edition in *BSM* xvi p. xl. S. wrote *aye when* on a lower level, below a speaker change symbol and offset to the right; thus, these two syllables form the new ending for l. 16, replacing *oh no* (albeit uncancelled), and introduce a new speaker. *Aye,*] aye *Nbk 21*.
16–18. Aye when ... den.] Cp. *Isaiah* xi 6–8:

> The wolf also shall dwell with the lamb, and the leopard shall lie down with the kid; and the calf and the young lion and the fatling together; and a little child shall lead them. And the cow and the bear shall feed; their young ones shall lie down together: ... And the sucking child shall play on the hole of the asp, and the weaned child shall put his hand on the cockatrice' den.

18. den.] den *Nbk 21*.
19–34. Yet Love ... heaven and hell;] This dialogue on the nature of love is reminiscent of Paul's discourse on 'charity'; see *I Corinthians* xiii 4–7.
19–27. These lines belong to one of the captive Greek women with her emphasis on 'country', freedom, and equality.
20. thee;] thee *Nbk 21*.
21. Love lives] Loves live *BSM. free ...*] free .. *Nbk 21*.
23. country's] countrys *Nbk 21*.
25. duties,] duties *Nbk 21. yoke*] yoke, *Nbk 21.* bind —] bind *Nbk 21*.
26. [?While]] Whom *BSM*. Decipherment of this word in *Nbk 21* is uncertain because of multiple layers. The progression seems to be *Which* then *Whom* then *While*.

And Heaven protests not — may love.

Fatima
O [wrong not love, O bind not] love,
O [say not love can be] —
30 Like aught but God's own light above
One for the bound and free
Through right or wrong, through good or ill
Which levels, lifts, and to its will
[Subdues not] heaven and hell; like me
35 The worm beneath the sod

27. *protests*] forbids *BSM*.
28-39. These lines belong to Fatima who rejects the description of love provided by the previous Maiden speaker and emphasises her lowly status.
28-9. Wispy, intermittent strokes cancel most of these two lines, but complete rhyming counterparts below in ll. 30-1 indicate that they were to be retained, making a quatrain for the first part of a nine line stanza response to the Maiden's nine line stanza (ll. 19-27) above.
30. *God's*] Gods *Nbk 21*. S. cancelled *Gods*, replacing it with *Heaven* above which was then also cancelled; *Gods* was then underscored, signalling stet.
32. Although the *BSM* editors transcribe this phrase, they omit it in their partial edition in *BSM* xvi p. xli. For the following line, they adapt their transcription of the last line on *Nbk 21* p. 93: 'Love is not love, that [shines] not still' (*BSM* xvi 99). The MS, however, shows *that* is cancelled as well as *shines*; the present editors find the word *BSM* reads as 'shines' to be illegible. The two final words, *not still* are uncancelled; it seems, however, that this incomplete line is superseded by the draft on the following page (p. 94). *through*] throug *Nbk 21*; throng *BSM*.
33-6. These lines appear in *Nbk 21* p. 94 after approximately seventeen line-drafts are begun and cancelled. The draft shows that S. was searching for an appropriate line to rhyme with 'ill' in l. 32.
33. A second set of seeming cancel strokes in this line may in fact be a stet; the line is necessary for sense and confirms the rhyme pattern. *levels*] The sense is '[t]o lower the position of, bring down' (*OED* 3c), the opposite of 'lifts'.
34. Just below this line's beginning is the rest of the line drafted in faint pencil that reads [?] *heaven & hell; like me* thus completing the rhyme with 'free' above in l. 30. *BSM* gives '[?Equal]ize]' as the reading for the illegible word, a word which in the present editors' view is ultimately cancelled. 'Equalize' is contrary to the intent of this speech. *[Subdues not]*] *BSM* reads '[Reduce] not' and indicates the phrase is cancelled. A second line through the two words is possibly a stet.
35-6. These two lines in *Nbk 21* p. 94 are adapted from *Epipsychidion* (no. 391) 128-9: 'The spirit of the worm beneath the sod / In love and worship, blends itself with God'. In the *Hellas*-related framework, Fatima characterises her lowly state

May hope, and mingle with its god.

Shall the swallow hate summer? Oh never
[?Can] I joy while he is in grief?
Sing sisters ...

Maidens
40 Shall we sing —
Wake that fierce and mighty strain
Whose mystic words are like a train
Of shadows! — dance that measure old

---

as that of the worm. On yet another occasion, S. further adapted these lines as the conclusion for his sonnet to Byron, *Lines to* — (no. 429) 13-14: 'Who dares these words. — The worm beneath the sod / May lift itself in worship to the God.' (See the note to those lines). Further draft lines associated with the Byron sonnet are found in *Nbk 21* p. 228 *reverso*.
35. This line initially read *Like me, the worm beneath the sod*, but when the emendation to the line above occurred in pencil with *like me* concluding that line, S. then cancelled — in pencil — the first two words of this line, touching up the *e* of *the* as well.
36. *god.*] god *Nbk 21*.
37-40. At this point, the draft in *Nbk 21* pp. 94-5 indicates a shift in Fatima's mood; rather than continuing her dispute with the Maidens regarding the nature of love, she describes her unhappiness. The last line cancelled at the bottom of p. 94 reads *My spirits are failing alas* and then at the top of p. 95 she starts to address the Maidens: [*Gentle sisters, let*]. Both attempts suggest a change of mood and focus. The next line is the successful l. 37 and a little further below is l. 38, both structured as questions. She addresses the women with 'Sing sisters ...' as if seeking a joyful distraction, and possibly their response is 'Shall we sing —' (l. 40).
37. *Oh*] oh *Nbk 21*.
38. This line began with *Shall I*, in *Nbk 21*, and then *Shall* was cancelled and the conjectural *Can* squeezed in above.
39. A more complete but cancelled line below l. 39 in *Nbk 21* reads: *Sing gentle sisters — that wild strain,* — The second half of that line, however, was recycled into the quatrain beginning at l. 41. *sisters* ...] sisters . . *Nbk 21*.
40. The plural *we* indicates that this is not a speech by Fatima but a chorus of the Maidens. *sing* —] sing *Nbk 21*.
41-4. Unlike the preceding lines, this quatrain, at the bottom of *Nbk 21* p. 95, is drafted with little trouble and few emendations.
41. Although *that* is partially cancelled, its retention seems necessary for metre and sense.
42. *train*] s train *Nbk 21*. The 's' is evidently a slip with 'strain' in l. 41 still echoing in S.'s composing.

Whose motions speak of things untold.
45 Come sisters of the dance …
    Weave the splendour of the dance

    As the Wind leads forth her clouds through the Heavens wild
                                                    and wide —

44. *Whose*] Which *Nbk 21*. S. first wrote *Which speaks*. Desiring a parallel structure with the phrase in l. 42, he cancelled *speaks* and replaced it with *motions speak* but failed to alter the now ungrammatical *Which* at the line's beginning. *untold.*] untold *Nbk 21*.

45–51. With nowhere else to continue this scene — the next pages are filled with already drafted *Hellas* material — S. might have turned over approximately 25 leaves to unused pages, *Nbk 21* pp. 149–151. Textual links such as *Now blithe compan* [for 'companions'] (p. 149), [*Dance blithe comp*] and *Come sisters of the dance* (p. 150) and *I lead ye to the dance* (p. 151) would seem to support this sequence. The invitation to the dance in these final lines is accompanied by the movement of a celestial dance. The motion of clouds before the wind and the appearance of the moon and stars at dusk feature regularly in S.'s verse. He imagines the dancing of stars in *Song of Pan* (no. 318), l. 25 and in *WA* (no. 341) 269, but for the dance of heavenly bodies in *I would not be a King* he seems particularly to have recalled *PU* (no. 195) IV 77–80 (see also l. 129), which include a long (twelve-syllable) line (79):

> But now — oh weave the mystic measure
>   Of music and dance and shapes of lights,
> Let the Hours, and the Spirits of might and pleasure,
>   Like the clouds and sunbeams, unite.

The portion of the notebook where these lines are found is a repository for a group of lyrics (*Autumn: a Dirge* (no. 415); *The Indian Girl's Song* (no. 412); *The flower that smiles today* (no. 417.)

45. This line is so neatly underlined that it does not appear to be a cancel stroke. It perhaps functions as the linking device to the *Nbk 21* p. 95 material, ll. 38–9. *dance …*] dance … . *Nbk 21*.

47–8. Lines of fourteen syllables are highly unusual in S.'s verse: see *Written at Cwm Elan* (no. 61). The sustained pulse might reflect the dance movements of 'the splendour of the dance'. Between these two lines on *Nbk 21* p. 151 is the cancelled line *Then come my bright Companions* — variations of which appear, also cancelled, on facing p. 150 and on p. 149.

As the moon leads forth her stars in the purple eventide
I lead ye to the dance
50   To the dance
I am dancing

K: 'Could Arethusa to her fountain run'

The untidy and much-cancelled draft of these ten lines occupies *Nbk 21* p. *261 reverso*, the page immediately following the fair draft of *Unfathomable Sea! whose waves are years* (no. 416). Written in the same ink and with a similar pen-cut, they are likely to date from, or close to, the time of *Unfathomable Sea*. Mary did not transcribe the lines into any of her copybooks; they were first published by Richard Garnett in *Relics* where they are grouped with 'fragments [that] appear to have been written originally for "Hellas"'. Garnett's text, which has been followed by subsequent *eds*, shows substantive variations from the *Nbk 21* draft in ll. 1, 2 and 4. It is collated with the MS in the notes below. Like the draft of *Unfathomable Sea*, the present lines continue with a few historical references that are almost entirely cancelled and left undeveloped:

[Though Rome]   its [destroyer]
[Macedonia, its young Conqueror]

The fragment, which might at first have been intended for another conception of *Hellas*, sets out a series of conditions for the re-establishment of ancient Greek freedom that are self-evidently impossible of fulfilment. The cumulative effect of these is comprehensively to deny the masternarrative of Romantic Philhellenism: that modern Greece might recover the political and artistic glory it enjoyed in time long past. In contrast, the final chorus of *Hellas* prefers a mode of prophecy which, 'indistinct and obscure' (*Hellas*, S.'s note 7), more adequately accommodates both the uncertainty of the current armed revolution and the general tendency of all human endeavour to deteriorate. Like *Unfathomable Sea*, the text of *Could Arethusa* comprises a stanza of ten lines, which shorten as they reach a concluding couplet.

48–9. An earlier draft on p. 149 reads: [*As*] *the moon leads the stars oer the smooth silent sea / Now blithe compan.*
51. Separated by a space from the preceding four lines, this may have been intended as a further line or part-line, or perhaps the beginning of a second stanza.

Text from *Nbk 21* p. 261 rev. Commas have been supplied in ll. 2 and 7; semicolons in l. 5 (replacing a comma) and l. 7.

Published in *Relics* 12; *Locock 1911* ii 81; *BSM* xvi 244-5 (facsimile and transcription of MS).

'Could Arethusa to her fountain run'

Could Arethusa to her fountain run
From Alpheus and the bitter Dorian,
Or could the morning shafts of purest light
Again into the quiver of the Sun
5   [Be gathered]; could one thought from its wild flight
Return into the temple of the brain

¶ **411 Appendix K** *1-2.* Ovid, *Metamorphoses* v 572-641 recounts how the nymph Arethusa, pursued by the river god Alpheus, fled from her home in the Peloponnese until Diana transformed her into a stream; Alpheus then mingled his waters with hers. She eventually reached Sicily, rising as a sacred spring on the island of Ortygia off Syracuse. See also Pausanias V vii 2. For S.'s continued treatment of the myth see also *Arethusa arose* (no. 311) and *Arethusa was a maiden* (no. 312).
1. Could Arethuse to her forsaken urn *Relics. Arethusa*] The terminal *a* is not completely closed in the MS — like the *a* in *shafts* (l. 3) — and can appear to be an *e*. The thickly-cut nib that S. was using makes some letters difficult to form clearly and to distinguish confidently. It is inherently unlikely that he would spell the name so as to make three syllables, leaving the line a syllable short. *fountain*] source.
2. From Alpheus and the bitter Doris run *Relics. bitter Dorian*] The briny Mediterranean which Arethusa passed through to reach Sicily. Cp. *From Virgil's Tenth Eclogue* (no. 167): 'So when thou [Arethusa] / Glidest beneath the green and purple gleam / Of Syracusan waters mayest thou flow / Unmingled with the bitter Dorian [*Doris amara*] dew'.
3-4. Largely cancelled lines include: *O could the pure and rapid* [?] */ Flow backward to its purest mountain* / [?] *Peneus.* The Peneus was a river flowing through the plains of Tempe in ancient Greece; traditionally Daphne was changed into a laurel on its banks. Cp. *Song of Pan* (no. 318) l. 13: 'Liquid Peneus was flowing — '. The sun-god Apollo is commonly represented as an archer loosing an arrow from his bow, as in *Song of Apollo* (no. 317) ll. 13-14: 'The sunbeams are my shafts with which I kill / Deceit'.
4. quiver] quivers *Relics.*
5. gathered];] gathered— *Relics.*
6. Both *unspotted* and *unstained* are cancelled after *Return* in *Nbk 21.*

Without a change, without a stain;
Could aught that is, ever again
Be what it once has ceased to be —
10   Greece might again be free.

L: 'A star has fallen upon the Earth — a torch'

These lines are drafted in *Nbk 21* pp. 260–57 *reverso* and immediately follow the draft of *Could Arethusa to her fountain run* (Appendix K). S. confidently begins the opening sestet (*abccab*) on p. 260 *reverso*. The following quatrain (*dede*) became more troublesome as he continued drafting in the lower half of p. 260 *reverso*. Dissatisfied with those starts, S. flipped over the page and began anew at the top of p. 259 *reverso* where a few promising lines emerge followed by a series of many cancelled line starts written below. The five successful lines in the upper third of the page were recopied with a few corrections at the top of facing p. 258 *reverso*; however, this more or less complete version was struck through with a diagonal cancel stroke. An apparent break in composition occurred, for S. returned to the lower half of p. 258 *reverso*, writing with a distinctly different ink and pen-cut. The new lines drafted here, drawn from elements found on pp. 260, 259, and upper half of p. 258, all *reverso*, finalise the quatrain and the first tercet (*fgh*). Turning over the leaf, he completed a second tercet (*fgh*) on p. 257 *reverso*, making a sestet. The final phase of the text is a set of three complete lines rhyming *h-i-i* ('Earth'–'breath'–'death'); the final half line ('A spirit of Life,') is left incomplete, and the text was apparently abandoned.

Because *Unfathomable Sea! whose waves are years* (no. 416) along with *Could Arethusa* and *A star has fallen upon the Earth — a torch* run consecutively in *Nbk 21*, Garnett (*Relics* 12) and the editors Reiman and Neth (*BSM* xvi) suggest that these verses are evolving preludes to *Hellas* inscribed in *Nbk 21*. They indicate that *A star has fallen* — like *Unfathomable Sea!* and *Could Arethusa* — was 'another failed attempt' to begin *Hellas*, and consequently date those attempts to the spring of 1821

7. *stain;*] stain,— *Relics*.
9. *be* —] be, *Relics*.
10. *free*.] free! *Relics*.

(p. xxxviii). The MS draft following *A star has fallen*, and separated only by stubs of three missing leaves is S.'s *Epitaph* (no. 420) for Keats, 'Here lieth one whose name was writ on water'. In assuming that *Epitaph* was written near the time of S.'s work on *Adonais* in May-June, Reiman and Neth reason that *Unfathomable Sea!* — and by extension *Could Arethusa* and *A star has fallen* — may have been drafted 'as early as February, but certainly during March' (*BSM* xvi p. xxviii). The headnote for *Epitaph* in the present edition demonstrates the error of that conclusion: that S. was certainly unaware of Keats's final wishes for his epitaph inscription in the spring of 1821; that S. probably drafted the epitaph near the time of his letter to Joseph Severn, 29 November 1821. (See the headnote to *Epitaph* in the present volume; see also Cian Duffy, 'Percy Bysshe Shelley's Other Lyrical Drama and the Inception of "Hellas"', *Studies in English Literature 1500–1900* lv (2015), 817–40.) As discussed in the introductory headnote above, because of the physical proximity of *Epitaph*, it is the view of the present editors that a much later date in 1821 is a more likely period for the composing of *A star has fallen*. A similar date could be applied as well to *Unfathomable Sea!* and *Could Arethusa* for several reasons. First, the page where the draft of *Unfathomable Sea!* commences, which is the first page in the *reverso* portion of *Nbk 21* (p. 264 rev.), actually begins with the cancelled line, *A spark of inextinguishable [fire] lightning*, a beginning very similar to the first draft of l. 1 of Appendix L on p. 260 *reverso*: *A spark has fallen upon the Earth*. Later, S. cancelled *spark*, emending it to *star*. Secondly, given the shared prosodic and metrical features of *Unfathomable Sea!* and *Could Arethusa* along with a possible prosodic link with *A star has fallen*, these three texts might be a related set or ensemble, amounting to another strand in S.'s determination to address the Greek crisis. Such a possibility is seemingly supported by their sequential nature — written one after another in uninterrupted succession — and the uniformity of the medium throughout the three drafts. Finally, despite the patchwork disposition of the *Hellas* drafts in *Nbk 21*, with little indication for their final arrangement as they appear in *HM 329*, the single organising principle for those drafts is that they were all composed in the right-side up, forward running direction of the notebook. The *reverso* direction of these three texts would thus seem to exclude them from the *Hellas* composing period.

Unfathomable Sea! and *Could Arethusa* establish their locus in terrestrial geography and phenomena while *A star has fallen* expands its perspective to encompass a celestial vision. The impulse for the cosmic imagery perhaps comes from *Revelation* viii 10: 'And the third angel sounded, and there fell a great star from heaven, burning as it were a lamp'. Similarly, *Revelation* ix 1 begins: 'And the fifth angel sounded, and I saw a star fall from heaven unto the earth'. *Revelation* ix continued to provide

S. with the language of prophecy early in the following year: a cancelled draft for one of Archy's prescient speeches in *Charles the First* (no. 426), composed sometime in January 1822, references *the battle of Abaddon* which is also described in *Revelation* ix (see note to I ii 395). In *A star has fallen*, S. assumes the prophetic voice of John, describing his vision of what would seem to be a hopeful outcome for Greece. It is a vision that is defined through a catalogue of earthly architectural and decorative features ('torch', 'cresset', 'temple-porch', 'floor', 'beam', 'well', 'prison', 'charnel', 'garment'). The complex stanza pattern and varying metres echo patterns found in *Ode to Naples* (no. 343). The constitutional revolution in Naples shares the challenge of political renewal and rehabilitation with Greece where political forces are threatening her future as an independent nation.

Text from *Nbk 21* pp. 260–257 rev. Commas have been supplied in ll. 2, 6, 8, 14 and 17; other punctuation deviating from MS is described in the notes. Indentation follows MS.

Published in *Relics* 12–13 (ll. 1–19 [in part]); *Locock 1911* ii 81–2 (ll. 1–19 [in part]); *BSM* xvi 240–5 (facsimile and transcription of MS).

'A star has fallen upon the Earth — a torch'

    A star has fallen upon the Earth — a torch
       Of Heaven has fallen mid the benighted nations,
    A quenchless atom of immortal light —
       A living spark of Night …
5   A cresset shaken from that temple-porch

¶ **411 Appendix L** *1–2. A star … fallen*] Cp. *Revelation* ix 1.
1. Earth —] earth *Relics*; Earth *Locock 1911*. *a torch*] Omitted in *eds*.
2. Of Heaven has fallen] Omitted in *eds*. *mid*] 'Mid *Relics, Locock 1911*. *nations,*] nations *Nbk 21*.
3. benighted] 'Overtaken by the darkness of the night; affected by the night' (*OED* 1). *light —*] light, *Relics, Locock 1911*.
4. Night …] Night, *Relics, Locock 1911*.
5. cresset] 'A vessel of iron or the like, made to hold grease or oil, or an iron basket to hold pitched rope, wood, or coal, to be burnt for light; usually mounted on the top of a pole or building, or suspended from a roof' (*OED* 1a). *that temple-porch*] the constellations. *Relics*; the constellations,— *Locock 1911*.
5–13. that temple-porch … birth —] *Eds* omit virtually all of these lines and publish instead the early drafts found in *Nbk 21* pp. 260–58 *reverso*. (See headnote for stages in S.'s composition and revision of earlier inscribed lines.) Although an incomplete fragment — lacking only the latter half line of the last line — the MS

>   Whose floor is the constellations,
>   Secret as a thought more fleet
>   Than the thunder beam, it fell
>   Where our world's slow pulses beat
> 10   Unextinct in that cold well —
>   Wielding this sphere which is its prison —
>   A ray of the eternal pent
>   In limbs of mortal birth —
>   Till, as a Spirit half unrisen

demonstrates S.'s repeated emendations to guarantee a deliberate metrical pattern and rhyme scheme that are not evident in *eds*. The version by Garnett (*Relics* 13) — which Locock follows, differing only in punctuation — reads:

>   A cresset shaken from the constellations.
>   Swifter than the thunder fell
>   To the heart of Earth, the well
>   Where its pulses flow and beat,
>   And unextinct in that cold source
>   Burns, and on   course
>   Guides the sphere which is its prison,
>   Like an angelic spirit pent
>   In a form of mortal birth,

6. *constellations,*] constellations *Nbk 21*.
8. *beam,*] beam *Nbk 21*; heaven *BSM*. *it*] of *BSM*. S. first wrote *Than the thunder it* [*past*]. Above this line he entered *shaft* canc., and then *beam* was added. Finally, [*past*] was replaced by *fell* just below.
9. *slow pulses beat*] [soul] pulses leap *BSM*. Cp. *My pulse beats temperately*, an uncancelled jotting note related to *Charles the First* cited in the note to I i 143 SD and found in *Nbk 19* p. 182 *reverso*.
11. *this sphere*] that sphere *BSM*.
12. *A ray*] As ray *Nbk 21*.
14. *Till,*] *Relics*, Locock 1911; Till *Nbk 21. unrisen*] arisen *Relics*, Locock 1911, *BSM*. In *Nbk 21* p. 258 *reverso*, S. initially ended this line with *newly risen*; he then cancelled *newly* and added *half un* above. Overleaf, on p. 257 *reverso*, he rewrote l. 14, and *unrisen* is clear.

15   Shatters its charnel, it has rent
            In the rapture of its mirth
         The thin and broidered garment of the Earth,
         A [desolation], [ruining] its chaos — a fierce breath
         Consuming all its forms of living death
20   A spirit of Life,

M: 'The pilot spirits the eternal stars'

Written in ink, this fragment is found at the 'back' of *Nbk 21* on p. 229 *reverso*. It follows S.'s reading notes for *Charles the First* (no. 426) from Hume and Whitelocke as well as the Keats *Epitaph* (no. 420), all of which date from late 1821, probably December, which is the likely period for this fragment as well. Although p. 229 *reverso* now faces p. 228 *reverso* containing the first three lines of a draft in pencil of S.'s sonnet to Byron, this was not always the case for five leaves have been removed, possibly because of a damaging liquid spill. S.'s fair copy of his sonnet to Byron is dated *Jan 22.* [1822], Byron's birthday, which would further confirm the late 1821 dating for this fragment. (See *BSM* xii 131–2 for a discussion and photofacsimile of the now lost MS of the sonnet; see *BSM* xvi p. 213 n. for B. C. Barker-Benfield's communication to the editors of *BSM* regarding the damage and the likelihood that p. 228 *reverso* contains what 'may be among his last compositions in the Notebook').

No clear link with *Hellas* has been established, and this line and a half may represent an entirely independent point of departure. Pilots are a

15. charnel,] *Relics, Locock 1911;* charnel — *Nbk 21.* rent] rent, *Relics, Locock 1911.*
16. mirth] mirth, *Relics, Locock 1911.*
17. broidered garment] painted garment *Relics, Locock 1911; BSM* records the first word as illegible. In *Nbk 21* p. 257 *reverso*, S. first wrote *painted raiment* then cancelled both, writing in *broidered* below and *garment* above the core line. *garment* is seemingly canc. and then stetted. There is a possible cancel stroke through *broidered.* Cp. *Paradise Lost* iv 701–2: 'Crocus, and hyacinth with rich inlay / Broidered the ground'. *Earth,*] Earth *Nbk 21* but a blot just below *Earth* makes any punctuation conjectural.
18. A [desolation], [ruining]] Ruining *Relics; Locock 1911.* chaos —] chaos: *Locock 1911.*
19. its forms] the forms *BSM.* death] death. *Relics, Locock 1911.*
20. Omitted in *eds.*

recurring theme in S.'s work, and, on the whole, tend to be flesh and blood characters (e.g. *L&C* (no. 143) 3209; *The Fugitives* (no. 369) 18; *Charles the First* I iii 20). The pilot here, however, is spiritual, or god-like in controlling the stars, rather than being guided by them.

Text from *Nbk 21* p. 229 rev.

Published in *BSM* xvi 212–13 (facsimile and transcription of MS).

'The pilot spirits the eternal stars'

> The pilot spirits the eternal stars
> Knows each in

412 The Indian Girl's Song

[Lines to an Indian Air]

Four complete MSS of this much-admired lyric are known to have survived; they exhibit minor differences, no one version being identical to another. *Nbk 21* (pp. 144–7, 153) contains an untitled draft of all three stanzas and there are a few lines of draft, also untitled, in *Nbk 19* (pp. 200 *reverso*–199 *reverso*). An autograph fair copy headed *The Indian girls song*, deriving from the *Nbk 21* draft, is now in the Fondation Martin Bodmer, Cologny (Genève) (*Bodmer*). Another copy was transcribed on the recto and verso of the first of two leaves damaged by seawater and mud; these, entitled *The Indian Serenade*, were recovered from the wreck of S.'s boat the *Don Juan*, which foundered on 8 July 1822, occasioning his death and that of Edward Williams (*MYRS* viii 329–35). One side of the second leaf carries a transcription of the libretto of the popular duet 'Ah

¶ **Appendix M** *1.* Before this line, there were three attempts to begin; the MS shows a shift in the number of actors and their nature:

> [*Blind pilots*]
> [*Blind pilots* [*?they*]]
> [*The spirits that pilot*[*s*] *every*]

By the time S. reached the first line, 'pilot' had moved from verb to noun and was singular rather than plural.

DOI: 10.4324/9781315779874-6

perdona' from the first act of Mozart's opera *La Clemenza di Tito* (1791). The MSS of both poem and libretto are now agreed to be in Mary's hand, though previously they were considered by some to be in S.'s (*BSM* xxiii p. ix). (See, e.g., *Reiman (1977)*, *Reiman (2002)*, *Chernaik* 248, *BSM* xvi pp. l–liii, *MYRS* viii 336–9; *L about S* 16–17). The libretto and the poem in this MS are held in the Morgan Library & Museum (*Morgan*). Mary also transcribed a fair copy into *Harvard Nbk 1*, again under the title *The Indian Serenade* (*MYRS* v 89).

A text of the poem (referred to here as *I arise from dreams of thee* because of its several MS versions whose single common feature is the first line) was first published in 1823, a few months after S.'s death, as *Song, Written for An Indian Air*, among the 'Minor Pieces' in *The Liberal: Verse and Prose from the South* (I ii 397), the short-lived literary magazine planned by S. and Byron and edited by Leigh Hunt. Judith Chernaik notes that *Morgan* 'appears to be the source of the *Liberal* text, and perhaps of *1824* as well. Since these transcripts were both made during Shelley's lifetime, they may conceivably have independent authority' (*Chernaik* 248). Mary mentions in a letter to Jane Williams of January 1823 that the version to appear in *The Liberal* had been 'altered' by Hunt (*Mary L* i 306). This seems likely to refer to the removal of 'die' from l. 15, so attenuating the sexual connotation of the line, and to the substitution of 'me' for the 'it' of all other witnesses in l. 23. A text differing slightly from *The Liberal* printing appeared without date in *1824* under the title *Lines to an Indian Air*. Mary included this version, with two minor variants, in *1839* and *1840*, grouped with poems of 1821. A date of composition in the latter half of that year would be consistent with the position of the complete draft in *Nbk 21* and with that of the few draft lines in *Nbk 19* (see *BSM* xii pp. lii–liii; *BSM* xvi pp. l–liii) — as well as with Medwin's recollection that the lyric was composed in summer 1821 for Jane Williams to sing 'adapted to the celebrated Persian air sung by the Knautch [or Nautch] girls, [professional Indian dancers], "*Tazee be tazee no be no*"'. Jane had learnt several airs of eastern origin during her time in India (*Medwin (1913)* 317–18; *Relics* 98–9). For his part, Trelawny recalled that the Scottish tenor John Sinclair (1791–1857), who in late 1821 and early 1822 was performing at the Opera House in Pisa (*Mary Jnl* i 388–9; *Mary L* i 215–18), had requested that S. and Byron each write a song for him. Apparently in response, Byron composed his *Stanzas to a Hindoo Air* on 1 January 1822 (*Byron PW* vii 511, 721; *MYR Byron* iii 443–7) while S.'s contribution was *I arise from dreams of thee* — both to be sung to 'an Indian air which Jane Williams had often played to them ... which begin[s] "Allah Malla punca"' (Iris Origo, *The Last Attachment* (1949) 298–9, 508).

S.'s song was evidently well known in the Shelley circle at Pisa. He replies in a letter of 31 March 1822 to Claire Clairmont, then living in Florence, that Mary will 'send you the Indian air', very likely the one including the refrain *Tazee be tazee no be no* that Medwin recalled as that to which *I arise from dreams of thee* was set (*L* ii 403). Claire transcribed this air — which is traditionally included as the third *ghazal* (lyric) in the *Divan* (collected poems) of the medieval Persian poet Hafiz (1315–90) — into her journal, headed *Indian Song* (*Claire Jnl* 286–8). The refrain *Tazee be tazee no be no* (or in the transliteration in *Claire Jnl, tazu bu tazu now bu now*) she gives variously (as they appear in a contemporary translation): 'ever fresh and ever gay', 'ever fresh and ever fine', 'ever fresh and ever sweet', 'ever fresh and ever young'.

A year after S.'s death, in a letter of August 1823, Mary writes from Paris to Leigh Hunt that, at a musical evening, she had been deeply disturbed to hear played on a harp the first notes of what may well have been the air (or one of them) associated with *I arise from dreams of thee* in the Pisan circle; these introduced

> the Indian air you have often heard me mention that [? Edward and] Jane used to sing together [...] It was the only air except one other of E's [Edward's]—in the world, I think, that I c^d not have heard through [...] but how could I hear the mimickry of that voice—the witch [sic] to recall such scenes.—Let me forget it—the very remembrance makes me melancholy. (*Mary L* i 374–5)

Against the substantial body of evidence in support of composition in late summer/autumn 1821 there needs to be set some indications of an earlier date which have influenced understanding of the poem's genesis and associations. In *Rossetti 1870* William Michael Rossetti discloses that he was in possession of

> a copy of the poem communicated to me by Mr. Catty [one of Sophia Stacey's two sons]. The verses were given to Miss Sophia Stacey in 1819, and perhaps written in 1818. They have hitherto been referred to the year 1821, and supposed to have had their origin in the oriental air to which Mrs Williams (whom Shelley did not know in 1819) sang them. (ii 565)

Sophia Stacey (see headnote to no. 271 and *Rossetti Papers 1862 to 1870* (1903) 392, 414–16), a relation of S.'s by marriage — who was still alive when her son passed to Rossetti a copy of *I arise from dreams of thee*, which he remembered as having been presented to his mother by S., made a stay in Florence from 8 November to 29 December 1819 on a tour of Italy, taking rooms in the same house in which the Shelleys were then lodging. During these weeks she and S. were frequently in each other's company and he gave her a number of original lyrics. According to Helen Rossetti Angeli, Sophia's diary — its location is now unknown — records that 'after hearing her sing on the evening of the 17th November [S.] handed her the exquisite verses, "I arise from dreams of thee", having promised to write her some poetry the day before' (*Shelley and his Friends in Italy* (1911) 98). Sophia's younger son Corbet Stacey Catty confirms this entry (see below). Nonetheless Rossetti, considering *1824* as more authoritative, takes that version as his text — the title of *The Indian Serenade* and two minor verbal changes apart. He does not include in his commentary any distinctive readings from the text of the poem he says he received from the Catty family. He does cite both *Relics* 98–9 and, from *Hunt Correspondence* ii 266–7, a letter of Robert Browning dated 6 October 1857 in which Browning notes a few differences between the *1824* text and the one (*Morgan*) recovered from the salvaged *Don Juan*, which he has just been able to examine. To these Rossetti tentatively adds two further variants which, he says, he has seen in 'what purports to be a verbatim copy of *The Indian Serenade*, as recovered from Shelley's corpse' (evidently *Morgan*):

From the first sweet sleep of night — (l. 2)

Where it *must* break at last (l. 24)

The first of these clearly differs from *Morgan* and the other surviving textual witnesses, as does the second, though it cannot be decisively compared to *Morgan* because line 24 (see note) has been damaged in that MS. Forman considered the first 'a clerical error' and the second to be the final two letters of 'must', a possible reading (*The Athenaeum* 4166 (31 August 1907) 240).

These two traditions of evidence for composition — in 1819 for Sophia Stacey, in 1821 for Jane Williams — can hardly be reconciled on the basis of such information as we now possess without recourse to indemonstrable hypotheses. For example, did S. compose *I arise from dreams of thee* in late 1819, present it to Sophia Stacey, then (having kept no copy or lost one he did keep) redraft the song, based on his memory of it, in the latter half of 1821 for Jane Williams to sing? Possibly. In *The Athenaeum* 4199 (18 April 1908) 478 Corbet Stacey Catty recalls that *I arise from dreams of thee* was for many years in her [Sophia's] possession, and which I constantly saw in the MS. Unfortunately, about the middle of the fifties, this was lost in a sale of [household] effects [following a fire], whether stolen or burnt I cannot say ... 'I arise from dreams of thee' ... she always accepted as specially written for her, and which she was never tired of singing when they were wedded to Salaman's beautiful music [published in *Six Songs* (1838) by Charles Kensington Salaman (1814–1901)].

Other conjectures in favour of composition in 1819 could be advanced (see, for example, *BSM* xvi pp. lii–iii), and there is no reason to suspect Sophia Stacey/Catty or her sons of either inaccurate recollection or deceit. But, resting largely on testimony rather than existing MS evidence, their claims can hardly weigh conclusively against those for 1821. That a complete draft exists in a notebook securely dated to the latter half of that year or early the next warrants a practical editorial decision in the matter of date of composition while not absolutely excluding the possibility that a version of the poem was first composed in 1819 and given to Sophia Stacey, the autograph MS then lost in the mid 1850's, and a copy that had been taken kept in the family and transmitted to Rossetti.

Forman 1876–7 accepts the title *The Indian Serenade* from *Morgan* as reported by Rossetti, as well as the 1819 date of composition, otherwise putting together a somewhat eclectic text from both MS and printed sources. The coming to light of an autograph MS (*Bodmer*) once in the possession of Sir Percy and Lady Shelley, which was sold at Sotheby's in 1962 and is now in the Fondation Martin Bodmer, Cologny (Genève), introduced a new title, *The Indian Girl's Song*. This MS has been taken as copy-text for the present edition; variants of interest from other witnesses are recorded in the notes.

In the months between the draft of *I arise from dreams of thee* and his death the song was evidently regularly performed in S.'s Pisan circle. The title of *The Indian Girl's Song* (*Bodmer*) in itself strongly suggests that that copy was indeed intended to be sung by Jane Williams, as Medwin recalled, and to an air she had acquired when living in India. As a girl, Jane had spent some years there and retained a fondness for the country and its culture. During the Pisan carnival season of 1822 she chose to put on Hindustani costume (18 February: *Gisborne Jnl* 131). If the song was at some stage meant to be, as *When the lamp is shattered* (no. 437) is very likely to have been, one of the lyrics for incorporation into *Fragments of an Unfinished Drama* (no. 436), it would suit the character of the Lady, the part that seems the most appropriate for Jane to have assumed. Certainly dreams and dreaming form an important theme of the play, which shares with the song both its melancholy tone and its sombre undertones. Whether there is any significant relation between *I arise from dreams of thee* and S.'s transcription of the duet 'Ah perdona' in the libretto of *La Clemenza di Tito* by Caterino Mazzolà (*MYRS* viii 338), for which Mozart furnished the music, appears uncertain. The dramatic situation of the duet is that the emperor Tito, unaware that the two are in love, has sent Annio to inform Servilia that he has chosen her to be his empress. The anguish of loving one on whom a higher claim exists will have resonated with S.'s feelings for the married Jane Williams. He in all probability encountered the duet in *La Clemenza di Tito* at least as early as July 1817 when the opera was staged in London and reviewed by Leigh Hunt in the *Examiner*, as H. B. Forman pointed out ('Shelley, Metastasio, and Mozart: "The Indian Serenade"', *The Athenaeum* 4175 (7 November 1907) 550–51). Forman considered that one might reasonably suppose Mozart's to have been the 'tune running in his head' when S. composed *I arise from dreams of thee*; and he goes on to speculate that Sophia Stacey's playing on the harp in 1819 together with 'the main melodic trend' of Mozart's music for the duet, associated both of these with the genesis of *I arise from dreams of thee*. The poem is one of S.'s that has been most frequently set to music, Burton R. Pollin's *Music for Shelley's Poetry* (1974) listing 150 different settings.

John Drew, *India and the Romantic Imagination* (1987) 231–82, traces S.'s acquaintance with representations of India and with its literary traditions, as does Nigel Leask, *British Romantic Writers and the East: Anxieties of Empire* (1992) 68–169; B. A. Park, 'The Indian Elements of the "Indian Serenade"', *K-SJ* x (1961) 8–12 examines the 'eastern' idiom of *I arise from dreams of thee*. Chauncy B. Tinker, 'Shelley's Indian Serenade', *The Yale University Library Gazette* xxv (1951) 70–72 describes a MS of music for the poem and proposes Moore's *Lalla Rookh* as the source of 'champak' in l. 11. For the numerous musical settings of *I arise from dreams of thee*, see Burton R. Pollin, *Music for Shelley's Poetry: An Annotated Bibliography of Musical Settings of Shelley's Poetry* (1974); 'More Music for Shelley's Poetry', *K-SJ* xxxi (1982) 31–6; and *The LiederNet Archive*.

Text from autograph fair copy now in the Fondation Martin Bodmer, Cologny (Genève). The apostrophes in the title and in l. 13, the commas in ll. 15 and 18, and the semicolon in l. 22 have been supplied.

Published in *The Liberal* I ii (1823) 397 (entitled *Song, Written For an Indian Air*); *1824* 163 (entitled *Lines to an Indian Air*); *MYRS* viii 332–3 (facsimile and transcription of MS).

The Indian Girl's Song

    I arise from dreams of thee
    In the first sleep of night —
    The winds are breathing low
    And the stars are burning bright.
5   I arise from dreams of thee —
    And a spirit in my feet
    Has borne me — Who knows how?
    To thy chamber window, sweet! —

    The wandering airs they faint
10 On the dark silent stream —

¶ 412 Title. Song, Written For an Indian Air *Liberal*; Lines to an Indian Air *1824, 1839, 1840*; The Indian Serenade *Morgan, Harvard Nbk 1, eds*. Although serenading one's beloved in the open air beneath her chamber window is traditionally a role for a male singer, the *Girl's* in the title of *Bodmer* is the only gender-specific indication in the language of the MSS witnesses.

1. [From dreams of thee beloved, I have risen wild & joyous] *Nbk 21*.

2. sleep] *Nbk 21, Nbk 19*; sweet sleep *Morgan, Harvard Nbk 1, Liberal, 1824, 1839, 1840, eds*.

3. The winds] *Chernaik, Reiman (2002)*; When the winds *Morgan, 1824, 1839, 1840, eds*; [When] The winds *Harvard Nbk 1*.

4. burning] *Nbk 21, Harvard Nbk 1, Liberal*; [?shin] *Morgan*; shining *1824, 1839, 1840, eds*.

7. Has borne] *Nbk 21, Harvard Nbk 1*; Hath led *Morgan, Liberal, Forman 1876–7, Hutchinson, Locock 1911*; Has led *1824, 1839, 1840*. Who knows] oh! who knows *Morgan*; [oh] who knows *Harvard Nbk 1*.

8. In the *Nbk 21* draft S. hesitated between *lattice* and *window*, finally preferring the latter. Beneath the *Nbk 21* p. 144 draft of the first stanza is the line: *Come forth, look forth I die away.*

9–10. [The airs around me faint on the flowers & the trees / The dewy odours die on the dewy dying breeze] *Nbk 21*.

10. *dark silent*] the dark & silent *Nbk 21*; the dark, the silent *Morgan, Harvard Nbk 1, Liberal, 1824, 1839, 1840, eds*. The draft in *Nbk 21* contains various attempts at this line: *on the flowers & the trees, on the bosom of the stream, upon the dewy* [?]; and see previous note.

The champak odours fail
Like sweet thoughts in a dream;
The nightingale's complaint —
It dies upon her heart —
15   As I must die on thine,
O beloved as thou art!

O lift me from the grass!
I die, I faint, I fail!
Let thy love in kisses rain
20   On my lips and eyelids pale.
My cheek is cold and white, alas!
My heart beats loud and fast;
O press it close to thine again
Where it will break at last.

11. The odours of my chaplet fail *Nbk 21.* And the Champak's odours fail *Morgan, Forman 1876–7.* The champak is a large evergreen tree of the magnolia family bearing fragrant flowers varying in colour from cream to orange. S. could have found references to it in Moore's *Lalla Rookh* (1817) and Sir William Jones's *Botanical Observations* (c.1770, repr. 1807). See articles by Park and Tinker above.
12. [on the dying / dewy wind / breeze] *Nbk 21.*
14. S.'s first attempt at the line in *Nbk 21* reads: *grows weak in [her wild dream].*
15. Harvard Nbk 1, 1839, 1840, Rossetti 1870, Rossetti 1878, Locock 1911; As I must on thine *Morgan, Liberal, 1824, Forman 1876–7, Hutchinson;* And I must die on thine *Nbk 21.*
17–18. B. A. Park (see above) cps Sir William Jones's *Hymn to Náráyena:* 'Oh! raise from cumbrous ground / My soul in rapture drown'd'.
19. [Let] thy [kisses] fall [like dew] rain *Nbk 21.*
21. [My breath is ebbing and my heart] *Nbk 21.*
23. press it close to thine] *Harvard Nbk 1, 1824, 1839, 1840, Rossetti 1870, Rossetti 1878, Locock 1911;* press it against [?this] *Nbk 21;* press it to thine own *Morgan, Forman 1876–7, Hutchinson;* press me to thine own *Liberal.*
24. it will break at last] *Harvard Nbk 1, Liberal, eds;* [?there] let it break at last *Nbk 21;* [?st] break at last *Morgan.*

413 'Which like a crane, its distant home pursuing'

This fragment is written *reverso* on *Box 1* f. 109ᵛ, part of the bifolium ff. 108–9 which also contains an untitled draft of *The Aziola* (no. 405). At the top of the leaf there are a series of false starts that are mostly heavily cancelled:

> *In* [*thunder & in fire*]
>   [*Thunder & lightning*]
>   [*Two spirits, instruct*]
>   [*pilot-spirits clothed*] *in*
>   [*The waves sounds*]

The opening of this fragment with the relative pronoun *Which* suggests that the run of similes, and the cancelled starts above, are a continuation of another composition. S. was writing *Hellas* (no. 411) at the same time as this fragment (see discussion of dating and imagery below), and it could be that these lines were intended for that poem. The lines are predominantly in iambic pentameter, aside from the shorter lines 5, 8, and the rhyme at lines 8–9. E. B. Murray dismisses the passage as 'often indecipherable' and 'largely incoherent' (*BSM* xxi 464), but the subjects and the sentiments of this fragment are typical of S.'s late poetry. S. had used sharks in similes of 1819 (*To S[idmouth] and C[astlereagh]* (no. 252) ll. 11–15) and 1820 (*A Vision of the Sea* (no. 321) ll. 56–8), and although avian imagery is common throughout S.'s verse, it becomes more pronounced in his final years. There are references to vultures in *TL* (no. 452) at ll. 262 and 497, and the migratory crane appears in three of S.'s late poems: *Hellas* 308, 480; tellingly in *To —* (*'The serpent is shut out from Paradise'*) (no. 430) l. 41 ('The crane o'er seas and forests seeks her home'); and in a run of similes in *Fragments of an Unfinished Drama* (no. 436) ll. 116–21:

> Since at the time the sea-swan built [her nest,]
> And the crane returned to her unfrozen home,
> And the false cuckoo [bade the] spring good morrow,
> And on a wintry bough the widowed bird,
> Hid in the deepest night of ivy leaves,
> Renewed the vigils of her inmost sorrow —

DOI: 10.4324/9781315779874-7

The second line of this extract from *Fragments of an Unfinished Drama* and the first line of the poem below ('Which like a crane, its distant home pursuing') have a striking parallel with Goethe, *Faust* 1099: 'Der Kranich nach der Heimat strebt' ('the crane struggles onwards to her home' (trans. *Hayward* 34)). S. had made a literal translation of the speech by Faust containing this line (*Faust* 1064–99) in May-September 1815 and renders the line as 'The crane to her home stretches' (see *They approach you again, fluctuating Shapes!* (Volume 6, Appendix B) l. 1099 and headnote). In his last two years in Italy, Goethe was again a central part of S.'s reading and thought: S. was reading *Faust* with Claire in October 1821 and probably translating passages *viva voce* to Byron that winter. S. then made further translations from *Faust* in early 1822 (see headnote to *May-day Night* (no. 440)), and a further echo from Faust's speech containing the crane-image also appears in *TL* 26–8 and 547–8. The crane is a large, long-legged and long-necked bird with two genera common in Europe (*Antigone* and *Grus*). Cranes differ from herons as they fly with their necks outstretched rather than pulled back, as if eager to reach their destination. The presence of so many birds of passage in S.'s late poetry may be related to visits with Claire and Mary to the Bay of Spezia in autumn 1821 (see *Claire Jnl* 248, *Mary Jnl* i 379, *Mary L* i 213) and S.'s and Mary's eventual residence there from April 1822. The bay was close to the wetlands of the Magra valley, which are the site of migrations by cranes, herons and mallards.

Dating this fragment is challenging. Mary used comparable paper to the bifolium on which it is written in the surviving leaves of the June-July 1821 'rough transcript' of her novel *Valperga* (1823), as did Edward Williams for Act IV of *The Promise* in June-July 1821 (see discussion in *BSM* xxiii 82). Murray seems correct to claim that differences in the ink used for the draft of *The Aziola* and *Which like a crane, its distant home pursuing* on this bifolium suggest they were written at different times (*BSM* xxi 464). B. C. Barker-Benfield's suggestion that 'it seems in principle more likely that a more careful draft for one piece would predate a rougher one for another' (*BSM* xxiii 81) plausibly indicates that this fragment post-dates *The Aziola*, which was written before 4 August 1821 (see headnote to that poem). This fragment could therefore have been written as early as June 1821 or as late as the following summer. But the proximity of the manuscript to *The Aziola*, and the presence of the crane (peculiar to the poetry of S. from *Hellas* onwards, and that he perhaps witnessed crossing the Bay of Spezia) point to a likely composition date of September or October 1821.

Text from *Box 1* f. 109ᵛ rev.

Published in *BSM* xxi 76–7 (facsimile and transcription of MS).

'Which like a crane, its distant home pursuing'

Which like a crane, its distant home pursuing
Floats onward — far [rejoicing in its] flight
A vulture's [?form] [?out] leaps at shout of War;
[Swift] as a shark when a ship mutinies
5   [Follows] and fattens, close behind;
When [in] the tropics one continuous wind
[?Flings] every wave and wind from seas and skies
And quells all calm and storm
But such as to its steady speed conform
10 And feeds the sail …

¶ 413 *1–3*. The sense of these lines is that 'Which … onward' refers to the crane, and 'far … War' refers to the vulture.
1. crane] Written after *Eagle* canc. in *Box 1*.
2. onward —] The dash is written over a comma in *Box 1*. *far … flight*] S. first wrote the words *far rejoicing in its shadow* in *Box 1*, cancelled them and wrote *far,* above. He then cancelled the comma and inserted *flight* below *shadow*.
3. Cp. Southey, 'The Triumph of Woman' (1797) ll. 258–62:

> The shout of war rings echoing o'er the vale:
> Far reaches as the aching eye can strain
>   The splendid horror of their wide array.
>   Ah! not in vain expectant, o'er
>   Their glorious pomp the Vultures soar!

vulture's] vultures *Box 1*. Before settling on *vultures* there are several false starts in *Box 1*, including the phrases *like an untethered* and *Swift as a shark*. War;] War *Box 1*.
5. behind;] behind *Box 1*.
6. When] Written before *And* canc. in *Box 1*. *wind*] Written beneath *storm* canc. in *Box 1* (after cancellations of both words).
7. [?Flings]] This barely legible word is cancelled in *Box 1*, with *Strips* as another cancelled alternative.
10. There are seven widely spaced suspension points at the end of this line that run all the way to the right margin of the page in *Box 1*.

414 'An archer stood upon the Tower of Babel'

The following fragment is one of three compositions that S. wrote in his copy of *Euripidis Tragœdiæ Viginti, cum variis lectionibus*, ed. Josuae Barnes, 6 vols bound as three (1811–12); the others are a partial draft of *Autumn: a Dirge* (no. 415) and *[?] / As when within a chasm of [?mighty] seas* (Appendix B). S.'s copy is in Eton College Library (shelfmark: Kl.4.20) and was the gift of Maurice Baring. Baring gifted the volumes to Edmund Gosse on 11 February 1921, who announced the discovery of the three compositions in a letter to the *TLS* 2711 (24 February 1921) 126 (*Gosse TLS*), which includes transcriptions of this item and the draft of *Autumn*, and a mention of *[?] / As when within a chasm of [?mighty] seas*. The volumes were returned to Baring in 1929 after Gosse's death. In *Some Book-Hunting Adventures: A Diversion* (1931) 46–54, R. S. Garnett claims that S.'s Euripides was on display at a London bookseller sometime before May 1920, and that this bookseller had acquired it 'from Bournemouth' (52). Bournemouth is the location of Boscombe Manor, the home built by Sir Percy Florence Shelley. Presumably, the bookseller acquired the Euripides from someone with access to the house or its owner, Shelley Scarlett, 5th Lord Abinger, to whom Jane, Lady Shelley had bequeathed the Euripides. Lady Shelley had possession of the book on the death of her husband Percy Florence Shelley who had inherited it from Mary (his mother); see *The Library of Edmund Gosse* (1924) 237. In a letter in *TLS* 2712 (3 March 1921) 143, in response to *Gosse TLS*, Garnett claims that he had written a promotional letter about this volume on behalf of the bookseller, which was sent to 'a leading firm of book auctioneers'. Having failed to be sold by these auctioneers, it was then 'transferred to another bookseller', from whom, it appears, Baring purchased the volumes.

The fragment is neatly and clearly written vertically in pencil on the recto of the lower endpaper of the second volume (comprising volumes 3 and 4 of Barnes's edition). *Gosse TLS* speculates that it is 'Perhaps [...] only an experiment of rhymes to "table."' A number of factors — the indentation of lines 2, 4 and 6, the periphrasis to provide the 'Abel' rhyme, and the colloquial 'loon' — suggest an attempt at a satirical or serio-comic stanza in *ottava rima*, a form that S. had used for *Hymn to Mercury* (no. 336), *WA* (no. 341) and *The Zucca* (no. 421).

DOI: 10.4324/9781315779874-8

The fragment refers to two parts of Genesis: the episode of Cain and Abel, and the later story of the Tower of Babel to which S. refers in *DP* (*Reiman (2002)* para. 7). S. was interested in the story of Cain throughout his poetic career (see headnote to *The Devil's Walk: A Ballad* (no. 83) and *MA* (no. 231) 139–46), and he was full of praise for Byron's closet drama *Cain* (1821), claiming in a letter to John Gisborne of January 1822 that it 'contains finer poetry than has appeared in England since the publication of Paradise Regained' (*L* ii 388). The enduring appeal of the Cain figure to S., and the apparent lack of a connection between Euripides' works and the biblical subject of the fragment, make establishing a date of composition difficult. S. read from his Euripides in 1818 on his journey to Italy and in summer 1820 (see headnote to [?] / *As when within a chasm of mighty seas*), but the tone of the piece and its hint at *ottava rima* suggest a later date. On 22 October 1821 S. wrote to Hogg that 'I […] wander about the edges of the hills sometimes with my book, and live in a total intellectual solitude […] I have employed Greek in large doses, & I consider it the only sure remedy for diseases of the mind. I read the tragedians, Homer, & Plato perpetually' (*L* ii 360). A few months after writing this letter S. wrote *Autumn: a Dirge*, a draft of which is also in this volume of Eton Euripides, and *The Zucca*, an unfinished experiment in *ottava rima* drafted in *Nbk 21* alongside another draft of *Autumn*. This was also the period in which S. read Byron's *Cain* (see headnote to *To —* ('*The serpent is shut out from Paradise*') (no. 430)). S. carried his Greek books with him on walks at this time, and the pencil medium and the writing of an original composition in a book would seem to indicate it was composed while out of doors. These factors, and the dating of *Autumn* and *To —* ('*The serpent is shut out from Paradise*'), allows for a tentative date range of October 1821 to January 1822 for the composition of this fragment.

Text from the recto of the lower endpaper of the second volume of S.'s copy of *Euripidis Tragœdiæ Viginti, cum variis lectionibus*, ed. Josuae Barnes, 6 vols bound as 3 (1811–12), Eton College Library, shelfmark: Kl.4.20. Reproduced by permission of the Provost and Fellows of Eton College.

Published in Edmund Gosse, 'New Fragments of Shelley', *TLS* 2711 (24 February 1921) 126; *Julian* iv 75; *MYRS* viii 274–5 (facsimile and transcription of MS).

'An archer stood upon the Tower of Babel'

An archer stood upon the Tower of Babel
And bent his bow against the rising moon,
There sate the brother of the murdered Abel
And grinned a wicked smile upon the loon
5 Under his arm, bored with the bloody cable
 The [?thorns]

415 Autumn: a Dirge

This short poem is the most ambitious and most resolved of the meteorological lyrics that S. attempted between October 1821 and March 1822, which also include *Rough wind that moanest loud* (no. 422) and *The rude wind is singing* (no. 438). The themes of *Autumn* are also in keeping with speeches in, and related to, *Hellas* (no. 411), for example the Phantom's speech at ll. 871–86, the semichoruses at ll. 1023–49, and the Maidens' chorus at the close of *I would not be a King: enough* (*Lines connected with Hellas* (no. 411 Appendix), Appendix J) ll. 45–51.

There is a rough draft of *Autumn* in S.'s copy of Euripides, *Euripidis Tragœdiæ Viginti, cum variis lectionibus*, ed. Josuae Barnes, 6 vols bound as three (1811–12) (*Eton Euripides*) now in the library of Eton College.

¶ 414 1. *An*] The *Gosse TLS, Julian. Archer*] This figure could be Nimrod, builder of the Tower of Babel, who is described as 'a mighty hunter before the LORD' (*Genesis* x 9).
2. *moon,*] moon *Eton Euripides*; moon; *Gosse TLS, Julian*.
3–4. S. alludes to the Christian tradition of seeing Cain's face in the moon; see *Inferno* xx 126 and *Paradiso* ii 49–51. Paget Toynbee first made the connection between these lines and the *Commedia* in a letter in *TLS* 2712 (3 March 1921) 143.
4. *loon*] loon; *Gosse TLS, Julian*. 'A boy, youth, lad' (*OED* 2b).
6. *[?thorns]*] There is underwriting beneath the *th* of [?thorns] in *Eton Euripides*. S. could be alluding to Dante's description of the setting moon as 'Caino e le spine' ('Cain with fork of thorns') at *Inferno* xx 126, which extends the Christian tradition of seeing Cain in the moon by relating the marks on the moon's surface to the bundle of thorns Cain was condemned to carry on his back. *Julian* and *MYRS* opt for 'thong', while 'throng' is favoured in *Gosse TLS*, but there does not appear to be the terminal 'g' required for either of these words.

DOI: 10.4324/9781315779874-9

On this edition and its provenance, see the headnote to *An archer stood upon the Tower of Babel* (no. 414). This draft is written in pencil across the free upper endpaper verso and the first flyleaf recto of the second volume. It is untitled and comprises fourteen lines (a first stanza and the first three lines of a second). At this stage S. has already decided on a lyric with lines of varied rhyme and metre, and established many of the elements, including the refrain on the 'year'. The numerous cancellations and alternatives on these pages, and the fact that *in mourning array* is written in the margin at right angles to the rest, show that this draft underwent heavy revision. A subsequent draft, which starts on p. 143 of *Nbk 21*, continues on p. 142, and ends on p. 141, includes a development of this phrase, with *your saddest* written above *mourning* canc. on p. 143. The *Nbk 21* draft is written in ink and begins neatly on p. 143, but becomes rougher in the second stanza on p. 142. The several mathematical calculations in S.'s hand on pp. 142–3 (see *BSM* xvi 144–5) are likely to have been in place before the poem was drafted. In this intermediate draft the lyric is titled *A Dirge*, and it differs from the later, apparently final, draft in *Box 1* f. 99 only slightly. The most significant variant is *Wrapt in azure and grey* instead of the reading in l. 18 below. On *Nbk 21* p. 141 S. wrote the following heavily cancelled lines and false starts, which may be an attempt at a third stanza:

> The [hoar white] hoar frost is [creeping], [the pale Sun is sleeping] the
> The snow falls
> [Rich]
> [The rich are now]
> [The lord is]
> [With]
> Drawn by
> [With cold hand]   [Comes winter, the [?]]
>   Of the year. —
> The poor man is pining, the richman is dining
> [The snow]

This appears to be a rough third stanza as the first line continues the progressive movement through the seasons of the earlier stanzas, from *warm sun* to *chill rain* on to *hoar frost*. It is impossible to say why S. chose not to complete the turn he makes to more human and political subjects in this unresolved stanza. As Carlene Adamson first deduced, the single leaf comprising the final draft, now in *Box 1*, was torn out of *Nbk 21* between p. 154 and p. 155 where a stub is now visible. The *Box 1* draft is written in ink and titled *Autumn A Dirge*; it is written neatly and contains only a few cancellations. S. also takes care over the line indentation and stanza spacing. (See the photograph on the page preceding the Contents of this volume which shows the manuscript of ll. 1–18 of the text below in *Box 1* f. 99^r). The *Box 1* draft could conceivably have been a presentation copy: the hand is clear, the lay-out is tidy, and the leaf has also been folded twice, which might suggest that it was enclosed in a letter. For another possible case of a presentation copy made from a page removed from a notebook see *Lines to — [Sonnet to Byron]* (no. 429) and headnote. However, a number of factors cast doubt on this hypothesis: the leaf appears to have been torn from *Nbk 21* quite roughly, the lay-out is not as neat as that of the presentation copies of poems given to Jane Williams and Edward Williams (see headnote to *To — ('The serpent is shut out from Paradise')* (no. 430)), and it is impossible to confirm whether the folds to the leaf were made by S. or someone else.

Lines 18–22 are copied at the top of p. 18 of *Mary Copybk 1*, which was used by Mary between autumn 1822 and autumn 1823 to transcribe S.'s unpublished verse. A collation of *Mary Copybk 1* by B. C. Barker-Benfield (see *BSM* ii 244) reveals that two leaves preceding p. 18 have been removed from this notebook, and presumably the page that immediately preceded it contained ll. 1–17 of the poem. In *Mary Copybk 1*, Mary transcribes l. 18 as

Wrapt in azure and grey / Put on white, black & grey

thus presenting the line first as it appears in *Nbk 21* p. 142, and then as it stands (apart from punctuation) in the final draft in what is now *Box 1*. This implies that Mary was unaware of the later draft when she began copying the poem in *Mary Copybk 1*, and that she transcribed this final reading later, when she had access to the *Box 1* leaf. The poem was first published in *1824* with the title 'Autumn: a Dirge' (166); in the Table of Contents, it is given as 'Autumn, a Dirge' (ix). In *1824* the reading of l. 18 is 'Put on white, black, and grey', suggesting Mary knew this was not a variant, but rather the final version of the line. Either she could have overlooked the *Box 1* leaf in her initial transcription in *Mary Copybk 1*, or, if S. had given the *Box 1* leaf to someone else, it was returned to Mary allowing her to add the later reading.

Given its material, themes, and formal characteristics, it is highly likely that *Autumn* was written in the last quarter of 1821. The original drafting of *Autumn* in S.'s copy of Euripides coincides with other compositions in the volume during this period, and its development in *Nbk 21* takes place alongside *Hellas* and other smaller lyrics dated after September 1821. The knotted composition and editorial history of *Autumn* has, however, led to some problems in dating this lyric. For example, in *1839* iv 40, Mary places it among poems written in 1820. In light of this dating, Forman went on to speculate that *Autumn* was one of the poems which S. asked 'to be added to the pamp[h]let of Julian & Maddalo' in a letter to Ollier of 10 November 1820 (see *Forman 1876-7* iii 132 and 153-4; *L* ii 246). Donald Reiman and Michael Neth plausibly suggest in *BSM* xvi p. xlix that Mary's date may result from the manuscript witness in *Eton Euripides* leading her to consult her journal in order to find the last time she recorded S. having read Euripides: June 1820 (*Mary Jnl* i 323). Locock also claims that this lyric has an earlier foundation than the last quarter of 1821, and speculates that *The death knell is ringing* (no. 357) 'reads like a study for *Autumn, A Dirge*' (*Locock Ex* 22; see also *Locock 1911* ii 228). However, as shown in the headnote to *The death knell is ringing*, while there are some similarities between that poem and *Autumn*, there is no material connection between them. The subject of *Autumn* suggests that it was composed during a period when an autumn was becoming a winter, and the 'blithe swallows' of l. 15 are typical of S.'s interest in migratory birds in late 1821 (see headnote to *Which like a crane, its distant home pursuing* (no. 413)). The metrical variety and playfulness have similarities with a number of later lyrics such as *The flower that smiles today* (no. 417), *To — ('The serpent is shut out from Paradise')*, and *Swifter far than summer's flight / Remembrance* (no. 433). A comparison between *Autumn* and *Dirge for the Year* (no. 381) shows S.'s stylistic development over the course of his final two winters. *Dirge for the Year* was written during a period of illness in the cold December of 1820, and while the poem shares the meteorological concerns of *Autumn*, it has none of the formal complexity or modulations of tone that are central to S.'s last lyrics.

As the title makes clear, the poem is a dirge: a mournful song traditionally performed at a funeral. But the title is also somewhat deceptive as the dirge is not for autumn, but for the passing year that S. personifies as female. Although a quite different poem in theme and voice, Keats's 'To Autumn' (published in *Lamia, Isabella, The Eve of St. Agnes, and Other Poems* (1820) that S. read avidly from October 1820 until his death) may have influenced the use of a female personification, the swallows of l. 15, and the eleven-line stanza in *Autumn*. As discussed above, the poem's subject is typical of the melancholy cast of many of S.'s works in late 1821, and shares the avian and meteorological images of his verse in this period. The poem makes a seasonal progress from an autumn of dying flowers and failing sun in stanza 1, to the rain and cold of winter in stanza 2, and finally to the vernal regeneration suggested in the last line. There is a complex rhyme scheme (*abcdbeeefff*), which is further tangled by the gerund rhymes in the first two lines of each stanza and the repeated refrains at lines 3, 5, 9, 10. The combination of repetitive musicality and the halting quality of the unrhymed lines 1, 3, and 4 creates the dolefulness appropriate for a dirge. The metre is similarly sophisticated, with the stanza split into two units divided after line 5. In the first part, lines 1, 2, and 4 of the stanza are hexameters, each with internal rhymes or half rhymes and strict medial caesurae, and these are balanced by the shorter lines 3 and 5. By contrast, the second half of the stanza creates a song-like quality through short iambic lines that share some rhymes ('away', 'bier', 'year') in both stanzas. The metrical variation between stanzas, provided by substituted feet and feminine endings, is highly characteristic of S.'s most accomplished lyrics such as *The Cloud* (no. 319) and *To a Sky-Lark* (no. 330).

Text from *Box 1* f. 99.

Published in *1824*; *BSM* xvi 156–9 (facsimile and transcription of MS).

Autumn: a Dirge

The warm sun is failing, the bleak wind is wailing,
The bare boughs are sighing, the pale flowers are dying,
      And the year,
On the earth her death-bed, in a shroud of leaves dead,
5   Is lying:
    Come months, come away,
    From November to May,
    In your saddest array;

¶ **415** *Title.* See headnote.
3. *year*] Year *BSM*.
4–5. *leaves ... lying*] The inversion and the delayed verb recalls *OWW* (no. 259) 2–3: 'the leaves dead / Are driven'.
4. See the burial of the 'Poet' in *Alastor* (no. 114) ll. 52–4 where 'the charmed eddies of autumnal winds / Built o'er his mouldering bones a pyramid / Of mouldering leaves'. The *Nbk 21* draft of this line reads: *In a shroud of leaves dead, on the earth her deathbed. the*] Written over *her* in *Box 1*.
6. *Come*] Come, *1824*. Alt. from *Comes* in *Box 1*.
8. *saddest array*] See Gray, *Elegy Written in a Country Churchyard* ll. 113–14: "'The next with dirges due in sad array / Slow through the church-way path we saw him borne'".

	Follow the bier
10	Of the dead cold year,
	And like dim shadows watch by her sepulchre.

           The chill rain is falling, the nipped worm is crawling,
           The rivers are swelling, the thunder is knelling
                      For the year. —
15   The blithe swallows are flown, and the lizards each gone
                      To his dwelling;
                 Come months, come away,
                 Put on white, black, and grey,
                 Let your light sisters play —
20   Ye, follow the bier
                 Of the dead cold year,
           And make her grave green with tear on tear.

10–11. Cp. OWW 23–5:

> Thou Dirge
> Of the dying year, to which this closing night
> Will be the dome of a vast sepulchre

11. like dim shadows watch] S. first wrote *like shadows sit down* in *Box 1* then cancelled *sit down,* wrote *watch* above, and inserted *dim* before *shadows. sepulchre.*] *1824*; sepulchre *Box 1*.
12. nipped worm] OED defines 'nipped' as 'pinched, compressed, tightly squeezed' and uses *Autumn* as an example of this definition. Lloyd N. Jeffrey in 'Shelley's "Plumèd Insects Swift and Free"', *K-SJ* xxv (1976) 105, claims that the worms 'evoke the gloomy cold of fall, particularly to those readers who have observed with Shelley that an early freeze often leaves large numbers of caterpillars lying numbed and feeble under the trees and shrubs'. Worms are cold blooded, and therefore their behaviour is highly affected by changes in temperature: S.'s worm is 'nipped' because in winter its movement is reduced.
13. is knelling] Written above *is yelling* canc. in *Box 1*.
14. year. —] year; *1824*.
15–16. These lines invert the spring imagery of *Adonais* (no. 403) ll. 157–62.
15. The blithe swallows are flown] Cp. Keats, 'To Autumn' l. 33: 'And gathering swallows twitter in the skies'. *lizards*] *1824*; lizards, *Box 1*.
17. Come] Come, *1824*. *months,*] *1824*; months *Box 1*. *away,*] away; *1824*.
18. white, black,] *1824*; white black *Box 1*; white, black *Mary Copybk 1*.
19. play —] play, *Mary Copybk 1*.
20. Ye,] Ye *Mary Copybk 1*. *bier*] Written after *year* canc. in *Mary Copybk 1*.
21. year,] *1824*; year *Box 1, Mary Copybk 1*.
22. tear.] *Mary Copybk 1, 1824*; tear *Box 1*.

416 'Unfathomable Sea! whose waves are years'

[Time]

These ten lines of untitled fair draft on p. 262 *reverso* of *Nbk 21* are a redaction of rough draft on the preceding pp. 264–3 *reverso*; a line of draft has been torn off, apart from the single cancelled word 'isles', at the top of the latter page. Mary transcribed the fair draft into *Mary Copybk 2* p. 47 (see *Massey* 120–1) without title — although 'Time' appears as an item in the Contents (see *Massey* 230) — then published it, undated, in *1824* (215) under that title; in *1839* she grouped it with poems written in 1821. Her text and the title have been adopted by succeeding *eds*. Further draft, heavily-cancelled and unresolved, on pp. 263–2 *reverso* furnishes the central image of the 'Ocean of Time' with a historical dimension; a tentative and selective transcription includes the following lines and phrases:

> *For they were clouds* [*that*] *faded in the wind*
> *Each wrecked to unrecognizable form*
> [*Behold where lies*]
> [*Many a mighty*]
> *India Assyria Egypt Athens* [*and*] *Rome*
> *Went forth like ships rejoicing in the ruin*
> [*Like Eagles*] *of Heaven & Earth & sea*
> *Like birds their whirlwind winged prey pursuing*

These jottings on the familiar theme of the ruins of empires indicate parallels between *Unfathomable Sea!* and the drafts of *Hellas* (no. 411) that occupy most of *Nbk 21* — as commentators have recognised (see Irving Massey, 'Shelley's "Time": An Unpublished Sequel', *SiR* ii (1962) 57–60 and *BSM* xvi pp. xxvii–xxviii). Resemblances of thought and language to the semi-choruses of *Hellas* 682–737, which are drafted on pp. 138–40 and 160–3 of *Nbk 21*, suggest that the present lines, together with *Could Arethusa to her fountain run* and *A star has fallen upon the Earth — a torch* (*Lines connected with Hellas* (no. 411 Appendix), Appendices K and L), might well represent a later literary response to the Greek War of Independence from Ottoman rule, which S. had developed amply in the dramatic poem. For further discussion, see headnote to *A star has fallen upon the Earth — a torch*.

The decided pessimism of both the present lines and *Could Arethusa to her fountain run* translates S.'s reservations on the prospects for lasting Greek liberty brought about by force, which he still entertained in September. His enthusiastic reception of news on the Greek advances (*L* ii 324) was tempered by his doubt that 'slaves can become freemen so cheaply' (*L* ii 350) and his fear that, the Greeks having resorted to bloody retribution on their Turkish oppressors, the cycle of violence would perpetuate itself: 'How should slaves produce any thing but tyranny—even as the seed produces the plant' (*L* ii 325) — or, as the Chorus in *Hellas* has it, 'Revenge and wrong bring forth their kind' (l. 729). Also influencing his partisan response were the uncertain issue of armed revolt in general and the dispiriting example of the failed Neapolitan and Piedmontese revolutions in spring 1821 (*L* ii 263, 276, 290–1).

Unfathomable Sea recovers and adapts some elements that can be found among S.'s drafts and completed poems set down over several months before 1821 and especially the central image of a treacherous ocean and its wreck-strewn shores. *LMG* (no. 325), for instance, composed in summer 1820, includes the lines (192–5):

> You are now
> In London, that great sea, whose ebb and flow
> At once is deaf and loud, and on the shore
> Vomits its wrecks, and still howls on for more.

For other borrowings from S.'s earlier verse in *Unfathomable Sea* see the notes below. If, as they appear to have been, the ten lines were intended as poetic unit, they display the characteristics of an irregular Spenserian stanza, of a kind that does not appear in *Hellas*. Lines 5–8 rhyme *cdde* rather than the orthodox *bcbc* and the twelve syllables of the regular terminal alexandrine are divided into a couplet of two lines of six syllables, so enhancing both the gnomic and the musical qualities of the conclusion.

Text from *Nbk 21* p. 262 rev. Commas have been supplied in ll. 1, 3, 6 (end), 7, 8, and 9.

Published in *1824* 215; Irving Massey, 'Shelley's "Time": An Unpublished Sequel', *Studies in Romanticism* ii (1962) 59; *Massey* 278; *BSM* xvi 246–7 (facsimile and transcription of MS).

'Unfathomable Sea! whose waves are years'

Unfathomable Sea! whose waves are years,
Ocean of Time, whose waters of deep woe
Are brackish with the Salt of human tears,
Thou [?Lifeless] flood, which in thy ebb and flow
5   Claspest the boundaries of mortality! —
And sick with prey, yet howling on for more,
Vomitest thy wrecks on its inhospitable shore,
Treacherous in calm and terrible in Storm,
       Who shall put forth on thee,
10   Unfathomable Sea? —

¶ **416** Title. See headnote.
4–5. Cp. *Methought I was a billow in the crowd* (no. 361), 'that stream without a shore, / That Ocean which at once is deaf and loud' (ll. 2–3), which is followed, in *Nbk 15* p. 21, by the cancelled line *Which stuns itself breaking on lifes bleak shore* (see *BSM* xiv 26–7).
4. *[?Lifeless]*] S. originally wrote *Shoreless*; then underlined it, apparently for revision, in order to avoid the repetition and contradiction of 'shore' in l. 7, later entering above the *Shore* of *Shoreless*, with a different pen-point and in a different ink, three or four barely legible letters, which could be *Lif* or *Life*. *1824* reads 'shoreless', followed by *eds*.
5. *boundaries*] Written in a different ink and with a differently cut pen above the line, replacing *limits*, the reading of *1824* and *eds*, which is cancelled with the same ink and pen as the insertion.
6–7. Cp. *LMG* 192–5 (quoted in the headnote above).
6. *with*] for *Mary Copybk 2*; *of 1824, eds*.
7. *its*] I.e. mortality's; Rossetti 1870 ii 584 cps *Ginevra* (no. 398) l. 160 in a passage (ll. 161–3) that likens our obscure idea of life beyond death to the ignorance, before they enter material existence, of pre-existing beings, who know 'no more / […] of this our life — before / Their barks are wrecked on its inhospitable shore'.

417 'The flower that smiles today'

[Mutability]

Nbk 21 contains a draft and a fair copy of this sombre lyric, both untitled: the draft on pp. 1, 2 and the front (originally the back) pastedown, and the fair copy on p. 154. Page 1 also carries S.'s draft of the first eight lines of *The Zucca* (no. 421) written crossways over the draft of the final stanza of *The flower that smiles*. As *The Zucca* dates from late December 1821 to January 1822, *The flower that smiles* must have been drafted earlier. Its position on pp. 1, 2 and the front pastedown is inapt to serve as evidence for assigning a date of composition early in the period when the notebook was in use (late summer 1821-January 1822). However (as Donald Reiman and Michael Neth point out in *BSM* xvi p. liv), because in some other instances S. left a small number of pages blank at either end when he began to write in a fresh notebook, he may have done so with *Nbk 21*. The fair copy, on the other hand, situated as it is in the midst of the drafts for *Hellas*, appears to have been entered towards the middle of October 1821, the month during which the lyric drama was composed. Mary transcribed the fair copy of *The flower that smiles* into *Mary Copybk 1* pp. 18–19 (*BSM* ii 38–41) without giving it a title, and published it in *1824* as 'Mutability', the title that S. had assigned to the 16-line lyric *We are as clouds that veil the midnight moon* (no. 113), which he included in *1816*.

GM argued that *The flower that smiles* should be recognised as a dramatic lyric intended 'for the opening of *Hellas*, to be sung by a favourite slave, who loves him, to the literally sleeping Mahmud before he awakens to find his imperial pleasures slipping from his grasp' ('Shelley's Lyrics' in *The Morality of Art: Essays Presented to G. Wilson Knight*, ed. D. W. Jefferson (1969) 205–06). It is possible that such was S.'s intention at some early stage in the composition of *Hellas*, the draft of which fills most of *Nbk 21*, but neither draft nor fair copy offers sufficient evidence to warrant a secure conclusion on the dramatic poem as original destination for the lyric. *The flower that smiles* shares the essential pessimism of such late pieces as *Swifter far than summer's flight / Remembrance* (no. 433) and *Rough wind that moanest loud* (no. 422); its peculiarity among these is specified in detail by *Chernaik* (155–6) in an illuminating exposition of the poem as a variant on the traditional theme of *carpe diem*.

Text from *Nbk 21* p. 154. Commas have been supplied at the end of ll. 6 and 19.

Published in *1824* 198; *BSM* xvi 156–7 (facsimile and transcription of MS).

'The flower that smiles today'

The flower that smiles today
Tomorrow dies;
All that we wish to stay
Tempts and then flies;
5   What is this world's delight?
Lightning, that mocks the night,
Brief even as bright. —

Virtue, how frail it is! —
Friendship, how rare! —
10   Love, how it sells poor bliss
For rich despair!
But these though soon they fall,

¶ **417** *Title*. Mutability *1824, eds*.
7. even as] In the draft on p. 2 of *Nbk 21* the line reads *Brief although bright*; S. carried this over to the fair copy on p. 154 before substituting *even as* for *although*.
9. how] too *1824, 1839, 1840, Rossetti 1870*.
10–11. Ironically altering the traditional sense of 'rich' and 'poor' in relation to the theme of 'Love' — as in *Romeo and Juliet* I i 212–13: 'O, she is rich in beauty, only poor / That when she dies, with beauty dies her store'.
11. rich] *rich* is the reading of the draft in *Nbk 21* front pastedown which S. transcribed into the fair copy on p. 154. He cancelled it in favour of *proud* written above the line, then underlined *rich* for retention. *1824* and *eds* prefer 'proud'. The draft also shows the alternative line: [*And leaves*] *despair*.
12–14. Virtue, Friendship, Love 'outlive the joy which they briefly occasion, and the illusion of possession. Love flowers as bliss, but lingers as despair' (*Chernaik* 156).
12. these] then *Mary Copybk 1*; we, *1824, 1839, 1840, eds*. *Rossetti 1870/1878* considered it 'almost certain' that the line should read: 'though *we* fall' or 'so soon they fall'.

	Survive their joy, and all
	Which ours we call. —
15	Whilst skies are blue and bright,
	Whilst flowers are gay,
	Whilst eyes that change ere night
	Make glad the day;
	Whilst yet the calm hours creep,
20	Dream thou — and from thy sleep
	Then wake to weep.

418 'A fresh fair child stood by my side'

[Love, Hope, Desire, and Fear]

(Translation of Brunetto Latini, *Il Tesoretto* xxi 82–156)

The draft of these lines, S.'s free translation of a passage from Brunetto Latini's *Il Tesoretto*, occupies the back pastedown and pages 155–9 of *Nbk 21*. The lines on pp. 155–9 (ll. 11–68 of the text given below) were first published by Richard Garnett in *Relics* 40–2 under the title 'Love, Hope, Desire, and Fear', omitting ll. 12, 17, 24 and 49. Garnett presents his text without comment, evidently not recognising its derivation from Brunetto Latini's original; neither does he connect it with S.'s rendering, on the back pastedown, of the ten lines immediately preceding in the Italian text, ll. 1–10 in S.'s text below, which were first published in *V&P* 5 under the title 'Eros'. The lines published in *Relics* are, however, headed by a row of asterisks, which may represent Garnett's conjecture that relevant preceding matter has been removed from the notebook or perhaps his signal that the abrupt beginning indicates that S.'s draft is an excerpt. Both *Forman 1876-7* and *Hutchinson* follow Garnett in presenting 'Love, Hope, Desire, and Fear' as a poem in its own right rather than

---

20–1. Cp. Caliban's words in *The Tempest* III ii 143–6: 'and then in dreaming / The clouds methought would open and show riches / Ready to drop upon me, that when I waked / I cried to dream again'.
21. to] and *Nbk 21* p. 1.

DOI: 10.4324/9781315779874-12

a translation, grouping it with poems of 1821 — unlike *Locock 1911* which places it with S.'s other translations and includes an English version by W. M. Rossetti of the relevant source passage in *Il Tesoretto*. This was identified by A. C. Bradley in 'Shelley and Brunetto Latini' (*The Athenaeum* 3729 (15 April 1899) 469). Bradley supplies the original Italian from 'the text of Zannoni, cap. xix, ll. 81-154', i.e. as it appears in *Il Tesoretto e Il Favoletto di Ser Brunetto Latini*, ed. Giovanni Battista Zannoni (1824); and he includes S.'s English version as transcribed in *Relics* (which, as illustrated in the notes, differs significantly from the text as edited here), concluding that 'Shelley's fragment cannot be called a translation of these lines, but it was evidently suggested by them'. Both GM and *BSM* xvi pp. lv–lvi argue that the position of the main draft of the translation in *Nbk 21* is consistent with composition in autumn 1821, during or just after the drafting of *Hellas* (no. 411), which fills most of the notebook. The translation on pp. 155-9 is the last in a series of drafts of shorter texts, including *Autumn: a Dirge* (no. 415), *The Indian Girl's Song* (no. 412), and *The flower that smiles today* (no. 417) which interrupt the main draft of *Hellas*, itself composed largely in October 1821; so that the translation from *Il Tesoretto*, at least the lines on pp. 155-9, might well have been completed in that month.

Brunetto Latini (*c*.1220–*c*.1294) was a Florentine scholar, poet, translator and rhetorician, who, following the defeat of the Guelph party in 1260, was exiled from his native city for the next six years. He spent most or all of this period in France where he wrote *Li livres dou Tresor*, an encyclopaedic work in French prose with notable sections on ethics and public discourse. Returning to Florence, where he lived until his death, he resumed an active involvement in civic affairs and held a number of prominent public offices. In Canto XV of *Inferno*, Dante, who was born in Florence in 1265, dramatises a meeting between his fictional self and the soul of Brunetto Latini, which has been damned for sodomy, or so the text of the canto seems strongly to suggest. In their conversation Brunetto addresses Dante as *figliuol mio* (my son) and predicts a glorious future for him, while Dante gratefully acknowledges the paternal kindness with which Brunetto treated him in life, in particular the older man's counsels on the way to achieve perpetual fame. The nature and extent of any pedagogical relation that Brunetto Latini might actually have exercised towards Dante has not been precisely established, but it was widely accepted that he acted as tutor and mentor to the young poet who was some 45 years his junior. So much is stated in, for example, John Taaffe's *Comment on the Divine Comedy* (1822, pp. xiv, 20) which S. read in proof in summer 1821 (*L* ii 293, 303-4) (see headnote to *A capering, squalid, squalling one* (no. 419)).

Il Tesoretto ('The little Treasure') is a visionary and didactic poem of nearly 3000 *settenari a rima baciata* (seven-syllable lines in rhyming couplets). The passage that serves as S.'s source runs to 74 lines, the final ones of numbered section XXI in the most recent of the editions that S. could have used, that published by Giuseppe Assenzio in the first of four volumes of *Raccolta di Rime Antiche Toscane* (1817; see no. 418 Appendix). The passage occurs in the same position in the same numbered section in the edition immediately preceding Assenzio's, *Tesoretto di Messer Brunetto Latini*, in *Parnaso Italiano ovvero Raccolta de' Poeti classici italiani*, III: Messer Brunetto Latini (1788); see Brunetto Latini, *Il Tesoretto*, ed. Julia Bolton Holloway (1981) pp. xxxv–vi. These 74 lines, which show no substantial variants in any of the four printed editions published before 1821, S. reduces to 68 — of varying lengths, largely in couplets but including some triplets and unrhymed lines. The English of the resulting poem rewards close comparison with the diction of its Italian source (no. 418 Appendix), from which it displays significant differences. S. also adds details of his own invention which elaborate upon and reinforce the principal theme of the original — the deceptions and failures of Love and Desire (see notes to ll. 9–10, 21–2, 28–31, 37–8, 43–4, 51–2, 53–4, 61–8). In the poem Brunetto portrays himself as the central character of a pedagogical narrative which recounts his initiation by the female figure of Nature into a true understanding of universal history on the Biblical plan of Creation, Fall, Incarnation and Redemption. She further apprises him that the operations of the physical universe and the functions of the human soul are harmoniously ordered and regulated by herself, subject to the Divine Will alone. Brunetto is then directed to set out on a journey through a symbolic landscape, protected by Nature's gift to him of a badge marked with her seal. Passing through a desolate country, he reaches a fertile plain presided over by the Empress Virtue and her offspring, one of whom, Generosity, he observes educating a young knight in the honourable conduct appropriate to his station. Eventually reaching the domain of Love, he is able to view its operations without danger, shielded by the seal bestowed upon him by Nature and with the guidance of the amatory poet Ovid. Here S.'s text begins. For brief commentary on the translation see *Webb* 304–5 and *BSM* xvi pp. lv–lix.

Text from *Nbk 21* back pastedown and pp. 155–9. Punctuation has been modified.

Published in *Relics* 40-2 (ll. 11-68 only, entitled 'Love, Hope, Desire, and Fear'); *V&P* 5 (ll. 1-10 only, entitled 'Eros'); *BSM* xvi 250-1, 159-63 (facsimile and transcription of MS).

'A fresh fair child stood by my side'

  A fresh fair child stood by my side
    In naked pride;
  He was arrayed [   ] —
  And held a bow and many a wingèd reed
5   Which without heed
  He shot around among the company;
    Stone blind was he —
  And yet where'er he bent his aim
  The arrow like a falcon tame
10 Knew its prey and struck the same.
  And many there were hurt by that strong bow
    And none knew how.
  His name, they said, was Pleasure —
  And near him stood, glorious beyond measure,
15 Four Ladies, who possessed all empery
    [?O'er] earth and air and sea
  And all that in them be: —

¶ 418 *Title.* Love, Hope, Desire, and Fear *Relics.*
1. *fresh*] fresh, *V&P.*
2. *pride;*] pride. *V&P.*
3. [   ] —] in pinions beautiful *V&P.* The second half of the line is unresolved in the draft. S. first wrote *in pinions wide*, cancelled the phrase, though *wide* may possibly be underlined for reinstatement, then wrote *beautiful* above the line.
4. *reed*] reed, *V&P.*
7. *Stone*] Tho' *V&P. he —*] he. *V&P.*
8. *aim*] aim, *V&P.*
9-10. The simile of the tame falcon is not in the original.
9. *arrow ... tame*] arrow, ... tame, *V&P.*
10. *same.*] ... *V&P.*
11. A mark in the MS after *hurt* may be a comma; S. perhaps intended to finish the line differently and neglected to remove the comma when he changed his mind. *bow*] boy *Relics.*
15. *possessed*] possess *Relics.*
16. *[? O'er]*] In *Relics.*

        Nothing that lives from their award is free.
            Their names will I declare to thee —
20   Love, Hope, Desire, and Fear,
            And they the regents are
        Of the Four elements, of that wild world the heart;
        And each diversely exercised her art
            For her own part
25   By force or circumstance or sleight
            To prove her dreadful might
            Upon that poor domain. —
        Desire, presented her enchanted glass, and then
            The spirit dwelling there
30   Was spellbound to embrace what seemed so fair
            Within the magic mirror. —
            Dazzled by that bright error
        It would have scorned the frown of the avenger
            And death and penitence and danger
35   Had not silent Fear
        Touched it with her palsy spear
        So that it stood mute as a frozen torrent;
        The life was curdled in its current.
        It dared not speak — not even in look, and motion

18. *award*] Judgement, sentence.
21-2. These two lines, as well as l. 27, are not in the original.
22. Of the Four elements that frame the heart *Relics*.
28-31. The image of the enchanted glass/magic mirror is not in the original.
28. *her*] *Relics*; [?*his*] *Nbk 21*; the masculine form may well be the accurate reading of the MS even though Desire figures among the Four Ladies of l. 15. If 'his' is correct, S. may momentarily have confused Desire with the (masculine) Pleasure of l. 13. *enchanted*] [false] *Relics*.
31. *the*] that *Relics*.
32. *Dazzled*] And dazed *Relics*.
33. *frown*] [shafts] *Relics*.
35. *not*] not then *Relics*.
36. Touched with her palsying spear *Relics*.
37-8. Neither the image of the frozen torrent nor that of the 'curdled … current' is in the original.
37. So that as if a frozen torrent *Relics*.
38. *life*] blood *Relics*.
39. *not even in look, and motion*] even in look or motion *Relics*.

40   But chained within itself its fierce [devotion].
       Between desire and fear, thou wert
           A wretched thing, poor heart ...
       Sad is the life of him who bears thee in his breast,
           Wild bird for that weak nest,
45   Till Love — even from the fierce Desire it brought
       And from the very wound of tender thought
       Drew solace ... and the pity of sweet eyes
       Gave strength to bear those gentle agonies
           They had inspired —
50   The loss, the doubt, the terror, and the sorrow.
       And Hope approached ... she who can borrow
           For poor Today, from rich Tomorrow
           And fear withdrew, as night when day
           Descends upon her orient ray. —
55   And after long and vain endurance
           The sad heart woke to her assurance —
           At one birth these four were born
           In the world's forgotten morn,
           And from Pleasure still they hold
60   All it circles, as of old. —
           When, as summer does the swallow,
           Pleasure lures the heart to follow —
           O weak heart of little wit! —
           The fair hand that wounded it,

40. *fierce*] proud *Relics*. *[devotion]*] Possibly not cancelled.
43-4. These two lines are not in the original.
43. Sad was his life who bore thee in his breast *Relics*.
45. *the fierce Desire it brought*] fierce Desire it bought *Relics*.
49-50. Surmount the loss, the terror, and the sorrow *Relics*.
51-2. *she ... Tomorrow*] Not in the original.
51. *And Hope*] Then Hope *Relics*.
53-4. *as ... ray*] Not in the original.
56. *sad heart woke*] poor heart woke *Relics*.
58. S. first wrote *While the world was yet unworn* in *Nbk 21*, then for the final three words substituted *forgotten morn*, neglecting to alter *world* to *world's*.
60. The *Relics* text ends with this line.
61-8. Apart from ll. 67-8 the ideas and images in this passage are S.'s own contributions.
64-5. Between these two lines is an uncancelled part-line: [?*Borne*], *as cloud upon*.

65   Taking like a panting hare
          Refuge in the lynx's lair,
          Love, Desire and Hope and Fear
          Ever still are near. —

418   Appendix

Brunetto Latini, *Il Tesoretto* xxi 82–156

Below is the source text of S.'s translation of the final 74 lines of section XXI in Brunetto Latini's *Il Tesoretto*, as it appears in *Raccolta di Rime Antiche Toscane* (1817) i 76–8. There are differences in spelling and punctuation as well as more significant lexical and syntactical differences between the text below and modern critical texts edited from manuscript such as that in Julia Bolton Holloway's edition, cited in the headnote to no. 418 above.

          I' vidi ritto stante
              Ignudo un fresco fante,
          Ch'avea l'arco, e li strali,
              Et avea penne, et ali.
5   Ma neente vedea:
              E sovente traea
          Gran colpi di saette;
              E là dove le mette,
          Convien, che fora paja
10   Chi, che pericol n'aja.
          E questi al buon ver dire
              Avea nome Piacire.
          E quando presso fui,
              I' vidi presso a lui
15   Quattro donne valenti
              Tener sopra le genti
          Tutta la signorìa.
              E de la lor balìa
          I' vidi quanto, e come;

20   E sovvi dir lor nome.
       È Amore, e Speranza,
         Paura, e Disïanza.
       E ciascuna 'n disparte
         Adopera sua arte,
25   E la forza, e 'l savere,
         Quant'ella può valere.
       Che Disïanza punge
         La mente, e la compunge,
       E forza malamente
30   D'aver presentemente
       La cosa disïata:
         Et è sì disvïata,
       Che non cura d'onore,
         Nè morte, nè romore,
35   Nè pericol d'avvegna,
         Nè cosa, che sostegna:
       Se non, che la paura
         La tira ciascun'ura
       Sì, che non osa gire,
40   Nè solo un motto dire,
       Nè fare pur sembiante:
         Però, che 'l fine amante
       Ritiene a dismisura.
         Ben ha la vita dura,
45   Chi così si bilanza
         Fra tema, e disïanza.
       Ma fine Amor sollena
         Nel gran disio, che mena;
       E fa dolce parere
50   E lieve a sostenere
       Lo travaglio, e l'affanno,
         E la doglia, e lo danno.
       D'altra parte Speranza
         Adduce gran fidanza
55   Incontro a la Paura;
         E tutt'or l'assicura
       D'aver lo compimento
         Del suo 'nnamoramento.
       E questi quattro stati,

60   Che son di Piacer nati
     Con esso sì congiunti,
        Che già ore, nè punti
        Non potresti trovare
        Tra 'l loro 'ngenerare.
65   Che quand'uomo 'nnamora,
        I' dico, che in quell'ora
     Desia, et ha timore,
        E speranza, et amore
     Di persona piaciuta:
70   Che la saetta acuta,
     Che muove di piacere,
        Lo sforza, e fa volere
     Diletto corporale:
        Tant'è l'amor corale.

419 'A capering, squalid, squalling one'

These incomplete lines parody the verse translation of Dante's *Inferno* by John Taaffe (1787/8–1862), a member of S.'s circle at Pisa. They are written in ink on the lower part of the recto of the first leaf of a bifolium (ff. 61–2) in *Box 1* and are marked off with a horizontal line. The verso of f. 61 and the whole of f. 62 are blank and the lower part of f. 62 and the bottom corner of f. 61 are torn away. The writing in the centre of the upper part of f. 61ʳ, also in ink, is in Edward Williams's hand. Williams wrote *Hellas / Hellas / a lyrical drama*, then, beneath a horizontal line, the Chorus's words in the original Greek from line 1080 of *Oedipus at Colonus*, μάντις εἴμ᾽ ἐσθλῶν ἀγώνων ('I predict a victory in the struggle!') and ended with *Soph:* (for Sophocles). Comparison of f. 61ʳ with f. 1ʳ of *HM 329* (Williams's press copy of *Hellas* (no. 411) in the Huntington Library, San Marino, CA) shows that the former was a draft design for the poem's title-page (for facsimiles, see *BSM* xxi 16 and *MYRS* iii 13). As well as serving as the epigraph to *Hellas*, the quotation from Sophocles was the motto that S., in a letter of 21 March 1821, asked Peacock to have engraved on two seals (*L* ii 277). The remainder of f. 61ʳ, also in ink, is in S.'s hand. It comprises, in the upper half of the leaf, doodles and calculations around Williams's writing and, beneath the word *Soph.*, scrawl that is difficult to decipher (E. B. Murray's extraction of the word 'Ant?igone' in *BSM* xxi 17 is dubious). Immediately beneath a doodle below this scrawl are some lines of roughly drafted verse which, though related to the six lines at the foot of the leaf that make up the present lines, are set apart from them by a space: *O / [?whiz], [?whiz], / Spurt, phiz; vomit, sweat, whine, / Caper, squalid, squalling; [?red]*. The dissonant, unpoetical idiom ('phiz' = grimace; 'whiz' = 'a sibilant sound somewhat less shrill than a hiss' (*OED*)) mimics Taaffe's lexis. Like the first of the present lines below, the first three words of the final line of this rough draft — *Caper, squalid, squalling* — echo the wording of a line from Taaffe's translation of *Inferno* (identified below) that for S. (and Byron, who had arrived in Pisa on 1 November (*Mary Jnl* i 381)), typified his deficiencies as a poet.

B. C. Barker-Benfield notes that the bifolium containing the present lines is 'very likely from the same stock' (*BSM* xxiii 83) of paper as *HM 329* on which Williams press-copied *Hellas* between 6 and 10 November 1821 (*Gisborne Jnl* 110–11). As Murray notes, the fact that the Dedication is dated 'November 1st 1821' in *HM 329* f. 5ᵛ (see facsimile in *MYRS* iii 22) and *1822* p. [v] 'may indicate that this fair copy pattern [i.e. Williams's title-page design on f. 61ʳ] was written either on that day or slightly earlier' (*BSM* xxi 444). S.'s writing on the leaf would appear to have been done fairly soon after that of Williams, perhaps in the first fortnight or so of November when meetings with Taaffe were frequent; Mary notes 'Taaffe in the evening' in her journal for 8 and 9 November and 'Taaffe calls' on 1 and 15 November (*Mary Jnl* i 381–2).

Of Irish descent, Taaffe had lived mostly at Pisa since 1815, disinherited by his family because of the legal consequences of an unfortunate marriage in Edinburgh in 1810. He was introduced to S., Mary and Claire, probably by Francesco Pacchiani, on 28 November 1820 (*Claire Jnl* 189; *L* ii 253 n.). Insight into his literary activities prior to the composition of the present lines is provided by a typescript based on the manuscript of his autobiography, *My Life* (1835, with an addendum of 1845) in Special Collections, The Claremont Colleges Library, Claremont, California (shelfmark: CT868.T33 A3 1845a). Encouraged at Stonyhurst 'to consider poetry the chief business of my life', he had been received by Scott in Edinburgh and mixed with writers including Germaine de Staël and A. W. Schlegel during winters at Pisa (*My Life* 31, 49b, 69). S. appears to have had some regard for him. The affectionate nickname he used for Taaffe, 'τάφος' (grave, tomb), recalled in *Medwin* ii 23, surfaces in the anglicised version *Taaphfe* which is cancelled at the foot of *Nbk 19* p. 142 *reverso* amidst draft of *Charles the First* (no. 426) (see *BSM* xii p. xxxii, 240 n. and 241). S. also respected Taaffe's critical abilities. In a letter of 26 December 1820, he acknowledged his 'generous approbation' of *Cenci (1819)* (*L* ii 253; for S.'s presentation copy to Taaffe, now in CHPL (shelfmark: *Pforz A-RD 10), see headnote to *The Cenci* (no. 209)). Another letter to Taaffe, of 4 July 1821, accepted his 'strictures' on the preface to *Adonais* (no. 403), the printing of which by Giovanni Rosini — dubbed 'Taaffe's printer' by Byron in a letter to Edward Dawkins of 28 April 1822 — S. oversaw (*L* ii 306; Valentina Varinelli, '"Accents of an Unknown Land": Percy Bysshe Shelley's Writings in Italian', *European Romantic Review* xxx (2019) 261; *Byron L&J* ix 150). However, Taaffe's poetic pretensions were clearly a source of mirth and irritation, particularly to Mary who, in letters to Maria Gisborne of 7 March and 9 February 1822, described him acidly as 'the poet laureate of Pisa', and said that he 'bores us out of our [senses] when he comes & writes complimentary verses' (*Mary L* i 223, 218). His published verse prior to 1822 includes *To the Baronness of Stael* (1816), printed at Pisa by Rosini, a copy of which is in CHPL (shelfmark: Pforz (Taaffe, J. To the Baronness of Stael)), and *Padilla: A Tale of Palestine* published in London in the same year. *The Literary Panorama* vi (1817) 414 noted the latter volume's 'peculiarities of diction, which though expressive in the first instance, yet too often indulged, offend the ear'. Taaffe's assessment of himself as 'a very indifferent and even worthless poet' (*My Life* 31) is thus not one from which his acquaintances demurred.

A further context of the present fragment is Taaffe's *Comment on the Divine Comedy of Dante Alighieri* which Mary notes reading on 19, 22, 23 and 31 March 1821 (*Mary Jnl* i 357-9). By then Taaffe appears to have had the first volume, on the first eight cantos of *Inferno*, printed by Rosini. S. enclosed proofs of this portion of *Comment* in a letter to Taaffe of 5 June 1821, noting that he had 'carefully looked over them' and was 'not so fortunate as to have found any errors' (*L* ii 293; see also *L* ii 303); the same day, Mary wrote to Taaffe saying that 'Shelley will be very glad to receive the next proof' (*Mary L* i 202). S. volunteered to read 'the remainder' in a letter to Taaffe from Lerici of 11 June 1822 on being 'agreably surprised by the intelligence of the completion of the *Comment*' (*L* ii 431). Taaffe had originally intended *Comment* to be accompanied by his own translation of the relevant cantos 'in terza rima', 'allow[ing] myself the liberty of varying my lines from eight to ten syllables [...] as well as of using double rhymes at pleasure' (*Comment* xxii, xxiv), features that are perhaps echoed in S.'s parody below. When S. first proposed *Comment* to Ollier for publication, in a letter of 16 June 1821, he praised the commentary as 'a most excellent work, & one without which the history & the spirit of the age of Dante as relates to him, will never be understood by the English students of that astonishing poet', and noted 'the great beauty of the typography: they are the same types as my elegy on Keats is printed from' (*L* ii 304). But his judgement of the verse was muted: 'there are certainly passages of great strength & conciseness' (*L* ii 303). Reservations concerning the verse, at which S. hinted in a further letter to Ollier the following month (*L* ii 311), were expressed more candidly by Byron (see below) who, between December 1821 and March 1822, demanded that John Murray publish *Comment* as a condition of making peace with him (see *Byron L&J* ix 81, 90, 122, 123, 126). Evidently Taaffe abandoned publication of his translation since the Preface to *Comment* states 'That translation of mine I have since suppressed: yet not until two Cantos were printed'; as a consequence, extracts from the translation 'occur to small amount, save in the comments on the two first Cantos' (xxii, xxv).

In a letter of 29 April 1821 to Claire, S. communicated the line of Taaffe's that he reworks in the first of the lines below: '*I Mantuan, capering, squalid, squalling* / a verse of Mr. T.'s translation of Dante' (*L* ii 288). Though this line does not appear among the instances of Taaffe's translation in *Comment*, it is likely to have been among 'the verses, up to the eighth Canto' of *Inferno* (*L* ii 303) that S. had read, according to his above-mentioned letter to Ollier of 16 June. Its source in *Inferno* is difficult to determine although Virgil's speech in i 64–9 is a possibility. While Dowden's suggestion that this line was '[p]erhaps [...] a jest made up at Taaffe's expense' (*Dowden Life* ii 364 n.) cannot be dismissed, it is significant that Medwin recalled Byron to have singled it out as well:

> 'There's Taaffe is not satisfied with what Cary has done, but he must be *traducing* him too. What think you of that fine line in the "Inferno" being rendered, as Taaffe has done it?
>
> "I Mantuan, capering, squalid, squalling."
>
> There's alliteration and inversion enough, surely! I have advised him to frontispiece his book with his own head, *Capo di Traditore*, "the head of a *traitor;*" then will come the title-page comment—Hell!"'
> (*Medwin (1824)* 196–7)

Taaffe was under the impression that a copy of *Comment* (presumably the proofs of 'the remainder' referred to in S.'s letter of 11 June 1822) had 'gone to the bottom with unfortunate Shelley and Williams' when the *Don Juan* sank on 8 July 1822 (*My Life* 81). Murray published *Comment* on 21 December 1822 (*The Letters of John Murray to Lord Byron*, ed.

Andrew Nicholson (2007) 434), its title-page omitting the author's name and 'VOL. 1' implying that further volumes would follow. The work was mentioned favourably by Leigh Hunt in 'Letter 1 – Pisa' of his 'Letters from Abroad' in *The Liberal* I i (1822) 111 n. However, in an acerbic review in *London Magazine* vii (1823), Henry Cary, as S. had done, epitomised Taaffe's extraordinary translation by giving an example of a single line. Cary selected 'Ho! charge, hurra, jolt, bound, rebound!' (*Comment* 430), Taaffe's rendition of the first two words of *Inferno* vii 28, 'Percotëansi 'ncontro' (translated by Cary as 'Both smote together'), as the review's 'motto' (317). No further volumes of *Comment* were published. For discussion of *Comment* and Cary's review, see Antonella Braida, 'Henry Francis Cary and John Taaffe Junior: The Translator of Dante and a Comment on the Divine Comedy', *Journal of Anglo-Italian Studies* vii (2002) 35–50.

Murray provides commentary on this fragment in *BSM* xxi 444–5. For accounts of Taaffe's life, his ignominious behaviour following the Masi affray in March 1822 and his fond, astute recollections of S., see: C. L. Cline, *Byron, Shelley and their Pisan Circle* (1952) 16–25 and *passim*; Richard Harter Fogle, 'John Taaffe's Annotated Copy of *Adonais*', *K-SJ* xvii (1968) 31–52; *Mary Jnl* ii 590–3; and Mario Curreli, *Una certa Signora Mason: Romantici inglesi a Pisa ai tempi di Leopardi* (1997).

Text from *Box 1* f. 61ʳ.

Published in *BSM* xxi 16–17 (facsimile and transcription of MS).

'A capering, squalid, squalling one'

  A capering, squalid, squalling one,
  Came from [   ]
  [   ] like a cat
  Whose stomach yerks forsooth with too much rat,
5 So beastly it might make a witch to spew,
  What then, O Taaffe, might it not do to you —

¶ 419 *1. capering,*] capering *Box 1*; capring *BSM. squalid,*] squalid *Box 1. one,*] one *Box 1* (written above *Mantuan* canc. in *Box 1*).
4. yerks] jerks; 'yerk' = 'to move with a jerk or jerks; to jerk' (*OED* 6b). *rat,*] rat *Box 1*.
6. then,] then *Box 1*. *O*] o *Box 1*. *Taaffe,*] Taaffe *Box 1*. *So beastly* to *you* is cancelled beneath this line in *Box 1*.

420 Epitaph

[On Keats]

These lines are drafted twice by S. in *Nbk 21*, with a rough initial pencil draft occupying the upper part of p. 256 *reverso*, and beneath it a more carefully realised but still obviously incomplete draft, written in ink and in S.'s neater and more compact hand. Centred above this neater draft S. has written *Epitaph*, clearly intended as a title. The lines were evidently prompted by the epitaph on Keats's gravestone in the Protestant cemetery in Rome, and use both the name and Spenserian stanza from *Adonais* (no. 403). The date of these lines offers something of a puzzle. Keats's wish that his gravestone should bear the simple epitaph 'Here lies one whose name was writ in water' was communicated by Joseph Severn to Charles Brown in a letter from Rome dated 8 February 1821, i.e. 15 days before Keats's death on 23 February. The original of this letter is lost and is known only through Brown's transcript which is incorporated into his 'Life of John Keats' (see *Keats Circle* ii 52–97; the epitaph is given on p. 91). Keats's request that this epitaph be on his gravestone was clearly widely known in literary London at least by early March. Keats's publisher John Taylor wrote to John Clare on 9 March 1821: 'We heard yesterday of Keats [...] In this last Letter we are told that Keats desires to have this Line put upon his Tombstone "Here lies one whose Name was writ on Water"' (quoted from *Shelley and Keats: As they struck their Contemporaries*, ed. E. Blunden (1925) 79). Blunden notes that 'The handwriting of Taylor is clear, and he certainly wrote the words as "*on* Water".' Severn and Brown, however, always concur in the wording *in* rather than *on*, and '*in* water' is how Keats's gravestone actually reads. Keats's wish that this line be his sole epitaph was not respected by Severn and Brown, who, against the wishes of Keats's executors, including Taylor, had a longer and tonally far different statement cut:

> This Grave contains all that was Mortal, of a YOUNG ENGLISH POET Who, on his Death Bed, in the Bitterness of his Heart at the Malicious Power of his Enemies, Desired these Words to be engraven on his Tomb Stone. HERE LIES ONE WHOSE NAME WAS WRIT IN WATER.

Keats's grave also bears the design of a Greek lyre with half its strings broken, which Severn at first stated was Keats's idea, and then subsequently

claimed as his own (see Robert Gittings, *John Keats* (1968) 434–5, and *Joseph Severn: Letters and Memoirs*, ed. Grant Scott (2005) 156, 216); cp. *Adonais* note to l. 324.
It is not known when or how S. learned of Keats's chosen epitaph. During the composition of *Adonais* S. definitely knew almost nothing of the detailed circumstances of Keats's death, as the closing paragraph of the Preface to that poem makes clear:

> The circumstances of the closing scene of poor Keats's life were not made known to me until the Elegy was ready for the press [...] He was accompanied to Rome, and attended in his last illness by Mr. Severn, a young artist of the highest promise, who, I have been informed "almost risked his own life, and sacrificed every prospect to unwearied attendance upon his dying friend." Had I known these circumstances before the completion of my poem, I should have been tempted to add my feeble tribute of applause to the more solid recompense which the virtuous man finds in the recollection of his own motives.

The circumstantial account referred to here must have been the letter from 'Colonel' Finch to John Gisborne (see notes to the Preface to *Adonais*), which was forwarded to S. in a letter dated 13 June 1821, and acknowledged as 'the heart rending account' in S.'s reply to Gisborne of 16 June (*L* ii 299). Finch's account however makes no mention of an epitaph. S. subsequently sent a copy of *Adonais* to Severn from Pisa with a letter dated 29 November 1821, which very directly emphasises that Finch's account remains the sole source of his knowledge about Keats's death:

> I send you the Elegy on poor Keats—and wish it were better worth your acceptance. You will see by the preface that it was written before I could obtain any particular account of his last moments; all that I still know was communicated to me by a friend who had derived his information from Colonel Finch; (*L* ii 366)

This statement could be read to imply that S. was informed of Keats's epitaph in Severn's reply to this letter, although no such letter is known to exist. Severn mentions to Charles Brown in a letter of 1 January 1822 that he has received *Adonais* from S. (*Severn: Letters and Memoirs* 185). This surmise might further imply that S.'s lines on Keats's epitaph were composed in

December 1821 or January 1822, in response to further information from Severn. However, S.'s letter of 29 November goes on to convey 'thanks for the picture you promise', clearly indicating receipt of an earlier letter from Severn, in which he could very well have communicated the information concerning Keats's epitaph. This also fits with the positioning of S.'s lines in *Nbk 21*, where they immediately precede, in *reverso*, S.'s working notes towards his drama of *Charles the First*, which he was working on in January 1822 (see headnote to no. 426). When Mary first published the lines in *1839* she grouped them with other 'Fragments' included under 'Poems written in 1822'.

A probable date in November 1821 runs counter to the assertion in *BSM* xvi that 'the lines on Keats provide the one composition on the pages [in *Nbk 21*] written *reverso* that can be dated with reasonable certainty before or at the same time as the printing of *Adonais* in July 1821'. There is no evidence to support this view, or the further statement that the lines on Keats's epitaph 'may have been intended as the beginning of an introductory poem to open the *Adonais* volume' (*BSM* xvi p. xxix). The fact that S. nowhere in *Adonais (1821)* makes any reference to the epitaph — whereas upon learning of it he was moved to compose about it — suggests that he did not know of it before the printing of *Adonais* in early July 1821, and the evidence of the Preface to *Adonais*, discussed above, demonstrates that he remained unaware of it after receiving Finch's information, which information by his own account was still his only source in late November when he wrote to Severn. There is also no evidence to support the hypothesis of an 'introductory poem to open the *Adonais* volume', which was complete and published by the beginning of July. S.'s subsequent apparent intentions for 'corrections', 'additions', or 'omissions' to be incorporated in a planned English edition, which was never in the event forthcoming in his lifetime or until 1829 (see headnote to *Adonais*), do not suggest any intervention so substantial and radical as an 'introductory poem', any more than they make the inclusion of an 'epitaph' likely. S.'s lines on the epitaph are self-contained in their metaphor, and do not suggest any structural or rhetorical integration with the published *Adonais*. There is a significant further inference in *BSM* xvi, that a July date for the lines on Keats implies that three unfinished poems preceding it in *Nbk 21* in the *reverso* direction, *Unfathomable Sea! whose waves are years* (no. 416), *Could Arethusa to her fountain run*, and *A star has fallen upon the Earth — a torch* (see *Lines connected with Hellas* (no. 411 Appendix), Appendixes K and L), must all date from before the composition period of *Adonais*. On this basis *BSM* xvi argues for a start on preliminary writings towards *Hellas* as early as March 1821, with a much earlier overall composition period for that major work than the usually accepted date of October 1821 (see headnote to no. 411). All of these datings depend on what seems a very improbable date for the lines on Keats's epitaph.

There still remains the mystery of how and when S. did learn of Keats's epitaph, and of whether his source was also the source of his '*on* water' rather than the '*in* water' of the actual gravestone (see correspondence in *TLS* 2460 (26 March 1949) 201, 2461 (2 April 1949) 217, and 217 (9 April 1949) 233). John Taylor, who makes the *on* for *in* mistake in his letter to Clare quoted above, seems an unlikely source for S.'s information, but in theory any number of S.'s friends could have passed on the information, accurately or inaccurately, at any time after July 1821 (conceivably through Byron, whom S. visited in Ravenna in August 1821); but S.'s letter of 29 November 1821 to Severn, quoted above, does very strongly suggest that he still did not know towards the end of 1821. The epitaph was probably suggested to Keats by a passage in Beaumont and Fletcher's *Philaster* V iii: 'all your better deeds / Shall be in water writ, but this in marble', but the phrase is a commonplace in classical literature with versions in Sophocles, Menander, Philostratus, Meleager, Plato, and Catullus, which versions are variously recalled in English Renaissance authors including Chapman and Donne (see Oonagh Lahr, 'Greek Sources of "Writ in Water"', *K-SJ* xxi–xxii (1972–3) 17–18). S., or his source, may have been influenced in their assumption about Keats's phrasing by the form of the commonplace in Bacon's *On Life*, which would have been familiar to S.: 'But limns on water or but writes in dust'. The five lines of the *Epitaph* develop a single complex metaphor which depends on S.'s '*on* water' rather than the almost punning ambivalence of Keats's '*in* water'.

Text from *Nbk 21* p. 256 rev.

Published in *1839* iv 183 under the title 'Fragment VII.—ON KEATS, who desired that on his tomb should be inscribed—' (see headnote to *To Stella* (no. 352) for discussion of a possible earlier (1834) date of first publication); *BSM* xvi 240–1 (facsimile and transcription of MS).

Epitaph

"Here lieth one whose name was writ on water":
But ere the breath that could erase it, blew,
Death, half repentant of so foul a slaughter,
   Death, the immortalising winter, flew
5   Athwart the stream — Time's printless torrent grew
A scroll of crystal blazoning the name
   Of Adonais: [   ] and knew

¶ **420** *Title.* See headnote.
1. *water":*] Water" *Nbk 21*; water!" *1839*.
2. *it,*] it *1839*.
3. Death, in remorse for that fell slaughter, *1839*. The line is not fully resolved in either draft version in *Nbk 21*. S. appears to develop the line from *half immortalizing* to *half-repentingly* in the rougher draft, to *half repentant of so foul* in the neater draft, above which is written *in response for that fell*. *BSM* transcribes both *half repentant of so foul* and *for that fell* as cancelled, but the cancelling lines are not carefully drawn and could in either case be read as underlinings indicating reinstatement. Mary's reading is evidently unmetrical in an obviously Spenserian stanza.
5. Athwart the stream, and time's monthless torrent grew *1839*. The neater draft in *Nbk 21* has *stream* above *flood* canc., and there appears to be an uncancelled colon or semi-colon after *flood* (although not recognised in the transcription in *BSM*), together with a mark that may represent an ampersand (and so transcribed in *BSM*). The draft line is left metrically unresolved, as reflected in the text of 1839. The dash in the present text is editorial. *printless*] This word, read as 'monthless' in *1839*, is written above *the* canc. Cp. *Darwin*, Part I, *The Economy of Vegetation* iv 380: 'printless steps of time'.
6–7. The rougher draft in *Nbk 21* reads *blazoning thy name / O Adonais!*; in the neater draft this is first copied exactly, and then *thy* is altered to *the*, and *O* (probably) to *Of*.
6. *crystal*] Chrystal *Nbk 21*; crystal, *1839*.
7. *Adonais:*] Adonais! *1839* (which ends the 'Fragment' at this point). S. clearly intended to continue the stanza, but various attempts to complete this line are all illegible at the foot of the page. The rough draft also peters out at this point, suggesting that S. perhaps gave up on the piece with his inability to continue from this line, which inability happened to coincide with the bottom of the page.

421 The Zucca

This substantial but uncompleted poem was published in *1824* where it is dated January 1822. S. drafted ll. 1–8 without title in *Nbk 21* p. 1 writing crosswise over reading notes for his unfinished drama *Charles the First* (no. 426), the initial draft of *The flower that smiles today* (no. 417), and some barely legible lines resembling *Autumn: a Dirge* (no. 415) which is drafted elsewhere in *Nbk 21* (pp. 141–3). Two further lines, which may have been intended as ll. 9–10, are written, also crosswise, on p. 2. The draft of the eleven stanzas printed here begins again at l. 1 on p. 198 *reverso* of *Nbk 19* under the title *The Zucca* and continues, skipping some pages, to p. 186 *reverso*. Written in the same ink and with a similarly cut pen as the *Nbk 21* draft, it was probably undertaken directly or shortly after it (see *BSM* xii pp. liii–liv). S. evidently transcribed his first draft of ll. 1–8 from *Nbk 21* into *Nbk 19*, though he disregarded or overlooked the two lines on the following page (see note to ll. 9–12 below). The *Nbk 19* draft is followed immediately by S.'s draft for the opening scene of *Charles the First*, which he made between 3 and 26 January 1822. The likelihood is therefore that he composed *The Zucca* in the period from late December 1821 to early January 1822, and circumstantial evidence would seem to confirm this date-range. Stanza 11 of the poem introduces a 'savage storm / Waked by the darkest of December hours' which 'Was raving round the [narrator's] chamber hushed and warm'. Commentators have linked these lines to Mary's letter to Maria Gisborne of 21 December (the day of 'the darkest of December hours') which mentions 'high wind and rain' in Pisa (*Mary L* i 212). Edward Williams's journal records 'violent' storms there between 25 and 30 December, the worst of them on the 27th and 29th, while S. himself evokes this 'tremendous weather' with 'Torrents of rain [...] The wind [...] beyond anything I ever remember' in a letter to Claire Clairmont of 31 December (*Gisborne Jnl* 120–1; *L* ii 370). To Peacock on 11 January he recalls 'the heavy gales [...] at Christmas', and no doubt reveals the source of details in stanzas 8 and 9 of the poem when he says that 'our windows are full of plants which turn the sunny winter into spring' (*L* ii 373–4).

The uncompleted sequence of 11 stanzas in *Nbk 19* consists of a mixture of fair draft (with corrections) and rough draft. The absence of a conclusion, the number of unfinished and unresolved lines and the sometimes tortuous syntax offer significant challenges to coherent reading, as indicated in the notes below. Mary must have made a transcript for *1824*; it is not known to survive though it may have occupied some of the pages now missing from *Mary Copybk 1* into which she transcribed material from *Hellas* (no. 411) and *Charles the First* (see *BSM* xvi p. lx). It seems clear that she based her subsequent editions of the poem in *1839* and *1840* on *1824*, just possibly also returning to the *Nbk 19* draft (see *BSM* xii 336 n.). Richard Garnett provided a correction to l. 38 in *Relics 95*. Rossetti, through Garnett's offices, was allowed to examine *Nbk 19*, and on that basis re-edited the entire text for *Rossetti 1870* (*BSM* xii pp. xxxv–vi). *Locock 1911* supplemented Rossetti's text of the incomplete final stanza with details which he said had come to him from Garnett (see note to ll. 81–2).

In a footnote to *1824* Mary translates the Italian word of the title as 'pumpkin'. It can also signify a gourd (see *Fragments of an Unfinished Drama* (no. 436) l. 197) and in comic-colloquial usage can designate the human head. S. recounts, in a letter to Peacock of November 1818, having seen farmyards with 'vast heaps of many coloured zucki or pumkins [sic] some of an enormous size piled as winter food for the hogs', on the road to Ferrara (*L* ii 45); while earlier that month Mary complains to Maria Gisborne of her antipathy to the dirt and smells of Venice, where, she adds, 'they carry zucche about to sell, the sight of which always makes me sick' (*Mary L* i 81). So the plant that S. chose as vehicle for his parable of ideal longing and erotic dejection had distinctly humble as well as negative associations for both him and Mary. In the poem, a melancholic narrator experiencing a winter of the soul rescues a dying *zucca* plant and restores it to health by carrying it indoors and watering it with his tears which are stirred by the sound of a voice (apparently a woman's) singing to the accompaniment of a stringed instrument. In elaborating this narrative S. modified and recombined familiar motifs from his own earlier poems: the lifeless blossom of *On a Dead Violet: To* ——— (no. 274), the decay of the *mimosa pudica* in *SP* (no. 296) after the lady who had tended it dies; the fugitive presence of an ideal being (glimpsed through the appearances of natural phenomena in the early stanzas of *The Zucca*) in *Hymn to Intellectual Beauty* (no. 123) and in *Epipsychidion* (no. 391) ll. 21–123. The narrator's susceptibility to music is shared by the poet in *Alastor* (no. 114) and by Lionel in *R&H* (no. 144); the power of the female voice in song is given lyrical expression in, for example, *To Constantia* (no. 155), *Music (I pant for the music which is divine)* (no. 273), and *With a guitar. To Jane* (no. 446).

Autobiographical resonances are clearly to be discerned throughout the poem. The narrator's despondency invites comparison with S.'s own during the winter of 1821–2 — the result of his ill-health, public indifference or hostility to his writings, his deteriorating relationship with Mary, and his developing attraction to Jane Williams. The absence of any obvious remedies for this perplexed and troubling set of circumstances no doubt finds an equivalent in the draft's incompletion. S.'s state of mind at this time is considered in greater detail in the headnote to *To* — (*'The serpent is shut out from Paradise'*) (no. 430). The numerous intimations of a human dimension in the life of the plant, in stanzas 6–9 especially, recall similar correspondences in *SP*, as does the portrayal of the *zucca* by a few striking details of shape and colour. The implicit analogy between a 'blighted' plant and a 'lorn' heart S. made explicit in a letter to Claire Clairmont of 11 December 1821, in which it appears that Claire had previously identified him with the Sensitive-Plant of his own earlier poem. He writes: 'The Exotic as you please to call me droops in this frost — a frost both moral & physical — a solitude of the heart [...] the Exotic [...] unfortunately belonging to the order of mimosa' (*L* ii 367–8). See also *The magnetic lady to her patient* (no. 449) ll. 29–30 where the 'lady' (a character based on Jane Williams) describes her 'patient' (based on S. himself) as a 'withered flower'.

S.'s attraction to Jane Williams constitutes an important context. The unidentified individual whose singing and playing on a *stringed instrument* cause the narrator to weep over the plant in stanzas 10–11 recalls other poems in which a character based on Jane Williams appears. Jane often sang to her own accompaniment on the guitar (see note to ll. 67–74; and *To Jane* (*'The keen stars were twinkling'*) (no. 453). S. also expanded and reworked the entire episode of the discovery and nurturing of the *zucca* in the drama that he began to write for his Pisan circle during the spring of 1822: see *Fragments of an Unfinished Drama*. In S.'s play, a female character patently inspired by Jane Williams, wakes from a dream to discover a mysterious plant growing in her chamber which she, like the narrator of *The Zucca*, nurtures through the winter, restoring it to health with tears prompted by her own singing (see *Fragments of an Unfinished Drama* ll. 188–237, and notes to ll. 67–74 and 69 below).

The Zucca continues a series of narrative poems which S. began to write in spring 1820 in *ottava rima* — the Italian verse form practiced by Ariosto, Boccaccio and Tasso, by Calderón, and by Byron in *Beppo* and *Don Juan* — which include *WA* (no. 341) and the translation of the Homeric *Hymn to Mercury* (no. 336). See headnote to *WA* (Genre). The present poem develops in quite another thematic direction and style the situation that S. imagines in *The Question* ——— (no. 288), also in *ottava rima*, in which, winter having suddenly turned to spring, the narrator dreams of gathering flowers from a riverbank for a nosegay.

The Zucca has received little critical attention. Brief notices include: Wasserman 189–90, 417–18; Thomas Frosch, '"More than ever can be spoken": Unconscious Fantasy in Shelley's Jane Williams Poems', *SP* cii (2005) 381–3; Timothy Webb, *Shelley: A Voice Not Understood* (1977) 239–45; Alan M. Weinberg, 'Shelley's Italian Verse Fragments: Exploring the Notebook Drafts', in *The Neglected Shelley*, ed. Alan M. Weinberg and Timothy Webb (2015) 304–6.

Text from *Nbk 19* pp. 198 rev.–194c rev. and pp. 190 rev.–186 rev. S.'s sparse pointing has been supplemented and somewhat modified after consulting *1824*, *1839* and later *eds*; important additions to and modifications of punctuation are recorded in the notes.

Published in *1824* 175–8; *Rossetti 1870* ii 363–5; *Locock 1911* ii 269–71; and *BSM* xii 351–342 and 337–328 (facsimile and transcription of MS).

The Zucca

1

  Summer was dead and Autumn was expiring
  And infant Winter laughed upon the land
  All cloudlessly and cold, — when I desiring
   More in this world than any understand,
5 Wept o'er the beauty which [like sea] retiring
   Had left the earth bare as the wave-worn sand
  Of my lorn heart, and o'er the grass and flowers
  Pale for the falsehood of the flattering hours.

¶ 421 *1*. S. did not head-number the first stanza in *Nbk 21* or *Nbk 19*.
2. laughed] Displayed a cheerful or pleasant appearance: 'laugh', 'to appear lively with movement, sound, or the play of light and colour, as if expressing joyous feeling' (*OED* 1b); typically found in the context of summer and harvest, the word here ironically describes a barren winter landscape.
3. desiring] desiring, *Nbk 19*.
5–8. Wept ... hours] The verb governs both 'beauty' (l. 5) and 'grass and flowers' (l. 7). The fundamental comparison is between the narrator's state of feeling and the landscape: it develops through a complex analogy that likens the earth from which beauty has almost disappeared as winter advances to the bare sand of a shore from which the sea has receded, then the shore itself to the narrator's desolate heart.

2

    Summer was dead, but I yet lived to weep
10   The instability of all but weeping —
    And on the Earth lulled in her winter sleep
      I woke, and envied her as she was sleeping.
    Too happy Earth! over thy face shall creep
      The wakening vernal airs, until thou leaping
15   From unremembered dreams, shall never see
    No death divide thy immortality ...

3

    I loved ... oh no, I mean not one of ye
      Or any earthly one, — though ye are dear
    As human heart to human heart may be;
20   I loved, I know not what, but this low sphere
    And all that it contains, contains not thee:

5. *[like sea]*] Cancelled in both *Nbk 21* and *Nbk 19*, suggesting that S. would have replaced the phrase had he proceeded to a fair copy.
6. Had left the earth dry as the sealess sand *Nbk 21*.
7. *lorn*] S.'s third attempt after 'poor' canc. and *rent* canc.; Mary gave *poor* in *1824* and *1839*. Rossetti *1870* restored *lorn* from *Nbk 19*. *grass and flowers*] pallid flowers *Nbk 21*.
8. *flattering*] false, misleading. Cp. *Charles the First* I i 127-8: 'Your worm of Nile [i.e. crocodile] / Betrays not with its flattering tears like they'. The first draft of the line in *Nbk 21*, *Deserted by the azure winged hours*, indicates the sense intended: 'the grass and flowers' had been deceived into thinking the warm days of spring and summer in which they flourished would never end.
9-12. Cp. *The flower that smiles today* (no. 417) ll. 20-1. S.'s first draft of ll. 9-10 in *Nbk 21* reads *A sorrow in which hope was not all* [ ] / *A winter gentle as a Celtic spring*.
14. *vernal airs*] Spring breezes.
15. From unremembered dreams shalt [ ] see *1824*, *1839*; shalt ... . see *Rossetti 1870*; shalt see *eds*. S. tried *shall find* and *shall be* before settling on *shall never see*, thus formulating the idea in lines 13-16: 'the seasonal cycle does not disrupt the Earth's continuous life, which returns in spring, its winter decay no more than a forgotten dream'. Cp. *Fragments of an Unfinished Drama* ll. 231-3, 250-4.
17. *not one of ye*] S.'s successive drafts, *not thee, although, not thee*, or *thee*, develop away from what might have been taken as a reference to an actual individual to contrast 'any earthly one' with an ideal beloved.

>   Thou, whom seen nowhere I feel everywhere,
>   By Heaven and Earth and all that in them are
>   Veiled art thou like a storm-extinguished star.
>
>
>   4
> 25   By Heaven and Earth, from all whose shapes thou flowest,
>   Neither to be contained, delayed or hidden,
>   Making divine the loftiest and the lowest
>   When for a moment thou art not forbidden
>   To live within the life which thou bestowest,
> 30   And leaving noblest things vacant and chidden;
>   Cold as a corpse after the spirit's flight,
>   Blank as the sea after the birth of night.
>
>   5
>   In winds and trees and streams and all things common,
>   In music, and the sweet unconscious tone

23. Dim object of my soul's idolatry *1824, 1839*. Mary's adoption of an uncancelled line in the draft violates the rhyme-scheme. *Rossetti 1870*, followed by *eds*, preferred the present line, which appears to represent a later stage in the unresolved draft. But Rossetti (again followed by *eds*) gives the first word as 'From', which is cancelled in the draft, what appears clearly enough to be *By* being written to the left of it. 'By', which the repetition in l. 25 appears to confirm, alters the sense of lines 23–24 to: 'the appearances of nature are animated by an ideal presence which they themselves conceal from view', a fundamental Shelleyan intuition. Cp. *Hymn to Intellectual Beauty* ll. 1–12; *My lost William, thou in whom* (no. 254) ll. 1–4; *Epipsychidion* ll. 21–2. Also in the *Nbk 19* draft, but cancelled, are: *Thou for whose love I walk in this despair* and *Thou goddeess [sic] of my soul's idolatry*.
24. Veiled art thou like — *1824*. Mary unaccountably omitted the entire line from *1839* and *1840*. *Rossetti 1870* reads 'Veiled art thou, like a [storm-benighted?] star', although *storm extinguished* is clear in the draft. His conjecture was not accepted by *Forman 1876–7* which gives 'Veiled art thou, like a   star' (which was followed by later *eds*).
30. *vacant*] vacant, *Nbk 19*. *chidden*] reproved, rebuked.
32. *sea*] sun *1824, 1839, eds*; *BSM* xii 344 also reads 'sea'. 'The word in the MS may be either "sun" or "sea"; I think the latter more probable but have followed Mrs Shelley's reading' (*Rossetti 1878* iii 421).
33. Recalling *Adonais* (no. 403) l. 163.
34–6. The untidy and unfinished draft records S.'s struggle to express the idea that, like the other examples evoked in stanzas 4 and 5, some ineffable and unintended quality in both animal and human utterance evinces the concealed presence of an ideal being.

35 Of animals, and [Voices which are human]
       Meant to express some feelings of their own,
    In the soft motions and rare smile of woman,
    In flowers and leaves, in the grass fresh shown
       Or dying in the autumn, I the most
40 Adore thee present or lament thee lost.

                           6
       And thus I went lamenting, when I saw
          A plant upon the river's margin lie,
       Like one who loved beyond his nature's law
          And in despair had cast him down to die.
45 Its leaves which had outlived the frost, the thaw
          Had blighted, as a heart which [?] eye
       Can blast not, but which Pity kills. The dew
       Lay on its spotted leaves like tears too true.

                           7
       The Heavens had wept upon it, but the Earth

35. *Of animals,*] Of animals & [men], *Nbk 19*.
37. *rare*] exquisite, excellent.
38. *leaves, in the grass fresh shown*] leaves and in the fresh grass shown *1824, 1839*.
Relics 95 restored what appears to be the correct order, *fresh shown*, from the draft.
S. first wrote *fresh* [   ] *shewn*, then entered *grass* above *fresh*, evidently intending
the noun to precede and so create a parallel between 'fresh shown' and 'dying' in the
following line. *Rossetti 1870* and *eds* adopt his correction but retain the 'and' from
1824/1839, which is not in the draft. The comma after 'leaves' has been supplied.
43–4. S.'s poetry regularly celebrates love unconstrained by social convention or customary prejudice, as in *L&C* (no. 143), *R&H* and *Epipsychidion*. In the dying zucca,
however, he represents the morbid consequences of the narrator's love for the ideal
being of stanzas 3–5, which the limits of human nature prevent him from satisfying.
46–7. *as a heart ... Pity kills*] Cp. the effects of hatred, scorn, indifference and pity in
To — ('The serpent is shut out from Paradise') ll. 9–16, a poem in which S. deals more
directly with the torment of mind consequent upon his feelings for Jane Williams.
46–8. *blighted ... spotted*] 'blighted' here means 'diseased', specifically any of a
number of fungal parasites that show as spots on the leaves of plants. S. introduces
blighted and speckled leaves as figures of more general disease and decay in
Mazenghi (no. 296) l. 88; *PU* (no. 195) I 173; *SP* iii 52.
46. *as*] Replacing *like* which is cancelled in *Nbk 19*, no doubt because 'like' also
occurs in l. 3 and l. 8 of this stanza. *1824* and *1839* read 'as'; *Rossetti 1870* and *eds*
read 'like'. The illegible word is given as 'Hatred's' in *1824, 1839* and *eds*. The *Nbk*

50   Had crushed it on her unmaternal breast.
          [   ]
            [   ]
          [   ]
            [   ]
          [   ]
          [   ]

                              8
        I bore it to my chamber and I planted
          It in a vase full of the lightest mould.
        The winter beams which out of Heaven slanted
          Fell through the window panes, disrobed of cold,
55   Upon its leaves and flowers; the star which panted
          In evening for the Day whose car has rolled

---

19 MS has been blotted by a clear liquid at this point and is impossible to decipher confidently though it may have been legible when Mary prepared copy for *1824*. GM conjectures 'the Unkind'.

47–8. Images of mourning involving flowers, tears and dew feature regularly in *Adonais* (no. 403): see ll. 46–9, 140–4, 289–300; and the note to ll. 69–71 below.

49–50. S. left stanza seven unfinished, drafting these lines at the foot of *Nbk 19* p. 190 *reverso*, then adding and cancelling a number of lines in continuation at the top of the following page: [*And the blue Winter's boundless*] eye [*of azure mirth / Laughed on it's ruin* [ ]; *It owed its welcome death / [Even as the rest who owe their bitter birth] / To that great mother, in law, even as the rest*. Rossetti's unannotated edition of *The Poetical Works of Percy Bysshe Shelley* (1870) reconstructs these cancelled lines and incorporates them into the stanza as follows: 'And the blue Winter's eye of boundless mirth / * * * * * * / It owed its welcome death [and] bitter birth / To that great mother-in-law, even as the rest'.

52. *mould*] soil.

53–5. *The winter beams ... flowers*] After passing through 'the window panes', the oblique beams of the winter sun warm the plant as they strike it, as if they had left off a cloak grown cold in the air outside. The commas in line 54 have been supplied. Cp. Keats, 'The Eve of St. Agnes' ll. 217–18: 'Full on this casement shone the wintry moon, / And threw warm gules on Madeline's fair breast'.

55–8. *the star ... night*] S. habitually associates the planet Venus (when seen as the evening star) with love: e.g., *R&H* 968–87, *TL* (no. 452) 414–19. The sun is represented in Greek and Roman myth as a beautiful young man who travels across the daytime sky in a chariot of fire, returning to the east during the night via subterranean passages. Cp. *Epithalamium* (no. 401) Text C ll. 17–22.

55. *flowers;*] flowers, *Nbk 19*. *panted*] The word carries the erotic sense it has in *Adonais* 168. Cp. Keats, *Hyperion* III 99–102:

Over the horizon's wave, with looks of light
Smiled on it from the threshold of the night.

9

The mitigated influences of air
60   And light revived the plant, and from it grew
Strong leaves and tendrils, and its flowers fair,
   Full as a cup with the vine's burning dew,
O'erflowed with golden colours, an atmosphere
   Of vital [   ] enfolded it anew
65 And every impulse sent to every part
The unbeheld pulsations of its heart.

10

Well might the plant grow beautiful and strong
   Even if the air and sun had smiled not on it,
For one wept o'er it all the winter long
70   Tears pure as Heaven's rain, which fell upon it
Hour after hour; for sounds of softest song
   Mixed with the stringèd melodies that won it
To leave the [gentle] lips on which it slept
Had loosed the heart of him who sat and wept;

———————

                              Point me out the way
          To any one particular beauteous star,
          And I will flit into it with my lyre,
          And make its silvery splendour pant with bliss.

58. Cp. Keats, *Hyperion*, I 203–4: 'Hyperion, leaving twilight in the rear, / Came slope upon the threshold of the west'.
59. *mitigated*] Made milder because sheltered from the winter climate outdoors.
63. *golden colours*] Cp. the 'golden eye' of the flower of the mysterious plant in *Fragments of an Unfinished Drama* 204.
64. *1824* and *1839* (followed by *eds*) supply 'warmth' to fill the gap in this line.
65–6. Cp. *Fragments of an Unfinished Drama* ll. 208–12 where the 'pulses' of the mysterious plant are 'almost' visible. There, as here, S. is humanising the plant.
66. *unbeheld*] unseen. Cp. *The Cenci* (no. 209) II i 192; *PU* III i 23, 45.
67–74. The plant is nourished by the tears of the narrator, the 'one' of l. 69, who is moved by the singing and playing of another individual (inspired, it would seem, by Jane Williams, who had a talent for music; see *With a guitar. To Jane*). Cp. *The magnetic lady to her patient* (no. 447) ll. 29–30 in which the lady of the title (based on Jane Williams) 'weeps healing rain' from her soul upon her patient (based on S.), who is cast as a 'withered flower'. Cp. also *Fragments of an Unfinished Drama* ll. 226–36, where a female character whom S. would appear to have written for

                          11
75   Had loosed his heart, and shook the leaves and flowers
       On which he wept, whilst the savage storm
       Waked by the darkest of December hours
         Was raving round the chamber hushed and warm;
         The birds were shivering in their leafless bowers,
80   The fish were frozen in the pools, the form
       Of every summer plant was d[   ]
       Whilst this [   ]

Jane Williams weeps over her plant while singing and playing 'wild songs', and *WA* 297–310 where the god Love plants a seed to produce a 'gourd-like fruit' which he fashions into the Witch's boat.
67. S.'s final intention is difficult to judge from the draft. He first wrote *Well might the plant grow strong & thrive*, revising the end of the line to *beautiful and strong* and writing above that *amain*, which is cancelled then underlined as if for restoration. *Yet* is written above and to the left of *Well*, neither being cancelled. *1824* and *1839*, followed by *eds*, opt for 'Well'. 'Yet well', though very awkward, would be possible metrically if 'the plant' were elided as a single syllable.
68. *air and sun*] sun and air *1824*, *1839*; corrected by *Rossetti 1870*, followed by *eds*.
69–71. The 'one' of l. 69 evidently refers in the third person to the first-person narrator of the poem, as in the cancelled lines for stanza 8: *I bore it to my chamber, and I fed / The plant with tears pure as the dew of Heaven*. S. modified the second of these for line 70. Lines 69–71 allude to Keats's 'Isabella; or, the Pot of Basil' (1820) ll. 409–32 in which the title-character nourishes with her tears the basil plant under which her murdered lover's head is buried. See the note to *Adonais* ll. 48–49.
71. *hour;*] *1824*, *1839*, *eds*. hour, *Nbk 19*.
72. *it*] i.e. the 'song' of line 71.
74. *Had*] And *BSM* xii. It is difficult to decipher the word which is added below a cancelled *Shook*. The 'Had loosed' at the beginning of the following stanza argues for 'Had' here.
76. *whilst the*] the while the *1824*, *1839*, *eds*.
77. *December*] December's *1824*, *1839*, *eds*.
78. *warm;*] warm, *Nbk 19*.
79–80. Cp. *It was a winter such as when birds die* (no. 285) ll. 1–3; *Fragments of an Unfinished Drama* ll. 127–34; *A widowed bird sate mourning for her love* (no. 427), which S. also composed in the *reverso* section of *Nbk 19* during January 1822.
81–2. S.'s draft ends here, on *Nbk 19* p. 186 *reverso*. The word that he left incomplete in line 81 invites completion as 'dead', which is the reading that Mary supplied in *1824* and *1839*, followed by *eds*. Locock gives lines 81–2 as 'Of every summer plant was dead and chill, / Whilst this tear-nurtured [   ] still', saying that these 'additions' were 'communicated' to him by Garnett (*Locock 1911* ii 527), but no more authoritative source for them has been identified. S. wrote '12' directly beneath his draft of the unfinished line 82, an indication that he meant to add at least one further stanza to the poem.

422 'Rough wind that moanest loud'

[A Dirge]

The sole MS source for these lines is Mary's transcription in *Mary Copybk 1* pp. 58–9, where ll. 1–8 are an item numbered '81', immediately following her transcription of part of *The Pine Forest of the Cascine, near Pisa* (no. 431/432 Appendix; see headnote and notes) which is numbered as '80'. Lines 9–15 are transcribed as a separate item numbered '82', which is then immediately followed by a transcription of further lines incorporated in *The Pine Forest of the Cascine* numbered as '83'. Mary's source for her transcription of *Rough wind that moanest loud* is not known, but her placement of the lines among draft for *The Pine Forest of the Cascine* suggests some probable connection with the manuscript source of that poem. GM conjectured that it is perhaps possible that the basis of Mary's transcription of *Rough wind*, as also that of *The Pine Forest of the Cascine*, was a now lost portion of *Nbk 20* (see headnotes to nos. 401 and 406). Lines 1–8 were first published in *1824* 219 under the title 'A Dirge'. They were then accidentally omitted from *1839* and *1840*, as is explained by Mary in a letter to Edward Moxon of 14 July 1841 (*Mary L* iii 17):

> I must mention that by an unaccountable oversight a poem of Shelley, printed in the Posthumous Poems is omitted in my editions it the [sic] one beginning
> Rough wind that moanest loud

The lines were next published in *1846*, and were reinstated in *1847* iii 205 where they were included among the 'Poems Written in 1822', further suggesting some connection, at least in Mary's mind, with the date of *Pine Forest of the Cascine*, part of which is dated 'Saturday. February 2nd 1822' in *Mary Copybk 1* p. 58 (see *BSM* ii 118–19). Mary never published ll. 9–15, and presumably considered them as a start on a separate poem, since she numbered them as a separate item in *Mary Copybk 1*. However there is a small ink 'X' to the right of the first line of her transcription (l. 9) on p. 58 (*BSM* ii 118), and GM persuasively conjectures (in a communication quoted in *BSM* ii 231): 'Surely a second stanza for "A Dirge". Doesn't Mary's X mean "return to this & try to do better"?'. The lines certainly appear to represent an unfinished second stanza repeating the metre and rhyme-scheme of ll. 1–8.

Text from *Mary Copybk 1* pp. 58–59.

Published in *1824* (ll. 1–8 only); *BSM* ii 118–121 (facsimile and transcription of MS).

'Rough wind that moanest loud'

    Rough wind that moanest loud
        Grief too sad for song,
    Wild wind when sullen cloud
        Knells all the night long!
5   Sad storm whose tears are vain,
    Bare woods whose branches stain,
    Deep caves and dreary main,
        Wail for the world's wrong.

    Ah me, my heart is bare
10   Like a winter bough;
    The same blast of frozen air
        Bared it then that breaks it now!
    Green leaves and crimson flowers
        Clothed in the azure hours
15   Death —

¶ **422** *Title*. Mary Shelley gave these lines the title 'A Dirge' in *1824*; a dirge is 'a song of mourning or lament' (*OED* 2).
1. *Rough*] Mary first wrote *Wild* then cancelled it and wrote *Rough* to the left in *Mary Copybk 1*. *wind*] wind, *1824*. *loud*] *1824*; loud, *Mary Copybk 1*.
2. *song,*] song *Mary Copybk 1*; song; *1824*.
3. *wind*] wind, *1824*.
4. *long!*] long; *1824*.
5. *storm*] storm, *1824*. *vain,*] *1824*; vain *Mary Copybk 1*.
6. *woods*] woods, *1824*. *stain,*] *1824*; stain *Mary Copybk 1*; 'My belief is that the word here ought to be "strain": but "stain" is not meaningless, as it may refer to the tints which come off on hands that touch soppy sprays of foliage' (*Rossetti 1870* ii 577).
8. Wail, for the world's wrong! *1824*. *Mary Copybk 1* reads *Wail for the worlds wrong* with two small and somewhat oddly spaced marks to the right of *wrong*, the second of which is show-through, but the first of which may be a period.
10. *bough;*] bough *Mary Copybk 1*.

423 'Alas, if I could feign'

These unfinished lines are written in ink in the upper half of the first page of *Nbk 22* in the forwards direction of the notebook as it has been paginated. In the lower half, also in ink, are some calculations and, beneath them, a list of months followed by the figure '30', probably a financial sum, not, as Forman supposes (*Huntington Nbks* iii 3), a day of the month. The months in all but the first instance have a number alongside: *April: 30 / May: 30. 2 / June 30. 3 / July 30 4 / August 30. 5 / Sep$^{t.}$ 30. 6. —*. Nora Crook and Timothy Webb compare these calculations and a list of months alongside numbers with 'March', 'April', 'June' and 'July' followed by the numbers 1–4, written next to calculations, in *Nbk 18* p. 149 *reverso* (see *BSM* xix 284–5). Their view that the *Nbk 18* calculations are most likely financial and that the months 'could cover the period that a sum of money was supposed to last' (*BSM* xix p. 284) may also explain the figures and dates on this page in *Nbk 22*. It is impossible to be certain whether the calculations and the list of dates were written into the notebook on the same occasion, and whether this was significantly earlier, later, or at a similar time to when these lines were drafted. On balance, however given the position of these lines in the page's upper half, they were probably drafted there before the other items.

S.'s usual habit of writing in a notebook was to begin at both ends. Hence it is possible that this fragment is one of its earliest entries. Mary Quinn suggests 'late summer or early fall of 1821 as the earliest time frame in which [Shelley] would have been working in this notebook' (*MYRS* vii p. xxxi). However, the present editors see no evidence that any of S.'s writing in *Nbk 22* was entered before late December 1821. The schema for *Charles the First* (no. 426), which occupies several pages at the start of the present reversed direction of the notebook (ff. *1^r–*4^r and *5^r), may have been in place before 3 January 1822 because on 8 January Edward Williams recorded in his journal that S. had 'sat down about 5 days since' to write the play (*Gisborne Jnl* 123). A date of composition for these lines of late December 1821 or early January 1822 is conceivable if the reason for S. writing them on this, the opening page at one end of the notebook was that he had already begun to use the pages at the other end for the larger project of *Charles the First*. However, if the figures after the dates measure the number of months from when the list was made, one might speculate that it could date from the end of March 1822, and thus, if these lines were written only slightly earlier than the list, they may possibly date from March too.

DOI: 10.4324/9781315779874-18

A context for these lines is difficult to identify. The nature of the MS evidence, including the fact that the rhyme-word at the end of the fourth line was written before the rest of the line was complete, suggests original composition rather than a translation. The possibility that the lines are an aborted attempt at a dramatic lyric for *Charles the First* cannot be ruled out. It should be noted that these verses share a number of characteristics with a speech by Archy addressed to the Queen in Scene ii (see that scene's note to ll. 426–30). Forman speculates in the following comment that they may a have biographical reference but does not substantiate his claim: 'There is a certain subtlety of suggestion in the little quatrain, but nothing to indicate whether its heroine was Mary or some one else' (*Huntington Nbks* iii 4).

Text from *Nbk 22* f. 1ʳ. Indentation follows the MS.

Published in *Huntington Nbks* iii 4; *MYRS* vii 4–5 (facsimile and transcription of MS).

'Alas, if I could feign'

    Alas, if I could feign
        A smile as you a tear —
    Sunshine [?in] the rain
        Would [   ] appear

424   'There was a star when Heaven was young'

This pencilled fragment occupies the top half of f. 3ʳ in *Nbk 22*; the bottom half has been left blank. Three false starts to lines, not obviously related to the fragment, are cancelled above it. It appears to follow a pattern of alternating eight- and six-syllable lines but neither the rhythm nor the rhyme-scheme envisaged can confidently be discerned on the basis of so slender a sample. The motif of a single star associated

¶ 423 2. S. first wrote *Smiles as you do tears*, then added a capital 'A' at the start of the line but omitted to change the capital at the start of the second word to a small letter. *smile*] Smile *Nbk 22* (alt. from *Smiles*). *a tear*] Alt. from *do tears* in *Nbk 22*.
3. *[?in]*] to *Huntington Nbks*. While *MYRS* reads the word written over *to* in *Nbk 22* as 'as', GM's reading of 'in' is more convincing.
4. *Would*] Written after *Would* canc. in *Nbk 22*.

with celestial music S. returned to in another fragment on f. 7ᵛ of *Nbk 22*: *By the music of Heaven* [?] / *A star out of*. A further fragment, of six heavily cancelled lines, on f. 8ᵛ (above a draft of the final line of *Swifter far than summer's flight* (no. 433)) introduces cosmic love to the pairing of star and heavenly music. The theme of a star penetrating the terrestrial sphere is developed in *A star has fallen upon the Earth — a torch* (*Lines connected with Hellas* (no. 411 Appendix), Appendix L) and elaborated at length in *Fragments of an Unfinished Drama* (no. 436) ll. 156–83, which appear to have been composed in late autumn 1821 and March–April 1822 respectively. The present lines, situated near the front of the forward sequence of *Nbk 22*, may tentatively be dated to late December 1821/early January 1822. In addition to those already indicated, there are interesting similarities to *WA* (no. 341) stanzas 32–3 and to *The Zucca* (no. 421) ll. 55–8.

Text from *Nbk 22* f. 3ʳ.

Published in *Huntington Nbks* iii 5; *MYRS* vii 12–13 (facsimile and transcription of MS).

'There was a star when Heaven was young'

> There was a star when Heaven was young
>   That twin with Hesper sprung —
> The music that without a lyre
>   Struck

425 'Though thou scatterest their ashes'

S.'s pencil draft of these lines on f. 5ʳ of *Nbk 22* closely resembles a fragment of six lines on the immediately preceding f. 4ᵛ, which it expands while altering some details. The lines on f. 4ᵛ read:

> *Scatter their ashes*
>   *The spark will burn —*
> *Like the death*

¶ **424** 2. *Hesper*] Hesperus or Vesper, the planet Venus as the evening star.
4. *Struck*] Written beneath *Wandered oer the sea* canc.

Darken their glory —
Their fame shall be
In song & in story

The position in the notebook of both fragments is consistent with their having been set down in late December 1821/early January 1822. There are verbal and thematic echoes of the chorus and antiphonal semi-choruses of *Hellas* (no. 411) 34–109. Both drafts reprise one of the foundation-principles of S.'s conception of political and literary history: that the power of Freedom as example and idea survives temporary eclipses to inspire hope in future ages. He develops the theme in, for example: *L&C* (no. 143) 3649–747; *OWW* (no. 259) 63–70; *Adonais* (no. 403) 406–14; *TL* (452) 206–7, and in *DP* (*Reiman (2002)* para. 48).

Text from *Nbk 22* f. 5ʳ; full stops have been supplied in ll. 4 and 8.

Published in *Huntington Nbks* iii 6; *MYRS* vii 20–1 (facsimile and transcription of MS).

'Though thou scatterest their ashes'

 Though thou scatterest their ashes
  The spark will yet burn
 [Like a star] [ ] flashes
  From [ ] the urn.

5 Though thou darken their glory
  Their names will yet be
 The far lights for story
  To [?] [ ] thee.

 Like stars through the rolling
10 [Of clouds]

¶ 425 *1–4.* Cp. the language of *Adonais* 359–60: 'Nor, when the spirit's self has ceased to burn, / With sparkless ashes load an unlamented urn.'
1. scatterest] S. wrote and cancelled *tramplest* before returning to the *scatter* of the draft on f. 4ᵛ.
7. far] The reading of *Huntington Nbks* iii and *MYRS*. GM reads 'fair'.

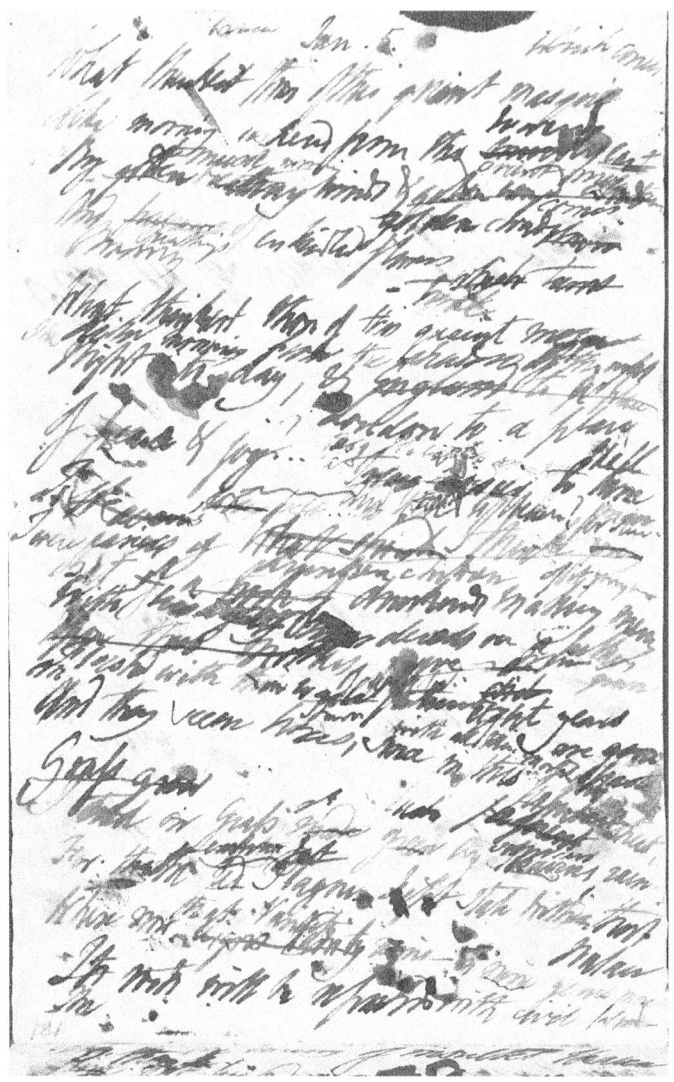

Shelley's draft of Act I, Scene i, lines 2–15 of *Charles the First*, from a manuscript notebook in the Bodleian Library (see Note on Illustrations).

Source: Bodleian MS. Shelley adds. e. 17, p. 181 rev., black and white. Reproduced by kind permission of The Bodleian Libraries, University of Oxford.

426 Charles the First

Date of composition. According to Edward Williams's journal entry of 8 January 1822, S. began composing *Charles the First* on, or around, 3 January:

> As to S[helley]'s "Charles the First"—on which he sat down about 5 days since, if he continues in the spirit [of] some of the lines which he read to me last night, it will doubtless take a place before any other that has appear[ed] since Shakspeare, and will be found a valuable addition to the Historical Pla[y.] (*Gisborne Jnl* 123)

However, S.'s plan for a tragedy about King Charles I, to be authored by Mary rather than himself, had been mooted several years previously, as she later recalled:

> He often incited me to attempt the writing a tragedy—he conceived that I possessed some dramatic talent, and he was always most earnest and energetic in his exhortations that I should cultivate any talent I possessed, to the utmost ... The subject he had suggested for a tragedy was Charles I., and he had written to me, "Remember, remember Charles I. I have been already imagining how you would conduct some scenes. The second volume of St. Leon begins with this proud and true sentiment, 'There is nothing which the human mind can conceive which it may not execute.' Shakspeare was only a human being." These words were written in 1818, while we were in Lombardy ... ('Note on The Cenci', *1839* iii 272–3; the citation is from S.'s letter to Mary of 22 September 1818, *L* ii 40)

The first evidence of S.'s intention to write such a tragedy himself is found in his letter to Thomas Medwin of 20 July 1820: 'I mean to write a play, in the spirit of human nature, without prejudice or passion, entitled "Charles the First"' (*L* ii 219–20). In the summer of 1820, his desire to write another tragedy is likely to be connected with *Cenci (1819)*, published in March 1820, sales of which were reportedly good (see headnote to no. 209). Soon after 25 September 1819, Peacock had submitted a copy of *Cenci (1819)* to Thomas Harris, the manager of Covent Garden Theatre (*Peacock L* i p. cxxv) only to elicit the following reaction, communicated by Peacock and later reported by Mary: 'He pronounced the subject to be so objectionable, that he could not even submit the part to Miss O'Neil for perusal.' But the fact that Harris 'expressed his desire that the author would write a tragedy on some other subject, which he would gladly accept' ('Note on The Cenci', *1839* iii 279) must have encouraged S. to believe himself capable of writing one suitable for the contemporary stage. Hesitation and doubt characterise his early 1821 letters to his publisher, Charles Ollier, concerning what he regarded as his next major composition (after *PU* (no. 195)): 'My next attempt (if I should write more) will be a drama, in the composition of which I shall attend to the advice of my critics, to a certain degree, but I doubt whether I *shall* write more' (*L* ii 258). A combination of ambition, concern at the amount of time required to complete such a large-scale endeavour, and a lack of confidence in the putative play's reception inform a further letter to Ollier the following month (dated 22 February 1821):

> I doubt about 'Charles the First'; but, if I do write it, it shall be the birth of severe and high feelings. You are very welcome to it, on the terms you mention, and, when once I see and feel I can write it, it is already written. My thoughts aspire to a production of a far higher character; but the execution of it will require some years. I write what I write chiefly to inquire, by the reception which my writings meet with, how far I am fit for so great a task, or not. And I am afraid that your account will not present me with a very flattering result in this particular. (*L* ii 269)

That S. had begun reading related to *Charles* by the early autumn of 1821 (at least in the form of the notes made from historical sources in *Nbk 21* — see 'Sources, genre and form' below) is likely given his comment to Ollier in a letter of 25 September 1821 that '*Charles the First* is conceived, but not born' (*L* ii 354) and the subsequent confident promise to his publisher in a letter of 11 October 1821 that he was to 'Expect Charles the 1st or Troilus & Cressida in the spring' (*L* ii 357).

Sustained work on *Charles* continued from around 3 January 1822 for at least a fortnight. Trelawny, having arrived at Pisa on 14 January (according to Williams; see *Mary Jnl* i 389, *Gisborne Jnl* 125), recalls S. telling him during a ride together to Leghorn that 'I am now writing a play for the stage' (*Recollections* 76) while Mary expresses her ambition for S.'s labours to Maria Gisborne in a letter of 18 January 1822: 'I hope Charles the 1st which is now on the anvil, will raise his reputation—' (*Mary L* i 215). S.'s familiar routine during periods of sustained, intense composition is captured in his letter to Peacock of 11 January 1822 describing life at Pisa:

> I have long been idle,—& as far as writing goes, despondent—but I am now engaged in Charles the 1ˢᵗ & a devil of a nut it is to crack.—... We live as usual tranquilly: I get up, or at least wake, early: read & write till two; dine,—go to Lord B's & ride or play at Billiards, as the weather permits, & sacrifize the evening either to light books or whoever happens to drop in.— (*L* ii 373-4)

His letter to Ollier of the same day communicates certainty that the play will be finished in a few months and acknowledges (again) that he is uncertain of its popular success:

> The Historical Tragedy of 'Charles the First' will be ready by the Spring. It is my intention to sell the copyright of this poem. As you have always been my publisher, I give you the refusal of it. — My reason for selling it, to speak frankly, is, that the Bookseller should have sufficient interest in its success to give it a fair chance. Should you not think it worth while to make any offer for it; of course you will absolve me from levity in applying to another publisher. I ought to say that the Tragedy promises to be good, as Tragedies go; and that it is not coloured by the party spirit of the author: How far it may be popular I cannot judge. (*L* ii 372)

This letter was followed by another to John Gisborne the next day (12 January) instructing him to ask Ollier 'whether he will buy the copyright of "Charles the First", what he will give me, and when he will pay me' (*L* ii 375). But less than a fortnight later, in his letter to Hunt of 25 January, S.'s tone is much less confident. He implores Hunt to seek an alternative publisher while also admitting that he is unable to compose; his hope to lend financial support for Hunt's journey to Italy (via the sale of his play's copyright) and for their planned, jointly edited journal (*The Liberal*) with Byron contributes to the letter's anxious tone:

> One thing strikes me as *possible*. I am at present writing the drama of Charles the 1st, a play which if completed according to my present idea will hold a higher rank that [than] the Cenci as a work of art—Would no bookseller give me 150 or 200 pounds for the copyright of this play? You know best how my writings sell; whether

at all or not, after they failed of making the sort of impression on men that I expected, I have never until now thought it worth while to inquire. This question is now interesting to me inasmuch as the reputation depending on their sale might induce a bookseller to give me such a sum for this play. Write to Allman your bookseller, tell him what I tell you of Charles the 1st and do not delay a post.—I have a parcel of little Poems also—the Witch of Atlas & some translations of Homers Hymns the copyright of which I would sell.—I offered the Charles I. to Ollier, & you had better write at the same time to learn his terms—Of course you will not delay a post in this.— / … My faculties are shaken to atoms & torpid. I can write nothing, & if Adonais had no success & excited no interest what incentive can I have to write? (*L* ii 380–2)

The following day (26 January), S. instructed Gisborne to terminate 'my connexion with Mr. Ollier' and noted that progress with *Charles* was so faltering that he had in effect suspended work: 'I write nothing but by fits. I have done some of Charles I. but although the poetry succeeds very well I cannot seize the conception of the subject as a whole yet, & seldom now touch the *canvas*' (*L* ii 387–8). The view that S. abandoned *Charles* because the imaginative effort it required was antipathetic to him is articulated by Medwin who offers the following summary of its fate: 'I shall hereafter have to speak of his Charles I., which at the earnest request of others he commenced, but which nothing could so far conquer his repugnance as to accomplish' (*Medwin (1913)* 221). Medwin certainly witnessed S.'s creative exertions (and was familiar with *Nbk 19*) but his assessment of why composition was so short-lived is incorrect in some aspects and incomplete in others:

> The task seemed to him an irksome one. His progress was slow; one day he expunged what he had written the day before. He occasionally shewed and read to me his MS., which was lined and interlined and interworded, so as to render it almost illegible. The scenes were disconnected, and intended to be interwoven in the tissue of the drama. He did not thus compose *The Cenci*. He seemed tangled in an inextricable web of difficulties, as to the treatment of his subject; and it was clear that he had formed no definite plan in his own mind, how to connect the links of the complicated yarn of events that led to that frightful catastrophe, or to justify it. … Shelley could not reconcile his mind to the beheading of Charles. He looked upon him as the

slave of circumstances, as the purest in morals, the most exemplary of husbands and fathers,—great in misfortune, a martyr in death; and could not help contrasting his character and motives with those of the low-minded, counterfeit patriots, the crafty, canting, bad men, who hatched that murderous conspiracy,—much less could he make a hero of that arch-hypocrite, Cromwell, or forgive him for aiming at the royal sceptre. ... He hated the Puritans,—not their tenets so much as their intolerance. (*Medwin (1913)* 341–3)

Certainly, the MS shows 'expunged' passages, but equally, persistent refinement and designs for an overall artistic integrity not expressed in Medwin's summation are apparent. Additionally, another more likely explanation for the suspension of work on *Charles* is that S. lost the incentive to continue since, having determined to break with Ollier, he had no publisher for it, at least in the short term. Gisborne's reply of 19 February 1822 to S.'s letter of 26 January, explained that he found himself 'obliged to temporize with' the Ollier brothers for lack of an alternative ('Barry Cornwall's publisher is become a bankrupt, and Keats's publisher, I understand from Hogg, is a vile Methodist'), and noted that '[t]hey decline paying any price whatever for "Charles 1st," so that the disposal of that work in the first instance might lay the foundation of a new and better connection' (*Gisborne Jnl* 80). S.'s letter to Hunt of 2 March 1822 is rueful both about his friend's lack of faith in his capacity to make progress with *Charles* and its inability to yield him financial benefit:

> So you think I can make nothing of Charles the 1st—Tanto peggio. Indeed I have written nothing for this last two months; a slight circumstance gave a new train to my ideas & shattered the fragile edifice when half built.—What motives have I to write.—I *had* motives—and I thank the god of my own heart they were totally different from those of the other apes of humanity who make mouths in the glass of the time—but what are *those* motives now? The only inspiration of an ordinary kind I could descend to acknowledge would be the earning £100 for *you*—& that it seems I cannot.— (*L* ii 394)

S.'s last recorded comment on the play (in a letter to Gisborne of 18 June 1822) confirms that just before his death it was a work he viewed as suspended rather than abandoned:

I do not go on with 'Charles the First'. I feel too little certainty of the future, and too little satisfaction with regard to the past, to undertake any subject seriously and deeply. I stand, as it were, upon a precipice, which I have ascended with great, and cannot descend without *greater*, peril, and I am content if the heaven above me is calm for the passing moment. (*L* ii 436)

Manuscript evidence. The MS of *Charles the First* is found in *Nbk 19*, a mutilated notebook originally containing approximately 142 leaves of which 112 are extant (including 19 with torn half-leaves). (For a detailed discussion of the notebook's homemade construction, its succession of repairs, the identification of misplaced or lost and recovered leaf fragments, see *BSM* xii pp. lxii–lxxviii and B. C. Barker-Benfield 'MS. Shelley adds. e. 17: description and collation, April 1988', in Departmental Files at the Bodleian Library, Refs. LVI. 16). The detached part of a leaf now located in *Box 1* (f. 136) was identified by Neville Rogers in 1952 as a fragment from *Charles the First*, Scene iii, and belongs to *Nbk 19* Stub K; together they would have formed the fourth leaf following the one now numbered as pp. 55/56 in *Nbk 19*. Although *Nbk 19* was used primarily by S., Mary also used it for her *Valperga* reading notes, as well as *Orpheus* (Appendix B in Volume 4 of the present edition), a possible collaborative work with S. Additionally, Medwin entered into *Nbk 19* his translation of a sonnet by G. Batista Felice Zappi, *Chi è costui, che in si gran pietra scolto.* S., Mary and Medwin all used *Nbk 19* in the same manner, as if it were a stenographer's notebook with 'upper' and 'lower' page use, rather than a left/right movement. The writing thus runs parallel to the spine, and S. often used the upper and lower pages as if they were one page, working back and forth across the gutter. One exception to this stenographer-style writing movement is the translated couplet from Petrarch's *Africa* on p. 54 *reverso*, *O thou whose cold hand tears the veils from error* (Appendix C); other rare exceptions are lines inserted along the left-hand margin when S. ran out of space on a given page (see *Nbk 19* p. 142 *reverso* (facsimile in *BSM* xii 241) for an instance of a crosswise entry). Besides the draft of *Charles*, S.'s drafts in *Nbk 19* include, among other material, his review in Italian of Sgricci's improvisation, 'The Death of Hector' (pp. 11–21), *The Boat on the Serchio* (no. 406), ll. 70–139 (pp. 218–217, 215–212, 210–208, all *reverso*), *Written on hearing the news of the death of Napoleon* (no. 407) (pp. 206–202, all *reverso*), and *The Zucca* (no. 421) (pp. 198–194c, 190–186, all *reverso*).

The contents of the notebook and its disposition of writings suggest that its use began with both S. and Mary drafting a variety of texts — translations, a review, reading notes, random jottings, and verse. All of these texts were entered from either the 'front' or the 'back' of the notebook (as now paginated), and progressed towards its centre. These varied texts thus embrace the draft of *Charles* and confirm that their composition preceded that of the play. Two 'streams' of the *Charles* draft are evident: Scene iii moves forward from the front of the notebook while the 'stream' of Scenes i, ii, and iv moves from the 'back' in *reverso* manner. Both 'streams' end with uncompleted scenes. The remaining pages, roughly in the middle of the notebook, are characterised by blank pages, stubs, mutilated half-leaves, and four brief items. *A widowed bird sate mourning for her love* (no. 427), *Art thou pale for weariness* (no. 428), and *O thou whose cold hand tears the veils from error* are clustered together on pp. 52–4 *reverso* while the sonnet to Byron, *Lines to —* (no. 429), occurs on a misplaced leaf (93c/94), which also belongs to this middle section of the MS, most likely between p. 72 *reverso* and Stub p. 73 *reverso* (see *BSM* xii 136 for further discussion.) *A widowed bird* was intended for insertion into Scene ii, and it is possible that *Art thou pale* might also have been destined for a position in the play (see headnotes to nos 427 and 428). The Petrarch translation, *O thou whose cold hand*, was probably entered around the time of the sonnet's composition, 22 January 1822, the date of Byron's birthday (see headnote to Appendix C). Thus, the middle, empty section of the notebook became a repository for either verses intended for insertion into *Charles the First* or writings composed near the end of January, a time when S. described his frustration with the play and suspended work on it. As noted by Nora Crook (*BSM* xii p. xliv), S. commemorates his progress through the play with two dates. In *Nbk 19* p. 181 *reverso*, at the top of the page, above the first line of Scene i is the notation *Jan. 5* confirming the remarks in Williams's journal cited above. (For a photofacsimile of this page which includes the draft of lines 2–15, see p. 318.) In similar fashion, S. inscribes *20th Jany* in the left-hand margin of the concluding speeches of Scene ii on p. 102 *reverso*. These two dates are consistent with the overall entering of materials in *Nbk 19*.

One exception to this order of materials is Medwin's translation of Zappi (p. 126 *reverso*) which interrupts a portion of *Charles* Scene ii. When Medwin entered his translation, the surrounding pages were undoubtedly empty; it seems unlikely that even Medwin would compose too closely to S.'s own drafts. Given that S. memorialises his completion of Scene ii with the notation *20th Jany.* (p. 102 rev.), Medwin must have entered his translation before this 1822 date, which supports Crook's conjecture that

Medwin 'transcribed this after his return to Pisa in November 1821 and before Shelley wrote the portion of "Charles the First"' (*BSM* xii p. lv). The translation also marks the second 'intrusion' of Medwin's presence in this notebook: the first, the Petrarch translation on p. 54 *reverso*, was most likely the result of a collaborative effort between him and S. (see headnote to Appendix C).

Scenes i, ii, and iv of *Charles*, including an abbreviated *Dramatis Personae*, stage directions, and jottings, run more or less continuously from the 'back' of the notebook, p. 185 *reverso* to p. 93b *reverso*; Scene iii runs from the 'front' of the notebook, p. 33 to p. 51, and then skips to p. 55. The two short lyrics and the scrap of the Petrarch translation described above are entered on pp. 52–4 *reverso*, which explains the skip, an indication of their earlier entry before that of the Scene iii material. *A widowed bird* on p. 52 *reverso* was intended as an insertion for Archy's final speech at the close of Scene ii as lines 478–85; the point for insertion is found on p. 101 *reverso*. The lyric is written in the same *reverso* direction as that of the rest of Scene ii despite the fact that the surrounding *Charles* Scene iii material runs in the forwards direction; the lyric's *reverso* position is another small indication of its link with Scene ii (see headnote to *A widowed bird*). Additional MS materials related to *Charles the First* are found in three other notebooks: *Nbk 21* pp. 255–547, 244–237 all *reverso* contain S.'s reading notes from *Hume* and *Whitelocke* (see *BSM* xvi 239–220 for facsimile and transcription; see 'Sources, genre and form' below for bibliographic details); S.'s schema and additional jottings for the play are in *Nbk 22* ff. *1^r-*4^r, *5^r (see *MYRS* vii 339–326, 323–322 for facsimile and transcription); and *Nbk 18*, front pastedown, contains a prose version of verse found in *Nbk 19* p. 34, which is possibly intended for a speech by Vane (see *And blushing / April is not a rebel to rude March* in *Lines connected with Charles the First* (no. 426 Appendix B)). *Nbk 18* also contains, on p. 160 *reverso*, a phrase — the wind's invisible tyranny — that is found twice in *Nbk 19*. It first appears on p. 185 *reverso* in jottings related to Hampden's character; the phrase is later incorporated into a speech by Laud on p. 132 *reverso* (ii 249 in the present edition); see *BSM* xix 4–5 and 302–3 for facsimiles and transcriptions of these two fragments.

With the exception of three, single-word emendations on p. 129 *reverso* in pencil, the medium throughout the *Nbk 19* draft is ink. Differences in pen-cut width accompanied by numerous layered variations in ink tones are evidence of S.'s frequent ongoing revisions during multiple composing periods. Several typically Shelleyan leafy sketches and trees occur throughout the draft; two boat hulls are roughly sketched on p. 183 *reverso*, and several architectural-like sketches appear on p. 40; a third sketch on

p. 182 *reverso* is discussed in more detail in the note to Scene ii 441–71. On pp. 147, 157–8 all *reverso* are several cone-like drawings with spiral markings, resembling a whirlwind or tornado shape. Given the repeated images of atmospheric turbulence in the play, it is perhaps tempting to regard these as emblems of the drama's political frame of reference.

To date, no transcript or press copy of *Charles* by Mary has been identified, but it is clear that she must have prepared a copy for publication. The edition in *1824* is greatly abridged, running to 277 lines only, compared to *Rossetti 1870* (approximately 802 lines) and the present edition (897 lines). Mary did, however, transcribe two stanzas of *A widowed bird* as an independent lyric and entitled it 'A Song' in *Mary Copybk 2* (*Massey* 76–7), apparently unaware of its position in the play. (See the headnote to no. 427 for further details of these two stanzas' independent publishing history). Because she seemed to have deliberately omitted Archy's speeches throughout the play — *1824* only allows him a half line — she might have overlooked the linking device in Archy's last speech and introduction to his song. On the other hand, the fact that she entitled it 'A Song' hints at the possibility that she had noted in *Nbk 19* p. 101 *reverso* that Archy identified his musical coda as *the song*.

Publication. An advance notice (first cited in *Peck* ii 260) of *Charles*'s publication appeared in *The London Magazine* iii (Jan. 1821) 68, just below the announcement of 'Lord Byron's New Tragedy', *Marino Faliero*; headed 'Mr. Shelley', it states:

> A friend of ours writes to us, from Italy, that Mr. Shelley, the author of that powerful Drama, "The Cenci," is employed upon an English historical Tragedy. The title, we believe, is to be *Charles the First*; at any rate that monarch is the hero, or principal person of the story. We hear that Mr. Shelley has expressed his determination to paint a true portrait of the unfortunate English King (it may be made a very captivating one) and to exclude from his work all prejudice, political as well as moral.

The 'friend' in Italy is perhaps Medwin who had spent the winter of 1820–1 with the Shelleys; S.'s letter to Medwin of 20 July 1820 mentions his plan for the drama, echoing some of the notice's phrasing: 'a play … without prejudice or passion, entitled "Charles the First"' (*L* ii 219–20). Despite the premature notice, the first publication of *Charles* did not appear until *1824*, and then in an abridged version of the incomplete drama. As noted above, Mary presented only 277 lines of *Charles the First* in the 'Fragments' portion of *1824* 237–48, where the running recto page headings read 'A Fragment.' Emphasising its fragmentary state, it is titled 'Charles the First. Fragments.' (237), and asterisks are placed in, and at the end of, scenes. Several other substantial writings in *1824* also lack surviving transcripts: the translation *The Cyclops* (no. 172), *The Zucca*, and two of the three scenes from *Cyprian* (no. 441). Such a group of texts, including *Charles*, represents a significant gap in the textual transmission that led to *1824*. Mary writes to Hunt on 18 September 1823 that 'I am now therefore fully occupied in preparing the MSS.' and adds, 'the present volume would consist of unpublished pieces' (*Mary L* i 384) although *1824* did include several previously published works. She was comprehensive in raking through approximately thirteen notebooks as well as numerous loose sheets in order to assemble the *1824* materials; however, she was less diligent in rescuing the entirety of *Charles* from oblivion. As Crook notes, Mary's extreme abridgements resulted in a drama where Queen Henrietta's part claimed 'greater prominence' than what the holograph demonstrates (*BSM* xii p. xxxv). All of Archy's speeches, except a half line, are omitted (as noted above), as well as large portions of the important discussion by Charles, Laud, and Wentworth in Scene ii; Scene iv is entirely excluded from her edition. Because she had virtually all of S.'s MS notebooks at hand, an asset that would be unavailable to subsequent editors for roughly the next 144 years, she was able to correlate his schema in *Nbk 22* with the draft in *Nbk 19*. R. B. Woodings in '"A Devil of a Nut to Crack:" Shelley's *Charles the First*', *SN* xl (1968) 216–37 (*Woodings (1968a)*) was the first to draw together *Nbk 19* and *Nbk 21* with Forman's transcripts of *Nbk 22* in *Huntington Nbks* iii 103–7. In her preface to *1824*, Mary clarifies that several of the writings — *The Cyclops*, *Cyprian* and *TL* (no. 452) — were not among the poems that had 'received the author's ultimate corrections' (vii). Notably, she omits to mention *Charles* in this context. (Interestingly the works she cites are among those for which, like *Charles*, her transcriptions are not extant.) For her 'Note on Poems Written in 1822' in *1839*, she comments on *Charles*, almost apologetically, as if acknowledging her silence about it in *1824*:

> Shelley had conceived the idea of writing a tragedy on the subject of Charles I. It was one that he believed adapted for a drama; full of intense interest, contrasted character, and busy passion. He had recommended it long before, when he encouraged me to attempt a play. Whether the subject proved more difficult than he anticipated, or whether in fact he could not bend his mind away from the broodings and wanderings of thought, divested from human interest, which he

best loved, I cannot tell; but he proceeded slowly and threw it aside for one of the most mystical of his poems, "The Triumph of Life," on which he was employed at the last. (*1839* iv 227)

Her phrase 'threw it aside' is possibly responsible for the inattention to, and relative lack of critical interest in, S.'s drama, a work which had consumed a great deal of his time and energy in sourcing materials and reading in 1820–2, evidenced by his numerous book orders, Mary's reading notes in her journals, the play's frequent mention in his letters, and records of discussions of *Charles* with Mary, Edward Williams, Trelawny, and Medwin.

As Charles Taylor demonstrates, both *1829* and *1834* served as copy text for Mary's *1839* edition of *Charles* (*Taylor* 34–46), a decision making it unlikely that she returned to the play's holograph or her transcripts in preparing *1839* (where it is titled 'Charles the First. A Fragment'). If she had returned and reviewed the MSS, she might not have made the comment in a note to the 'Note on Poems Written in 1822', that 'no omissions have been made', particularly with regard to *Charles*. Nevertheless, it seems that she retained a clear memory of the state of the MSS for she adds, all in the past tense:

> Did any one see the papers from which I drew that volume, the wonder would be how any eyes or patience were capable of extracting it from so confused a mass, interlined and broken into fragments, so that the sense could only be deciphered and joined by guesses, which might seem rather intuitive than founded on reasoning. Yet I believe no mistake was made. (*1839* iv 226 n.)

Such an acknowledgement of the challenges might explain the resort to unauthorised editions in her preparation of *1839*.

Richard Garnett's cordial relationship with Sir Percy Florence Shelley and his wife Jane, Lady Shelley, allowed him access to the Shelley archive at Boscombe. The result was *Relics* which included an unpublished, albeit cancelled, passage connected to *Charles* found on what was then a loose leaf now housed in *Box 1* (f. 136^v) (see headnote to *Lines connected with Charles the First* (Appendix A)). Curiously, he did not publish the uncancelled lines overleaf (now Scene iii 94–103); furthermore, although he had access to *Nbk 19*, he did not feel compelled to include any other of the lines for *Charles* that Mary omitted.

In preparation for his Memoir and edition of Shelley, William Michael Rossetti contacted Garnett, and on 8 March 1869 recorded in his diary:

Dined with Garnett, who gave me a transcript of a few fragments by Shelley not yet published, and a MS. book of his containing some unpublished portions of *Charles the First,* which I shall read through, and may use as I like— (*Rossetti Papers: 1862–1870* (1903) 385)

The following day he notes, 'Began deciphering the Shelley MS. book [*Nbk 19*]; I see there are (*inter alia*) considerable pickings of *Charles the First* to be got out of it.' Several days later, 12 March, Rossetti describes to William Allingham, Irish poet and friend of D. G. Rossetti, the new material and his task: 'Some scraps extracted by Garnett, and as yet unpublished, and ... one of Shelley's MS. books, which contains, I find, a considerable bulk of *Charles the First* as yet unprinted, and which I am deciphering—no easy job' (*Rossetti Papers* 429). On 17 March, Rossetti records in his diary that Garnett called on him to 'take back the Shelley MS.' (386). Rossetti's nine days of work on the 'considerable pickings' resulted in a remarkable addition of approximately 525 lines to Mary's *1824* edition of *Charles.* Rossetti shaped the drama much as it is viewed even into the twenty-first century, serving as the basis for the *OSA* text. Without access to *Nbk 22,* Rossetti was unaware that the Hampden/Vane dialogue had been designated by S. as Scene iii; Rossetti placed it as 'Scene iv' and moved the Star Chamber scene into place as 'Scene iii'. He correctly identified *A widowed bird* as Archy's song which had appeared in *1824* as an independent poem; however, he misplaced it as the opening of a 'Scene v', a scene which never existed in S.'s drafts, notes or schema. In an attempt to include Garnett's newly published lines from *Charles,* he conjecturally inserted them into a speech by Bastwick in Scene iv, admitting in a note that 'I have not found them in the notebook, and cannot affirm that I am right in here introducing them; but I see no other place for them equally plausible' (ii 586). (See 'Manuscript evidence' above for Rogers's identification of the leaf separated from *Nbk 19* which Garnett published in *Relics.*) None of these structural flaws, however, would be identified until the middle of the twentieth century when the MS evidence became more accessible. Rossetti's unannotated edition of 1870 corrected 'Gynaeocoenic' to 'Gynaecocoenic' (see ii 393 and note), which seems to be the only emendation to the text of *Charles* in *Rossetti 1870* that he made at that time. Of this one-volume edition he writes to Garnett, 16 January 1870:

> The very day THE Shelley [two-volume edition] was out I received the proof of the little notice I wrote of him for the cheap series to be published in July. I SUPPOSE by the bye that that cheap book ... will reproduce the guinea text verbatim, with the sole omission of

my own Notes etc.: so that Shelleyites who care for the revisions and don't want to pay a guinea will soon be accomodated.— (*L about S* 34)

He also bemoaned what he termed 'pestiferous misprints', and citing an example from *TL*, he indicates that he made other corrections at that time for the unannotated 1870 edition (*L about S* 34). Despite the virtues of Rossetti's labour, *Rossetti 1870* did not find contemporary favour from either the Shelley family or Shelley scholars. The Shelleys were, in the main, unhappy with his prefacing 'Memoir'. Rossetti records (16 May 1870), 'Allingham tells me that (as I had always anticipated) some passages in my Memoir of Shelley do not please the Shelley family, but he has not broached the subject in its minutiae to them' (*The Diary of W. M. Rossetti: 1870-1873*, ed. Odette Bornand (1977) 8-9). Others were unhappy with what they perceived as his cavalier editorial method 'of punctuation, printing, and conjectural emendation' (*Edinburgh Review* xxxiii (1871) 448). On the other hand, Mathilde Blind, although offering a series of corrections in her unsigned review, also acknowledged Rossetti's great achievement, characterising his work 'as the first *critical* edition of the poet's works' (*The Westminster Review* xxxviii (1870) 77). That reputation has persisted until the present day. Crook notes that the texts critiqued by Rossetti's contemporaries did not include writings — like *Charles* — deriving from *Nbk 19*; Rossetti's access to the notebook 'gave his work authority and made subsequent editors reluctant to go over that ground again' (*BSM* xii p. xxxvii). Chastened by the criticisms of his peers, Rossetti made some emendations in *Rossetti 1878*, e.g. the correction of 'court' for 'count' in Archy's speech (ii 476), which was perhaps based on Forman's conjecture of '*count* for *court*' in *Forman 1876-7* iii 326. In *Charles*, overall, there were few changes, but Rossetti did accept Forman's lower case emendations for reverential pronouns, i.e. 'he' rather than 'He' in referring to a deity. *Forman 1876-7* noted also the absence of most of the line at i 203 which Rossetti corrected in *Rossetti 1878*. (Other instances of alternative readings in *Rossetti 1878* are provided in the notes.)

In large part, *Hutchinson* followed *Rossetti 1870* but did incorporate two if not three conjectures found in *Forman 1876-7*; *Hutchinson* also introduced one reading for which there is no authority ('ample' for 'ampler' in Scene ii 225 in *Hutchinson*; ii 259 in present edition). With evolving access to MS materials in the twentieth- and twenty-first centuries, more recent scholars have been allowed a view of MS witnesses comparable to that of Mary's in 1822-3 during her preparation for *1824*. The result has been a few revised transcriptions of several brief passages (see *Woodings (1968a)*; R. B. Woodings, 'Shelley's Sources for "Charles the First"', *MLN* lxiv (1969) 267–75 (*Woodings (1969)*); and Nora Crook, 'Calumniated Republicans and the Hero of Shelley's "Charles the First"', *K-SJ* lvi (2007) 155–72 (*Crook (2007)*). Crook's meticulous transcription of *Nbk 19* with insightful discussions of S.'s methods and likely intentions for organisation in *BSM* xii represents a significant step to arrive at an edition of this incomplete work. Helpful in understanding the impact of Shelley's key editors on S.'s texts, including *Charles*, are Mary Quinn's discussion in her Introduction to *MYRS* iv pp. xxxvi–xlvii; Nora Crook's preface in *BSM* xii pp. xxxiv–xxxvii; and Michael Rossington, 'Editing Shelley' in *The Oxford Handbook of Percy Bysshe Shelley*, eds Michael O'Neill and Anthony Howe (2013) 645–56.

Sources, genre and form. Godwin describes, in a letter to S. of 8 June 1818, his plans for a book 'to be called The Lives of the Commonwealth's Men' as well as who should write it:

> But in my bed this morning I thought, Mary perhaps, would like to write it, and I should think she is perfectly capable. The books to be consulted would be comparatively few, Noble's Memoirs of the Protectorate House of Cromwel, Whitlock's Memorials of English Affairs under Charles the First, Ludlow's Memoirs, Colonel Hutchinson's Memoirs, the Trials of the 29 Regicides, the Trial of Sir Henry Vane, & the Dying Speeches of Corbet, Okey and Barkstead. In a few instances, as I have observed in my Letter of Advice, the references of these authors might lead to further materials. (Bodleian MS. Abinger c. 66 f. 45^r)

The emphasis in Godwin's suggested list of materials focuses on the 'Commonwealth's Men'; Godwin's intention was to re-evaluate the rebels and regicides who had been loaded 'with all the abuse and scurrility that language can furnish.' The outcome of such an examination might demonstrate that 'perhaps they will be found equal to any ten men in the annals of the Roman Republic' (Bodleian MS. Abinger c. 66 f. 44^v). By the end of the 1818 summer, S. had already transformed Mary's writing task into a play rather than a collection of biographical sketches; he even indicates to her that he has thoughts on how she could 'conduct' some scenes (*L* ii 39–40; see also 'Date of composition' above). Consequently, S.'s own evolving reading list includes a more wide-ranging set of sources, confirming a different viewpoint and purpose: the reign of Charles and the overthrow of monarchy by a republican revolution. This narrative formulation was coupled with his determination to craft a drama 'not coloured by the party spirit of the author' (*L* ii 372). Thus, the historical sources begin to cluster into two groups: Godwin's recommendations and S.'s own preferences. Godwin's list is comprised mostly of Commonwealth rebel and regicide accounts: Mark Noble, *Memoirs of the Protectorate House of Cromwell*, 2 vols (1784) (*Noble Memoirs*); Bulstrode Whitelocke, *Memorials of the English Affairs or, an Historical Account of What passed from the beginning of the Reign of King Charles the first, to King Charles the Second His Happy Restauration* (1682) (*Whitelocke*); Edmond Ludlow, *Memoirs of Edmund Ludlow*, 3 vols (1698–9) (*Ludlow 1771*); Lucy Hutchinson, *Memoirs of the Life of Colonel Hutchinson*, ed. J. Hutchinson (1806) (*Hutchinson Life*); [Heneage Finch, Earl of Nottingham], *The Indictment, Arraignment, Tryal, and Judgment, at large, of Twenty-Nine Regicides, the Murtherers of His Most Sacred Majesty King Charles I* (1739) (published anonymously in 1660); Henry Vane, *The Tryal of Sir Henry Vane, K$^{t.}$, at the Kings Bench, Westminster, June the 2d. and 6th 1662* (1662) (*Vane*); and *The Speeches, Discourses, and Prayers, of Col. John Barkstead, Col. John Okey, and Mr. Miles Corbet* (1662). Of this list, only *Whitelocke* provides a detailed history of the era rather than a personal memoir. S.'s notes, along with Mary's reading lists and journal entries, indicate that three of these sources, *Hutchinson Life, Ludlow 1771* and *Whitelocke*, were read by both Mary and S.

Mary read *Memoirs of the Life of Colonel Hutchinson* by Lucy Hutchinson (1620–81) between 15 and 17 July 1821 (*Mary Jnl* i 374); on 7 August 1821, Claire records her reading of it (*Claire Jnl* 245). It seems reasonable to assume that, with Godwin's recommendation, S. too would have examined Hutchinson's account of the life of her husband John. He was the son of Sir Thomas Hutchinson by his first wife Lady Margaret, who was daughter of Sir John Byron of Newstead, which perhaps made Hutchinson's *Memoirs* even more interesting to S. Thus, three members of the Pisan circle — Byron, as well as Williams, a lineal descendant of one of Cromwell's daughters, and S. himself, 'kinsman' of Algernon Sidney according to Medwin (*Medwin* ii 165) — had family links to central actors in the tumultuous years of the Civil War and the Restoration. As a Member of Parliament for Nottinghamshire, Colonel Hutchinson accepted an invitation to act as one of the King's judges, and on 22 December 1648, 'in his conscience that it was his duty to act as he did, he, upon serious debate, both privately and in his addresses to God, and in conferences with conscientious, upright, unbiassed persons, proceeded to sign the sentence against the king' (*Hutchinson Life* 304). In June 1660, Hutchinson was expelled from Parliament as a regicide but escaped the fate of other regicides in part through the influence of Lord Byron and

Sir Allen Apsley, his kinsmen. The historian Catharine Macaulay (1731–91) had appealed to Lucy Hutchinson's family to publish her memoirs for the unique view she had of this period, but was unsuccessful in her request. Her *Life* did not appear until 1806, edited by a relative, Rev. Julius Hutchinson.

The *Memoirs of Edmund Ludlow* is another account by an English parliamentarian who, like John Hutchinson, was a judge in the trial of Charles and signed the warrant for his execution. Blair Worden (*Roundhead Reputations: The English Civil War and the Passions of Posterity* (2001) 39–121) determines that *The Memoirs of Edmund Ludlow* was in large part a fabrication created by John Toland, a deist, who based the so-called *Memoirs* on Ludlow's manuscript of his autobiography, *A voyce from the watch tower*, a portion of which is now in the Bodleian Library, Oxford (MS. Eng. hist. c. 487). S., however, would not have known of this deception. Although S. might have acquired the 1698–9 first edition, the quarto edition of 1771 would probably have been more accessible; this latter source is the one cited here. Mary first records reading *Ludlow 1771* on 15 and 25 July 1821 (*Mary Jnl* i 374–5). Ludlow, a republican and supporter of the Commonwealth, recognised his perilous situation at the Restoration. He fled abroad, eventually settling in Vevey, Switzerland, where he died in 1692. S. and Byron visited Vevey in June 1816 during an excursion around Lake Geneva seeking out spots linked to Rousseau's life and writings. Although S. remarks that 'Vevai is a town more beautiful in its simplicity than any I have ever seen' (*L* i 487), he makes no mention of Ludlow's exile or memorials there. Byron, however, in his 'Alpine Journal' written for Augusta Leigh, recounts his return to Vevey that following September, accompanied by Hobhouse. He describes Ludlow's monument of black marble in St. Martin's Church and comments that Ludlow was 'one of the King's (Charles's) Judges—a fine fellow.—I remember reading his memoirs in January 1815 ... the first part of them very amusing—the latter less so' (*Byron L&J* v 97). Ludlow's memoir begins with only a brief account of events during Charles's reign; the memoir's focus was primarily on events after 1649. S.'s interest would have been on the earlier period, and perhaps it is this 'first part' that Byron found amusing. Ludlow's anti-monarchist position was clear:

> the question in dispute between the king's party and us being, as I apprehended, "Whether the king should govern as a God by his will, and the nation be governed by force like beasts: or whether the people should be governed by laws made by themselves, and live under a government derived from their own consent?" (*Ludlow 1771* 114)

But equally, Ludlow records his dissatisfaction with the resulting interregnum and the dangers it brought: 'Men may learn from the issue of the Cromwellian tyranny, that liberty and a standing mercenary army are incompatible' (*Ludlow 1771* 376). Acknowledging such complexities could have been useful for S. in pursuing a play 'without prejudice or passion' and is consistent with his own comments in *PVR* on the perils and consequences of civil war:

> War, waged from whatever motive, extinguishes, the sentiment of reason & justice in the mind. ... A sentiment of confidence in brute force & in a contempt of death and danger is considered as the highest virtue, when in truth and however indispensible to the [ ] [,] they are merely the means & the instruments, highly capable of being perverted to destroy the cause they were assumed to promote. (Text based on *SC* vi 1063-4)

Among Godwin's recommendations, the *Memorials* by Bulstrode Whitelocke (1605-75) was a key source in providing S. with the lively London scene which opens his drama as well as the basis for several speeches. S.'s reading notes from *Whitelocke* collated with Hume's history occur in *Nbk 21* which also contains the draft of *Hellas*, thus indicating autumn-winter 1821 for the entering of those notes. (See discussion of Hume below for location in MS, transcription and facsimile details.) Although the masque passages in *Whitelocke* are not recorded in the *Nbk 21* reading notes, S. adopts vocabulary, phrases and a great number of details for the colourful masque progression in Scene i. *Whitelocke*'s account also describes the antimasque with its procession of 'Projectors' (i.e. promoters of 'bogus or unsound business ventures', *OED* 1b), each espousing an absurd Patent of Monopoly:

> First in this Antimasque, rode a Fellow upon a little Horse, with a great Bit in his mouth, and upon the man's head was a Bit, with Headstall and Rains fastned, and signified a Projector, *who begged a Patent, that none in the Kingdom might ride their Horses, but with such Bits as they should buy of him.* (*Whitelocke* 20)

Whitelocke notes that the antimasque 'pleased the Spectators' for it served as a covert signal to the King 'of the unfitness and ridiculousness of these Projects against the Law' (20). S.'s antimasque (i 180-203) with its 'troop of cripples, beggars and lean outcasts' is likewise commented upon by a

Spectator in the role of the Old Man who, in deciphering the meaning of the antimasque when the Young Man fails to catch its implications, provides a catalogue of England's sins and failures. *Whitelocke*'s account is also the basis for first speeches by the King and Queen in Scene ii as well as Bastwick's opening salvo in his confrontation with Archbishop Laud in the Star Chamber, Scene iv. Crook's statement in *BSM* xii p. xix that S. used the new edition of *Whitelocke* by Tonson of 1732 because the 'pagination matches PBS's notes in MS. Shelley adds e. 7' would appear to be inaccurate. S.'s notes in *Nbk 21* match exactly the original 1682 edition but do not match the 1732 edition. This is further confirmed by what Crook assumed was a possible 'homophonic error' on S's part in the antimasque description, Scene i 199 (*BSM* xii 270 n.). In *Nbk 19* p. 157 *reverso*, S. writes *keys & tongues* as in the 1682 edition ('Keys & Tongues', p. 19) rather than the corrected 'Keyes and Tongs' of 1753, p. 20. A key question is how S. had access to the 1682 edition which must have been somewhat rare. The earliest possible evidence of S.'s use of *Whitelocke* is autumn 1821, and thus it seems likely that it was included in the box that arrived in June 1821 (discussed below).

Whether S. had access to, and read, the other four sources recommended by Godwin is somewhat less certain. As discussed above, Mary's 1816 reading notes record that S. read 'Life of Cromwell', but this may not have been Noble's book on Cromwell that Godwin recommended two years later (*Mary Jnl* i 141). The editors of *Mary Jnl* suggest that Mary's note refers rather to *Memoirs of Oliver Cromwell and his Children, Supposed to be Written by Himself* (1816). Peacock's list of S.'s books to be sold by Wise in 1829 includes two relevant entries: '*Life of Oliver Cromwell*. 2.' (Pforz MS (S'ANA) f. 6ʳ) and '*Memoirs of Cromwell* 2 vol.' (Pforz MS (S'ANA) f. 10ʳ). With the scant information supplied by the Peacock lists, one could conjecture that the '*Memoirs of Cromwell* 2 vol.' may well be *Noble Memoirs* while the '*Life of Oliver Cromwell*' may be the supposed autobiography that the *Mary Jnl* editors propose. This conjecture is perhaps validated by the fact that there is no reference after 1816 to either of these volumes in the letters and journals of Mary or S.'s letters; furthermore, it is clear these volumes were no longer with the Shelleys once they left England in March 1818.

Crook (2007) plausibly suggests that S. based his character of Sir Harry Vane on Vane's *Tryal*. Given the resonance between Vane's commentary and meditations before his death and his speeches in S.'s Scene iii, it seems very likely that S. had consulted this source, despite the fact that no record of it appears in any of the primary materials. This volume is undoubtedly one of those sources that was packed in the long-awaited box sent from England sometime after February 1821. (See discussion below, regarding the details of the Shelleys' box.) No evidence has been established that S. consulted Finch's *Twenty-Nine Regicides* or the collected speeches of Barkstead, Okey, and Corbet although these accounts should not be excluded from consideration as source materials.

Godwin's list of materials for a projected book by Mary has generally been viewed as the starting point for S.'s own consideration of King Charles, the Civil War, and the Commonwealth. However, some time before Godwin's prompt, S. had already reflected upon the Civil War's aftermath with anger and impatience. In a letter from Dublin to Elizabeth Hitchener, 27 February 1812, S. writes:

> I cannot bear to hear people talk of the glorious Revolution of 1688. — was that period glorious when with a presumption only equalled by their stupidity, and a shortsightedness incomme[n]surable but with the blindest egotism Parliament affected to pass an act delivering over themselves and their posterity to the remotest period of time to Mary and William and their posterity. — I saw this Act yesterday for the first time: and my blood boils to think that Sidney's and Hampden's blood was wasted thus, that even the defenders of liberty as they are called were sunk thus low, and thus attempt[ed] to arrest the perfectibility of human nature. — (*L* i 264)

John Hampden was to become a central figure in S.'s drama ten years later. In another instance of S.'s independent interest in the Civil War, Mary records on 13-14 October 1816 that 'Shelley reads life of Cromwell' while she herself was reading during the same period (29 September–27 October) Edward Hyde, Earl of Clarendon's *The History of the Rebellion and Civil Wars in England, Begun in the year 1641*, 3 vols (1702-4) (hereafter *Clarendon*) (*Mary Jnl* i 137-42).

In fact, *Clarendon* was one of a group of three histories the Shelleys were reading in a rather structured fashion from 1818 onwards that provided a range and focus of events quite different from that of Godwin's initial list. Included in this group are David Hume, *The History of England from the Invasion of Julius Caesar to the Revolution in 1688*, 6 vols (1754-62), read June-August 1818 (*Mary Jnl* i 215-23); the aforementioned *Clarendon*, read October-November 1819 (*Mary Jnl* i 298-301); and Catharine Macaulay, *The History of England from the accession James I to that of the Brunswick Line*, 8 vols (1763-83) (*Macaulay*), read July-September 1820 (*Mary Jnl* i 326, 329, 331). A fourth history, Gilbert Burnet's *Bishop Burnet's History of His Own Time* 2 vols (1724–34) was ordered by S. in a letter to Ollier of 22 February 1821 (*L* ii 270); previously, in a letter of (?)7 July 1820, he had tried to order Burnet's history with the help of the Gisbornes who were in London at that time (*L* ii 212). Burnet's account focuses primarily on the span of time from the Restoration of Charles II until the reign of Queen Anne and the signing of the Treaty of Utrecht in 1713 and touches only very briefly on the period of Charles I and the Commonwealth.

As early as 1812, S. had attempted to order from Hookham 'Hume's Hist of England (Cheapest poss. Edit.)'. S.'s bookseller indicates, however, with an asterisk next to the Hume entry in S.'s letter, that he was unable to fulfil S.'s request (*L* i 342), though it is possible that Hookham was eventually able to provide S. with an edition of Hume. By the time the Shelleys arrived in Italy, they had acquired an edition because in the summer of 1818 at Bagni di Lucca, perhaps inspired by Godwin's 8 June 1818 letter, Shelley began a marathon reading of Hume on 19 June, tackling it almost daily and often aloud throughout that summer (*Mary Jnl* i 215–23). The edition he read in 1818 was obviously not the 1819 edition he used when he made his *Nbk 21* notes on *Hume* and *Whitelocke*: the page numbers in the 1819 Regent's edition of *The History of England from the Invasion of Julius Caesar to the Revolution in 1688* (hereafter *Hume*) correspond to S.'s page notations in his notes. For S.'s *Hume* and *Whitelocke* notations see *Nbk 21* pp. 255, 253, 251–247, 244–237 all *reverso* (facsimile and transcription in *BSM* xvi 238–220); see also *Woodings (1969)*, which includes a partial transcription of these notes.

The questions that now remain are why and how S. comes to use this later edition of Hume. Given the financial constraints during S.'s residence in Pisa, it seems unlikely that he would have ordered another Hume, and this time a 16-volume edition. One possible explanation is that with Byron's arrival in Pisa on 1 November 1821, S. would have had access to Byron's library. By this time, S. had completed his principal composition of that autumn for, on 6 November, Williams records: 'Commence writing out for S[helley] a fair copy of his Hellas' (*Gisborne Jnl* 110). With the completion of *Hellas* (no. 411), he now had time to move ahead with the historical drama. If S. were using a copy of Byron's *Hume*, it could go some way towards explaining the rather atypical set of reading notes found at the end of *Nbk 21*. Such a scenario also offers a possibility for focusing the dating of these notes. Against this possibility, however, is S.'s tentative and cryptic comment to Ollier in a letter of 25 September 1821:

> *Charles the First* is conceived, but not born. Unless I am sure of making something good, the play will not be written. Pride, that

ruined Satan, will kill *Charles the First*, for his midwife would be only *less than him whom thunder has made greater.* I am full of great plans; and, if I should tell you them, I should add to the list of these riddles. (*L* ii 354)

If these comments point to a more active engagement with Hume's *History* in September, before Byron's arrival, the acquisition and/or access to a second *Hume* edition of 1819 is still unexplained. One additional curiosity in the Hume story is that Peacock's list of S.'s books includes 'Humes History of England 6 vol.' (Pforz MS (S'ANA) f. 9ʳ) suggesting that Hookham was eventually successful in acquiring the Hume edition for S. Eight and ten-volume editions of Hume had been published, and it is possible that S. took only the last two (or possibly four) volumes with him to Italy, which included the reigns of James I, Charles I, the Commonwealth, and James II. If, however, S. did not take to Italy a portion of the volumes of the edition noted in the Peacock list, it would mean that the Shelleys had access to three different sets of Hume's multi-volume edition.

As noted above, Mary records her almost daily reading of *Clarendon* (*Mary Jnl* i 137–42) in the autumn of 1816. Despite the fact that Clarendon's history usually appears as three volumes, the editors of *Mary Jnl* conjecture that 'Shelley and Mary probably possessed the 1816 edition, which contained an additional volume, *The History of the Rebellion and Civil Wars in Ireland* first published 1719–20' (*Mary Jnl* i 137n); Mary's reading list for 1816 records '4 Vols. of Clarendon's History' (*Mary Jnl* i 93). S. began an equally assiduous reading of *Clarendon* in autumn 1819, from 2 October until 9 November, and Mary notes that he often read it aloud (*Mary Jnl* i 298–301). The lively first-hand account by Clarendon, who survived two Kings, one Lord Protector, and one civil war could easily lend itself to engaged readings by S. Archy's speech at the departure of the court near the end of Scene ii, seems indebted to Clarendon's description of young Prince Charles and a scheme devised by the Duke of Buckingham to travel to Spain in order to woo the Infanta. James, apoplectic at the perils of such a journey by his son, with all its potential for failure and even the possible loss of the young prince's life, responds with an emotional outburst including his utterance, 'baby Charles' (*Clarendon* i 47), the epithet that Archy uses in Scene ii 421. Hume closely follows Clarendon's account of this incident, but Hume's version is perhaps less memorable in its retelling (vii 62–3).

Mary had read Catharine Macaulay's *History of England* regularly from 29 June to 29 July 1820 followed by S. who read her work on 18–25

August and 4 September (*Mary Jnl* i 324–31). Macaulay's history came with high recommendation: in *A Vindication of the Rights of Woman* (1792), Mary Wollstonecraft describes Macaulay (1731–91) as 'The woman of the greatest abilities, undoubtedly, that this country has ever produced' (*The Works of Mary Wollstonecraft*, eds Janet Todd and Marilyn Butler, 7 vols (1989) v 174–5). Macaulay's fearless, almost gothic descriptions of the torture and punishment of religious and political opponents must have forcefully struck S.: such incidents serve at key moments of high drama in Scenes i and iv of his play. Macaulay's anti-monarchist position is clear, but she reserves particular vitriol for Thomas Wentworth, Earl of Strafford. In part, she is arguing against Hume's more sympathetic evaluation of Wentworth, but her main criticism of him is his apostasy, a key point that Bastwick in Scene i articulates as the royal procession moves through the streets of London. Instrumental in passing the Petition of Right, Wentworth attracted the attention of the court, and, as Macaulay writes, 'They had at this time, with the bribe of a peerage, and the presidentship of the council in the northern parts, bought off from the popular party Sir Thomas Wentworth' (ii 23–4). In her character summary, following the account of his execution, Macaulay returns to this theme:

> His patriotism dissolved on the first beam of court favour; he was intoxicated on the first taste of power, and became a more bold and zealous instrument of tyranny than any minister this country ever produced. He was of a revengeful, insolent disposition; but his supreme vice was an insatiable ambition, directed to false and unlawful objects. (ii 432)

Wentworth seems to dominate Macaulay's second volume: she describes with numerous precise details his character, more so than her generalised descriptions of Charles or Laud. Wentworth's long speeches and important presence in Scene ii reflect that emphasis. Furthermore, S.'s notes in *Nbk 22* f. *4^r show that he intended to conclude Act II with Wentworth's execution, a shockingly swift reversal of fortune for a key figure. Macaulay frequently cites from Wentworth's collection of personal documents and letters. Although there is no mention in any of the primary materials or in S.'s notes of *The Earl of Strafforde's Letters and Dispatches*, ed. William Knowler, 2 vols (1739) (hereafter *Strafforde*), it is just possible that he might have decided to acquire this edition for himself.

Another source which S. might have acquired was *Killing No Murder: Briefly Discoursed In Three Questions* by Edward Sexby (who wrote under the name of William Allen) (1657) (hereafter, *Killing (1689)*) of which Medwin remarks:

> I must now speak of his Charles the First. He had designed to write a tragedy on this ungrateful subject as far back as 1818, and had begun it at the end of the following year, when he asked me to obtain for him that well-known pamphlet, which was in my father's library,— "Killing no murder." (*Medwin* ii 162)

Whether Medwin acquired the pamphlet for S. is unknown, but given the fact that it was 'well-known' and reprinted regularly since its first publication, it seems likely that S. could have acquired a copy through his bookseller. The pamphlet boldly lays out the argument for tyrannicide, and Cromwell is the author's target. Sexby brazenly dedicates the tract to 'His Highness Oliver Cromwell'. Drawing on, among others, Aristotle, Plato, and Tacitus, as well as Exodus, Judges, 1 Chronicles and 2 Chronicles from the Old Testament, the author lays out his argument framed by three questions:

> That I may be as plain as I can, I shall first make it a question (which indeed is none) whether my Lord Protector be a Tyrant or not? Secondly, if he be, Whether it is lawful to do Justice upon him without Solemnity, that is, to kill him? Thirdly, If it be lawful, Whether it is likely to prove profitable or noxious to the Common-Wealth? (*Killing (1689)*).

S.'s incomplete play has no speech for Cromwell, but he was to appear in Scene iii (see note to the first stage direction in Scene iii); in the schema notes for that scene, S. writes, *a pursuivant comes with an order of council to prevent their embarkation — Cromwells speech on that occasion* — (*Nbk 22* f. *1ᵛ*). S.'s desire to seek out a tract such as *Killing No Murder* is consistent with his desire to craft a play 'without prejudice or passion' for it would offer a counterbalance to the laudatory portrait of Macaulay's history or of *Noble Memoirs* which describes Cromwell in the following manner: 'one of whom, it has been justly remarked, was the greatest man that has owed his existence to this island' (i p. iii). These two extreme positions — one calling for Cromwell's death, the other calling for his veneration — are captured in Medwin's account of S.'s dilemma:

> He [S.] was not blind to the energy of Cromwell's foreign policy, nor insensible to the greatness to which he raised England, but reprobated

his unconstitutional use of power, his trampling on all law, by a military despotism more odious than the worst acts of his predecessor. (*Medwin* ii 164–5)

Among the accounts and histories of rebels, regicides, and revolutionaries which S. read, the King's voice is missing, but that was supplied in part by *Reliquiae Sacrae Carolinae* (1651) and *Eikon Basilike* (1649), the former a collection of official documents and letters written by and to Charles, the latter the thoughts and meditations of the presumed author King Charles. S.'s copy of these two works, bound into one volume, is now in CHPL (PBS 0282). Peck first described the annotations and pencilled markings, possibly made by S., in this volume (*Peck* ii 361–4). Peck was made aware of the existence of this volume by a brief letter from R. S. Garnett published in the *TLS* 998 (3 March 1921) 144. R. B. Woodings first linked that volume with S.'s notation from the *Eikon Basilike* found on p. 1 of *Nbk 21*, the same notebook that includes S.'s reading notes from *Hume* and *Whitelocke* (*Woodings (1969)* 273–5). S.'s note, *Page 154 Eikon Basilike — Effects of the Uxbridge treaty. 158.*, matches the pages in the CHPL volume on that topic and confirms his reading of the *Eikon Basilike* as well as *Reliquiae Sacrae Carolinae*. The *Eikon Basilike* serves as Charles's apologia for his actions, but at the same time he claims responsibility for his failed endeavours and errors of judgement. Appearing in the year of the king's execution, 1649, the *Eikon Basilike* went through numerous reprintings in that year alone; its attempted suppression by the Commonwealth government could only guarantee its continued popularity and assured Charles's position as a martyr. The famous emblem frontispiece by William Marshall is a striking engraving depicting a kneeling Charles, and on the floor is his crown inscribed with 'Vanitas'; his right hand is extended and holding up a crown of thorns. If the Pforzheimer volume included this frontispiece, it is now missing, and one cannot ascertain if S. had known of its existence; however, Charles's own words reiterate the theme. On p. 35 of the Pforzheimer *Eikon*, S has apparently marked with a pencilled marginal stroke the following: 'nor will I be brought to affirme that to men, which in My Conscience I deny before God. I will rather chuse to wear a Crown of Thorns with My Saviour, then to exchange that of Gold … for one of lead'. S.'s Charles also makes a similar allusion to his Christ-like suffering: 'O, it shows well / When subjects twine flowers of observance / With the sharp thorns that line the English crown' (ii 5–7).

Milton's response in his *Eikonoklastes* (1649) is an intellectual appeal meant to invalidate the emotional appeal of Charles's *Eikon Basilike* and would certainly have been read by S. Indeed, Milton's presence and voice describing the very events S. was examining in his drama must have played a significant role in driving him towards a dramatic analysis of the rise and fall of a king. Late in 1819, S. had announced to the Gisbornes his intention to 'journey across the great sandy desert of Politics' (*L* ii 150), and *PVR* was the result of that journey. In Chapter I of *PVR*, S. discusses the effects of the Reformation on England, applying Milton's words to the contentious issue of the execution of Charles I:

> The exposition of a certain portion of religious imposture, drew with it an enquiry into political imposture, and was attended with an extraordinary exertion of the energies of intellectual power[.] Shakespeare & Lord Bacon & the great writers of the age of Elizabeth & James the Ist were at once the effects of this new spirit in men's minds, & the causes of its more complete developement. By rapid gradation the nation was conducted to the temporary abolition of aristocracy & episcopacy, & the mighty example which "in teaching nations how to live," England afforded to the world of bringing to public justice one of those chiefs of a conspirasy of priviledged murderers & robbers whose impunity has been the consecration of crime. (Text based on *SC* vi 966–7)

S.'s citation is from Milton's preamble to *The Doctrine & Discipline of Divorce* (1643): 'Let not England forget her precedence of teaching nations how to live' (*Complete Prose Works of John Milton*, Volume II: 1643–1648, ed. Ernest Sirluck (1959) 232). The above passage resonates with Milton's view, and indeed, the structure of this section of Chapter I of *PVR* follows that of Milton's historical discussion of cause and effect in *The Doctrine*. Milton's voice persists in S.'s letters and his reading; during the period when S. was preparing to begin his work on *Charles the First*, he requests the Gisbornes in England to add to a shipment 'Miltons prose works' which he notes were 'among my own books' (?7 July 1820) (*L* ii 212); (these may have been the volumes he ordered from Hookham on 29 July 1812 (*L* i 319)). Almost two weeks later he writes to Medwin of his plans to write a play on Charles the First (*L* ii 219–20). Another essay by Milton, written in the same year as *Eikonoklastes*, similarly addresses the dangers of monarchical governments. *The Tenure of Kings and Magistrates* (1649) presents the argument for the justification of the murder of a tyrant; one passage, with its powerful citation from Seneca followed by Milton's translation, could serve as a précis for the views of the regicide accounts which S. sought out:

The *Greeks* and *Romans*, as thir prime Authors witness, held it not onely lawfull, but a glorious and Heroic deed, rewarded publicly with Statues and Garlands, to kill an infamous Tyrant at any time without tryal: and but reason, that he who trod down all Law, should not be voutsaf'd the benefit of Law. Insomuch that *Seneca* the Tragedian brings in *Hercules* the grand suppressor of Tyrants, thus speaking,

> _____ *Victima haud ulla amplior*
> *Potest, magisque opima mactari Jovi*
> *Quam Rex iniquus* _____
> _____ There can be slaine
> No sacrifice to God more acceptable
> Then an unjust and wicked King _____ _____ (*The Complete Works of John Milton*, Volume VI: Vernacular Regicide and Republican Writings, eds N. H. Keeble and Nicholas McDowell (2013) 162)

Mary's reading of both *Ludlow* and *Hutchinson 1806* (see above; *Mary Jnl* i 374–5) within a day of each other is perhaps an indication of the arrival of the long-awaited box from England aboard the ship *Amy*. On 28 May 1821, Mary writes to Maria Gisborne, 'We have heard that the Amy is arrived, and as it contains a most interesting Box for us, let me intreat you to send it, (the parcel, not the Amy) directed to Casa Silva, as quickly as you can —' (*Mary L* i 200). Again, on 1 June, she mentions the all-important box to Maria Gisborne: 'Perhaps by this time our parcel from the Amy is on its way to us — but we have yet heard nothing about it, and are anxious to see it' (*Mary L* i 201). Importantly, in a 5 June letter to the Gisbornes, S. bemoans the fact that the box had not yet arrived, writing, 'My unfortunate Box! it contained a chaos of the elements of Charles the first' (*L* ii 294) which gives reason to assume the *Hutchinson Life* and *Ludlow 1771* volumes might well have been among S.'s 'elements of Charles the first'. Three days later, Mary writes to Maria Gisborne, 'Our box has been found on board the "Amy."' (*Mary L* iii 400), and it can be conjectured that sometime around 8 June the Shelleys received their box. It can also be assumed that the box contained Godwin's answer to Malthus. In a 21 February 1821 letter to Maria Gisborne, Mary writes, 'We are promised soon several boxes from England — containing (one of them) Papa's answer to Malthus which perhaps you are curious to see —' (*Mary L* i 184). It was not until months later, 18–22 June, that Mary records reading Malthus followed by

Godwin's answer to Malthus on 23–4 June, a period which coincides with the arrival of the long-awaited box earlier that month (*Mary Jnl* i 370–1). Although an inventory is missing for the important box that the Shelleys finally received in June 1821, it seems likely that several items not listed in Mary's journals or reading lists may well have been included among the 'chaos of the elements of Charles the first'. Such items would probably have included *Vane, Whitelocke, Reliquiae Sacrae Carolinae, Eikon Basilike* as well as those materials both S. and Mary began reading in summer 1821, *Hutchinson Life* and *Ludlow 1771*.

The preoccupation of criticism with historical sources for S.'s drama has tended to obscure S.'s literary influences and models of inspiration. In a conversation recorded by Trelawny, S. acknowledged that his key literary influence for *Charles the First* was Shakespeare:

> I am now writing a play for the stage. It is affectation to say we write a play for any other purpose. The subject is from English history; in style and manner I shall approach as near our great dramatist as my feeble powers will permit. King Lear is my model, for that is nearly perfect. (*Recollections* 76–7)

S. had previously noted his admiration for *Lear* in *DP*, writing '*King Lear* … may be judged to be the most perfect specimen of the dramatic art existing in the world'. In particular, S. remarks that 'the comedy should be as in *King Lear* universal, ideal, and sublime' (*Reiman (2002)* para. 15). Consequently, S. models Archy the Fool on *Lear's* Fool in his use of riddles, puns, songs, and visionary truth-telling. Medwin notes that Archy's character was also inspired by Calderón, whose works S. had been reading and translating contemporaneously with the conception and composition of *Charles the First*:

> Shelley meant to have made the last of king's fools, Archy, a more than subordinate among his dramatis personæ, as Calderon has done in his *Cisma de L'Ingalaterra*, a fool *sui generis*, who talks in fable, "weaving a world of mirth out of the wreck of all around." (*Medwin* ii 166)

That S. would have been crafting a role for a fool who was 'more than subordinate' seems inevitable given the analysis of that role by August Schlegel in *A Course of Lectures on Dramatic Art and Literature*, trans. John Black, 2 vols (1815) (*Schlegel (1815)*), which S. read aloud to Mary and Claire, 16–21 March 1818, during their journey to Italy (*Mary Jnl* i 198–9). (See headnote for *Cyprian* for a discussion of S.'s view of Shakespeare and Calderón through the lens of Schlegel.) More than merely the 'mirth' (ii 104) that Medwin notes, it is Archy's wisdom which resonates in his speeches, a feature that Schlegel discerns in Shakespeare's fools:

> It is well known that they frequently told such truths to princes as are never now told to them. Shakspeare's fools, along with somewhat of an overstraining for wit, … have for the most part an incomparable humour, and an infinite abundance of intellect, enough to supply a whole host of ordinary wise men. (*Schlegel (1815)* ii 145)

While the Fool in *Lear* and Pasquín in *La cisma* certainly contributed to Archy's characterisation, Macaulay's and Hume's accounts of Archibald 'Archy' Armstrong's presence in Charles's court fleshed out S.'s portrait of Charles's jester. The jottings in *Nbk 19* found on p. 33 and p. 182 *reverso*, which precedes S.'s first lines for Scene i and iii, include more notes for Archy than any other character, demonstrating his essential role in S.'s overall plan. It could be argued that Archy's significant position in S.'s drama might be the voice that is most akin to S.'s own. Archy alone has two sets of entrances and exits in Scene ii; he spars with two central figures, Wentworth and Laud; he has a strong relationship with both the King and Queen; he is the single figure who is allowed a wide range of spoken discourse, including lengthy prose passages, blank verse, and lyrics and songs with varying prosodic forms. Armstrong purportedly published his own account of the events leading to his ejection from court that S. refers to in Scene ii. *Archy's Dream* (1641), a quasi-autobiographical work, includes a vision of the Archbishop's voyage to hell, presumably in retaliation for the punishment Laud had inflicted on him. It seems unlikely, however, that S. would have known of this pamphlet (for a discussion of Archy's position and role in the courts of James and Charles see Andrea Shannon, '"Uncouth language to a Princes ears": Archibald Armstrong, Court Jester, and Early Stuart Politics', *Sixteenth Century Journal* xlii (2011) 99–112).

Discussions of Shakespeare's influence on S. usually focus on poetic language (see Newman Ivey White, 'Shelley's *Charles the First*', *JEGP* xxi (1922) 439; hereafter *White (1922)* and David Lee Clark, 'Shelley and Shakespeare', *PMLA* liv (1939) 270–1; hereafter *Clark*). For example, John of Gaunt's speech (*Richard II* II i 45–74) provides language and imagery for the dialogue between Hampden and Vane in Scene iii; however,

Shakespeare's influence extends to other compositional features. S. himself describes his play as 'The Historical Tragedy of "Charles the First"', thus indicating Shakespeare's historical dramas as apposite models with their examination of contentious religious and political questions and the scope of their settings and structure (*L* ii 372). Among S.'s reading notes from *Hume* and *Whitelocke*, he comments on the issue of monopolies and taxes, adding 'See Richard 2^d. —' (*Nbk 21* p. 251 rev.). Richard's eager grasping for money to fund a war, taxing the people, and fining the nobles are the same crimes of overreach committed by Charles. In terms of character, Richard's moments of arbitrary and changeable behaviour are echoed in Charles's arbitrariness and reversal of decision, particularly in his suddenly succumbing to Laud's call for war in Scotland in Scene ii. Moreover, Richard's trajectory from king to murdered prisoner would offer a parallel to Charles's reign, imprisonment, and execution. *Richard II*, however, is not the only play of Shakespeare that S. could have drawn from; themes of patriotism, English nationalism, loyalty, treachery, war, peace, and court intrigue are all explored in the history plays which S. kept returning to throughout 1818 to 1820, including *Henry IV*, Parts 1 and 2, *Henry V*, *Henry VI*, Parts 1, 2, and 3, *Henry VIII*, *King John*, and *Richard III*. Of these history plays, Schegel writes:

> This mirror of kings should be the manual of young princes: they may learn from it the inward dignity of their hereditary vocation, but they will also learn the difficulties of their situation, the dangers of usurpation, the inevitable fall of tyranny, which buries itself under its attempts to obtain a firmer foundation; lastly, the ruinous consequences of the weakness, errors, and crimes of kings, for whole nations, and many subsequent generations. (*Schlegel (1815)* ii 218)

Such a distillation of drama's 'mirror' of monarchy could have hardly failed to impress S., with its outline for characterisation, political realities, and dramatic arc.

Milton's poetical works related to the political upheavals of his time addressed the complex nature of establishing a just government, and his set of republican sonnets were particularly apropos to S.'s play. For example, Sonnet xvi, addressed to Cromwell (first published in 1694), sets out the great work achieved and yet to be done in turning from war to peace. Possibly contributing to S.'s characterisation of Vane is Sonnet xvii, which Milton sent to Vane on 3 July 1652. Here, the poet honours 'Vane, young in years, but in sage counsel old' for his ability to balance the demands of 'spiritual power and civil' (ll. 1, 10) (John Milton, *Complete Shorter Poems*, ed. John Carey, 2nd edn (1998) 330–1). That same balance which Milton discerns also appears in S.'s portrait of the young Vane. Challenging Hampden's determination to escape the tyranny of England for the New World, Vane contends that remaining in England is the difficult but more responsible action; he asks of Hampden:

> What — wilt thou leave thy mother in her woe?
> What — canst thou desert this dear nurse of men,
> This land, this home, this England, — this appointed
> Station for death and life? — (iii 41–4)

S. would also have known Wordsworth's 'Sonnets dedicated to Liberty', inspired by a reading of Milton's sonnets by his sister Dorothy in 1801 (*The Fenwick Notes of William Wordsworth*, ed. Jared Curtis (2007) 73). Philip Connell ('Wordsworth's "Sonnets Dedicated to Liberty" and the British Revolutionary Past', *ELH* lxxxv (2018) 747–74) examines Wordsworth's 'ideological retrenchment' (749) against the background of the French Revolution, the Napoleonic threat, and differing revaluations of England's Glorious Revolution of 1688. It is just this 'ideological retrenchment' that S. found unconscionable in Wordsworth when he told Peacock in a letter of 25 July 1818, 'What a beastly and pitiful wretch that Wordsworth! That such a man should be such a poet!' (*L* ii 26). While S. would have concurred with Wordsworth's depiction of the nobility of 'Sydney, Marvel, Harrington, / Young Vane, and others who call'd Milton Friend' (Sonnet 15: 'Great Men have been among us; hands that penn'd', ll. 3–4, in *Poems, in Two Volumes* (1807) (hereafter *Wordsworth (1807)*) i 141), S. chafed at the older poet's blind adherence to English nationalism and his abandonment of democratic ideals for a personal security guaranteed by power and privilege. One passage in *Charles* Scene iii appears to be a riposte to Wordsworth's apostasy: Hampden's speech, beginning at 'Fair star' (iii 23–38) transposes and subverts Wordsworth's 'Fair Star of Evening, Splendor of the West' (Sonnet 1: 'Composed by the Sea-side, near Calais, August, 1802' in *Wordsworth (1807)* i 127). Hampden, looking towards the western sky, is anxious to set sail for the New World and escape the tyranny of an England whose 'vaporous horizon' is 'like a dungeon's grate'; Wordsworth anxiously looks towards England from France's shore, seeing 'my Country' (l. 2) as a refuge of peace and stability. Where Hampden's evening star's 'beam lies o'er the wide Atlantic', Wordsworth's 'hangest, stooping, as might seem, to sink / On England's bosom' (ll. 3–4). Where

Wordsworth's star reassures with its immobility, Hampden's inspires with kinetic energy.

Godwin's *Mandeville. A Tale of the Seventeenth Century in England*, 3 vols (1817) — set some years after the action of *Charles* but coloured by those events — created a powerful reaction in S. Writing to Godwin on 7 December 1817 after reading the novel (*L* i 573–4), he was fulsome in his praise; so much so that Godwin, pleased by his comments, forwarded them to the *Morning Chronicle* which published them as 'Extract of a Letter from Oxfordshire' ((9 December 1817) 3). S. reacted immediately (11 December 1817), writing to Godwin, 'As it is, I cannot but be gratified that you should think any opinion of mine relating to your book worthy of being presented to the public' and adding that he had written 'a more copious statement' (*L* i 577) which he had sent to the *Examiner* where it was published on 28 December 1817 (826–7). Signing himself 'E.[lfin] K.[night]', S. writes of *Mandeville* that 'It is a wind which tears up the deepest waters of the ocean of mind' (*Prose Works* 279). Charles Mandeville, a student at Winchester College is an innocent victim of planted evidence: a book of subversive anti-royalist prints is found in his room. Mandeville vividly describes several prints, all mocking the murdered Charles, and one seems particularly relevant to Wentworth's view of Parliament in the second scene of S.'s play:

> Another print represented Charles with a sword drawn, a dragon with many heads opposite, and Strafford standing near the king, to lend him his aid. The dragon erected its crest with conscious superiority, and thrust out its forked tongue; while the king shrunk frightened at his own temerity, and seemed preparing to seek his safety in flight. Underneath was written, "As for that hydra, the parliament, take good heed! You know I have found it here cunning, as well as malicious." (*Godwin Novels* iii 98)

Besides Shakespeare's plays, S. was reading other theatrical works from the period, a seemingly natural preparation in developing his own play of the Caroline era. S. wrote to Ollier, 22 February 1821, requesting '"Old English Drama", 3 vols.' In this same letter he also discusses his drama: 'I doubt about "Charles the First"; but, if I do write it, it shall be the birth of severe and high feelings' (*L* ii 269–70). It seems likely that the three-volume set of dramas that S. had ordered in February was also included in the Shelleys' box: in the flurry of Mary's reading Malthus, Godwin, *Hutchinson 1806* and *Ludlow 1771* from mid-June to mid-July 1821, she also records reading 'Old Plays' on 14–17, 25 June, and continuing until

17 July (*Mary Jnl* i 370–4). (Mary records reading '2 plays in the ancient drama' on 26 February 1818, but this was during their stay in lodgings in London before their departure for Italy, and it is likely this volume had been lent to her by the Hunts or Peacock for she records no other reading of old dramas until the 1821 summer (*Mary Jnl* i 195)). *The Ancient British Drama*, 3 vols (1810) (hereafter *British Drama*), generally agreed to be edited by Sir Walter Scott, was a collection of plays written during the 'reigns of ELIZABETH, JAMES, and CHARLES THE FIRST' and selected in large part from an earlier publication, *A Select Collection of Old Plays* (1744) edited by Richard Dodsley (*British Drama* i p. vi). The editors of *Mary Jnl* note that it was probably the three-volume Scott edition rather than Dodsley's twelve-volume edition which S. intended to order. (They and the editor of *L* entitle *British Drama* incorrectly as *Ancient English Drama*.)

Beyond the Scott collection of sixteenth- and seventeenth-century plays, Mary records S.'s frequent reading from Beaumont and Fletcher (*The Dramatic Works of Ben Jonson, and Beaumont and Fletcher*, 4 vols (1811), hereafter *Dramatic Works*) (*Mary Jnl* i 218–19, 295, 298, 317). During the same period as his reading of Hume's *History* in the summer of 1818, S. read Beaumont and Fletcher's *A Maid's Tragedy* (9 July; *Mary Jnl* i 218). Stuart Curran identified a likely link between Beaumont and Fletcher's use of the masque and S.'s play: '*Charles the First*, whose promising first scene, enacted before a masque, establishes its radical perspective with an immediate paraphrase of the satiric lines from *The Maid's Tragedy*' (*Curran (1975)* 189). Act I opens with two gentlemen, Cleon and Strato discussing the upcoming mask with Lysippus; Lysippus asks,

> Stato, thou hast some skill in poetry,
> What think'st thou of the masque? will it be well? (I i 4–5)

With an almost identical question, 'What thinkest thou of this quaint masque ... ?', S. opens his Scene i (l. 2); furthermore, a similar question is asked in the last third of Scene i at ll. 136–7. Even among S.'s jotting notes preceding the play, a partial version of this question appears: *What think you* (*Nbk 19* p. 183 rev.). The importance of the question posed about the masque becomes apparent: it is the framework for Scene i and is the topic for the King's and Queen's first speeches in Scene ii. S.'s first scene, a reconstruction of the four Inns of Court progression as described by Whitelocke, includes an antimasque, a characteristic of the masque genre. Whitelocke makes clear that there were two presentations of both the progression and the masque performance: the first progression moved through the London streets beginning at *'Ely-house* in *Holborn'* and then 'down *Chancery-Lane* to *Whitehall'* where the masque would be performed in the Banqueting House (19). Whitelocke provides the reason for the second performance:

> The *Queen* who was much delighted with these Solemnities, was so taken with this Show and Masque, that she desired to see it acted over again: whereupon an Intimation being given to the Lord Mayor of *London*, he Invited the *King* and *Queen*, and the *Inns of Court Masquers* to the *City*, and entertained them with all state and magnificence, at *Merchant-taylors Hall.*
>
> Thither marched through the *City* the same Show, that went before to *Whitehall,* and the same *Masque* was again presented to them in the *City*; (*Whitelocke* 21)

Among S.'s initial jottings for the drama, his SD notes (*Nbk 19* p. 184 rev.) give *Scene the pageant [at the] to please [arrival] of the Queen* which makes clear that it was this second presentation which framed S.'s first scene as well as the opening to Scene ii. Crook provides a helpful discussion on the probable progression route through the City of London (*BSM* xii 130). Whitelocke never mentions James Shirley, the author of *The Triumph of Peace. A Masque, presented by the Foure Honourable Houses, or Innes of Court* (1633) or the stage designer, Inigo Jones, and thus S. was probably unaware of the masque's authorship. Moreover, as Cameron notes, it seems unlikely 'that Shelley would have an edition of Shirley's work with him in Italy, as Shirley is a writer in whom he had little if any interest' (Kenneth Neill Cameron, 'Shelley's Use of Source Material in *Charles I', MLQ* vi (1945) 197–210 (*Cameron (1945)*), 199 n.). Shirley's MS 'stage directions' and choreography for the masque's progression, 'The manner of the progression of the masque, [The triumph of peace] [manuscript], 1634' is located in the Folger Shakespeare Library (Hamnet call number: Z.3.1 (25)).

Although Shirley's authorship of the masque was probably unknown to S., he was familiar with Leigh Hunt's masque, *The Descent of Liberty* (1815) (*Hunt 1815*); the volume is included in the Marlow book sale list (Pforz MS (S'ANA) f. 3^r). Writing from Surrey Jail, Hunt states in his preface, 'The following piece was written … chiefly to express the feelings of hope and delight, with which every enthusiastic lover of freedom must have witnessed the downfall of the great Apostate from Liberty' (*Hunt 1815* v). Hunt's decision to present the defeat of Napoleon as a masque was adopted by S. four years later to address a national tragedy, the Peterloo massacre.

Hunt's pastoral treatment of the genre couched in cloudy vistas and floral catalogues contrasts sharply with S.'s rousing quatrains, vigorous, popular language and unleashed outrage in *MA* (no. 231). Nevertheless, despite these differences, both Hunt's and S.'s treatment of the masque removed it from the aristocratic audience for whom most masques were traditionally intended, resulting in a democratisation of the genre. Similarly, in *Charles the First*, S. takes advantage of Whitelocke's antimasque description to give the people a compelling voice that counterbalances the nobles' sophisticated but deadly speeches in the following Whitehall scene. Hunt's *Descent of Liberty* volume also included a history of the masque genre that would have been of interest to S. as well. Hunt singles out several works including Beaumont and Fletcher's *The Masque of the Inner-Temple and Gray's Inn* (*Dramatic Works* iv 569–74) and *The Maid's Tragedy* (*Dramatic Works* ii 1–36). In fact, Hunt includes the opening scene between Lysippus and Stato cited above, with the line which S. adapts for the opening of his Scene i (*Hunt 1815* xxxv).

S.'s varied and constant reading of plays from Shakespeare, Beaumont and Fletcher, Goethe, and Calderón would certainly inform his attention to dramaturgy, but another likely source of influence in constructing a drama for the stage was his frequent attendance at not only plays but also operas (for a list of performances seen by S., see Jacqueline Mulhallen, *The Theatre of Shelley* (2010) 243–56). According to Ronald Tetreault, S.'s own opera-going repertoire reflects the musical tastes of Regency London ('Shelley at the Opera' *ELH* xlviii (1981) 144–71); however, it also reflects Peacock's musical preferences. Just prior to S.'s departure from England in spring 1818, he attended the opera regularly, often in the company of Peacock. In fact, after Peacock's introduction to it, opera-going became a regular habit for the Shelleys during their peripatetic life in Italy; Mary's and Claire's journals for 1817–22 record S.'s attendance at approximately forty opera performances. Of S.'s first experiences in London, Peacock writes:

> In the season of 1817, I persuaded him to accompany me to the opera. The performance was *Don Giovanni*. Before it commenced he asked me if the opera was comic or tragic. I said it was composite,—more comedy than tragedy. After the killing of the Commendatore, he said, 'Do you call this comedy?' By degrees he became absorbed in the music and action. ... From this time till he finally left England he was an assiduous frequenter of the Italian Opera. He delighted in the music of Mozart, and especially in the *Nozze di Figaro*, which

was performed several times in the early part of 1818. (*Peacock Works* viii 81–2)

S. also saw the first London performance of Rossini's *Barber of Seville*, but it was Mozart's *Don Giovanni* which he saw on five occasions (*Mary Jnl* i 170, 192–7, *Claire Jnl* 83–6), suggesting that he overcame his concerns about the mixing of comedy with tragedy. His comments in *DP* already noted above might well have been provoked by this discussion with Peacock, and it is possible that Archy's key role in Scene ii demonstrates S.'s attempt to create an acceptable dramatic form possessing a 'blending of comedy with tragedy'. More obvious, however, is that the attention to dramatic structure and scene construction in *Charles the First*, evidenced in his schema in *Nbk 22* and the draft in *Nbk 19*, reflect that interest and preoccupation with operatic and theatrical strategies. The play's four scenes alternate from outdoor venues to interiors: the formal, courtly 'chamber in Whitehall' scene follows the energetic London street scenes of the Masque progression; the exterior scene on the Thames with its London cityscape backlit by the evening's western horizon precedes the claustrophobic and menacing interior scene set in the Star Chamber. Moreover, there is an operatic quality in the disposition of the speeches, with duets, trios, quartets and choruses alternating and playing off one another. The Old Man's speech at the start of the play, serves as a kind of overture, presaging themes and foretelling outcomes, much as Mozart's overtures prefigure the scenes and melodies of *Don Giovanni*. In Scene ii, the argumentative trio of Charles, Laud and Wentworth eventually resolves; Archy sings a departing song and then leaves the stage to a duet between Charles and Henrietta. The close of Scene ii is one that narrows the public world of the earlier rancorous political drama to a quiet and intimate domestic scene.

The discussion in *Medwin* of S.'s design 'to write a tragedy on this ungrateful subject' was the first to bring together three different types of sources for *Charles the First*: a seventeenth-century pamphlet (*Killing No Murder*), an historical account (*Hume*), and a dramatic text (Calderón's *La cisma de Inglaterra*). It was not until the twentieth century that scholars began to evaluate the contributions of S.'s preparatory reading and to acknowledge the seriousness with which he approached the historical drama; however, that work has primarily focused on historical sources rather than literary ones. *Cameron (1945)* identifies S.'s key historical texts read in preparation for his play as *Whitelocke*, *Clarendon*, *Hume* and *Macaulay*. Woodings in *Woodings (1969)* challenges what he perceives to be Cameron's emphasis on *Macaulay*; linking S.'s reading notes in *Nbk 21* and his schema in *Nbk*

22 to the draft MS in *Nbk 19*, Woodings finds that *Hume* represents a more important source. To insist too strongly on any one source, however, does not seem warranted, especially in the light of S.'s documented, vigorous search for a variety of materials, his admitted strategy to present an unprejudiced view, and the prehensile nature of his reading habits.

Historical context. S.'s seventeenth-century sources generally employed the Julian calendar; although the New Year was celebrated on 1 January, the legal calendar determined the year's official start for royal and parliamentary affairs. Consequently, in that context, the year began on 25 March, the Annunciation, also known as Lady Day. *Whitelocke*, for example, follows the legal year when assigning dates and, in keeping with the Parliamentary record, gives the execution of Charles as 30 January 1648. Later historians, like Hume and Macaulay writing after the adoption of the Gregorian calendar in 1752, adjust the date of Charles's execution to 1649.

Although S. would not be rigorously constrained by those well-researched histories — he often compresses time and conflates events — in general, he follows the sequence of Charles's 'Historical Tragedy' beginning in the tenth year of his reign. The play's first scene opens in February 1634, or 1633 in Whitelocke's account where he writes, 'The time for presenting of this Masque at *White-Hall*, was agreed to be on *Candlemas* Night to end *Christmas*' (19). Candlemas is normally 2 February, forty days after 25 December, marking the end of Epiphanytide. The King's fool Archy refers to 'the last day of the holydays' (ii 425) confirming this seasonal setting for the first two scenes as well.

The political themes of Scene ii— ship-money, Scottish resistance, the recall of Parliament, and the thwarting of the planned immigration to America by a group of 'rebels', discussed by Charles, Laud, Strafford and Cottington — belong to a more expanded period of time, roughly 1634–8. In the first case, although the tax via ship-money had been introduced during Charles's reign as early as 1626, the decision to expand its reach in 1634 was seen as 'unlawfull', thus causing much dissent. Whitelocke records this ill-advised change to the tax:

> And by advice of his Privy Council, and Council Learned, the King requires *Shipmoney*. The Writ for it was at first but to Maritime Towns and Counties; but that not sufficing, other Writs were Issued out, to all Counties to levy *Shipmoney*. (*Whitelocke* 22)

Military plans to punish Scotland for her stubbornness in resisting proposed changes to the liturgy and the Church's organisation are recommended by Laud in the play (ii 364–72) and were eventually carried out in the Scottish wars in 1639 and 1640. Charles had dissolved Parliament in 1626 which explains Cottington's and Laud's arguments for 'the assembling of a parliament' (ii 375) in order to help secure funds for the treasury. Historically, the King did finally call for a Parliament (known as the Short Parliament) in April 1640 only to dissolve it three weeks later. Following the Crown's defeat in the second Scottish war, the King once again called for a Parliament in the autumn of 1640 (known as the Long Parliament). The order for the detention of the rebels which Laud demands (ii 404–8) establishes the characters and setting for Scene iii and is recorded in Hume as an event of 1637 (vii 216), The Scene iv fragment set in the Star Chamber — the trial of Bastwick and Williams, Bishop of Lincoln — is taken from events of 1637 (*Whitelocke* 24–5).

S. seems to have deliberately brought together in Act I the issues of ship-money, the Scottish wars, the calling of Parliament (Scene ii), and the rebels' attempted flight (Scene iii) in order to form the main threads for action in Act II as outlined in his schema in *Nbk 22*. With regard to Act $2^{d.}$, S. writes, *This Act to open [after] between the two Scotch Wars* (*Nbk 22* ff. *3ʳ, *4ʳ). On f. *3ʳ he provides more details: *Act $2^{d.}$ Scene 1 Chiefs of the Popular Party, Hampden's trial & its effects*. John Hampden, the eloquent rebel voice of Scene iii who seeks exile, challenged the imposition of ship-money, and his trial in 1637 ended somewhat inconclusively. Hume notes:

> Notwithstanding these reasons, the prejudiced judges, four excepted, gave sentence in favour of the crown. Hambden, however, obtained by the trial the end for which he had so generously sacrificed his safety and his quiet: the people were roused from their lethargy, and became sensible of the danger to which their liberties were exposed. (vii 223)

The MS schema concludes Act II with the phrase *The End — Straffords death* (*Nbk 22* *f. 4ʳ) which is anticipated in Scene ii by Wentworth's repeated appeals to the King to 'assemble not / A parliament' or, at the very least, to delay it (ii 341–2; see also ll. 309–14, 380–3). His distrust of Parliament was justified. One of the first actions of the Long Parliament of 1640 was to impeach Wentworth, who, only months before (January 1640), had been created Earl of Strafford by the King. When the impeachment failed, the Commons launched a bill of attainder against him, which was successful; as a result of the bill, Wentworth, Earl of Strafford, was executed on 13 April 1641.

S. is inconsistent in naming this key character in the MS: *Wentworth* and *Strafford* are both arbitrarily employed in speaker headings as well as names by which he is addressed throughout the play. Despite Crook's view that this change is deliberate because S. 'is applying "double time" similar to the later (1849–50) theorized solution to the temporal anomalies that perplexed critics of *Othello*' (*BSM* xii p. xlvi), there does not seem a need for such a complex interpretation. S. was moving among numerous sources which used both names, and ahistorical slips were likely; furthermore, no apparent pattern emerges in his denomination of Wentworth/Strafford. Given that none of the play's extant scenes depict events of 1640 by which time Wentworth was given the title 'Earl of Strafford', 'Wentworth' is used in the present edition, following Mary's decision in *1824* as well as S.'s historical sources. Hume and Macaulay generally use 'Wentworth' until Charles created him 'Earl of Strafford' in January 1640.

Criticism. Hazlitt's judgement of the *1824* text in *Edinburgh Review* xl (1824) 509 is somewhat reserved: 'In the unfinished scenes of Charles I., (a drama on which Mr Shelley was employed at his death) the *radical* humour of the author breaks forth, but "in good set terms" and specious oratory. We regret that his premature fate has intercepted this addition to our historical drama. From the fragments before us, we are not sure that it would be fair to give any specimen'. The principal critical accounts of the play and its sources since the late C19 are as follows: H. S. Salt, *A Shelley Primer* (1887) 77–8; *White (1922)* 431–41; Walter Francis Wright, 'Shelley's Failure in *Charles I*', *ELH* viii (1941) 41–6; *Cameron (1945)*; Raymond D. Havens, '*Hellas* and *Charles the First*', *SP* xliii (1946) 545–50; *Woodings (1968a)*; *Woodings (1969)*; *Cameron (1974)* 411–21; Joan Mandell Baum, *The Theatrical Compositions of The Major English Romantic Poets* (1980) 203–16; Richard Cronin, *Shelley's Poetic Thoughts* (1981) 51–3; David Norbrook, 'The reformation of the masque', in *The Court Masque*, ed. David Lindley (1984) 94–110; Kenneth Johnston and Joseph Nicholes, 'Transitory Actions, Men Betrayed: The French Revolution in the English Revolution in Romantic Drama', *The Wordsworth Circle* xxiii (1992) 76–96; Steven Jones, '"Choose Reform or Civil War": Shelley, the English Revolution, and the Problem of Succession', *The Wordsworth Circle* xxv (1994) 145–9; William Jewett, 'History's Lethean Song: *Charles the First* and *The Triumph of Life*', in *Fatal autonomy: Romantic Drama and the Rhetoric of Agency* (1997) 205–53; Greg Kucich, '"This Horrid Theatre of Human Sufferings": Gendering the Stages of History in Catharine Macaulay and Percy Bysshe Shelley', in *Lessons of Romanticism: a critical companion*, eds Thomas Pfau and Robert F. Gleckner (1998) 448–65; Timothy Morton and Nigel Smith, 'Introduction', in *Radicalism in British Literary Culture, 1650–1830: From Revolution to Revolution*, eds Timothy Morton and Nigel Smith (2002) 5–7; Jeffrey N. Cox, 'The dramatist', in

The Cambridge Companion to Shelley, ed. Timothy Morton (2006) 65–84; Michael Rossington, 'Shelley's republics', in *Repossessing the Romantic Past*, eds Heather Glen and Paul Hamilton (2006), 63–79; *Crook (2007)*; *Crook (2009)*; Jacqueline Mulhallen, 'Turning History into Art — Charles the First', in *The Theatre of Shelley* (2010) 115–46.

Text from *Nbk 19* pp. 182 rev.–156 rev. (Scene i); *Nbk 19* pp. 156 rev.–127 rev., 125 rev.–116 rev., 114 rev.–101 rev., 52 rev. (Scene ii); *Nbk 19* pp. 41–3, 45–51, 55, Stub K (Scene iii 1–91, part of 93, part of 103); *Box 1* f. 136 (Scene iii 92, part of 93, 94–102, part of 103); *Nbk 19* pp. 101 rev.–95 rev., 93b rev. (Scene iv). MS punctuation has, in general, been followed; departures are indicated in the notes. Verse indentation follows the MS. *Dramatis personae* adapted from *Forman 1876–7* with additions from *Nbk 22* schema and *Nbk 19* scene headings; additions to the *Dramatis personae* include speakers and addressees in speeches who are otherwise omitted in MS and *Forman 1876–7*. Stage directions and speaker assignments are supplied from *Nbk 19, 1824* and *Rossetti 1870*; omitted but necessary stage directions and speakers are added editorially and are so indicated in the notes. S. is inconsistent in his designation of 'King Charles' using both *King* or *Charles* throughout the draft; *1824* and *Rossetti* standardise as 'King'. The present edition employs both title and proper name; that same standardisation applies to 'Queen Henrietta'.

Published in *1824* 237–48 (Scene i 1–5, 10–19, 22–33, 35–9, 41–2, 44–8, 67–74, 76–7, 79–80, 83–7, 90–1, part of 133, 134–7, 147–52, 154–61, part of 162, 163–9, 174, 177–97, 200–7, part of 208; Scene ii 2–3, part of 5, part of 10, 11–18, 20, 23–4, part of 25, 89–93, 100–2, part of 103, 104–20, 132–46, part of 147, part of 264, 265–77, 280, part of 284, 285, 489–93, part of 494–5, 496–518, part of 519; Scene iii 1–5, 13–40, 47–9, part of 50, 54–7, part of 60, 61–9; Scene iv omitted); *Relics* 91 (Scene iii part of 93); *Rossetti 1870* 373–94 (Scene i 40, 43, 49–60, part of 62–3, 64–5, 81–2, 92–3, 95–101, 105–12, 115–30, part of 140, part of 162, 175–6; Scene ii 2–3, part of 5, 6–10, 21–2, 27–33, 35–65, part of 66, 67–88, part of 103, 121, part of 147, 148–64, 172–208, 212–23, part of 225, 226–31, part of 232, 236–57, 259–63, part of 264, 278–9, 281–3, part of 284, 286–98, part of 299, part of 301, 302–79, part of 380, 381–96, 398–420, part of 421–2, 423–57, 459–88, [part of 475, 476–88 published as 'Scene v'], part of 519, 520–23; Scene iii [published as 'Scene iv'] 70–2; Scene iv [published as 'Scene iii'] 1–31, part of 32, 33–63; *Woodings (1968a)* 224–5, 231–2 (Scene ii 4; Scene iii 6, part of 7, 8, 11–12, 42–3, part of 44, part of 45–6, 47–8, part of 49, 76–9, 83–5, part of 93); *Crook (2009)* 302–3 (Scene iii 73–4,

85–91); *BSM* xii 70–109, 114–15, 120–3, 144–207, 210–327 (facsimile and transcription of MS).

Charles the First

DRAMATIS PERSONAE

KING CHARLES I.
QUEEN HENRIETTA.
LAUD, ARCHBISHOP OF CANTERBURY.
WENTWORTH, EARL OF STRAFFORD.
LORD COTTINGTON.
LORD WESTON.
LORD ESSEX.
SIR HENRY VANE, THE ELDER
LORD KEEPER COVENTRY.
NOY, ATTORNEY GENERAL.
WILLIAMS, BISHOP OF LINCOLN.
LITTELTON, SECRETARY.
JUXON.
SIR JOHN FINCH.
ARCHY, THE COURT FOOL.
HAMPDEN.
PYM.
CROMWELL.
CROMWELL'S DAUGHTER.
SIR HARRY VANE, THE YOUNGER.
HAZELRIG.
LEIGHTON.
BASTWICK.
PRYNNE.
PURSUIVANTS, MARSHALMAN, GENTLEMEN OF THE INNS OF COURT, CITIZENS, CLERK.

¶ **426** *Title.* See headnote 'Date of composition' and 'Publication'.
Dramatis Personae. S. provides only the briefest list as a DP in *Nbk 19* p. 185 *reverso.* Arranged in two columns, the first reads *Charles / Henrietta / Laud* and the second *Pym / Hampden / Cromwell / Sir H. Vane.* However, as Crook notes, it is 'Not so much a Dramatis Personae as a lining-up of Royalists and Republicans' (*BSM* xii 326). As discussed in the Headnote, *Forman 1876-7* was the first edition to provide a more inclusive DP that has been followed by subsequent *eds*. The present DP emends Forman's list to include characters who speak or are spoken to, or whose presence is indicated by S.'s own stage directions in the *Nbk 19* draft or the *Nbk 21* schema. *Forman 1876-7* omits LORD ESSEX, SIR HENRY VANE, the elder, NOY, Attorney General, SIR JOHN FINCH (who replaces ST. JOHN), and HAZELRIG. Descriptions of personages will be provided in subsequent notes on their first appearance.

ACT I

Scene i

The Masque of the Inns of Court before the Temple Bar: the Pageant to please the Queen. Enter BASTWICK, CITIZENS *including* OLD MAN, YOUNG MAN, LAW STUDENT. *Enter* LEIGHTON *who stands upstage in shadow. Enter a* PURSUIVANT.

Pursuivant
Place for the Marshal of the Masque!

Young Man
What thinkest thou of this quaint masque which [turns]
Like morning from the shadow of the night,
The night to day, and London to a place

SD. *Act I*] Omitted *Rossetti 1870*. *Nbk 22* f. *1ʳ schema gives: 'Act. 1.ˢᵗ The Masque / Scene 1. st —'. *The Masque ... Queen.*] Scene the pageant to please the Queen *Nbk 19* p. 184 rev.; The Pageant to [celebrate] the arrival of the Queen *1824*; The Masque of the Inns of Court *Rossetti 1870*. *Enter* BASTWICK ... *shadow.*] omitted in *Nbk 19* but some entrances noted during course of the scene: enter Leighton Bastwick & a citizen *Nbk 19* p. 172 rev.; omitted in *1824, Rossetti 1870*. Schema in *Nbk 22* f. *1ʳ gives: *Bastwick & citizens — to him enter Leighton: & afterwards An old man & a Law student. Enter* a PURSUIVANT.] Omitted in *Nbk 19, 1824, Rossetti 1870*.
1. SD. *Pursuivant*] A Pursuivant *1824, Rossetti 1870*. Omitted in *Nbk 19*. 'A royal or state messenger, esp. one with the power to execute warrants; a warrant officer' (*OED* 2a).
2. SD. First Speaker *1824*; First Citizen. *Rossetti 1870*. Omitted in *Nbk 19*. The speaker of ll. 2–5 is addressed as 'young man' in l. 6. Subsequent *eds* have tended to follow *Rossetti 1870* in speaker assignments in this scene as well as in the following three scenes.
2. *masque which [turns]*] masque, which turns, *1824, Rossetti 1870*. *What thinkest thou of this quaint masque which comes* is an earlier, uncancelled version of this line found at the top of *Nbk 19* p. 181 *reverso*. Curran (1975) identifies a parallel with Beaumont and Fletcher, *The Maid's Tragedy* I i 5: 'What think'st thou of the masque?' (see 'Sources, Genre and Form' in headnote).

5   Of peace and joy?

    Old Man
                        And Hell to Heaven?
    What should I think of it, young man, for sure,
    But of drunken children making merry
    With [?] [?] [?] on a father's grave,
    [?Are] flushed with our [?wasted] patrimony.
10 With all their mortal [?spoils], nine years are past,
    And they seem hours, since in this [populous] street,
    I trod on grass [made] lush by summer's rain,
    For the [red] Plague kept state within that palace
    Where now that Vanity reigns — in [nine] years more
15 The roots will be refreshed with civil blood. —
    I thank the mercy of insulted [Heaven]

5. SD. Omitted in *Nbk 19*; Second Speaker *1824*; Second Citizen *Rossetti 1870*.
5. *Heaven?*] Heaven, *1824*; Heaven! *Rossetti 1870*.
6–10. Omitted in all *eds*.
6. *What should I think of it*] A response and linking device to the Young Man's question in line 2.
7. The line originally began with *But of* [*a troop of drunkards*].
8. Blots and cancels make the MS particularly illegible here. *BSM* gives 'devils' for the third illegible word. *grave,*] grave *Nbk 19*.
9. *our [?wasted]*] their [?wasted] *BSM*. *patrimony.*] patrimony *Nbk 19*.
10. *1824* and *Rossetti 1870* give only part of this line, 'Eight years are gone'; however, *eight* is cancelled, and replaced by *nine* above, and *gone* canc. and replaced by *past* below. *[?spoils]*] [?sport] *BSM*. *nine*] [?fresh] *BSM*.
11. *[populous]*] populous *1824, Rossetti 1870*; replaced by *fragrant* in *Nbk 19* which is also cancelled. *street,*] street *1824, Rossetti 1870*.
12. *grass [made] lush*] Cp. the account of the London plague of 1625 in *Whitelocke* 2: 'he drove fast through the Streets, which were empty of People and overgrown with Grass'. *summer's rain*] Alt. from *Heaven's rain* in *Nbk 19*.
13. *the [red] Plague*] the red plague *1824*; the red Plague *Rossetti 1870*.
14. *Where now that Vanity reigns —*] Where now reigns vanity — *1824*; Where now that vanity reigns. *Rossetti 1870*. *in [nine]*] in nine *1824*; In nine *Rossetti 1870*. S.'s calculations of nine years before and after the date — 1633 (Gregorian) or 1634 (Julian) — of this scene's events, probably refer to the London plague in 1625 and the Civil War in 1642. *Whitelocke* uses the Gregorian calendar, which could explain the seeming discrepancy in S's calculation of the date.
15. *blood. —*] blood — *Nbk 19*; blood; *1824*; blood: — *Rossetti 1870*.
16. *I thank*] And thank *1824, Rossetti 1870*. *[Heaven]*] *Eds* do not indicate the cancellation of this word.

The sin and wrongs [?wound], as an orphan's cry,
The patience of the great avenger's ear. —

Young Man
Yet, father, 'tis a happy sight to see,
20 When [all] the fierce cares of [?furious] life
Keep Sabbath in the weary heart of man;
Avarice and tyranny, vigilant fear

17. *The*] That *1824, Rossetti 1870. sin and wrongs*] *1824, Rossetti 1870*; sin wrongs *Nbk 19*. *[?wound],*] wound *1824*; wound, *Rossetti 1870*.
18. *avenger's ear.* —] avenger's ear — *Nbk 19*; avenger's ear. *1824*; Avenger's ear. *Rossetti 1870*.
19. *SD*. Omitted in *Nbk 19* although large gap indicates speaker change; Third Speaker (*a youth*) *1824*; A Youth *Rossetti 1870*.
19. *to see,*] to see, — *Rossetti 1870*.
20-1. Omitted in all *eds*. These two lines, written at the bottom of *Nbk 19* p. 180 *reverso*, are linked to l. 19, in the page's upper quarter, by the words *A sabbath*, possibly cancelled, written just below *Yet father*. Repeatedly, on this page, S. tried out versions with *Sabbath*: *A sabbath of the cares of daily life* canc. and *When in a sabbath of the cares of life* canc. *BSM* xii 312 n. considers that these two lines, as well as several lines at the top of p. 179 *reverso*, were replaced by draft on p. 178 *reverso*.
21. *man;*] man *Nbk 19*.
22-6. *Avarice ... gift.* —] All *eds* detach these lines from the rest of the Young Man's speech, separated by a series of asterisks, and place them after the present edition's l. 37. The editors of the present volume, however, concur with *BSM* xii 312n., that the lone word *When* above *Avarice* in *Nbk 19* p. 178 *reverso* is a linking device to ll. 19-20 on p. 180 *reverso*.
22-4. *Avarice ... hell's threshold*] See *Aeneid* vi 273-81 where the entrance to Hell is described:

> vestibulum ante ipsum primisque in faucibus Orci
> Luctus et ultrices posuere cubilia Curae,
> pallentesque habitant Morbi tristisque Senectus
> et Metus et malesuada Fames ac turpis Egestas,
> terribiles visu formae, Letumque Labosque:
> tum consanguineus Leti Sopor et mala mentis
> Gaudia, mortiferumque adverso in limine Bellum
> ferreique Eumenidum thalami et Discordia demens,
> vipereum crinem vittis innexa cruentis.

('Just before the entrance, even within the very jaws of Hell, Grief and avenging Cares have set their bed; there pale Diseases dwell, sad Age,

And open-eyed conspiracy, lie sleeping
   As on hell's threshold; and all gentle thoughts
25 Waken to worship him who giveth joy
   With his own gift. — Surely it is a joy,
   Beautiful, innocent, and unforbidden
   By God or man ... 'tis like the bright procession
   [Of] skiey visions in a solemn dream
30 From which men wake as from a Paradise,
   And draw new strength to tread the thorns of life. —
   If God be good wherefore should this be evil?

and Fear, and Hunger, temptress to sin, and loathly Want, shapes terrible to view; and Death and Distress; next, Death's own brother Sleep, and the soul's Guilty Joys, and, on the threshold opposite, the death-dealing War, and the Furies' iron cells, and maddening Strife, her snaky locks entwined with bloody ribbons.')

22. *Avarice and tyranny,*] When avarice and tyranny, *1824*; When Avarice and Tyranny, *Rossetti 1870*. *fear*] fear, *1824*; Fear *Rossetti*.
23. *open-eyed*] open eyed *Nbk 19*. *conspiracy,*] conspiracy *1824*; Conspiracy, *Rossetti 1870*. *lies sleeping*] When Aeneas arrives at the gates of Hell, the Sibyl offers Cerberus, the three-headed dog guarding the entrance to Hades, a drugged morsel which causes him to sleep, thus allowing Aeneas to enter the underworld safely (see *Aeneid* vi 417–25).
24. *hell's*] Hell's *1824*.
25. *him*] Him *Rossetti 1824*. *joy*] joys *1824, BSM*; joys, *Rossetti 1870*.
26. *gift.* —] gift. *1824, Rossetti 1870. Surely it is a joy,*] Omitted in *eds.*
28. *man ...*] man; — *1824*; man. *Rossetti 1870*. An earlier version of the second half of this line appears in *Nbk 19* p. 180 *reverso*: *'tis like the brief Paradise*. That version is repeated on p. 179 *reverso* where it is emended to the present reading. *'tis*] 'Tis *Rossetti 1870*.
29. *dream*] dream, — *Nbk 19. skiey*] 'Of, relating to, located in, or emanating from the sky.' (*OED* 1a). Cp. *The Cloud* (no. 319) 17: 'Sublime on the towers of my skiey bowers' and *OWW* (no. 259) 50–1: 'As then, when to outstrip thy skiey speed / Scarce seemed a vision'; also Keats, *Endymion* iv 558: 'A skyey masque, a pinioned multitude –'.
30. *Paradise*] paradise *1824, Rossetti 1870*.
31. *the thorns of life*] Cp. *OWW* 54: 'I fall upon the thorns of life! I bleed!'. *life.* —] life. *1824, Rossetti 1870*.
32. *good*] good, *1824, Rossetti 1870*. *evil?*] evil *Nbk 19*.

And if this be not evil, dost thou not
[Blas]pheme, [old man], and transform good to [ill]?
35 O, kill the serpent creed, nor let it [?draw]
Unseasonable poison from the flowers
Which bloom so rarely in this barren world.

Old Man
How young art thou in this old age of time!
How green in this grey world! Canst thou discern

33-7. These lines in *Nbk 19* p. 179 *reverso* draw on abandoned draft on p. 178 *reverso*. Both *1824* and *Rossetti 1870* prefer the variants found on p. 178 *reverso* and *Rossetti 1870* reorders thusly:

> And, if this be not evil, dost thou not draw
> Unseasonable poison from the flowers
> Which bloom so rarely in this barren world?
> Oh! kill these bitter thoughts which make the present
> Dark as the future! —

Rossetti's version overlooks several cancelled words and includes incomplete lines given in the note to l. 35 below.
33. *thou not*] thou not draw *1824, Rossetti 1870*. *Eds* have taken *draw* from a line below in *Nbk 19* p. 179 *reverso*, omitting the following, partially cancelled, l. 34 to which it belongs.
34. Omitted in *eds*. It is likely that the cancelled words in *Nbk 19* were meant to be retained: once the revisions on the facing p. 178 *reverso* were abandoned, S. returned to p. 179 *reverso*, emending and concluding the line. *[ill]?*] [ill] *Nbk 19*. The apparent cancel stroke through *ill* might simply be the t-bar stroke of *to* just below.
35-6. For these lines, *Rossetti 1870* gives instead 'Oh! kill these bitter thoughts which make the present / Dark as the future!—' (*1824* reads 'O, kill ... ') based on a draft in *Nbk 19* p. 178 rev.:

> *O kill [?the] thoughts which make the present*
> *Dark as the future ... mangle that serpent creed*
> *Which transforms innocence to ill [   ]*
> *Which makes a death [of] life, and [   ] sucks*

These incomplete and metrically irregular lines were replaced by the emended and complete lines on p. 179 *reverso*.
35. *O,*] *1824*; Oh! *Rossetti 1870*; O *Nbk 19*.
37. *world.*] world? *1824, Rossetti 1870*. The punctuation in *Nbk 19* is indeterminate because of smeared and blotted ink.
38. *SD*. Omitted in *Nbk 19*; Second Speaker *1824*; Second Citizen *Rossetti 1870*.
39. *Canst thou*] *1824, Rossetti 1870*; canst you *Nbk 19*. *discern*] not think *1824*.

40 The signs of seasons, yet perceive no hint
    Of change in that low scene in which thou art
    Not a spectator but an actor, or
    Art thou a puppet moved by [?enginery]?
    The day that dawns in fire will die in storms,
45 Even though the noon be calm. My travel's done —
    Before the whirlwind wakes I shall have gained
    My inn of lasting [rest], but thou may'st still
    Be journeying on in this inclement air. —
    Wrap thy old cloak about thee, clench [?thy] [?staff],

40. Omitted in *1824.*
41. low scene] low scene, *1824*, stage-scene *Rossetti 1870.*
42. actor, or] actor? [   ] *1824*; actor? or *Rossetti 1870.*
43. Omitted in *1824. moved*] The word functions kinetically rather than emotively as in *Q Mab* (no. 92) v 71: 'These puppets of his schemes he moves at will'. *[?enginery]*] Crook argues (*BSM* xii 130) that Rossetti's 'enginery' is 'impossible', and proposes a queried 'mummeries'. The MS is particularly marred at this point, so readings are conjectural; however, *enginery* or even *engineries* is certainly possible. See also *LMG* (no. 325) 107: 'Plotting dark spells and devilish enginery' and *Hellas* 819: 'The shock of crags shot from strange engin'ry.'
44–5. Another draft of these lines appears in *Nbk 19* p. 183 *reverso* among early jottings:

> [*The day that dawns in cloud*] *fire* [*will die*] *in storms*
> *Even though the noon be calm:* [*gather thy cloak*]
> *About thee:*

45. My travel's done —] my travel's done — *Nbk 19*; My travel's done; *1824*; My travel's done,— *Rossetti 1870.*
46. have gained] have found *1824, Rossetti 1870.*
47. [rest],] rest; *Rossetti 1870. may'st*] must *1824, Rossetti 1870*; mayest *BSM*. An apostrophe seems present but *BSM*'s 'mayest' is also possible.
48. air. —] air. *1824, Rossetti 1870.*
49–60. Omitted in *1824.*
49. A variant of *Wrap thy old cloak about thee* occurs in *Nbk 19* p. 183 *reverso*; see note to ll. 44–5. Cp. *Othello* II iii 96: '[Then] take thy auld cloak about thee.' *thee, clench [?thy] [?staff],*] thy back; *Rossetti 1870*; thee[:] [?dark] [?thy] st[?ar] *BSM*.

50 [And ?make thy] brow as rugged [as the] [?lion's];
    Nor leave the broad and plain and beaten road,
    Although few flowers smile on its trodden dust,
    For the violet paths that seest not Pain.
    Masked in an angel's likeness, this Charles of England

50. Omitted in *eds*. There is much blotting here so decipherment is conjectural. Below *[And ?make]* are possibly two words, seemingly uncancelled. *BSM* gives 'storm cloud'.
51–3. The Old Man's advice (ll. 49–53) to the Young Man about his choice ahead, either a 'beaten' or a 'violet' path is echoed in *TL* 62–5:

> But more with motions which each other crossed
> Pursued or shunned the shadows the clouds threw
> Or birds within the noonday ether lost,
>
> Upon that path where flowers never grew, ...

51. *road,*] road *Nbk 19*.
52. *few flowers*] no flowers *Rossetti 1870*. *dust,*] dust *Nbk 19*.
53–4. For the violet paths of pleasure. This Charles the First *Rossetti 1870*. Failing to notice the additions to 53–4 at the bottom of *Nbk 19* p. 176 *reverso*, Rossetti conflated the two line halves of 53 and 54 in the upper half of the page. Line 53 originally read *For the violet paths of pleasure,* — then *of pleasure* was cancelled while the following line's ending was offset to the right, leaving space for infilling of l. 53's second half, and the first half of 54. At the bottom of p. 176 *reverso* are the completions of ll. 53 and 54: *that seest not [Satan] Pain / Masked in an an angel's likeness*. (The second *an* is certainly a slip.) A long horizontal line separates these emendations from the last line of the Old Man's speech just above. *BSM* reads the draft at the bottom of the page as: 'that seest not Peters *canc*. Rome / Masked in an angels [helm] of'.
53. *Pain.*] Pain *Nbk 19*.
54. *this Charles of England*] This Charles the First *Rossetti 1870*. *Locock 1911* ii 476 noted the anachronism in Rossetti's edition for normally the regnal number 'I' or 'First' is not used for the first ruler with that name during his or her reign. Only with the coronation of a later monarch with the same name is the 'First' then applied. It seems that S. initially wrote *This Charles the first* in *Nbk 19* p. 176 *reverso*, and then perhaps recognised the Old Man's anachronous usage. Added below is *This   of England* which leaves a large gap for *Charles*, written just above as part of the first phrase.

55 Rose like the equinoxial sun [?]
    By threatening vapours, through whose ominous veil
    Darting his altered influence, he has gained
    This height of noon ... from which he must decline
    Amid the darkness of conflicting storms
60 To dark extinction and to latest night.

                                          Enter a PURSUIVANT.
    Pursuivant
    Room for the King ... [fall] back, [thou ragged knave]!

55–6. Bacon's essay 'Of Seditions and Troubles' draws a parallel between the likelihood of storms occurring when days and nights are of the same length and rulers being vulnerable to civil unrest if the social order becomes less hierarchical: 'Shepherds of people had need know the calendars of tempests in state; which are commonly greatest when things grow to equality; as natural tempests are greatest about the *Equinoctia*' (Francis Bacon, *The Major Works*, ed. Brian Vickers (1996) 366). On S.'s view of Bacon, see note to i 63–4 below.
55. *equinoxial sun*] When the sun crosses the equator during the vernal or autumnal equinox, higher tides result, accompanied by proverbial storms. Crook (*BSM* xii 308) notes Charles's accession to the throne on 25 March 1625, a period of the vernal equinox. [?]] [<mas>k]ed *BSM*. The word is illegible in *Nbk 19*. A large blot here seems to have caused this page to be stuck to facing p. 177 *reverso*, and once they were pulled apart, some of the paper on p. 177 *reverso* was torn away. The word appears to end in *od* or *ed*; a possible reading is 'shrouded'.
56. By vapours, through whose threatening ominous veil *Rossetti 1870*. *threatening* was the third and final alternative adjective for *vapours* (*fiery* canc. and *ominous* canc. were rejected choices).
57. *influence,*] influence *Rossetti 1870*.
58. *noon ...*] noon — *Rossetti 1870*.
59. *storms*] storms, *Rossetti 1870*.
60. *dark*] dank *Rossetti 1870*. *BSM* prefers 'dark' noting that 'obliteration seems the point here, not decay' (308). Rossetti's 'dank' is certainly possible; stylistically, S. may have found the repetition with 'darkness' in l. 59 was undesirable.
61. SD. *Enter* a PURSUIVANT] enter a pursuivant ... *Nbk 19*; omitted in *eds*. Found in *Nbk 19* p. 174 *reverso* along with first half of l. 61, the only uncancelled elements on this page. The pursuivant's interruption shifts attention to historical figures, beginning with Bastwick and his comments on key members of the royal party. *Pursuivant*] Omitted in *Nbk 19* and *eds*.
61. Omitted in all *eds*. This line, mostly uncancelled, is found in *Nbk 19* pp. 174–3 *reverso* among many cancelled lines occurring over three pages (175–3 *reverso*) and appears to be addressed to the Old Man, the previous speaker (see *BSM* xii 304). Another SD on p. 175 *reverso*, also uncancelled, reads: *Circumstances / then enter Masque*. S. probably recognised the need for the royal party to arrive at the

Bastwick
There goes the apostate Strafford — who poisons
[The King's dull ear with] whispered aphorisms
From Machiavel and Bacon, and if Judas

Merchant-Taylor's Hall to await the masque progression. *Whitelocke* 21 outlines the organisation of this second presentation of the masque *to please the Queen*; see 'Sources, Genre and Form' in the headnote. Thus S. postponed the masque's entry until after the royal party's procession, perhaps indicated by the *Circumstances* he noted on p. 175 *reverso*. The preparation for the masque progression begins at l. 133, and the progression itself begins with Marshalman's announcement at ll. 158–9 Another possible version of l. 61 reads *Room for the King ... [thou ragged insolence!]*; l. 61 is perhaps S.'s signal that he needed to provide an entry for the King. *Woodings (1968a)* 233–4 argues that the breakdown in composition evident in pp. 175–3 *reverso* represents a disruption when S. reconsidered the structure of Scene i and 'replaced the original opening of the Mask scene' (233).
62. SD. *Bastwick*] *Nbk 19*; omitted in *eds*. John Bastwick (1593–1654), a Puritan, is mentioned in *Whitelocke, Macaulay* and *Hume*. See *Whitelocke* 21: 'Dr. Bastwick a Physician was brought into the High Commission Court, for his book *Elenchus [Religionis] Papisticae, & Flagellum Pontificis & Episcoporum Latialium* [A Confutation of Popery, and a Scourge for the Pope and the Latin Bishops]'. He reappears in Scene iv at his sentencing trial overseen by Archbishop Laud and Wentworth, the Earl of Strafford. Bastwick describes both men here with contempt.
62–7. Omitted in *1824*. Rossetti orders ll. 62–5 differently, with two incomplete half lines:

>   .   .   .   There goes
> The apostate Strafford; he whose titles ...
>   .   .   .   whispered aphorisms
> From Machiavel and Bacon: and, if Judas
> Had been as brazen and as bold as he. ...

Cp. *3 Henry VI* III ii 191–3: 'I can add colors to the chameleon, / Change shapes with Proteus for advantages, / And set the murtherous Machevil to school.'
62. *the apostate Strafford*] Thomas Wentworth, 1st Earl of Strafford (1593- 1641), was regarded as an apostate in abandoning the cause of the popular party for that of the crown. Initially, he was an outspoken advocate of the Petition of Right (1628) which limited some powers of the Crown; however, once the Petition was accepted, he supported the authority of the King. Hume records that 'the king ... made him president of the council of York, and deputy of Ireland; and regarded him as his chief minister and counsellor' (vii 195). Macaulay writes, 'The frail man [Wentworth before his preferment] was at first ashamed of his apostacy, and concealed his change of sentiments; but at length pretended to justify himself by condemning the principles of his former associates' (*Macaulay* ii 26). *Hutchinson Life* 68 also notes his apostasy. See 'Historical context' in the headnote as well as note to ii 220–5.
63–4. *aphorisms / From Machiavel and Bacon*] S. refers to Niccolò Machiavelli (1469–1527) in 'On Learning Languages' (1816) (*Prose Works* 164); Claire read

65 Had been as brazen and as bold as he,
    He might have changed his halter for a scourge,
    Outfacing scorn to be a terror ...

First Citizen
                                    That
    Is the Archbishop?

Machiavelli's novel *Belfagor* (1545) on 30 November and *Discourses on Livy* (1531) on 11 December 1820 (*Claire Jnl* 190, 193). S. granted the status of poet to Francis Bacon (Viscount St Alban, 1561–1626 and Lord Chancellor (1617–21)) in *DP* (*Reiman (2002)* para. 36). His *Essayes or Counsels, Civill and Morall*, 3rd edn (1625) was his most popular work; Peacock read it on 3–5 September 1818 probably in an edn of William Willymott (?1672–1737) (*Peacock Letters* i 139, 144 n. 101). The book list for the sale of S.'s Marlow library includes both 'Bacon on Government' and 'Bacons Essays' (Pforz MS (S'ANA 1082) f. 6^r), the latter, possibly the volume Peacock records reading. The figure of Bacon reappears in *TL* as one of the 'mighty phantoms of an elder day' (l. 253). The influence of Bacon and Machiavelli on Wentworth is evident in his speeches and letters that often echo the aphoristic style and sense of the two writers. (See 'Sources, Genre and Form' in headnote regarding the possibility that S. might have acquired *Strafforde's Letters*.) S. perhaps links the two writers because Bacon himself frequently cites Machiavelli; see his essay 'On Seditions and Troubles' referred to in the note to i 55–6 above.

64–7. *and if Judas ... be a terror*] Following his betrayal of Jesus for thirty pieces of silver, Judas hanged himself (see *Matthew* xxvii 3–5).

66. Omitted in *eds*.

67. SD. *Rossetti 1870*; omitted in *Nbk 19* but a long medial dash just below the first part of l. 67 denotes a speaker change; First Speaker *1824*. Although *Nbk 19* does not indicate an SD here, the SD entrance for a different, second citizen at l. 76. indicates it must be the First Citizen who addresses Bastwick.

67–91. *1824* resumes Scene i.

67. *Outfacing ... terror*] Omitted in *eds*. 'Outfacing' = staring down (see *OED* 1a). That] That *1824, Rossetti 1870*.

68. SD. Omitted in *Nbk 19*; Second Speaker *1824*; Second Citizen *Rossetti 1870*.

68–9. *Rather ... Rome*] William Laud (1573–1645), the Archbishop of Canterbury, was feared and hated by the Puritans as well as other Protestant groups for his zealous enforcing of high-church ceremonies and traditions which many regarded as too Catholic: 'the discontented puritans believed the church of England to be relapsing fast into Romish superstition; the court of Rome itself entertained hopes of regaining its authority ...; and, in order to forward Laud's supposed good intentions, an offer was twice made him ... of a cardinal's hat' (*Hume* vii 197–8).

68. *Archbishop?*] Archbishop? . . *Nbk 19*; Archbishop. *1824, Rossetti 1870*. Pope.] Pope: *Rossetti 1870*.

Bastwick
                    Rather say the Pope.
London will be soon his Rome; he walks
70 As if he [trod upon] the heads of men.
He looks elate, drunken with blood and gold —
Beside him moves the Babylonian Woman
Invisibly, and with her, as with his shadow,
Mitred adulterer, he is joined in Sin;
75 How he proceeds elate, swollen with the pride
That turns heaven's milk of mercy to Revenge.

Second Citizen   [*Lifting up his eyes.*
O, good Lord! rain it down upon him —

69. *Rome; he walks*] Rome, he walks *Nbk 19*; Rome: he walks *1824*; Rome. He walks *Rossetti 1870*.
70. *men.*] men: *Rossetti 1870*.
71. *elate*] 'puffed up, self-satisfied' (*Concordance*). *blood and gold*] S.'s notes in *Nbk 22* f. *2ʳ include the phrase, *Lauds excessive thirst for gold & blood*. A frequent collocation in S.'s writings; see, e.g., *Q Mab* iv 195, *WA* (no. 341) 191, *Written on hearing the news of the death of Napoleon* 34–5 and *TL* 287. *gold —*] gold; — *1824*; gold. *Rossetti 1870*.
72. *the Babylonian Woman*] The Whore of Babylon is described in *Revelation* xvii 1–5: 'I will shew unto thee the judgment of the great whore that sitteth upon many waters: With whom the kings of the earth have committed fornication, and the inhabitants of the earth have been made drunk with the wine of her fornication. … And upon her forehead *was* a name written, MYSTERY, BABYLON THE GREAT, THE MOTHER OF HARLOTS AND ABOMINATIONS OF THE EARTH'.
73. *her,*] her *1824*, *Rossetti 1870*.
74. Mitred adulterer! he is joined in sin, *1824*, *Rossetti 1870*. *Mitred*] A mitre is 'a tall deeply-cleft headdress worn by a bishop … as a symbol of episcopal office' (*OED* 3a).
75–6. Omitted in *eds*. Although 'elate' appears in both ll. 71 and 75, its repetition is perhaps intentional.
76. *That turns heaven's*] Which turns Heaven's *1824*, *Rossetti 1870*.
77–101. Omitting ll. 88–9, *Rossetti 1870* assigns ll. 77–101 to 'Third Citizen' only.
77. *O,*] O *Nbk 19*; Oh *BSM*. *There,*] [   ] *1824*; omitted in *Rossetti 1870*.
77. *SD. Second Citizen … Lifting up his eyes*] enter Citizen (lifting up his eyes) *Nbk 19*; Another Citizen *1824*; Third Citizen *Rossetti 1870*. *Bastwick*] Omitted in *Nbk 19*; omitted in *eds*. Neither Mary nor Rossetti noted that l. 77 was completed by the next speaker with 'There' echoing Bastwick's first comment above at l. 62. *1824* closes the line with empty brackets, on the assumption that the line was incomplete.

Bastwick
                                There,
Girt by [?the] [?maiden] ladies of her court
And disguised Jesuits, walks the papist queen
80   As if her nice feet scorned our English earth; —
The Canaanitish Jezebel! I would be
A dog if I might tear her with my teeth.
There's old Sir Henry Vane, the Earl of Pembroke,

78–80. Girt by … earth] Henrietta Maria (1609–69), youngest daughter of Henry IV of France and sister to the future Louis XIII, was mother to Charles's successors, Charles II and James II; her Catholicism was a source of discontent for the public. Hume writes, 'Her religion, likewise, to which she was much addicted, must be regarded as a great misfortune, since it augmented the jealousy which prevailed against the court, and engaged her to procure for the catholics some indulgences which were generally distasteful to the nation' (*Hume* vii 195).
78–9. Girt by … queen] Amid her ladies walks the papist queen, *1824*; queen *Rossetti 1870*. Eds select a cancelled half-line in *Nbk 19* p. 171 *reverso*, conflating ll. 78–9 into one line. For the first half of l. 78, Crook reads 'Asif by her window' (*BSM* xii 298). *Girt by* is legible; however, the next two words are very uncertain. [?*the*] might be *BSM*'s 'her' for overwriting is evident.
79. And disguised Jesuits] Omitted in eds.
80. nice] 'finely dressed, elegant' (*OED* 2d) and 'fastidious' (*OED* 3b), but also 'lascivious' 'wanton' (*OED* 2b) in light of the next line. *earth; —*] earth. *1824, Rossetti 1870*.
81–2. Omitted in *1824*. These two lines are in the jottings section in *Nbk 19* p. 182 *reverso*. Rossetti was first to place them in this speech. A similar phrase occurs in *Whitelocke* 14: 'Dr. Leighton a Scotch-man, for his Book Intituled, *Sions Plea*, dedicated to the last Parliament, counselling them "to kill all the Bishops, by smiting them under the fifth Rib", and railing against the Queen, calling her a "Canaanite and Idolatress"'. Bastwick would have been familiar with Leighton's book, as Crook notes (*BSM* xii 320). *I would be … my teeth*] After Jehu orders Jezebel to be defenestrated, only her skull, feet and palms of her hands are buried, her flesh having been eaten by dogs, as prophesied by Elijah (2 *Kings* ix 33–6).
81. Canaanitish] 'Resembling the Canaanites or their practices and beliefs; alien, heathen' (*OED* 2). *Jezebel*] Phoenician wife of Ahab, accused of trying to lead the Israelites into idolatry and a symbol of sexual immorality (see 1 *Kings* xvi 31, xix 1, 2; 2 *Kings* ix 30–7; *Revelation* ii 20).
82. teeth.] teeth! *Rossetti 1870*.
83. old Sir Henry Vane] Vane (1589–1655), known as 'the Elder' and father to Sir Harry Vane, the younger who appears in Scene iii, held various roles in Charles's court including treasurer of the household and secretary of state. He does not appear in any other scene. *Earl of Pembroke*] Philip Herbert (1584–1650), 4th Earl of Pembroke, was an acknowledged patron of art and culture and shared with Charles a deep interest in painting. Vane and the Earl of Pembroke were among those acting as advisors for the Masque; see *Whitelocke* 19.

Lord Essex, and Lord Keeper Coventry,
85 And others who make base their English breed
By [vile] participation of their honours
With papists, atheists, tyrants and apostates. —

First Citizen
[A Pursuivant passed now with wingèd] speed:
[The] temple lawyers' masque will short be here.

Bastwick
90 When lawyers mask, 'tis time for honest men
To strip the vizor from their purposes; —

84. *Lord Essex*] Robert Devereux, 3rd Earl of Essex (1591-1646) soldier and Parliamentarian who was one of three generals leading the King's army to Scotland in 1639. Essex is listed in the DP for Scene ii but has no assigned speech. *Lord Keeper Coventry*] Thomas Coventry (1578-1640) was made Lord Keeper of the Great Seal in 1625. Like Vane the elder and Pembroke, he does not appear in any other scene.
85. *make*] made *1834, 1839, Rossetti 1870*. Crook notes that *1839*'s 'made' was 'prob. derived from Asch.'s [Asch. = *1834*] independent error, not re-consultation of [MS]' (*BSM* xii 296).
86. *By [vile] participation*] By vile participation *1824, Rossetti 1870*. S. probably cancelled *vile* for metrical reasons when the line concluded with *with apostates*; once the line ending was revised, *vile* was perhaps meant to be retained. White (1922) 439 notes that 'vile participation' recalls *1 Henry IV* III ii 87.
87. *tyrants and apostates.* —] tyrants, and apostates. *1824, Rossetti 1870*.
88. SD. Omitted in *Nbk 19* and *eds*.
88-9. Omitted in *eds*. The apparent cancellation of much of l. 88 might instead be a 'ruling-off' line to separate this brief interruption from Bastwick's speech. Another line underscores l. 89. These lines neatly set up Bastwick's sardonic comment in ll. 90-1.
89. *[The] temple lawyers' masque*] There are four Inns of Court: Middle Temple, Inner Temple, Lincoln's Inn and Gray's Inn. Presumably, the First Citizen is noting the imminent arrival of the first two groups of lawyers from the Middle and Inner Temple: 'After him followed one hundred Gentlemen of the Inns of Court, five and twenty chosen out of each house, of the most proper and handsom young Gentlemen of the societies' (*Whitelocke* 19).
90. SD. Omitted in *Nbk 19* and in *Rossetti 1870* where ll. 90-101 are treated as a continuation of his Third Citizen's speech above.
90. *mask,*] mask *1824*; masque, *Rossetti 1870*.
91. *purposes;* —] purposes. *1824, Rossetti 1870*; purposes — *Nbk 19*.

A seasonable [?tide] for masques — [in] truth,
When Englishmen and Protestants should [sit]
In ashes and in sackcloth, penitent
95   To avert the wrath of [?] whose scourge is felt
For the great sins which have drawn down from Heaven
On our home, wars and foreign overthrow.

Second Citizen
The remnant of the martyred Saints in Rochefort
Have been abandoned by our faithless allies
100   To that idolatrous and adulterous torturer
Lewis of France — the Palatinate is lost,

92–158. Omitted in *1824*.
92. [*?tide*]] time *Rossetti 1870*; written above *time* canc. Crook persuasively argues that *tide* refers to Shrove-tide, 'a period of licensed excess offensive to Puritans and immediately succeeded by the penitential Ash Wednesday' (*BSM* xii 129). *for masques — [in] truth,*] for masquers this! *Rossetti 1870*.
94. Although various parts of this line are cancelled in *Nbk 19* p. 170 *reverso*, an underlining stroke restores the entire line. Rossetti's incomplete line, '. . . dust on their dishonoured heads,' is assembled from emendations to the various cancels in the stetted line below. To sit 'in ashes and in sackcloth' is the Old Testament demonstration of repentance and humility in the face of natural disasters or sinful actions; see *Jonah* iii 5–6.
95. [?]] Him *Rossetti 1870*; [fire] *BSM* (GM suggests 'one').
96. *Heaven*] heaven *Rossetti 1870*.
97. . . . and foreign overthrow *Rossetti 1870*. *home,*] home *Nbk 19*; house *BSM*.
98. *SD*. Omitted in *eds*. Following *overthrow* (l. 97) in *Nbk 19* p. 169 *reverso* is an apparently cancelled full-stop followed by an unusual series of notations that almost certainly signify a speaker change.
98. *Saints*] saints *Rossetti 1870*. *Rochefort*] Crook (*BSM* xii 294) plausibly suggests that S.'s error of *Rochefort* for 'Rochelle' was due to their adjacent listing in the unpaginated index in *Ludlow 1771*. In 1627 the enclave of French Huguenots at La Rochelle requested English aid and liberation from the French who sought to suppress their religion. The English attempts failed because of error, cowardice and treachery; see *Hume* vii 176.
101. *Lewis of France*] Louis XIII (1601–43). *France* —] France,— *Rossetti 1870*. *Palatinate*] A cluster of fragmented territories in present-day central Germany but which, at the time of Charles's reign, were part of the Holy Roman Empire. The Palatinate was actually 'lost' not by Charles but by his father, James I, who failed to support the Protestant Frederick V, the Elector Palatine, who had accepted the throne of Bohemia in 1619 which initiated the Thirty Years War; the following year, 1620, he was evicted from Bohemia, thus abdicating both roles of Elector and King. He was exiled to the Dutch Republic in 1622. *lost,*] lost. . . . . *Rossetti 1870*.

Our embassy to the Pope —

[LEIGHTON *moves downstage.*

Bastwick
What thing comes here?
What [image] of our lacerated country?
Filling in the gap of speech with speechless horror,
105 Canst thou be — art thou?

Leighton
I was Leighton; what
I am, thou seest ... yet turn thine eyes away,
And with thy memory look on thy friend's mind
Which is unchanged — and where [is] written deep

---

102. Omitted in *eds.* This line is squeezed in among two and a half cancelled lines in *Nbk 19* p. 169 *reverso*:

> *Our flag which was the terror of the ocean*
> *Is now the scorn of every pirate keel*
> *That rounds its borne —*

For the last half-line above, *BSM* gives 'That wounds its [form]', and Crook gives 'That wounds its honour' (*Crook (2009)* 305). The long dash following *Pope* and the large space separating this half-line from its second half below indicates a speaker change. (See *Crook (2009)* 305–6 for a discussion of S.'s dramatic strategy in this passage.)
102. SD. Leighton *moves downstage*] Omitted in *Nbk 19*; long dashes and large gaps in MS indicate speaker changes. *Nbk 19* p. 172 *reverso* shows Leighton's presence on stage at the start of Bastwick's first speech (ll. 62–7), but he is unrecognised until this moment. After l. 101, *Rossetti 1870* gives: 'Enter LEIGHTON (who has been branded in the face) and BASTWICK'. *Bastwick*] Omitted in *Nbk 19* and *Rossetti 1870*. *BSM* xii 294 suggests that '1st Citizen (Bastwick's companion)' is the likely speaker of ll. 102–5. Because Leighton pleads for him to 'look on thy friend's mind', it is, however, more likely to be Bastwick; furthermore at l. 121 Bastwick, in return, addresses Leighton as 'friend'.
102–4. Omitted in *eds.*
104. horror,] horror *Nbk 19.*
105. be —] be, *Nbk 19. art thou?*] art thou ...? *Rossetti 1870*; Rossetti assigns this half line to 'Third Citizen'. *was Leighton;*] was Leighton: *Rossetti 1870.*
106. I am,] I am *Nbk 19*; I *am Rossetti 1870. seest ...*] seest. *Rossetti 1870. yet turn thine eyes away,*] And yet turn thine eyes, *Rossetti 1870.*
107. mind] mind, *Rossetti 1870.*
108. unchanged —] unchanged, *Rossetti 1870.*

The sentence of my judge.

Bastwick
                          Are these the marks which
110   Laud thinks improve the image of his Maker
       Stamped on the face of man?

First Citizen
                              Curses upon
        The impious Archbishop!

Second Citizen
                          It is said, too,
        That he] has published by authority
        [?   ] books of pastimes which invite
115   All lewd and papist drunkards [?to] profane

109–11. Are these … of man? Rossetti 1870 assigns this sentence to 'Third Citizen' but Bastwick would be the more appropriate speaker, his horror registered in a second question in response to Leighton (see l. 105). Just below this passage, S. clearly indicates First and Second Citizen in *Nbk 19* p. 168 *reverso*.
109. SD. Omitted in *Nbk 19*; Third Citizen *Rossetti 1870*.
109. marks] The result of the punishment of Alexander Leighton (c. 1570–1649) for publishing *An Appeale to the Parliament, or, Sions Plea Against the Prelacy* (1628): 'he was severely whipped, then put in the pillory, where he had one of his ears cut off, one side of his nose slit, branded on one cheek with a red-hot iron with the letters S. S. [for 'sower of sedition']' (*Macaulay* ii 99). *which*] with which *Nbk 19, Rossetti 1870*.
110–11. See *Genesis* i 26–7: 'And God said, Let us make man in our image, after our likeness … So God created man in his *own* image, in the image of God created he him'.
110. Laud thinks improve] Laud thinks to improve *Rossetti 1870*.
111. SD. Citizen 1ˢᵗ *Nbk 19*; omitted in *Rossetti 1870*.
111–12. Curses … Archbishop! Rossetti assigns these two half-lines to the 'Third Citizen' (see note to ll. 109–11).
111. Curses upon] Curses upon him, *Rossetti 1870*.
112. SD. *Rossetti 1870*; 2ᵈ· Citizen *Nbk 19*.
112. The impious Archbishop!] The impious tyrant! *Rossetti 1870. said, too,*] said besides *Rossetti 1870*.
113–14. Omitted in *eds*. For 'books of pastimes' see *Ludlow 1771* 3: 'several new holy-days introduced, and required to be observed by the people with all possible solemnity, at the same time that they were encouraged to profane the Lord's day, by a book commonly called, the Book of Sports, printed and published by the

The Sabbath with their [ri]otous orgies
And has permitted that most heathen custom
Of dancing round a pole dressed up with flowers
At May-day morn upon [the] village [gree]ns.
120 A man who thus twice crucifies his God
May well [?behead] his brother. —

Bastwick

                                      In my mind, friend,
The root of all this ill is Prelacy.

---

king's special command.' S. notes *the Kings orders for sports on a Sunday, & other wickednesses* from his reading of Hume, and adds, *A droll thing that the nation should be compelled to amuse itself* (*Nbk 21* pp. 242-1 rev.; *BSM* xvi 224-7).
114. [?]] [?Im] [?pious] *BSM*.
115. *All lewd*] That lewd *Rossetti 1870*. [?*to*] *profane*] may profane *Rossetti 1870*.
116. *The Sabbath with their* ... *Rossetti 1870*. The Second Citizen's use of *Sabbath* demonstrates his Puritan sympathies; Hume writes, 'They [House of Commons] also enacted laws for the strict observance of Sunday, which the puritans affected to call the Sabbath, and which they sanctified by the most melancholy indolence' (*Hume* vii 131).
117-18. Hume notes the parliamentary ordinance (18 April 1644) with 'a clause for the taking down of may-poles, which they called a heathenish vanity' (*Hume* viii 84 n. 53).
117. *heathen*] heathenish *Rossetti 1870*; alt. from *heathenish* in *Nbk 19*.
118. *flowers*] wreathes *Rossetti 1870*.
119. On May-day. *Rossetti 1870*.
121. *SD*. Omitted in *eds*. The speaker changes here and in ll. 123-4 are indicated in *Nbk 19* by mid-page horizontal strokes between lines. Because few names are assigned, the order was determined by ll. 123-4. *Bastwick* appears at the end of l. 121 and is cancelled, an indication perhaps that he was the intended speaker.
121. *May well [?behead]*] May well ... *Rossetti 1870*. In *Nbk 19* p. 167 *reverso*, there is only a large space between *well* and *his*; however, the reading '[?behead]' is based on a cancelled line just above: *Behead his fellow men*. — The long dash following *brother* and the offset, lower placement of the line's second half indicate a speaker change which *Rossetti 1870* does not recognise.
121-3 *In my mind ... the root*] *Rossetti 1870* assigns these lines to the Second Citizen.
122. *Prelacy*.] Prelacy *Nbk 19*; prelacy. *Rossetti 1870*. Prelacy: 'The system of church government by prelates or bishops ... Frequently *derogatory*' (*OED* 4).

Leighton
I would cut up the root …

Bastwick
                      And by what means?

Leighton
Smiting each Bishop under the fifth rib.

Second Citizen
125 You seem to know the vulnerable place
     Of these same crocodiles. —

Leighton
                        I learnt it in
Egyptian bondage, Sir. Your worm of Nile

---

123. SD. Leighton] Omitted in *Nbk 19* but for speaker dash; omitted in *eds*. First half-line assigned to previous speaker 'Second Citizen' in *Rossetti 1870*. *Bastwick*] Omitted in *Nbk 19* but for speaker dash; Third Citizen *Rossetti 1870*.
123. root …] root. *Rossetti 1870*.
124. SD. Omitted in *Nbk 19*; Second Citizen *Rossetti 1870*. Speaker dash in *Nbk 19*.
124. 'Dr. Leighton a Scotchman, for his Book Intituled, *Sion's Plea*, dedicated to the last Parliament, counselling them "to kill all the Bishops, by smiting them under the fifth Rib"' (*Whitelocke* 14). Cp. 2 *Samuel* ii 23: 'wherefore Abner with the hinder end of the spear smote him under the fifth *rib*, that the spear came out behind him'. Cancelled versions of this line appeared earlier, on p. 180 *reverso*: *Smiting the Bishops* canc. and *the 5th rib* canc. Cp. S.'s note in *Nbk 21* p. 255 *reverso*: *Dr Leighton proposes to kill the Bps by smiting them under the fifth rib* — (*BSM* xvi 238–9).
125. SD. Omitted in *Nbk 19*; Third Citizen *Rossetti 1870*. Speaker dash *Nbk 19*.
126. SD. Omitted in *Nbk 19*; Second Citizen *Rossetti 1870*. All of l. 126 in *Nbk 19* p. 167 *reverso* was originally to have been spoken by the Second Citizen: *Of these same crocodiles, [whose lamentations]*. However, S. cancelled the last two words, thus shortening the Citizen's second line. He then appears to have added a dash allowing Leighton to reply at the caesura.
126. crocodiles. —] crocodiles, — *Nbk 19*; crocodiles. *Rossetti 1870*. Crocodiles proverbially wept as they devoured their young; thus 'a person who weeps or makes a show of sorrow hypocritically or with a malicious purpose' (*OED* 2b). Cp. *MA* 24–5: 'Hypocrisy / On a crocodile rode by.'
127. Egyptian bondage, Sir] Leighton equates his imprisonment to the bondage of the Israelities in Egypt as recounted in *Exodus*. That fact that he addresses the previous speaker as 'Sir' suggests he speaks to one of the interested Citizens rather than Bastwick who he had previously told to 'look on thy friend's mind' in l. 107.
bondage, Sir] bondages, sir. *Rossetti 1870*. The conjectural 'bondage' in *Forman*

Betrays not with its flattering tears like they;
For when they cannot kill, they whine and weep —
130 Nor is it half so greedy of men's bodies
As they of soul and all; nor does it wallow
In slime as they in simony and lies. —

Bastwick
And foul lusts of the flesh. —

Marshalman
       Give place, give place!
You torch-bearers advance to the great gate

1876–7 was adopted in *Locock 1911*. *Your worm of Nile*] Another expression for 'crocodiles' (l. 126) or the Nile crocodile, indigenous to northern and central Africa. It is possible, however, that S. has conflated aspects of a crocodile with those of an asp, more generally known as 'the worm of Nile'. See *2 Henry VI* III i 227–8: 'Gloucester's show / Beguiles him, as the mournful crocodile / With sorrow snares relenting passengers' and Cleopatra's reference to the asp: 'Hast thou the pretty worm of Nilus there, / That kills and pains not?' (*Ant. & Cl.* V ii 243–4).
129. For when] For, when *Rossetti 1870. weep* —] weep. *Rossetti 1870*.
132. simony] 'The buying or selling of ecclesiastical or spiritual benefits; *esp.* the sale or purchase of preferment or office in the church.' (*OED* 1a). *lies.* —] lies *Rossetti 1870*.
133. SD. Bastwick] Omitted in *Nbk 19* and in *eds*. *Rossetti 1870* gives this half-line as the conclusion of the Second Citizen's speech but the full-stop and dash following *lies* in *Nbk 19* p. 166 *reverso* as well as another long dash above *flesh* indicate a speaker change. Bastwick's voice, with his hatred of the corrupt clergy, is appropriate to close this portion of Scene i which he opened above at l. 62. *Marshalman*] *Nbk 19*; Fourth Speaker (a pursuivant) *1824*; A Marshalman *Rossetti 1870*.
133. foul] close *Rossetti 1870*. S. first wrote *And the foul lusts* but then cancelled *the foul* and added *close* above in *Nbk 19* p. 166 *reverso*. He then underlined *foul* indicating its reinstatement; *close* is thus an uncancelled alternative. Above a cancelled line preceding l. 133 is *dark*, which might be a third uncancelled alternative; equally, however, it might be an emendation for that cancelled line. *flesh.* —] flesh. *Rossetti 1870. place!*] place *Nbk 19*; place!— *1824*. *1824* resumes Scene i at the caesura.
134–6. See *Whitelocke* 19: 'The first that marched were twenty Footmen, ... each one having his Sword by his side, a Baton in his hand, and a Torch lighted in the other hand; these were the Marshal's-men who cleared the Streets, made way, and were all about the Marshal, waiting his Commands. After them, and sometimes in the midst of them came the Marshall, then Mr. Darrel, afterwards Knighted by the King'.
134. torch-bearers] torchbearers *Nbk 19*, torchbearers, *Rossetti 1870. the great gate*] probably the gate at Temple Bar, historically the site of pageants and processions, separating The City of London from The City of Westminster. *gate*] gate, *1824*, *Rossetti 1870*.

135   And then attend the Marshal of the Masques
      [Into the royal presence.]

      A Law Student
                           What think'st thou
      Of this quaint show of ours, my agèd friend?
      Even now ye see the redness of the torches
      Inflame the night to the eastward, and clarions

---

135. attend] 'To follow, escort, or accompany, for the purpose of rendering services. (Used specifically of those who act as ladies or gentlemen in waiting to royal personages.)' (*OED* 8). *Masques*] All *eds* give 'Masque' singular. Above this line in *Nbk 19* p. 166 *reverso*, S. writes again the plural form (*The Marshal of the Masques* canc.), but elsewhere in *Nbk 19*, among jottings on p. 182 *reverso*, he also gives the singular form: *Place for the marshall of the masque!* (see also Scene ii 3, *your gay masque*).

136. SD. A Law Student] *Nbk 19*; Fifth Speaker (a law student) *1824*.

136–208. Because of the repetition of the phrase *What think'st thou / Of this quaint* in ll. 2–3 and ll. 136–7, *Woodings (1968a)* 233–4 argues that the Law Student and Old Man's dialogue (ll. 136–47) is another version of the Young Man and Old Man's dialogue (ll. 2–60) and is evidence 'that Shelley replaced the original opening of the Mask scene, and planned a new beginning …' In Woodings's view, with the first sixty lines removed, the play would open with Bastwick's speech (beginning at l. 62) and the 'descriptions of the characters'. (See 'Sources, Genre and Form' in the headnote for more on the phrase's repetition and likely source.) With the deliberate reiteration of the phrase, however, S. formalises this scene's return to the voices of the first group of non-historical speakers.

136. [Into the royal presence.]] The retention of this cancelled half-line in all *eds* seems correct: the second half is neatly completed by the beginning of the Law Student's question. *royal*] Royal *1824*. *think'st*] thinkest *1824*, Rossetti *1870*. Above the *es* of *thinkest* in *Nbk 19* p. 166 *reverso* is a large apostrophe, indicating a contraction.

137. show] Preceded by *pageant* canc. and then *masque* canc. in *Nbk 19*. This line recalls l. 2 above and foreshadows the Queen's comments in Scene ii 11: 'the quaint pageant'. The fact that the Law Student addresses his speech to 'my agèd friend' (the Old Man) returns the action to the opening group of characters. Given that the 'Inns of Court should present their service to the King' with a Royal Masque (*Whitelocke* 18), the Law Student views it personally: 'this quaint show of ours'.

138–46. Omitted in *1824*.

138. ye see] we see Rossetti *1870*.

139. Inflame] Cp. the *[inflamed] electric fountains* in *Cyprian* ii 36 (*Nbk 18* p. 62). *and clarions*] and the clarions Rossetti *1870*.

140   Rouse up the astonished air — 'tis at hand,
      And the loud music seems a magic stream
      On which the pageant floats. — And you, grave Sir —
      Does not your blood boil yet?

140–6. Despite the roughness of the MS in the upper quarter of p. 165 *reverso* in *Nbk 19*, Rossetti chose to retain much of that material which resulted in a jumbled and incomplete passage:

> Gasp (?) to us on the wind's wave. It comes!
> And their sounds, floating hither round the pageant,
> Rouse up the astonished air.

A revision, missed by Rossetti, appears to emend the end of the Law Student's speech in *Nbk 19* p. 165 *reverso* and gives the Old Man's response as well. The revision (ll. 140–7) is found several pages later, ruled off at the bottom of *Nbk 19* p. 161 *reverso*, and continues on to facing p. 160 *reverso*. Rossetti thus omits ll. 141–6 and erroneously allows the First Citizen to reply to the Law Student's address to 'my agèd friend'.

140. the astonished air] See *Lines connected with Hellas* (no. 411 Appendix A) (*It is the period when all the Sons of God*) l. 66: 'Cling in the astonished air. —'. *'tis at hand,*] Omitted in *Rossetti 1870*. This half-line is found in a ruled-off section at the foot of *Nbk 19* p. 161 *reverso*.

141–2. And the loud … floats. —] In *Nbk 19* p. 161 *reverso*, these one and a half lines adapt and resolve several images and phrases from the p. 165 *reverso* passage: [*sound to us upon the wind*] and then [*floats*] *to us on the wind's wave — it comes / And their sounds floating* [?*welter*] *round / the pageant comes*. See *TL* 97–8: 'I heard alone on the air's soft stream / The music of their ever-moving wings.'

141. magic stream] magical stream *BSM* (the *al* is emended and cancelled in *Nbk 19* p. 161 *reverso*).

142–6. And you, grave Sir — … seething. —] Omitted in *eds*. This half-line and the next four lines are found *in Nbk 19* p. 160 *reverso* facing *'tis at hand … floats.*— on p. 161 *reverso*. A descending line of dots on p. 165 *reverso* (right-hand side) and an ascending line of dots on p. 160 *reverso* (right-hand side) might be a linking symbol, tying the material on pp. 161–160 *reverso* to that on p. 165 *reverso*. *BSM* xii 276 indicates that these lines probably belong to the Law Student and the Old Man but links them to an earlier passage.

142. And you,] and you *Nbk 19*.

143. SD. Omitted in *Nbk 19* and *eds*. On a jottings page in *Nbk 19* p. 182 *reverso* are two and a half lines that would make a suitable response by the Old Man to the Law Student at this juncture with his query, 'Does not your blood boil yet?'. They read:

> I thank the reason shrewd within my head
> That in this general fever of the world
> My pulse beats temperately.

Old Man
                                                     Tears for men's folly
         Might kill [the] fire lit in youth's heart of straw,
145   But it goes out — and the virtuous fury
         Dies in smoke and foam of its own seething. —

Young Man
         I will not think but that our country's wounds

The Old Man's *reason* and temperate *pulse* set in contrast to the world's *fever* would seem to silence the student's estimation of the Old Man's patience. Cp. *Hamlet* III iv 140–1: 'My pulse as yours doth temperately keep time, / And makes as healthful music.' A suitable position for the lines on p. 182 *reverso* is not evident given their metrical structure. While they could fit in at the start of the Old Man's speech, just before l. 143, insertion of the passage would leave the Law Student's last line, also at 143, incomplete. On the other hand, if they were added to the end of the Old Man's speech, following l. 146, his last line *My pulse beats temperately* would then be incomplete.
143–6. *Tears for … seething.* —] Cp. the second stanza of the ballad sung by Davie in Walter Scott, *Waverley; Or, 'Tis Sixty Years Since*, 3 vols (1814), I, ch. xiv:

> The young man's wrath is like light straw on fire;
> *Heard ye so merry the little bird sing?*
> But like red-hot steel is the old man's ire,
> *And the throstle-cock's head is under his wing.*

S. and Mary read *Waverley* between 23 February and 9 April 1817 and Mary records reading it again on 15–16 December 1821 (*Mary Jnl* i 166, 388). In the Preface to his tragedy *Marino Faliero*, published on 21 April 1821 (*Byron PW* iv 523), Byron cites the first and third lines above, followed by part of Syphax's speech from Joseph Addison, *Cato, A Tragedy* (1713), II v 136–7: 'Young men soon give, and soon forget affronts; / Old age is slow in both'. Neither quotation in Byron's Preface is entirely accurate (*Byron PW* iv 302). Byron had read *Marino Faliero* to S. during the latter's stay in Ravenna in August 1821. S. told Mary in a letter of 7 August: 'I have read only parts of it, or rather he himself read them to me & gave me the plan of the whole' (*L* ii 317). S.'s letter to Peacock of ?10 August indicates that he may by then have read the whole himself: 'I have not seen [Byron's] late plays, except "Marino Faliero", which is very well, but not so transcendently fine as the "Don Juan"' (*L* ii 330).
144. *straw,*] straw *Nbk 19*.
147. *SD*. Omitted in *Nbk 19*; First Speaker *1824*; First Citizen *Rossetti 1870*. The Young Man's 'I will not think' echoes as a reply to the Law Student's initial question, 'What think'st thou' at l. 136.

May yet be healed — the King is just and gracious
Though wicked counsels now pervert his will;
150 These once cast off —

Old Man
                As adders cast their skins
And keep their venom, so Kings often change
Councils and counsellors that, tagged together,
Hang on the limbs of the foul dwarf ambition
Like the base patchwork of a leper's rags ...

148–9. the King is just ... his will] Cp. Macaulay ii 45 citing a supporter of the King: 'I know we have a good king, and this is the advice of his wicked ministers'; *Hutchinson Life* 68 notes, 'there were two [Laud and Wentworth] above all the rest, who led the van of the king's evil counsellors'.
148. healed — the King] healed — The King *1824*; healed. The king *Rossetti 1870*. *gracious*] gracious, *1824, Rossetti 1870*.
149. will;] will, . . *Nbk 19*; will: *1824, Rossetti 1870*.
150–4. As adders ... leper's rags] Initially, the Old Man's speech here was one and a half lines; then S. entered the next speaker heading, *Young Man*. On second thought, S. cancelled the Old Man's short speech and started again, composing a longer speech of four and a half lines but failing to cancel the Young Man's speech heading.
150. SD. Omitted in *Nbk 19*; Second Speaker *1824*; Second Citizen *Rossetti 1870*. Crook is probably correct in suggesting that the curious set of zig-zag strokes overlaid with three dots and then underlined is S.'s symbol for the Old Man (*BSM* xii 283).
150. off —] *1824, Rossetti 1870*; off — . . . *Nbk 19*.
151. so Kings often change] so kings often change; *1824; Rossetti 1870*.
152–4. Councils ... leper's rags] Cp. a cancelled passage in the press copy of *Hellas* in Edward Williams's hand (*HM 329* p. 10):

                or with men
        Who have put off those filthy general rags
        Which make the soul leprous

152. that,] that *Nbk 19*. *1824* and *Rossetti 1870* give 'Councils and counsellors hang on one another,' an extant line certainly; however, squeezed in above it is the phrase *that* [?] *tagged together* emending the line so as to work with the new l. 153 which is infilled above at the start of this speech in *Nbk 19* p. 164 *reverso*.
153. 'Hiding the loathsome [   ]' *1824*; 'Hiding the loathsome …,' *Rossetti 1870*. The line in *Nbk 19* p. 164 *reverso* originally read *Hiding* [*ambitions*] *the loathsome ambition* [*deformity*]. These images were resolved in the completed line infilled above, before the start of this speech: *Hang on the limbs of the foul dwarf ambition*.
154. rags ...] rags. *1824, Rossetti 1870*.

Young Man
155 O, still those dissonant thoughts … list how the music
Grows on the enchanted air — and see the torches
Restlessly flashing, the crowd divided
Like waves before an Admiral's prow —
                              [*The Masque approaches.*

Marshalman
                                        Give place
To the Marshal of the Masques!

Young Man
                              How glorious
160 Even in a vision! See those thronging chariots
Rolling like painted clouds before the evening sun

155. SD. Third Speaker *1824*; The Youth *Rossetti 1870.* The SD *Young Man* was entered prematurely in the middle of *Nbk 19* p. 164 *reverso*, but then S. developed the Old Man's speech. The Young Man's speech finally begins at the bottom of the same page.
155. O, still] Oh! still *Rossetti 1870. thoughts … list how the music*] thoughts— List! loud music *1824*; thoughts!— List how the music *Rossetti 1870.*
156. air — and see] air — And see *Nbk 19*; air! And see, *1824, Rossetti 1870.*
157. flashing, the crowd] flashing, and the crowd *1824, Rossetti 1870.*
158. SD. The Masque approaches] Omitted in *eds. 1824* indicates a lacuna. Twice in *Nbk 19* p. 163 *reverso*, S. squeezes in a possible SD: [?*the*] masque [?*app*] and *and the masque approaching.* Marshalman] Omitted in *Nbk 19*; Another Speaker *1824*; A Marshalman *Rossetti 1870.* Whitelocke notes there was a 'Marshal of the Masque' as well as an entourage of 'Marshal men'; see note to ll. 134–6.
158. Admiral's prow —] Admiral's prow. *1824*; admiral's prow! *Rossetti 1870. Give place*] Give place— *1824.*
159. SD. Omitted in *Nbk 19*; Third Speaker *1824*; The Youth *Rossetti 1870.*
159. Masques!] Masque! *1824, Rossetti 1870.* See note to l. 135. Between this line and the Young Man's speech below, *Rossetti 1870* inserts an SD and half-line located in *Nbk 19* p. 174 *reverso* ('A Pursuivant / Room for the King!'); in the present edition these elements are found at l. 60 SD. and l. 61. *How glorious*] *1824* and *Rossetti 1870* conflate with part of next line: 'How glorious! See those thronging chariots'. It seems certain, however, that 'How glorious' is the Young Man's conclusion of the Marshalman's last half-line.
160–73. See those … chosen land] S. follows closely Whitelocke's description of the chariots, the riders and horses; see *Whitelocke* 19–20.
160. Even in a vision!] Omitted in *eds.* The second half of this line is found just below, on the facing *Nbk 19* p. 162 *reverso*.
161. Rolling] Rolling, *Rossetti 1870. the evening sun*] the wind: *1824*; the wind, *Rossetti 1870.*

Behind the[ir] [solemn] steeds — how some are shaped
[Like] curved [shells] dyed with the azure silence
Of Indian seas, some like the new-born moon,
165 And some like cars in which the Roman climbed,
Canopied by Victory's eagle-wings outspread,
The Capitolian. — See how [gloriously]
The mettled horses in the torchlight [stir],
Their gallant riders [?shouting] while they check
170 Their foaming speed, — how beautiful [?they] [?seem],

162. Behind the[ir] [solemn] steeds —] Behind their solemn steeds: *Rossetti 1870*; omitted in *1824*. *how some are shaped*] Some are *1824*.
163. [Like] curved [shells]] Like curved sea-shells *Rossetti 1870*. Rossetti's 'sea-shells', queried by *Forman 1876-7*, can be explained: *seas*, an emendation for *waves* canc. in the line below, is squeezed in and sits underneath *[shells]*. *azure silence*] azure depths *1824*, *Rossetti 1870*.
164. seas,] seas; *1824*, *Rossetti 1870*. *moon,*] moon; *1824*, *Rossetti 1870*.
165-7. And some ... outspread] S. seems to have drawn the depiction of the 'cars' and the triumphant Roman shaded by 'Victory's eagle-wings' from his description of the Arch of Titus: 'Titus is represented standing on a chariot drawn by four horses ... & surrounded by the tumultuous numbers of his victorious army; ... Behind him stands a Victory, eagle-winged' (Nora Crook, 'Arch of Titus' in 'Shelley's Jewish "Orations"', *K-SJ*, lix (2010) 58-9; the MS of this passage is found in *Box 1* f. 207^r; for a facsimile see *BSM* xxi 246).
165. Roman] Romans *1824*, *Rossetti 1870*. S. is possibly referring specifically to Titus; see note to ll. 165-7 above.
166. All eds enclose this line in parentheses. *eagle-wings outspread*] The eagle, a symbol of courage, was represented on standards carried by the Roman legion.
167-75. See how [gloriously] ... English air] See *Whitelocke* 19: 'The richness of their Apparel and Furniture glittering, by the light of a multitude of torches attending on them, with the motion and stirring of the mettled Horses, and the many and various gay Liveries of their Servants; but especially the personal beauty and gallantry of the handsome young Gentlemen, made the most glorious and splendid shew that ever was beheld in England.'
167. Capitolian. —] Capitolian — . *Nbk 19*; Capitolian— *1824*; Capitolian! *Rossetti 1870*. The Capitolian (The Capitolium or Capitoline Hill, one of the seven hills of Rome) was visited several times by the Shelleys during their stay in Rome (March-June 1819). On 10 March 1819 Mary recorded: 'Visit the Capitol & see most divine statues' (*Mary Jnl* ii 252).
168. mettled] 'lively, eager, spirited, frisky' (*OED* 2b). *[stir,]* stir *1824*, *Rossetti 1870*.
169. [?shouting] while they check] while they check their pride *1824*; while *they* check their pride *Rossetti 1870*.
170. Omitted in *eds*. *Their foaming speed* was cancelled and then stetted. Another version reads *Their [foaming] pride*. This is probably the source of 'pride' in the *eds* version of l. 169.

How full of spirit, beautiful and brave,
How far excelling even their former selves
Shows the graceful flower of this chosen land,
Like shapes of some diviner element
175   Than English air, and beings nobler than
The envious and admiring multitude.

A Law Student
These are the lilies glorious as Solomon,
Who toil not, neither do they spin: unless
It be the webs they catch poor rogues withal ...

171–3. Omitted in *eds.*
171. How full of spirit] Followed by a caret symbol in *Nbk 19* p. 162 *reverso,* possibly indicating the place for one and a half lines above on facing p. 163 *reverso* to be inserted.
173. graceful] Written above *chosen* in *Nbk 19.*
174–6. Like shapes ... multitude] Found at the top of the page overleaf, *Nbk 19* p. 161 *reverso.*
174. element] element! *1824.*
175–6. Omitted in *1824.*
177. SD. Omitted in *Nbk 19*; Second Speaker *1824*; Second Citizen *Rossetti 1870.* The Law Student seems the most likely speaker of the three speakers: the tone is not that of the naïve Young Man. The Old Man's bitter response to the comment (l. 180) confirms this.
177–9. These are ... withal] Both *1824* and *Rossetti 1870* postpone these lines to follow l. 185 below. On *Nbk 19* p. 161 *reverso*, lines similar to these and following the Young Man's last line at 176 are incomplete and seemingly added in during an initial composing period:

> the [gay] bright lilies
> *That toil not neither do they spin — except*
> *Such [webs] toils of law as catch poor rogues, yet Solomon*
> *In all his glory is not like one of these*

However, when the facing leaf (pp. 160–159 rev.), which is half torn away, is flipped up against p. 161, the final draft of these lines on p. 159 *reverso* neatly fits into place just below l. 176 on p. 161 *reverso.* The first line of the Old Man's response (l. 180) confirms this order by continuing the *flower/lilies* image of ll. 173, 177.
177. the lilies glorious as Solomon] Cf. *Matthew* vi 28–9: 'Consider the lilies of the field, how they grow; they toil not, neither do they spin: And yet I say unto you, That even Solomon in all his glory was not arrayed like one of these.'
178. toil not,] toil not *Nbk 19, Rossetti 1870.* spin:] spin,— *1824*; spin— *Rossetti 1870.*
179. withal ...] withal. *1824, Rossetti 1870.*

Old Man

180 Aye, these are they who bloom upon his dunghill,
Nobles and sons of nobles — patentees,
Monopolists, and stewards of this poor farm
On whose lean sheep sit the prophetic crows;
Here is the Pomp that strips the houseless orphan,
185 Here is the Pride that breaks the desolate heart,
Here is the Surfeit which to them who earn
The niggard wages of the earth, scarce leaves
The tithe that will support them till they [crawl]
Back to her cold hard bosom — here is Health
190 Followed by grim Disease ... Glory by Shame,

180. SD. Omitted in *Nbk 19*; Second Speaker *1824*; Second Citizen *Rossetti 1870*.
180. Aye, there they are—*1824*; Ay, there they are— *Rossetti 1870*.
181-2. *patentees ... Monopolists*] Cp. S.'s notes in *Nbk 21* p. 251 *reverso*: *Monopolies & taxes. See Richard* 2^d — *See Hume 206. & consider the present times* (*BSM* xvi 234-5). *Hume* records 'Monopolies were revived; an oppressive method of buying money being unlimited, as well as destructive of industry. ... The manufacture of soap was given to a company who paid a sum for their patent' (vii 206). *Ludlow 1771* also notes, 'Patents and monopolies of almost every thing were granted to private men, to the great damage of the publick' (i 12).
181. *Nobles*] Nobles, *1824, Rossetti 1870*. *nobles* —] nobles, *1824, Rossetti 1870*. *patentees*] Persons 'granted a privilege, title, land, etc., by letters patent' (*OED* 1). 'Letters patent' are open letters 'issued by a monarch or government to record a contract, authorize or command an action, or confer a privilege, right, office, title, or property. In later use *esp*.: such a document which grants for a set period the sole right to make, use, or sell some process, invention, or commodity' (*OED* 'patent' *adj*. 1a).
182. *Monopolists*] Those who possess a trading monopoly (see *OED* 1). *farm*] farm, *1824*.
183. *prophetic crows*] The crow's prophetic powers are referenced in Ovid, *Met*. ii 550: 'ne sperne meae praesagia linguae!' ('Scorn not the forewarning of my tongue'). In ll. 184-92 the crows prophesy poverty, famine and death. *crows;*] crows — *Nbk 19*; crows. *1824, Rossetti 1870*.
184. *Pomp*] pomp *1824, Rossetti 1870*. *orphan,*] orphan — *Nbk 19*.
185. In *eds*, this line is followed by ll. 177-9 of present edition. *Pride*] pride *1824, Rossetti 1870*. *heart,*] heart *Nbk 19*; heart. *1824, Rossetti 1870*.
186. *Surfeit*] surfeit *1824, Rossetti 1870*. Above this line in *Nbk 19* p. 159 *reverso* is the phrase *Here is the Pride* [*that*] which is the linking device to the complete line on p. 161 *reverso*.
187. *niggard*] scanty (see *OED* 4). *earth,*] earth *Rossetti 1870*.
189. *to her*] to its *1824*. *bosom* —] bosom. *1824, Rossetti 1870*. *Health*] health *1824, Rossetti 1870*.
190. *Disease ... Glory by Shame,*] disease .. Glory by Shame *Nbk 19*; disease, glory by shame, *1824, Rossetti 1870*.

Waste by lame Famine, Wealth by squalid Want
And England's Sin by England's Punishment;
And, as the Effect pursues the Cause foregone
So, giving substance to my words, behold — [*Enter Antimasque.*
195 At once the sign and the thing signified —
A troop of cripples, beggars and lean outcasts
Horsed upon stumbling jades, carted with dung,
Advance to filthy tunes and the [?vile] twang
Of keys and tongues, [jews' harps and marrow bones],
200 Dragged for a day from cellars and low cabins
And rotten hiding-holes, to point the moral
Of this presentment, and bring up the rear
[Of painted Pomp] [with] Misery —

191. All *eds* give 'Waste by lame famine, wealth by squalid want'.
192. England's Sin] England's sin *1824, Rossetti 1870. England's Punishment;*] England's punishment *Nbk 19*; England's punishment. *1824, Rossetti 1870.*
193. Effect] effect *1824, Rossetti 1870. Cause*] cause *Nbk 19, 1824, Rossetti 1870.*
194. SD. Omitted in *Nbk 19*. The Old Man's personification of evils in England is given *substance* with the arrival of the antimasque which he describes in the following lines.
194. behold —] behold *Nbk 19, 1824, Rossetti 1870.*
196–9. S.'s description faithfully follows *Whitelocke* 19:

> After the Horsemen came the Antimasquers, and as the Horsemen had their Musick, … so the first Antimasque being of Cripples, and Beggers on horseback, had their Musick of Keys and Tongues, and the like, snapping and yet playing in a Consort before them.
>
> These Beggers were also mounted, but on the poorest leanest Jades that could be gotten out of the Dirt-carts, or elsewhere …

196. beggars] beggars, *1824, Rossetti 1870. outcasts*] outcasts, *1824, Rossetti 1870.*
197. jades] shapes *1824*. A jade is 'a sorry, ill-conditioned, wearied, or worn-out horse' (see *OED* 1a).
198. Omitted in *eds*. The complex tangle of layers with letters hidden among them undoubtedly accounts for this line's omission in *eds*. The line began promisingly in *Nbk 19* p. *157 reverso* with *Advance to the* [*villainous*][*tunes*] then [*villainous dissonance*], but cancels and elaborate strokes give the impression S. was trying to disguise the latest revisions.
201. hiding-holes,] hiding-holes *1824.*
202. presentment] presentiment *1824.*
203. SD. Omitted in *Nbk 19*; Speaker *1824*; The Youth *Rossetti 1870.*

> *Young Man*
>
>   It is but
> The antimasque and serves as discords do
> In sweetest music; who would love spring flowers
> If they succeeded not to winter's flaw —
> Or day unchanged by night, or joy itself
> Without the touch of sorrow?
>
> *Old Man*
>
>   I and thou ...

203-5. It is but ... sweetest music] The effect of the contrast between the masque and the antimasque is noted in *Whitelocke* 19: 'and the variety and change from such noble Musick, and gallant Horses, as went before them, unto their proper Musick, and pitiful Horses, made both of them the more pleasing'.
203. Of painted pomp with misery! *1824*. Omitted in *Rossetti 1870* presumably because of the cancel stroke. Forman, however, followed *1824*, noting Rossetti's omission of this phrase (*Forman 1876-7* iii 297); Rossetti corrected the line for *Rossetti 1878* iii 189. The line initially read, *Of painted Pomp with its own miscreance*. *Nbk 19* p. 157 *reverso* shows two additional attempts to replace it, the final version being *Of all but the dread consequence*. S. then began the opening to Scene ii with *Enter King Queen / Laud; Wentworth Archy &*. However, all these stage directions were cancelled because he possibly decided the new scene start was premature. Perhaps the unusual wavy strokes are meant to reinstate the cancelled l. 203 along with the later emendation of *misery* added in above [*with its own miscreance*]. *It is but*] 'Tis but *1824, Rossetti 1870*.
204. *antimasque*] anti-masque, *1824, Rossetti 1870*.
205. *music; who*] music. Who *1824, Rossetti 1870*. The reading in *Nbk 19* p. 156 *reverso* is unclear; it seems as if a colon was altered, overwritten by a long comma. *spring flowers*] May flowers *1824, Rossetti 1870*. Both *May* and *spring* are cancelled, where *May* is the second choice inserted below *spring*. The next line in *Nbk 19* p. 156 *reverso* dips below *May* at *winter's* (l. 206) so it seems likely that S. cancelled *May*, intending to reinstate the cancelled *spring*, preferring the parallel comparison of season to season with 'spring' and 'winter'.
206. *winter's flaw* —] Winter's flaw; *1824*; winter's flaw? *Rossetti 1870*. 'flaw' = 'a sudden blast or gust, usually of short duration' (*OED n.*^{2} 1a). Cp. *Hamlet* V i 215-16: 'O that that earth which kept the world in awe / Should patch a wall t' expel the [winter's] flaw!'.
207. *night,*] night; *1824*.
208. *SD*. Omitted in *1824*; Second Citizen *Rossetti 1870*. One of the rare occasions that the Old Man's SD, written out, appears in *Nbk 19* (p. 156 rev.).
208. *I and thou ...*] Omitted in *1824*, however, a lacuna is indicated. The Old Man's response echoes the latent *sorrow* revealed in *discords* demonstrated by his own existence and that of the Young Man. The number notation, *180*, written

Scene ii

A Chamber in Whitehall

Enter PURSUIVANT.

Pursuivant
Place, give place!

Enter the KING, QUEEN, LAUD, WENTWORTH, LORD COTTINGTON, LORD KEEPER COVENTRY, LORD TREASURER WESTON, LORD ESSEX, ARCHY. *To them enter* SIR JOHN FINCH, ATTORNEY NOY, *and* GENTLEMEN OF THE INNS OF COURT.

King Charles [*To* FINCH, NOY *and* GENTLEMEN.

Thanks, Gentlemen, we heartily accept

---

after this line near the page edge (*Nbk 19* p. 156 rev.) might be S.'s line count for this scene (as suggested by Crook, *BSM* xii 268). If so, it would mean that the first 60 lines were to be included in S.'s conception of Scene i; just below these lines on p. 156 *reverso* are the stage directions and first lines of Scene ii. The discrepancy between this edition's scene of 208 lines and the 180 notation might be explained by the possibility that 180 serves as an approximate count because several brief passages are out of sequence and/or located on mutilated leaves. After this line, Rossetti appends an SD and a half line, 'A Marshalsman. Place, give place!' which belong, in fact, to the next scene. *Place, give place* appears below S.'s scene close, marked by a long centred dash and positioned just above the Scene ii SD (*Nbk 19* p. 156 rev.).

SD. Scene ii] Scene 2. *Nbk 22* f. *1ʳ; omitted in *Nbk 19*. A Chamber in Whitehall] Scene Chamber in Whitehall *Nbk 19* p. 156 rev.; The interior of Whitehall. — *Nbk 22* f. *1ʳ.
1. SD. Pursuivant] Omitted in *Nbk 19* and *eds*. Despite its absence, a pursuivant, or royal messenger must be the speaker of this half-line; see note to Scene i 1. SD above.
1. Omitted in *1824*; *Rossetti 1870* includes this line at the end of Scene i. *place!*] place. *Nbk 19*. Line 1, squeezed in between the Old Man's last line in Scene i and the speakers of Scene ii in *Nbk 19*, is probably a later addition when S. recognised the need to formalise the King's entrance with the royal party followed by the entrance of the Masque committee and the Gentlemen of the Inns of Court.

2. SD. Enter King Queen. Laud / Wentworth Archy *Nbk 19*; The interior of / Whitehall. — The King / Wentworth, Laud, L$^{d.}$ Keeper / Coventry Lord Essex Archy / to them enter S^r [or D^r (*MYRS* vii 154)] John, Noy, & the lawyers — *Nbk 21* f. *1^r; *Enter the* King, Queen, Laud, Wentworth, and Archy *1824*; Enter the King, Queen, Laud, Lord Strafford, Lord Cottington, and other Lords; Archy; also St John, with some Gentlemen of the Inns of Court *Rossetti 1870*. *Lord Treasurer Weston*] Richard Weston, 1st Earl of Portland (1577–1635) was instrumental in seeking out and sustaining the King's sources of revenue. *Clarendon* notes: 'he had a full share in his master's esteem, who looked upon him as a wise and able servant, and worthy of the trust he reposed in him, and received no other advice in the large business of his revenue' (i 87). *Lord Essex*] Robert Devereux, 3rd Earl of Essex (1591–1646), was an experienced soldier. In the first Scottish war, 'The earl of Essex, a man of strict honour, and extremely popular, especially among the soldiery, was appointed lieutenant-general' (*Hume* vii 244). However, only three years later, in 1642, he was to oppose the King in leading the Parliamentarian army as Captain-General and Chief Commander. *Sir John Finch*] Rossetti reads 'St John' for *Sr John* in *Nbk 19* p. 154 *reverso* despite the fact that just below, *Sir Johns* is legible. Accepting Rossetti's reading, Cameron concluded that S. 'makes the spokesman for the delegation not Sir John Finch but Oliver St. John.' Thus, according to Cameron, St. John's presence with his 'Puritan sympathies' makes him a target of Henrietta's anger at Puritan strictures on masques, mummeries, and dancing (*Cameron (1945)* 202). *BSM* xii 264 concurs with this assessment. The MS, however, shows no such deviation from Whitelocke's account that it is Sir John Finch who is present in this scene. Indeed, his name appears twice in *Nbk 19* and once in *Nbk 21* as described above. Finch was one of the key organisers of the Masque, the lead committee member for Gray's Inn; it is to him that the King offered his official public thanks to the Inns of Court for their masque (*Whitelocke* 21). It seems unlikely S. would have deviated so far from his sources as to allow a Puritan to be the organiser of the Masque, an entertainment that Puritans railed against. Furthermore, the formal and gracious opening of this scene is a counterpoint to the previous scene with its harsh and contemptuous Puritan attacks on the court's participation in, and encouragement of, such frivolities as plays and masques. See note to ll. 21-2 for the events that precipitated the decision to launch a particularly elaborate and costly Masque in 1634. *Attorney Noy*] The King's attorney, named a Grandee for the Masque preparations along with Sir John Finch (*Whitelocke* 19). To FINCH, NOY and GENTLEMEN] Omitted in *Nbk 19* and eds. 2-5. S. here follows closely Charles's response quoted in *Whitelocke* 21: 'Gentlemen, pray assure those from whom you come, that we are exceeding well-pleased with that Testimony which they lately gave us, of their great respect and affection to us, which was very acceptable, and performed with that Gallantry, and in so excellent a manner, that I cannot but give them thanks for it'.

2. *Gentlemen,*] gentlemen, *1824*; gentlemen. *Rossetti 1870*. we heartily] I heartily *1824*, *Rossetti 1870*. *Nbk 19* p. 156 *reverso* shows *I* canc. with several strokes; 'we' follows *Whitelocke* 21 (see note to ii 2-5 above), as the majestic plural and is perhaps meant also to include Queen Henrietta.

This token of your service, your gay masque,
When in the envious winter, its glory
5 Was performed gallantly. — O, it shows well
When subjects twine flowers of observance
With the sharp thorns that line the English crown.
The kingly heart enjoys what it confers
Even as it suffers that which it inflicts

3. *service;*] service: *1824, Rossetti 1870. masque,*] masque *1824, Rossetti 1870.*
4. Omitted in *eds*. This line is infilled in *Nbk 19* p. 156 *reverso* above l. 1 and just below the SD; it is then ruled off to separate it from the surrounding material. The reading in *Woodings (1968a)* 225 is: 'Where, in the envious winter [of this] its glory'.
5. *gallantly.* —] gallantly — *Nbk 19;* gallantly. *1824; Rossetti 1870. O, it shows well*] Omitted in *1824;* And it shows well *Rossetti 1870.*
6–10. Omitted in *1824.*
6. *twine flowers*] twine such flowers *Rossetti 1870. observance*] observance (?) *Rossetti 1870.* BSM indicates an ampersand following *observance* which is possible but unnecessary given that the following line is clear. Cp. Clarendon's description of the realities of being a ruler: 'and above all, that whosoever may have a thought of ruling in this land, may be throughly convinced in his own judgment, that it is a crown of briars and thorns that must be set on his head, without he can satisfy all reasonable men, that it is his fixed principle and resolution, inviolably to defend our religion, and preserve our laws' (*Clarendon* i 7).
7. *that line*] that deck *Rossetti 1870.* Below *deck* canc. (*Nbk 19* p. 156 rev.) is *line* which *BSM* indicates is attached to *brow* canc.; however, *line* is an independent emendation to l. 7 above and is not cancelled. *crown.*] crown *Nbk 19.*
8–10. Below l. 7 are two uncancelled lines: *A gentle heart which feels what it inflicts / Though justice guide the stroke, enjoys no less* (*Nbk 19* p. 156 rev.). However, these two lines as well as a third line are re-worked several pages later on p. 150 *reverso.* Rossetti understood that the re-worked lines found there were to be fitted into the p. 156 *reverso* draft.
8. *The kingly heart*] A gentle heart *Rossetti 1870.* At bottom of p. 150 *reverso* is a cleanly written *The [gentle] kingly heart.*
9. *inflicts*] inflicts, *Rossetti 1870.*

10   Though Justice guide the stroke. —

Queen Henrietta
                              And, Gentlemen,
     Call your poor Queen your debtor — the quaint pageant
     Rose on me like the figures of past years
     Treading their still path back to Infancy —
     More beautiful and mild as they draw nearer
15   The quiet cradle: I could have almost wept
     To think I was in Paris, where these shows
     Are well devised — such as I was ere yet
     My young heart took a portion of the burthen
     Of married love and my [?] [   ]

10. SD. Omitted in *Nbk 19*; Queen *1824*, *Rossetti 1870*.
10. guide] guides *Rossetti 1870*. stroke. —] stroke — *Nbk 19*; stroke. *Rossetti 1870*. Cp. Charles's phrase when defending Wentworth: 'yet I could never be convinced of any such criminousnesse in him as willingly to expose his life to the stroke of Justice' (*Eikon Basilike* 7). *Rossetti 1870* gives a different incomplete line before Henrietta's interjection: *Accept my hearty thanks*, a half-line that occurs at the top of p. 155 *reverso* just before her speech. Because it belonged to the sequence of lines in the first draft at bottom of p. 155 *reverso*, it seems likely it was abandoned because of the new lines on p. 150 *reverso* which included a new half-line *Though Justice guide the stroke.*— making a complete line with the Queen's response. *And, Gentlemen,*] And, gentlemen, *1824*, *Rossetti 1870*.
11. debtor —] debtor. *1824*, *Rossetti 1870*. the quaint] Your quaint *1824*, *Rossetti 1870*. For l. 3 above, S. cancelled *quaint* and emended it to *gay* perhaps to avoid repetition with its use here in the Queen's speech. See also Scene i 2, *quaint masque* and 137, *quaint show*.
12. years] years, *1824*, *Rossetti 1870*.
13. Infancy —] infancy, *1824*, *Rossetti 1870*.
15. cradle:] cradle. *1824*, *Rossetti 1870*. The draft in *Nbk 19* p. 155 *reverso* shows complicated punctuation following *cradle*: a set of three suspension points overlaid by a long dash; above that, a dash and colon.
18–19. *My young ... my [?]*] Layers of emendations and cancels in *Nbk 19* p. 155 *reverso* make for conjectural readings here; *eds* omit l. 19 entirely.
18. My young heart shared with [   ] the task, *1824*; My young heart shared a portion of the burthen, *Rossetti 1870*. All the elements of these readings (except *1824*'s 'task') are present in the *Nbk 19* draft; however, what seems to be a later emendation, *took a portion of the burthen*, over-writes a mostly illegible cancelled phrase.

20 The careful weight of this great Monarchy ...
    In Paris, ribald censurers dare not move
    Their poisonous tongues against these sinless sports.
    There, Gentlemen, between the sovereign's pleasure
    And that which it regards, no clamour lifts

    19. Omitted in eds. [?]] work BSM. The rest of the line remains incomplete in *Nbk 19*.
    20. *weight*] weight, *1824, Rossetti 1870. Monarchy* ...] monarchy. *1824, Rossetti 1870.*
    21-9. The youngest sister of Louis XIII, Henrietta here describes how 'sinless sports' like plays and masques reminded her of her youth in Paris, but more importantly, these entertainments are neither censured nor deemed immoral there, unlike the Puritan outrage levelled against such activities in London. She ends with a comparison of the French and English monarchs, implying that if Charles had the riches of Louis, his gifts — 'golden deeds' (l. 29) — would be more generous. The question of Charles's depleted treasury is also signalled by Henrietta describing herself as 'your poor Queen your debtor' in l. 11.
    21-2. Lines 21-2 are omitted in *1824*. Rossetti inserts ll. 21-2 after the first half of the present edition's l. 25: 'Its proud interposition'. Although ll. 21-2 are found at the bottom of p. 155 *reverso* — just below l. 25 — and continue at the top of p. 154 *reverso*, they should follow l. 20 instead, completing Henrietta's Paris and London comparison. In addition, they are separated from l. 25 by three centred horizontal strokes; their insertion point is signalled by the word *censurers* left uncancelled amidst the line endings for 18–19 and just above *Monarchy* followed by three suspension points. Henrietta's mention of 'ribald censurers' refers generally to the Puritans who believed that plays and masques were immoral, and specifically to William Prynne (1600–69) and his book, *Histrio-Mastix, the Players Scourge ... wherein it is largely evidenced, by divers Arguments ... that popular stage-playes ... are sinfull, heathenish, lewde, ungodly spectacles, and most pernicious corruptions. ...* (1632). *Whitelocke* 19 recounts how 'the Queen acted a part in a Pastoral at Somerset house'. Not long afterwards, a group of Prelates, perhaps including Laud, showed the King and Queen the book where Prynne wrote that '"Women actors notorious Whores", and informed the royal couple that Prynne had purposely written the Book against the Queen and her Pastoral'. Laud launched an attack on Prynne by taking 'scandalous' extracts from his book to 'Mr. Attorney Noy ... and charged him to prosecute Prynne for this book; which Noy afterwards did, rigorously enough in the Star Chamber'. S.'s SD for the incomplete Scene iv in the Star Chamber includes Prynne who historically received a punishment similar to that of Bastwick and Leighton. The Masque depicted in Scene i was instigated by 'principal Members of the societies of the four Inns of Court' for the express purpose of challenging Prynne's religious views in the *Histrio-Mastix* 'because this action would manifest the difference of their opinion from Mr. Prynne's new learning, and serve to confute his *Histrio Mastix* against enterludes' (*Whitelocke* 18).

25 Its proud interposition — and his smile
    Warms those who bask in it ... as ours would do. —
    [Yet] — take my heart's thanks — add them, Gentlemen,
    To those good words which were he King of France
    My royal lord would turn to golden deeds.

    Sir John Finch
30 Madam, the love of Englishmen can make

21. *ribald*] irreverent (see *OED adj.* 2).
23.*There, Gentlemen*] There, gentlemen *1824*; *There*, gentlemen *Rossetti 1870*.
25. *interposition* —] interposition. *1824, Rossetti 1870. and his smile*] Omitted in *1824*; *Rossetti 1870* published this line as two independent and incomplete half-lines: the first half follows this edition's l. 24, while the second half follows l. 22. In *Nbk 19* p. 155 *reverso*, the cancelled *and his smile* is then underlined, an example of S.'s linking devices. On the facing page 154 *reverso* the same phrase, *and his smile* reappears, offset to the right, followed by its completed thought: *Warms those who bask in it ...*
26–88. Omitted in *1824*.
26. *it ...*] it, *Rossetti 1870*. *do.* —] do *Rossetti 1870*.
27. *[Yet] — take*] If ... Take *Rossetti 1870*. S. followed l. 26 in the top third of *Nbk 19* p. 154 *reverso* with *Yet take my heart's thanks, add them dear Gentlemen / To what my royal husband would* then all were cancelled. He then skipped over a set of three wavy lines and one and a half lines of cancelled verse which probably were entered earlier in anticipation of a scene closing. They read [*And thus conclude / These dreams & so these pomps have vanished*]. Cp. *Whitelocke* 21: 'Thus these Dreams past, and these Pompes vanished.' Below this phrase is a revised version of l. 27 beginning with a majuscule *Y*, a short-hand for *Yet* as in the first draft above; however, *Rossetti 1870* and *BSM* decipher the *Y* as the word 'If'. S.'s first version beginning with *Yet* works grammatically with adjacent complete lines.
thanks — add them, Gentlemen,] thanks: add them, gentlemen, *Rossetti 1870*.
28–32. Several apparently abandoned lines found in *Nbk 19* p. 152 *reverso* share some similarities in phrasing with this exchange between the Queen and Sir John. A partial transcription reads:

> Your majesty, too [poor] meanly rates the love
> [?Touching] your poor servants, in this paragon. —
> Th[e love of English hearts] [makes] adorns
> Less than yourself. —

28. *which*] which, *Rossetti 1870*. *France*] France, *Rossetti 1870*.
30. SD. St. John *Rossetti 1870*. Rossetti read the superscript *r* as a 't'. (See note to l. 2. SD. above.)
30–2. *Madam ... despot's*] *Whitelocke* 21 cites Finch's fulsome thanks to the King and Queen. Finch's response in S.'s play retains the notion of loyalty to the King, where Englishmen do not need 'a despot's' treasury when 'The lightest favour' of

The lightest favour of their lawful king
Outweigh a despot's. —

               [*Aside of* LORD COVENTRY *to* LAUD, *overheard by* ARCHY.
Lord Coventry
               My Lord Archbishop,
Mark you what spirit sits in Sir John's eyes?

---

their King is more than sufficient payment. At the same time, however, he also corrects the Queen's seeming preference for the French court. This correction earns him the disdainful remarks of Lord Coventry and Laud which follow in ll. 32-7.

32. SD. Aside] Omitted in *Nbk 19* and *eds*. Rossetti concludes the first half of l. 32 with a brief passage found several pages away in *Nbk 19* p. 149 *reverso*: 'We humbly take our leaves, / Enriched by smiles which France can never buy.' (The present edition places these lines at ll. 64-6, following the conclusion of the sparring among Laud, Wentworth and Archy.) It seems certain, however, that l. 32 is concluded by Lord Coventry's aside to Laud, *My Lord Archbishop*, found just below on p. 154 *reverso* and offset to the right, a usual indication of speaker change. S. had first written then cancelled *My Lord of Essex* on the *verso* of this page, p. 153. Then he entered *Archy* as speaker heading and began his speech; however, that premature start was cancelled, and the exchange between Laud and Coventry was fitted in among Archy's cancelled lines. Archy's long response that follows demonstrates his attention to their private exchange. Rossetti's SD gives '*Exeunt* ST JOHN *and the Gentlemen of the Inns of Court*.' However, it seems more likely that the King and Queen continue their conversation with Finch and the Gentlemen on stage during the dialogue by Archy, Laud, and Wentworth. Crook provides an insightful discussion regarding the theatrical advantage of 'simultaneous discourse' in this scene (see *BSM* xii 254). *Lord Coventry*] King *Rossetti 1870*. Omitted in *Nbk 19* but Laud's response, l. 36, confirms this speech attribution is correct.

32. Originally read *Outweigh a despot's treasury* in *Nbk 19* — which makes the meaning transparent. However, apparently for metrical reasons, S. cancelled *treasury* once the second half of the line was composed. The half-line, *My Lord Archbishop* follows Finch's speech in sequence, on the same page (p. 154 rev.). *Rossetti 1870* assigns the half line and l. 33 to the King.

33. Sir John's] St John's *Rossetti 1870*; St Johns *BSM*. *Sir Johns* is written out reasonably clearly at very bottom of *Nbk 19* p. 154 *reverso*; the first draft of this line, [*What do you see sitting in Sr Johns eyes?*] is found just above l. 33. *Mark*] Observe (see *OED* 'mark' 26: 'To notice or perceive physically; to observe; to look at or watch'). To Laud's reiteration of 'I mark' in l. 34, Archy responds with a sustained play on the theme of eyes and seeing in ll. 38-51.

Laud
I mark. —
35 Methinks it is too saucy for this presence,
And doubt not this, my Lord of Coventry:
We will find time and place for fit rebuke.

Archy
Yes, pray, your Grace, look, for like an unsophisticated [eye]

34-7. I mark ... rebuke] The order of the lines in this speech is conjectural. They are fitted in among cancelled lines for Archy's speech in *Nbk 19*, and it is difficult to know which was the first intended line for Laud. 'I mark' would seem to respond directly to Sir John's query, 'Mark you what spirit sits in Sir John's eyes?' and is typical of S.'s linking device between speeches; additionally, 'it' in l. 35 needs to be near the referent, 'spirit' in l. 33.
34. Omitted in *Rossetti 1870.* Perhaps a deliberately short line, theatrically establishing Laud's self-righteousness and egotism, which is described in *Hutchinson Life* (68) and *Hume* (vii 196).
35. saucy] 'Of persons, their dispositions, actions, or language: Insolent towards superiors; presumptuous' (*OED* 2a). It is Sir John's presumption in his address to the Queen which particularly displeases Laud. *Rossetti 1870* assigns this line to the King, following l. 33 of the present edition. *presence,]* presence. *Rossetti 1870*
36-7. Rossetti 1870 places these two lines after l. 88 in the present edition.
36. Coventry:] Coventry, *Rossetti 1870.*
37. rebuke.] rebuke. — *Rossetti 1870.*
38. SD. Archy *Nbk 19*, *Rossetti 1870*. (See also the note to 32. SD.) The King's fool is mentioned in all of S.'s materials for the drama: *Nbk 21* p. 248 *reverso* (*poor Archy the* [*fool*] / *King's fool is dismissed by Laud*); *Nbk 22* f. *1^r (listed in SD for Scene ii); and throughout the text in *Nbk 19*. While Archy was inspired by the Fool in *King Lear*, S.'s characterisation is also closely based on both Hume's and Macaulay's record of the actual incident prompting Laud's fury with Archy. Macaulay (ii 225) writes:

> On some disagreeable news coming to court, Archibald Armstrong, the King's jester, seeing the prelate pass by, called out, "Whaws feule now:" [i.e. 'Who's fool now?" as if spoken with a Scottish accent] For this offence the harmless buffoon, who by his office had the privilege of passing jokes with impunity, was ordered, by a sentence of the council, to have his coat pulled over his head, and to be dismissed the King's service. (ii 251)

See also 'Sources, genre and form' in headnote for Armstrong's continued dispute with Laud.
38. Yes, pray, your Grace, look,] Yes pray, your Grace, look *Nbk 19*; Yes, pray your Grace look: *Rossetti 1870. unsophisticated [eye]]* unsophisticated ... *Rossetti 1870*; unsophisticated [eye] *Rossetti 1878*. Although cancelled in *Nbk 19*, 'eye' seems necessary for sense.

which sees everything upside down as those just come from the
40　outside of this [?empty] world, you who are wise will discern
the shadow of an idiot in lawn sleeves and a rochet setting springes
to catch woodcocks in haymaking time. — Poor Archy,
whose owl
eyes are tempered to the error of his age, and because he is
a fool and by special ordinance of God forbidden ever to see
himself
45　as he is, sees now in that deep eye a blindfold devil
sitting on the
ball, and weighing words out between King and subject. — One
scale is full of promises and the other full of protestations,
and then another devil creeps behind the first out of the dark
[?windings] [of a] pregnant lawyer's brain, and takes the
bandage

39–40. as those just … world] Omitted in *Rossetti 1870*. This phrase is squeezed in between previously written lines in *Nbk 19*.
41–2. springes / to catch woodcocks] Cp. Polonius's speech to Ophelia in *Hamlet* I iii 115: 'Ay, springes to catch woodcocks'; 'springes' are snares used to trap small game.
41. lawn sleeves and a rochet] References to ecclesiastical garments. 'lawn' = 'A kind of fine linen, resembling cambric … used for the sleeves of a bishop' (see *OED* 1 and 2.) A 'rochet' = 'An ecclesiastical vestment similar to a surplice, typically of white linen and chiefly worn by a bishop' (*OED* 1a). Archy here mocks Laud's well-known obsession with elaborate vestments. Chief-Justice Richardson, who earned the ire of Laud, 'complained that he had been almost choked with a pair of lawn sleeves' (*Macaulay* ii 148–9).
42. time. —] time. *Rossetti 1870*. *Poor Archy*] The first instance when Archy applies the epithet to himself. The King, when describing or addressing his Fool throughout Scene ii, most commonly uses it; see ll. 93, 113, 424, 437, and 458.
43–5. tempered … deep eye] *Nbk 19* p. 152 *reverso*, where these lines as well as ll. 51–6 are found, seems to have been a repository for various speeches entered at different times, and any ordering of them must be conjectural. The tenor and themes of several abandoned lines suggest they are related to the earlier exchange between the Queen and Sir John; see note to ll. 28–32.
44. fool] fool, *Rossetti 1870*.
45–6. sitting on the ball] 'the ball' might refer to the orb that the monarch holds along with the sceptre during coronations as in *Henry V* IV i 260: ''Tis not the balm, the sceptre, and the ball'.
46. King and subject. —] king and subjects. *Rossetti 1870*; King & subjects *BSM*.
47. promises] promises, *Rossetti 1870*. *protestations,*] protestations: *Rossetti 1870*.
49. [?windings]] windings *Rossetti 1870*, *BSM*. *pregnant*] 'full of ideas; imaginative, inventive; resourceful' (*OED* 2a).

50 from the other's eyes and throws a sword into the left-hand scale for all the world like my Lord of Essex's there ...

Wentworth
A rod in pickle for the fool's back!

Archy
Aye, so it shall turn out, and some are now smiling whose tears will make the brine; for the fool sees.

50. *eyes*] eyes, Rossetti 1870.
51. *Lord of Essex's there* ...] Lord Essex's there. *Rossetti 1870.* The reading *Essex* in *Nbk 19* p. 152 *reverso* is certain, and his speaker heading appears below on this page; however, that heading is cancelled and *Wentworth* written beneath. The question is why would Wentworth take such offence to Archy's mention of Essex? It seems possible that when S. cancelled the *Essex* speaker heading, he forgot to emend *Essex* to *Wentworth* at the end of Archy's speech. Wentworth needs to be introduced here for he and Laud control the direction of the scene from this point. Although S. included Essex in the SD for scene ii, he has no apparent speaking role (but see note to ii 53–4).
52. SD. [Essex] Wentworth *Nbk 19*; Strafford. *Rossetti 1870.* Rossetti's speaker assignment seems correct given the following exchange between Archy and Wentworth regarding turncoats (ll. 53–8). The possibility, however, that the cancelled *Essex* is the speaker should not be ruled out.
52. *A rod in pickle*] 'a punishment kept in reserve, ready to be inflicted when required' (*OED* 'pickle' *n.¹* 1c).
53. SD. *Rossetti 1870.* Omitted in *Nbk 19* but there is a tell-tale gap before infilling, indicating a speaker change.
53–4. If Essex were to speak l. 52, Archy might turn to the smiling Wentworth, who conceivably is enjoying Archy's chastisement, and warn him of future tears. Wentworth's angry response for his insolence in the next line seems natural. Archy's salt brine of tears develops the 'pickle' reference of l. 52 as well as his 'owl eyes' (ll. 42–3) of his earlier speech. An early version read *tears will make the brine [to salt the flesh]* but the last four words were smeared out. *BSM* xii 129 comments: 'Rossetti is also forced to end Archy's speech with the cryptic "for the fool sees"' and argues that the object of 'sees' is, in fact, the phrase 'a blindfold devil' of l. 45. Archy's abrupt ending, however, with 'sees' as an intransitive verb, is in keeping with his prophetic acumen, much like the Fool in *King Lear*.
53. *Aye, so it shall turn out, and some*] Ay, and some *Rossetti 1870.* Rossetti assumes underlining of *so it [may] shall turn out* as a cancel stroke. However, the retention of the phrase with 'turn' neatly sets up 'coat turned' and 'turncoats' in the following lines. The MS caret just after *turn out* indicates where the phrase above (*and some are now smiling whose*) needs to be inserted.
54. *fool sees.*] Fool sees ... *Rossetti 1870.*

Wentworth
55 Insolent, you shall have your coat turned and be whipped
out of the palace for this. —

Archy
If all turncoats were whipped, poor Archy would be disgraced
in good company. — Let the knaves whip the fools, and all
                                            the fools
laugh at holy divines, and the godly slit each other's noses
60 and ears, as having no need of any sense of discernment in
                                            their craft;
and the knaves to marshal them all, and then join in a
                                     procession to Bedlam
to entreat the madmen to omit their sublime Platonic
                                                  contemplations,
and manage the state of England. —

---

55. SD. Strafford *Rossetti 1870*. Omitted in *Nbk 19*. It is possible that the speaker might be Laud; see note to ii 89–93 below.
55–6. *Insolent, you*] Insolent! You *Rossetti 1870*. *this.* —] this. *Rossetti 1870*.
57. SD. *Rossetti 1870*. In *Nbk 19* p. 151 *reverso*, *Archy* is squeezed in at the right-hand page edge confirming this speech assignment.
57. *Rossetti 1870* includes the jumbled sentence, 'When all the fools are whipped, and all the protestant writers, while the knaves are whipping the fools ever since a thief was set to catch a thief.' However, it seems that this passage in *Nbk 19* pp. 151–2 *reverso* was replaced by l. 57 and the following lines below on p. 152 *reverso*. *turncoats*] 'turncoat' = 'A person who deserts one party or cause in order to join an opposing one' (*OED* 1a). Archy refers here to Wentworth as a turncoat, and thus makes it clear that he would 'be disgraced / in good company' with the Lord Deputy.
59. *laugh at holy divines, and the godly slit*] laugh at it. [Let the] wise and godly slit *Rossetti 1870*. See Macaulay's description of punishments by mutilation in the note to i 109.
60. *ears, as ... craft;*] ears (having ... craft); *Rossetti 1870*.
61. *knaves to marshal them all, and then join*] knaves, to marshal them, join *Rossetti 1870*. *Bedlam*] 'The Hospital of St. Mary of Bethlehem, used as an asylum for the reception and treatment of the mentally ill; originally situated in Bishopsgate' (*OED* 2). Cp. *May-day Night* (no. 440) ll. 170–1: 'The way is wide, the way is long, / But what is that for a Bedlam throng?'.
62. *omit*] 'abandon' (*OED* 3). *Platonic*] 'Confined to words, theories, or ideals, and not leading to practical action; ineffectual' (*OED* 3).
63. *England.* —] England: — *Nbk 19*; England. *Rossetti 1870*. Rossetti adds to this passage the following lines in *Nbk 19* p. 150 *reverso*: 'Let all the honest men who

Sir John   [*To* KING *and* QUEEN.

                              We humbly take our leave
65 Enriched by smiles which France can never buy.

Gentlemen
We humbly take our leave —

                    [*Exeunt* SIR JOHN, ATTORNEY NOY *and*
                    GENTLEMEN OF THE INNS OF COURT.

Enter SECRETARY LITTLETON *with papers which the* KING *looks over.*

King Charles
                                   These stiff Scots
His Grace of Canterbury must take order
To force under the Church's yoke. — You, Wentworth,
Shall be myself in Ireland, and shall add

---

lie pinched (?) up at the prisons or the pillories, in custody of the pursuivants of the High-Commission Court, marshal them' (in *Rossetti 1878*, 'penned' replaces the conjectured 'pinched'.) A partial transcription of the MS (which shows much more instability than that reflected in Rossetti's text) reads:

> let all the honest / men [can] who be [found] [?picked] up at the [Fleet] prisons, or in / the [plantations] [?court ?] pillories & [pillory], [or in the wardship] in custody / [of] the pursuivants of the High Commission / court marshall [?them]

It appears that the above passage was abandoned, while a better conclusion (ll. 61-3 of the present edition) was fitted at the bottom of p. 151 *reverso* and the top of p. 150 *reverso*, just above this fragment.
64-5. SD. The several SDs are omitted in *Nbk 19* and *Rossetti 1870*. Rossetti places ll. 64-5 after l. 32 above. It seems likely, however, that the exit is in sequence in the draft. Lines 64-6 are found in *Nbk 19* p. 149 *reverso*. No specific speaker is named but the numeral *1* appears above ll. 64-5 and *2* is above l. 66. The empty space surrounding them suggests S. hoped to add an additional speech. *Exeunt* etc.] Omitted in *Nbk 19* and *eds. Enter* etc.] Enter Secretary Littleton with / [a letter] papers which looking over the / King says. *Nbk 19*; Enter Secretary Lyttelton, with papers. / King (looking over the papers). *Rossetti 1870*. Edward Littleton (1590-1645) was appointed Solicitor General by the King in 1634. *King Charles*] Omitted in *Nbk 19* but *King says* appears in SD just above in *Nbk 19* p. 148 *reverso*; King *Rossetti 1870*.
68-71. *You, Wentworth ... wanting.*] See note to i 62.
68. yoke. — *You,*] yokes — you Wentworth *Nbk 19*.

70 Your wisdom, gentleness and energy
   To what in me were wanting. — My Lord Weston,
   Look that those merchants draw not, without toll,
   Their bullion from the Tower; urge on the payment
   Of ship-money; take fullest compensation
75 For violation of our royal forests,
   Whose limits from neglect have been o'ergrown
   With cottages and cornfields; the uttermost
   Farthing exact from those who claim exemption
   From knighthood: that which once was a reward

70. wisdom, gentleness and energy] wisdom gentleness & energy *Nbk 19*; wisdom, gentleness, and energy, *Rossetti 1870*.
71. Weston] As Lord Treasurer, Weston is the key figure to exact payments throughout the kingdom; the payments were to come from the various means which Charles goes on to describe in the following lines.
72. draw not, without toll,] draw not, without toll *Nbk 19*; draw not without loss *Rossetti 1870*.
73. Hume's description of the many avenues the King pursued in his relentless quest for money includes the following example: 'A loan of forty thousand was extorted from the Spanish merchants, who had bullion in the Tower, exposed to the attempts of the king' (vii 259). *Tower; urge on*] tower, urge on *Nbk 19*; Tower; and, on *Rossetti 1870*.
74. ship-money] shipmoney *Rossetti 1870*. Ship-money, the most divisive and hated tax of Charles's reign, was normally paid by maritime towns and counties during war time, but for it to be exacted in inland counties during peace time without Parliamentary approval was unacceptable, provoking 'the discontents of the people' (*Hume* vii 259).
75. our royal forests] Hume notes that 'heavy fines, were required for encroachments on the king's forests; whose bounds, by decrees deemed arbitrary, were extended much beyond what was usual' (vii 211).
76. limits from neglect] limits, from neglect, *Rossetti 1870*.
77–8. the uttermost / Farthing exact] See *Matthew* v 26: 'Thou shalt by no means come out thence, till thou hast paid the uttermost farthing.'
77. cornfields; the uttermost] cornfields. — the uttermost *Nbk 19*; cornfields. The uttermost *Rossetti 1870*.
78–80. from those who … a punishment] Landholders earning a certain amount from their lands were obliged 'to receive the order of knighthood' (*Hume* vii 204) which involved payments to the crown; consequently, many attempted to claim exemption from this *antient honour*, a phrase S. wrote in a cancelled version of this passage. Hume notes that 'Edward VI., and queen Elizabeth, who had both of them made use of this expedient for raising money, had summoned only those who were possessed of forty pounds a-year and upwards to receive knighthood, or compound for their neglect; and Charles imitated their example, in granting the

80 Shall thus be made a punishment, that subjects
    May learn how majesty can wear at will
    The rugged nature. — My Lord Coventry,
    Lay my command upon the courts below
    That bail be not accepted for the prisoners
85 Under my warrant of the Star Chamber;
    The people shall not find the stubbornness
    Of parliaments a cheap or easy method
    Of dealing with their rightful sovereign.
    My Lord of Canterbury —

---

same indulgence' (vii 204). In this way, the 'reward' of knighthood 'Shall thus be made a punishment' requiring 'the uttermost / Farthing'.
80. *punishment,*] punishment; *Nbk 19.*
81. *May learn*] May know *Rossetti 1870.*
82. *The rugged nature*] The rugged mood *Rossetti 1870.* The draft here is difficult, so readings are conjectural. Rossetti prefers 'mood' which is interlined above the core line and is a possible reading. However, below is *The rugged [nature]* and below that *Of* [?] *natur[es]* (*BSM* reads 'Of [baser] natures'). *My Lord Coventry,*] My Lord of Coventry *Rossetti 1870.* Thomas Coventry (1578–1640) was made Keeper of the Great Seal in 1625.
83. *courts*] Courts *Rossetti 1870.*
84. Hume remarks several instances of the arbitrary withholding of bail; contemporaneous with other events in this scene, Hume writes that, 'on a commitment by the king and council, bail or releasement had been refused to Jennings, Pargiter, and Danvers', who presumably had launched complaints that the petition of right had been violated (vii 217).
85. *my warrant*] the warrant *Rossetti 1870. Star Chamber;*] Starchamber, *Nbk 19;* Star Chamber. *Rossetti 1870.* A high court originating in the medieval king's council, the Star Chamber in 1633 'extended its authority; and it was matter of complaint, that it encroached on the jurisdiction of the other courts; imposing heavy fines and inflicting severe punishment, beyond the usual course of justice' (*Hume* vii 207).
87. *Of parliaments*] Of Parliament *Rossetti 1870.*
88. *sovereign.*] sovereign: *Rossetti 1870.* Between this line and the next, l. 89, Rossetti inserts ll. 36–7, which the present edition assigns to Laud.
89. The King, who was just about to assign Canterbury further tasks, is interrupted by Archy's rude, punning interjection. *1824* resumes the text at 'The fool is here —' (with some exceptions to be noted) until l. 147 where another long interruption occurs. *Lord of Canterbury* —] lord of Canterbury *1824;* Lord of Canterbury. *Rossetti 1870.*
89–93. S. takes an anecdote related by both *Hume* (vii 219–20) and *Macaulay* (ii 251) as the basis for the exchange between Archy and Laud. In S.'s version, Archy's joke on Laud only earns him a penance of 'Ten minutes in the rain' ordered by the Queen in ll. 111–12 instead of dismissal from the King's service (see note to 38. SD.).

Archy
                    The fool is here —

Laud
90 I crave permission from your Majesty
    To order that this insolent fellow be
    Chastised for he mocks my sacred character,
    Scoffs at the state, and —

King Charles
                  What, my poor Archy!
    [?Be] my intercession that your Grace weighs [?not]
95 Your gravity with the lightness of a fool.
    His prerogative is above the king's:
    [?Enthroned in] [?the] scorner's chair, he but laughs

89. SD. *1824, Rossetti 1870*. In *Nbk 19*, a curious, almost vertical squiggle in front of *The* could be *Archy*. Resuming the play at this point, *1824* also gives the SD 'KING.' for the first half of l. 89.
90. SD. *1824, Rossetti 1870*. Omitted in *Nbk 19*.
90. *permission from*] permission of *1824, Rossetti 1870*. *Majesty*] majesty *Nbk 19*.
92. *Chastised for he*] Chastised, he *1824*; Chastised: he *Rossetti 1870*. *my sacred*] the sacred *1824, Rossetti 1870*.
93. SD. King *1824, Rossetti 1870*. Omitted in *Nbk 19*.
93–110. *What, my ... philosophy.*] Of these seventeen lines, *1824* and *Rossetti 1870* give eleven. The draft is much cancelled, overwritten, and disordered in *Nbk 19* pp. 145–4 *reverso*, so the reading and organisation are conjectural. It seems, however, that S. returned to the passage on at least one further occasion, emending and extending the King's speech.
93. *state*] stake *1824* (an error noted and corrected in *Relics* 95). *What, my poor Archy!*] what my Archy! — *Nbk 19*; What, my Archy? *Rossetti 1870*. S. first wrote [*O poor*] *Archy!* — in *Nbk 19* p. 145 *reverso* where *poor* is only partially cancelled; a second stroke skimming below seems to reinstate it.
94–9. Omitted in *eds*.
96. *prerogative*] 'A special right or privilege possessed by any particular person, group, class, or institution' (*OED* 2b).
97. *[?the] scorner's chair*] 'the position of a mocker' (see *OED* 'scorner' 1b). An allusion to *Psalms* i 1: 'Blessed *is* the man that walketh not in the counsel of the ungodly, nor standeth in the way of sinners, nor sitteth in the seat of the scornful'. Cp. *Lines connected with Hellas* (Appendix A) (*It is the period when all the Sons of God*) l. 138: 'whose throne a chair of scorn —'.

> At what we weep and fear ... our very person
> Is butt of his wild archery ... poor Ape,
> 100 He mocks and mimics all he sees and hears,
> Yet with a quaint and graceful licence. — Prithee,
> For this once do not as Prynne would, were he
> Primate of England; — with your Grace's [?leave],
> He weaves about himself a world of mirth,
> 105 Out of the wreck of ours — and, like a parrot
> Hung in his gilden prison from the window

99–108. poor Ape ... with a bird's mind; —] Cp. *WA* 633–7:

> The king would dress an ape up in his crown
> And robes, and seat him on his glorious seat,
> And on the right hand of the sunlike throne
> Would place a gaudy mock-bird to repeat
> The chatterings of the monkey. —

99. wild archery] A play on Archy's name; the theme of feathered arrows continues in this scene (see ll. 108–9 and 116–17).
100. This line follows l. 93 in *1824* and *Rossetti 1870*. In *Nbk 19* p. 145 *reverso*, the MS originally read, *Poor Ape he mimics all he sees & hears.*
101. licence. — Prithee,] license — prithee *Nbk 19*; license— Prithee *1824*; license. Prithee *Rossetti 1870*.
102. Prynne] See note to ii 21–2. 'This same Prynne was a great hero among the puritans; ... The thorough-paced puritans were distinguishable by the sourness and austerity of their manners, and by their aversion to all pleasure and society' (*Hume* vii 208). The King counts on Laud's antipathy towards the Puritans, in the figure of Prynne, asking him to overlook Archy's mockery and mimicry, something Prynne would never do.
103. England; — with] England, — with *Nbk 19*; England. *1824*; England. With *Rossetti 1870*. *1824* omits the rest of this line. *[?leave],*] [?leave] *Nbk 19*.
104–5. He lives in his own world; and, like a parrot *eds*. However, the first half of the line as published in *eds* is cancelled in *Nbk 19*. At the bottom of the page (p. 144 rev.) is the re-worked line, *He weaves about himself a world of mirth,* along with another half-line, *Out of the wreck of ours —*. It seems that this phrase is to be fitted into the passage above, on the same page, with *& like a parrot* completing l. 105. *Eds* place this line and a half after 'Poor Archy!' at l. 113. *the wreck*] this wreck *1824*. *and, like a parrot*] and, like a parrot, *1824*. See note to ii 99–108.
106. gilden prison] gilded prison *1824*, *Rossetti 1870*. I.e. cage made of gold. The word 'gilden' had become obsolete by the early C19 (see *OED*). S. first wrote *gilded* in *Nbk 19* p. 144 *reverso*, but he carefully and repeatedly over-wrote the *d* with an *n*.

Of a queen's bower over the public way,
Blasphemes with a bird's mind; — his words like arrows
Which know no aim beyond the archer's wit
110 Strike sometimes what eludes philosophy.

Queen Henrietta
Go, sirrah, and repent of your offence
Ten minutes in the rain ... be it your penance
To bring news how the world goes there —

                [*Exit* ARCHY.

King Charles
          Poor Archy!

Laud
I take with patience, as my master did,

---

107. public way] Inserted above the uncancelled alternative *common street* in *Nbk 19*. Cp. *TL* 43: 'Methought I sate beside a public way'.
108. mind; —] mind:— *1824, Rossetti 1870*. *Nbk 19* p. 144 *reverso* shows a possible full-stop and a set of dots overlaid by a dash. *words like*] words, like *1824, Rossetti 1870*.
109. wit] wit, *1824, Rossetti 1870*.
110. what eludes philosophy] An echo of *Hamlet* I v 166–7: 'There are more things in heaven and earth, Horatio, / Than are dreamt of in your philosophy.' *eludes*] Written beneath the uncancelled word *escapes* in *Nbk 19*. *philosophy.*] philosophy.— *Rossetti 1870*.
111. SD. Queen *1824*. Omitted in *Nbk 19*.
111–13. Rossetti 1870 assigns these lines to the King (l. 111 is preceded by the SD [*To Archy*.]). The large gap between ll. 110 and 111 in *Nbk 19* p. 144 *reverso* indicates a speaker change, and it seems clear that these lines belong to the Queen. Here, she gives Archy two instructions: to spend 'Ten minutes in the rain' and 'To bring news how the world goes'. Later in this scene, when Archy returns, the Queen asks 'Is the rain over, sirrah?' (l. 426) and then 'What news abroad? how looks the world this morning?' (l. 431). The perfect match of diction and action confirm Mary's decision to assign these lines to the Queen.
112. rain ...] rain: *1824, Rossetti 1870*.
113. SD. Exit ARCHY] [exit Archy] *Nbk 19*. *Rossetti 1870* places this SD after 'Poor Archy!' *King Charles*] Omitted in *Nbk 19*. The King's brief interjection here seems appropriate, for the next response is by Laud, presumably to the King, where he accepts the level of indulgence that the King shows towards Archy.
113. there —] there. *1824*; there.— *Rossetti 1870*. *Poor Archy!*] poor Archy *Nbk 19*. See note to ii 42 and 104–5.
114. master] Master *Rossetti 1870*.

115   All scoffs permitted from above —

King Charles
                                My lord,
Pray overlook these papers ... Archy's words
Had wings, but these have talons, —

Queen Henrietta
                                And the Lion
That wears them must be tamed. — My dearest lord,
I hail the new-born courage in your eye
120   Armed to strike dead the spirit of the time
Which spurs to rage the many-headed beast. —
These councils look up and [   ]

115. SD. Charles Nbk 19; King *1824, Rossetti 1870.*
115. above —] above. *1824, Rossetti 1870. My lord,]* Rossetti *1870;* My lord *Nbk 19;* My Lord, *1824.*
116–17. Archy's words / Had wings] S. first wrote *Archy's words / Had feathers [?in] their* in *Nbk 19* p. 143 *reverso* and then cancelled the last three words which recall the image in l. 108: 'his words like arrows'.
116. overlook] read through, examine (see *OED* 2). *papers ...]* papers. *1824, Rossetti 1870;* 'papers' = documents.
117. SD. The Queen *Nbk 19;* Queen *1824, Rossetti 1870.*
117–47. Henrietta's impassioned speech to her husband, applauding his courage and resolve and encouraging him to further decisive action, is in keeping with accounts of her character. Hume writes, 'Charles reserved all his passion for his consort, to whom he attached himself with unshaken fidelity and confidence. By her sense and spirit, as well as by her beauty, she justified the fondness of her husband; though it is allowed, that, being somewhat of a passionate temper, she precipitated him into hasty and imprudent measures' (vii 195).
117. talons, —] talons. *And the Lion]* and the Lion *Nbk 19;* And the lion *1824, Rossetti 1870.*
118. tamed. —] tamed. *1824, Rossetti 1870.*
119. I hail] I see *1824, Rossetti 1870. your eye]* y.ʳ eye *Nbk 19;* thine eye *Rossetti 1870.*
120. spirit of the time] spirit of the time . . *Nbk 19;* spirit of the time. *1824;* Spirit of the Time, *Rossetti 1870.*
121. Omitted in *1824. many-headed beast]* A reference to the Hydra of Lerna which it was the second of Hercules' labours to destroy. The phrase is commonplace — see, e.g., Horace, *Epistles* I i 76 and *Faerie Queene* I VIII vi 2. *beast. —]* beast — *Nbk 19;* beast. *Rossetti 1870.*
122–31. Omitted in *eds. 1824* indicates the lacuna with five asterisks. The decision to omit these lines in *eds* was certainly the result of the rough state of the MS.

[?Thy] bearing now shows well, [and I prize less]
The partnership of greatness which I owe
125 To thy sweet love than this resolve, which shall
Lift thy disdained [throne out of the dust]
Even to the height where your great [ancestors]
Left it [all radiant] as a star that [?w   ],
The prophet of thy dawn that makes it pale,
130 Transmitting it to those who follow you,
Not like a spendthrift's patrimony. — Only
Do thou persist — for faint but in resolve
And it were better thou hadst still remained
The slave of thine own slaves, who cur-like tear
135 The fugitive, and flee from the pursuer;
And Opportunity, that empty wolf
Flies at his throat who falls. — Subdue thy actions

123. [?Thy]] The word is obscured by a large blot in *Nbk 19. bearing*] livery *BSM*. The apparent cancel stroke through *and I prize less* might be a linking device for the following line; see *BSM* xii 240.
127–30. your great [ancestors] … to those who follow you] Henrietta reminds Charles of his relation to both the Tudor and Stuart dynasties; his father James I was the first to be monarch of both England and Scotland. The sense here seems to be that Charles is elevated by the past glory of his 'ancestors' marked by a 'star' that now pales in the 'dawn' of his own reign. His 'greatness' will not be lost for it is passed on to his children. See also the Old Man's description in i 54–5: 'this Charles of England / Rose like the equinoxial sun.'
127. [ancestors]] Possibly accidentally cancelled in *Nbk 19* p. 142 *reverso* when the line below was cancelled by a long continuous stroke. It is at this point that the two sideways-written lines (128–9) are probably to be inserted.
128. The final word is mostly covered by an offset blot in *Nbk 19* p. 142 *reverso*; *BSM* tentatively suggests 'w[<?ane>]d' however, it might be 'wakened' which also makes sense with the following line. The first draft of this line read: *Left it all radiant, a star, [pale] in thy pallid dawn*.
131. a spendthrift's patrimony] Cp. the Old Man's speech in i 7–9.
132. persist —] persist: *1824, Rossetti 1870. for faint*] for, faint *1824. resolve*] resolve, *1824, Rossetti 1870*.
134. who cur-like tear] who tear like curs *1824, Rossetti 1870*. Mary's and Rossetti's version is present but cancelled in the emended draft in *Nbk 19* p. 142 *reverso*. Another cancelled draft reads, *like empty wolves*; a similar phrase will reappear in l. 136.
135. pursuer;] pursuer, *Rossetti 1870*.
136. And Opportunity] And opportunity *Rossetti 1870*.
137. falls. —] falls — *Nbk 19*; falls. *1824, Rossetti 1870*.

Even to the disposition of thy purpose,
And be that tempered as the Ebro's steel;
140 And banish [weak-eyed] Mercy to the weak
Whence she will greet thee with a gift of peace
And not betray thee with a traitor's kiss
As when she keeps the company of rebels
Who think that she is Fear; this do, or we
145 Should fall as from a glorious pinnacle
In a bright dream, — and wake as from a dream
Out of our worshipped state.

King Charles
       Belovèd friend,
God is my witness, that this weight of power,
Which he has made my earthly task to wield

---

139. tempered as the Ebro's steel] The region of the Ebro river in Spain has a long tradition in metallurgy and steel-making, and Spain was renowned for the quality of its swords.
140. The cancelled *weak-eyed* has been retained — which is also followed by *eds* — to give a metrically regular line. *Mercy*] mercy *Nbk 19*.
141. peace] peace, *1824*; peace, — *Rossetti 1870*. Written below this line in *Nbk 19* p. 142 *reverso* is *Taaphfe* (a reference to one of S.'s sobriquets for John Taaffe, a member of the Pisan circle; see *A capering, squalid, squalling one* (no. 419)). This random notation was perhaps prompted by an encounter with Taaffe during the period of composition of *Charles*; he called on the Shelleys during the evenings of 18, 22 and 31 January 1822 (*Mary Jnl* i 390, 392–3).
142. kiss] kiss, *1824, Rossetti 1870*.
143. rebels] rebels, *1824, Rossetti 1870*.
144. Fear; this do, or we] fear. This do, lest we *1824*; Fear. This do, lest we *Rossetti 1870*.
146. dream, —] dream, *1824, Rossetti 1870*. *wake as from a dream*] wake, as from a dream, *Rossetti 1870*.
147. SD. Charles ... Nbk 19; King. *Rossetti 1870*. Omitted in *1824* along with the second half of l. 147.
147–264. Belovèd friend ... Add mutilation;] Omitted in *1824*.
147. Belovèd friend,] *Rossetti 1870*; beloved friend *Nbk 19*.
148. witness,] witness *Rossetti 1870*.
149. Which He sets me my earthly task to wield *Rossetti 1870*; Which he has set me my earthly task to weild *BSM*.

150   Under his law, is my delight and pride
      Only because thou lovest that and me. —
      A monarch bears the office of a God
      To all the underworld, — and to his God
      Alone he must deliver up his trust
155   Unshorn of its permitted attributes. —
      [And] now, as if the baser elements
      Had mutinied against the golden Sun
      That kindles them to harmony and quells
      Self-destroying rapine, the wild million
160   Strike at the eye that guides them, like the humours
      Of a distempered body that conspire
      Against the spirit of life throned in the heart,
      And these become the prey of one another
      And last of death; — and, when thus, the spirit

150. his law] His law *Rossetti 1870*.
151. me. —] me. *Rossetti 1870. that*] Refers to 'this weight of power' (l. 148) and echoes an earlier speech of Henrietta (ll. 18–20).
152–5. A monarch … permitted attributes] Charles is setting out the hierarchy of relationships between himself, his subjects ('the underworld') and God; as God's subject, a monarch relinquishes all of himself to God in delivering 'up his trust'. In *Eikon Basilike* (S.'s copy of which, now in CHPL, is discussed in 'Sources, Genre and Form' in the headnote) the purported author Charles often reflects on this reciprocal relationship: 'God gives Me a heart frequently & humbly to converse with him, from whom alone are all the traditions of true glory and majesty' (136).
152. A monarch bears] For a king bears *Rossetti 1870*.
153. underworld, —] under world; *Rossetti 1870.* 'underworld' = 'the sublunary or terrestrial world' (*OED* 1).
154. trust] trust, *Rossetti 1870*.
155. attributes. —] attributes. *Rossetti 1870*.
156. [And] now, as if the] [It seems] now as the *Rossetti 1870*.
157. Sun] sun *Rossetti 1870*.
158. harmony and quells] harmony, and quells *Nbk 19*, *Rossetti 1870*.
159. Self-destroying] Their self-destroying *Rossetti 1870. rapine, the wild million*] rapine. The wild million *Rossetti 1870*. Above *wild* is an alternative, *palsied* uncanc. in *Nbk 19* p. 140 *reverso*. Cp. Vane's last speech in iii 94: 'Of the dull million, my eternal fame'.
160. them, like the humours] them; like as humours *Rossetti 1870*.
161. Of a] Of the *Rossetti 1870*.
162. heart,] heart,— *Rossetti 1870*.
163. And these] And thus *Rossetti 1870. another*] another, *Rossetti 1870*. Rossetti omits the rest of this line.
164. last] lastly. *death; —*] death.... *Rossetti 1870*.
164–71. and, when thus … perils.] Omitted in *Rossetti 1870*. These lines are ruled off in the lower third of *Nbk 19* p. 140 *reverso*. They appear to be a re-working of

165 Survives its ruin, and like monarchy
     Renews itself even to the brink of time.
                                    [*To* WENTWORTH, *etc.*
     Yet know, ye, the pillars of my shaken state,
     [And] were it not thus, yet I now would arm
     My common nature with a kingly sternness
170 For as I am a man and vulnerable
     I [stand exposed to] a thousand perils.

Wentworth
That which would be ambition in a subject
Is duty in a Sovereign ... for on him

---

earlier draft on p. 139 *reverso* although *BSM* xii 236 suggests they were intended to be worked into the p. 139 *reverso* material. They provide the needed link to prompt Wentworth's response, grounding both the King's lines here and Wentworth's in the architectural imagery of 'pillars', 'keystone' and 'arch'.
164-6. The sense here is that the 'spirit', already mentioned above in l. 162 ('the spirit of life'), outlives the conspiring 'humours' which threaten to take over the body; however, they end by destroying each other, leaving behind the spirit, still intact. Life and monarchy thus outlive the turbulence of self-destroying 'humours'.
166. SD. Omitted in *Nbk 19*. This SD is determined by the shift of addressee of this part of Charles's speech. Previously, he had been addressing Henrietta, but the 'ye' (l. 167) indicates now a wider audience. The final five lines here are particularly addressed to Wentworth, who then picks up and adapts the architectural imagery near the beginning of his speech ll. 174-5 as well as confirming the 'thousand perils' (l. 171) with a new one: 'the peril of the unseen event' (l. 182).
167. The first draft in *Nbk 19* p. 140 *reverso* reads: [*And know you*], *the* [*columns*] *of my shaken state.*
171. perils] fiends *BSM*.
172. SD. Wentworth ...] *Nbk 19*; Strafford. *Rossetti 1870*.
173-5. for on him ... strength;] See Wentworth's speech of December 1628 to the Council of the North, cited in *The Academy* vii (1875) 582: 'Subjects ... ought with solicitous eyes of jealousy to watch over the prerogatives of a Crown; the authority of a King is the key-stone which closeth up the arch of order and government, which contains each part in due relacion to the whole, and which once shaken, infirm'd, all the frame falls together into a confused heap of foundation and battlement of strength and beauty'. The similarity between this speech and Charles's address to Wentworth (ll. 167-71) followed by Wentworth's reply (ll. 172-5) suggests that S. had knowledge of this speech although it does not appear in any of his known sources. The preface to *The Academy* article (581) indicates it was copied from a Bodleian Library MS and had not been previously published.
173. Sovereign ...] sovereign; *Rossetti 1870*; sovereign, *Woodings (1969)* 272. *him*] him, *Rossetti 1870, Woodings (1969)* 272.

As on a keystone hangs the arch of life
175 Whose safety is its strength; degree and form
And all that makes the age of reasoning man
More glorious than a beast's, depend on this —
That Right should fence itself inviolably
With power; in which respect [the] state of England,
180 From usurpation by the insolent commons,
Cries for reform; — nor let your Majesty
Doubt here the peril of the unseen event,
For all your brother Kings, coheritors
Of your high interest in the subject earth,

174. keystone] keystone, *Rossetti 1870*, *Woodings (1969)* 272. 'A central stone at the summit of an arch or vault, locking the whole together' (*OED* 1a). *life*] life, *Rossetti 1870*.
175. strength; degree] strength. Degree *Rossetti 1870*.
177-8. More memorable than a beast's, depend / On this—that Right should fence itself inviolably *Rossetti 1870*; More memorable than a beast's, depend on this— / That Right should fence itself inviolably *Forman 1876-7*. Forman notes 'both lines are marred by the arrangement of Mr. Rossetti's edition,—the first by poverty, and the second by redundancy' (*1876-7* iii 304-5). In *Nbk 19* p. 138 *reverso*, the progression of emendations to line starts and endings and the deliberate underlining of [*glorious*] replacing *memorable* in l. 177 suggests that much of Forman's conjecture is probably correct.
177. glorious] memorable *Rossetti 1870*, *Forman 1876-7*, Hutchinson, *Woodings (1969)* 272. *depend*] depends *Nbk 19*. *on this* —] [on this] *Nbk 19*. Omitted in *Rossetti 1870* and *Woodings (1969)*, 272.
178. That Right] On this—that Right *Rossetti 1870*; On this: that Right *Woodings (1969)* 272.
179. power] Power *Woodings (1969)* 272. *England,*] England *Rossetti 1870*.
180. commons,] commons *Rossetti 1870*. *commons* = the House of Commons.
181-97. nor let ... have thee do:] *Rossetti 1870* inserts these lines after l. 208 in the present edition.
181. reform; —] reform. *Rossetti 1870*, *Woodings (1969)* 272. *nor*] Nor *Rossetti 1870*.
182. event,] event. *Rossetti 1870*.
183-91. For all ... or arms] The 'brother Kings' are those referred to in ll. 188-9: Philip II of Spain (1527-98), Louis XIII of France (1601-43) and Ferdinand II, Holy Roman Emperor and King of Bohemia (1578-1637); only the latter two monarchs were contemporaries of Charles. S. perhaps takes his cue from Hume who describes two of these monarchs thus: 'the king of Spain, possessed of the greatest riches and most extensive dominions of any prince in Europe' and 'the emperor Ferdinand, hitherto the most fortunate monarch of his age, who had subdued and astonished Germany by the rapidity of his victories' (vii 122).
183. For all] How did *Rossetti 1870*. *Kings*] kings *Rossetti 1870*.
184. earth,] earth *Nbk 19*.

185 Rose past such troubles to that height of power
    Where now they sit, and awfully serene
    Smile on the trembling world. — Such popular storms
    [Philip] the Second of Spain, [Lewis] of France,
    And late the German head of many bodies,
190 And every petty lord of Italy
    Quelled, or by arts or arms ... is England poorer
    Or duller; or art thou who wield her power
    Tamer than they? — or shall this island be,
    Moated by its inviolable waters,
195 To the world present and the world to come
    Sole pattern of extinguished monarchy?
    Not if thou dost as I would have thee do:
    Get treasure, and spare treasure ... fee with coin

185. Rose past] Rise through *Rossetti 1870*.
187. world. — Such] world — Such *Nbk 19*; world? Such *Rossetti 1870*.
188. [Philip] the Second] Philip the second *Rossetti 1870*. *[Lewis]*] this Lewis *Rossetti 1870*.
190. Italy] Italy, *Rossetti 1870*.
191. Quelled,] Quelled *Rossetti 1870*. *or by arts or arms*] I.e. 'either by arts or arms'. For this collocation, see Jonson, 'To Penshurst' 98, *Paradise Regained* iv 368 and *Sonnet: Political Greatness* (no. 342) l. 2: 'Nor peace nor strength, nor skill in arms or arts'. *arms ... is*] arms. Is *Rossetti 1870*.
192. Or duller;] Or feebler? *Rossetti 1870*. S. first wrote *feebler* in *Nbk 19* p. 137 *reverso* then cancelled it and wrote *duller* above. *who wield*] who wield'st *Rossetti 1870*.
193. they? —] they — *Nbk 19*; they? *Rossetti 1870*. *be,*] be— *Rossetti 1870*.
194. Moated by] [Girdled] by *Rossetti 1870*. *waters,*] waters— *Rossetti 1870*.
197. This line sets up the list of actions that Wentworth desires Charles to carry out. *do:*] do . . *Nbk 19*; do. *Rossetti 1870*.
198. Get treasure] Get treason *Rossetti 1870*. Locock queried Rossetti's reading (*Locock 1911* ii 477), suspecting a lacuna in text. *treasure ... fee*] treasure. Fee *Rossetti 1870*. 'fee' = bribe (see 'fee' *v.¹ OED* 3b).
198-208. Get treasure ... [?themselves]] In *Rossetti 1870* this passage follows l. 181 of present edition. See notes to ll. 181-97 above. In *Nbk 19* p. 136 *reverso* between ll. 197 and 198, is a large space, ruled off and enclosing a brief note by S. The resulting break in the draft here is perhaps the reason Rossetti assumed that the verses below the note were out of place and needed insertion elsewhere. S.'s note reads: *The Queen Mother Mary of Medicis / see Whitelocke — 1st. scene perhaps.* On p. 171 *reverso* in *Nbk 19*, appears the notation *Mary di Medicis* written vertically alongside the text where Bastwick describes the royal party's procession. (See *BSM* xii 228 for further discussion of a possible insertion point.) *Whitelocke*'s date

                The loudest murmurers, feed with jealousies
200   Opposing factions ... be thyself of none; —
                Borrow gold of many, for those who lend
                Will serve thee till thou payest them, and thus
                Keep the fierce Spirit of the hour at bay;
                Till Time amid its coming generations
205   Of nights and days unborn, shall bring some chance,
                Or War or Pestilence or Nature's self,
                By some distemperature or terrible sign
                Rise as an arbiter [?betwixt] [?themselves]
                In which those now knit against thee, an isthmus

---

for her appearance in England is 1638: 'In *October, Mary de Medices* the Queen Mother of *France* came into *England*, the people were generally discontented at her coming, and at her followers; which some observed to be the Sword, or Pestilence; and that her restless Spirit Imbroyled all where she came' (28). S. entered in *Nbk 22* f. *3ᵛ yet another notation about the Queen Mother among his schema for Act II: *Mary de Medici the Queen came to England in 1638. It was observed that the sword & pestilence followed.*
199. *murmurers,*] murmurers; *Rossetti 1870.*
200. *factions ...*] factions,— *Rossetti 1870. none; —*] none — *Nbk 19*; none; *Rossetti 1870.*
201. *Borrow*] And borrow *Rossetti 1870.*
202. *them,*] them; *Rossetti 1870.*
203. The first draft of this line in *Nbk 19* p. 137 *reverso* reads: *Keep the fierce spirit of the age. Spirit of the hour*] S.'s emendation of *age* to *hour* recalls the title of a speaker in *PU* III iii 75–6; iv 98–204. The 'Spirit' there is associated with the inevitability of revolutionary change and may imply the same force here. Wentworth's plan to keep the 'Spirit' 'at bay' is perhaps his denial of those inevitable forces of change. *Spirit*] spirit *Rossetti 1870. bay;*] bay *Nbk 19*; bay, *Rossetti 1870.*
204. *Till Time amid*] Till time, amid *Rossetti 1870*; Till time, and *Forman 1876-7, Hutchinson.*
205. Following this line, Rossetti indicates a lacuna with five dots. *shall bring some chance*] bring some one chance *Rossetti 1870.*
206–8. These three lines are found at the bottom of *Nbk 19* p. 136 *reverso* and are offset slightly to the right of the preceding lines, suggesting they were meant to be inserted elsewhere. As a series of unpredictable events, their position after 'chance' in l. 205 seems correct.
206. *Or War or Pestilence*] Or war or pestilence *Rossetti 1870.*
207. *distemperature*] 'Derangement, disturbance, disorder' (*OED* 4); an archaic usage in S.'s day. *sign*] sign, *Rossetti 1870.*
208. *[?betwixt] [?themselves]*] betwixt themselves *Rossetti 1870.*
209–11. Omitted in *eds*. The sense here is that the enemies who are 'knit against' the King will be divided eventually by the vagaries of time and chance. Cp. *Sonnet:*

210 Of [mountains rocky] on the Earthquake's [?]
    Shall start asunder for a little word. —

    King Charles
    Your words shall be my deeds;
    You speak the image of my thought. My friend —
    If Kings can have a friend, I call thee so —
215 Beyond the large commission which thou bearest
    [Under the great seal] of the realm, [take this],
    And for some obvious reasons let there be
    No seal on it except my kingly word
    And honour as I am a gentleman; —

Political Greatness ll. 9–10: 'What are numbers, knit / By force or custom?'. Line 210 is conjectural: *mountains* and *rocky* are cancelled individually, and then two underlining strokes seem to restore them. The incompleteness of the line could also suggest that it is a set of emendations for the complete l. 211 below. Another possible reading might be 'Shall start asunder on the Earthquake's word. —'.
212. SD. Charles *Nbk 19*; King. *Rossetti 1870.*
212. A short line which might be intentional for impact; the MS shows no attempt to complete the line. The echo of Wentworth's 'word' (l. 211) in the King's 'words' neatly links the two speeches. S. initially wrote *Thy word* in *Nbk 19* p. 135 *reverso* making the link even more obvious. *words ... deeds*] Cp. *Cyprian* i 219: 'If there were words, here is the place for deeds.' *deeds;*] deeds *Nbk 19*; deeds: *Rossetti 1870.*
213. image of my thought] This phrase is also found cancelled in the draft for a speech by Justina in *Nbk 18*; see the note to *Cyprian* iii 105. Between *thought* and *My friend* there is a large space in *Nbk 19* p. 135 *reverso*, some of it filled with a dialogue between the King and Laud. With second thoughts, S. must have decided to delay that discussion (ll. 231–5) and to develop further the King/Wentworth exchange, a dialogue that foreshadows and develops with devastating dramatic irony S.'s planned outcome for Act II; his notes read: *The End — Straffords death* (*Nbk 22* f. *4ʳ). friend —*] friend *Rossetti 1870.*
214. (If kings can have a friend, I call thee so), *Rossetti 1870.*
215. which thou bearest] which belongs (?) *Rossetti1870.*
216. Under the great seal of the realm, take this: *Rossetti 1870.* What appears to be a cancel line through the last two words of this line might be a single bar-stroke for both *t*'s in *take this. [take this]*] Having presented Wentworth with a 'commission' bearing 'the great seal', the King perhaps extends his hand to Wentworth, a gesture that 'for some obvious reasons' will carry 'No seal'.
217. And for] And, for *Rossetti 1870. reasons*] reasons, *Rossetti 1870.*
218. on it] on it, *Rossetti 1870.*
219. gentleman; —] gentleman. *Rossetti 1870.*

220 Be as thou art within my heart and mind
    Another self, here and in Ireland. —
    Do what thou judgest well; take amplest licence
    And stick not even at questionable means
    To the nigh end wherein our common safety
225 Is. — Hear me, Wentworth: my word is as a wall
    Between thee and this world of enemies ...
    They hate thee for thou lovest me. —

Wentworth
                                                I own
    No friend but thee — no enemies but thine;
    Thy [lightest] thought is my eternal law.
230 How weak, how short is life to pay. —

220–5. Be as ... Is.] Hume describes Wentworth's elevation to Baronet, Viscount, and finally Earl of Strafford. Beyond the titles, Hume notes that Wentworth's loyalty and judgement were recognised by the King: 'By his eminent talents and abilities, Strafford merited all the confidence which his master reposed in him: his character was stately and austere; more fitted to procure esteem than love: his fidelity to the king was unshaken' (vii 195–6).
220. Be as] Be— as *Rossetti 1870. mind*] mind— *Rossetti 1870.*
221. Ireland. —] Ireland: *Rossetti 1870.*
222. well;] well, *Nbk 19*, *Rossetti 1870. licence*] license, *Rossetti 1870.*
223. stick] hesitate, scruple (see *OED* 19a). *means*] means. *Rossetti 1870.* Rossetti's omission of l. 224 explains his full-stop.
224. Omitted in *eds. nigh*] right *BSM*. Written above *great* canc. in *Nbk 19* p. 134 *reverso*. 'nigh' = 'close at hand' (see *OED adj.* 1a).
225. Is. —] Omitted in *eds. Hear me, Wentworth:*] hear me Wentworth *Nbk 19*; Hear me, Wentworth. *Rossetti 1870. my*] My *Rossetti 1870.*
226. of enemies ...] [thine] of enemy *Nbk 19*; thine enemy— *Rossetti 1870.* A cancelled draft above this line is *thine enemies ...*
227. They hate thee] That hates thee, *Rossetti 1870. me.* —] me. *Rossetti 1870.*
227. SD. Omitted in *Nbk 19*; Strafford. *Rossetti 1870.* The speaker change is indicated by the space at bottom of *Nbk 19* p. 134 *reverso* and at the top of p. 133 *reverso* where Wentworth begins his response.
228. thee —] thee, *Rossetti 1870; thine;*] thine *Nbk 19*; thine: *Rossetti 1870.*
230. SD. Omitted in *Nbk 19*; King. *Rossetti 1870.*
230. How weak, how short] How weak how short *Nbk 19*; How weak, how short, *Rossetti 1870. pay.* —] pay .. *Rossetti 1870. Peace, peace* —] Peace peace — *Nbk 19*; Peace, peace! *Rossetti 1870.*

King Charles
                                        Peace, peace —
Thou owest me nothing yet.
                                                 [*To* LAUD.

                          My lord, what say
Those papers?

Laud
                 That we have been too mild,
Too patient; — if the cause had been our own,
That were but Christian patience which is now
235 Guilty remissness in the things of God. —

King Charles
O be our feet still tardy to shed blood,

231. SD. Omitted in *Nbk 19*. *Rossetti 1870* inserts the SD into the line.
231–5. The second half of l. 232 and ll. 233–5 are omitted in *eds*. *My lord, what say / Those papers* is found in *Nbk 19* p. 133 *reverso*; an earlier cancelled draft on p. 135 *reverso*, however, is followed by Laud's response. Next to *Laud* (l. 232 SD), a set of deliberate indicator symbols — an oval shape encircling a circle and dot — are matched by similar symbols found twenty pages later (p. 114 rev.) showing the place for Laud's speech to be inserted. Below this second symbol, S. redrafted the first one and a half lines of Laud's speech, left a large space and began writing the King's response, ll. 236–9, in the bottom half of *Nbk 19* p. 114 *reverso*. Crook (*BSM* xii 186) describes the sequence of composition.
232–3. Not recognising that these lines are linked to the King's speech just before, Woodings (1968a) 226 publishes and conflates them into one line, 'We have been too mild, too patient' and omits the rest of l. 233 and ll. 234–5.
232. mild,] mild *Nbk 19*.
233. patient; —] patient — *Nbk 19*. *own,*] own *Nbk 19*.
236. SD. Charles *Nbk 19*, *Woodings (1968a)* 226; King. *Rossetti 1870*.
236–40. O be ... hand. —] This speech is placed by Rossetti much later in Scene ii, following l. 386 in the present edition. See note to ll. 231–5 above for the repositioning of Laud's speech, ll. 232–5. Laud's last line (l. 235) includes the phrase 'Guilty remissness' which is picked up by the King in his second line (l. 237), 'Guilty though it may be' and further confirms their speeches' adjacent position despite being 20 pages apart. Hume describes Charles's conflicting attitudes towards Scotland:

> So great was Charles's aversion to violent and sanguinary measures, and so strong his affection to his native kingdom, that it is probable the contest in his breast would be nearly equal between these laudable passions, and his attachment to the hierarchy. (vii 243)

236. O be] Oh be *Rossetti 1870*. *blood,*] blood *Nbk 19*, *Woodings (1969)* 272.

        Guilty though it may be ... I would still spare
        The stubborn country of my birth, and ward
        From countenances which I loved in youth
240 [The wrathful Church's lacerating hand. —]

        Laud
        Your Majesty has ever interposed,
        In lenity towards your native soil,
        Between the heavy vengeance of the Church
        And Scotland; — mark the consequence of warming
245 This brood of northern vipers in your bosom.
        [The rabble] instigated, can we doubt,

237. be ...] be! *Rossetti 1870*; be. *Woodings (1968a)* 226; *Woodings (1969)* 272.
237-40. I would still spare ... lacerating hand. —] Charles, born in Scotland in 1600, remained there until 1604; here, he expresses his love for his native country and requests mercy towards its people.
240. hand. —] hand — *Nbk 19*; hand. *Rossetti 1870, Woodings (1969)* 272. This complete line (*Nbk 19* p. 113 rev.) is cancelled; its retention, however, seems essential to completing the sense of the previous lines. The continuation of this scene is found on p. 132 *reverso*, picking up on Laud's grievances against Scotland. The King's use of 'stubborn' is repeated by Laud in a cancelled passage on p. 132 *reverso* further confirming the textual relationship despite the 19 pages separating them in *Nbk 19*:

        [*Your Majesty has ever so interposed*]
        [*Between the Church & the rebellious Scots*]
        [*To spare that stubborn land* canc. *people. — mark the*]

241. SD. Omitted in *Nbk 19*.
242. soil,] soil *Nbk 19*.
244. Scotland; — mark] Scotland. Mark *Rossetti 1870*. The dash (*Nbk 19* p. 132 rev.) is written over three suspension points.
246-53. Laud's reference here is to the 'outrage' (l. 251) manifested in Scotland because of the Church's imposition of a standard *Book of Service* and reiteration of a set of canons. Hume writes that 'The king's great aim was to complete the work so happily begun by his father; to establish discipline upon a regular system of canons, to introduce a liturgy into public worship, and to render the ecclesiastical government of all his kingdoms regular and uniform' (vii 232). It was determined to introduce the 'first reading of the service in Edinburgh' on Easter day 1637. (S.'s note for this event is in *Nbk 22* f. *3^v.) The reading however, was delayed until 23

By Hume and Loudon, Linsey and false Argile —
For the waves never menace Heaven until
Scourged by the wind's invisible tyranny —
250   Have in the very temple of the Lord
Done outrage to his chosen ministers. —
They scorn the liturgy of the holy Church,

July in hopes that Scottish opposition would abate. Hume describes how those hopes were dashed:

> But no sooner had the dean opened the book, than a multitude of the meanest sort, most of them women, clapping their hands, cursing, and crying out, *A pope! a pope! antichrist! stone him!* raised such a tumult, that it was impossible to proceed with the service. The bishop, mounting the pulpit, in order to appease the populace, had a stool thrown at him: the council was insulted: and it was with difficulty that the magistrates were able, partly by authority, partly by force, to expel the rabble, and to shut the doors against them. (vii 233–4)

246. The rabble, instructed no doubt *Rossetti 1870*.
247. By Loudon, Lindsay, Hume, and false Argyll, *Rossetti 1870*. *Loudon*] John Campbell, Earl of Loudon (1598–1663) variously spelled Loudon, Louden and Loudoun. *Linsey*] John Lindsay, Earl of Lindsay, afterwards known as John Crawford-Lindsay (1596–1678) variously spelled Lindsay, Lindsey and Lindesey. *Hume*] James Home, 3rd Earl of Home (d. 1666). *Argile*] Archibald Campbell, Marquis of Argyll, 8th Earl of Argyll (1598–1661). These nobles represent the Scottish Covenanters who rejected the innovations of Laud and the King to impose changes in the liturgy and the canons of the church. *false Argile*] *false Traquair* is an uncancelled alternative in *Nbk 19* p. 132 *reverso*. Both Argile and Traquair were liable to accusations of double-dealing. Argile (variously spelled Argyle, Argylle, and Argyll) had seemed to be on the King's side in the disagreement between the Covenanters and the Crown, but *Whitelocke* indicates his shifting loyalties, 'who now began to shew himself for the Covenanters party' (27). John Stewart, 1st Earl of Traquair (*c*.1600–59) (also variously spelt Traquaire, Trequayre. Trequair, Trequaire) was named Treasurer of Scotland and then in 1639 named the King's new Commissioner (*Whitelocke* 29).
248–9. For the ... *tyranny*] *Rossetti 1870* encloses these lines in parentheses.
248. *Heaven*] heaven *Rossetti 1870*.
249. Two other versions of this line appear elsewhere in S.'s notebooks: *Vexed by the winds invisible tyranny* (*Nbk 19* p. 183 rev.) and *The winds invisible tyranny* (*Nbk 18* p. 160 rev.). *tyranny* —] tyranny *Nbk 19*; tyranny) *Rossetti 1870*; tyranny), *Locock 1911*.
251. *to his*] to His *Rossetti 1870*. *ministers.* —] ministers. *Rossetti 1870*.
252. *Church,*] church *Nbk 19*.

Refuse to obey her canons, [and] deny
The Apostolic grace with which the Spirit
255 Has filled its elect vessels, even from him
Who held the keys with power to loose and bind
To him who now [pleads] in this royal presence
The cause of *Him* who is your King and mine.
Let ampler powers and new instructions be
260 Sent to the high commissioners in Scotland.
To death, imprisonment and confiscation,
Add torture, add the ruin of the kindred
Of the offender, — add the brand of infamy,
Add mutilation; and if this suffice not,

253. *to obey her canons*] to obey to her canons *Nbk 19*. The line with emendations and cancels reads: *Refuse [obedience] to obey to [the] her canons, [mock] [and] deny.*
254. *Apostolic grace*] apostolic power *Rossetti 1870. grace*] Written above *power* canc. (*Nbk 19* p. 131 rev.).
255. *vessels*] Vessels *Nbk 19.*
256. *bind*] bind, *Rossetti 1870.*
257. In the series of cancels for the last half of this line, S. perhaps omitted to stet *pleads* but it seems essential for meaning. *presence*] presence.— *Rossetti 1870.*
258. Omitted in *eds. of* Him] The underlining of *Him* in *Nbk 19* p. 130 *reverso* would seem to emphasise the difference between 'him' (l. 257) and the divine '*Him*'.
259. *ampler powers*] ampler powers, *Nbk 19*; ample powers *Hutchinson.*
260. *high commissioners*] High Commissioners *Rossetti 1870.*
261–66. The violent energy of Laud's speech appears in Hume's description of his character:

> His zeal was unrelenting in the cause of religion; that is, in imposing, by rigorous measures, his own tenets and pious ceremonies on the obstinate puritans, who had profanely dared to oppose him. In prosecution of his holy purposes, he overlooked every human consideration; or, in other words, the heat and indiscretion of his temper made him neglect the views of prudence and rules of good manners. (vii 196)

261. *imprisonment*] imprisonment, *Rossetti 1870.*
263. *offender, —*] offender, *Rossetti 1870.*
264–85. *1824* resumes here and includes ll. 264–77, 280, 284–5 of the present edition.
264. *Add mutilation;*] Omitted in *1824*; Add mutilation: *Rossetti 1870. and if*] And if *1824*; and, if *Rossetti 1870.*

265   Unleash the sword and fire, that in their thirst
      They may lick up that scum of schismatics.
      I laugh at those weak rebels who, desiring
      What we possess, still prate of Christian peace —
      As if those arbitrating messengers
270   Which play the part of God 'twixt right and wrong
      Should be let loose against the [innocent] sleep

265. fire] Fire *Nbk 19. that in their thirst*] that, in their thirst, *Rossetti 1870. thirst*] Written above *hunger* canc. in *Nbk 19* p. 130 *reverso.*
266. schismatics] I.e. those guilty of the sin of schism (see *OED* 'schismatic' *n.* a.).
267–76. In this passage, Laud's criticises the intransigence of the Scottish Covenanters who rejected all of the Crown's attempts at compromise regarding the imposition of the liturgy; the Covenant was 'a renunciation of popery' and 'a bond of union ... to resist religious innovations' (*Hume* vii 236). Moreover, Hume notes that the 'covenanters found themselves seconded by the zeal of the whole nation: above 60,000 people were assembled in a tumultuous manner in Edinburgh and the neighbourhood'. With the power of such national unity on their side, when demanded by Charles's ministers to renounce their position, the Covenanters replied:

> With what peace and comfort it had filled the hearts of all God's people; what resolutions and beginnings of reformation of manners were sensibly perceived in all parts of the nation, above any measure they had ever before found or could have expected; how great glory the Lord had received thereby; and what confidence they had that God would make Scotland a blessed kingdom. (vii 237)

It is this Christian 'peace' by which Laud frames his response to the Covenanters, accusing them of inconsistency in their faith: although they 'prate of Christian peace' (l. 268) they fail to react with 'Christian charity' (l. 275) by accepting the 'smiter's hand' of the Crown and Church, a perverse reading of the New Testament, but characteristic of Laud's ability to twist scripture for his own ends. See notes to l. 276 and ll. 286–9.
268. Christian peace —] christian peace, *1824*; Christian peace: *Rossetti 1870*.
269. arbitrating messengers] dreadful messengers *1824*; dreadful arbitrating messengers *Rossetti 1870.* In *Nbk 19* p. 129 *reverso, executing Angels* was cancelled and emended to *mighty messengers*; then, *mighty* cancelled and *dreadful* added above. Finally, *arbitrating* was added leaving the line with two uncancelled alternatives. *1824* retains two cancelled words at the end of the line, 'As if those dreadful messengers of wrath'.
270. God] god *Nbk 19*. An earlier cancelled version reads *God. wrong*] wrong, *1824.*
271. against the [innocent]] against innocent *1824*; against the innocent *Rossetti 1870.*

        Of templed cities, and [?earth's] smiling fields
        For some poor argument of policy
        Which touches their own profit or their pride,
275   When it indeed were Christian charity
        To turn the cheek even to the smiter's hand.
        And when our great Redeemer, when our God,
        When He who gave, accepted, and retains
        Himself in propitiation of our sins
280   Is scorned in [his] immediate ministry

272. Of templed cities and the smiling fields, *1824, Rossetti 1870* (Rossetti omits the comma). The reading by Mary and Rossetti is how the line initially appeared, although *the* is clearly cancelled. In *Nbk 19* p. 129 *reverso*, an emendation is added, in ink, above *the* canc. which *BSM* conjecturally reads as '[?on] [?the]'. The present edition's conjectural reading '[?earth's]' fits the morphology of the extant letters in the emendation; at the end of the line, *earth,* in pencil, is added just below the underlined *fields. fields]* fields, *Rossetti 1870*.
274. Which touches our own profit or our pride *1824, Rossetti 1870*. In *Nbk 19* p. 129 *reverso*, the first *our* is cancelled and *their* added below in pencil. The second *our*, although uncancelled, has *their*, also in pencil, added above. Laud refers here to 'those weak rebels' (l. 267), i.e. the Covenanters, who rejected episcopacy, or the rule by bishops.
275–6. *Rossetti 1870* encloses these lines in parentheses.
275. When] Where *1824, Rossetti 1870*. *Where* altered to *When*, but perhaps possible that *Where* was reinstated. *Christian]* christian *1824*.
276. See *Matthew* v 39, 'But I say unto you, That ye resist not evil: but whosoever shall smite thee on thy right cheek, turn to him the other also', and *Luke* vi 29. hand.] hand: *1824*; hand); *Rossetti 1870*.
277. And] And, *Rossetti 1870*. God,] God *Nbk 19, 1824*.
278–9. Omitted in *1824*.
278. He] *Rossetti 1870*; he *Nbk 19*. retains] retained *Rossetti 1870*. The reverential pronoun 'He' refers to Christ, or 'our great Redeemer' (l. 277). See note to l. 279 regarding a third reference to Christ.
279. Based on *1 John* ii 2, 'And he is the propitiation for our sins'; this line appears in the service for Communion in *The Book of Common Prayer*: 'If any man sin, we have an Advocate with the Father, Jesus Christ the righteous; and he is the propitiation for our sins'. It was this book which Laud tried to impose on the Scottish churches. *propitiation]* 'The action of propitiating someone; appeasement, conciliation; atonement, expiation; an instance of this' (*OED*). sins] sins, *Rossetti 1870*.
280. [his] immediate ministry] his immediate ministers, *1824*; His immediate ministry, *Rossetti 1870*. The pronoun *his* is clearly cancelled, possibly unintentionally, when the following start of a word, *inestima*, was cancelled; *inestimable* reappears in the next line. Presumably, because the multiple emendations of *ministers/*

With hazard of the inestimable loss
Of all the truth and discipline which is
[Salvation] to the extreme generation
Of men innumerable — they talk of peace ...
285   Such peace as Canaan found, let Scotland now. —
And by that Christ who came to bring a sword
Not peace upon the earth, and gave command

---

ministry became illegible, S. neatly wrote in *ministry* above. Laud's point here is that the attacks on the bishops, or the 'immediate ministry', are attacks on Christ.
281-4. With ... innumerable —] Omitted in *1824.*
281. With hazard of] The sense here is 'with the risk of'.
283. [Salvation]] Salvation *Rossetti 1870. extreme*] extremest *Rossetti 1870*; written above *utmost* canc. in *Nbk 19*. 'extreme' = 'latest of all' (see GM's gloss to the instance of this word in *Adonais* (no. 403) 51 and *OED* 3).
284. Of men innumerable —] Omitted in *1824*; Of men innumerable, *Rossetti 1870. they talk of peace ...*] They talk of peace! *1824*; they talk of peace! *Rossetti 1870*. Laud's agitation is apparent here with his reiteration of the Covenanters' need to 'prate of Christian peace' in l. 268.
285. Such peace as Canaan found] The *Book of Joshua* records Joshua leading the Israelites into the Promised Land and overthrowing the Canaanites, as well as other tribes. Joshua's vengeance in Canaan is that desired by Laud in Scotland with his ironic use of *peace*: 'And they utterly destroyed all that *was* in the city, both man and woman, young and old, and ox, and sheep, and ass, with the edge of the sword' (*Joshua* vi 21). A cancelled passage on the same page as this line in *Nbk 19* p. 128 *reverso*, partially transcribed here, shows an even closer link to the biblical description of the razing of Jericho:

> *Goodwill and peace thus was Canaan won*
> *But her idolatrous women were ript up*
> *Her infants and her hoary elders* [?]
> *Their brains dashed out, and for the fugitives*
> *Hell was enkindled by the breath of God*
> *Such peace as Canaan found*

now. —] now. *1824*; now: *Rossetti 1870.*
286-489. Omitted in *1824.*
286-9. Cp. *Matthew* x 34: 'Think not that I am come to send peace on earth: I came not to send peace, but a sword', and *Luke* xxii 36: 'Then said he unto them, But now he that hath a purse, let him take *it*, and likewise *his* scrip: and he that hath no sword, let him sell his garment, and buy one.' Laud naturally selects perhaps the only verses where Christ appears to promote lethal arms.
286. And by] For, by *Rossetti 1870. sword*] sword, *Rossetti 1870.*
287. peace] peace, *Rossetti 1870.*

> To his disciples at the Passover
> That each should sell his robe and buy a sword;
> 290 Once strip that minister of naked wrath
> And it shall never sleep in sheath again
> Till Scotland bend or break. —
>
> *King Charles*
>   My Lord Archbishop,
> Do what thou wilt and what thou canst in this. —
> Thy earthly, even as thy heavenly king,
> 295 Gives thee large power in his unquiet realm.
> But we want money, and my mind misgives me

288. *Passover*] passover *Nbk 19*, *Rossetti 1870*.
289. *robe*] robes *Nbk 19*. *sword;*] sword,— *Rossetti 1870*.
290–2. To remove ('strip') the sword from its scabbard, means it will never be returned to its 'sheath' until Scotland submits or is defeated.
290. *minister of naked wrath*] The sword Christ commanded his disciples to buy. *wrath*] wrath, *Rossetti 1870*.
291. *sheath*] peace *Rossetti 1870*.
292. SD. *Charles* canc. *Nbk 19*; King. *Rossetti 1870*.
292. *break. —*] break. *Rossetti 1870*; breaks — *BSM*. Lord Archbishop,] Lord archbishop *Nbk 19*; lord archbishop . . . *BSM*.
293. *this. —*] this. *Rossetti 1870*.
294. *earthly,*] earthly *Rossetti 1870*. *king,*] king *Nbk 19*; King *Rossetti 1870*.
295. *his unquiet realm*] Cp. Archy's 'your unquiet kingdom' later in this scene (l. 413).
296–8. These lines are separated by an SD, *Laud*, seemingly cancelled and then stetted, then draft of two cancelled lines, followed by l. 296, all typical indications of a speaker change in *Nbk 19*. Additionally, along the right-hand page edge is a large curly bracket, seeming to link the line ends of 295 and 296. *BSM* conjectures, however, that these lines belong to Laud. In support of the speech assignments here and throughout ll. 299–334, Macaulay records Sir Henry Vane's notes of the key council debate that were presented at Strafford's trial in 1641. S. closely follows in sense, speakers, and structure Vane's notes which are entitled 'No danger of a War with Scotland, if offensive, not defensive'. They open with the King's request for money:

> *King Charles.* How can we undertake offensive war, if we have no money?
>
> *Lord Strafford.* Borrow of the city one hundred thousand pounds. Go on vigorously to levy ship-money. Your majesty having tried the affections of your people, is absolved and loosed from all rules of government, and to do what power will admit. Your majesty having tried all ways, and being refused, shall be acquitted before God and man;

That for so great an enterprise, as yet
We are unfurnished —

Wentworth
       Yet it may not long
 Rest on our wills.

Cottington
      Our attempts to levy
300 Taxes without a parliament produced
 Small profit to the treasury; the expenses

---

 and you have an army in Ireland that you may employ to reduce *this* kingdom to obedience; for I am confident the Scots cannot hold out five months.

 Archbishop Laud. You have tried all ways, and have always been refused; it is now lawful to take it by force.

 Lord Cottington. Levies abroad there may be made for the defence of the kingdom. The lower house are weary of the King and church. All ways shall be just to raise money by, in this inevitable necessity, and are to be used, being lawful.

 Archbishop Laud. For an offensive, not defensive war.

 Lord Strafford. The town is full of lords: Put the commission of array on foot; and if any of them offer to stir we will make them smart.

            (*Macaulay* ii 456–7)

297. *yet*] yet, Rossetti 1870.
298. *SD.* Strafford *Nbk 19*, Rossetti 1870.
298. *unfurnished* —] unfurnished. Rossetti 1870.
299. *SD.* Cottington *Nbk 19*; Rossetti 1870. Francis Cottington (1578?–1652), secretary to Prince Charles, was requested by King James to accompany the Prince of Wales on his journey to Spain in order to negotiate a marriage to the Infanta, a business which ultimately came to nothing. Once King, Charles appointed him Chancellor of the Exchequer. He figures in Vane's notes used for the impeachment of Wentworth (see note to ii 296–8.)
299–301. *Our attempts … treasury*] Except for *Small profit to the treasury,* Cottington's lines are cancelled in *Nbk 19* and then underlined (indicating restitution). See Cottington's speech cited in note to ll. 296–8.
299. *Our attempts to levy*] Omitted in *eds*.
300. Omitted in *eds*.
301. *Small profit to the treasury;*] Omitted in *eds*. *the expenses*] The expenses Rossetti 1870; [to] expenses *BSM*.

Of gathering ship-money, and of distraining
For every petty rate — for we encounter
A desperate opposition inch by inch
305 In every warehouse and on every farm —
Have swallowed up the gross sum of the imposts.
So that though felt as a most grievous scourge
Upon the land, they stand us in small stead. —
As touches the receipt ...

Wentworth
                        'Tis a conclusion
310 Most arithmetical, for thence you infer
Perhaps the assembling of a parliament.
Now, if a man would call his dearest foes
To sit in lawful judgement on his life,
His majesty might wisely take that course. —

                                          [*Aside to* COTTINGTON.

302. *gathering*] Underlined in *Nbk 19* signalling a possible cancel; no alternative indicated. *ship-money*] shipmoney *Rossetti 1870*. See note to ii 74.
302-3. *distraining / For every petty rate*] I.e. seizing property if even for only a small return. distrain = 'to compel the defaulter, by detention of the thing seized, to pay money due or perform an obligation' (see *OED* 8a).
303-5. *— for we ... farm —*] (for we ... farm), *Rossetti 1870*.
306. *gross*] entire (see *OED* 6a). *imposts.*] imposts; *Rossetti 1870*. 'imposts' = taxes or duties (see *OED*).
307. *that though*] that, though *Rossetti 1870*.
308. *stead. —*] stead *Rossetti 1870*.
309. *touches*] See note to ii 274. *receipt ...*] receipt. *Rossetti 1870*.
309. *SD.* Strafford *Rossetti 1870*. *Nbk 19* p. 124 *reverso*, a torn half-leaf, shows both *Strafford* and *Wentworth*.
310-11. Wentworth's meaning here is that according to Cottington, despite all the expedients to gain money, the balance has fallen short; however, as Cottington infers, calling a parliament would reinforce the levy of taxes.
310. *arithmetical,*] arithmetical: *Rossetti 1870*. *for thence*] and thence *Rossetti 1870*.
311. *parliament.*] parliament *Nbk 19*.
312-14. In dissuading the King from calling a parliament, Wentworth uses an analogy that foreshadows the final outcomes for both men.
312. *would*] should *Rossetti 1870*. *foes*] enemies *Rossetti 1870*. Written above enemies canc. in *Nbk 19*.
313. *in lawful*] in licensed *Rossetti 1870*.
314. *majesty*] Majesty *Rossetti 1870*. *course. —*] course — *Nbk 19*; course. *Rossetti 1870*.

315 It is enough to expect from these lean imposts
That they perform the office of a scourge
Without more profit; —
[*To* KING *etc.*

fines and confiscations
And a forced loan from the refractory city
Will fill our coffers ... and the golden love
320 Of loyal gentlemen and noble friends
[?For] thee, the worshipped father of our country,
With contribution from the Catholics
Will make rebellion pale in our excess ...
Be these the expedients, until time and wisdom

315–19. Wentworth admits to Cottington their policy failings, while to the larger group including the King, he is eager to insist on their future success.
315. SD. Rossetti 1870; aside to Cottington *Nbk 19.*
316. scourge] scourge, *Rossetti 1870.*
317. SD. Omitted in *Nbk 19*; Aloud *Rossetti 1870* (inserted at caesura).
317. profit; —] profit; *Nbk 19*; profit. *Rossetti 1870. fines and confiscations*] Fines and confiscations, *Rossetti 1870.*
318. See Wentworth's speech cited above in the note to ii 296–8. *refractory*] 'Obstinate, stubborn; unmanageable, rebellious' (*OED* 1). *city*] city, *Rossetti 1870*; City, *Locock 1911*. Locock adds a note: 'The City of London, as I have indicated by the added capital' (ii 477).
319. coffers ...] coffers: *Rossetti 1870.*
321. [?For] thee, the worshipped] For the worshiped *Rossetti 1870. our country,*] our common country; *Nbk 19*; our common country, *Rossetti 1870. worshipped*] Written above *hallowed* canc. in *Nbk 19.*
322. Hume notes that Henrietta's faith was key in guaranteeing Catholic assistance:

> The queen had great interest with the catholics, both from the sympathy of religion, and from the favours and indulgences which she had been able to procure to them. She now employed her credit, and persuaded them, that it was reasonable to give large contributions as a mark of their duty to the king, during this urgent necessity. (vii 243–4)

contribution] contributions *Rossetti 1870. Catholics*] catholics, *Rossetti 1870.*
323. rebellion] Rebellion *Rossetti 1870. excess ...*] excess. *Rossetti 1870.* The gloss in *Concordance* is 'violence'; however, the sense seems to be of 'superabundance' (see *OED* 7a).
324. expedients,] expedients *Rossetti 1870.*

325   Shall frame a settled state of government.

Laud
And weak expedients they … Have we not drained
All [sources of supply], till the punished which seemed
A mine exhaustless —

Wentworth
                              And the love which is, —

Laud
If loyal hearts could turn their blood to gold;
330   Both now grow barren. — And I speak it not
As loving parliaments, who, as they have been
In the right hand of bold, bad mighty kings
The scourges of the bleeding Church, I hate. —
Methinks they scarcely can deserve our fear.

325. Terminal punctuation in *Nbk 19* is uncertain.
326–8. *Have we not drained … A mine exhaustless*] In reply to Laud, Wentworth's meaning is that unlike the 'sources of supply' which only 'seemed' to be endless, the love of the people for their King is 'exhaustless'.
326. *they …*] they! *Rossetti 1870.*
327. *Rossetti 1870* gives an incomplete line: 'All, till the … which seemed'. The pale *p* in *punishment* overlaps a cancelled word start, possibly [*the*].
328. SD. Wentworth *Nbk 19*; Strafford *Rossetti 1870.*
328. *exhaustless* —] exhaustless? *Rossetti 1870.* which is, —] which *is*, *Rossetti 1870.*
329. SD. Omitted in *Nbk 19*; Strafford *Rossetti 1870.*
329. Rossetti assigns this line to 'Strafford', along with the second half of l. 328, but it must be Laud who speaks here for 'blood' and 'gold' are his trademark. He values the 'love of loyal hearts' only if it results in 'gold'. Cp. i 71 and note. *gold;*] gold *Nbk 19*, gold. *Rossetti 1870.*
330. *barren.* —] barren — *Nbk 19*; barren: *Rossetti 1870. And*] and *Nbk 19, Rossetti 1870.*
331. *who,*] who *Nbk 19*; which, *Rossetti 1870.*
332. *bold,*] bold *Rossetti 1870.*
333. *hate.* —] hate. *Rossetti 1870.*

Wentworth

335 [O my dear liege], take back the wealth thou gavest ...
With that, take all I held, but as in trust
For thee, of my inheritance; leave me but
This unprovided body for thy service
And a mind dedicated to no care
340 Except thy safety — but assemble not
A parliament; ... hundreds will bring like me
Their fortunes as they would their blood before. —

King Charles

Not so — thou judgest, thou art but one. — Alas,
We should be too much out of love with Heaven
345 Did this vile world show many such as thee,
Thou perfect, just and honourable man. —
Never shall it be said that Charles of England

---

335. SD. Strafford *Nbk 19*, *Rossetti 1870*.
335. [*O my dear liege]*] O my dear liege *Rossetti 1870*. *gavest ...*] gavest: *Rossetti 1870*.
336. *With that,*] *Rossetti 1870*; With that *Nbk 19*.
337. *my inheritance;*] mine inheritance: *Rossetti 1870*.
338-9. Wentworth relinquishes all of his fortune to the King, and he is left with only his 'body' and 'mind' with which to serve.
338. *unprovided*] 'Not provided for in terms of financial maintenance' (*OED* 3c). *service*] service, *Rossetti 1870*.
340. *safety —*] safety:— *Rossetti 1870*.
341. *parliament; ... hundreds*] parliament. Hundreds *Rossetti 1870*. *bring like me*] bring, like me, *Rossetti 1870*.
342. *fortunes*] fortunes, *Rossetti 1870*. *blood before. —*] blood, before ... *Rossetti 1870*. 'blood' = 'boldness, courage, fighting spirit' (*OED* 12b).
343. SD. Charles *Nbk 19*; King. *Rossetti 1870*.
343. The sense of the King's response is that he rejects Wentworth's assurance that others will make the same sacrifices of 'fortune' and 'blood' as he has done; the King recognises that Wentworth's judgement can only apply to himself. *Not so —*] No! *Rossetti 1870*. *thou judgest, thou art*] thou who judgest them art *Rossetti 1870*. *one. — Alas,*] one . . — Alas *Nbk 19*; one. Alas! *Rossetti 1870*.
344. *Heaven*] heaven *Rossetti 1870*.
345. *thee,*] thee *Nbk 19*.
346. *perfect,*] perfect *Nbk 19*, *Rossetti 1870*. *man. —*] man — *Nbk 19*; man! *Rossetti 1870*. Of the King's regard for Wentworth, see note to ii 220-5.

Stripped those he loved for fear of those he scorns;
Nor will he so much misbecome this throne
350 As to impoverish those who most adorn
And best defend it ... what you urge, dear Strafford,
Inclines me rather —

[*Enter* ARCHY.

Queen Henrietta
                              To a parliament?
Is this thy firmness that thou wilt preside
Over a knot of [?rabid] censurers

348. *Stripped*] Dispossessed (see *OED* 'strip' *v.*¹ 2a). *scorns*;] scorns *Nbk 19*.
349. *this throne*] his throne *Rossetti 1870*.
351. *And best*] And most *BSM*. *it ... what*] it. That *Rossetti 1870*. *Strafford*,] *Rossetti 1870*; Strafford *Nbk 19*.
352. *SD. Enter* ARCHY] Omitted in *Rossetti 1870*. In the *Nbk 19* draft, S. gives three entrances for Archy, arriving from his penance in the rain: here, on p. 120 *reverso*; on p. 119 *reverso*; and on p. 113 *reverso*. Rossetti selects the p. 113 *reverso* entry, which follows l. 387. *BSM* suggests that the entrance here, on p. 120 *reverso*, is revised on p. 119 *reverso*, thus preferring that position — when the Queen weeps following l. 361 — for Archy's entrance. On the other hand, Archy's presence during the Queen's impassioned speech, with her tearful conclusion, seems a valid argument for its earlier position as here. *Queen Henrietta*] Queen *Nbk 19*, *Rossetti 1870*.
352. *rather* —] rather ... *Rossetti 1870*. *Nbk 19* p. 120 *reverso* shows three suspension points overlaid by a long dash, an indication the King is interrupted by the Queen who worriedly anticipates that he is about to reject Wentworth's advice, 'assemble not / A parliament' (ll. 340–1).
353. *thy*] *Rossetti 1870*; your *Nbk 19*. *firmness that thou*] firmness? and thou *Rossetti 1870*. The draft shows *Is this your firmness that you* and then above that is *thou wilt preside* indicating S. was undecided about the pronoun form. Later in this speech, however, he consistently uses 'thy' and 'thou' in the Queen's address to the King.
354. *of [?rabid] censurers*] of ... censurers, *Rossetti 1870*. Crook conjectures persuasively that S. wrote *ribad* as '*sic* for *rabid*; vowels transposed under influence of *ribald*' in l. 358 (*BSM* xii 196). Cp. a similar phrase reworked several times in the drafts of ii 21: [*insolent censurers*] and [*Unpunished*] *ribald censurers* (*Nbk 19* p. 155 rev.). 'rabid' = 'Furious, raging' (*OED* 1a). Cp. *L&C* 1774.

355 [?For] [?the] unswearing of thy best resolves?
    To choose the worst when the worst comes too soon?
    O plight to the worst before the worst must come?
    O wilt thou smile whilst our ribald foes,
    Dressed in thine own usurped authority,
360 Sharpen their tongues on Henrietta's fame?
    It is enough — thou lovest me no more —

[QUEEN *weeps*.

King Charles
O, Henrietta! —
                                           [*They talk apart.*

Cottington   [*To* LAUD.
            Money we have none,

355. *[?For] [?the]]* To the *Rossetti 1870*; [?To] [?this] *BSM*. The conjectural readings in *Nbk 19* p. 120 *reverso* by eds are the result of the rough state of the draft. *unswearing*] Retracting. *resolves?*] resolves, *Rossetti 1870*; resolve[s]? *BSM*.
356–7. The anaphora 'worst' is also suggested in S.'s schema for the play in *Nbk 22* f. *3ᵛ: *Worse than the worst is indecision*. This might be S.'s gloss on a comment by Hume: 'It is evident that Charles had fallen into such a situation that, whichever side he embraced, his errors must be dangerous: no wonder, therefore, he was in great perplexity. But he did worse than embrace the worst side: for, properly speaking, he embraced no side at all' (vii 246).
356. *To choose the worst*] And choose the worst, *Rossetti 1870*.
357. *O plight to*] Plight not *Rossetti 1870*; O [fl]ight *BSM*. 'plight' = 'To pledge or bind oneself to do or give (something)' (*OED* 3). *come?*] come *Nbk 19*; come. *Rossetti 1870*.
358. *O wilt*] Oh wilt *Rossetti 1870*. *ribald*] See note to ii 21. *foes,*] *Rossetti 1870*; foes *Nbk 19*.
359. *thine*] their *Rossetti 1870, Forman 1876–7, Hutchinson*. *Rossetti 1878* emends to *thine*, which is followed in *Locock* ii 113. *authority,*] authority *Nbk 19*.
360. *Henrietta's fame*] I.e. common talk about Henrietta (see *OED* 'fame' 1a). *fame?*] *Rossetti 1870*; fame — *Nbk 19*.
361. *enough —*] enough! *Rossetti 1870*. *more —*] more! *Rossetti 1870*.
362. SD. QUEEN *weeps*] weeps. *Nbk 19*; Weeps. *Rossetti 1870*. *King Charles*] Charles *Nbk 19*; King. *Rossetti 1870*. *They talk apart.*] (they talk apart) *Nbk 19*; They talk apart. *Rossetti 1870*. *Cottington ... To* LAUD] Cottington *Nbk 19*; Cottington [to Laud] *Rossetti 1870*.
362. *O, Henrietta! —*] O Henrietta! — *Nbk 19*; Oh Henrietta! *Rossetti 1870*. *none,*] none *Nbk 19*; none: *Rossetti 1870*.

And all the expedients of my lord of Strafford
Will scarcely meet the arrears. —

Laud
                                                            Without delay
365 An army must be sent into the North,
      Followed by a commission of the Church
      With amplest power to quench in fire and blood,
      And tears, and terror, and the pity of Hell,
      The intenser wrath of heresy. — God will give
370 Victory, and Victory over Scotland give
      The lion England tamed into our hands.
      That will lend power, and power bring gold. —

Cottington
                                                                Meanwhile
We must begin first where your Grace leaves off;
Gold must give power [?or] —

---

363. my lord] my Lord Rossetti 1870.
364. arrears. —] arrears. Rossetti 1870.
365. North,] North Nbk 19; north; Rossetti 1870.
366. commission of the Church] Commission of the Church, Rossetti 1870.
367. blood,] Rossetti 1870; blood Nbk 19.
368. And tears,] And tears Rossetti 1870. Hell,] Hell Nbk 19; hell, Rossetti 1870.
369. heresy. —] heresy — Nbk 19; Heresy. Rossetti 1870.
370. Victory, and Victory] Victory; and victory Rossetti 1870.
372. SD. Cottington Nbk 19.
372. power,] power Nbk 19. gold. —] gold — Nbk 19; gold. Rossetti 1870.
373. off;] off. Rossetti 1870.
374. SD. Omitted in Nbk 19. However, a large gap and right-hand offset for the second half of l. 374 in Nbk 19 p. 118 reverso indicates a new speaker.
374–80. I am not averse ... dissolves them. —] Laud's speech here probably refers to the anticipation of events in the spring of 1640. Ludlow writes, 'Thereupon, hoping that a Parliament would espouse his quarrel, and furnish him with money for the carrying on of his design, he summoned one to meet at Westminster on the 3d of April, 1640, which, sitting but a little time, thereby obtained the name of the Short Parliament' (Ludlow 1771 i 14). This Parliament, however, refused to grant the King his subsidies, and thus, as a 'word dissolves them' (l. 380), 'the King put a period to their sitting the fifth of May; the Earl of Strafford, and others of his Council advising him so to do, and to make use of other means for his supply' (Ludlow 1771 i 14).
374. power [?or] —] power, or ... Rossetti 1870.

Laud

I am not averse
375 From the assembling of a parliament. —
Strong actions and smooth words might teach them soon
The lesson: to obey. — [And] are they not
A bubble fashioned by the Monarch's mouth —
The birth of one light breath? — If they serve no purpose,
380 A word dissolves them. —

Wentworth

Let this parliament
But be deferred until I can bring over
The Irish regiments; they will serve to assure

375. *parliament.* —] parliament. *Rossetti 1870.*
377. *The lesson: to obey.* —] The lesson; to obey. — *Nbk 19*; The lesson to obey. *Rossetti 1870. [And]*] [and] *Nbk 19*; And *Rossetti 1870.*
378. *bubble*] 'Anything fragile, insubstantial, empty, or worthless; a deceptive show' (*OED* 2a). *Monarch's mouth* —] monarch's mouth, *Rossetti 1870.*
379. *breath? — If*] breath — if *Nbk 19*; breath? If *Rossetti 1870. purpose,*] *Rossetti 1870*; purpose *Nbk 19.*
380. SD. Strafford *Nbk 19, Rossetti 1870.*
380. *them.* —] them — *Nbk 19*; them. *Rossetti 1870. Let this parliament*] The engine of parliaments *Rossetti 1870.* Rossetti arrived at his reading by conflating parts of two different lines which earned Forman's comment, 'This phrase seems to me inconceivable' (i 312). *Nbk 19* p. 117 *reverso* gives *Parliaments might be / The engines of* which is left incomplete and uncancelled. Another draft below gives [*Let us rather seek*] / [*By arts & negotiation to defer*]; yet another attempt begins, [*Let this Scottish war*] / [*Not be*]. Finally, squeezed in, among these cancelled lines is *Let this parl* the last word an abbreviation for 'parliament'.
381-3. See note to ii 296-8 above for the context of Wentworth's recorded statement, 'and you have an army in Ireland that you may employ to reduce *this* kingdom to obedience; for I am confident the Scots cannot hold out five months'. All of S.'s key sources — *Whitelocke, Clarendon, Ludlow 1771, Macaulay* and *Hume* — cite Wentworth's words, and their import becomes clear. The charge of treason against Wentworth hinged, in large part, on the understanding of the italicised *this*: his enemies chose to interpret it as the kingdom of England rather than the kingdom of Scotland. Despite witnesses denying any treasonous intent by Wentworth, the ambiguity in Sir Henry Vane's notes remained. Wentworth's case was lost, and the charge of treason stood.
381. *But be deferred,*] Might be deferred *Rossetti 1870.*
382. *regiments;*] regiments: *Rossetti 1870.*

The issue of the war against the Scots. —
And this game won, which if lost, all is lost.
385 Gather these chosen leaders of the rebels,
And call them, if you will, a parliament.

King Charles [*To* LAUD.
Have you o'erlooked the other articles?

Laud
Hazelrig, Hampden, Pym, young Harry Vane,
Cromwell, and other rebels of less note,

---

383. *Scots.* —] Scots. *Rossetti 1870*
384. *And this game won,*] And, this game won— *Rossetti 1870*. *is lost.*] is lost— *Rossetti 1870*.
385. *leaders of the rebels*] This phrase is written just below *rebels in Westminster* which was cancelled and then underlined (as if for restitution) in *Nbk 19* p. 116 *reverso*. Thus, another possible reading of this line is: *Gather these chosen rebels in Westminster*. *rebels,*] *Rossetti 1870*; rebels *Nbk 19*.
386. *them,*] *Rossetti 1870*; them *Nbk 19*. *parliament.*] *Rossetti 1870*; parliament *Nbk 19*.
386–7. Line 386 is the last line written in the upper third of *Nbk 19* p. 116 *reverso*. The continuation of this scene with the King's query directed at Laud is found three pages later, on p. 113 *reverso*.
387. *SD. King Charles*] Omitted in *Nbk 19*. *To* LAUD] Omitted in *Nbk 19*.
387. *Rossetti 1870* attached this line to an earlier speech by Charles (ll. 236–40); see note to ii 236–40 for discussion of the placement of that earlier speech. *o'erlooked*] See note to ii 116.
388. *SD. Laud Nbk 19*. Rossetti gives '*Re-enter* ARCHY.' as SD following l. 387. See note to ii 352. SD. above for S's multiple entrances for Archy in this scene.
388–408. *Hazelrig ... detention*] For this portion of the scene, S. draws extensively on Hume's description of the rebels' thwarted departure for America:

> Eight ships, lying in the Thames, and ready to sail, were detained by order of the council; and in these were embarked sir Arthur Hazelrig, John Hambden, John Pym, and Oliver Cromwell, who had resolved for ever to abandon their native country, and fly to the other extremity of the globe: where they might enjoy lectures and discourses of any length or form which pleased them. (*Hume* vii 216)

S. adds to this list 'young Harry Vane', an important figure in Scene iii. The descriptions by Macaulay (ii 253–4) and Hume are very similar, but Hume spells 'Hambden' rather than *Hampden*, S.'s spelling in *Nbk 19*. S.'s note *15* in *Nbk 21* p. 249 *reverso* outlines this scene: *Hazlerig Hambden Pym & Cromwell, are restrained*

390   Intend to sail with the next favouring wind
       For the plantations —

Archy
              Where they think to make
       A commonwealth like old Gonzalo's in the play,
       Gynaecocoenic and pantisocratic. —

---

from embarking for America, & following the political & religious puritans, who had there already laid the foundation[s] of a free government; — First scene (date unknown) (see *BSM* xvi 232-3).
391. *SD.* Archy *canc.* in *Nbk 19* although *Enter Archy* appears just above second half of l. 391. See note to ii 352 SD.
391. *plantations* —] Plantations. *Rossetti 1870.* to *make*] to found *Rossetti 1870.* Rossetti's reading is certainly possible: S. initially ended the line with *found canc.*, adding *make* above; however, a second *found* is cancelled below the first which is then possibly stetted.
392. *like old Gonzalo's*] like [?old] Gonzago's *Nbk19*; like Gonzalo's *Rossetti 1870*; like o<ld> Gonzaga's *BSM*. 'But the allusion is indisputably to a speech of Gonzalo in *The Tempest*' (*Rossetti 1870* ii 586). While the reading in *Nbk 19* p. 112 *reverso* is unmistakably *Gonzago's*, the cancelled first draft of l. 392 on the facing p. 113 *reverso*, however, reads, *What old Gonzalo in the play would call*. Certainly 'Gonzalo' was also intended for the line's second draft on p. 112 *reverso*. S.'s substitution of *g* for *l* was perhaps a slip explained by the repeated alliteration of the G's in *Gonzalo* and *Gynaecocoenic* in the next line. Shakespeare's Gonzalo muses 'Had I plantation of this isle, my lord—' (*The Tempest* II i 144), echoing l. 391 above. After an interruption by Sebastian and Antonio he continues:

> I' th' commonwealth I would by contraries
> Execute all things; ...
> No occupation, all men idle, all;
> And women too, but innocent and pure;
> No sovereignty— (II i 148-9; 155-7)

393. *Gynaecocoenic*] Gynaeocoenic *Rossetti 1870* (error corrected in Rossetti's unannotated 1-vol. edn of 1870). 'gynaecocoenic' = a compound, combining γυναικο- (woman, female) and κοινός (common), i.e. 'having women in common'; this is the only instance of this word in *OED*. *pantisocratic*] Pantisocracy = a compound of the combining form of παντο- (all) and ἰσοκρατία (equality of power or political rights). 'Pantisocracy' was how Southey and Coleridge styled the community they intended to establish in America in 1794 to which Coleridge refers in *The Friend*, 3 vols (1818): 'I ... formed a plan, as harmless as it was extravagant, of

King Charles
What's that, sirrah?

Archy
                  New Devil's politics
395 From Hell, the old pattern of all commonwealths.

---

trying the experiment of human perfectability on the banks of the Susquehannah' (*Collected Works of Coleridge* vi Pt 1, ed. Barbara E. Rooke (1969) 224). The ironic tone of Archy's speech (and the blatant anachronism in respect of the time-frame of S.'s play) can be compared with Byron's mockery in *Don Juan* iii 833–4: 'All are not moralists, like Southey, when / He prated to the world of "Pantisocrasy"'. Cp. *PB3* (no. 239) Prologue 36 and S.'s note and editorial notes.
394. SD. *King Charles*] Omitted in *Nbk 19*; King. *Rossetti 1870*. *Archy*] Omitted in *Nbk 19*.
394. *sirrah?*] *Rossetti 1870*; Sirrah? *Nbk 19*. *Devil's politics*] devil's politics. *Rossetti 1870*.
394–8. *New Devil's ... Merlin's prophecy*] Archy's speech is wide-ranging, with materials drawn from the Bible, Shakespeare, political theory, pagan and national mythologies. The general thrust, directed towards the King, prophesies the end of absolute monarchy and the rise of Cromwell's republican Commonwealth. *Ludlow 1771* records the resolutions (February, March 1649) of the House of Commons following the execution of Charles:

> 'That the House of Peers was useless and dangerous, and ought to be abolished;' and an Act was soon after passed to that effect. After this they proceeded to declare, 'That the office of a King in this nation is unnecessary, burdensome, and dangerous to the liberty, safety, and publick interest of the people, and therefore ought to be abolished; and that they will settle the government of the nation in the way of a Commonwealth.' (i 221)

The overturning of old orders expressed in these bold acts of 1649 would seem to be at the heart of Archy's jumbled patter.
395. *From Hell, the old pattern*] Hell is the pattern *Rossetti 1870*. *commonwealths.*] commonwealths *Nbk19*; commonwealths: *Rossetti 1870*. A previous draft of this line and two more read:

> *Hell is the pattern of all commonwealths*
> [*And Heaven of monarchies — Merlin*]
> [*Says that before the battle of Abaddon*]

This cancelled draft sets out another prophetic image of cataclysmic change: Abaddon whose kingdom is 'the bottomless pit' commands an army of locusts; their orders are to hurt 'only those men which have not the seal of God in their foreheads' (*Revelation* ix 11, 4).

Lucifer was the first republican;
He bore Heaven's light down to the darkness.
Will you hear Merlin's prophecy, how three poets,
All in one brainless skull,

396–7. The 'republican' Lucifer evokes the figure of Prometheus, another who dared to bring light 'to the darkness' and challenged the authority of the sovereign power. Such overthrow, whether it is of God, Jupiter, or the King, and the resulting discord is the theme of the Fool's song in *King Lear* to which Archy refers in l. 398 (see note). See also *DP* where S. describes Dante as 'the Lucifer of that starry flock which in the thirteenth century shone forth from republican Italy, as from a heaven, into the darkness of the benighted world' (*Reiman (2002)* para. 19).
396. Lucifer] Written beneath *Satan was* canc. and *the Anarch Satan* canc. in *Nbk 19* p. 112 *reverso*. 'Lucifer' was Satan's name (meaning 'light-bearer' in Latin) in *Paradise Lost* (vii 131) before his rebellion and fall. *republican;]* republican, *Rossetti 1870*. An advocate of 'a state in which power rests with the people or their representatives; [specifically] a state without a monarchy' (*OED* 'republic' *n.* 2a).
397. Omitted in *eds. down]* Queen *BSM. darkness.]* darkness *Nbk 19.*
398. prophecy,] prophecy *Nbk 19. three poets,]* three poets *Nbk 19*; three posts (?) *Rossetti 1870*. Forman conjectures the reading 'poets' rather than Rossetti's 'posts (?)' in *Forman 1876–7* 313 n. *Locock 1911* ii 477 accepts Forman's conjecture and suggests that 'three poets' allude to Coleridge and Southey (see note to ii 393), and 'perhaps Wordsworth'. For S.'s jibes at this same trio see *Proteus Wordsworth, who shall bind thee?* (no. 243):

> Proteus Wordsworth, who shall bind thee?
> Proteus Coleridge, who shall find thee?
> Hyperprotean Proteus, Southey,
> Who shall catch thee, who shall know thee? (1–4)

Merlin's prophecy] Archy refers here to the Fool's song in *Lear* III ii 81–94 which he says is a 'prophecy Merlin shall make' (95). Another possible source for Merlin's role as prophet and enchanter is Thomas Malory's *Le Morte Darthur* (1485). New editions of this work had appeared in 2 vols and 3 vols in 1816 and Southey edited another edition in 2 vols in 1817.
399–403. All in … at full] Eds conflate ll. 399 and 400 into one line: 'In one brainless skull, when the whitethorn is full,' and enclose all five lines in double quotation marks. Indentations and lineation in the present edition follow *Nbk 19*.
399. All in one] "In one *Rossetti 1870*; [?Wh] in a one *BSM. skull,] Rossetti 1870*; skull *Nbk 19*.

400   When the moon is at full,
Shall sail round the world and come back again,
Shall sail round the world in a brainless scull,
And come back again when the moon is at full.

Laud
            Where, in spite of the Church,
405 They will hear homilies of whatever length
Or form they please, [and will defy our power];
So please your Majesty to sign this order
For their detention —

400. *When the moon is at full*] when the whitethorn is full *Rossetti 1870*. In *Nbk 19* p. 112 *reverso*, the adjective *white*, inserted above *moon*, is only faintly cancelled which possibly explains Rossetti's reading. *full,*] *Rossetti 1870*; full *Nbk 19*.
401. *world*] world, *Rossetti 1870*. *again,*] again *Nbk 19*; again: *Rossetti 1870*.
402. *scull,*] scull *Nbk 19*; skull, *Rossetti 1870*. Archy continues in wordplay with 'skull' and 'scull'; a 'scull' is 'a boat propelled with a scull [oar] or a pair of sculls' (*OED* 2).
403. *full.*] full *Nbk 19*; full:" *Rossetti 1870*.
404. SD. Omitted in *Nbk 19* and *Rossetti 1870*. Rossetti assigns ll. 404–6 to Archy, as part of his speech above, ll. 394–403. The large gap between ll. 403 and 404 and the deep offset to the right of l. 404, however, are two signals of a speaker change.
404. This half-line is a continuation of Laud's speech at l. 391. Ignoring Archy's interjection, Laud picks up the thread of his vengeful plans for the 'rebels'. *Where*] When *Rossetti 1870*. *Church,*] Church *Nbk 19*.
405–6. *homilies ... please*] See the note to ii 388–408 for Hume's accounts of the imminent departure of the rebels, including the phrase 'where they might enjoy lectures and discourses of any length or form which please them' (vii 216). Earlier in this scene, Laud has raged against the Scottish churches for scorning the liturgy (l. 252); the fact that the escaping Puritans could establish their own liturgy ('homilies of whatever length') would have particularly angered Laud.
406. *please,*] please, — *Nbk 19*; please. *Rossetti 1870*. *[and will defy our power];*] Omitted in *eds*. A strip of the right-hand edge of *Nbk 19* p. 111 *reverso* is torn away and repaired with a piece of mending tissue; it is thus impossible to know the end punctuation of ll. 406–7 (*BSM* xii 179 n., 181 n.). Below l. 406 is a complete extant line: *Schism and sedition to prosperity*. Omitted in *eds*, it seems impossible to connect it grammatically with adjacent lines. A conjectural meaning might be that the Puritans' escape would 'defy our power' and thus guarantee that *Schism and sedition* would prosper.
407–8. *So please ... detention*] *Rossetti 1870* conjecturally assigns this speech to Cottington; however, no speaker break is evident in *Nbk 19* p. 111 *reverso*. That they belong to Laud is evident because he is the one examining 'the … articles' (l. 387), which name the fleeing rebels, and he desires Charles's consent and signature.
408. *detention —*] detention. *Rossetti 1870*.

Archy
If your majesty were tormented night and day by fever, gout,
rheumatism
410 and stone and asthma, etc., and you should [?] these
diseases had secretly
entered into a conspiracy to abandon you, should you think it
necessary
to lay an embargo on the port by which they meant to
dispeople your unquiet kingdom of man?

King Charles
If fear were made for Kings the fool mocks wisely, —

409. SD. Omitted in *Nbk 19*.
409-13. Archy's foresight querying the wisdom of the order for embargo echoes Byron's comment on the phenomenon of 'so great an effect from so slight a cause' in his preface to *Marino Faliero*; citing this embargo incident, Byron writes, 'that an order to make Cromwell disembark from the ship in which he would have sailed to America destroyed both King and Commonwealth' (*Byron PW* iv 302).
409. rheumatism] rheumatism, *Rossetti 1870*. S.'s list of maladies may owe something to Clarendon's vivid description of the death of King James, Charles's father: 'who, in the spring following [March 1625], after a short indisposition by the gout, fell into an ague, which, meeting many humours in a fat, unwieldy body of fifty-eight years old, in four or five fits, carried him out of the world' (*Clarendon* i 55). For a body similarly corrupted by disease, see the King's speech, ii 160-4.
410. stone] stone, *Rossetti 1870*. 'A hard morbid concretion in the body, esp. in the kidney or urinary bladder, or in the gallbladder (gall-stone *n.*) ... Also, the disease caused or characterized by the formation of such a concretion' (*OED* 10a). See headnote to *The magnetic lady to her patient* (no. 447) for a discussion of S.'s concern that his health problems were caused by kidney stones. *you should* [?] *these diseases*] you found these diseases *Rossetti 1870*; you should [reason] these diseases *BSM*.
413. unquiet kingdom of man] White (1922) 439 compares *Julius Caesar* II i 67-8 ('the state of a man, / Like to a little kingdom') and *Macbeth* I iii 140 ('my single state of man'). Cp. l. 295: 'Gives thee large power in his unquiet realm'.
413. man?] *Rossetti 1870*; man. — *Nbk 19*; them? *Forman 1876-7*.
414. SD. Charles *Nbk 19*; King *Rossetti 1870*.
414. wisely, —] wisely — *Nbk 19*; wisely; *Rossetti 1870*.

415 But in this case —   [*Writing.*
                                       [*To* LORD KEEPER COVENTRY.
         here, my lord, take the [?warrant]
      And [see] it duly executed forthwith. —

                            [*Exit all but* KING, QUEEN *and* ARCHY.

      That imp of malice and mockery shall be punished.

      Archy
      Aye, there's Laud, solicitor for the crown. I am the physician
                                                         of whom Plato

415. SD. *To* LORD KEEPER COVENTRY] Omitted in *Rossetti 1870*. In *Nbk 19* p. 110 *reverso*, *Coventry* appears centred mid-page, indicating the recipient of the King's signed warrant. Also possible but less likely is that *Coventry* is a speaker heading for l. 417.
417. SD. Exit Laud *Nbk 19*; Exeunt all but King, Queen, and Archy. *Rossetti 1870*.
417. It is possible that this line is spoken by Laud on his departure.
418-25. *Aye, ... the holydays.* —] Archy's speech provides a list of the departing players and, like his previous one (ll. 398-403), is framed by prophecy.
418-21. *I am the physician of whom Plato ... without benefit of clergy.*] *Locock 1911* ii 478 cps Archy's lines with Socrates' speech in Plato's *Gorgias* 521e-522a:

> For I'll be judged the way a doctor would be judged by a jury of children if a pastry chef were to bring accusations against him. Think about what a man like that, taken captive among these people, could say in his defense, if somebody were to accuse him and say, "Children, this man has worked many great evils on you, yes, on you. He destroys the youngest among you by cutting and burning them, and by slimming them down and choking them he confuses them. He gives them the most bitter potions to drink and forces hunger and thirst on them. He doesn't feast you on a great variety of sweets the way I do!" What do you think a doctor, caught in such an evil predicament, could say? (trans. Donald J. Zeyl, in Plato, *Complete Works*, ed. John M. Cooper (1999) 864)

A cancelled portion of this speech in *Nbk 19* p. 110 *reverso* following the phrase *a jury of children* continues *of cutting some & burning others* [*& giving some bitter drink, and forbidding others to eat sweet things*] and confirms that S. had *Gorgias* 522a in mind. S. told Hogg in a letter of 22 October 1821 that he read 'Plato perpetually' and that 'The Gorgias is now open before me, and I shall read it with double interest from the views which you suggest about it' (*L* ii 360). Crook and Webb suggest that the reference to *Gorgias* 502b-504e in *Nbk 18* back pastedown (*BSM* xix 312-13) may have been entered at this time (see *BSM* xix p. xl).

prophesied — who was to [?be] accused by the confectioner
before a jury
420 of children, who [found] [him] guilty without waiting for the
summing up —
and hanged without benefit of clergy. — [?There's] baby
Charles and the pretty
Twelfth Night queen of hearts, and the overgrown schoolboy
Cottington (and that

418. *Aye,*] Ay, *Rossetti 1870*. *there's Laud, solicitor for the crown*] Omitted in *Rossetti 1870*; there's Laud solicitor for the accuser[s] *BSM*. Archy's riposte to the departing Laud is fitted in above what was initially the start to Archy's speech: *I am the physician of whom*. The comma after 'Laud' is editorial.
419. *confectioner*] Although the word can mean a 'compounder of medicines, poisons, etc.' the *Gorgias* passage referred to in the note to ii 418–21 above suggests the meaning here is 'One who makes confections, sweetmeats ... etc.' (*OED* 1 and 2). *prophesied* —] prophesied. — *Nbk 19*; prophesied, *Rossetti 1870*.
420. *summing up* —] summing-up, *Rossetti 1870*.
421. *benefit of clergy*] 'The advantage of belonging to a privileged order which was exempted from the jurisdiction or sentence of the ordinary courts of law' (*OED* 'benefit' *n*. 3c). By this mechanism, defendants escaped the death penalty, earning a lesser punishment. *clergy*. —] clergy. *Rossetti 1870*. *[?There's]*] Thus *Rossetti 1870*. Although 'There's' is a conjectural reading, it is supported by the previous 'there's' in l. 418, establishing a catalogue of personages, much as Bastwick does in i 62, 77 and 83. *baby Charles*] Baby Charles *Rossetti 1870*. Clarendon records King James's conversation with Cottington regarding the upcoming journey to Spain by Charles in order to woo the Infanta: '"Cottington, here is baby Charles"'; once Cottington begins to describe the possible hazardous outcomes of the journey, 'the King threw himself upon his bed, and said, "I told you this before," and fell into new passion and lamentation, that he was undone, and should lose baby Charles' (*Clarendon* i 47). *pretty*] omitted in *Rossetti 1870*; [motly] *BSM*.
422. *Twelfth Night*] Refers to the twelfth day after Christmas, 6 January, marking the end of Advent and the beginning of Epiphany. The Masque of Scene i was set to occur at Candlemas, marking the end of Epiphany (see *Whitelocke* 19). *Twelfth Night queen of hearts*] twelth night queen of hearts *Nbk 19*; Twelfth-night Queen of hearts, *Rossetti 1870*.
422–4. *(and that little ... composition)*] Parentheses omitted in *Rossetti 1870*; *BSM* also omits, deciphering the open parenthesis as 'O'.
422–3. *that little urchin Laud*] All of these personages are 'little' or diminutive in some feature, as befits 'a jury of children'. Both *Macaulay* and *Hume* cite the account of a letter confiscated from the home of the Bishop of Lincoln. Hume writes:

> These letters were written by one Osbaldistone, a schoolmaster, and were directed to Williams. Mention was there made of *a little great*

little urchin Laud who would reduce [?a] verdict of "guilty,
                                  death" by famine if it
were impregnable by composition) all empanelled against
                                  poor Archy for presenting
425 them bitter physic the last day of the holydays. —

    Queen Henrietta
    Is the rain over, sirrah?

---

      man; and in another passage, the same person was denominated *a little urchin*. By inferences and constructions, these epithets were applied to Laud. (vii 217)

These same letters are the evidence used by Laud in the case against Williams in Scene iv; see note to iv 39–43. See also 'Sources, genre and form' in headnote for Godwin's treatment of this episode in *Mandeville* (1817) i 278 (*Godwin Novels* vi 97–8). *Cottington (and]* Cottington, and *Rossetti 1870*.
423. *reduce]* bring back (see *OED* 5). *"guilty, death"]* guilty death *Nbk 19*; "guilty, death," *Rossetti 1870*. Rossetti's presentation of this phrase as if a pronouncement of the verdict and the punishment seems appropriate. In a letter of 19 July 1821, S. writes to Gisborne, employing a similar phrase:

    The decision of the cause whether or no *I* am a poet is removed from the present time to the hour when our posterity shall assemble: but the court is a very severe one, & I fear that the verdict will be guilty death.— (*L* ii 310)

Rossetti cites this same letter in his 'Memoir of Shelley' (*Rossetti 1870* i p. cxxxvi), printing the last phrase as, 'the verdict will be, *Guilty—Death*.'
424. *impregnable by composition]* For 'composition' meaning 'agreement', see *OED* 22. 'Composition' / 'compounding' means to accept terms of settlement in lieu of prosecution; it tends to result in a reduction of the initial penalty. In this case, if 'impregnable', the verdict could not be compounded. Archy recognises Laud's devious strategy: he 'would reduce' a verdict only if he knew it could not, in actual fact, be reduced. *composition)]* composition— *Rossetti 1870*. *empanelled]* I.e. formed as a jury (see *OED* 'empanel' *v.*)
425. *bitter physic]* Archy's truth-telling in his speeches serves as the 'bitter physic' for his audience ('physic' in the sense of a '[m]ental, moral, or spiritual remedy' (see *OED* 2b)). See the note to ii 418–21 above. *holydays]* holidays *Rossetti 1870*. A reference to this scene occurring at Candlemas, the formal end of the Christmas season. See note to ii 421 and 'Historical context' in headnote.
426. *SD. Queen Henrietta]* Queen *Nbk 19*, *Rossetti 1870*. *Archy]* King *Rossetti 1870*. Rossetti possibly assumed the pentameters (ll. 426–8) belonged to the King

Archy
When it rains
And the sun shines, 'twill rain again tomorrow,
And therefore never smile [till] you've done crying.
But 'tis all over now.
430 Like the April anger of woman, the gentle sky has wept itself
serene. —

Queen Henrietta
What news abroad? how looks the world this morning?

Archy
Gloriously as a grave covered with virgin flowers. There's a
rainbow in the
sky — let your Majesty look at it — for a rainbow in the
morning is the [?good]

---

rather than Archy; however, Archy often begins his speeches in pentameters and then dissolves into prose (see note to ii 429–30 below). Additionally, the Queen addresses him as 'sirrah', a term used only for Archy by his superiors. Finally, the Queen's earlier admonition to him, 'Go, sirrah, and repent of your offence / Ten minutes in the rain …' (ll. 111–12) is now here fulfilled.
426–8. *When it rains … crying*] The interaction of 'sun', 'rain', 'smile' and 'crying' echo a quatrain *Alas, if I could feign* (no. 423) found in *Nbk 22* which also contains S.'s schema for *Charles*. Given its physical proximity to *Charles* material in *Nbk 22*, one could conjecture the quatrain might be intended for insertion in the drama.
427. *tomorrow,*] to-morrow: *Rossetti 1870*.
428. Archy's response here indicates he was a witness to the earlier moment in this scene when the Queen weeps (ll. 361–2). *you've*] youre *BSM*.
429–30. *But 'tis … serene*] Although Archy's previous two and a half lines are pentameters in response to the Queen's question in l. 426, S. formats these two lines as prose in *Nbk 19* p. 109 *reverso*. Nevertheless, the second half of l. 430 falls back into a true pentameter, blurring the line between prose and poetry, a characteristic of Archy's discourse. His speeches starting at ll. 448, 459, 462, and 477 complete a pentameter begun by a previous speaker and then slip into prose. *now. / Like*] now: like *Rossetti 1870*.
429. Rossetti assigns this line and the next to Archy, assuming that he would speak only in prose.
430. *serene. —*] serene — *Nbk 19*; serene. *Rossetti 1870*.
431. SD. Queen *Nbk 19*, *Rossetti 1870*.
432. SD. Archy *Nbk 19*.
432–71. *Gloriously … ghost of this ass*] The conception of Archy's role and the emblems he employs in his speeches throughout this passage were established

shepherd's warning, and the flock of which you are the pastor
are scattered among the
435 mountains, where every drop of water is a flake of snow, —
and the breath of May pierces like a January blast. —

---

early on in S.'s plans for the play: a set of jottings for Archy's speeches here is found in *Nbk 19* p. 182 *reverso*, a page just before the start of Scene i: *Archy — a mitre, & a crown / rainbow, clouds / a buggy ditch* (For *buggy*, *BSM* reads 'buzzing'.) On this same page of jottings is a sketch that *BSM* xii 321 notes is 'perhaps suggested by the idea of a rainbow spanning a river'. A wavy descending line (the Thames river) in the middle of what seems to be a landscape horizon with an emphatic arch ('rainbow') almost touching the horizon line ('North to South'), intersected by a tall vertical line ('balance') with a looping squiggle wrapped around it ('congregated lightnings') does indeed seem like a visual illustration of Archy's speeches in this passage. As he recounts his journey to claim the 'treasures' found at the rainbow's ends, he repeatedly describes the rainbow in detail, mentioning it seven times, either as 'rainbow' or 'bow'. The tips of the rainbow are marked by the 'crown' on the 'North' tip, and the 'mitre' on the 'South' tip. Both Charles and Henrietta repeatedly interrupt Archy, oblivious to his coded message presaging the deaths of the King and the Archbishop.

433–6. *for a rainbow … warning*] In *Nbk 19* p. 109 *reverso* this phrase is written as prose, but *Rossetti 1870* formats as a couplet thus:

> "A rainbow in the morning
> Is the shepherd's warning;"

Archy's words refer to the adage 'Red sky at night, / Sailor's delight. / Red sky in morning, / Shepherd's warning' (see *Matthew* xvi 2–3) and undoubtedly prompted Rossetti's lineation here. Cp. *Venus & Adonis* ll. 453–6, which echoes even more of Archy's speech:

> Like a red morn, that ever yet betokened
> Wrack to the seaman, tempest to the field,
>   Sorrow to shepherds, woe unto the birds,
>   Gusts and foul flaws to herdmen and to herds.

433. *sky — let your Majesty look at it — for*] sky. Let your Majesty look at it, for *Rossetti 1870*.
434–5. *and the flock … mountains*] Cp. *Matthew* xxvi 31: 'Then saith Jesus unto them, All ye shall be offended because of me this night: for it is written, I will smite the shepherd, and the sheep of the flock shall be scattered abroad.'
434. *flock*] flocks *Rossetti 1870*.
435. *mountains*] mountain-tops *Rossetti 1870*. snow, —] snow, *Rossetti 1870*.
436. *pierces like a January blast*] A reference perhaps to the date of Charles's execution, 30 January 1649. *blast*. —] blast. *Rossetti 1870*.

King Charles
The sheep have mistaken the wolf for the shepherd my poor
                                                                         fellow —

Archy
And the shepherd the wolves for the watch-dogs. —

Queen Henrietta
But the rainbow was a good sign: it says that the waters of the
                                                                         deluge are gone
440 and can return no more. —

Archy
Aye, the salt-water one ... but that of tears and blood must yet
                                                                      come down and

---

437. SD. Charles *Nbk 19*; King *Rossetti 1870*.
437. my poor fellow —] my poor boy; *Rossetti 1870*. In *Nbk 19* p. 108 *reverso*, S. wrote *boy* — and then cancelled *boy*, adding in *fellow* upon the heavy dash.
438. SD. Archy *Nbk 19*; omitted in *Rossetti 1870*.
438. Rossetti 1870 assigns this line to the King as a continuation of his l. 437. Archy's meaning here is that like the 'sheep', the 'shepherd' (the King) is mistaken as to the identity and purposes of the 'wolves' (councillors) that he believes to be benign, protective 'watch-dogs'. *And the shepherd*] and the shepherd, *Rossetti 1870. watch-dogs.* —] watch dogs. — *Nbk 19;* watchdogs. *Rossetti 1870*.
439–41. But the rainbow ... salt-water one] The Queen refers to the story of Noah, the flood, and its aftermath: 'And God said ... I do set my bow in the cloud, and it shall be for a token of a covenant between me and the earth ... And I will remember my covenant, which *is* between me and you and every living creature of all flesh; and the waters shall no more become a flood to destroy all flesh' (*Genesis* ix 12–15). The Queen understands the rainbow as a symbol of peace and reconciliation; however, Archy makes clear the rainbow he saw is a symbol of 'tears and blood'.
439. SD. Queen *Nbk 19, Rossetti 1870*.
439. sign:] sign, Archy: *Rossetti 1870*. Rossetti interpreted a centred *Archy* as an addition to the Queen's first line, however, it is more likely a speaker heading for l. 438. *waters of the deluge*] *Rossetti 1870;* waters [that] the deluge *Nbk 19*.
440. more. —] more. *Rossetti 1870*.
441-2. but that of tears .. fire follows,] While the previous two lines refer to the first book of the Bible, these would seem to refer to the cataclysmic events involving 'tears', 'blood' and 'fire' described in the last book, *Revelation*. At the same time, they also are a prophecy of the imprisonment and execution of Charles and the Civil Wars.
441. SD. Archy *Nbk 19*.
441. Aye, the salt-water one ...] Ay, the salt-water one: *Rossetti 1870. down*] down, *Rossetti 1870*.

that of fire follows, if there be any truth in lies. — The
                                   rainbow hung over the city
     with all its shops, roofs and steeples from North to South like
                                                      a bridge of
     congregated lightnings [?pierced] by the masonry of Heaven,
                                             or like a balance in
445 which the Angel that distributes the coming hour was
                                            weighing that heavy one
     whose poise is now felt in the lightest hearts before it bows
                                                the proudest heads
     under the meanest feet —

     Queen Henrietta
     Who taught you this trash, sirrah?

     Archy
                                       A torn leaf
     Out of an old book ... trampled in the dirt. —

442. *fire follows*] fire follow *Rossetti 1870*.
443–4. *like a bridge of congregated lightnings*] Cp. *OWW* 25–6: 'Vaulted with all thy congregated might / Of vapours'.
443. *shops, roofs and steeples*] shops, .. and churches, *Rossetti 1870. North to South*] north to south, *Rossetti 1870*.
444–6. *like a balance ... poise*] The image of a balance and weights recalls Archy's earlier speech at ii 45–51.
444. *lightnings [?pierced]*] lightning pieced *Rossetti 1870*; lightnings pie[r]ced *BSM*. *Heaven, or like*] heaven — like *Rossetti 1870*.
445. *the Angel*] the angel *Rossetti 1870*.
446. *poise*] 'weight' (*OED* 1). *hearts*] hearts, *Rossetti 1870*.
447. *feet —*] feet. *Rossetti 1870*.
448. SD. *Queen Henrietta*] Omitted in *Nbk 19*; Queen *Rossetti 1870*. *Archy*] *Rossetti 1870*; omitted in *Nbk 19*.
448–9. *A torn leaf ... dirt*] *Rossetti 1870* formats the first line and a half of Archy's speech as prose. See the headnote to *Swifter far than summer's flight / Remembrance* (no. 433) which includes a transcription of S.'s note accompanying that poem: 'Do not say it is mine to any one even if you think so; — indeed it is from *the torn leaf of a book out of date*' (emphasis added). The date-range of the composition of *Swifter far* (January-May 1822), overlaps with the period of composition of the *Nbk 19* draft of this play (January 1822).
448. *trash, sirrah?*] *Rossetti 1870*; trash sirrah — *Nbk 19*.
449. *Out of an old book ...*] out of an old book *Rossetti 1870*.

450   But first the rainbow — it moved as the sun moved and
                                        [?turns] until the
      top of the Tower [?burned] like the [pinnacle] of a cloud
                                        before the [?] of [?the]
      [?sun] through its left-hand tip, and Lambeth Palace looked
                                        as dark as
      a rock [?under] the [?other] ... Methought I saw a crown
                                        figured upon one tip and a
      mitre on the other. — So, as I had heard treasures were
                                        found where the rainbow
455   quenches its points upon the earth, I set off and at the
                                        Tower ... but I shall not tell
      your Majesty what I found close to the closet window on
      which the rainbow had glimmered.

      King Charles
      O my poor Archy, speak out ... some make their
                                        consciences fools;
      I will make my fool my conscience.

      Archy
                                        I saw there

450. *But first*] But for *Rossetti 1870*. *moved and [?turns]*] moved, and . . *Rossetti 1870*; moved and [?turned] *BSM*.
451-2. *top ... Lambeth Palace*] top of the Tower . . of a cloud through its left-hand tip, and Lambeth Palace *Rossetti 1870*. *Nbk 19* p. 106 *reverso* includes three tiny levels of emendations fitted in between two lines making for conjectural readings. *[?burned]*] [beamed] *BSM*. *before the [?] of [?the] [?sun]*] [before] [the] [noble] [?grace] of the [Sun] *BSM*.
453. *[?under] the [?other] ...*] before the other. *Rossetti 1870*. *tip*] tip, *Rossetti 1870*.
454. *other.* —] other. *Rossetti 1870*.
455. *off*] off, *Rossetti 1870*. *Tower ...*] Towers . . *Nbk 19*; Tower— . *Rossetti 1870*. A terminal *s* is added in *Nbk 19* p. 106 *reverso* (probably an unintentional slip); see *Tower* sing. in l. 451. *but I*] But I *Rossetti 1870*.
456. *closet window*] closet-window *Rossetti 1870*.
458. SD. Omitted in *Nbk 19*; King *Rossetti 1870*.
458. *O my poor Archy, speak out ...*] Speak: *Rossetti 1870*. *Rossetti 1870* omits the second half of this line, substituting instead the next line, 'I will make my Fool my conscience.'
459. *my fool*] my Fool *Rossetti 1870*. Just before Archy's 'I saw there', *Rossetti 1870* inserts a phrase, 'Then conscience is a fool, —' for which there is no authority in the *Nbk 19* draft. Rossetti seems to have constructed it from pieces of the phrase *some make their consciences fools* in l. 458 which he had omitted.

460   a cat caught in a rat's trap. I heard the rats squeak behind the
                                                                                     wainscot;
     it seemed to me that the very mice were consulting on the
                                                                       manner of her death. —

Queen Henrietta
Archy is shrewd and bitter —

Archy
                                                 Like the season,
     So blow the winds. — But at the other end of the bow, where
                                                                      the grey rain
     [?above] the grass and leaves was tempered by a tender
                                                                  interfusion of violet
465   and gold, in the [?] meadows beyond Lambeth, what think
     you that I found instead of a mitre? —

King Charles
Vane's wits perhaps —

460. *rat's trap*] rat-trap *Rossetti 1870*. *wainscot;*] wainscots: *Rossetti 1870*. 'Panel-work of oak or other wood, used to line the walls of an apartment' (*OED* 2).
461. *death.* —] death. *Rossetti 1870*.
462. SD. *Queen Henrietta*] Queen *Nbk 19, Rossetti 1870. Archy*] *Nbk 19*.
462. *bitter* —] bitter. *Rossetti 1870*. *White (1922)* 439 finds an echo of *Lear* I iv 136: 'A bitter fool!'. *season,*] season *Nbk 19*.
463. *So*] so *Rossetti 1870*. *bow,*] [rain]bow *Nbk 19*; rainbow, *Rossetti 1870*.
464–5. *violet and gold*] A reference to the Archbishop Laud; see iv 20 and note.
464. *[?above] the grass and leaves was tempered*] was tempered along the grass and leaves *Rossetti 1870*.
465–6. *Lambeth ...mitre*] Lambeth Palace was the London residence of Laud, the Archbishop of Canterbury. See i 74 and note.
465. *gold,*] gold *Rossetti 1870*. [?]] A faint dry-quilled word is an emendation above another cancelled word or word start (?*fre*) in *Nbk 19* p. 105 *reverso*, possibly 'fresh'.
466. *mitre?* —] mitre? *Rossetti 1870*.
467. SD. *King Charles*] King *Nbk 19, Rossetti 1870. Archy*] *Nbk 19*.
467. *Vane's ... vain.* —] Vane's ... vain. *Rossetti 1870*. It is unclear if 'Vane's' refers to Vane the elder or the younger; young Sir Harry Vane appears in Scene iii with more word play on 'vane', as in weather vanes. *perhaps* —] perhaps. *Rossetti 1870*.

Archy
                    Something as vain. — I saw
A [?dim] vapour hovering in a stinking ditch over the carcass
                                of a dead ass, some
rotten rags and broken dishes, the wreck of what once
                         administered to the stuffing-out
470 and the ornament of a worm of worms ... His grace of
                           Canterbury expects to enter the
new Jerusalem some Palm Sunday in triumph on the ghost of
                                    this ass —

King Charles
Enough, enough! —

468. *[?dim]*] gross *Rossetti 1870*; dizzy *BSM* (see *BSM* xii 166, 129 for an explanation of this reading).
469-70. *rotten rags ...worms*] The images here ('rags', 'broken dishes', 'ornament') are possible references to Laud's preoccupation with ostentatious episcopal garments and Communion accoutrements and innovations. An earlier version of these lines in *Nbk 19* p. 105 *reverso* reads, *some rotten rags and broken dishes, this scouring of* [*the table and the wardrobes of his*] and lends support to this reading. (For *table BSM* reads 'trash'.) Hume writes:

> Orders were given and rigorously insisted on, that the communion-table should be removed from the middle of the area, where it hitherto stood in all churches, except in cathedrals. It was placed at the east end, railed in, and denominated an ALTAR ...

> The kneeling at the altar, and the using of copes, a species of embroidered vestment, in administering the sacrament, were also known to be great objects of scandal, as being popish practices ... (*Hume* vii 200)

Macaulay describes at length Laud's sacrament theatrics: toying with the napkin covering the host (wafer or bread), ostentatiously approaching, retreating and bowing to the cover and cup three times (ii 102).
469. *rags*] rags, *Rossetti 1870. dishes,*] dishes— *Rossetti 1870. stuffing-out*] stuffing out *Nbk 19.*
470-1. *to enter ... this ass*] Cp. Christ's entry into Jerusalem on an ass, *Matthew* xxi 5-9. Archy transforms the humble entrance of Christ into the spectral and corrupt entrance of Laud.
470. *worms ...*] worms. *Rossetti 1870. grace*] Grace *Rossetti 1870. expects*] excepts *Nbk 19.*
471. *new*] New *Rossetti 1870. Sunday*] Sunday *canc.* in *Nbk 19. ass* —] ass. *Rossetti 1870.*
472. *SD. King Charles*] Omitted in *Nbk 19*; Queen *Rossetti 1870.* Queen Henrietta] Omitted in *Nbk 19.*

Queen Henrietta
                                Go desire Lady Jane
        She place my lute, together with the music
        Mari received last week from Italy,
475   In my boudoir —

        Archy
                        And I'll go hide

472–3. The combination of *Lady Jane, lute* and *music* recalls S.'s poems of spring 1822 associating Jane Williams and music; see *When the lamp is shattered* (no. 437) and *With a guitar. To Jane* (no. 446).
472. Rossetti 1870 assigns all of this line to the Queen; however, a centred horizontal stroke — S.'s speaker change symbol — and the offset second half of the line indicate that the line is shared between the King and Queen. Thus the King tires of Archy's relentless skewering of the Archbishop, and the Queen diplomatically distracts Archy with another task. *Enough, enough!* —] Enough enough, — *Nbk 19*; Enough, enough! *Rossetti 1870*.
474. *Mari*] Marturin Marye (surname also spelled Marie) French musician, described as one 'of the most excellent Musicians of the Queens Chappel' in *Whitelocke* 19. See Ian Spink, 'The Musicians of Queen Henrietta-Maria: Some Notes and References in the English State Papers', *Acta Musicologica* xxxvi (1964) 177–82.
475. SD. Omitted in *Nbk 19*; *King Rossetti 1870*.
475–88. *And I'll go hide … light*] *Rossetti 1870* edits these lines as the opening to a 'Scene v'; however, S. developed no such scene. R. B. Woodings, in attempting to correct Rossetti, ascribes these lines 'to the conclusion of Scene ii' as a soliloquy following the exit of the King and the Queen ('Shelley's Widow Bird', *RES* n. s. xix (1968) 412 (*Woodings (1968b)*)). The middle of *Nbk 19* p. 104 *reverso* draft, however, shows S. changing his plan for speakers and providing indicator links for ll. 475–7, 486–8 found on p. 101 *reverso*. Ultimately, further indicator links on p. 101 *reverso* tie p. 52 *reverso* (containing ll. 478–85) to this scene as well (see note to l. 477). The Queen's response in ll. 489–94 confirms that Archy's departure speech is embedded in the scene.
475. The reading of this line and the SDs in *Rossetti 1870* is:

                In my boudoir, and ..   [*Exit Archy.*]
                    King.   I'll go in.

Rossetti attributed the phrase 'I'll go in' to a centred SD *Charles*, misreading *lie* as 'in'. While moving back and forth among non-adjacent pages, S. forgot to cancel SD *Charles*, a premature start for the King's next speech. The *Nbk 19* p. 104 *reverso* phrase *and I'll go lie / Under* is a linking device to p. 101 *reverso* where *I'll go [lie] hide* appears along with ll. 476–7. *boudoir* —] boudoir, and .. *Rossetti 1870*. *And I'll go hide*] I'll go live *Rossetti 1870*, *Woodings (1968b)* 412; I'll go hide *Crook (2009)* 304.

under the ivy that overgrows the terrace, and count the tears
                 I shed on
its old roots as [?she] plays the song of —
                 [*Sings.*
  A widowed bird sate mourning for her love
    Upon a wintry bough,
480 The frozen wind crept on, above
    The freezing stream below —

  There was no leaf upon the forest bare,
    No flower upon the ground —
  And little motion in the air,
485   Except the mill-wheel's sound.

476. *terrace*] terace *Nbk 19*; ter[r]ace Crook (2009) 304. *count*] court Rossetti 1870 (Rossetti's one-vol. unannotated edition of 1870 corrects 'court' to 'count'). On the basis of Rossetti 1870, Forman 1876–7 printed 'court' but conjectured 'count' in a note (iii 326). *tears I shed*] tears shed Rossetti 1870, Woodings (1968b) 412.
477. *roots*] roots (?) Rossetti 1870. *as [?she] plays the song of —*] as the [wind?] plays the song of Rossetti 1870; as the [illegible] plays the song of Woodings (1968b) 412; as the [ ] plays the song of — Crook (2009) 304. Although conjectural, 'she' is reasonable given the Queen's order for Archy regarding her lute and music (ll. 473–5): he plans to listen, hidden 'under the ivy' to her playing. What eds read as the article 'the' (followed by a conjectural word or lacuna) might simply be 'she' instead, with an elongated misstroke of the 's'. There is no lacuna in the MS. Other handwriting slips here in *Nbk 19* p. 101 *reverso* include *as* attached to [?she] the omission of *r* in *terace* and the missing stroke in *count*, all indications of S.'s composing haste in this passage. The slip of the feminine pronoun (or the omission of 'Queen' before *plays*) seems to be part of this pattern.
478. SD. Rossetti 1870; omitted in *Nbk 19*.
478–85. *A widowed bird ... sound*] *Nbk 19* p. 101 *reverso* gives most of the song's first two lines, *A widowed bird, sate mourning / Upon a wintry bough* followed by a series of six underlined points, which serve as the linking device to the complete lyric found in *Nbk 19* p. 52 *reverso*. Rossetti publishes this phrase as if a title in double quotation marks; Woodings (1968b) publishes the phrase as part of the same sentence, continuing on from l. 477: 'the widowed bird, Sate mourning on a wintry bough.' Given that the p. 52 *reverso* version of the first line is complete, the present edition regards the p. 101 *reverso* phrase as merely a linking device not meant to be repeated. See *A widowed bird sate mourning for her love* for collations and discussion of these two stanzas as well as a third, almost complete stanza. The context for the lyric's position at this point in the drama poignantly anticipates the Queen's future widowed state and echoes the winter season of Scene ii as well as the season for Charles's execution.

Heigh-ho — the lark and the owl; one flies the morning
and one flies the night. Only the nightingale, poor fond soul,
sings like the fool through darkness and light. —

[*Exit* ARCHY.

Queen Henrietta
               My own beloved lord,

486–8. *Heigh-ho ... light*] *Rossetti 1870* publishes these lines as a first quatrain of the *widowed bird* lyric. However, *Nbk 19* p. 101 *reverso* shows them to be presented as prose following the insertion point for the lyric.
486. *Heigh-ho* —] Heigho! *Rossetti 1870*. Cp. *Lear* III ii 75: 'With heigh-ho, the wind and the rain —'. *owl;*] owl! *Rossetti 1870*. *one flies*] One flies *Rossetti 1870*. *morning*] morning, *Rossetti 1870*.
487. *flies the night*.] [lulls] flies the night; *Nbk 19*; lulls the night: — *Rossetti 1870*; [lulls] [?flies] the night; *BSM*.
488. *sings*] Sings *Rossetti 1870*. *light*. —] light *Rossetti 1870*.
489–519. *1824* resumes the play with the Queen's speech at this point.
489. *SD. Exit* ARCHY] The SD *exit* is centred, mid-page, in *Nbk 19* p. 104 *reverso*, among the linking devices for Archy's final song; omitted *Rossetti 1870*. See note to l. 477 above. *Queen Henrietta*] Omitted in *Nbk 19*; Queen *1824, Rossetti 1870*.
489. *My beloved lord, 1824, Rossetti 1870, Woodings (1969)* 271. The line, offset to the right in *Nbk 19* p. 104 *reverso* links back to and metrically completes the Queen's last line, 'In my boudoir —' at l. 475. Initially, a speech here was to be for the King, following Archy's exit and picking up where the Queen's speech (ll. 472-5) left off:

               [*And*] *let* [*Sir* [?] *Vandyke know*]
        [*I cannot sit*]
        [*That I will sit to him tomorrow*]
        [*That today no*]

Although cancelled, these lines indicate another aspect of the monarch that S. develops in this scene. Charles's interest in art would demonstrate that he was also a man of taste and refinement in contrast to the barbaric acts and calamitous events surrounding him. *Hume* records: 'He was possessed of an excellent taste in all the fine arts, and the love of painting was in some degree his favourite passion' (vii 194). The mention of *Vandyke* is significant: Sir Anthony Van Dyck (or Vandyke) (1599–1641) was knighted by the King in 1632 and given the title 'Principal Painter in Ordinary'. It is estimated he painted about 40 portraits of the King, 30 of the Queen, several of Wentworth and of Laud. Cp. ii 510 for a reference to Vandyke in a different context.

490　Have you not noted that the fool of late
　　　Has lost his careless mirth, and that his words
　　　Sound like the echoes of our saddest fears: —
　　　What can it mean? I should be loth to think
　　　Some factious slave had tutored him. —

　　　King Charles

　　　　　　　　　　　　　　　　　　　　Oh no —
495　He is but occasion's pupil — partly 'tis
　　　That our minds piece the vacant intervals
　　　Of his [wild] words with their own fashioning,
　　　As in the imagery of summer clouds,
　　　Or coals of the winter fire, idlers find
500　The perfect shadows of their teeming thoughts;
　　　And partly that the terrors of the time
　　　Are sown by wandering rumour in all spirits,

490-1. *Have you ... mirth*] Cp. *Hamlet* II ii 295-6: 'I have of late but wherefore I know not lost all my mirth'.
490. *fool*] Fool *Rossetti 1870*.
492. *fears: —*] fears? *1824, Rossetti 1870, Woodings (1969)* 271. Cp. *To — [the Lord Chancellor]* (no. 333A) 32: 'Source of the sweetest hopes, the saddest fears —'.
493. *loth*] loath *Woodings (1969)* 271.
494. SD. Omitted in *Nbk 19*; King *1824, Rossetti 1870*.
494. *factious*] 'mutinous, dissenting, partisan' (see *OED* 2). *him. —*] him. *1824, Rossetti 1870, Woodings (1969)* 271. *Oh no —*] Omitted in *1824*; Oh no! *Rossetti 1870*; Oh no, *Woodings (1969)* 271. For the first line of the King's response, *1824* publishes only the phrase 'It partly is,' a variation of the next line's ending but fails to note the completing foot for l. 494, *Oh no —*, squeezed in just above, at the top of the page in *Nbk 19* p. 103 *reverso*.
495. Omitted in *1824*. *occasion's pupil — partly*] Occasion's pupil. Partly *Rossetti 1870, Woodings (1969)* 271.
496-7. *the vacant intervals ... fashioning*] The sense is that his listeners' 'minds' fill the silent pauses between Archy's words with meaning.
497. *[wild]*] wild *1824, Rossetti 1870, Woodings (1969)* 271. *fashioning,*] fashioning; *1824*; fashioning,— *Rossetti 1870*; fashioning ... *Woodings (1969)* 271.
498. *clouds,*] *Rossetti 1870*; clouds *Nbk 19*.
499. *coals of*] coals in *1824*.
500. *thoughts;*] *Rossetti 1870*; thoughts. *Nbk 19*; thoughts: *1824*.
501. *And partly*] And partly, *1824*; And, partly, *Rossetti 1870*.
502. *rumour*] Rumour *1824, Rossetti 1870*. *spirits,*] spirits; *1824*.

And in the lightest and the least may best
Be seen the current of the coming wind.

Queen Henrietta
505 Your brain is overwrought with these deep thoughts.
Come, I will sing to you; let us go try
These airs from Italy — and you shall see
A cradled miniature of yourself asleep,
Stamped on the heart by never-erring love,
510 Liker than any Vandyke ever made;
A pattern to the unborn age of thee,
Over whose sweet beauty I have wept for joy
A thousand times, and now should weep for sorrow

503-4. *And in ... wind*] On a jottings page for *Charles* in *Nbk 19* p. 183 *reverso*, the idea of wind as a harbinger of change is similarly developed:

> *The multitude is a stagnant lake —*
> *Vexed by the winds invisible tyranny*
> *And Hampden sits,: the mover of the storm*

The phrase 'the wind's invisible tyranny' appears earlier in this scene at l. 249.
503. *least*] least, *1824*.
505. SD. Omitted in *Nbk 19*; Queen *1824, Rossetti 1870*. A long, centred dash in a large gap between l. 504 and l. 505 indicates a speaker change.
505. *thoughts.*] thoughts; *1824*.
506. *Come,*] *1824, Rossetti 1870*; Come *Nbk 19*.
507. *Italy* —] Italy,— *1824*; Italy; *Rossetti 1870*. *and you shall see*] Omitted from this line by *Rossetti 1870* and inserted inexplicably as the second half of the King's last line: 'Whose reign is men's salvation. And you shall see'. In place of the second half of l. 507, Rossetti inserts the second half of l. 519 ('and as we pass') followed by ll. 520-3. Consequently, he assigns ll. 519-23 to the Queen rather than to the King. *Nbk 19* p. 103 *reverso*, however, makes clear that the Queen's lines (ll. 507-11) follow regularly without interruption.
508. On their departure to their private chambers, Charles and Henrietta will pass the nursery: the 'cradled miniature' would refer to one of Charles's sons, either the future Charles II (b. 1630) or James II (b. 1633) but most likely the former given the Queen's next lines, ll. 511-18, with their possible reference to the Restoration. The double meaning of 'miniature' — either small model or tiny portrait — leads thematically to the references to Vandyke in l. 510 and Correggio in l. 520.
509. *love,*] love — *Nbk 19*; love; *1824, Rossetti 1870*.
510. *Vandyke*] See note to ii 489 above. *made;*] made, *1824, Rossetti 1870*.
513. *times,*] times,— *Rossetti 1870*. *sorrow*] sorrow, *1824, Rossetti 1870*.

>   Did I not think that after we were dead
> 515 Our fortunes would spring high in him, and that
>   The cares we waste upon our heavy crown
>   Would make it light and glorious as a wreath
>   Of Heaven's beams for his dear innocent brow. —
>
>   *King Charles*
>   Dear Henrietta ... and as we pass
> 520 The gallery we'll decide where that Correggio

514. *Did I not*] *1824, Rossetti 1870*; Did not *Nbk 19*. Apparently an accidental omission of *I* for an earlier version of the line, cancelled above, gives: *Did I not think our heavy anxious cares*.
515. A line through *would* in *Nbk 19* p. 102 *reverso* is actually the long dash that separates the conclusion of the Queen's speech from that of the King.
518. *Heaven's*] heaven's *1824, Rossetti 1870. brow.* —] brow — *Nbk 19*; brow. *1824, Rossetti 1870.*
519. *SD.* Charles *Nbk 19*; King *1824, Rossetti 1870.*
519-23. *and as we pass ... salvation*] Omitted in *1824*; *Rossetti 1870* assigns these lines to the Queen, inserting them after the first half of l. 507: 'These airs from Italy'.
519. *Dear Henrietta* ...] Dear Henrietta ... *Nbk 19*; Dear Henrietta! *1824, Rossetti 1870*. Eds assumed the scene concluded here with only this half line. *and as we pass*] Omitted in *1824*; and, as we pass *Rossetti 1870*. See note to ll. 519-23.
520. *Correggio*] Italian painter, Antonio Allegri known as Correggio (1489-1534). S. might have had in mind Correggio's painting *Madonna in adorazione di Gesù Bambino* (*Adoration of the Christ Child*) which he could have seen in his visits to the Uffizi in autumn 1819 (*Mary Jnl* i 298 and ff.; *L* ii 126). Provenance details on the Uffizi Gallery website indicate that 'The work came to the Uffizi in 1617 and was located in the Tribuna, where it remained until 1848' (https://www.uffizi.it/en/artworks/correggio-virgin-adoring-child). In a letter to Peacock from Bologna, 9 November 1818, S. describes with energetic detail two paintings by Correggio that he and Mary had viewed. His description of *Christ beatified* was the basis for 'that immortal shape' in Panthea's dream (*PU* II i 73-4). He adds, 'I do not think we saw any other of Correggio's, but this specimen gives me a very exalted conception of his powers' (*L* ii 50). In *Nbk 19* p. 102 *reverso* is a date notation in the left-hand margin at the start of this line which reads *20th Jany. Jany* is written in a second time just below. *BSM* xii p. xliv reasons that S.'s notation here marks the date he completed this scene. The notation's position next to the last lines of the last speech also confirms the reordering of these lines here. See 'Date of composition' in headnote. *gallery*] gallery, *Rossetti 1870.*

Shall hang — the virgin mother of [sweet sorrow]
With her child, born the King of Heaven and Earth
Whose reign is men's salvation.

[*Exit* KING *and* QUEEN.

Scene iii

Enter HAZELRIG, HAMPDEN, PYM, CROMWELL, *his* DAUGHTER, *and young* SIR HARRY VANE.

521. *virgin mother*] Virgin Mother *Rossetti 1870. of [sweet sorrow]*] Omitted in *Rossetti 1870*. Drafts of alternative line-endings staircase down the page: [*with the child*] then [*born to sorrow*] then [*sweet sorrow*]. The preposition 'of' seems a later addition indicating that *sweet sorrow* was to be retained. The King's speech compliments and balances that of the Queen, both finding in the sleeping children and the painting reflected images of each other. The reference to the 'virgin mother' emphasises as well Henrietta's Catholicism, which Hume commented 'must be regarded as a great misfortune' (vii 195).
522. *Heaven and Earth*] heaven and earth, *Rossetti 1870*.
523. A short line, but not atypical for a scene's conclusion.
SD. Omitted in *Nbk 19*; omitted in *1824, Rossetti 1870*. *1824* concludes this scene with a series of asterisks, suggesting that the scene was incomplete. The MS evidence in *Nbk 19* p. 102 *reverso*, however, indicates otherwise in the dignified elegance of the King's last lines, and the date memorialising its completion. The next page overleaf, p. 101 *reverso*, is the linking passage for Archy's departing words and the cue for his song (ll. 475–88). Below that is a large space and then the notation for Scene iv set in the Star Chamber.

SD. *Scene iii*] Scene iv *Rossetti 1870*. Omitted in *Nbk 19*; Scene 3[d.] *Nbk 22* f. *1[v]. S.'s reading notes on the intended departure of the rebels, probably from *Hume*, are in *Nbk 21* p. 249 rev.: *Hazelrig Hambden Pym & Cromwell are restrained from embarking for America, & following the political & religious puritans, who had there already laid the foundation[s] of a free government; — First scene (date unknown)*. The scene setting, although not indicated by S. in any of the MS, was described as 'Eight ships, lying in the Thames, and ready to sail' in both *Macaulay* (ii 254) and *Hume* (vii 216). The outdoor Thames scene with 'the North wind', 'the evening star' and 'cloud', would allow for Vane's comments when looking back on the city's skyline, 'the Abbey towers' and 'St. Margaret's' (ll. 15–19). *Enter* HAZELRIG, HAMPDEN, PYM, CROMWELL, *his* DAUGHTER, *and young* SIR HARRY VANE] Hampden, Pym, Cromwell, and the younger Vane *1824*; Hampden, Pym, Cromwell, his Daughter, and young Sir Harry Vane *Rossetti 1870*. *Nbk 19* gives: [Hazelrig] . Hamden, Pym, Cromwell his daughter — *& young* S[r]/ H. Vane — [enter to them Sir Ar. Hazelrig] —. The schema in *Nbk 22* f. *1[v] gives: *Pym Hazlerig / Cromwell, young Sir H. Vane, Hampden &[c]*. HAZELRIG] Arthur Hazelrig (c.1601–61) (variously spelled Hesilrige,

Heslerig, Haselrigge, Hessilrigge, Haselrig and Haslerig among the sources) is present in the *Nbk 21* notes, the *Nbk 22* schema and the *Nbk 19* draft, indicating that he would be a part of this scene at some point. HAMPDEN] John Hampden (1595-1643) was among the most outspoken opponents of the King's demand for ship money who 'denied the payment of Shipmoney, as an illegal Tax' (*Whitelocke* 24). Although the case for ship-money went against Hampden, his elegant articulation of its illegality remained in the people's minds; it was eventually repealed in 1640 (*Whitelocke* 37). PYM] John Pym (1584-1643), a member of Parliament, was instrumental in organising the successful case of treason against Wentworth, the Earl of Strafford; in 1641, the King brought an accusation of treason against him as well as Hazelrig, Hampden and two others, who were known as the Five Members. Ultimately, the King lost this suit. CROMWELL] Oliver Cromwell (1599-1658) at this point had previously served as a Member of Parliament until its dissolution in 1629, and he had become a Puritan actively working to rid the Church of its Roman Catholic tendencies. Although *Nbk 19* has speeches only for Hampden and Vane in Scene iii, S.'s schema in *Nbk 22* indicates that Cromwell may have concluded the scene with a speech: *a pursuivant comes with an order of council to prevent their embarkation — Cromwells speech on that occasion —* (f. *1ᵛ). his DAUGHTER] Cromwell's daughter could have been either Bridget (1624-62) or Elizabeth (1629-58) or 'a composite character' (*BSM* xii 71 n.); both women held critical views on Cromwell's increasingly radical agitation and his abandonment of republicanism (see *Hume* viii 297). young SIR HARRY VANE] Although S.'s reading notes in *Nbk 21* do not include Sir Henry Vane, the younger (1613-62) (he is not mentioned in either *Whitelocke* or *Hume* as a member of that rebel party), by the time of the schema (*Nbk 22* f. *1ᵛ) and the drafting of Scene ii 388 in *Nbk 19*, Vane is described as one of the departing rebels. His commitment to joining his fellow Puritans, however, is not supported by his speeches in Scene iii, which argue for remaining in England (see *BSM* xii p. xlv). Whether or not S. intended him to commit to exile, his dialogue with Hampden polemically allows for exposition of two positions for dealing with tyranny. Curiously, of this group, Vane is the only one who actually spent time in America (1635-7), following his Puritan allegiance and helping to set up like-minded communities. Perhaps S. intended to develop Vane's experience: that flight from England would resolve nothing and would only end in disillusion. At the top of *Nbk 19* p. 33, where the draft of this scene starts, is the phrase *Archy the fool* separated from the players' SD by a centred long dash and offset to the right. *BSM* xii 71 asks, 'is he a mute unregarded witness?'. Although not impossible, it seems unlikely that Archy would appear 'unregarded' and alone; his position, like the Fool in *King Lear*, has always been as companion to the King, appearing onstage with him at the same time. Such a notation, however, might be a linking device: although not technically the last speech of Scene ii, Archy's speech is the last portion of Scene ii draft, found in *Nbk 19* p. 101 *reverso*, and is intended to be fitted in earlier in that scene as his exit device. Perhaps *Archy the fool* is a place-holder indicating that the Scene iii Hampden/Vane dialogue is to be inserted after the Archy material on p. 101 *reverso*, but before the Scene iv draft found in the lower half of that same page.

Hampden
England, farewell! thou, who hast been my cradle,
Shall never be my dungeon or my grave! —
I held what I inherited in thee
As pawn for that inheritance of freedom
5 Which thou hast sold for thy despoiler's smile ...
Thy love can tempt those whom thy fears betray;
Proud in the want of that immortal cincture
Which girds the front of kingless states, and dims
The tyrant's gilded crest ... too cheaply bought,

1. SD. Hampden occurs only once as a speaker heading (*Nbk 19* p. 35) in the third version of S.'s six drafts for the following opening lines of this scene.
1-4. England ... freedom] Six versions of these opening lines occur in *Nbk 19* on pp. 33 (two drafts), 35, 37, 39, and 41. Only the first draft on p. 33 is cancelled (with a series of five zig-zag strokes). *1824* published the sixth version on p. 41, a decision followed by *Rossetti 1870*; the present edition concurs with that decision. *Woodings (1968a)* 230-1 offers partial transcriptions of the first three drafts; *BSM* xii 71-83 provides complete transcriptions of all versions.
1. England, farewell!] *1824, Rossetti 1870*; England farewell, *Nbk 19, Woodings (1968a)* 231. *thou,*] Thou, *1824, Rossetti 1870*; thou *Nbk19, Woodings (1968a)* 231. *cradle,*] *1824, Rossetti 1870*; cradle *Nbk 19, Woodings (1968a)* 231. The appearance of 'cradle' in this scene's first line recalls the Queen's last speech in the previous scene ii 508 ('A cradled minature') as well as her first speech, ii 15 ('The quiet cradle') when remembering her infancy in Paris.
2. Shall] Shalt *1824, Rossetti 1870*. *grave!* —] grave! *1824, Rossetti 1870*.
3-5. The sense here is that Hampden has given up to England his inheritance in the expectation of 'freedom', but that 'freedom' has been sold for a mere 'smile'. The despoiler in this case is the King: see Scene ii 25, 65, 187, 358 and Scene iv 53 for 'smile' or 'smiles' associated with the power of monarchs or bishops. A previous version reads *I held what I possess, life wealth, honour / In pawn for what thou hast not liberty ...* (*Nbk 19* p. 39).
3. thee] *Rossetti 1870*; thee, *Nbk 19, 1824*.
5. thy despoiler's] thy false despoiler's *Woodings (1968a)* 231. *smile ...*] smile: — *1824*; smile: *Rossetti 1870*; smile. *Woodings (1968a)* 231.
6-12. Thy love ... of this] Omitted in *1824, Rossetti 1870*. *Woodings (1968a)* 231 gives a version of these lines, but one which fails to recognise that several lines were recast and others added in the top quarter of the page.
6. betray;] betray *Woodings (1968a)* 231.
7. Proud in the loss of that [too cheap unction] *Woodings (1968a)* 231. *cincture*] 'That which encircles or encompasses' (*OED* 3).
8. front] forehead (see *OED* 1a). *kingless*] King less *Nbk 19*. Hampden's use of 'kingless' here and 'Edens' below (l. 27) recalls *Hellas* 1047: 'Between Kingless continents sinless as Eden'. *states, and dims*] [?might] *Woodings (1968a)* 231.
9-10. The tyrant's ... beg] Omitted in *Woodings (1968a)* 231.

10   Though thou dost scorn and we despair to beg,
     By noblest blood — such as even now convulses
     The hearts that break for freedom — stripped of this,
     How can I call thee England or my country?
     Does the wind hold?

     Vane
                        The vanes wait steady yet
15   Upon the Abbey towers. The silver lightnings
     Of the evening star, spite of the city's smoke,
     Tell that the North wind reigns in the upper air. —

13. England] England, *1824, Rossetti 1870. country?*] country! Woodings (1968a) 231, *BSM.*
14. SD. 1824, Rossetti 1870. Omitted in *Nbk 19.*
14-19. The vanes ... St. Margaret's] The present edition follows *1824* and *Rossetti 1870* in assigning these lines to Vane, and given the initial mention of 'The vanes', that seems correct in order to identify Vane to the audience. However, in the MS (*Nbk 19* p. 41) a long dash and a space follows *towers* (l. 15); the line continues overleaf, offset to the right as *[And] the silver lightnings.* Although the long dash and space are usual indications for a speaker change at the caesura — such a speaker might be Pym, Cromwell, or his daughter — the attribution by *1824* and *Rossetti 1870* of ll. 15-19 to Vane seems correct. These lines' graceful evocation of the London skyline at twilight reflects Vane's quiet regard for his homeland that appears in subsequent speeches in this scene. (See also note to l. 19.)
14. The vanes sit steady *1824, Rossetti 1870.*
15-19. Upon ... St. Margaret's] Vane's gaze is towards the west and the London skyline from his and his compatriots' position on the Thames. The 'Abbey towers' (Westminster Abbey) and 'St. Margaret's' are all located near the Palace of Westminster where Parliament would meet. 'Abbey towers' is anachronistic for, although familiar to S., they were not added to the Abbey until 1722-45.
15. Abbey towers.] abbey towers — *Nbk 19;* Abbey towers. *1824;* Abbey-towers. *Rossetti 1870.*
16. star,] star *Nbk 19.* The 'evening star', or Venus, lit by the setting sun, signaling Vane's westerly regard, becomes the focus continued in Hampden's response in ll. 22-9. Cp. *Evening. Ponte a Mare, Pisa* (no. 324) l. 24: 'Which the keen evening star is shining through'. *smoke,*] smoke *Nbk 19.*
17. North] north *1824, Rossetti 1870. air. —*] air — *Nbk 19;* air. *1824, Rossetti 1870.*

Mark too that fleet of fleecy wingèd cloud
Sailing athwart St. Margaret's.

Hampden

Hail, fleet herald

18. *fleet of fleecy wingèd*] flock of fleecy winged *1824*; fleet of fleecy-wingèd *Rossetti 1870*; flock of fleecy-wingèd clouds *Forman 1876–7*. Forman restores *1824*'s 'flock' because 'Mrs. Shelley's is surely the better reading, avoiding the accidental play upon the word *fleet*, in the next line' (iii 323 n.). The MS, however, disproves Forman and shows S. deliberately fine-tuning the lines so as to guarantee the customary linking device between speeches. Moreover, 'fleet' complements the maritime imagery of 'Sailing' in the next line.
19. SD. *1824, Rossetti 1870*. Omitted in *Nbk 19*. The long dash following *St. Margaret's*, a large gap, and the rest of the line offset to the right, indicate a speaker change.
19. *St. Margaret's*] Perhaps an indication of Vane's and his companions' Puritan faith. Sitting in the shadow of Westminster Abbey, St. Margaret's was the parish church of the Palace of Westminster and where members of the House of Commons took the sacrament before commencing business. By late 1640, with the weakening hold of the monarchy and the church on national life, the Puritan members of Parliament were more open in their faith and ambitious in overturning Laud's innovations, one of which was his moving the communion table to churches' eastern walls. Hume records that 'they [the Commons] ordered, as a necessary preliminary, that the communion-table should be removed from the east end of St. Margaret's into the middle of the area' (vii 285). See note to ii 469–70 for Laud's other 'innovations' described by Hume.
20–36. *Of tempest ... blasphemies*] Several iterations of this passage occur in *Nbk 19* on pp. 42, 43, 44, and finally 45–6 where S. seems to have resolved most of the themes and images from pp. 42–4. Like Hampden's first speech, which developed over six variations, abandoned material is not cancelled. Rossetti includes some of that uncancelled but seemingly abandoned material in his edition. Between the present edition's 'tyranny' and 'and thou' (l. 22) Rossetti inserts:

> Beyond the webs of that swoln spider. ...
> Beyond the curses, calumnies, and lies (?)
> Of atheist priests! ...

These lines, however, belong to a series of other uncancelled lines; a partial transcription of p. 42 reads:

> *Beyond the arrows of a tyrant's eye*
> *Beyond the shot of [linked] thunderbolts*
> *Which mitred priests vibrate upon the land*
> *Linking our spirits to the wrath of God*
> *The Procrustean faith of Prelacy*

20 Of tempest! that wise pilot who shall guide
   Hearts free as his to realms as pure as thee,
   Beyond the shot of tyranny; and thou,
   Fair star, whose beam lies o'er the wide Atlantic
   Athwart its zones of tempest and of calm,

Infilled at the top of the page are the two and a half lines cited above from *Rossetti 1870*. Most of this passage, however, is reworked again on pp. 43 and 44, indicating that the above lines were premature and unstable. Finally, on pp. 45–6, the passage is resolved with much retained from the earlier pages but in a more concise, controlled manner.
20. *wise*] wi[d]se *Nbk 19*; wild *1824*; rude *Rossetti 1870*. Rossetti's reading of 'rude' appeared in two earlier versions of this line on pp. 42–3.
21. *his*] his, *1824*. *thee,*] *1824, Rossetti 1870*; thee *Nbk 19*.
22. *tyranny;*] tyranny, *Nbk 19, Rossetti 1870*; tyranny! *1824*. *and thou,*] and thou *Nbk 19*; And thou, *1824*; And thou *Rossetti 1870*.
23–38. *Fair star ... home —*] In *Nbk 19* p. 45, a large space between l. 22 and l. 26 signals the insertion point for ll. 23–5, drafted on p. 43 and indicated by a long vertical line beside them in the left-hand margin. They are a response to Wordsworth's sonnet 'Composed by the Sea-side, near Calais, August, 1802', inverting Wordsworth's themes of England and unabashed nationalism:

> Fair Star of Evening, Splendor of the West,
> Star of my Country! on the horizon's brink
> Thou hangest, stooping, as might seem, to sink
> On England's bosom; yet well pleas'd to rest,
> Meanwhile, and be to her a glorious crest
> Conspicuous to the Nations. Thou, I think,
> Should'st be my Country's emblem; and should'st wink,
> Bright Star! with laughter on her banners, drest
> In thy fresh beauty. There! that dusky spot
> Beneath thee, it is England; there it lies.
> Blessings be on you both! one hope, one lot,
> One life, one glory! I, with many a fear
> For my dear Country, many heartfelt sighs,
> Among Men who do not love her linger here. (*Wordsworth (1807)* i 127)

See 'Sources, Genre and Form' in headnote for further discussion. Havens (*SP* xliii (1946) 547–8) notes that the 'Fair star' serving as a guide to 'the isles of th' Evening land' is an echo of *Hellas* 1027–30 and 1038–41.
23. *lies o'er*] lies on *1824, Rossetti 1870, BSM*. *Atlantic*] Atlantic, *1824, Rossetti 1870*.

25 Bright as the path to a belovèd home —
     O light us to the isles of th' Evening land! —
     Like floating Edens cradled in the glimmer
     Of sunset, through the distant mist of years
     Touched by departing hope, they gleam; lone regions,
30 Where power's poor dupes and victims yet have never
     Propitiated the savage fear of Kings
     With purest blood of noblest hearts; whose dew
     Is yet unstained with tears of those who wake
     To weep each day the wrongs on which it dawns;
35 Whose sacred silent air owns yet no echo
     Of formal blasphemies; nor impious rites
     Wrest man's free worship from the God who loves
     Towards the worm who envies us his love. —

25. *belovèd home* —] beloved home — *Nbk 19*; beloved home, *1824*; belovèd home, *Rossetti 1870*.
26. *O light*] Oh light *Rossetti 1870*. *th' Evening*] th' evening *1824*; the evening *Rossetti 1870*. *land!* —] land — *Nbk 19*; land! *1824, Rossetti1870*.
27. *Edens*] Edens, *1824*.
29. Tinged by departing Hope, they gleam! Lone regions, *1824*; Touched by departing hope, they gleam! lone regions, *Rossetti 1870*. A draft of this line, incomplete, first occurs in *Nbk 19* p. 44, *Tinged by [departing] fled hope they [burst on me] shine,* — and explains Mary's reading.
30. *victims*] victims, *1824*.
31. *Kings*] kings *1824, Rossetti 1870*.
33–4. *who wake / To weep each day*] A frequent collocation in S.; e.g. *Hellas* 20, *The flower that smiles today* (no. 417) 19–20 and *TL* 430.
34. *weep each day*] *1824, Rossetti 1870*; weep, each day, *Nbk 19*.
36. *blasphemies;*] *1824, Rossetti 1870*; blasphemies, *Nbk 19*.
37. *worship*] worship, *Rossetti 1870*. *loves*] loves *Rossetti 1870*.
38. *Towards the worm*] Towards the worm, *1824*; To the poor worm *Rossetti 1870*. Rossetti's version appears in a first draft, *Nbk 19* p. 40. *worm*] 'serpent' (*OED* 1) and, as used here, an allusion to the serpent in *Genesis*. Cp. *Paradise Lost* i 34–6: 'The infernal serpent; he it was, whose guile, / Stirred up with envy and revenge, deceived / The mother of mankind'. In a different vein, cp. *Lines to — [Sonnet to Byron]* 13–14: 'The worm beneath the sod / May lift itself in worship to the God.' The sonnet's last line is also found in *Nbk 19* on Stub p. 73 *reverso* facing p. 94 *reverso* where the rest of the sonnet is drafted. (See note to i 62–3 for discussion of the misplaced leaf 94/93c.) The nearest writings in this portion of the nbk are Scene iii 95–104 (stray leaf in *Box 1* f. 136ᵛ but belonging to Stub Kʳ) and Scene iv 62–3 (p. 93b rev.). Given the date of the Byron sonnet, *c*.22 January 1822, these lines were composed within the same month, possibly within days of each other. *love.* —] love, *1824*; love! *Rossetti 1870*.

Receive, [?thou] young [   ] of Paradise
40   These exiles from the old and [sinful] world.

Vane
What — wilt thou leave thy mother in her woe?

39. *Receive,*] Receive *1824*. Both *1824* and *Rossetti 1870* acknowledge the line's lacuna.
40. *world.*] world! *1824, Rossetti 1870*.
41-70. *What — wilt ... Like eaglets*] These lines, found in *Nbk 19* pp. 46-8, are unstable and particularly difficult with layers of emendations, cancels, and evidence of at least three different composing periods. *1824* selected out, rather randomly, the more legible lines and assigned them all to Hampden; in general, *Rossetti 1870* followed that lead but did extract several additional lines. The assignment of speakers in the present edition is at times conjectural but is supported by the clearly defined language and positions of Hampden and Vane. Hampden's speeches employ a diction that is combative, dark and sombre; Vane's speeches are illumined by patience, hope and sacrifice. The editorial sequence is determined by debate structure where a premise is contradicted by the next speaker who applies the same images and metaphors but subverts them to an opposing view.
41-60. *What — wilt thou leave ... England's air.*] The dialogue between Hampden and Vane draws its language, imagery and argument, as noted by *White (1922)* 439, from John of Gaunt's speech *Richard II* II i 40 ff. For example, cp. Vane's 'What — canst thou desert this dear nurse of men, / This land, this home, this England' (ll. 42-3) with Gaunt's 'This blessed plot, this earth, this realm, this England, / This nurse' (II i 50-1). Gaunt's expression of loss at the debased state of England, 'This land of such dear souls ... Is now leas'd out ... Like to a tenement or pelting farm' (II i 57-60) echoes in Hampden's despairing vision of England as 'a den for slaves to gender in. —' (l. 46). Hamlet's speech to Rosencrantz and Guildenstern, as (noted by *Clark* 271) captures the opposing visions of England's surrounding atmosphere held by Hampden and Vane. Vane's 'This glorious clime, — this firmament, whose lights / Dart mitigated influences through their veil / Of moist and pale-blue atmosphere' (ll. 47-9) echoes Hamlet's 'this most excellent canopy the air, look you, this brave o'erhanging firmament, this majestical roof fretted with golden fire' (*Hamlet* II ii 299-301); however, in his next breath, he adds, 'why, it appeareth nothing to me but a foul and pestilent congregation of vapours' (II ii 301-3), a suffocating description which Hampden expresses as 'This vaporous horizon ... Presses upon me like a dungeon's grate' (ll. 54-6).
41. *SD.* In *Nbk 19* p. 47, [*Harry*] *Vane* appears, offset to the right and opposite a cancelled phrase, *This glorious*, which was a premature start for l. 47. S. began again, infilling ll. 41-4 during at least two different composing periods based on significant differences in ink and pen-cut.
41-9. *What — wilt ... tears*] Lines 41-6 omitted in *1824* and *Rossetti 1870*. *Woodings (1968a)* 224-5 published an edition of ll. 42-3, 45-9.
41. *woe?*] woe *Nbk 19*.

What — canst thou desert this dear nurse of men,
This land, this home, this England, — this appointed
Station for death and life? — [   ]

Hampden
45 That which was England, English sufferance,
[Is grown] a den for slaves to gender in. —

Vane
This glorious clime, — this firmament, whose lights

42. What cannot then learn this dearest nurse of men *Woodings (1968a)* 224.
43. *England, —*] England, *Woodings (1968a)* 224.
43-4. *appointed / Station*] appointed station— *Woodings (1968a)* 224.
44. *Station*] 'A place at which a stop or temporary stay is made in the course of a journey' (*OED* 20b) but also implied is 'Station of the Cross': 'Each of a set series of images or pictures representing successive incidents of Jesus' Passion from his condemnation to his burial' (*OED*). *for 'death and life?'* —] Omitted in *Woodings (1968a)*. S.'s order of 'death and life' and the association with Christ's suffering conforms with Vane's acceptance of the place of death in life:

> Death is not to be feared and fled from, as it is by most, but sweetly and patiently to be waited for, as a thing natural reasonable, and inevitable. It is to be looked upon as a thing indifferent, carrying no harm in it. (*Vane* 126)

life? —] life . — *Nbk 19*.
45. SD. Omitted in *Nbk 19*.
45. *England, English sufferance,*] England. Our dear country *Woodings (1968a)* 225. *sufferance*] 'Patient endurance, forbearance, long-suffering' (*OED* 1).
46. *a den for slaves to gender in*] Cp. *Othello* IV ii 61-2: 'a cistern for foul toads / To knot and gender in'. *den*] [*illegible*] *Woodings (1968a)* 225. *gender*] copulate (*OED* 1). *in.* —] in. *Woodings (1968a)* 225. The line began as *Is grown a sink* then *sink* canc. and *den* added, presumably for assonance with *gender in*. 'Sink' in this instance = 'A pool or pit formed in the ground for collecting waste water, sewage, etc.; a cesspool' (*OED* 1a). In describing London in 1637, Clarendon writes of the City, 'the sink of all the ill humours of the kingdom' (*Clarendon* i 270).
47. SD. Omitted in *1824* and *Rossetti 1870* who assign all the rest of the lines for this scene to Hampden. Vane's name occurred just above these lines (*Nbk 19* p. 47) before Hampden's lines were fitted in; see note to 41. SD. Vane is the most obvious speaker, deliberately reversing Hampden's grotesque scenario: while Hampden looks downward to the *sink* or 'den', Vane looks up to the 'firmament'.
47. *clime, —*] clime, *1824, Woodings (1968a)* 225; clime; *Rossetti 1870*. *firmament,*] firmament *Woodings (1968a)* 225.

Dart mitigated influences through their veil
Of moist and pale-blue atmosphere, whose gentle tears
50 Are the robes of this all-feeding earth —
This pendulous air, fraught with golden plenty,
Multiplies wealth throughout the silent night
Till crested cities, and [   ]

Hampden
This vaporous horizon, whose [dim] round
55 Is bastioned on the circumfluous sea,
Presses upon me like a dungeon's grate.

48. *mitigated influences*] Cp. the similar reference to a temperate and benevolent environment in *The Zucca* l. 59. *influences*] influence *1824*, *Rossetti 1870*. *their veil*] the veil *1824*, *Woodings (1968a)* 225.
49. *Of moist and pale-blue*] Of pale blue *1824*; Of pale-blue *Rossetti 1870*. *atmosphere,*] atmosphere; *1824*. *whose gentle tears*] whose tears keep green *1824*, *Rossetti 1870*; omitted in *Woodings (1968a)*.
50. *1824*; The pavement of this moist all-feeding earth *Rossetti 1870*.
51–3. *This pendulous ... cities, and*] Omitted in *1824* and *Rossetti 1870*. The reiteration of 'This' (as in 'This glorious clime, — this firmament') with 'This pendulous air' would appear to link rhetorically the two sections of Vane's speech.
51. Cp. *Lear* III iv 67–8: 'Now all the plagues that in the pendulous air / Hang fated o'er men's faults light on thy daughters!', and also *PU* III i 11. *with golden*] with the golden *Nbk 19*.
53. *crested cities*] Cp. the cancelled version of a draft for ll. 180–1 of *Lines connected with Hellas* Appendix A (*It is the period when all the Sons of God*): *In lurid drops upon the crested cities* (*Nbk 21* p. 32).
54. SD. Omitted in *Nbk 19*. Assigned to Hampden in *1824* and *Rossetti 1870*.
54. *vaporous*] Hampden's word, meaning 'Filled with, thick or dim with, vapour; foggy, misty' (*OED* 3a), is the antithesis of Vane's salubrious and light-filled 'atmosphere' and 'air'. Cp. *Lines Written among the Euganean Hills, October, 1818* (no. 183) ll. 91–2: 'The waveless plain of Lombardy, / Bounded by the vaporous air'. *horizon,*] horizon; *1824*. Both *1824* and *Rossetti 1870* place this line after l. 50 of the present edition.
55. Below the start of this line, at the bottom of *Nbk 19* p. 47 is *Impregnably* which could be an alternative start to this line: *Impregnably bastioned on the circumfluous sea*. Cp. *Hellas* 'bastioned impregnably' (l. 774). Both *1824* and *Rossetti 1870* insert a line ('Repelling invasion from the sacred towers;') after l. 55 but which the present editors conjecture belongs to Vane (see note to l. 69 below). *on*] by *1824*, *Rossetti 1870*.
56–8. *Presses ... alive*] Cp. *The Cenci* (no. 209) V iv 48–51: 'So young to go / Under the obscure, cold, rotting, wormy ground! / To be nailed down into a narrow place'.
56. *Presses*] [It] presses *Woodings (1968a)* 231. *dungeon's grate.*] dungeons grate — *Nbk 19*; dungeon's grate, *1824*, *Rossetti 1870*; dungeon grate, *Woodings (1968a)* 231.

A low dark roof — a damp and narrow wall —
A fearful grave to one buried alive
Would stifle less the inmost spirit of life
60   Than England's air. The boundless Universe
[Becomes] a cell too narrow for the soul
That owns a master —

Vane
                    While the loathliest ward
Of this wide prison, England, is a nest
Of cradling peace built on the mountain's top

57. *roof* —] roof, *1824*, *Rossetti 1870*, Woodings (1968a) 213. *wall* —] vault: *1824*; wall, *Rossetti 1870*; wall. Woodings (1968a) 231.
58–9. *A fearful ... life*] Omitted in *1824*, *Rossetti 1870*.
60–2. *Than England's ... master*] This passage in *Nbk 19* p. 48 is a series of layered emendations and cancels, possibly the reason why *1824* publishes another uncancelled version of this passage, slightly more legible, found on p. 46 (*1824* with MS collation):

The mighty universe becomes a cell	Universe *Nbk 19*
Too narrow for the soul that owns no master.	a master *Nbk 19*
But he whose	omitted in *1824*

This p. 46 version, however, is incomplete while the re-working on p. 48 is resolved and gives the usual indications for a speaker change in the middle of l. 62 (a long dash, a gap, and offset to the right) which is ignored in both *1824* and *Rossetti 1870*. Consequently, all of Vane's lines here (ll. 62–9) are assigned to Hampden in both editions. *Crook (2009)* also assigns ll. 60–2 to Vane but allows for the possibility that Hampden is the speaker (302 n.). *Rossetti 1870* generally follows the p. 48 version; see note to l. 60.
60. *Than England's air.*] Omitted in *1824*, *Rossetti 1870*, *Crook (2009)*. *Universe*] universe *Rossetti 1870*, *Crook (2009)*.
61. The line through *Becomes* in *Nbk 19* p. 48 might not be a cancel but an underlining stroke.
62–3. *While ... prison, England*] Cp. Hamlet's speech to Rosencrantz and Guildenstern: 'Denmark's a prison. ... A goodly one, in which there are many confines, wards, and dungeons' (*Hamlet* II ii 243–6).
62. SD. Omitted in *Nbk 19*. Omitted in *1824*, *Rossetti 1870*, *Crook (2009)*.
62. *master* —] master; *Rossetti 1870*. Omitted in *1824*; see note to ll. 60–2 for *1824*'s version. *While the loathliest ward*] While the loathliest spot *1824*; while the loathliest ward *Rossetti 1870*, *Crook (2009)*. *ward*] 'Each of the divisions or separate departments of a prison' (*OED* 17b).
63. *prison,*] prison *Nbk 19*. *England,*] England, .. *Nbk 19*; England, ... *Crook (2009)*.
64. *cradling*] cradled *1824*. *mountain's top*] mountain tops, *1824*; mountain tops,— *Rossetti 1870*.

65   To which the eagle spirits of the free,
     That range through Heaven and Earth, and scorn the storms
     Of time, and gaze upon the [light] of truth,
     Return to brood on thoughts that cannot die,
     And cannot be repelled —

65. *eagle spirits*] eagle-spirits *1824. free,*] free *Nbk 19.*
66. *That range*] Which range *1824,* Rossetti *1870. Heaven and Earth,*] Heaven & Earth *Nbk 19*; heaven and earth, *1824,* Rossetti *1870. storms*] storm *1824,* Rossetti *1870.*
67. *truth,*] *1824,* Rossetti *1870*; truth *Nbk 19.*
68. *1824* breaks up most of this line into two lines and adds the half line l. 69 in the present edition:

> Return to brood over the [   ] thoughts
> That cannot die, and may not be repelled.

These two lines conclude *1824*'s scene iii and the entire play as well. *die,*] die Rossetti *1870.*
69. Following *repelled* (at the bottom of *Nbk 19* p. 48) are several attempts to complete the line which are all cancelled: *and soon / when growing ?eag.* S. then seems to have decided to end Vane's speech mid-line with a dash. (Hampden's response beginning at the caesura was drafted and then cancelled on the facing half-leaf, p. 49; those cancelled lines were to reappear several pages later, on p. 55, and form the basis for ll. 83–5 in present edition.) Infilled at the top of *Nbk 19* p. 48 are two extant lines, *Repels invasion from the [sacred] towers / When usurpation is all source of change* — which are indented to the right and in a distinctly different ink tone and wider stroke than lines just below; they do, however, match the ink tone and strokes of l. 69 at the bottom of the page. Both *1824* and Rossetti *1870* incorporated an edited version of the first line into Hampden's speech following l. 55 in present edition: 'Repelling invasion from the sacred towers,' (*1824*; the final punctuation in Rossetti *1870* is a semi colon). The image of these two lines, however, would seem to belong to Vane who repeatedly acknowledges the mechanism of change; moreover, the reiteration of *Repels* and *repelled* (l. 69) suggests that perhaps these two lines were an alternative conclusion to Vane's speech below (ll. 62–9). As S. arrived at the bottom of the page, it is possible that he fitted in the two additional lines in the small space at the top of the same page, a typical habit of S.'s to guarantee that all of a single speech was on one page. Perhaps, as he became absorbed in Hampden's response drafted on the following pages, S. omitted to resolve the conclusion of Vane's speech. *repelled* —] repelled. Rossetti *1870.*

Hampden
70 Like eaglets floating in the heaven of time,
    They soar above their quarry and shall stoop
    Through palaces and temples thunderproof,
    As prey-birds through a forest or a [?storm]
    On the triumphant powers of Fraud and Wrong.
75 Meanwhile — [   ]
    As wouldst thou judge a Mother who should say

70–103. Like eaglets … [?Till] [?it]] Omitted in *1824*.
70. SD. Omitted in *Nbk 19*.
70–4. eaglets] Hampden adopts Vane's eagle image, but overturns it by characterising eagles as 'prey-birds' who arrive with 'Fraud and Wrong' rather than the 'eagle spirits' who seek out 'cradling peace'. Crook assigns this line and the following ll. 72–5 to Vane (*Crook (2009)* 302).
71. quarry] quarry, *Rossetti 1870. stoop*] 'Of a hawk or other bird of prey: To descend swiftly on its prey, to swoop' (*OED* 6a).
72. This line concludes Rossetti's edition of Scene iii (although he designates it as 'Scene iv'). *Nbk 19* p. 49, where ll. 70–2 occur, is a mutilated leaf, the verso of which contains ll. 73–5. *thunderproof,*] thunderproof. *Rossetti 1870*; thunderproof *Crook (2009)* 302.
73–103. As prey-birds … [?Till] [?it]] Omitted in *Rossetti 1870*.
73. prey-birds] fiery birds *BSM, Crook (2009)* 302. Cp. *Hellas* 255: 'The prey-birds and the wolves are gorged and sleep'.
76–82. As wouldst …England] The meaning of this passage is that one would judge poorly the Mother who required her sons to be either willing participants (presumably in denying freedom) or obedient victims. Her 'mutineers' would be the rebels, who have judged her, and found her 'ragged and pale and cold' and unworthy of love or loyalty. All neatly contained in *Nbk 19* p. 51, these lines must certainly belong to Hampden with his view of England's failure to uphold individual freedom. It is possible, however, that S. might have intended them to be inserted earlier in this scene as a response to Vane's lines (41–4) found on *Nbk 19* p. 47 where he describes England as *mother* and *nurse*. They are placed here because of their proximity to surrounding Hampden material; additionally, none of the usual symbols for insertion are present on this page or p. 47.
76. As] [How] *Woodings (1968a)* 232. The line (*Nbk 19* p. 51) began as *[What wouldst]* then a new line starts:

> How wouldst thou judge *[a Mother who should say]* of Eve had she assembled
> Abel & Cain

Then, S. cancelled most of the second half of the first line and *Abel & Cain*. He wrote in again his original line ending, cancelling *How* and adding *As* above. That

To her assembled Sons — 'Obey or serve,
Deceive or be deceived, inflict or suffer,
Leave freedom to the scoffing winds of Heaven' —
80 And who [?should] [?] among her [?mutineers]
In her old age, ragged and pale and cold,
So judge this England, — [   ]
And thus wilt thou behold with patient eyes,
And with tame hand and heart, and silent lip
85 Endure the oppression of the time? —

Vane

                                         Even this
Most bitter cup would I not put away —
If from the hand whence the redeemer drank;
[Blind is the eye] that sees not in this world
All things maturing to a mighty end,

---

emendation was probably determined by the last line on this page, l. 82; thus, *As wouldst thou judge ... So judge this England.*
77. *assembled Sons*] assaulted sons Woodings (1968a) 232. *'Obey or serve,*] "obey or serve *Nbk 19*; obey or serve, Woodings (1968a) 232.
78. *deceived,*] deceived — *Nbk 19*, Woodings (1968a) 232. *suffer,*] suffer *Nbk 19*, Woodings (1968a) 232.
79. *Heaven'* —] Heaven *Nbk 19*; Heaven ... Woodings (1968a) 232 (the suspension points probably indicate omission of the following lines).
81. *cold,*] cold *Nbk 19*.
82. No connecting half-line to complete this line is apparent. The following pages include the draft for Archy's song *A widowed bird sate mourning for her love* overleaf (*Nbk 19* p. 52 rev.), the draft of *Art thou pale for weariness* (*Nbk 19* p. 53 rev.) and the Petrarch translation, Appendix C (*Nbk 19* p. 54 rev.). Finally, in *Nbk 19* p. 55, S. resumes the last lines of Hampden's speech (ll. 83–5) followed by Vane's response.
83. *And thus wilt*] And wilt Woodings (1968a) 232. *eyes,*] eyes *Nbk 19*, Woodings(1968) 232.
84. *tame hand*] torn hand Woodings (1968a) 232. *lip*] lip, Woodings (1968a) 232.
85. SD. Vane *Nbk 19*.
85. *time?* —] time. — *Nbk 19*; time Woodings (1968a) 232.
87. *the hand*] the head BSM; Crook (2009) 302. *drank;*] drank — *Nbk 19*, Crook (2009) 302.
88. The seeming cancel here might belong to the pale brown writing underneath *Blind is the eye* for the rest of the line is successfully worked out and leads naturally to l. 89. In this line as well as ll. 87 and 90, Vane addresses Hampden's accusation of docile, unresponsive features: 'patient eyes, / ... tame hand and heart, and silent lip'.
89. *end,*] end *Nbk 19*, Crook (2009) 302.

90   And dead the soul that bears no feeling heart
     In the great action of the growing work.
     England is but the station to gained grace;
     *   *   *   *   *   *
     Hisses and scorn, even as my master did,

90. S. first wrote *And dead the heart* but *heart* canc. and replaced by *soul* just below.
92–103. *England* ... *[?Till] [?it]*] These lines are drafted on a leaf that had become detached from this notebook and is now identified as *Box 1* f. 136. (Because the second half of l. 93 acquired a misleading textual history in *Relics*, it has resulted in the anomaly of the line appearing here, in Scene iii as l. 93, and again in *Lines connected with Charles the First* (Appendix A) as the first line.) These lines are separated from the previous lines (ll. 83–91) by what would have originally been nine pages (pp. 56–60, modern stub, Stub J); the 'stray leaf' would have been attached to Stub K. The adjacency of ll. 91 and 92 here is therefore artificial. It could be conjectured that S. had hoped to develop further the Hampden/Vane dialogue. While pp. 56–60 are blank, the stubs, however, do show evidence of writing. Given that l. 93 seemingly begins mid-thought, it can be conjectured that at least the page facing f. 136ᵛ, represented by Stub Jᵛ, would have included *Charles the First* material.
92. *station*] See ll. 43–4: 'This land, this home, this England, — this appointed / Station for death and life?'. It is possible that l. 92 is a reworking of the earlier two lines although the temporality is different; ll. 43–4 express a current situation while this line projecting into the future. In any event, 'station' still carries the same religious connotations; see note to iii 44 above. *gained grace*] [?garnered] [grace] *BSM*.
93–4. *Hisses* ... *fame*] The view that the 'Hisses and scorn' ... 'Of the dull million' are silenced in the 'blameless grave' is an echo of a theme in Vane's work. In the section 'Meditations on Death' he writes, 'This [Death], that is all the hurt enemies can do us, is that which we should desire and seek after, as the onely Haven of Rest, from all the Torments of this life; and which, as it gives us a fuller fruition of Christ, is a very great gain, that the sooner we are possessors of, the better' (*Vane* 126). See also the note to iii 44 above.
93. First published in *Relics,* this line is found at the top of f. 136ᵛ, at the level where the leaf has been torn away; the first three words are dissected by the tear. The line is probably a continuation of material on the facing but missing 'page' witnessed by Stub Jᵛ and its writing. This line appears to be connected to the overleaf material on f. 136ʳ because of the tell-tale linking words, *the* [*scoffs*] *scorn* found there, just above l. 95 showing the same emendation of *scoffs* canc. and emended to *scorn.* Conjecturally, the line before l. 93 might have included something like 'I would gladly suffer'. *Hisses and scorn,*] Omitted in *Relics*; ... scorns, *Woodings (1968a)* 232. *even*] Even *Relics. master*] Master *Relics. did,*] did *Nbk 19*, *Woodings (1968a)* 232.

>   Of the dull million, my eternal fame;
> 95 [The] blameless grave, the quiet place of rest;
>   Of what in me, he whom I serve, forbids:
>   To find repose under a tyrant's frown. —
>   A summer's fruit maturing to decay,
>   An autumnal seed laid in the wintry earth,
> 100 A flower which decks the spring of that great year;
>   What is [the] [spirit] which the storm of [?time]
>   Shakes to the lap of ruin, what is [?mine]
>   [?Till] [?it]

94. million,] million *Nbk 19. fame;*] fame — *Nbk 19.*
95. grave,] grave *Nbk 19. rest;*] rest *Nbk 19.*
96. forbids:] forbids *Nbk 19.*
97. frown. —] frown — *Nbk 19.*
98-100. A summer's ... year] The cycle of seasonal references ('summer', 'autumnal', 'wintry', 'spring') recalls Vane's metaphor in his analysis of the power shifts among the three estates: 'Nay, though this Representation (as hath fallen out) be restrained for a season, to the Commons House, in the single actings, into which (as we have seen) when by the inordinate fire of the times, two of the three Estates [the clergy and the nobility] have for a season been melted down, they did but retire into their Root, and were not hereby in their Right, destroyed, but rather preserved, though as to their exercise, laid for a while asleep, till the season came of their Revival and Restoration' (*Vane* 45).
98. A cluster of blots pepper the end of this line as well as 97 and 99, so terminal punctuation is conjectural. *BSM* xii 123 notes an echo of this line's theme of decay and regeneration in Vane's work: 'Nothing perishes or is dissolved by Death, but the Vail and Covering, which is wont to be done away from all ripe fruit. It brings us out of a dark dungeon, through the crannies whereof, our sight of Light is but weak and small, and brings us into an open Liberty, an estate of Light and Life' (*Vane* 127).
99. seed] reed *BSM*; *earth,*] earth *Nbk 19.*
100. year;] year *Nbk19.*
102. Shakes to the lap of ruin although an incomplete line and thought, is possibly a reflection of Vane's view that the suffering brought by 'ruin' is paradoxically, the very thing that brings him closer to God and salvation: 'God's strength may appear in the Prisoner's weakness; and the more all things carry the face of certain ruine and destruction unto all that is near and dear to him in this world, the more will divine deliverance and salvation appear; to the making good of that Scripture' (*Vane* 26).
103. At this level, the page (*Box 1* f. 136) was torn away leaving Stub K in the notebook; both the stub and the leaf contain parts of the last two conjectural words.

Scene iv

The Star Chamber. LAUD, JUXON, WENTWORTH, etc. *as Judges.* CLERK, OFFICER. *Enter* BASTWICK, PRYNNE.

Laud
Bring forth the prisoner Bastwick: let the clerk
Recite his sentence. —

SD. *Scene iv*] Scene. *Nbk 19*; omitted in *1824*, Scene III *Rossetti 1870*. *The Star Chamber*] the Star chamber *Nbk 19*. Located in the Palace of Westminster, the Star Chamber was so-called because its ceiling was decorated with a pattern of gilt stars. Originally a just and useful higher court evolving out of the King's Council from medieval times, under the Stuarts it became a court able to abridge and override lower courts, to levy taxes arbitrarily, and to serve as the King's personal weapon in dealing with opponents. The Chamber became a substitute for Parliament for eleven years once Charles I had suspended that body; however, with the return of the Long Parliament, it was abolished in 1641. In extended and figurative use it refers to 'an institution or body considered as constituting an 'inner circle', as having special authority in some matter, or as taking arbitrary or unconstitutional decisions' (*OED* 2b); see *Merry Wives* I i 1–2: 'I will make a / Star Chamber matter of it.' LAUD, JUXON, WENTWORTH, etc. *as Judges.* CLERK, OFFICER. *Enter* BASTWICK, PRYNNE.] Laud &^{c}.as Judges. enter Bastwick Prynne *Nbk 19* (see also note to l. 1 below); LAUD, JUXON, STRAFFORD, and others, as Judges. PRYNNE as a prisoner, and then BASTWICK *Rossetti 1870*. The scene itself is taken from events in 1637, described in *Whitelocke* (24–5), *Clarendon* (i 270–2), *Macaulay* (ii 242–9) and *Hume* (vii 214–15). S.'s schema for this scene is in *Nbk 22* f. *2^r (see *MYRS* vii 334–5). This scene commences (SD and ll. 1–2) in the lower half of *Nbk 19* p. 101 *reverso* where the upper half contains Archy's exit speech, his song title, and his final lines of Scene ii. The ink and pen-cut in both halves are the same greyish brown ink suggesting they were contemporaneous. See note to ii 475.
1. SD. Laud *Nbk 19*.
1. *Bastwick:*] *Rossetti 1870*; Bastwick. . *Nbk 19*. Clustered together at the end of this line are [*Bastw*] [*officer*] and [*Clerk*]. The seeming cancel stroke is typical of S.'s SD symbol for a character's entrance or speech.
2. SD. See note to l. 1.
2–6. *That he … court*] Regarding this punishment, S. closely follows *Whitelocke* 25: 'Burton and Bastwick were fined five thousand pounds apiece, to loose their Ears in the Pillory, and to be imprisoned, the one in *Launceston Castle*, and the other in *Lancaster Castle*'. Bastwick's sentencing recalls his horror in finally recognising Leighton who was disfigured by these same punishments (see i 102–11).
2. *sentence.* —] sentence — *Nbk 19*; sentence. *Rossetti 1870*. *That*] "That *Rossetti 1870*. Rossetti encloses the Clerk's speech in quotation marks.

Clerk
     That he pay five thousand
Pounds to the King, lose both his ears, be branded
With red hot iron on the cheek and forehead,
5 And [imprisoned] within Lancaster Castle
During the pleasure of the court. —

Laud
     Prisoner,
If you have aught to say wherefore this sentence
Should not be put into effect, now speak.

Juxon
If you have aught to plead in mitigation,

3. *King*] king *Rossetti 1870.*
4. *red hot*] red-hot *Rossetti 1870. forehead,*] *Rossetti 1870*; forehead *Nbk 19.*
5. *And [imprisoned]*] And be imprisoned *Rossetti 1870.*
6. *SD.* Laud *Nbk 19.*
6. *court.* —] court — *Nbk 19*; Court." *Rossetti 1870. Prisoner,*] *Rossetti 1870*; — Prisoner *Nbk 19.*
8. *speak.*] *Rossetti 1870*; speak *Nbk 19.*
9. *SD.* [Cott] Juxon *Nbk 19.* William Juxon (1582–1663) had succeeded Laud as President of St. John's College, Oxford, and then Bishop of London; the King named him Lord High Treasurer following the death of Richard Weston. Of Juxon, Hume notes that he 'was a person of great integrity, mildness, and humanity, and endued with a good understanding' (vii 236), but Hume adds elsewhere that the Puritans 'were much dissatisfied with Juxon … because he was a lover of profane field-sports, and hunting' (vii 210). His reputation for integrity held him in good stead throughout the coming turbulent years. The King asked that Juxon give him the sacrament before his execution, and Juxon accompanied him to the scaffold where the King's last words were exchanged with him. *Whitelocke* 370 records:

> King. *I go from a corruptible to an incorruptible Crown, where no disturbance can be.*
>
> Dr. Juxon. *You are exchanged from a temporal to an eternal Crown, a good exchange.* Then the King took off his cloak, and his *George* which he gave to Dr. *Juxon,* saying *Remember* — some other small ceremonies were past, after which, the King stooping down, laid his Neck upon the block, and after a very little pause, stretching forth his hands, the Executioner, at one blow, severed his head from his Body.

Despite the Puritans' distaste for Juxon's passion for hunting, he was never called before Parliament on charges during the Civil War. In the Restoration that followed, Charles II named him Archbishop of Canterbury.

10   Speak. —

Bastwick
            Thus, my lords: if like the prelates, I
    Were an invader of the royal power,
    A public scorner of the word of God,
    Profane, idolatrous, popish, superstitious,
    Impious in heart, and in tyrannic act,
15 Void of wit, honesty and temperance; —
    If Satan were my lord, as theirs, and our God
    Pattern of all I should avoid to do —
    Were I an enemy of my God and King
    And of good men, as ye are — I should merit

---

10. SD. *Rossetti 1870*; B *Nbk 19*. The majuscule B for Bastwick is centred on the page.
10-19. *Thus, my lords ... ye are*] For this speech, S. follows very closely Whitelocke's citation of Bastwick's written response to the accusations against him:

> That the Prelates are Invaders of the King's Prerogative Royal, Contemners and Despisers of the holy Scriptures, Advancers of Popery, Superstition, Idolatry, and Prophaneness: Also they abuse the King's Authority, to the Oppression of his loyalist Subjects, and therein exercise great Cruelty, Tyranny, and Injustice; and in execution of those impious Performances, they show neither wit, honesty, nor temperance. Nor are they either Servants of God, or of the King, but of the Devil, being Enemies of God and the King and of every living thing that is good. (*Whitelocke* 25)

10. *Speak.* —] Speak — *Nbk 19*; Speak. *Rossetti 1870*. *lords: if like*] lords: — If like *Nbk 19*; lords. If, like *Rossetti 1870*. *prelates*] Bastwick's diatribe on *prelates* echoes his speech in i 121-2.
11. *royal*] Replaces *Kingly* canc.
13. *Profane, idolatrous,*] *Rossetti 1870*; Prophane[s] idolatrous *Nbk 19*. *superstitious,*] *Rossetti 1870*; superstitious *Nbk 19*.
14. *heart,*] heart *Rossetti 1870*. *act,*] *Rossetti 1870*; act *Nbk 19*.
15. *wit, honesty*] wit honesty *Nbk 19*; wit, honesty, *Rossetti 1870*. *temperance; —*] temperance — *Nbk 19*; temperance; *Rossetti 1870*.
16. *theirs, and our God*] theirs and our God *Nbk 19*; theirs, — our God *Rossetti 1870*. For this last phrase, *BSM* gives '& if our God'.
17. *do —*] do; *Rossetti 1870*.
19. *are —*] are;— *Rossetti 1870*.

20 Your purple state and gilt prosperity
    Which, when ye wake from the last sleep, shall turn
    To crowns and robes of everlasting fire. —
    B[ut] as I am, I [prithee] grudge me not
    The only earthly honour[?s] ye can yield,
25 Or I think worth acceptance at your hands: —
    Scorn, mutilation and imprisonment.

Laud
Officer, take the prisoner from the bar
And be his tongue slit for this insolence.

Bastwick
Whilst this hand holds a pen —

20. *purple state*] fearful state *Rossetti 1870*. Purple, the liturgical colour assigned to bishops, is also the colour worn by priests during Advent and Lent. The pairing of *purple* and *gilt* here echoes S.'s reading notes for this scene in *Nbk 21* f. *2ʳ: *Lauds excessive thirst / for gold & blood*.
21. *Which,*] Which *Nbk19*.
22. *crowns*] cowls *Rossetti 1870*. Both *cowls* and *crowns* are cancelled and then underlined in *Nbk 19*. BSM notes that 'stet for *crowns* clear and more appropriate' (*BSM* xii 154) and cites a similar set of images in *PU* I 286–91. Against this is the fact that *cowls* and *robes* are ecclesiastical regalia and would apply to both Laud and Juxon, unlike *crowns* which are royal emblems.
23. But, as I am, I bid ye grudge me not *Rossetti 1870*.
24. *honour[?s]*] favour *Rossetti 1870*.
25. *hands:* —] hands; — *Nbk 19*; hands,— *Rossetti 1870*. A very long dash follows the full-stop. At this point Rossetti inserts six lines based on Garnett's edition (*Relics* 91) of lines taken from the 'stray leaf' (*Box 1* f. 136ᵛ) and published in the present edition as *Lines connected with Charles the First* (Appendix A). Because Rossetti, like Garnett, was unaware of the original location and position of this 'stray leaf' — in *Nbk 19* — he was also unaware that it belonged to the Hampden/Vane dialogue of Scene iii.
27. Laud's address to the 'Officer' here provides the rationale for the editorial application in stage directions at ll. 38 and 49. *bar*] bar, *Rossetti 1870*. Bastwick's bravura and 'insolence' that Laud remarks on is noted in *Hume*: 'the very answers which they gave in the court were so full of contumacy and of invectives against the prelates, that no lawyer could be prevailed on to sign them' (vii 215).
29–34. *Stop ... away*] See the note to iv 9 SD for Juxon's reputation as a kind but astute actor. In this speech, having heard Laud's orders for the tongue mutilation and anticipating the amputation of Bastwick's hands, he diplomatically seeks leniency for Bastwick under the guise of looking out for the best interests of church and state.
29. *Whilst*] While *Rossetti 1870*. *pen* —] pen ... *Rossetti 1870*. *hands* —] hands ... *Rossetti 1870*. *Stop* —] Stop! *Rossetti 1870*.

Laud

       Be his hands —

Juxon

            Stop —
30 Forbear, my lord! The tongue which now can speak
 No terror, would interpret, being dumb,
 Heaven's thunder to our harm [in every heart],
 And hands which now write only their own shame,
 With bleeding stumps might sign our blood away.

Laud
35 Much more such mercy would there be in men
 Did all the ministers of Heaven's revenge
 Flinch thus from earthly retribution. I
 Could suffer what I would inflict.

          [*Exit* BASTWICK *with* OFFICER.

30. *Forbear, my lord! The*] *Rossetti 1870*; Forbear my lord, the *Nbk 19*. *tongue*] tongue, *Rossetti 1870*.
31. *dumb,*] dumb *Nbk 19*.
32-4. The meaning here is that the brutal punishments of Bastwick and others would produce a sense of revulsion among the population, to the detriment of the government, which in fact turned out to be the case. *Hume* records, 'The rigors, however, which they underwent, … gave general offence; and the patience, or rather alacrity, with which they suffered, increased still farther the indignation of the public' (vii 215).
32. *harm*] harm; *Rossetti 1870*. *[in every heart]*] Omitted in *Rossetti 1870* who leaves second half of line as a lacuna.
33. *hands*] hands, *Rossetti 1870*. *shame,*] *Rossetti 1870*; shame *Nbk 19*.
35-8. *Much more … inflict*] Macaulay describes at length Laud's zeal in prosecuting these cases and the speech he gave at that time where 'he railed with the utmost gall and bitterness against the unhappy prisoners, whilst he magnified his own religious patience in bearing injuries' (*Macaulay* ii 246).
35. Much more such "mercy" among men would be, *Rossetti 1870*.
38. SD. Omitted in *Nbk 19*; Exit Bastwick guarded *Rossetti 1870*.
38. *inflict.*] *Rossetti 1870*; inflict, — *Nbk 19*.

                             Bring up
The Lord Bishop of Lincoln. —
                                      [*To* WENTWORTH.
                     Know you not
40   That in distraining for ten thousand pounds
     Upon his books and furniture at Lincoln,
     Were found these scandalous and seditious letters
     Sent from one Osbaldistone, who is fled?
     I speak it not as touching this poor person,
45   But of the office which should make it holy
     Were it as vile as it was ever spotless. —

39. SD. Omitted in *Nbk 19*; To Strafford *Rossetti 1870*. The direction change of Laud's speech seems indicated by a particularly long, thick dash following *Lincoln*.
39–43. *Know you ... fled?*] The account of the Bishop of Lincoln and Osbaldistone is recorded in *Whitelocke* (25) *Macaulay* (ii 240-1) and *Hume* (vii 217). S. seems to have followed most closely *Hume*, both here and in scene ii 422:

> In order to levy the fine ... some officers had been sent to seize all the furniture and books of his episcopal palace of Lincoln; and in rummaging the house, they found in a corner some neglected letters, which had been thrown by as useless. These letters were written by one Osbaldistone, a schoolmaster, and were directed to Williams. (vii 217)

The letters contained comments that apparently mocked Laud. (See note to ii 422.) In *Nbk 21* p. 249 *reverso*, S.'s reading note no. *17* also records the Bishop's story: *Bp. Williams fined & imprisoned by Laud. Laud had owed his 1$^{st.}$ promotion to the good offices of that prelate with James. The most odious violation of private correspondence — see Hume 217.*
39. *Lincoln.* —] *Rossetti 1870*; Lincoln — *Nbk 19*.
40. *That*] That, *Rossetti 1870*. *distraining*] see note to ii 302. In this case, the distraining of Williams was for his failure to pay a fine of 'ten thousand pounds' which had been previously levied against him for various charges, one of which was betraying the King's counsel, a charge fabricated by Laud (*Macaulay* ii 236–42).
41. *Lincoln,*] *Rossetti 1870*; Lincoln. *Nbk19*.
43. *Osbaldistone*] Osbaldisdone *Nbk 19*. The present edition's spelling is as in *Macaulay* and *Hume*; *Whitelocke* gives 'Osbaldston'.
44. *person,*] person *Nbk 19*; person; *Rossetti 1870*.
45. *holy*] holy, *Rossetti 1870*.
46. *spotless.* —] spotless. *Rossetti 1870*.

Mark too, my [lord], [his] [ex][pressi]on strikes not
[His] majesty, [if] I misinterpret it. —

        [*Enter* OFFICER *with* WILLIAMS, BISHOP OF LINCOLN.

Wentworth
[?'Twere] politic and just that Williams taste
50 The bitter fruit of his connection with
The schismatics. But you, my lord Archbishop,

47–8. *Mark ... it*] Lines 47–8 have a similarity to Laud's comments in ii 34–7. There, Laud replies to Lord Coventry's comment with 'I mark' and then continues to interpret the 'spirit' or expression in Sir John's eyes, noting that it is inappropriate for 'this presence', by which he means the King. Here he is asking Wentworth to 'mark' the 'expression' of the Bishop touching 'His majesty'.
47. *[his expression] strikes not*] that this expression strikes *Rossetti 1870*.
48. *[His] majesty*] His Majesty *Rossetti 1870*. *[if] I misinterpret it. —*] if I misinterpret not. *Rossetti 1870*.
49. SD. Enter OFFICER *with* WILLIAMS, BISHOP OF LINCOLN.] *Enter* BISHOP WILLIAMS *guarded. Rossetti 1870*; [Bishop of Lincoln] *Nbk 19*; below the speaker heading *Strafford* (here given as 'Wentworth') is *Bishop of Lincoln* with two strokes through it, a common device by S. to note an SD. *Wentworth*] Strafford *Nbk 19*; *Rossetti 1870*.
49. *[?'Twere]*] Twere *Rossetti 1870, BSM*.
50–1. *The bitter fruit ... / The schismatics*] Wentworth is here referring to the earlier judgement against the Bishop which resulted in fines and imprisonment in the Tower. *Macaulay* notes:

> On some advice that he [Williams] gave how to allay the animosity of the Commons, it was determined that a degree of indulgence should be shewed to the Puritans. This inflamed Laud's malice to such a height, that Williams was persecuted without ceasing by the tools of this prelate. ... (ii 236)

Wentworth's presence in this scene is S.'s invention. Serving as Lord Deputy and Council of Ireland at this time, Wentworth was, however, aware of the Star Chamber's procedings against Williams. In a letter of 7 February 1637/8, George Garrard, the newsletter writer who apprised Wentworth of events in and around the City and the Court, wrote to Wentworth: 'I have heard some Propositions have been offered to the Bishop of *Lincoln*, he must pay his Fine of ten thousand Pounds, resign up his Deanry of *Westminster*, resign up his Bishoprick of *Lincoln*, accept one either in *Ireland* or *Wales*: All which he refuseth' (*Strafforde* ii 149).
51. *But you,*] but you *Nbk 19*. *lord Archbishop,*] lord Archbishop *Nbk 19*; Lord Archbishop, *Rossetti 1870*.

Who owed your first promotion to his favour,
Who grew beneath his smile —

Laud
         Would therefore beg
The office of his judge from this high court,
55 [That] it shall seem, even as it is, that I,
In my assumption of this sacred robe,
Have put aside all worldly preference,
All sense of all distinction of all persons,
All thoughts but of the service of the Church.
60 Bishop of Lincoln —

Williams
       Peace, proud hierarch —
I know my sentence, and I own it just. —
Thou wilt repay me less than I deserve
In stretching to the utmost [   ]

---

52. *your first promotion*] 'Laud, however, had owed his first promotion to the good offices of that prelate [Williams] with king James' (*Hume* vii 217). In *Nbk* 22 f. *2ʳ, S.'s reading notes closely follow *Hume*: '& Williams committed to the Tower to whom Laud owed his first promotion'. *favour,*] *Rossetti 1870*; favour *Nbk 19*.
54. *high court,*] High Court,— *Rossetti 1870*.
55. *I,*] *Rossetti 1870*; I *Nbk 19*.
57. *preference,*] *Rossetti 1870*; preference *Nbk 19*.
58. *persons,*] *Rossetti 1870*; persons *Nbk 19*.
59. *Church.*] Church *Nbk 19*; Church.— *Rossetti 1870*.
60. *Lincoln —*] Lincoln ... *Nbk 19*; Lincoln! *Rossetti 1870*. *Peace, proud hierarch —*] Peace proud hierarch — *Nbk 19*; Peace, proud hierarch! *Rossetti 1870*.
61. *just. —*] just. *Rossetti 1870*.
62-3. *Thou ... utmost*] These two lines are found in *Nbk 19* p. 93b *reverso*, a mutilated leaf (93b/93) which would originally have been facing p. 95 *reverso*

where ll. 50–61 appear. At some point, however, leaf 94 /93c, was erroneously inserted between 95 and 93b. *BSM* xii presents the relevant pages as they would have been when S. used the notebook; the misplaced leaf 94/93c appears there between stub p. 74 and p. 72 and contains the draft of *Lines to — [Sonnet to Byron]*. Williams's bravery and resignation to his 'just' punishment were also shared by the three men who had been tried before Williams. When they appeared on the scaffold to receive their punishment, *Macaulay* records:

> The cruel sentence passed on Prynne, Burton, and Bastwick, was yet more cruelly executed: The hangman performed his bloody office with an approved barbarity. Burton's ears were taken off so close, that a considerable branch of the temporal artery was wounded, and the blood streamed down the scaffold. Prynne's were hacked barbarously; he lost a large piece of his cheek with the reminder of his ears, and the executioner applied the burning iron twice to the branding of one cheek. The patient and even magnanimous behaviour of the sufferers heightened the pity and inclination of the people: They crouded with impatience round the scaffolds, and every wound given by the executioner produced an universal groan and lamentation. (ii 247)

That 'patient … magnanimous behaviour' angered Laud even more, who threatened to add 'farther censure' to all the accused (*Macaulay* ii 248 n.).
62. *deserve*] deserve, *Rossetti 1870*.
63. This line is left incomplete.

Appendix

Lines connected with Charles the First

A: 'Hisses and scorn, even as my master did'

These lines are written in ink on a leaf in *Box 1* (f. 136ᵛ). Richard Garnett first published them in *Relics* as the last item in 'Miscellaneous Fragments', recognising that they belonged to *Charles the First* (no. 426) but giving no indication that all but the first line are cancelled. Additionally, he did not include the first half of the first line. Rossetti acknowledged Garnett's understanding that the lines belonged to the play, attributed them to Bastwick, and inserted them after l. 26 in Scene iv, the Star Chamber scene in the present edition ('Scene iii' in *Rossetti 1870*) noting:

> These lines are given in the *Relics of Shelley* as pertaining to the drama of *Charles the First*. I have not found them in the notebook, and cannot affirm that I am right in here introducing them; but I see no other place for them equally plausible. (*Rossetti 1870* ii 586)

Since 1870, these lines have erroneously appeared in the Star Chamber scene in all editions. In a note dated 15 December 1952 in *Box 1*, Neville Rogers determined that the tear of f. 136 matched a stub in *Nbk 19* (see B. C. Barker-Benfield, 'MS. Shelley adds. e. 17: description and collation' (April 1988), Bodleian Libraries, REFS. LVI 10, p. 12); this stub is now designated 'written stub K' (see the quiring chart for Quire II in *BSM* xii p. lxxiii). In Nora Crook's edition of *Nbk 19*, the stray leaf is restored to its original position and placed alongside written stub K (see the photofacsimiles in *BSM* xii 120 and 122). The leaf's physical context makes clear that five of these six lines, cancelled with four continuous vertical zig-zag strokes, were abandoned and then re-worked overleaf on f. 136ʳ in draft that is the basis of *Charles the First* iii 91–101 in the present edition. (See *Charles the First*, note to iii 92–103 for a discussion of the drafting of these lines and their position in the play.) R. B. Woodings in '"A Devil of a Nut to Crack:" Shelley's *Charles the First*', *Studia Neophilologica* xl (1968) 232 (*Woodings (1968a)*) was the first to note the consistency of these lines with Vane's speeches.

Text from *Box 1* f. 136ᵛ.

Published in *Relics* 91; R. B. Woodings, "'A Devil of a Nut to Crack:'" Shelley's *Charles the First*', *Studia Neophilologica* xl (1968) 232; *BSM* xii 120–1 (facsimile and transcription of MS).

Hisses and scorn, even as my master did
[Until Heaven's kingdom shall descend on Earth,]
[Or Earth be like a shadow, in the light]
[Of Heaven absorbed; — some few tumultuous years]
5 [Will pass, and leave no wreck of what opposes]
[His will whose will is power. —]

¶ **426 Appendix A** *1. Hisses and scorn,*] Omitted in *eds*; … scorns, Woodings (1968a). The word *scorn* is written above *scoffs* canc. in *Box 1* f. 136ᵛ. The cancellation of *scoffs* and its replacement with *scorn* is repeated overleaf on f. 136ʳ. *even as my master did*] Even as my Master did, *Relics, Rossetti 1870*; even as my Master did, *Hutchinson, Locock*. Written in *Box 1* between ll. 1 and 2 are the following cancelled, incomplete lines: *And add one subject to the King / And if the Kingdom / Heaven's Kingdom / Heaven or Earth / Let Earth and*. The present editors have determined that while most of this passage (i.e. ll. 2–6) was abandoned, S. intended to retain the first line, using *scoffs* and *scorn* as a linking device to the successful continuation overleaf on f. 136ʳ which is incorporated in *Charles the First* iii 94 (see notes to iii 93 and iv 25).
2. [Earth,]] [Earth] *Box 1*; earth, *Relics, Rossetti 1870*; earth *Woodings (1968a)*. Written in *Box 1* between ll. 2 and 3 are one and a half lines, entirely cancelled: *Or Earth be lifted & made one with Heaven / And discord*.
3. [Earth]] earth *Relics, Rossetti 1870*. *[shadow,]*] shadow *Relics, Rossetti 1870*. *[in the light]*] Written beneath *absorbed in* canc. in *Box 1*.
4. [Heaven absorbed; — some]] Heaven absorbed — . some *Box 1*; heaven absorbed—some *Relics*; Heaven absorbed. Some *Rossetti 1870*; Heaven absorbed—some *Hutchinson*. *[tumultuous]*] *Woodings (1968a)* regards this word as illegible.
5. [wreck]] mark *Woodings (1968a)*.
6. [power. —]] power. *Relics, Rossetti 1870*.

B: 'And blushing / April is not a rebel to rude March'

These lines in ink are drafted in *Nbk 19* p. 34 among passages for *Charles the First* I iii. Crook (*BSM* xii 73 n.) remarks that the cancelled phrase of l. 6, *Or Englishmen* points to its link with that play and describes this fragment as a probable 'version of [the] Law Student's speech' (see i 203–8), a speech that the present editors ascribe to the Young Man. Steven Jones ('"Choose Reform or Civil War": Shelley, the English Revolution, and the Problem of Succession', *The Wordsworth Circle* xxv (1994) 146) accepts Crook's view that the fragment is probably a precursor to the youth's speech, noting it 'argues a natural precedent for change.' Given its position among material for the Hampden-Vane dialogue coupled with Vane's rejection of rebellion as a means for change, it is also plausible that this fragment was intended for the play's third scene rather than the first. Indeed, there is a particular resonance with some of Vane's last lines:

> A summer's fruit maturing to decay,
> An autumnal seed laid in the wintry earth,
> A flower which decks the spring of that great year; (iii 98–100)

As noted in *BSM* xix 5 n., the vocabulary and theme of this fragment echo the prose fragment written on the front paper pastedown in *Nbk 18*: *the spring rebels not against / winter but it succeeds it — / the dawn rebels not / against night but it / disperses it —*. See especially ll. 2 and 5 and the cancelled line above l. 1, *Winter is not a rebel to the Spring*.

Text from *Nbk 19* p. 34.

Published in *BSM* xii 72–3 (facsimile and transcription of MS).

[   ] And blushing
April is not a rebel to rude March

¶ **Appendix B** *1. And blushing* was apparently added after the completed lines below were entered: ll. 2–7 are written with a very fine pen-cut and a light brown-black ink while this phrase is done with a wider stroke and a more watery brown ink. Above and below this incomplete first line are the following cancelled lines in *Nbk 19*: *Winter is not a rebel to the Spring / Because its / The Spring*. These cancelled lines (the first of which is complete) are written with the same pen-cut and ink as that of ll. 2–7.
2. rude] 'Chiefly of the sea, winds, and seasons: turbulent, violent, boisterous, rough' (*OED adj.* 6a). Cp. *The rude wind is singing* (no. 436).

Because it weeps like Pity on the earth
Till it unlocks all its imprisoned flowers; —
5 Nor day to night though it disperses it; —
N[or truth] to error though it scatters it —
Or [Englishmen]

427 'A widowed bird sate mourning for her love'

[A Song]

This lyric is drafted in ink on *Nbk 19* p. 52 *reverso*. The first two stanzas appear to have been written in one sitting with only the third line of the opening stanza having been re-worked; the last two lines of the second stanza are written around a patch of ink bleeding through from the other side of the leaf (p. 51) containing draft of *Charles the First* (no. 426) iii 76–82. The third stanza, at the foot of the page, shows much re-working and its several abandoned starts, along with cancel strokes through the first two words of its third line and the overwritten word at the start of the fourth, testify to its unfinished state. The darker ink of this third stanza and the fact that it is offset to the left with the writing beginning closer to the edge of the page than the stanzas above, suggests it was composed at a later point than they were. The horizontal lines after ll. 4 and 8 signal stanza breaks, and a second, long and thick line in dark ink beneath l. 4 was perhaps added at the time the third stanza was drafted.

4. *imprisoned flowers*] Cp. the flowers in *The Question* (no. 288) 37–8: 'Kept these imprisoned children of the Hours / Within my hand …'. *flowers;* —] flowers. *BSM*.
7. *Or*] [Or] *BSM*. Written above *Nor* canc. in *Nbk 19*. *Or* is written in the same wide stroke and medium brown ink of the first line, as well as the long dashes at the end of ll. 5–6. This set of wide, medium brown strokes appear to belong to a later stage of emendations. [*Nor Englishmen*] and a further incomplete, cancelled line below — *Nor love to hate scorn* (where *hate* was cancelled and replaced by *scorn* before the whole line was cancelled) — are all in the fine strokes and light brown-black ink of ll. 2–6.

DOI: 10.4324/9781315779874-23

There is no evidence to support R. B. Woodings's claim in 'Shelley's Widow Bird', *RES* n. s. xix (1968) 411–14 that this poem could have been written as early as 'late 1821' (413). Instead a date of composition on, or shortly after, 20 January 1822 is likely for the first two stanzas (which were probably in place before *Art thou pale for weariness* (no. 428) on the page opposite, p. 53 *reverso*, was drafted). S. wrote '20th Jany.' in a small hand between the draft of ll. 521 and 522 of Charles's concluding speech to Scene ii in *Nbk 19* p. 102 *reverso* (see *BSM* xii 160–1). Assuming 20 January to be the date on which S. had reached that point on the page, Archy's final speech on the following page (p. 101 *reverso*; see *BSM* xii 158–9) must have been written slightly later, after S. realised the need to have Archy exit in order to leave Charles and Henrietta alone on stage for a closing dialogue to the scene. The draft of Archy's song and his preface to it (see *Charles the First* ii 475–88) on p. 101 *reverso* also includes a conclusion (in prose, not verse), which differs starkly in tone as well as form from the abandoned third stanza on p. 52 *reverso*. On p. 101 *reverso*, the punctuation of the MS after *A widowed bird, sate mourning upon a wintry bough* . . . . . . (with a long dash beneath the six suspension points) suggests S.'s possible shorthand cross-reference to the draft of ll. 1–8 on p. 52 *reverso*. (For a discussion of S.'s linking devices, Archy's preface and conclusion, and the significance of this lyric's first two stanzas in Scene ii of *Charles the First* see note to ii 475–88 and following notes through to 489 SD). Nora Crook states that the lyric on p. 52 *reverso* 'is written in the same grayish brown ink and scratchy quill as Archy's exit speech on p. 101 *reverso*, which suggests that the two were written about the same time' (*BSM* xii p. xlviii). However, while the MS evidence Crook adduces is accurate concerning the first eight lines on p. 52 *reverso*, the third stanza may have been written at a later time, though possibly not much later than 26 January when S. wrote to John Gisborne claiming of *Charles the First* that, 'I cannot seize the conception of the subject as a whole yet, & seldom now touch the *canvas*' (*L* ii 388).

The poem was transcribed in *Mary Copybk 2* (*Massey* 76–7) under the heading 'A Song' and published under that title in the 'Miscellaneous Poems' section of *1824* apparently indicating that Mary was unaware of its destination in *Charles the First* immediately prior to Henrietta's speech in Scene ii beginning at l. 489 which is printed after a line of asterisks in *1824* 245. She placed it among 'Poems written in 1822' in *1839* iv 180. Probably as a result of the loan of *Nbk 19* by Richard Garnett for nine days in March 1869 (see *Rossetti Papers 1862 to 1870* (1903) 385–6), Rossetti was able to propose that this song belonged to *Charles the First*: '[t]he lyric "A widow bird," & c. has hitherto been printed separately, not as forming any part of the action'. Of the draft on p. 101 *reverso*, he commented: 'This fragment of a scene appears to belong to a much later portion of the drama than those which have preceded; perhaps to the period of King Charles's captivity, or even after his death' (*Rossetti 1870* ii 586). In placing the p. 101 *reverso* lines in a separate scene ('Scene V') at the end of his edition of *Charles the First* (*Rossetti 1870* ii 394), Rossetti failed to recognise their correct position in Scene ii. In his edition, he added the stage direction '[*Sings*]' to Archy's song, placed ll. 488–91 before 480–7, and enclosed the present lines within speech marks.

The *abab* rhyme and the metrical pattern of the first two quatrains — iambic pentameter in the first line, iambic tetrameter in the third, and iambic trimeters in the second and fourth — are also evidently followed in the three completed lines of the third quatrain. Woodings's suggestion that this poem re-purposes Archy's song for *Charles the First* as a 'personal love lyric' reflective of S.'s 'emotional situation' regarding Jane Williams ('Shelley's Widow Bird', 414) may be supported by echoes of the motif of the 'widowed bird' in *To —* (*'The serpent is shut out from Paradise'*) (no. 430) and elsewhere in S.'s poetry of late January and February 1822 (see the note to l. 1). Crook takes issue with Woodings in *BSM* xii pp. xlvii–xlviii and 127.

Text from *Nbk 19* p. 52 rev. Indentation follows the MS.

Published in *1824* 217 (ll. 1–8 only); *Rossetti 1870* ii 394 (ll. 1–8 only); *Massey* 242 (ll. 1–8 only); *BSM* xii 108–9 (facsimile and transcription of MS).

'A widowed bird sate mourning for her love'

A widowed bird sate mourning for her love
    Upon a wintry bough;

¶427 *Title*. See headnote.
1. See *To —* (*'The serpent is shut out from Paradise'*) ll. 4–6 ('The widowed dove must cease to haunt a bower / Like that from which its mate, with feignèd sighs, / Fled in the April hour —') and *Fragments of an Unfinished Drama* (no. 436) i 119–21 ('And on the wintry bough the widowed bird, / Hid in the deepest night of ivy leaves, / Renewed the vigils of her inmost sorrow —'). Cp. also *O Mary dear, that you were here* (no. 177), ll. 3–5: 'And your sweet voice, like a bird / Singing love to its lone mate / In the ivy bower disconsolate —'. *widowed bird*] widow bird *1824, eds. sate*] sat *Mary Copybk 2*.
2. *bough;*] *Mary Copybk 2, 1824*; bough *Nbk 19*.

> The frozen wind crept on, above
>   The freezing stream below —
>
> 5 There was no leaf upon the forest bare,
>   No flower upon the ground —
>   And little motion in the air,
>   Except the mill-wheel's sound.
>
>   And as she sung upon the smooth bright snow
> 10   I copied from my heart
>   [Her] [name], which [   ]
>   Whose music made me start —

428 'Art thou pale for weariness'

[To the Moon]

This unfinished lyric was drafted in ink in *Nbk 19* p. 53 *reverso* after the top of the leaf had been torn away. It is found among draft of *Charles the First* (no. 426) which was written between 3 and 26 January 1822 (see headnote to that play). Nora Crook suggests that it may 'have been written on

3. There are several mostly cancelled starts to this line in *Nbk 19*: [*And the frozen stream it*] / *The* [*frozen*] [*frozen wind it fle*]. *frozen*] Written above [*icy*] *wind*, [*it*] in *Nbk 19*; [*icy*] is faintly underlined suggesting S. considered reinstating it. *crept*] 1824 *Errata*, 1834, 1839, 1840; kept 1824, 1829. *on, above*] on above, Mary *Copybk 2, 1824*.
4. *below* —] below. Mary *Copybk 2, 1824*.
5. *There*] Written beneath *The* canc. in *Nbk 19*. *bare*,] Mary *Copybk 2, 1824*; bare *Nbk 19*.
6. *ground* —] ground; Mary *Copybk 2*; ground, *1824*.
7. *air,*] air *1824*.
9. There are several false starts to this line in *Nbk 19*: *I would not be a bird* / [?*And* canc.] [?*the* canc.] / [*Sung as forever*]. *And as she sung*] Written above *Passing along the* canc. in *Nbk 19* (with *as* written over another *she*). *smooth bright snow*] Written above *upon the snow* canc. and beneath *misery* canc. in *Nbk 19*.
10. *copied*] Written after *traced the* canc. in *Nbk 19*.
11. The cancelled words [?*is*] and [?*was*] are written in the margin before the start of this line in *Nbk 19*. *which*] Written above *which uttered* canc. in *Nbk 19*.
12. *Whose*] Written over *Which* canc. in *Nbk 19*.

DOI: 10.4324/9781315779874-24

the same occasion' though 'slightly before' (*BSM* xii 110) *A widowed bird sate mourning for her love* (no. 427), also in ink on the facing page (p. 52 rev.). However, the cramped writing of the incomplete second stanza, at the bottom of the page, near the gutter, indicates that *A widowed bird* was probably in place before this lyric's composition. For the possibility that both lyrics were written on, or soon after, 20 January, see the headnote to *A widowed bird*. Crook speculates that this poem 'could be a dramatic lyric, conceived as a lute-song for an unwritten scene [of *Charles the First*]; if sung by the Queen [Henrietta], it voices her deepest fears, and prophesies her future, wandering companionless as an exiled widow' supporting her conjecture with the claim that 'a dry-quilled word at the top of the page looks like a speech heading and could be "Queen"' (*BSM* xii pp. xlviii-xlix). However, the present editors are unsure of her reading of the hardly legible word, which may possibly be *Thou* (see ll. 1 and 7) or *Those*.

Mary transcribed ll. 1–6 in *Mary Copybk 2* pp. 28–9 (see *Massey* 76–9) under the heading 'To the Moon' and published the poem under this title in the same section of *1824* ('Fragments') as *Charles the First*. In *1839* iv 45, she placed it among 'Poems written in 1820', a mistaken dating accepted by late C19 and early C20 editors. Rossetti added ll. 7–8 in *Rossetti 1870* 'from Shelley's own MS' (ii 582) but failed to reproduce the space between l. 6 and l. 7 in *Nbk 19* which seems to signal a stanza-break. Forman divided the eight lines into two stanzas (*Forman 1876–7* iii 61) and, with no MS authority, inserted stanza number-headings (which are reproduced in *Hutchinson* and *Locock 1911*).

The first stanza, a sestet with a rhyme scheme of *ababcc*, combines iambic pentameters (ll. 2, 4–6) and slightly irregular tetrameters (ll. 1, 3) with the pulse varying through the feet. The incomplete second stanza seems as if it were going to continue in the same manner. Addresses to the moon are frequent in S.'s verse. See, e.g., *And like a dying lady lean and pale* (no. 225), *Tell me star, whose wings of light* (no. 454) and *Bright wanderer, fair coquette of Heaven* (no. 456) ll. 7–14.

Text from *Nbk 19* p. 53 rev. Indentation follows S.'s apparent intentions in the MS.

Published in *1824* 263 (ll. 1–6); *Rossetti 1870* ii 340–1 (ll. 1–8); *Massey* 243 (transcription only); *BSM* xii 110–11 (facsimile and transcription of MS).

'Art thou pale for weariness'

Art thou pale for weariness
   Of climbing Heaven, and gazing on the earth,
Wandering companionless
   Among the stars that have a different birth,
5 And ever changing, like a joyless eye
That finds no object worth its constancy?

Thou chosen sister of the spirit
   That gazes on thee till in thee it pities
The woe

¶ **428** *Title.* See headnote.
1–3. Cp. *Tell me star, whose wings of light* ll. 5–8.
1. There is a faint line over the first word and the first two letters of the second word in *Nbk 19*; it is difficult to determine whether it is a cancel stroke or a quill slip.
2. Cp. the description of the moon in *Tell me star, whose wings of light* l. 6: 'Pilgrim of Heaven's homeless way'. S. first wrote, then cancelled, *Lady of the spheres* at the start of this line in *Nbk 19*. *Heaven*] heaven *1824*. *earth,*] *1824*; earth *Nbk 19* (written above *world* canc.); Earth? *Mary Copybk 2*; earth,— *Rossetti 1870*
4. birth,] birth *Nbk 19*; birth; *Mary Copybk 2*; birth,— *1824*.
5. ever changing,] *Mary Copybk 2, 1824, Rossetti 1870*; ever changing *Nbk 19*; ever-changing, *1839, 1840*.
6. its constancy?] *1824*; its constancy — *Nbk 19*; its' constancy. *Mary Copybk 2*.
7. S. wrote, then cancelled, *Sole s* (possibly the *s* was a beginning for 'spirit' or 'sister') at the start of this line in *Nbk 19*. *Thou chosen*] Thou [spi] chosen *Nbk 19*. *sister of the spirit*] On spiritual sisterhood, see *Epipsychidion* (no. 391) 1 and *Adonais* (no. 403) 145. The moon is described as the sun's 'weak sister' in *Cyprian* (no. 441) ii 169. *spirit*] spirit, *Rossetti 1870*.
8. gazes on thee till in] Written above *pitys and loves and* canc. in *Nbk 19*. *pities*] pities … *Rossetti 1870*.
9. The woe] These words are cancelled and underlined in *Nbk 19* suggesting reinstatement.

429   Lines to —

[Sonnet to Byron]

This well-known sonnet, which has served as an important source for assessing S.'s relation to Byron as poet, has had a complex textual history. Lines 1–3 and the first two words of line 4 are drafted in pencil, without title, on p. 228 *reverso* of *Nbk 21* — a page that lies among drafts for *Hellas* (no. 411), though these are written in the forward direction of the notebook. S. carried this opening over to an ink draft on p. 94 *reverso* of *Nbk 19* where it is entitled *To* — and continued to a 12th line. Between the title and the body of the poem are the words, partially obscured by doodling, 'I am afraid these verses will not please you but'. The first eight lines of the *Nbk 19* ink draft are nearly identical to lines 1–8 in S.'s fair copy (see below) from which the present text is taken; not so lines 9–12 of the same draft, which read:

> But such is my regard, that nor your power
>   To soar, above the heights where others [   ]
> Nor fame, that shadow of the [unborn] hour
>   Cast from the envious future on the time

There is no draft of a 13th line on the page, but a variant of the final line in the finished poem has survived on the stub of the missing p. 73 *reverso*, which appears to have been contiguous to p. 94 *reverso* before it was removed from its place in the original sequence of pages (see *BSM* xii 136). It is possible that S. continued the draft or made a revised draft on that missing page, while the word 'to' on the stub of p. 68 *reverso* may indicate that it carried part or all of a fair draft or even a fair copy. The entire sonnet, dated *Jan 22* and entitled *Lines to —*, does exist in a fair copy, transcribed in S.'s hand on what is now British Library Zweig MS. 188, a single leaf which may have been detached from *Nbk 19*. Mary transcribed S.'s fair copy into *Mary Copybk 1* ff. 95–6, expanding his notation of the date to 'Jan[ry] 22 – 1822', and an entry in the Contents to *Mary Copybk 2*, 'To Lord B', may well refer to another transcription on a page now missing from that notebook.

Although she transcribed it, Mary never published the sonnet. Lines 1–7 first appeared in print, without title and showing a number of variants, in *The Athenaeum* 248 (28 July 1832) 488–9 in an instalment of Thomas Medwin's 'Memoir of Shelley'. Medwin presents the lines as S.'s considered judgement of his fellow poet:

> What his real opinion of Byron's genius was, may be collected from a sonnet he once showed me, and which the subject of it never saw. The sentiments accord well with that diffidence of his own powers—that innate modesty which always distinguished him. It began thus—
>
> > If I esteemed him less, envy would kill
> > Pleasure, and leave to wonder and despair
> > The ministration of the thoughts that fill
> > My soul, which, as a worm may haply share
> > A portion of the unapproachable,
> > Marks his creations rise as fast and fair
> > As perfect worlds at the Creator's will.

The most important of Medwin's variants from S.'s autograph copies alter the relation between poet and subject by changing the address from the second person to the third — 'him' for 'you' in line 1 and 'his' for 'your' in line 6. Medwin concludes: 'Shelley used to say, that reading Dante produced in him the same despair'. The seven lines are reprinted in *Medwin (1833)* 37, as they are given above; but 14 years later an expanded text of twelve lines appeared in *Medwin* ii 35 where it follows a garbled account, derived from S.'s letter to Peacock of 17 or 18 December 1818 (*L* ii 58), of the low regard in which S. held *Childe Harold's Pilgrimage*. Medwin continues: 'that he thought Byron a great poet, is proved by a sonnet, of which I forget two of the lines, but which Byron never saw':

> If I esteemed thee less, Envy would kill
> Pleasure, and leave to Wonder and Despair
> The ministration of the thoughts that fill
> My soul, which even as a worm may share
> A portion of the Unapproachable,
> Marks thy creations rise as fast and fair
> As perfect worlds at the Creator's will;
> But not the blessings of thy happier lot,
> * * * * * * *

> Nor thy well-won prosperity and fame,
> * * * * * * *
> Move one regret for his unhonoured name,
> Who dares these words—the worm beneath the sod
> May lift itself in homage of the God.

Medwin had certainly seen *Nbk 19*, no doubt during his stay in Pisa between 15 November 1821 and 9 March 1822: witness his description of the MS of *Charles the First* (no. 426) that it contains (*Medwin* ii 162–3) and a translation from the Italian on p. 126 in his hand. As indicated above, the notebook may have included, in addition to the twelve lines of the draft on p. 94 *reverso*, both an intermediate draft (if such was made) and the fair copy of the sonnet. Medwin must have seen one or even both of these, whether in the notebook or in another MS, as the final four lines of his 1847 text establish. But, besides admitting that he cannot recall two lines, he has imported line 8 — apparently, as Nora Crook suggests (*BSM* xii 136), a reminiscence of the fifth line of Keats's 'Ode to a Nightingale'. So, either he had transcribed the lines inaccurately from his source or, what is more likely, his memory of S.'s lines or of a transcription of them, which he had taken and lost, was at fault. Certainly, the texts of S.'s poems that Medwin incorporates into his writings are often unreliable, their inaccuracies owing to faulty transcription, failures of memory, deliberate alterations — or combinations of these. In the circumstances one cannot regard the 1832 or 1847 variants from S.'s surviving autographs (the draft on p. 94 *reverso* of *Nbk 19* and his fair copy) in Medwin's texts, which differ one from the other, as originating in an intermediate text which has not survived — rather than being mistakes of Medwin's own. He had seen such an intermediate draft and/or the fair copy, but that is all that may be said with confidence.

With their incompletions, inaccuracies and substitutions, Medwin's two texts remained the only published forms of the sonnet until a fourteen-line version appeared in *Rossetti 1870* where it is dated 1821 and given the title *Sonnet to Byron*, by which it has since become known. Through the mediation of Richard Garnett, Rossetti had been allowed to examine *Nbk 19*, which was kept with the collection of Shelley's manuscripts at Boscombe Manor by S.'s son Sir Percy and his wife Jane, Lady Shelley. Rossetti clearly did not see S.'s fair copy of the sonnet but only his 12-line draft. 'From these two sources' (*Medwin* and *Nbk 19*), he says in his note to the poem, 'I have put together the fourteen lines needed for the sonnet-form, and can offer my version to the reader as being at all events less imperfect than the one heretofore printed'. The resulting text, although it corrects Medwin in some particulars, marries an earlier and (via Medwin) a later version of the sonnet to create a hybrid with an imperfect rhyme-scheme. Rossetti also prints, in reduced type, the preliminary prose in the *Nbk 19* draft, 'I am afraid these verses will not please you but', which he sets in square brackets before the body of the poem. Though obviously and admittedly defective, Rossetti's text was widely reprinted by *eds*, with or without the introductory prose, as the most authoritative version of the poem available.

Having previously transcribed S.'s fair copy into *Mary Copybk 1* and perhaps *Mary Copybk 2* (see Burling, below, p. 21), Mary gave the original as an example of her late husband's autograph to an acquaintance, Charlotte Murchison (*Mary L* ii 127). It was subsequently sold at Sotheby's, in December 1931; William J. Burling reproduces a photograph of it from the Sotheby's sale catalogue in *K-SJ* xxv (1986) to accompany his article 'New Light on Shelley's "Lines To ———"' (20-3). It is also reproduced in *BSM* xii 132. The *Mary Copybk 1* transcription was itself first published in *Robinson* 201-2. S.'s autograph, whose whereabouts had been unknown since its sale at Sotheby's, was relocated in the Zweig Collection at the British Library by Donald H. Reiman who published a facsimile and transcription with commentary in *MYRS* viii 246-53.

If, rather than month and year, the *Jan 22* on S.'s fair copy records a day of the month, as it seems to do and as Mary believed it did in her transcription in *Mary Copybk 1*, then not only the finished copy but also the drafting of the sonnet may have been completed on 22 January 1822. This was Byron's birthday, his thirty-fourth. The hypothesis of composition in a single day would be strengthened if the leaf on which the autograph fair copy is transcribed were to be confirmed as having been part of *Nbk 19*, in which several pages near the draft on p. 94 *reverso* are missing. Both Crook (*BSM* xii 131) and Reiman (*MYRS* viii 247) conclude that such manuscript evidence as can be adduced short of bringing together *Nbk 19* (held in the Bodleian Library) and MS Zweig 188 (in the British Library) for close comparison does not exclude the possibility of S.'s autograph fair copy having been transcribed on a leaf of the notebook — though further study of each would be necessary to establish the connection definitively.

Other evidence supports composition on or just before the 22 January date given by S. on the fair copy. Crook (*BSM* xii p. lvi) notes that the position of the *Nbk 19* draft of the sonnet near the end of the second scene of *Charles the First* — the play on which S. worked between 3 and 26 January (see headnote) — suggests a date around 20 January. She also points out that while composing his tragedy S. would have had reason to keep *Nbk 21* (where he first drafted lines 1–3 of the sonnet among drafts for *Hellas* that date from autumn 1821) to hand in order to consult the historical notes on Charles I and his times that he had entered in that notebook. For his part, Medwin, in a later addition to his *Medwin*, maintained that the poem was composed in a single day and sketched the particular circumstances of its inception:

> This Sonnet was written one day after reading *The Corsair* from the perusal of which he rose with strong expressions of its beauty and force—and I remember his saying that it was the finest specimen of Couplets in our language:—that no one wielded that most difficult of metres with so much of variety and power as Byron—(*Medwin (1913)* 258)

There is no other record of S. re-reading *The Corsair* around this time, nor does he ever include it among the poems of Byron that he especially admired, while the impact on him of Byron's *Don Juan* and *Cain* demonstrably contributed to the sonnet — thus challenging the accuracy of the scene of composition reported by Medwin which proposes a direct and immediate link between Byron's romance and S.'s address to the author. Medwin's recollection is not without relation to the latter half of January 1822, however. The resemblance between Edward Trelawny, who arrived in Pisa on 14 January, and the pirate chief in Byron's poem was remarked upon by Byron himself, had become current coin in the Byron-Shelley circle in Pisa by the 21st of the month, and might have prompted S. to take up *The Corsair* again — at least to speak of it to Medwin at the time he wrote the sonnet or to have mentioned his poem in connection with Byron's in a later conversation (*Byron L&J* xi 236; *Mary Jnl* i 392).

Whatever impact *The Corsair* may have had on S.'s idea of Byron's achievement in January 1822, his estimate of *Don Juan* and *Cain* especially had confirmed him in the view that Byron was the pre-eminent poet of the age. From the beginning of their association in summer 1816 in Switzerland S. had urged Byron to undertake a poem of epic scope that should stand in relation to the revolutionary age they were living through as the great works of Homer, Shakespeare and Milton did to theirs and to all time — thereby (he wrote on 29 September 1816) 'being the parent of greatness, and of goodness, which is destined, perhaps, to expand indefinitely' (*L* i 507). In autumn 1816 S. was himself contemplating such a poem, which he would complete the following year, *L&C/*

RofI (no. 143; see headnote), and which since publication had gone all but unnoticed save for an abusive personal attack on him in the *Quarterly Review* and Leigh Hunt's subsequent defence of work and author in the *Examiner*. S. renewed his petition to Byron in April 1821. Byron had, he wrote, reached the age and perfected his art to the point at which he was now equipped to 'subdue yourself to the great task of building up a poem containing within itself the germs of a permanent relation to the present, and to all succeeding ages!' (*L* ii 284). In little more than a week Byron had distanced himself from S.'s design for providing the time with its definitive representation in poetry: 'You want me to undertake a great Poem—I have not the inclination nor the power' (*Byron L&J* viii 104). During a visit to him in Ravenna the following summer, however, S. became persuaded that his hopes for Byron's genius were after all, and after a fashion, being realised. The second instalment of *Don Juan* was published in England on 8 August; in a letter of that date from Ravenna S. related to Mary the effect on him of hearing Byron read aloud from Canto V:

> He has read to me one of the unpublished cantos of Don Juan, which is astonishingly fine.—It sets him not above but far above all the poets of the day: every word has the stamp of immortality.—I despair of rivalling Lord Byron, as well I may: and there is no other with whom it is worth contending. This canto is [...] sustained with incredible ease & power [...] it fulfills in a certain degree what I have long preached [to him] of producing something wholly new & relative to the age—and yet surpassingly beautiful. (*L* ii 323)

And on receiving the volume containing Cantos III-V in October he wrote to assure Byron of his increased admiration, alluding again to his own earlier exhortations: 'This sort of writing only on a grand plan & perhaps in a more compact form is what I wished you to do when I made my vows for an epic' (*L* ii 358). The conviction in the Pisan circle of the supremacy of Byron's literary achievement only intensified in response to *Cain* which appeared to Mary 'almost a revelation from its power and beauty' (*Mary L* i 209). For his part, S. told Edward Williams that Byron's play was 'second to nothing of the kind' (*Gisborne Jnl* 109) and wrote to John Gisborne that: 'it contains finer poetry than has appeared in England since the publication of Paradise Regained.—*Cain* is apocalyptic—it is a revelation not before communicated to man' (*L* ii 388). At the height of his powers in summer and autumn 1821, Byron appeared to S. to have attained a station comparable to that of the great ancient and modern poets — to have rivalled sacred scripture itself. By contrast, his own poetry had gained neither popular success nor critical esteem. In his letters of the period to his friends he repeatedly wonders why he persists in writing poetry in the face of such indifference, confessing to Peacock on 11 January 1822, as he struggled to advance with the composition of *Charles the First*, that he has lost all confidence in his prospects as an author: 'I wish I had something better to do than furnish this jingling food for the hunger of oblivion, called *verse*' (*L* ii 374). *Adonais* (no. 403), which he intended for the 'enlightened public', and of whose excellence he was convinced, had yet to elicit any positive response; while his expectations for *Hellas*, which might hope to find a wider resonance because of its engagement with the continuing revolution in Greece, were decidedly muted, not least because of his publisher's delay in sending it to press (*L* ii 363–4, 372). He imagines his lot to be composed of 'Hatred', 'scorn' and 'indifference' in the gloomy stanzas of *To —* ('*The serpent is shut out from Paradise*') (no. 430) which he sent to Edward Williams on 26 January, and in which the ruin of his poetic ambitions is embittered by the loss of domestic peace and affection that attended his estrangement from Mary. He finds distraction in such social intercourse as he is able to tolerate, but altogether, like his depleted purse, he 'drags on a sort of life in death' (*L* ii 374).

By the time he came to write his sonnet on and to Byron, then, S. had situated himself at the bottom of a scale of contemporary poetic status the summit of which was inaccessible to him and occupied by another. That scale measured both literary excellence and popularity. He wished to be a poet who could both speak to his time and transmit its true image to posterity but the first of these conditions depended upon finding some considerable number of readers, which he had been unable to do. Writing in August to Leigh Hunt of Byron's proposal that the three of them should co-operate to produce a new journal, *The Liberal*, and share profits from it equally, injured pride prompts him to dissociate himself from the other two. Byron and Hunt, each in his way, would bring to the enterprise that large measure of celebrity and regard in the modern literary world 'which the universal voice of my contemporaries forbids me either to stoop or aspire to. I am, and I desire to be, nothing' (*L* ii 344).

Writing to John Gisborne on 12 January S. playfully takes up the analogy between divine and poetic creation which he had elaborated about a year previously in *DP* (*Reiman (2002)* para. 42):

> What think you of Lord Byron now? Space wondered less at the swift and fair creations of God, when he grew weary of vacancy, than I at

the late works of this spirit of an angel in the mortal paradise of a decaying body. So I think—let the world envy while it admires, as it may. (*L* ii 376)

The passage alludes to Byron's *Cain* — for S. a counter-revelation to *Genesis*, *Paradise Lost* and *Paradise Regained* — which supplies the major thematic elements that he appropriated for his sonnet: the worship due to the creator, the abasement of the worshipper, the nature and scope of creation, the plurality of worlds. These he has assimilated to the mode of a personal address on the extremes of literary success and failure that had troubled him for months past. For the language of the poem he has, to a quite unusual degree, mined his own letters of the previous five months, to Byron and others. The letter to John Gisborne of 12 January displays especially close parallels, but (setting synonyms aside) almost all the significant words of the poem are to be found in the letters which deal with the antipodal literary positions of himself and Byron: 'wondered', 'creations', 'fair', 'name', 'fame', 'power', 'worm', 'despair', 'share', 'God'. The concluding line and a half is a variation on a couplet he had already formulated on two previous occasions. See note to ll. 13–14.

Byron does not appear ever to have mentioned the sonnet, and there is no reason to doubt Medwin's assertion that he never saw it. The prose apology at the head of the *Nbk 19* draft — *I am afraid these verses will not please you but* — would seem to indicate that S. had at first planned to send the poem to him but changed his mind. The prose is not carried over to the fair copy where the *Jan 22* date raises the possibility that S. had intended the piece as a birthday greeting to Byron. The *To —* of the draft and the *Lines to —* of the fair copy both signal that the poem involves a private transaction, and Mary's withholding it from publication would seem to confirm that she thought so too. Bieri speculates that S. might have written the sonnet to accompany a set of commemorative medals representing major events in Napoleon's career which S. presented to Byron, perhaps on his thirty-fourth birthday (*Bieri* ii 277).

Text from British Library Zweig MS. 188. Variants from Medwin's texts already given in the headnote are not repeated in the notes.

Published in *The Athenaeum* 248 (28 July 1832) 489 (ll. 1–7); *Medwin* ii 35 (ll. 1–7, 11–14); *Rossetti 1870* (preliminary prose, ll. 1–8, 9–11 (from draft), 12–14); *Robinson* 201–2; *MYRS* viii 250–1 (facsimile and transcription of MS).

Lines to —.

If I esteemed you less, Envy would kill
  Pleasure, and leave to Wonder and Despair
The ministration of the thoughts that fill
  My mind, which, like a worm whose life may share
5   A portion of the Unapproachable,

¶ 429 *Title*. Immediately above the title is the notation *Jan 22*. See headnote.
4–8. The elements of these lines are present in a passage on the essential unity of nature in *Q Mab* (no. 92) i 264–74:

> Spirit of Nature! here!
> In this interminable wilderness
> Of worlds, at whose immensity
> Even soaring fancy staggers,
> Here is thy fitting temple. [...]
>   Yet not the meanest worm
> That lurks in graves and fattens on the dead
>   Less shares thy eternal breath.

4–5. See the headnote for S.'s persuasion that his assurances to Byron that he was fitted to become the great original interpreter of the age in poetry were being carried out in *Don Juan*. Conversely, S. felt reluctant, he wrote to Leigh Hunt in August 1821, 'to share in the profits, and still less in the borrowed splendour' by associating himself with Byron and Hunt in the journal they proposed to initiate, *The Liberal* (*L* ii 344).
4. worm] In older usage 'worm' = a snake or serpent and in particular the serpent that tempted Eve, as in *Paradise Lost* ix 1067–8. Cp. *L&C* 399. Hence this personal reference to S. himself whom Byron jokingly referred to as the tempter serpent: *L* ii 368–9; *Byron L&J* ix 81, and *To —* ('*The serpent is shut out from Paradise*') (no. 430). S. likens his talent to a glow-worm extinguished by Byron's sun in *L* ii 423. Cp. also S.'s letter to John Gisborne of 22 October 1821 concerning an attack on Godwin in the *Edinburgh Review*: 'compared with these miserable sciolists he is a vulture [...] to a worm' (*L* ii 364); and Lucifer's mocking of Cain's aspirations in *Cain* II i 83–5:

> What are they, which dwell
> So humbly in their pride, as to sojourn
> With worms in clay?

5. Unapproachable] In addition to its primary signification, 'one who [...] cannot be approached or equalled' (*OED*), the word here seems to carry something of its more recent meaning, 'one who resists confidence and intimacy', a sense not inappropriate to the relations between S. and Byron. 'The demon of mistrust & of pride lurks between two persons in our situation poisoning the freedom of their intercourse', S. wrote of Byron to Mary in August 1821; and to Leigh Hunt

Marks your creations rise as fast and fair
As perfect worlds at the creator's will,
And bows itself before the godhead there.

But such is my regard, that, nor your fame
10   Cast on the present by the coming hour,
Nor your well-won prosperity and power

---

later that month: 'He has many generous and exalted qualities, but the canker of aristocracy wants to be cut out' (*L* ii 324, 345). Byron wrote to Mary of his 'very limited' capacity for friendship with men, even for S., in November 1822 (*Byron L&J* x 34).
7. *perfect worlds*] Complete and fully finished celestial bodies. The plural is significant. In Act II of *Cain* Byron had followed *Q Mab* in making the spectacle of the innumerable *worlds* that constitute the heavens as seen from space serve as the theatre for instruction on the past, present and future of the human race which challenges orthodox religious teaching. Others, Thomas Moore and Medwin among them, detected a strain of Shelleyan irreligion in *Cain* — which both Byron and S. denied: *L* ii 412, *Medwin (1913)* 334, *Records* i 80, *Robinson* 196–8.
8. Humbling itself before the godhead there *Nbk 19*. *Rossetti 1870* chooses not to include this line even though the final word completes the rhyme-scheme of the octave. *godhead*] 'The character or quality of being God or a god; divine nature or essence; deity' (*OED*).
9. *fame*] To Peacock in August 1821 S. declared his disdain for popularity, which in any case Byron's success had denied to other contemporary poets:

> My motive was never the infirm desire of fame; and if I should continue an author, I feel that I should desire it. This cup is justly given to one only of an age; indeed, participation would make it worthless: and unfortunate they who seek it and find it not. (*L* ii 331)

Rossetti adopts the ninth line of his text from the draft in *Nbk 19*, supplying the missing final word: 'To soar above the heights where others [climb]'.
11. *prosperity*] Flourishing condition generally but including the sense 'well supplied with money'. S. was ill-at-ease that the project of *The Liberal* was dependent on Byron's financial contribution, his own comparatively modest resources having prior claims on them and Hunt being unable to contribute (*L* ii 344, 380). Byron continued to sell his writings to the publisher John Murray for substantial sums (*L* ii 323–4) and, like S., had a considerable inheritance in prospect.

Move one regret for his unhonoured name
Who dares these words. — The worm beneath the sod
May lift itself in worship to the God.

13–14. The worm ... the God. This truncated couplet is adapted from *Epipsychidion* (no. 391) 128–9 which S. composed in January–February 1821 and which was published later that year: 'The spirit of the worm beneath the sod / In love and worship, blends itself with God'. In autumn 1821 he varied the lines in *I would not be a King: enough* (*Lines connected with Hellas* (no. 411 Appendix), Appendix J) where they are addressed by the character Fatima to a group of maidens, captives of the Ottoman Sultan Mahmud, in praise of the freedom to love despite social distinction and political obstacles: 'like me / The worm beneath the sod / May hope, and mingle with its god' (ll. 34–6). The present variant excludes any reference to love, the principal theme of the couplets in *Epipsychidion* and *I would not be a King: enough*. The formulation here also departs from the two previous ones and from S.'s draft for this poem (see the following note) in its concluding words, 'the God' — which are susceptible of various interpretations. The capital G notwithstanding, they could be taken as signifying a deity of the classical pantheon but might also denote the Biblical One God consistently with 'the Unapproachable' of line 5 and 'the creator's' of line 7 — as in the words of Adah (daughter of Adam and Eve) in Byron's *Cain* I i 502–4: 'Our father / Saith that he has beheld the God himself / Who made him and our mother'. Lucifer in *Cain*, who delivers visionary revelations to the title-character, also claims divine status; hence the aptness of 'the God' to Byron whose play, Shelley and Mary agreed, might claim the status of a new revelation: see headnote.
14. [ ]e worm in worship lifts itself to God *Nbk* 19 p. 73 *reverso*.

Appendix A

The Order of the Poems in *1822*

Hellas
Written on hearing the news of the death of Napoleon

Appendix B

'[?] / As when within a chasm of [?mighty] seas'

The following fragment is one of three compositions that S. wrote in his copy of *Euripidis Tragœdiæ Viginti, cum variis lectionibus*, ed. Josuae Barnes, 6 vols bound as three (1811–12), which is now in Eton College Library (shelfmark: Kl.4.19, hereafter *Eton Euripides*). On this edition and its provenance, see headnote to *An archer stood upon the Tower of Babel* (no. 414). Edmund Gosse announced the discovery of the fragments and drafts in S.'s Euripides in a letter to the *TLS* 2711 (24 February 1921) 126, and notes 'There is a third fragment [i.e. the present item], apparently in verse, but the pencil is so faint and agitated, that I fail to decipher it'. This fragment appears in the first volume (comprising volumes 1 and 2 of Barnes's edition). There is one further piece of writing in this volume not noted by Gosse: S. neatly wrote κρημνός (Greek for 'river bank', 'crag', 'cliff') in the middle of the recto of the first lower endpaper. This word occurs twice in the plays of this volume, in *Phoenissae* l. 1315 (which there is no evidence that S. read), and in *Hippolytus* l. 124, when the Chorus announces Phaedra's sickness.

This fragment is written in pencil on the recto of the second lower endpaper of the first volume of *Eton Euripides*. Like *An archer stood upon the Tower of Babel*, the lines are written at right angles to the book's spine. S.'s writing is large and very rough and there is substantial water damage to the page. Given that these lines appear in a foreign language text they could be a translation in the vein of *A belated sleep fell on his eyelids then* (Volume 6, Appendix D) but no plausible source has been found. The fragment begins with indecipherable writing (either one word or two), with the first letter apparently a majuscule. This first line is centred suggesting either a heading or possibly the proper name of a character in a drama. The fragment is typical of S.'s mature poetry: 'chasm' occurs frequently, and the image of 'Lightning [...] throned in darkness' combines a characteristic use of figurative language to explain a contrast of light and dark.

The fragment may tentatively be dated to a period when S. consulted the Euripides he had with him in Italy. *An archer stood upon the Tower of Babel* and a draft of *Autumn: a Dirge* (no. 415) appear in the second volume of

Eton Euripides and can tentatively be dated to between October 1821 and January 1822, but S. appears to have used the first volume (which contains *Hecuba, Orestes, Phoenissae, Medea, Hippolytus, Alcestis, Andromache*) in the summer of 1820. Mary records that S. 'read Euripides' from 19 to 23 June (*Mary Jnl* i 323), and his notebooks from around this time contain remarks on, and quotations from, *Hippolytus* (see the quotation of *Hippolytus* 1012–15 in *Nbk 17* p. 1, and notes on Hippolytus' interest in watching sexual intercourse at *Nbk 14* pp. 68–9). It is likely that the writing of κρημνός on the leaf before the fragment is contemporary with this reading of *Hippolytus*. A summer 1820 date is further suggested by the fact that it was around this time that S. wrote *Within a cavern of man's inmost spirit* (no. 323), which has verbal similarities to this fragment. Another possible date of composition is during S.'s journey to Italy in spring 1818, when he read 'two or three plays of Euripides' (*L* ii 15) before translating Euripides' *Cyclops* (no. 172) in June 1818 — one of the plays to which he refers could have been from the first volume of his Euripides (the unsteadiness of a coach journey would explain the rough hand).

Text from the recto of the lower endpaper of the first volume of S.'s copy of *Euripidis Tragœdiæ Viginti, cum variis lectionibus*, ed. Josuae Barnes, 6 vols bound as 3 (1811–12), Eton College Library, shelfmark: Kl.4.19. Reproduced by permission of the Provost and Fellows of Eton College.

Unpublished.

[?]
As when within a chasm of [?mighty] seas
Lightning is [?thron ed] in darkness

¶ **Appendix B** *2–3*. Cp. the description of the 'dome of Death' in Southey's 'The Vision of the Maid of Orleans' i:

> It was a spacious cavern, hewn amid
> The entrails of the earth, as tho' to form
> The grave of all mankind: no eye could reach,
> Tho' gifted with the eagle's ample ken,
> Its distant bounds. There, thron'd in darkness, dwelt
> The unseen POWER OF DEATH. (*Poems* (1799) 24)

4. *Lightning*] The pencil lead in the upstroke of the first letter has faded in *Eton Euripides* such that only the base remains.

Appendix C

'O thou whose cold hand tears the veils from error'

(Translation of Petrarch, *Africa* vi 901–2)

The draft of this couplet, unlike the rest of the material in *Nbk 19*, is written sideways, in landscape direction, on the mutilated p. 54. This couplet along with *A widowed bird sate mourning for her love* (no. 427) p. 53 reverso and *Art thou pale for weariness* (no. 428), p. 52 reverso interrupt an unresolved dialogue between Vane and Hampden in *Charles the First* (no. 426) found on pp. 51 and 55. The ink is dark, seemingly thick, and S.'s writing is compressed making decipherment difficult. Approximately one third of the leaf has been torn away. The fact that the line ends slope slightly downward as they near the torn edge suggests that the third of the leaf was torn off before the couplet was entered. Nora Crook identified this fragment as a translation from Mago's final speech in Petrarch's *Africa* in 'Shelley and his Waste-Paper Basket: Notes on Eight Shelleyan and Pseudo-Shelleyan Jottings, Extracts, and Fragments', *K-SR* xxv (2011) 76–8 (hereafter *Crook*).

Petrarch's epic *Africa* recounts the story of the Second Punic Wars and his hero Publius Cornelius Scipio Africanus. The context for this couplet is found in Book vi, where Mago, a Carthaginian commander and brother of Hannibal, is dying and uttering his last words. The Latin that forms the basis of S.'s translation from Petrarch's *Africa* vi 901–2 — which was begun in 1338–9 and published posthumously in 1397 — is given in most modern editions (e.g. Francesco Petrarca, *Rime, Trionfi e Poesie Latine*, ed. F. Neri et al. (1951) 688) as follows: 'tu retegis sola errores, et somnia vitae / discutis exactae' ('you [Death] unveil the errors and dispel the dreams of completed life', trans. Nicholas Havely). The position of this couplet in *Nbk 19* and Crook's identification of the circumstances surrounding its composition allow for some precision in dating. For the reasons discussed below, it is likely to have been written around 22 January 1822, rather than the 1820 date indicated in *BSM* xxiii 278.

The background for this fragment, summarised in *Crook*, is as follows. Byron received a letter from his publisher John Murray in January 1822 requesting a translation from Petrarch as a contribution to Ugo Foscolo's

Essays on Petrarch (1823) which included seven appendices all loosely related to Foscolo's four essays. Appendix I, entitled 'Specimens of the Latin Poetry of Petrarch' (209), includes an extract headed 'From The Africa. — Book VI / The Death of Mago', with the text of the Latin original and an English translation of this, the final episode in *Africa* vi, on facing pages (214–17); the English translation is signed 'Lord Byron'. Byron replied to Murray in a letter of 22 January 1822: 'In a post or two I shall send you a version of the extract from "Petrarch" as you wished— but you must not expect it to be good, I have not the turn for those things' (*Byron L&J* ix 90). Medwin recounts Byron's lack of enthusiasm for the project:

> "I have just got a letter," said he, "from Murray. What do you think he has enclosed me? A long dull extract from that long dull Latin epic of Petrarch's, *Africa*, which he has the modesty to ask me to translate for Ugo Foscolo, who is writing some Memoirs of Petrarch, which he has got Moore, Lady Dacre, &c. to contribute to. What am I to do with the Death of Mago? I wish to God, Medwin, you would take it home with you, and translate it; and I will send it to Murray. We will say nothing about its being yours or mine; and it will be curious to hear Foscolo's opinion upon it. Depend upon it, it will not be an unfavourable one." (*Medwin (1824)* 113)

Medwin, only too happy to take care of the 'dull extract', writes, 'In the course of the day I turned it into couplets, (and lame enough they were,) which he forwarded by the next courier to England' (*Medwin (1824)* 113). Given the almost daily contact between Medwin and S. during January 1822, Crook suggests that it is likely 'that Shelley was a willing participant in the trick played on Murray' (*Crook* 77). Mary then helped expedite the return of the finished work that Byron had promised Murray, by copying Medwin's translation. Mary's press copy of 'The Death of Mago', dated 'J[anuar]y 1822' with several minor corrections in another hand, generally agreed to be Byron's, is in the John Murray Archive, National Library of Scotland (NLS MS 43348, f. 50). Between 17 and 25 January, Mary had been 'copying' (*Mary Jnl* i 390–2) — probably Byron's *Werner* — almost daily, so transcribing the additional translation on Byron's behalf must have been added to her brief. Whether or not she knew of Byron's joke on Murray has not been established, but because she was undoubtedly working from Medwin's draft, she is likely to have known the deception. Moreover, Mary's handwriting in the press copy would not have aroused Murray's suspicions. Roughly two weeks later, on 8 February 1822, she wrote in her journal: 'When I would tear the veil from this strange world & pierce with eagle eyes beyond the sun', suggesting, perhaps, that the labour of copying was more than a mere rote experience for her (*Mary Jnl* i 396).

A cancellation in the *Nbk 19* p. 54 draft is further evidence of S. and Medwin's possible collaboration on the Petrarch extract. Medwin's version of the couplet as published by Foscolo reads:

> Oh, thou, whose cold hand tears the veil from error,
> Whose hollow eye is our delusion's mirror! (*Essays on Petrarch* (1823) 217)

In the *Nbk 19* version, S. begins the second line with *Whose hollow eye*, but after several attempts he cancels this start and begins with *Whose empty eyes*. S.'s version differs from Medwin's in several other particulars (see note to l. 1). Despite these differences, however, the *Nbk 19* version and the one Medwin published in *Essays on Petrarch* share the same structure, metre, and rhyme (*error/mirror*) and both avoid an overly literal translation of Petrarch's original. As Crook notes, they are 'a free imitation' of the Latin original: the details of the cold hand, the mirror, the hollow/empty eye in the two versions are absent in Petrarch's poem (*Crook* 77). The original translation by Medwin which Mary copied has not survived so it is impossible to compare S.'s and Medwin's MS versions. Several scenarios are possible: Medwin may have plagiarised most of S.'s couplet with, or without, S.'s knowledge, or he may have asked S. to tackle a few lines in the original that were troublesome. Perhaps they worked together to accede promptly to Byron's request, or perhaps S. was interested in Petrarch's text and worked with it independently. Medwin's account does not mention S.'s assistance and implies that credit for Foscolo's praise of what was published was due to himself alone: 'Almost by return of post arrived a furiously complimentary epistle in acknowledgment, which made us laugh very heartily' (*Medwin (1824)* 113-4).

It seems possible that Medwin's diversion might have offered a welcome respite from S.'s challenges with *Charles the First* of which he wrote to John Gisborne, at the end of that same week, on 26 January: 'I ... seldom now touch the *canvas*' (*L* ii 388). Prior to *Crook*, Massey had conjectured that these two lines might have belonged to *Art thou pale for weariness* (*Massey* 243) overleaf, and Crook in *BSM* xii had described them 'as a hypermetric heroic couplet' that '*might* record an idea for a dramatic lyric' (p. xlix). Michael Bradshaw treats them briefly in 'Reading as Flight: Fragment Poems from Shelley's Notebooks', in *The Unfamiliar Shelley*, ed. Alan M. Weinberg and Timothy Webb (2009) 21.

Text from *Nbk 19* p. 54 rev.

Published in *Massey* 243 (transcription of MS); Tatsuo Tokoo, 'The Contents of Shelley's Notebooks in the Bodleian Library', *Humanities: Bulletin of the Faculty of Letters, Kyoto Prefectural University* xxxvi (1984) 29 (part of l. 1 only); Nora Crook, 'Shelley and his Waste-Paper Basket: Notes on Eight Shelleyan and Pseudo-Shelleyan Jottings, Extracts, and Fragments', *K-SR* xxv (2011) 76; *BSM* xii 112–13 (facsimile and transcription of MS).

'O thou whose cold hand tears the veils from error'

O thou whose cold hand tears the veils from error
Whose empty eyes our delusions mirror

¶ **Appendix C** *1.* Others ?whose ?word [?rent] have torn the veils from ?man Massey. *hand*] Written above *heart* canc. in *Nbk 19*. *tears*] The final letter *s*, barely visible in *Nbk 19*, is required by sense and grammar. Medwin gives 'veil' rather than *veils*, but S.'s terminal *s* seems to be added as an afterthought.
2. eyes] eyeis *Nbk 19*; eye s *BSM*; eye is *Massey, GM, Crook*. The general confusion is understandable: *Whose hollow eye is* (which also occurs in Medwin's printed version) is cancelled along with another variation to that half-line, *empty eye*. S. begins another new line below with that same phrase, *Whose empty eye is*, and then *our delusions mirror* is added to complete the couplet. Finally, S. overwrites, with an exaggerated loop, the second *e* of *eye* and the *i* of *is*, creating a single word, *eyes*. The resulting line lacks S.'s usual fluency (and may thus be suggestive of Medwin's influence) where his earlier variant, *Whose empty eye is our delusions mirror*, is a more successful iambic pentameter. As noted by Nicholas Havely (email communication to the editors), S.'s use of *delusions* here (and Medwin's 'delusion's') for the Latin *somnia* indicates that they had access to an authorised Latin text and one which was different from that of the Latin version in *Essays on Petrarch* which gives *crimina* ('misdeeds') instead of *somnia*. Why neither Foscolo nor Murray noticed the discrepancy between *crimina* and its translation as 'delusions' is unclear; however, W. P. Mustard's description of the 'special history' of the 34 lines that Byron was asked to translate goes some way towards explaining why Foscolo selected this passage and how a second, less authoritative Latin version might have appeared in his 1823 publication (see 'Petrarch's *Africa*' in *The American Journal of Philology* xlii (1921) 111–12 n. 14).

Index of Titles

'A capering, squalid, squalling one' 292
A Dirge 312
'A fresh fair child stood by my side' [Love, Hope, Desire, and Fear] 284
A Song 482
'A widowed bird sate mourning for her love' [A Song] 482
'Alas, if I could feign' 314
'An archer stood upon the Tower of Babel' 271
'Art thou pale for weariness' [To the Moon] 485
'As the sunrise to the night' [Fragment: To Italy] 5
'[?] / As when within a chasm of [?mighty] seas' 501
Autumn: a Dirge 273

Charles the First 319

Epitaph [On Keats] 297

Fragment: To Italy 5

Hellas 7

'In the great morning of the world' 3
'It is the period when all the Sons of God' [Prologue to Hellas] 204

Lines to — [Sonnet to Byron] 488

Lines to an Indian Air 260
Love, Hope, Desire, and Fear 284

Mutability 282

'O thou whose cold hand tears the veils from error' 503
On Keats 297

Prologue to Hellas 208

'Rough wind that moanest loud' [A Dirge] 312

Sonnet to Byron 488

'The flower that smiles today' [Mutability] 282
The Indian Girl's Song [Lines to an Indian Air] 260
The Zucca 302
'There was a star when Heaven was young' 315
'Though thou scatterest their ashes' 316
Time 279
To the Moon 485

'Unfathomable Sea! whose waves are years' [Time] 279

'Which like a crane, its distant home pursuing' 268

Index of First Lines

A capering, squalid, squalling one 296
A fresh fair child stood by my side 287
A star has fallen upon the Earth — a torch 257
A widowed bird sate mourning for her love 484
Alas, if I could feign 315
An archer stood upon the Tower of Babel 273
And blushing / April is not a rebel to rude March 481
And like that star, the Shepherd of true stars 239
Art thou pale for weariness 487
As the sunrise to the night 6
[?] / As when within a chasm of [?mighty] seas 502

Could Arethusa to her fountain run 254

'Here lieth one whose name was writ on water' 301
Hisses and scorn, even as my master did 480

I arise from dreams of thee 266
I would not be a King: enough 246
Ibrahim — / Stab that pernicious slave who talks of fear 243
If I esteemed you less, Envy would kill 496
In the great morning of the world 4
It is the period when all the Sons of God 208

Like an exhalation 238

O thou whose cold hand tears the veils from error 506

Place for the Marshal of the Masque! 359

Rough wind that moanest loud 313

Summer was dead and Autumn was expiring 305
Suns and stars are rolling ever 233

The clouds of every heart and every mind 245
The flower that smiles today 283
The pilot spirits the eternal stars 260
The warm sun is failing, the bleak wind is wailing 277
There are two fountains in which spirits weep 242
There was a star when Heaven was young 316
Though thou scatterest their ashes 317

Unfathomable Sea! whose waves are years 281

We pass, outspeeding the thunder 237
We strew these opiate flowers 60
Which like a crane, its distant home pursuing 270

Youngest of the Destinies 229

For Product Safety Concerns and Information please contact our EU
representative GPSR@taylorandfrancis.com
Taylor & Francis Verlag GmbH, Kaufingerstraße 24, 80331 München, Germany

www.ingramcontent.com/pod-product-compliance
Lightning Source LLC
Chambersburg PA
CBHW061339300426
44116CB00011B/1923